Thunder & Lightning

The Fighting Gatti Brothers

By
Joe Botti

Win By KO Publications
IOWA CITY

Thunder & Lightning

The Fighting Gatti Brothers

By Joe Botti

(ISBN-13): 978-1-949783-08-7

(softcover: 50# acid-free alkaline paper)

Includes endnotes.

© 2023 by Joseph J. Botti. All Rights Reserved.

No part of this book may be reproduced, or transmitted in any form or by any means, graphic, electronic or mechanical, including photocopying, recording, taping, or by any information storage retrieval system without the written permission of Joseph J. Botti or Win By KO Publications LLC.

Cover photos courtesy of Joe Gatti and Mario Costa

Cover design by Gwyneth Flowers ©

Manufactured in the United States of America.

Win By KO Publications LLC

Iowa City, Iowa

winbykopublications.com

Dedicated to
Arturo "Thunder" Gatti
&
"Lightning" Joe Gatti
Apart in flesh, but together in spirit

Contents

Acknowledgements 6

Introduction 7

Part 1

Chapter 1: Death in Brazil 11

Chapter 2: Growing up in Montreal 14

Chapter 3: The Fighting Hilton Brothers 27

Chapter 4: Bufano's Gym & Jersey City Boxing 46

Chapter 5: Main Events & the Duvas 53

Chapter 6: Arturo Moves to New Jersey 59

Chapter 7: The Junior Middleweight Championship 78

Chapter 8: Arturo's First Professional Belt 102

Chapter 9: Charging to the World Title 117

Chapter 10: A Dream Realized 136

Chapter 11: The Rodriguez War 144

Chapter 12: The Patterson Rematch 167

Chapter 13: Ruelas 179

Chapter 14: Manfredy 202

Chapter 15: Robinson I & II 223

Chapter 16: Gamache 255

Chapter 17: The Golden Boy 291

Chapter 18: The Battle for Montreal & Millett 309

Chapter 19: Ward I 320

Chapter 20: Ward II 333

Chapter 21: Ward III 348

Part 2

Chapter 22: A Second Title 402

Chapter 23: Battling Depression & Leija	422
Chapter 24: Buildup to a Superfight	435
Chapter 25: Mayweather	453
Chapter 26: Damgaard	472
Chapter 27: Baldomir	493
Chapter 28: Gomez & Retirement	511
Chapter 29: Life After Boxing	537
Chapter 30: Tragedy in Brazil	556
Chapter 31: Burying a Legend	577
Chapter 32: Amanda Returns to Canada	598
Chapter 33: The Hall of Fame	615
Epilogue	623
Endnotes	631

Acknowledgements

There are many people who helped to make this book a reality. There are those, however, whom without their help this book could not have been possible. First of all, my wife Michelle and my children Katrina, Michael, Joshua, and Jenna. They have sacrificed much from my passion for the sport of boxing. My mother, Patricia McGinnis-Caputo, who passed in 2013. She handled the entrance gate at every amateur boxing show I promoted. She was my biggest supporter. My father, Robert Botti, for instilling the passion of boxing in me. Adam Pollack, for his assistance in publishing this book. Joe Gatti, who summoned the strength to relive difficult life memories. Henry Hascup, boxing historian, for his meticulous historical review. Vikki Gatti, Mario Costa, Sal Alessi, Mike "Mikey Red" Skowronski, Pete Maino, Donny Jerie, Andre Kut, Lou Duva, Teddy Cruz, Buddy McGirt, Diego Rosario, Ivan Robinson, Alfonso Gomez, Gabriel Ruelas, Angel Manfredy, Benjy Esteves, Joe Goosen, Ron Katz, Bob Rooney Sr., Scott DePompe, Michael DePompe, Paul Dunleavy, Barry Porter, Michelle & Jack Sprague, Omar Hernandez, Ricardo Ocasio, William Peer, Dominick DePinto, John Slater, Hugh Holguin, Steven Sandoval, Danny McDermott, Omar Sheika, Greg Speciale, Michael Strange, Eric Huard, Barrington Francis, Don Elbaum, Johnny Bos, Tommy Gallagher, Wayne Witkowski, Stanley Janousek, Travis Hartman, Sugar Ray Bailey and so many others who helped to make this book possible.

Introduction

It was in 1990, while I was training amateur boxers in Hudson County, New Jersey, when I first heard the names Joe and Arturo Gatti. Joe was a professional fighter with a record of 10-2 with 8 knockouts. Arturo Gatti was still boxing as an amateur.

It was common knowledge that both brothers had extensive experience in the sport of boxing. It was also well known that they were related, by marriage, to the Hilton boxing family. The Hilton brothers were boxing celebrities in Canada. They were also well known in Hudson County, as they spent time training in Jersey City. The Gatti brothers made many friends quickly. It was as though the Hudson County community adopted them as their own. The brothers had no parents or guardians with them when they arrived. Hudson County, with all of its positive and negative attributes, became their surrogate father and mother.

Growing up in Montreal, Canada, Joe and Arturo were not your typical Canadian boys. While most boys their ages were suiting up in hockey gear and dreaming of Stanley Cup glory, the Gatti boys had other dreams. Their dreams, infused by their father, were of glory in a boxing ring. They were naturals in the ring. Joe moved from Montreal to Jersey City, New Jersey in 1989. He brought his brother Arturo down soon after.

Joe and Arturo's careers, and lives, would take two entirely different paths. The brothers' careers were, in essence, a study on professional boxing. If a scientist in a lab wanted to study the effects of professional boxing, the two brothers would be the perfect samples. Both were world-class professionals, although one realized his dreams, while the other did not.

Almost without exception, everyone close to Arturo Gatti whom I interviewed asked the same question at the beginning of the interview: *"You're going to write a good book about Arturo, right?"* Even in death everyone wanted to protect Arturo's reputation and image. The loyalty that he commanded from his friends was, and still is, amazing.

While Joe was the fashionable, fun-loving older brother that everyone wanted to hang out with, Arturo was the mischievous, care-free younger brother that everyone felt the need to protect.

Arturo "Thunder" Gatti was involved in some of the sport's most entertaining and brutal fights. Anyone who saw those fights will never forget them.

"Lightning" Joe Gatti was the matinee idol and rising star well before anyone knew who Arturo was. Joe was a fast-handed, fleet-footed boxer who possessed a devastating left hook. Joe had matinee-idol looks and an infectiously personable demeanor that helped make him a local box-office attraction.

Both brothers dreamed of superstardom. Joe was a promoter's dream. His fan base had grown into a cult-like following in Northern New Jersey. The boxing ring appeared paved with gold and glory for Joe.

The story of Arturo and Joe Gatti is a fascinating look at the two sides of boxing. In this book I will dissect both careers and how they affected each brothers' lives outside of the ring, and also how their lives outside the ring affected their careers.

Jersey Journal reporter Wayne Witkowski described what he felt was the difference between Joe and Arturo. *"It was always said in ringside conversations that Joe was tough to get into the gym for training for his fights, but once Arturo was under contract, he was ready to go to work."*[1] Although both brothers tasted the canvas several times in their careers, Arturo was able to rise to his feet and partake in some of the most dramatic boxing finishes of all time.

Boxing is like a dog- or cock-fight. The tough ones that sacrifice their all to have their hands raised, the ones who keep coming back are the winners, or are they? Are the ones who fall to the wayside quickly the real winners? Gladiators like Arturo, who refuse to quit, are rewarded with a never-ending onslaught of blows from an all too eager line of fighters trying to improve their lot. Boxing mirrors life in many ways, but in this most cruel way, boxing, like life, is not fair. Unlike fairytales, these brave and fierce warriors are likely to be cut to ribbons before their careers are completed.

Boxers risk life and limb with every punch they throw and receive. What many of them do not realize though, is that the effects of their ring wars may bring with it severe consequences in the months or years after retirement. Hearing problems, vision problems, arthritic hands, deviated septums, a loss of gait when walking, TMJ jaw injuries, and worst of all, internal brain injuries. Internal brain injuries and concussions don't just lead to forgetfulness, they lead to painfully excruciating migraine headaches, tremors, and depression. When retired fighters who attend boxing shows display these signs of injuries they are disregarded by young rising athletes and their trainers. The up-and-coming prospects shrug off these telltale signs of what their future might hold with a "that's not going to happen to me" attitude. The prospect and his trainer will point to "a lack of defense," "sticking around the game too long" or "repeated drug use" as the reason why the old-timers suffer from boxing related ailments.

I interviewed Joe Gatti in his former home in Northern New Jersey. When we discussed boxing his eyes lit up like a child on Christmas morning. Joe stood up and started shadow boxing while he described some of his matches. He still displayed the quick feinting, footwork, and rapid hand-speed that was his prizefighting signature. I attempted to interview Pat Lynch, Kathy Duva, and Amanda Rodrigues-Gatti, but they declined to be interviewed.

In this book, I hope to shed light on the business of boxing as it affected both brothers. I explore the Northern New Jersey fight scene, as well as the gyms, trainers, managers, and promoters to whom the brothers were exposed. One brother succeeded and one brother fell short of the biggest prize. One had all of his dreams come true and one did not. One got out before the game ground him into nothingness, while one could not. One lived the dream inside of the ring and a nightmare outside of it. This is the story of Thunder and Lightning.

Part 1

"Now is the time to think of only one thing. That which I was born for."

Ernest Hemingway
The Old Man & The Sea

Chapter 1
Death in Brazil

It is July 11, 2009, in Fort Lauderdale, Florida. Anna-Maria Gatti is finalizing the details of her wedding when she receives a phone call from her sister-in-law, Amanda Rodrigues-Gatti. Amanda tersely advised Anna, *"Something serious happened. Your brother is dead."* Anna-Maria thought Amanda was joking.[2] Arturo's mother, Ida, was standing next to Anna. When Ida was told what Amanda had said, her first words were, *"She did it."*

Cell phones started ringing, tears were being shed from Montreal to New Jersey, as word of the tragedy spread. The responses mirrored each other. *"It can't be true. Arturo would never leave his kids. Arturo was not a quitter."* Many of the conversations ended with the same hypothesis, *"She must have murdered him or at least arranged the murder."*

Arturo's older brother Joe was in his home in Northern New Jersey when the phone call came. He was devastated, but not shocked. This was the culmination of a premonition he had long feared would come true. He always felt that this day was a possibility. Joe picked up the phone and called Mario Costa. When Costa answered, Joe spoke, *"Mario, they finally did it. They killed my brother."*[3] Word quickly spread across the news wires. The Associated Press, CNN, ESPN and every other major news network covered the tragedy.

On July 12, 2009, Amanda Rodrigues-Gatti was taken into custody by Brazilian authorities as a result of what they stated were *"contradictions in her interrogation."*[4]

Arturo's mother, Ida, was devastated. She cried uncontrollably for days. Everyone was blaming Amanda. Arturo and Amanda's marriage had been on the rocks. The couple fought incessantly. After Arturo's retirement, Amanda and Arturo were forced to move back to Arturo's native Montreal because Amanda had been threatened with deportation from the United States.

They lived in a penthouse condominium in a high-rise structure owned by Arturo's building company. Their son, Arturo Jr., lived with them in the condo on Jarry Street. The couple fought often. Sometimes when the domestic disputes escalated, Arturo would sleep in the basement of his mother's home. Arturo's stepfather,

Gerardo di Francesco, described the situation, *"The fighting started. They were separated. He was coming here to sleep. And she would come here to yell at him, 'Why don't you come back to the house.' It was quite the drama."*[5] According to Gerardo, the relationship began to sour not long after Arturo Junior's birth on September 9, 2008. However, their relationship had major problems well before that.

The couple had decided one last time to try and salvage their marriage. A second honeymoon was planned. The couple vacationed alone in Amsterdam and Paris, apparently without incident.

After Europe, they rented an oceanfront apartment in Porto de Galihnas, Brazil. Amanda flew down to Brazil from Europe while Arturo returned to Montreal for a few days before flying to New Jersey to pick up his son. Arturo and Junior flew down to Brazil to be reunited with Amanda. When Arturo was in Montreal, he asked his stepfather Gerardo to join him in Brazil. Di Francesco later expressed, *"I had decided to stay in Montreal to keep an eye on the house. But Arturo told me, 'If you aren't going to the wedding, come with me after to Brazil.' I don't know what would have happened if I'd gone with him to Brazil."*[6] Arturo apparently had reservations about going to Brazil.

Arturo had gained a reputation as a partier. Some claimed that he partied as hard as he fought. Some had hoped that moving back to Montreal would curb his appetite for the fast life. Unfortunately, the move only substituted the faces from the Jersey City party crowd to the Montreal one. The birth of his son, however, seemed to mellow the fighter. According to Di Francesco, *"Early on [when he returned to Montreal] he was going out a lot. His friends always wanted to go out with him. They would drink and get in late. But he had calmed down recently."*[7]

Arturo's frustrations were not confined to his marriage. After meeting Amanda and retiring from boxing, he severed most of his ties to the boxing world and his adopted hometown of Jersey City. His North Jersey friends claimed that Amanda was the cause for Arturo cutting them out of his life.

Arturo was a fighter in life. The fighting associated with his name would not end with his death. Arturo's boxing friends had broken into two warring factions. One faction was led by Arturo's manager, Pat Lynch. The other faction was led by the man who was responsible for relocating Arturo and Joe Gatti to Jersey City, Mario

Costa. Both factions held their own memorial services for the boxer.

Some of Arturo's friends claimed that he had been physically abused by his wife. Some extremely disturbing events occurred just prior to Arturo's death. Arturo's will had been changed abruptly. Originally, Arturo had signed a prenuptial agreement prior to his marriage with Amanda. His boxing fortune was willed to his mother Ida and his daughter Sofia. Sofia was born from a previous relationship. Two weeks prior to Arturo's death, he had changed his will, allocating nearly all of his wealth to his wife Amanda.

Chapter 2
Growing up in Montreal

Giovanni Gatti wasn't a big man. He stood 5 foot 8 inches tall and weighed around 140-pounds. In 1964, Giovanni had moved from San Pietro, Italy to Canada with his young wife Ida and their infant daughter Anna-Maria. Anna-Maria was born in 1963. Giovanni had learned to be an electrician in his native country, taught by his uncle, also named Giovanni.

San Pietro Infine is located in the Province of Caserta in the region of Campania in Southern Italy. It is located approximately 43 miles Northwest of Naples and 31 miles Northwest of Caserta. San Pietro is today known in Italy as the Pompeii of World War II, for the fierce battle that was fought there between the United States 5th Army and the German 10th Army's XIV Panzer Corps. The battle raged for ten days, from December 8 to December 17, 1943. The town was completely destroyed during the battle. It was rebuilt several hundred meters from its original location. The battle was crucial to the ultimate liberation of Rome.

During the battle, townspeople were forced to flee their homes and take up refuge in the many mountainous caves that surrounded the area. 140 of the 1,412 residents of San Pietro were killed during the battle. Giovanni Gatti, then only a year old, survived, as did many women and children, by taking up refuge in a cave.

John Huston, embedded with the U.S. Armies 143rd Regiment, would create a military documentary about the battle titled *The Battle of San Pietro*. The film was controversial in that it showed the many horrors of war with its graphic display of deceased soldiers. The film later would be used for training purposes, to show new recruits the reality of war.

Upon arrival in Canada, Giovanni and his family stayed with his sister Gilda in Calgary. After a few months, Giovanni moved his family to the Mile End section of Montreal, where his sister Filomena and her family were located. The Mile End section was heavily industrialized and home to a thriving garment district in the early part of the Twentieth Century. In the early 1980s, the section would become home to budding artists, filmmakers, musicians, and writers. Giovanni had no problem finding work, as there was a large contingent of Italian immigrants in the area. He started his own business called Gatti Electric.

Before long, Giovanni's budding business was employing fifteen workers. Giovanni eventually would have enough business to warrant four work vans. The vans were red in color, with the words "Gatti Electric" boldly written in white on the side. One of the vans would later be used to transport young Joe and Arturo to the local gyms and boxing shows in the area.

Giovanni was a rough character. He had a stern countenance and a "don't mess with me" look about him. Giovanni had a passion for boxing, but he was unable to pursue the sport in his native Italy.

On August 20, 1965, Giovanni and Ida welcomed their second child into the world, Giuseppina Gatti. Giuseppina was baptized at the Romanesque church, Notre-Dame-de-la-Defense. The church was named by French-Canadians. The church was also called Madonna della Difesa by the Italian-Canadians. The church was built in 1919 by Roch Montbriant and Guido Nincheri. The interior of the church has a fresco of Benito Mussolini, painted by Nincheri prior to World War II, to commemorate the Lateran Accords. Besides Giuseppina, the church would be the baptism location for siblings Giuseppe, born April 12, 1967, Mirella, born in 1968, Arturo, born April 15, 1972, and lastly Fabrizio, born in 1978. Unfortunately, in 2009, the site also would be the location of Arturo's funeral mass.

In 1972, the year Arturo was born, another birth was taking place. This one was in the boxing ring. In an outside parking lot of the Harbor Hotel in Lynn, Massachusetts, a 7-year-old Irish-American boy named Micky Ward entered the boxing ring for the first time. The gloves went all the way up to the elbows of the terrified 50-pound boy, who was facing a 12-year-old opponent named Joey Roach. Joey, from Dedham, Massachusetts, was the younger brother of Freddie Roach. The bout was stopped two rounds later due to rain. Ward, who loved football and baseball more than boxing, took up the sport because he looked up to his older brother Dickey. This 7-year-old would become "Irish" Micky Ward, and he would continue fighting for the next 33 years.

After moving to several different apartments, Giovanni purchased the family's first home at the corner of Drolet and St. Zotique Streets. The house was in the rough-and-tumble neighborhood of St. Michel, in Northern Montreal. It was at this location that the sport of boxing was injected into Joe by his father.

Giovanni set up a mini boxing gym in the family garage. He created a speed bag by utilizing a wooden electrical wire reel. Giuseppe, known in the neighborhood as Joe, explained, *"My father was an electrician. He had his own company. So you know those reels with the wires on it? The big reels? We put two of these circles, the spools together, and we made the speed bag."*[8] The heavy bag was created by using a post-office mail bag, as Joe describes, *"We put sawdust, but it was too light. We didn't know how to make it [laughs]. So we stuffed other stuff. I remember putting some bricks in-between the saw dust."* Arturo recalled the makeshift punching bag, *"We found a mail sack and hung it up like a heavybag. Lucky for the mailman, he wasn't inside."*[9] After Joe had conquered the basics of boxing, Giovanni sought out neighborhood kids for Joe to try his new skills on. *"My father would stop boys in the streets and give them a couple of dollars to spar with me. And I beat them up."*[10]

Joe was a natural righty, yet his father taught him to box with his right hand in front. Joe explains, *"I started southpaw. He taught me lefty."*[11] Kids that begin boxing naturally want to have their strong hand in front. Some trainers, however, purposely "turn the kids around" because they want the arm with strength to be in front to deliver the hook.

Giovanni trained Joe in the make-shift gym on a daily basis from age 6 to 9. Arturo was too young to box at the time. He would sit and watch as his father trained his brother.

In 1976, when Joe turned 9, Giovanni brought him to a real boxing gym to train for the first time. The gym was an hour drive away from the Gatti house, as Joe recalls, *"I was nine, we moved, and then when we moved, of course where we lived my father didn't know there was a gym. Where we lived the gym was half an hour away. When we moved, now it was an hour away! You know, but we ended up going there. My sister [Anna] used to take me there because I was too young. We used to take the bus. It was too far away."*[12] Giovanni would sometimes spar with his young sons. Arturo later recalled that he disliked sparring with his father, *"because my father didn't have a good defense."*[13]

Giovanni brought Joe to the Olympic Boxing Gym. Joe described the gym. *"It was an old theater. Like if you go to New York. It's an old building, like an old brownstone, and you go three stories up. We're like shot by the time we got to the top. We was like, 'Now we got to train!' It was old, you know the Rocky movie? When he walks up those stairs to get to the gym? It's all old like that, but a little bigger. It was like that."*[14]

Joe described what he remembered most about that first day in the gym. *"The smell and all the fighters. It was exactly what you saw in Rocky. The sweat, the humidity. It was hot. There was no breeze and you see all these guys fighting. Exactly if you went to Philly, that's what it looked like."*[15]

Joe recalled who was training in the gym at the time. *"There was a couple of fighters... Donato Paduano was still there, he was heavy, he was making a comeback. He was there and Ricas Zamberdini and Guerra Chavez."*[16]

Joe's father, like most fathers, wanted to give his son an edge. Giovanni had Joe drink an Italian dessert drink called Zabaione. The Italian drink was a mix of Marsala wine, egg yolks, and sugar. Marsala is a sweet, fortified wine similar to Sherry. It was intended to produce energy, but the alcohol content often had the 9-year-old Joe tipsy.

One of the trainers in the Olympic Gym, the one who would coach Joe and Arturo as amateurs, was Dave Campanile. Campanile had been a trainer since 1968. Although he did not box himself, Dave learned the trade from the great Roger Larivee. Larivee had been a professional boxing trainer, manager, and promoter. Campanile would eventually take over the gym when Larivee passed away in 1980. When Campanile saw that Joe was fighting lefty he turned him around to an orthodox stance. *"When we went to the gym they didn't know how to train lefties. So that's why I can change. Maybe that's why I have a good left hook."*[17] Many trainers at the time, and even today, will turn lefties into righties because they feel that lefties do "everything backwards."

Arturo, who was 5 years old at the time, was not as interested in the sport as Joe was. *"When he started he was 5 or 6. Then he started training. We used to fool around, some sparring. We used to use him as a clown. We used to tease him, chase him. He used to run on top of the ring. Then after we used to mess around a little bit before training. After that it was like a comedy club."*[18]

Although Arturo was allowed to play soccer and hockey with his friends, sports he loved and excelled in, he was now required to train in boxing at home. Giovanni attended most of Arturo's soccer matches and proudly shouted encouragement to his son.

When Giovanni returned home from work, Joe and Arturo were forced to stop playing with their friends and enter the house for dinner. After dinner, they proceeded to the makeshift gym in the garage with their father, where they received their boxing lessons. Arturo would have preferred to continue playing hockey or soccer, but there were no such options in Giovanni Gatti's household.

In 1979, when Arturo turned 7, he started training regularly at the Olympic Club. Anna-Maria would take her two younger brothers to the gym. The 7-year-old Arturo and the 12-year-old Joe were still too young to travel alone. They needed to travel by bus to the gym.

In the gym, Arturo would follow his big brother everywhere, mirroring his every move. Pierre Leclerc, a trainer at the Olympic Club, recalled Joe taking care of his little brother in the gym. Leclerc recalled that he never saw a love that was as pure as that between Joe and Arturo. Arturo sparred with 12-year-old Mike Moffa, who later recalled the sessions. *"He knew how to box like a man."*[19] The Olympic Club came in first place for amateur boxing gyms in Quebec from 1982 to 1985.

Giovanni would often call the gym to confirm that his boys were attending. The pressure on Joe was relentless. Even Joe's coach, Dave Campanile, would try to conceal the location of the competitions so Giovanni would not attend. The loud and often intoxicated Giovanni frequently distracted Joe's performances. He would shout out instructions to Joe from the back of the gym.

Giovanni would disparagingly call Joe, *"Scrap,"* if he lost a fight. Joe felt that his father's barrage of insults made him lose confidence in himself. Joe recalled, *"Everything I did was wrong, 'You're no good. He's better than you.' When I lost he kept pushing, pushing, pushing."*[20] Many years later, one of Arturo's friends would say that Giovanni was also tough on Arturo. At home, Giovanni occasionally faked having a heart attack to get attention from Ida. Ida would tell the kids to ignore their father and go to bed.

Russ Anbar, president of Boxing Quebec, recalled the first time he saw a young 7-year-old Arturo at the Olympic Boxing Gym. *"You could see that he was so adept at what he was doing. He looked like a professional at that age. He turned out to be that good."*[21]

Joe recalled that the Hilton brothers also trained in the gym. *"Yes, they were there too. That's how I met them, but they were not there in the beginning. They were there towards the end. I was still young; I think 15, when they came around. They were off and on because they used to go to the Shamrock Gym. I used to look up to the Hiltons a little bit. I was an amateur. I'm a little kid, but then I started sparring and that was it.*

"My father bought me the best gloves. The best headgear. I started with the M & Ms, the red, no, that might have been Reyes. I ended up with Shevlins and Dave had these old gloves we used to spar with

at first. They had the horsehair inside that used to come out. These were hairy. There was hair inside and I put my [hands inside] ahhh!! What is that! [The liner] was ripped. I was dropping guys. I would drop more guys in the gym than the fights [laughs]. The horsehair inside the Shevlins were good. They were light and they were hard, but they hurt. I got hit with an uppercut a couple of times; they almost ripped my nose off."[22]

The Shevlin gloves that Joe was referring to were made in Queens, New York, by retired Police Detective Al Shevlin. Shevlin modeled his gloves after the Everlast boxing gloves of the 1960s. Al wanted to break into the boxing glove business, but no one would teach him. He decided to take apart a pair of old Everlast gloves and use them as a template for his own design. Al started his company in the basement of his home in the early 1970s. He would visit area gyms in New York to sell his gloves and other equipment. Shevlin was known for making top quality sparring gloves, headgear, cups, bag gloves and focus pads. Shevlin used thick leather and his equipment was known to last. Al would even make special gloves with a leather shell front and crocodile skin palm back.

Some of the world's top fighters used Shevlin equipment in the 1970s, including Larry Holmes and Roberto Duran. The most memorable thing about the Shevlin gloves was the padding. Al originally used horse hair, then later a synthetic horsehair material, that would spread out after continued use, leaving the knuckle area in the middle of the glove with very little padding. The padding would get very heavy from the sweat and moisture. This would turn the area around the fist into a veritable cast. The gloves were known as "brain scramblers." You were guaranteed to have bloody noses and wobbly knees in the gym when sparring with the Shevlin gloves.

When Arturo was 8 years old his father took him to the Gentile Café in Montreal's Little Italy section. His father would order a drink, stand Arturo on the seat of the chair, and proclaim to his friends, *"Here he is, look. Look at him closely. One day he will be a champion."*[23]

Joe reminisced on his amateur career, which included a gold medal at the Acropolis Cup in Greece. *"My first amateur fight, I think it was in the Hotel Lowes. Every month we fought there. I won like thirty fights in a row. In my amateur career I won, I think, four or five gold medals and golden gloves. Two silvers, one bronze, two nationals, one international. At the internationals, I took the Acropolis Cup, which put me in the trials for the Olympics in 88."*[24]

In the Greece tournament, the Acropolis Cup, Joe won every fight in his weight class and was voted the best fighter of the tournament. Joe was wearing headgear, but his opponents weren't. Each country had to follow its own amateur rules. Joe wound up losing in the Canadian National Championships to Olympian Howard Grant in the 139-pound weight class. Grant would advance to the World Championships and eventually represent Canada in the 1988 Olympics.

Joe described how his father would shout advice to him and Arturo when they trained and fought. *"My father's best thing was 'PSHHT! PSHHT! Joe! PSHHT!' With the left hook he used to go, 'AH SINISTRO!!!' [Sinistro means left in Italian] You know, in Italian, and he'd go like this, 'PSHHT!'"*[25]

While Joe's father made the sound, he would show the boys the proper way he wanted the left hook thrown. He would throw the left hook across his own body with his left hand. While he was throwing the punch across his body, Giovanni would smack the bottom of his left elbow upward with his right palm. By doing this he meant to relate to the boys that he wanted the arm in a horizontal posture while it was coming across the body. Thus, the famous Gatti left hook was born.

At home, Giovanni and Ida struggled to pay the bills and provide their five children with food. Although Gatti Electric was a thriving business, there were seven mouths to feed on a middle-class income, in addition to all the expenses of a large family. The Gattis lived like most Italian-Canadian families at the time. Joe described the food they ate. *"Pasta fazul. Pasta, steak, tripe. I couldn't stand tripe. My father liked it a lot. If there was one steak left, I got it."*[26]

Joe explained that his father would give him any extra food, especially steaks, to help Joe's strength when he fought. Years later it would be revealed how envious Joe's sisters were that he was given preferential treatment because he was a boxer. Joe explained, *"Everyone was jealous. I couldn't believe it. I was devastated. I [later] heard they hated me because I was spoiled."*[27] Giovanni would cut off pieces of his own steak for Joe, to help give him the strength to become a champion.

Did this preferential treatment, in the presence of Arturo, help to fuel Arturo's desire to be more successful as a boxer than his brother? Could this tension, early in life, have led to the brothers becoming estranged later in life? Did it cause Arturo to grow closer to his mother Ida? Years later, when Arturo became a world champion, some family members would proclaim that it was poetic justice that he became the champion instead of the Giovanni-favored Joe.

Giovanni was known to have a short temper, and he liked to drink alcohol. When the two were mixed together, Giovanni's temper could be explosive. Neighborhood children were not allowed in the Gatti home, so his outbursts were mostly contained within the immediate family. Giovanni's weapon of choice when he became enraged was a strip of thick gauge electrical wire. Two-year-old Arturo was whipped on his shoulders for spilling water. Giovanni believed he was "educating," not beating, his children. Giovanni would whip Joe and Arturo for not jogging properly. After Giovanni beat Joe, he would make Joe run through the neighborhood without a shirt on to show the neighbors that he had been punished for doing wrong. Ida was not exempt from the beatings, as she also suffered at the hands of her husband.

Giovanni was known as a womanizer. Ida would spend her time inspecting his clothing for traces of perfume or hair follicles from other women. This behavior only led to Giovanni and the entire family being "on edge" while awaiting the next explosive outburst. Although Giovanni rarely exposed his temper in public, he was known to display his aggressive behavior at the Olympic Athletic Club if Joe and Arturo were not training or sparring to his satisfaction.

Giovanni often would start his day with cognac-infused coffee or a beer. You could count on one hand the amount of times that Giovanni was not in an intoxicated state. Joe recalled when he and his sister, Giuseppina, who was nicknamed Pina, were sent to the store for a loaf of bread. They took their time returning to the house, enjoying the freedom of being outside. Upon arriving home, Giovanni proceeded to beat Joe with a belt. Giovanni would force the children to hold out their hands as though they were going to be handed something. Giovanni would then whip the leather belt across the palms of their hands. Once, Pina refused to hold out her hands and was thrown across her bedroom as a result. Young Arturo, even if not subject to the beatings himself, must have been affected by the violence he witnessed his siblings receiving.

The day after the bread incident, Giovanni, still angry, tied Joe and Pina to the back porch. He forced them to kneel on pebbles for hours. Pina would start crying for mercy, but Joe silenced her by reminding Pina that cries of pain would only lead to them staying tied up longer.

Christmas in the Gatti house was filled with mixed emotions. Pina recalled, *"Without exaggeration, we have never known one happy Christmas."*[28] Each Christmas would start rather well, until it was ruined by Giovanni's drinking. The tradition of family dysfunction at Christmas-time continued even after Giovanni's death. Christmas for the Gatti kids was much different than at most homes. They did not receive the gifts that most children did. They received shoes or clothing that they needed instead of toys. Most of the clothing was sewn by their mother, who was a seamstress.

The Gatti kids were controlled with an iron fist by their father. A strict curfew was in place, if and when the children were allowed out at all. This type of environment restricted the friends that the Gatti kids had. When Giovanni had guests over he would make his three daughters, Anna-Maria, Pina, and Mirella, lace on sparring gloves and spar with Joe. He did this to show his company just how sharp Joe was becoming with his boxing technique. Giovanni's dream was to have a world champion boxer in his family.

Giovanni often would relate stories of his childhood in Italy to his children. He told his children that he had knocked out a mule in his youth. When Joe and Arturo were alone they would laugh at their father's apparently fabricated story.

On June 20, 1980, the Gatti brothers' hometown was treated to "big-time" boxing. Roberto Duran 71-1 (57 KOs) faced "Sugar" Ray Leonard, 27-0 (18 KOs), at the Olympic Stadium in a welterweight showdown. Duran defeated Leonard in an action-packed superfight to take Leonard's WBC title. On the undercard, Toronto light heavyweight "Hurricane" Eddie Melo 20-3 (18 KOs) fought to a draw with Fernand Marcotte 47-10-3 (32 KOs). Melo had eight first-round knockouts in his career. Arturo admired Melo when he was growing up. Arturo explained, *"I used to watch Eddie Melo. Somebody told me that I reminded them of Eddie Melo, the way I fight."*[29] Melo was a heavy puncher with a dynamite left hook.

One hot summer day, Giovanni was upset with Joe. He forced Joe to run behind his car for the 10-mile ride to the boxing gym. Arturo smiled at Joe from the back seat of the car. Joe gave Arturo the finger. Arturo tried as best as he could to contain his laughter. To tease Joe, Arturo picked up a bottle of water and with his best Hollywood impression started drinking it as though it was the most refreshing liquid on earth. Sweat was pouring down Joe's face as he tried to keep up with the car. Arturo couldn't contain himself and let out a laugh. Giovanni turned to Arturo and smacked him in the face. *"Oh, you think it's funny? You go out and run with him."*[30] The door swung open and Joe and Arturo were dripping sweat together as they ran behind their father's car.

On September 15, 1980, at the age of 8, Arturo shared the stage with the Hilton brothers. As he later recalled, *"I fought in the Paul Sauvé Arena... where the Hilton brothers fought... All five Hilton brothers were on that card. I boxed a special exhibition... People were very impressed. I wish I had the tape. After the fight I was the talk of the gym."* Arturo later embellished that there were *"twenty thousand people"* at the event. Arturo weighed in at only 45-pounds for the exhibition match against Eric Huard. The Arena packed in over 6,000 fans for the Quebec versus United States event. Arturo already was dreaming big. *"I always wanted to be a world champion since I was eight. I also wanted to be a professional soccer player."* Arturo and Huard would box two times at that age, with the second contest taking place in Valleyfield, Quebec. Huard recalled Arturo as being *"a very good boxer."*[31]

In 1980, Anna-Maria Gatti and Davey Hilton Jr. grew attracted to each other. Anna-Maria was forced to take her younger brothers to the gym. In doing so she would frequently see Davey when he trained at the Olympic Gym. Anna-Maria had many other things she would have liked to do instead of take her brothers to the gym, but she had no choice. Both Anna-Maria and Davey Jr. were 17 years old at the time. They would be married two years later, on April 17, 1982.

As Joe gained experience and added more amateur titles to his resume, the dream that he would one day become a world champion boxer became a real possibility. Joe had developed fast footwork and hand speed to go along with his powerful left hook. Arturo, on the other hand, was less polished and more of a rugged, aggressive type fighter.

In amateur boxing, when fighters are between the ages of 8 and 15, it is nearly impossible to gauge if the boxer might one day become a successful professional. The two biggest "acid tests" that a boxer must pass to be successful on a professional level are the ability to take a punch and punching power. Both of these qualities cannot be accurately gauged at an early age because the boxers haven't yet, or are just starting to, go through puberty.

When a boxer competes at the adult, open class, amateur level, it becomes clearer if the athlete has some professional potential. Open class is the title designated to boxers who reach a certain experience level of ten bouts or more. Prior to reaching this level they are designated as novice boxers. Even attaining many open-class national titles, however, is no guarantee of professional success, as several important changes occur when amateur boxers turn professional.

The professional debutant must box without a headgear, which exposes the boxer to harder impacts to the temple area. The lack of headgear also exposes the fighter to head-butts, as well as exposing the eyebrow bones. If a boxer has "soft skin" and is susceptible to swelling or cutting this will be exposed with the headgear off.

The gloves that are used are smaller in weight, from 12 ounces to 10 ounces for super welterweights and above, and from 10 ounces to 8 ounces for boxers weighing 147-pounds or less. The padding is more evenly distributed throughout the professional glove, whereas the amateur glove has a majority of the padding located in front of the knuckle area. These changes greatly impact the power of a blow.

The smaller gloves, coupled with the ability to utilize much more gauze on the hands, leads to the exposure of a "glass jaw" rather quickly in the pros. It is not uncommon in pro debuts to see world-class amateurs, who were never hurt before, have their knees buckled and occasionally even get knocked down.

Giovanni believed in both of his sons' potentials. He would proudly proclaim to friends and neighbors that his sons would be champions of the world someday.

The Gatti children were proficient in several languages; including French, Italian, and English, but they were required to use Italian when speaking to their parents at home.

Both Gatti brothers were considered open-class level boxers very early in their careers, as they were piling up bouts at very early ages. Giovanni discouraged Joe from participating in others sports as a child. Joe recalled, *"[I played] a little bit of hockey, but I never joined the team. I wasn't able to. I had to go from school to the gym. I remember one time I wanted to play football in high school. I needed to be 112-pounds with the equipment. I was not heavy enough [laughs]."*[32] Arturo, however, was allowed to play organized soccer.

Although Joe was considered the favorite in his father's eyes, and he benefited from this position, he was also held to a higher standard in regards to his boxing achievements. Joe couldn't fail. He had to win. He had to become a champion. There was a question as to whether Joe would have even taken up boxing at all if his father hadn't pushed him. Joe wasn't considered a "tough" kid around the gym. He was, as his former stablemate Pietro Napolitano recalled, *"a playboy."*[33] Most fighters would proudly display their battle marks after sparring. As a pro, years later, Joe carried a blow-dryer in his gym bag and would style his hair after sparring sessions. Joe felt pressure at home as well as at the gym. Family members, including his mother, appeared jealous of his relationship with his father.

Joe loved music. He would listen to the Beatles, Barry White, Engelbert Humperdink, and Tom Jones. Not only would he listen, he would sing along as well. Arturo loved the same music as his older brother.

Giovanni's favorite fighters were Ray "Boom-Boom" Mancini, Roberto Duran, Vito Antuefermo, Danny "Little Red" Lopez, "Sugar" Ray Leonard and Giovanni "Nino" Benvenuti. Joe admired the same fighters that his father did.

In 1982, the Gatti family returned to Italy to visit friends and relatives. Joe relates an incident that occurred on the trip. On the way to Italy, Giovanni again reminisced about his knocking out a mule. *"We were laughing about it and I was like, 'Yeah ok, you knocked out a mule.' And we were in Italy on a trip and this guy comes out and we were by the bar. We were kids and [the bartender was] like, 'Whose these kids?' [A guy sitting at the bar] was like, 'That's Johnny Gatti's kids.'"*[34] The bartender looked at the man with a puzzled expression while shrugging his shoulders. He still did not know who the man was talking about. Joe continued, *"[The man replied], 'Gatti! Gatti! The guy who knocked out the mule!' Then me and my brother, we were looking at each other [with eyes and mouths wide open]. Oh shit, it's true! I was 15 and he was 10."*[35]

Arturo started competing in organized hockey at the age of 10 and he would continue participating in the sport for the next 7 years. Arturo played the forward position and would later reveal that he never got into a fight while competing on the ice.

In 1983, at the age of 16, Joe Gatti won the Junior Championships in Quebec. In the same year, Arturo landed his first job, part-time, in a supermarket's fruit-and-vegetable department. Arturo was 11 years old. Although he was known as Arturo by his family at home and by his stablemates in the boxing gym, to his friends, including his best friend Christen Santos, he simply was known as Arthur.

Arturo already was known to be a wise guy and a troublemaker.

He would confront older kids and then run home to get Joe. Joe was only 112-pounds, but he would beat up anyone who picked on his little brother. The brothers would sneak to a public pool when their father wasn't around. At the pool, kids teased Arturo by telling him that his brother Joe was a fish. This was because Joe spent many hours in the water. Arturo ran home one day to get Joe because the kids wouldn't stop teasing him about his "fish" brother. Joe came back and lit up the kids who were teasing Arturo. After Joe had pummeled one of the kids against a fence, little 11-year-old Arturo jumped in and finished the kid off with a few parting blows.

The brothers found many ways to excite themselves. Joe enjoyed jumping ramps with BMX bicycles. Joe decided it was boring just jumping the ramps, so he asked Arturo to lay sideways in front of the ramp. After easily jumping over Arturo, Joe had Arturo turn length wise, with his head furthest from the ramp. The fearless Arturo obliged and Joe jumped over his brother, landing inches from Arturo's head. Giovanni would have been outraged if he knew what Joe was doing.

The French and Italian kids would often rumble in school. For the most part, though, Joe and Arturo kept out of the fights because they had both Italian and French friends.

Chapter 3
The Fighting Hilton Brothers

Although Joe and Arturo were outstanding amateurs in Canada, they were not the biggest or the most famous boxing family there. That status was held by the Hilton boxing family, which was led by their father Davey Hilton Sr., a former professional boxer who competed from 1958 to 1976. Hilton Sr. won the featherweight and junior middleweight Canadian titles in a career that saw him compile a 67-16 record with 49 knockouts. The Hilton family's fighting history predated Hilton Sr. His father and grandfather had participated in bareknuckle and gloved matches throughout Canada.

Davey Hilton Sr. was father to five boys, all of whom competed as amateur boxers. Davey Jr. was born in 1963, Alex followed in 1964, Matthew was born in 1965, Stewart in 1968, and Jimmy in 1971. The Hiltons arguably were one of the most successful amateur boxing families of all time. Davey compiled an amateur record of 133-2. Matthew's amateur record was an outstanding one of 108-0. Alex held an amateur record of 104-1. Stewart's amateur record was 60-7. Jimmy rounded out the brothers with an amateur record of 6-1. The brothers held a combined amateur mark of 411-11.

With all of their accolades, none of the Hilton brothers would compete for the Canadian Olympic boxing team. Davey Jr. and Stewart turned professional when they were 17 years old. Alex and Matthew turned pro at the age of 18. Jimmy was the only brother who would not box professionally, but he would go on to open his own boxing gym in 2014 called Team Hilton. The Canadian Olympic boxing team has had only one Olympic gold medalist in its history: Lennox Lewis. Lewis won the super heavyweight title while representing Canada in the 1988 Olympic Games in Seoul, South Korea. Being an Olympic boxer in Canada apparently does not hold the same earnings potential that it does in England or the United States.

Like the Gatti brothers, the Hiltons also had a father who would spare no expense to support his sons' boxing careers'. While the Gatti boys would travel to the fights in their father's red 'Gatti Electric' van, the Hiltons traveled from show to show in a trailer that the family owned. Matthew recalled, *"We'd travel all over Canada to amateur boxing tournaments in that trailer of Dad's. We'd travel hundreds of miles in a day just to get to a tournament. The trailer was big enough for just two beds. Mom and Dad would be in one, and all five brothers would be in the other. Mom cooked meals on a hot plate."*[36]

On Sunday, August 9, 1981, CBS televised a 10-round junior middleweight bout between Roberto Duran, 72-2 (57 KOs), and Bayonne N.J.'s Mike "Nino" Gonzalez, 24-1 (13 KOs). Nine months earlier, Duran had lost his WBC title to Ray Leonard in the famous "No Mas" rematch fight when Duran quit in the 8th round. The Duran-Gonzalez match was being held in Cleveland, Ohio and was promoted by Don King Promotions. Gonzalez' purse was $50,000 for the match, while Duran earned approximately $150,000.

Gonzalez was trained and managed by Bob Rooney Sr. and assisted by 71-year-old Carl Duva. Duva was a former professional boxer who compiled a 44-9-4 record as a middleweight from 1930 to 1940. Duva had made the Duran match. Carl was the brother of Lou Duva. Carl started Lou in boxing at the age of 10. Lou would have a 6-10-1 record as a middleweight. Duran was scheduled to fight a different opponent, but when that fight fell apart, Gonzalez was selected as the fill-in.

Matchmaker Don Elbaum recalled that Gonzalez was selected because *"he was the cheapest fight out there."*[37] Gonzalez had been offered $40,000 to take on Wilfredo Benitez for the WBC 154-pound title, but he turned down that offer because Don King offered him $10,000 more to fight Duran. Gonzalez had sparred with Duran and had a photo of him hanging in his house. Carl Duva stated, *"We were offered $40,000 for Benitez, so what am I crazy? Take less money to go 15 rounds with a guy who's also 22 and stronger or go 10 rounds with an old man? The thing was I know Nino's got Duran's picture on his wall so I asked him, 'Now you and Duran are friends, are you willing to fight him?' And he says, 'Carl, he's in my way, he's got to go.'"*[38]

Watching the Gonzalez-Duran bout in his hometown of Jersey City was Mario Costa, a man who eventually would become deeply involved with the Gattis' careers. Gonzalez lost a close, hard-fought decision to Duran. Costa was so impressed with the way Gonzalez fought, he decided to get involved with Nino's career. *"I saw the fight with [Nino and] Duran and I just thought Nino was a real good fighter from a small town. I managed Nino. I don't think I had it on paper. I might have had it on paper, but I never took no money. I managed Nino after the Duran fight. And still today, he sees me today, I'm like his dad."*[39] Costa was introduced to Gonzalez through Tony DiGilio. Tony's brother, John, was a former Bayonne boxer and also a "made man" in the Genovese crime family.

Gonzalez wanted to quit boxing after the Duran fight. He voiced his displeasure at his take-home cut from the match. Costa talked him into continuing. Costa assured Gonzalez that he would not take any money from Nino's purses. If his manager took his 33% and his trainer 10% that would have left Nino with only $28,500, before taxes, for the Duran fight. Costa recalled that Gonzalez was surrounded by mobsters, such as John DeGilio, at the time.

Costa wanted to change Gonzalez's direction. He hired a new trainer. Costa had been introduced to former middleweight champion Vito Antuofermo. Antuofermo was being trained by Carlos "Panama" Lewis at the time. Costa met Lewis through Antuofermo and asked him to train Gonzalez. After taking over Gonzalez's career, Costa opened the Ringside Gym in New York City. Panama Lewis started training Gonzalez at the gym, which was located at 40th Street and 8th Avenue. Costa owned the gym from 1983 to 1985.

Besides running a gym, Costa owned the White Mana Diner and the Ringside Lounge, which were both located in Jersey City. Costa purchased the White Mana in 1979 and the Ringside Lounge in 1982. Tony DiGilio frequented the Ringside Lounge.

There were those in the Hudson County boxing community who thought that John DiGilio was responsible for Bayonne fighters getting big fights on Don King's Cleveland cards. Gonzalez's fight against Duran and Chuck Wepner's fight against Ali were two of the examples cited. However, both Don Elbaum and trainer Tommy Gallagher believed that trainer/manager Al Braverman was the person who secured the Ali fight for Wepner as Braverman had a longstanding relationship with King. Elbaum, a close associate of Don King, recalled that both Gonzalez and Wepner were selected because they were "low-cost, low-risk" matches.

On June 1, 1984, "Nino" Gonzalez traveled up to Montreal to take on 11-0 (9 KOs) Matthew Hilton. Gonzalez was only 5-3-1 since the Duran loss. Still, Gonzalez was considered Hilton's toughest test to date. The 5'8" Gonzalez, who had started his career at junior lightweight, captured the N.J. welterweight title in 1979 with a 5th round knockout over Paterson N.J.'s Joe Grier.

Matthew Hilton had just defeated Reggie Ford of Guyana by 1st round knockout in Quebec City on April 30. Ford, although 10-14-1 going into the bout, had lost seven fights in a row.

Accompanying Gonzalez on the trip, and working his corner were Carl Duva, and his new manager, Mario Costa. Gonzalez had split with Bob Rooney Sr. over what he claimed were *"personal reasons."*

The Hilton-Gonzalez bout was the main event on the Montreal Forum card. After the main event ended, the Ray-Mancini-Livingstone Bramble and Johnny Bumphus-Gene Hatcher championship fights would be shown via closed circuit TV from Buffalo, New York. Bramble and Bumphus were both managed and trained by Carl Duvas' brother, Lou. Before the fight, Mario Costa called the "Nino" Gonzalez-Matthew Hilton match *"child abuse,"* because of the vast experience the 25-year-old Gonzalez held over the 18-year-old Hilton.[40] Hilton had only 11 fights and had never been past 6 rounds in a match. Gonzalez had been stopped by future world champion Duane Thomas a year prior, but Costa countered that Gonzalez was standing when that bout was stopped.

Hilton spoke of the importance of the Gonzalez match. *"He has the experience I need to go up against. It's going to be a tough fight. I have no choice but to fight a smart fight. A win means a big boost to my career and that's how I'm looking at it. I know I really have to prove myself for the first time."*[41] Gonzalez was hoping a win would put him in line for a fight with either Mark Medal or Alex Hilton.

Matthew Hilton defeated Gonzalez by 8th round knockout. He landed a short right hand in the 8th that dropped Gonzalez for the count. Matthew described the moment. *"I heard his corner yelling at him, 'Double jab him and then hook him with the right!' I told myself, 'That's a good idea. I'm gonna beat him to it.' That's what I did and he went down. That's the first time I've ever taken a guy out with my right hand."*[42]

After the win, Matthew had 107 knockouts in 118 pro and amateur fights combined. He had yet to lose a bout. Matthew was known for his powerful left hook that was taught to him by his father. Gonzalez would carry a reminder of Hilton's power, as he later recalled, *"He chipped two of my teeth in that fight."*[43]

Mario Costa was mesmerized by Matthew's punching power. Costa recalled the fight, and meeting a young amateur. *"It all started on June 1, 1984 in Montreal. I brought Nino Gonzalez to box Matthew Hilton. Also part of the Hilton team, as a sparring partner, was Joe Gatti. After the fight they all came to New Jersey at my invite. Joe introduced me to Arthur, who was 12 years old. I'll never forget those eyes, like two shining stars. He'd always follow me around at the fights and say, 'Please take me to America when I am old enough.'"*[44]

Costa was sold on Matthew's abilities due in part to comments that "Nino" Gonzalez made to him after the match. Costa recalled, *"After Matthew knocked Nino out I was in the ring. And Nino, right in the ring, says, 'Bro, he hits harder than Duran.' And Nino wasn't bullshit. Nino was a tough kid. So I go up to the Hiltons' father and I said, 'Listen, we came here to beat your son. We didn't come here to take a dive or get beat up. We came here to beat your son up. And Nino just told me your son hits harder than Duran. So if you want to come to America I'll help you.' One week, two weeks, the whole family was here [in Jersey City]. He fought Nino June 1, 1984. We were back in Canada July 10, 1984. We went back and fought a kid from my gym [Ronald Thermidor]."*[45]

Costa invited Davey Hilton Sr. and his sons to come live with him in Jersey City and train in his gym in Manhattan. Davey Sr. accepted the invitation and brought his wife and family to Jersey City the week after the Gonzalez fight.

Around the same time, 12-year-old Arturo suffered his first broken hand, in an amateur fight. When asked years later, after retiring, his earliest memory of boxing, Arturo would recall the broken hand, stating that he was *"very young, twelve,"* when the injury occurred. It would not, however, be the worst injury Arturo suffered that year as Gatti explained, *"Dislocated right shoulder. Happened... on a sled... doing jumps off ramps. Swollen pretty bad. The doctor didn't know what it was. Finally, a lady cracked my arm, twisted my arm three different ways. I passed out it was so painful."*[46]

Arturo's childhood heroes were Wayne Gretzky and Muhammad Ali. Describing Gretzky, Arturo stated, *"Just a simple guy, but he was a great hockey player. You wouldn't think he was as great as he was by just looking at him."* Arturo liked to watch certain fighters. *"Before I used to watch Roberto Duran, the movement, punches he threw. Ray Leonard, his movement, his intelligence. Julio Cesar Chavez, I like the guys I think I fight like. Take tips from them. Alexis Arguello. Aaron Pryor. 'Boom-Boom' Mancini."* Arturo's all-time favorite fighter was Roberto Duran, *"because I resembled him, I think, as a young kid."*[47]

Costa was a soccer player in school and didn't get involved in boxing until meeting "Nino" Gonzalez. *"I was helping the amateur kids in Jersey City and Bayonne PAL's Bob Rooney."*[48] Costa teamed up with New York's Jimmy Glenn, who ran a Gym on 42nd Street in Manhattan. Glenn, born in 1949, mentored Costa with his over thirty years of experience in the game. Glenn was a trainer and a cutman. He had worked with the likes of Floyd Patterson, Terrance Alli, and Howard Davis Jr.

Costa became good friends with Mike Tyson through the Hiltons as he explained. *"After the fight with Matthew the Hiltons lived here. They stayed here five years. And that's how Arthur and Joe came; first Joe. Davey Hilton was married to Joe's sister, Anna-Maria. Anna-Maria lived over here too. So they came over here with Matthew. I was a little closer with Matthew, and he was Mike's favorite. Matthew and David, they were always close friends with Mike [Tyson]. So one Sunday, here in the White Manor, Matthew says, 'Mario can we take a ride up to the Catskills.' 'Catskills!' I said, 'What are you fuckin' crazy, that's like two or three hours from here! Matt,' I said, 'You want to go to the Catskills?' He said, 'Yes.' He says, 'I used to live there and I want to go say hello to Camille Ewald [the owner of the house Tyson lived in].' And I said, 'Tyson?' He said, 'Yeah, I was there.' I didn't know. I didn't have no fucking idea.*

"In the beginning, Matthew fought on Mike's undercard because it was under Don King. The night that Mike became the youngest champion we was in the ring before Mike. I was walking out, they were coming in, at the Hilton, and I said to Matthew, 'I'm gonna walk Mike to the ring.' And I walked to the ring with them. And I stayed back in the corner. I knew Mike since I went to the Catskills. I became real close to Camille Ewald. That was his [adoptive] mom. I went to the funeral. I knew Mike the same time, since '84 when I started with Matthew. That's how far back I go."^{49} Mike Tyson would become so close to Costa that Mario let him build a pigeon coop on the roof of his bar.

Costa recalled Tyson asking him for a special request. *"Mike Tyson thought Nino was great. One day Mike was here and Mike goes to me, 'Mario, you know a fighter named Nino Gonzalez?' I said, 'Yes Mike, I know a fighter named Nino Gonzalez.' 'Can you please call him. Tell him to come here?' I said, 'Okay champ.' So I called Nino. I said, 'Nino, come over here. Mike wants to see you.' I didn't know anything. Nino didn't know nothing either. So Nino comes with his girl. So we're coming back from the pigeons and Nino's out front on the sidewalk. Mike gives him a hug like he really, really knew him. Never met him before. So Mike goes, 'I'm gonna tell you something.*

I was a young kid. I don't know 14 or 15. I was living in the Catskills with Cus D'Amato. Cus said to me, 'I want you to watch the fight with me tomorrow. I thought he meant that he wanted me to watch Duran. Because I loved Duran. That was like one of my idols. So Cus said to me, 'I want you to watch this Puerto Rican kid from Bayonne, Nino. He has a heart like a lion.' So Cus and Mike sat and watched the fight. And Cus liked Nino because of the body, remember Nino always went to the body. Before he went to the head, he went to the body. And Cus said, 'I want you to go to the body too.' Cus liked the style. He was very rough, Nino. And he'd never take a step back. Always putting the guy on the ropes and banging the shit out of the guy. And Cus said, 'I want you to watch this kid. He's got a heart like a lion.' And every time he sees Nino now he comes up to him."[50]

Jersey City was and still is an immigrant community. The city is the second-most populated in the state behind Newark. The city is broken down into several sections. The "Marion Section," where the Ringside Lounge is located, is made up mostly of Caucasian and Hispanic working-class residents. The "Marion Section" bordered the "Heights" to the north and the "Westside" to the south. The "Marion Section" got its name from the old Marion Hotel.

Other sections include "Downtown" and "Greenville." The "Downtown" section, by the waterfront, is made up mostly of white-collar residents who are New York business and art professionals. This section has a New York "Village" feel to it. Downtown has direct access to New York through the Holland Tunnel and is basically an extension of the Hoboken residential area. The "Greenville" section is made up mostly of African-Americans and includes some very tough, crime-ridden areas around Martin Luther King, Jr. Drive.

The "Greenville Section" was home to the Jersey City Recreation boxing gym, Dupree's Boxing World, founded by former light heavyweight contender Jimmy "The Cat" Dupree. The "Greenville Section" borders the heavily Polish- and Caucasian-populated Bayonne.

Bayonne is home to former heavyweight contender Charles "Chuck" Wepner, who was affectionately known as the "Bayonne Bleeder" for his blood-spilling ring encounters.

Jersey City and Bayonne were tough, urban areas. The New York City skyline overshadows the area, as it is directly across the Hudson River to the east. Bob Rooney Sr., Gonzalez's former manager, had been an assistant trainer and chief sparring partner for Chuck Wepner when he fought Muhammad Ali for the heavyweight title in 1975.

Back in Montreal, in early 1985, Joe Gatti went on a wild tear, disappearing from his family for months. Giovanni had made a terrible error in trusting Davey Jr. to chaperone Joe around. Davey introduced Joe to the club scene, drug parties, and bars. Joe started running the streets with Davey and boxer Serge Cusson. Joe and Serge were much wilder than both Davey and Arturo ever would be. Joe slept in motels and had no trouble wooing the women at the clubs. Joe already had been labeled as a boxing prospect in Canada, so finding drugs and women was very easy. When Joe finally decided to return home, he was shocked at what he found. A new family was moving into the Gatti home. Giovanni had sold the house and moved the family to another location. When Joe finally tracked his family down, he expected a near-death beating from his father. To Joe's surprise, Giovanni didn't say a word about Joe's disappearance. Giovanni's lack of anger shocked and puzzled Joe. Soon after, Joe left Montreal for Jersey City to spar with Matthew Hilton.

After Matthew reconnected with Tyson in the Catskills, he traveled with Joe Gatti, Davey Sr., and Mario Costa to Cus D'Amato's gym in Catskill, New York. Joe was Matthew's main sparring partner. Matthew, 19-0, had just defeated Vito Antuofermo on October 20, 1985 by 4th round retirement in Montreal. The 32-year-old Antuofermo, who held the WBA and WBC middleweight titles from 1979 to 1980, retired after the loss.

Matthew was preparing for a bout against Wilfredo Benitez on February 15, 1986. The fight would be held in Montreal. Benitez, 49-4-1 with 30 KOs, was a three-division champion. Benitez had won his first world title at the age of 17. The 5'10" Benitez, still only 27 years old, had only been stopped twice, by "Sugar" Ray Leonard and Davey Moore. Benitez would have a 2½-inch height advantage over Hilton. Benitez had trained in the Catskills, and Hilton may have been trying to get "inside information" on how to beat him.

Davey Jr. and Matthew started utilizing the D'Amato peek-a-boo style. Jimmy Ellis, former WBA heavyweight champion, was brought on board to train Matthew. Although only 5'7½" in height, Matthew was known for his aggressive style behind a crushing left hook. Joe Gatti reminisced about his first visit to the Catskills in late 1985. *"When D'Amato passed away I went there and that's when I met Mike [Tyson] and we were watching Mike's fights.*"[51]

Tyson was climbing the heavyweight ladder at the time as a young 19-year-old, with a record of 13-0, with all 13 wins by knockout. While at the Catskills, Joe Gatti grew closer to Mario Costa. Mario was a huge fan of Matthew's. As Joe described, *"Mario loved the Hiltons, especially Matthew. He spent so much money on these guys, you have no idea, and never got nothing back. He helped them... He got Matthew Hilton to fight for the championship."*[52]

Joe and Mario would become good friends. Anna-Maria had moved down to Jersey City with Davey Hilton. Arturo came down in 1985 to visit his sister. It was his first visit to Jersey City.

In December 1985, in New Jersey, the State Commission of Investigations or SCI, recommended that professional boxing be abolished in New Jersey. Main Events boxing promotional company president Dan Duva responded, *"They are discriminating against boxing. It is an inflammatory report designed to make headlines. In eight years of promoting fights, I have never seen any evidence of anyone allegedly connected to organized crime having any influence in boxing. In the last eight years, there have been jockeys convicted of wrongdoing in the participation of their sport. We've had two major college basketball scandals involving players. Baseball players have admitted to drug use. To my knowledge, in that time, no fight manager, boxer, trainer, or state official has been accused or convicted of any crime in participation of the sport. Their statement on organized crime having undue influence in boxing is absolutely false. It is totally incorrect. Why are they picking on boxing? There are 10 times more injuries in football, even at the high school level. If a boxer in New Jersey is knocked out, he cannot resume physical activity by law for 60 days. And then he must take a brain scan before he's allowed back in the ring. In football, a high school quarterback can get knocked out and the coach could put him back into the game three plays later. What's the difference? A knockout is a knockout.*

"Boxers in the State of New Jersey are examined before and after every fight. They have to pass physicals. On any given Sunday, if you gave physicals to both teams playing at Giants Stadium, a large percentage wouldn't be able to pass. It comes down to a moral judgment. They're saying football is okay, but boxing isn't. I don't think a state legislator should be able to say, 'I don't like that sport, so you're not going to be able to take part in it.' This report will get headlines. But when the legislators take the time to study it, they will

find there is not much substance to it. They said in the report that boxing produced 'no viable social or economic benefits.' It provides the same things that other sports do. It gives athletes a chance to earn an income. It brings revenue to an area and it gives entertainment to fans. Who are the SCI to say it's okay to entertain with football and not boxing?"[53]

The recommendation was brought on by a 137-page report by the SCI called "Organized Crime in Boxing." The report stated that organized crime had an "undue influence" on the sport and the commission called boxing "legal savagery." The SCI, which was created in 1968 to oversee organized crime and corruption, planned on asking the N.J. State Legislature to abolish the sport in New Jersey.

Boxer Bobby Czyz commented, *"That stuff about organized crime, that was gone years ago. That was in the thirties and forties. That makes no sense now. Nobody throws fights anymore. How many football players receive serious injuries every year? We're talking about paralysis, knee injuries, concussions, broken bones. But it would be unpopular to ban 'Monday Night Football.' Something like 87 people were killed hang-gliding last year. It would take a century of boxing to kill that many people. If boxing was abolished it would just be forced out of state. Millions of dollars would be lost. If it ever became a federal law, boxing would just go underground, bare-knuckle boxing. In the end, I think in this case, the public will just bury this [report]."*[54]

By May 1986 no action had been taken on the report. Those who supported boxing did so because the sport brought tax revenue into the state, and it gave urban youth a positive alternative to the streets. Former light heavyweight champion and N.Y. State Athletic Commissioner Jose Torres remarked, *"It's hard for other people to understand that fighters come from areas like Bedford-Stuyvesant, Harlem, Elizabeth, Paterson, and Newark. What options do they have? Drugs, alcohol, gangs, and the boxing gym. Boxing has to be the best option. You learn through boxing's hard work and discipline that there is another side of life. Boxing saves lives."*[55]

The SCI report disagreed with Torres' assessment. *"Some journalists have defended boxing on the grounds that people have the right to choose their destiny. Not exactly. Society has the right to set some rules. When a man dangles from a window ledge, the police try to pull him back. We don't let promoters sell tickets in the street below. If the same mob presence we have found in boxing existed, for example, in professional baseball or football, it would constitute a massive public scandal. The Commission believes that no truly viable social or economic benefits can be derived from such legal savagery. Too many boxers retire as physical or mental derelicts.*"[56]

The report targeted several promoters and managers by name; including promoter Carlo Dee and manager Al Certo. The report claimed that Dee was a close friend of an alleged Lucchese crime family associate, Andrew Licari. The report further claimed that Licari and Andrew Dembrowski paid Bobby Czyz Sr. $300,000 for a piece of Bobby Czyz Jr.'s management contract. The pair were allegedly guaranteed 26% of Czyz's earnings up until November of 1985 and 5% thereafter up until 1991. Lou Duva was the manager of record for Czyz.

Dan Duva added, *"If [Giants quarterback] Phil Simms was knocked out in the first quarter, he would be looked at on the sidelines and would be back in the game in the third quarter. The fans would cheer. If Larry Holmes gets knocked out, he can't get back into the ring for 60 days... There have been a lot of misconceptions developed by the press accounts of the SCI report. The Atlantic City casinos are very sensitive to those kinds of [organized crime influence] accusations. The casinos aren't anti-boxing, but they have become cautious about boxing."*[57]

The American Medical Association, or AMA, stated that 87% of professional fighters suffered chronic brain damage due to boxing. The American Association of Neurological Surgeons, or AAN, added that continued blows to the head were likely to lead to long-term brain injuries. The head of the AAN, Doctor Nelson Richards, stated, *"To call something a sport, where the best intention is a knockout, is wrong. It's barbaric. It's just not a sport. It's just something terrible."*[58]

Jose Torres countered, *"In the last three years, New York has examined 300 fighters who had been knocked out and none of them had any significant head injuries. Name me one fighter who is punch-drunk from boxing. Rocky Graziano? He makes $1 million a year talking like that. Anybody who knew Graziano before he was a boxer will tell you that he talked worse than that before he was a fighter."*[59]

Although few people actually believed boxing would be outlawed, many did believe more restrictions would be put in place that could strangle the sport. The SCI wanted to require promoters who worked in Atlantic City to have a casino vendors license which would guarantee a thorough criminal background check.

New Jersey boxing commissioner Larry Hazzard opined, *"Certain health and safety aspects must be addressed, but boxing should not be outlawed. Boxing has been around for more than 100 years and I have the greatest confidence it will be around for another 100 years."*[60]

On February 15, 1986 in Montreal, Matthew Hilton knocked out Wilfredo Benitez in the 9th round. Joe Gatti returned to Montreal with the Hiltons. Matthew, who had turned pro in the welterweight class, was now competing in the junior middleweight division. Joe was boxing in the welterweight class and regularly sparred with Matthew in the mid and late 1980s.

On November 22, 1986, the Gattis' and Hiltons' good friend, Mike Tyson, won the WBC heavyweight title when he knocked out Trevor Berbick in the 2nd round in Las Vegas. He became the youngest heavyweight champion of all time with his victory. Matthew fought on the undercard, knocking out Franklin Owens in the 2nd round for his 24th straight victory as a pro. Within a year, the 20-year-old Tyson would add the WBA and IBF titles to his ledger.

On April 29, 1987, at the Paul Suave Arena in Montreal, 146-pound Joe Gatti turned professional, with a 2nd round knockout of James McNee, 3-1, of Toronto. Joe's trainer was Davey Hilton Sr. In the co-main event of that card, 162-pound Matthew Hilton scored a 2nd round knockout over Muhammad Eltassi. The victory put Matthew, now 26-0 (21 KOs), in line for a shot at the IBF junior middleweight title.

Matthew would become the first Hilton brother to fight for and win a world title, when he defeated Buster Drayton for the IBF junior middleweight title on June 27, 1987 in Montreal. The fight was named "TV Fight of the Year" by *KO* magazine. Matthew became the first Canadian born boxer to win a world title since the 1940s.

On the undercard of the Hilton title fight, in his second professional bout, 148½-pound Joe Gatti defeated debuting Joe Doby by knockout in the 2nd round of a scheduled 4-round contest. Joe would not fight for another year, as he struggled with his identity. He had dreams of becoming an electrical engineer, but was forced to abandon those dreams to help with the family business when his father took ill. He disappeared for days on end without anyone knowing his whereabouts. He was 20 years old.

All the visions of grandeur that Joe dreamed about when he was an amateur ran into the roadblock of reality. After two professional wins by knockout, no one was offering him a big-money contract. He had barely earned a hundred dollars a round in his pro fights.

At that time, Joe was finding ways to relieve himself from the pressures of his father and the sport of boxing. A few days before Christmas, Joe was hanging out with friends at the Metropole Hotel. He partied so heavily with cocaine that his friends thought he was trying to kill himself. He had accomplished everything his father had asked of him, yet his life was going nowhere. To make matters worse, when he returned home, his father had disowned him.

Arturo was having troubles of his own. He did not want to attend Louis Joseph Pepino High School. He told his teacher that he wanted to drop out of school and fight for the Canadian amateur boxing team. Arturo stated, *"I don't want to waste time. I want to be a champion."*[61] The school's principal spoke with Ida and told her to tell Giovanni to straighten Arturo out. The principal told Ida to stop letting Arturo watch so many *Rocky* movies. *"I wasn't a wise guy,"* Arturo later recalled, *"I even tried night school later on, but it wasn't for me. My father made me go to work for him as an electrician. I wasn't very good. If it weren't for boxing I could have been responsible for burning down all of Montreal."*[62]

On October 16, 1987 in Atlantic City, Matthew defended his title against 23-0 (11 KOs) Jack Callahan of Indiana. Matthew knocked Callahan out in the 2nd round. Joe recalled the fight. *"He got $435,000 for the first defense... At that time it was a lot of money. Now it's a different story."*[63] The Matthew Hilton-Jack Callahan fight was on the undercard of the Mike Tyson-Tyrell Biggs championship match.

In late February 1988, 46-year-old Giovanni fell off of a ladder while working on electrical wiring. Giovanni refused to go to the hospital. Instead, he tried to heal by resting at home. Three days after the accident, Giovanni's deterioration continued. His skin took on a yellowish tint. Davey Hilton Sr. stopped by, and after seeing Giovanni's condition, drove Giovanni to the Santa Cabrini hospital emergency room. Giovanni's condition continued to worsen. He asked for his son Joe, who was nowhere to be found.

As Giovanni's condition declined, he became delusional and started hallucinating. Giovanni started telling his family, *"Joe needs help. Go help Joe. He needs help."*[64] He kept repeating this over and over.

Although Giovanni had no way of knowing, Joe indeed was in

trouble. Joe was hanging around with Serge Cusson. Serge was a lightweight boxer and brother of Mario Cusson. Joe also was hanging out with Hilton brothers Davey Jr. and Alex, both of whom were wild. Matthew was the calmest, but would struggle with alcoholism after losing his title. Davey Jr. would pick fights in bars for fun. You couldn't stare at Davey Jr. He took that as an invitation to fight. Davey was a bad influence on the younger Joe. Serge was wilder and crazier than all of the Hiltons and Gattis. Joe had been arrested while with Serge, and was in jail. After several days, Joe was released.

When he first heard that his father was in the hospital, Joe thought it was a joke. When he discovered it was true, he rushed to the hospital to see his father. Joe was hoping to spend time alone with his father, talking about the one thing that Giovanni loved most, Joe's boxing career. It was not meant to happen. When Joe arrived at the hospital on March 2, his father had already died.

The entire family took the loss hard. All of a sudden the Gatti children were fatherless. Giovanni was laid out at the Rivieres-des-Prairies funeral complex in Montreal. After the wake, the family flew the body back to San Pietro Infine in Italy, where Giovanni was laid to rest in the village cemetery.

One must wonder how Joe and Arturo absorbed the fact that their father refused to go to the hospital for so many days. Could Giovanni's lack of desire to receive medical treatment be perceived by Arturo and Joe as their father giving up on life? It was more likely that Giovanni was holding true to the tough guy mantra that men never go to doctors.

Joe was 20 years old when his father died. Arturo was 15. Arturo had not taken boxing as seriously as Joe, in part, because he wasn't forced to do so. Arturo would begin dedicating himself to the sport like never before. Knowing that his deceased father loved boxing more than anything else, Arturo used the sport as a way of holding on to his father. Arturo would return to the ring less than two weeks after his father's death, winning a decision in Schenectady, New York.

Arturo's renewed dedication to the sport led to his first national title only two months later, on April 24, when he won the Canadian junior championships. It was apparent that Arturo was now fighting for more than himself. Arturo would not be the first boxer to dedicate his accomplishments to a deceased parent. James "Buster" Douglas used the death of his mother to motivate him to win the heavyweight championship, and possibly the greatest upset in boxing history, when he came off of the floor to knock out Mike Tyson.

Joe became unstable after his father died. He felt as though he couldn't stay in Montreal any longer. Joe explained his feelings. *"I go back to Canada and John passed away and I go nuts. This is my father. So I was like, I can't stay here. He was the only one who controlled me. My brother [Arturo] was so young. He was 15. He wanted to go to the Olympics. He was a good amateur. So I called Mario and asked, 'Mario, if I come there can you get me a trainer? You gonna help me?' He said, 'Come on down. I'm gonna help you.' So I came down with my duffel bag, my training stuff. When I got here I stayed here. He got me involved with Pat Lynch. I already saw Pat at Triple Threat. He already knew who I was. Pat was involved with Triple Threat for a while and he was buying himself out. Marc Roberts bought him out. So he already knew who I was. They wanted to get their own thing going. Him, Richie Seibert and Mario Costa were the three guys."*[65]

Giovanni's death appeared to be the catalyst for both brothers to take chances with their lives and careers that they might not have otherwise taken. Joe decided to move to New Jersey. If Giovanni had not fallen victim to his tragic fall, Joe never would have moved to Jersey City. This meant that Arturo never would have moved to New Jersey either. Arturo later revealed that he probably would have followed his father and become an electrician.

When Giovanni died, the electrical company that he owned became Joe's. Ida asked Joe what he wanted to do with the business. Joe told his mother to sell the company. *"I don't care about the business or money. You need it more than I do."*[66] Ida kept the company. The family fell on hard times financially with the death of their breadwinner.

Arturo was becoming a standout amateur, and people were beginning to take notice. Coaches at the Olympic Boxing Club were seeing the possibility that Arturo could make the Canadian Olympic team if he continued his winning ways. He would be 20 years old when the 1992 Barcelona Summer Olympics took place. Dave Campanile took up the financial slack of paying for Arturo's boxing expenses.

On June 25, 1988 in Atlantic City, Joe returned to the ring with a 4-round decision victory over 3-0 Lemark Davis. The bout was Joe's first in the junior middleweight division. Azumah Nelson headlined the card with a 9th round knockout victory over Lupe Suarez in defense of his WBC super featherweight belt.

In June 1988, at only 16 years of age, Arturo traveled to the Guild Hall in Londonderry, Northern Ireland, with the Canadian national team. A boxer was supposed to be 17 to travel with an open class team, but Arturo was quietly taken on the trip because of his talent. The Canadians were taking on the Irish national team. Arturo was matched against 17-year-old Wayne McCullough, who had a vast amateur background. The boxers fought in the 126-pound weight class. McCullough dominated the fight with his reach. He landed at will, but Arturo refused to quit. Gatti had yet to develop his man strength. The Canadian coaches had to throw the towel in after Gatti received two standing-eight-counts in the 1st round. A few days later, Arturo fought in Belfast, winning by knockout.

Joe followed up his June win with a 2nd round knockout victory on July 29, over 2-0 Calvin Christensen, in Las Vegas. The bout was televised live on ESPN. Davey Hilton Sr. and Mario Costa worked Gatti's corner. The 6' tall Christensen attacked Joe right at the opening bell, landing a jab. Al Bernstein, ESPN's announcer, praised Gatti's left hook. Right after Bernstein's statement, Joe landed a double left hook to the body and head. Gatti landed several more hard hooks in the round. He followed with a hard right hand that stunned Christensen near the end of the round. Joe tried to finish Christensen but Calvin survived the round.

Gatti came out fast in the 2nd, landing hard hooks to the body and head. Bernstein broadcast that Joe showed good power in both hands with his compact punches. Joe followed with a right hand to the head that dropped Christensen to his knees. Christensen was up at the count of five. After the mandatory eight-count the action continued. Joe landed another hard right cross and the referee, Richard Steele, waived the bout over without a count.

Matthew Hilton, 28-0, also fought on the card, scoring a 4th round knockout over 23-1 Paul Whitaker in a non-title fight at 163-pounds. Matthew wouldn't hold the crown for long, losing the title by decision to Robert Hines in a major upset on November 4, 1988 in Las Vegas. Matthew knocked Hines down twice early in the contest, but faded as he complained to his father between rounds that he injured his left hand. After the fight, he revealed that he had suffered a rib injury while training for the contest. Matthew hurt his ribs while sparring with Francisco DeJesus. There are those who felt that the fight should have been postponed. It was rumored that the Hilton team disregarded the rib injury and let the fight go on as planned because of financial reasons. Matthew was observed drinking heavily on several occasions leading up to the Hines match.

The card was headlined by Michael Nunn, who defended his IBF middleweight title with an 8th round knockout over Juan Domingo Roldan. In the co-main, Thomas Hearns won the WBO super middleweight title with a 12-round majority decision over James Kinchen.

Joe was the swing bout on the card. He watched as his idol Matthew lost his title. Joe later recalled that he was so shocked by Matthew's loss he could not get his mind focused on his own fight. Davey Hilton Sr. noticed that Joe was unraveling in the dressing room and tried, to no avail, to motivate him.

At the start of the match, Joe was dropped almost immediately. He never recovered. He lost by 1st round knockout at the hands of Donnie Giron, a 1-1 boxer from Denver. The loss was his first defeat as a professional. To make matters worse, Top Rank matchmaker, Bruce Trampler, was scouting Joe for a possible contract offer. The loss to Giron ended any chance Joe had of being signed by Top Rank. Giron would retire in 2001 with a 17-7-2 record with 13 KOs.

In Montreal, Ida Gatti met and started dating Gerardo di Francesco, a mason from Montreal. They later would wed.

In February 1989, Arturo had competed in his 25th amateur bout. His record was 18-7. The 16-year-old was gaining a reputation for his aggressive, warrior-like style. Although Arturo had only 25 bouts up to that point, he had a relaxed, experienced style that belied his actual number of bouts. This was due to the fact that he had started boxing so young and had spent so many years in and out of the gym.

On June 27, 1989, Joe Gatti returned to the ring at the Paul Suave Arena in Montreal. He scored a 2nd round knockout over the 5-12-2 Jacques DeBlois of Montreal. Davey Hilton, 26-0-1, headlined the card with a 1st round knockout over Quebec's Richard Gagnon.

On October 10, 1989, Matthew returned to the ring with a 10th round knockout over Tim Williams, 16-10-1. The win helped put Matthew in line for the WBO middleweight title held by Doug DeWitt. In preparation for the DeWitt fight, Davey Hilton Sr. brought Matthew down to New Jersey to train. Joe Gatti was to be Matthew's main sparring partner again. Joe stayed with Matthew at the Embassy Suite in Secaucus N.J. Arturo came down and stayed with Joe and the Hiltons briefly, but returned to Montreal. Arturo was unable to turn professional because he was not yet 18.

Mike Skowronski started boxing in Bufano's Boxing Gym in 1986 when his friend, Don Dunleavy, brought him to the gym. He was still training in the Jersey City gym in 1989 when Joe Gatti and Matthew Hilton arrived. Skowronski recalled, *"It was always a problem for Matthew because he was so big. Half the battle in the gym for him was getting his weight down. I envision Matthew training with plastic on, plastic, and one of those neoprene suits to lose the weight. He would be like 205-pounds going back down to 155 every fight. That's when I met Joe. Joe was a welterweight and Joe was sharp. Joe could box you. Now you have to picture me, I was only 16 or 17 years old when I started doing it. I didn't get the luxury of starting at 6 or 7 years old. So I'm behind the eight ball. I am an average amateur local kid and I get to see a guy like Joe who started at 7 or 8 years old. Joe is sharp. He's staying with Matthew. I seen Matthew knock Bobby Joe Young out. I was there for that, a left hook. After the gym, Bobby Joe Young, the sad thing is, I was walking out and he was walking out. 'Yo Red, help me find my car.'"*[67]

Skowronski described what it was like to see Matthew hitting the heavybag, *"He was awesome. To describe it would be, picture two-inch pipe with a twelve-inch [punching bag] frame [at Bufano's gym], and you knew when Matthew was on the bag because you could hear that whole structure banging. It just looked like and sounded like damage. He would let that bag swing and just work on that bag with those big left hooks of his. You picture an 80- or 100-pound bag swinging and just coming to a dead stop when he landed that left hook. Never seen anything like it. Buddy McGirt was different. He moved around the bag. He looked like an artist, whereas Matthew just did damage on it. The only way I could describe it is damage. When I was young, I was so in awe of these guys.*

"I thought Joe was gonna be a world champion. I really did. You don't realize how hard it is to get a guy to that level. You have to navigate a career and I only grew to respect it after trying to move a couple of pros myself. Matthew would use whoever, like Francisco DeJesus, his brothers, and Joe. I was impressed because remember I got to see these guys on TV, and back then it was a big deal to see someone on TV."[68]

Skowronski talked of the experience gap between himself, Joe Gatti, and Matthew Hilton. *"I'm lucky to have fourteen or sixteen amateur fights and these guys had that many fights at 8 or 10 [years old]. You're fearless when you're a kid like that."*[69]

Sal Alessi, a veteran boxing trainer and manager, who trained fighters out of the Bayonne boxing club, recalled Matthew working on the heavy bag. *"I'm coming up the stairs to Bufano's on a Saturday morning and you hear the heavy bag and I knew Matthew Hilton was hitting the heavy bag cause it didn't sound like anybody else. The heavy punches, you could hear power in the punches. He just dented the bag. Unbelievable the way he beat a bag up. He had really big punching power."*[70]

Pete Maino, who along with Al Tarantula, trained boxers at Bufano's, recalled when the Hilton's came to Jersey City, *"It was like the circus came to town. They took their boxing seriously, but they just had a different way about them. They were raised to be fighters. Matthew Hilton was a sweetheart. He was the star of that show. He could hit like a fucking mule that kid, boy could he go to the body."*[71] Maino recalled first meeting Joe Gatti, *"Joe was the sweetest guy in the world. Joe was just so friendly and personable."*[72]

Chapter 4
Bufano's Gym & Jersey City Boxing

Bufano's boxing gym was located at 82 Beacon Avenue in Jersey City Heights, across town from Mario Costa's Ringside Lounge. The gym was opened by Dominic Bufano. He ran it until it closed in 1995. Bufano had opened his first gym in 1935 on Tuers Avenue and Broom Street in Jersey City. He moved to Beacon Avenue in 1946. In 1975, Bufano spent eight weeks in camp with Chuck Wepner as Chuck trained for his heavyweight championship bout with Muhammad Ali. Wepner was the inspiration for Sylvester Stallone's Rocky Balboa character, and many believe that Dominic Bufano was the inspiration for the Mickey Goldmill character played by Burgess Meredith.

Some of the fighters who trained in the gym over the years included Sonny Liston, Marvin Hagler, Eddie Gregory, Jimmy Dupree, Frankie Depaula, Mark Medal and Gus Lesnevich. Sal Alessi described Bufano, *"Dominic was a sweetheart. He could be a cantankerous guy. I mean, in the movie Rocky, Burgess Meredith played him to a hilt. The eye and everything. He had the one eye ramped down and he was a little guy with these big fore-arms. He was always friendly to me but he was a funny kinda guy. If he liked ya he'd give you the shirt off his back and if he didn't like ya he didn't want you in the gym. He didn't give a fuck about money. He didn't give a fuck about your reputation; he didn't care about nothin'. Dom, he had that little base of hair on the top of his head. Bobby Rooney told me a story one time when Chuck was fighting Ali. They brought Bufano in as a Sicilian witch doctor and he perched all his hair up in the center and he stood it up with some gel. He was putting the muluka on Ali at the fight and they told Dom that the Muslims were coming to get him. He was shitting his pants, and with pillow and blanket he showed up at Bobby Rooney's room and he wanted to sleep with Bobby cause he was scared that the Muslims were coming for him."*[73]

Mike Skowronski recalled Dominic, *"Bufano was an old ornery type guy. He was just like Mickey from Rocky. All of today's fighters stunk except Buddy [McGirt]. He loved Buddy and some other guys. It was just a good gym where all the local kids would come and train."*[74] Skowronski described the monthly dues. *"He was the best. Say it was 15 or 20 bucks a month. You wouldn't pay for like two or three months and he would say, 'Hey, you owe me dues.' And then you were on his good side again. He had no filing system. Whenever he realized that, 'Hey, I didn't get money from this guy in a while.' And then you would pay him and you would be a good guy. He'd give you an evil look and you'd be like, 'Dom, what's up?' 'You didn't pay your does this month,' in a whiny voice. And then when you gave him twenty bucks you were good to go.*"[75]

Pete Maino added, *"Dominic was like an elf. He was about 5 foot and two hearing aids. He looked like Gollum from Lord of the Rings. A big nose and one eye half closed. He always needed a shave. He would terrorize the biggest heavyweight. He was like Mickey from Rocky on steroids. He made Mickey look like Troy Donahue."*[76]

Bufano's gym was located on the second floor of a two-story house. The ring was small, only around twelve-feet-square. There were two heavy bags in the gym and there was an old pool room on the opposite side of the gym that hadn't been used in years. Buddy McGirt believed that the smaller ring helped make him a better fighter because it forced him to work more on defense.[77] Pete Maino had been told that the gyms main room was once a small ballroom dance hall prior to being converted to a boxing gym. Once in the 1990's, after the gym suffered a fire, Maino was cleaning up when he found a sign that read, *"No Spitting Out The Window."* The sign appeared to be from the 1940's. Maino often wondered, with a chuckle, what the story was behind the sign. *"It was probably a day in 1949 when somebody took a big swig of water and washed it around their mouth and spit it out the window and somebody must have gotten a shower down on the sidewalk."*[78]

At the time that Matthew Hilton and Joe Gatti arrived at Bufano's, some of the boxers who could be seen training there during various times of the day included Buddy McGirt, Bobby Joe Young, Mustafa Hamsho, Rip Rettig, Mark Medal and Mark DiGiovanni. Joe Gatti met Mike Skowronski in Bufano's and the pair became fast friends. Skowronski described Bufano's gym. *"Bufano's had a long stairwell going up and the pool tables were covered and you couldn't sit on the tables. Dominic wouldn't even let you put your bag on them. And when you would walk up, there would be a little room with a coffee table, where all the old-timers would sit and hang out and talk, a little round table. And from there you used to walk into the little changing room and locker area and from there you went into the gym. If it was 30' by 50' it was a lot. I mean it wasn't a big gym. Two heavy bags, a speed bag and a double-end bag that you could put up or take down in-between the two heavy bags. And it had a rail system, like piping, let's say two-inch conduits, that would come off the walls that bags were hung to. So it was free-standing framing that the bags were hung to. It was an old-school gym."*[79]

Sal Alessi fondly recalled Bufano's Gym. *"You could see your breath and steam came out of your prick when you pissed because there was no heat in the bathroom downstairs. It was so fucking cold that you pissed steam. And it was a billiard hall. And I can't remember the date but George Thorogood and the Destroyers were up there shooting a video, 'Bad to the Bone.'"*[80] Indeed, if you watch the *Bad to the Bone* video that was filmed in 1982, you can see the pool hall and boxing gym. Dominic Bufano was featured in the video, along with Bo Diddley and Willie Mosconi.

In May 1986, Matthew Hilton and his younger brother Stewart were the first Hiltons to arrive at Bufano's Gym. Mario Costa brought them to the gym. They were trained by Jimmy Ellis. Buddy McGirt sparred with Matthew nearly every day for the first month in the summer of 1986.[81]

Stewart Hilton died in September of 1986, when the car he was driving struck a bridge abutment, killing him and his girlfriend Luce Diotte. Both Stewart and his girlfriend were 17 years old. Stewart was 4-0 as a professional at the time of his death. Stewart's pallbearers included his brothers Davey, Matthew, Alex, and Jimmy.

McGirt was by far the best fighter in Bufano's when Joe Gatti and Hilton arrived. McGirt lived in Long Island but traveled to Jersey City by subway every day. The ride was over an hour in one direction. McGirt did not originally train in Bufano's. McGirt had his first pro fight on March 2, 1982, against Lamont Haithcoach, 2-0 (2 KOs). Haithcoach was managed by Al Certo. Certo would later manage McGirt. McGirt was brought in as an opponent on a week's notice. The two fighters fought to a draw.

McGirt's manager, Stuey Weiner, was impressed with Haithcoach's trainer Dominic Amoroso. All of Amoroso's fighters won on the card except Haithcoach. Weiner asked Amoroso to train McGirt. Amoroso was training fighters out of the Mile Square Gym in Hoboken at the time. McGirt took the Path train-ride from Long Island to Hoboken on a daily basis. After exiting the train, McGirt would walk two miles to the Mile Square Gym.

After a year, the Mile Square Gym closed down. Amoroso decided to start training his fighters at Bufano's Gym in Jersey City. McGirt was forced to change trains and walk in a different direction. Occasionally, Amoroso would pick up McGirt from the Path station, especially if it was raining. McGirt would leave high school early to catch the 12:27 train. Some days Amoroso would not be there waiting. McGirt believed that Amoroso was testing his desire to be a fighter.[82]

Matthew Hilton took a last-minute tune-up fight on December 19, 1989, against club fighter Fermin Chirino, 11-4-1. Taking a tune-up one month before a title fight was risky. Besides a possible loss, Matthew was risking a cut or injury, which could have ruined his title opportunity. Matthew was lucky to come away with a controversial draw in the Atlantic City contest. It was becoming apparent that Matthew had lost his hunger for boxing after the Hines loss.

Up in Canada, Arturo Gatti continued his domination in the ring. He fought, and won, all eleven of his amateur bouts in 1989, and capped the year off with his second straight national junior title in December. Every time that Mario returned to Canada to work a Hilton corner, little Arturo would approach him at the fights and ask Costa if he would take him to Jersey City when he was old enough. Costa, like Arturo's best friend Christen Santos, would affectionately call him Arthur.

In the United States, Joe and Matthew were sparring regularly at the Triple Threat gym in Newark, N.J. The Triple Threat Gym Enterprises boxing team was founded by former New York stock broker and sports agent, Marc Roberts, in 1988. Roberts, a native of Newark, was a former division 1 basketball player. He had signed U.S. Olympian heavyweight "Merciless" Ray Mercer, as well as junior welterweight Charles "The Natural" Murray, and light heavyweight Al "Ice" Cole, who both competed in the Olympic box-offs.

Roberts had several investors in his project, including Patrick Lynch, a ticket agent, who would eventually become Joe and Arturo's boxing manager. Al Cole later recalled that Lynch, who was a young 30-year-old when he became involved with Triple Threat, was so close in age to the fighters that he would want to hang out with them. Cole added that Lynch often would pick up the tab when he went out with the fighters.

Lynch was a native of Hudson County. He grew up in Union City. Union City was an active fight town in the fifties and sixties. The town was home to strings of taverns, nightclubs, go-go bars, and burlesque theaters. The "transfer station" on Paterson Plank Road was home to some of the roughest bars in Hudson County. Some of the counties' toughest boxers; such as Chuck Wepner, Frankie DePaula and Jimmy Dupree, frequented the "station." DePaula and Dupree's manager, Gary Garafola, owned a go-go bar called the Rag Doll on the strip. DePaula would be murdered in what would later be described as a mob hit. Some believed his death was caused by his domestic abuse of a 'made man's' family member.

Lynch got started in the ticket brokerage business when he worked for an older man who owned the ticket business. After the business was burglarized a few times, the man retired and gave the business to Lynch. The unmarried Lynch used his spare money to invest in the Triple Threat boxing team.

On January 15, 1990 in Atlantic City, N.J., Matthew Hilton lost his WBO title fight to champion Doug DeWitt when he failed to come out for the 12th and final round. Matthew's father partly blamed Joe for the loss. Joe and Matthew had been staying at the Embassy Suite in Secaucus N.J. Davey Hilton Sr. expected Joe to monitor Matthew, but Joe, being younger than Matthew, couldn't control his behavior. Joe recalled, *"His [Matthew's] father blamed me. I don't know why. Matthew wasn't training. He's up all night on the phone with his girlfriend in Canada."*[83]

The Hiltons returned to Montreal and would never come back. Joe returned with them, but soon realized that he no longer had a desire to live in Montreal. He longed to return to Jersey City. He called Mario and asked if he could come back.

Costa recalled, *"After Matthew lost to Doug DeWitt. That's when they came, Joe and Arthur. Joe started telling me, 'Mario, Mario, please let me come.' And then they came back right after the Doug DeWitt fight. Cause the Hiltons left. It was over for the Hiltons. Arturo would come and go back. I think on Christmas. Sometimes he would go back and people like Manny, my bartender, actually took him over the border and had him in the back of the car. Manny put a cover over him so he could sneak him back into Canada."*[84]

Marc Roberts bought Pat Lynch and Richard Seibert out of their shares of Triple Threat for $80,000. Seibert worked with Lynch at his ticket agency. The pair decided to form their own boxing management group with Mario Costa. They named the company East Coast Boxing Management. In April 1990, Joe Gatti signed a managerial contract with the newly-formed management group.

Costa was the president of East Coast Boxing, Lynch the vice president, and Seibert the secretary. Joe was given a $5,000 signing bonus. The managerial contract was the standard three-year contract. New Jersey does not allow contracts to exceed three years, the only exception being if the boxer wins a world title. In that event, the contract is extended one or two additional years. Costa recalled that Lynch would spend time at the Ringside Lounge asking Mario questions about the business side of boxing.

Joe signed a standard management agreement. The standard percentages in boxing were 33% for management, 10% for the trainer, and 1 to 3% for the cutman. Those percentages did not include training expenses, which could include meals, gas and tolls, training equipment, and gym fees. Some managers deduct the expenses from the fighter's purse after they take their cut, leaving the boxer with less than 54%. Joe recalled that the East Coast management group did not cut his purse during the first few fights.

In boxing, most investors lose money, because fighters rarely make it to a world title. Even if they did, that didn't guarantee the fighter would be popular and a money maker. It is only the rare ones who, as Jimmy Dupree liked to say, *"Hit the lottery."*

Joe's good friend, "Iron" Mike Tyson, lost his heavyweight title on February 11, via a shocking 10th round knockout loss to James "Buster" Douglas in Tokyo, Japan. Douglas was a 42-1 betting underdog going into the contest. Douglas won the contest even though he recently had suffered several personal distractions, including his son's mother suffering from a severe kidney ailment, his contracting the flu shortly before the match, and probably the biggest distraction but possibly a motivator for Douglas, the death of his mother, Lula Pearl, only 23 days before the fight. Douglas would dedicate his victory to his mother. Boxing journalist and ringside announcer, Reg Gutteridge, called the fight, *"The biggest upset in the history of the fight game, bar none!"*[85] HBO commentator, Larry Merchant, added that Mike Tyson, who loved pigeons, may have thought he found a pigeon in the Douglas bout, but it didn't turn out that way.

On March 16, 1990, Joe, 5-1, returned to the ring at the Essex County Community College in Newark N.J. He knocked out 2-2 Ferris Christian, of the Bronx, in the 1st round of his first scheduled six-round contest.

On March 31, Arturo traveled with the Canadian national team to Grand Forks, North Dakota, to take on the U.S. National Team. On the U.S. squad were Shane Mosley, Vernon Forrest, and Kirk Johnson. Arturo lost to American Tony Gonzales in the 119-pound weight class by a 2-1 decision. Arturo's teammate, Michael Strange, lost a 2-1 decision to Oscar De La Hoya in the 125-pound division. Strange recalled that he and Arturo *"both lost controversial split decisions. And then after the matches, Arturo and myself ended up at a Frat House at the University of North Dakota at a keg party. And we drank our sorrows away and had some fun with some of the university kids."*[86]

One of Arturo's teammates fondly recalled that at the nationals, on team trips, or at any amateur boxing show that Arturo attended, you always knew where Arturo was. He was always surrounded by a group of fighters who were laughing at his jokes.

Most Canadian amateur boxers, including Arturo and Strange, idolized Matthew Hilton while he was on the rise. Matthew, however, was now on the slide. The boxers who were now admired in Canada were professionals Donny LaLonde, Willie DeWitt and Shawn O'Sullivan. LaLonde was the former WBC light heavyweight champion, while O'Sullivan and DeWitt both were former silver medalists in the 1984 Olympics. O'Sullivan, a light middleweight, and DeWitt, a heavyweight, both had successful professional careers, though never winning world titles.

In the 1988 Olympics, Lennox Lewis won the gold medal for Canada in the super heavyweight class, after losing in the quarter-finals in the 1984 games. Lewis was allegedly disappointed that he wasn't given the same hero's status in 1988 that O'Sullivan was given in 1984 when he won the silver medal. Some felt that Canadians didn't embrace Lewis because he was born in London, England.

On April 7, 1990, Joe returned to the ring in West Virginia, where he knocked out Charlotte, North Carolina's, Dwayne Lattimore, 0-3, in the 1st round. Joe followed up that win with another knockout victory on May 8 over 0-1 Lynn Robertson in Atlantic City.

Chapter 5
Main Events & the Duvas

Main Events is a boxing promotional company based out of Totowa, N.J. It was one of the most successful boxing promotional companies in the world. The organization was founded by Dan Duva in 1978 with $500,000 that he earned representing heavyweight champion Leon Spinks in a legal matter. Dan was the son of legendary trainer and manager Lou Duva.

Lou spent his early years learning the sport at New York's famous Stillman's gym. Duva would go on to lead nineteen boxers to world titles.

The Duvas originally were from Paterson N.J. Dan was an attorney and a graduate of Seton Hall University. Dan's wife, the former Kathy Martone, would help run the family business as a publicist. Unlike Dan, who came from a large family, Kathy was an only child. Dan and Kathy both attended Passaic Valley High School. The couple started dating after they graduated. Kathy began working for a local newspaper after graduating from Montclair State college.

Main Events started out by running club shows at the Ice World Arena in Totowa in 1978. The shows ran through 1986 and had a cult-like following. They showcased local talent such as Bobby Czyz, Livingstone Bramble, Kevin Smith, Kenny Bogner, Scott Frank, Joe Grier, Diego Rosario, Mike "Nino" Gonzalez, Johnny Verderosa, and James Green. They also signed former Irish Olympian Christie Elliot.

Ice World held approximately 3,000 people. The Duvas built up a steady following with their shows. The family sold every single ticket themselves. Family friends worked the gate. Kathy's father would cut the tickets at the door and prevent people from sneaking in for free. Dan's friends and family helped set up chairs and the ring. They also worked the concession stands and the box office.[87]

Lou Duva once recalled with a laugh, that on many of the Ice World shows, they only broke even because of the concession stands. Kathy helped the company by writing press releases. Lou was reluctant to use Kathy as the company's publicist. Initially, he paid Murray Goodman to do the job. After Lou observed one of Kathy's freelance bylines for the *Daily News*, he was so impressed he decided to give her a shot at the publicist job.[88]

In 1979, Main Events formed a relationship with ESPN and started promoting shows for the television network. They followed that up by signing amateur standout Rocky Lockridge.

Dan and Lou formed a relationship with former music promoter turned boxing manager, Shelly Finkel. Finkel and Lou Duva signed experienced amateurs Alex Ramos, Johnny Bumphus, Tony Ayala Jr. and Tony Tucker to managerial contracts. Duva and Finkel signed a deal with Bob Arum's Top Rank, who would promote the boxers and showcase them on the NBC network. In 1981, the company landed its first mega-fight promotion when they won the purse bid for "Sugar" Ray Leonard's showdown against Thomas "Hitman" Hearns. The superfight grossed $40 million dollars. Kathy Duva credited Finkel's connections for helping to land the fight.[89]

Andy Olsen, a former publicist at Caesars Palace, which held the fight, recalled working with Kathy. *"She comes from Totowa Ice Rink in New Jersey. And she had opinions. And we weren't used to that. We were Caesars Palace. We had the feeling we knew what was going on."*[90] Olsen would grow to respect Kathy's work in the sport. It was Kathy's idea to make a circular logo to promote the fight, so neither Leonard nor Hearns would appear to get top billing over the other. The logo would be featured on everything from billboards and magazines to the casino letterhead and even buttons worn by the casino's card dealers. Main Events would follow up by landing the 1983 superfight rematch between Alexis Arguello and Aaron Pryor.

The promotional company suffered a shocking setback on New Year's Day 1983. One of their rising stars, Tony "El Torito" Ayala, 22-0 (19 KOs), the #1 ranked junior middleweight, broke into a West Paterson N.J. woman's home and brutally raped her at knife point. In June, the 20-year-old Ayala, who previously had assaulted two other women, was sentenced to 35 years in prison. Ayala had sexually assaulted one woman when he was only 15 years old, in the bathroom of a drive-in theater in San Antonio, Texas. That crime was squashed due to his age and his boxing talent. After Ayala signed with Main Events, he gave $40,000 of his signing bonus to the San Antonio victim as compensation.[91]

In 1984, Main Events would have its biggest year. They crowned three world champions when Johnny Bumphus, Rocky Lockridge, and Mike McCallum all became world champions. Perhaps bigger than that, however, was the signing of five 1984 U.S. Olympians. Main Events signed Gold Medalists Mark Breland, Tyrell Biggs, Pernell Whitaker, and Meldrick Taylor. They also added Bronze

Medalist Evander Holyfield. In 1988, the promotional group added Olympic Gold Medalist Lennox Lewis.

Holyfield joined Main Events even though it was believed he could make more money with Top Rank or Don King. Holyfield chose Main Events because he believed they would make him a winner.

Finkel would come under fire for bringing all of his fighters, which including Alex Ramos, Mike McCallum, Evander Holyfield, Meldrick Taylor, and Pernell Whitaker, to Main Events. Thomas Hauser questioned how Finkel could deny being tied to one promoter when, for years, he brought virtually every fighter he had to that one promoter.[92] That would be like a baseball agent bringing all of his clients to one team. This could possibly hurt a fighter's earning potential by denying him access to the free market.

Finkel responded to the allegations by denying that he was a silent partner in Main Events. He stated that Main Events didn't have the cash to sign the 1984 Olympians. Finkel brokered a partnership between Main Events and two builders from Connecticut. He was adamant that he didn't gain anything from the financing. Finkel added that there weren't many options. He trusted that Main Events would provide his fighters with maximum exposure.[93]

N.J. based promoter Andre Kut recalled Duva's gym in Paterson. Former fighters Paul and Joe Cavaliere helped Lou run the gym along with cutman Ace Marotta. Kut recalled training alongside Tony Ayala and Bobby Czyz in Duva's gym. He described Ayala as, *"Scary, as he had no mercy. He always came charging out throwing bombs. Gym courtesy was always a must for Czyz. If he caught you with a good shot he backed off, never taking advantage. If Ayala caught you with a good shot he would just continue until Joe [Cavaliere] or Ace [Marotta] yelled at him to back off. No doubt he was destined to be a world champ. He had all the tools and a killer instinct."*[94]

On July 8, 1990, Joe Gatti was 8-1 with 7 knockouts going into his match against 5-1 (3 KOs) Michael Ward of Maryland. Ward dropped Joe in the first round and won the 6-round contest by decision. Ward would go on to win 13 out of his next 14 contests before losing a 10-round decision to future world champion Verno Phillips.

Joe bounced back on August 17, 1990 in Newark N.J., with a 2nd round knockout win over Philadelphia's Eric Holland, 6-8-2 (0 KOs). Local promoter Gabe LaConte recalled, *"Joe Gatti was a tall, handsome kid who looked like he had a great future. Everyone loved him. He was Italian and White, who could be matched with the best in the up-and-coming Black community. Ethnic considerations in a racist industry often went into the matching up of fighters."*[95]

After the Holland win, the East Coast Boxing team signed Joe with Philadelphia, Pennsylvania's most active promoter, J. Russell Peltz.[96] Richie Seibert brokered the deal to sign Joe with Peltz. Peltz ran shows regularly in Philadelphia and Atlantic City.

In boxing, management and promotional contracts are separate entities. The promoter books fights for the boxer and is supposed to "promote" him, while the manager is supposed to control the training and living arrangements for the fighter while accepting or declining matches and purses offered by the promoter.

Arturo's Junior National Championship in December earned him the right to represent Canada at the World Junior Boxing Championships in Lima, Peru in October 1990. The 18-year-old Arturo lost his first fight against Puerto Rican Gilberto Otero in the 119-pound category. The scoring of the bout was 22-22, a tie. Amateur boxing recently had adopted the computerized scoring system after the 1988 Seoul Olympics, to help discourage terrible decisions like the one that led to Roy Jones being robbed of an Olympic gold medal. The new computerized scoring method consisted of three or five ringside judges with scoring buttons. If all of the judges pressed their button within a three-second time frame, that boxer would earn a point. In the event of a tie, as was the case with Arturo's bout, the total times each judge pressed the button would be added up. The total tally was 122-119 in favor of Otero. Arturo returned to Montreal and moved up to the 125-pound weight division.

The new scoring system would completely change the face of amateur boxing. Athletes quickly adopted a hit and run style to be successful. This gave an enormous edge to tall, fast boxers. Even though they were supposed to, almost no judges scored body blows. Power and effectiveness meant nothing; only clean obviously landed head blows from the outside. There were judges who didn't even score jabs. Arturo tried to adapt to this new style by boxing and moving, but the new scoring system would destroy any chances the 5'7½" Arturo had at becoming an Olympian.

On October 22, 1990, at the Trump Plaza Hotel in Atlantic City, Joe won an 8-round unanimous decision over Cali, Columbia's Brinatty Maquilon, 11-7 (5 KOs). The *Press of Atlantic City's* Dave Bontempo commented on the bout, *"Jersey City middleweight Joe*

Gatti won an uncharacteristic eight-round decision over Brinatty Maquilon of New York. Gatti, 10-2, with eight knockouts, wasn't able to display the firepower leading to his previous knockouts. Maquilon's awkward style forced Gatti to jab and retreat."[97]

On November 3, 1990 in Hull, Quebec, Canada, Arturo fought for the last time as an amateur in Canada. Arturo had won the provincials in Quebec, and was representing that province in the nationals. He met future three-time Canadian Olympian Michael Strange in the semi-finals. Strange, a seasoned international-level amateur, had a flurrying style with a tight defense, which gave Arturo fits. Arturo lost a decision to Strange.

Knowing he could never defeat Strange with the amateur scoring system, and having only three rounds with which to work, Arturo decided he would fare better as a professional. Strange later recalled fighting Arturo in the amateurs. *"Arturo was more of a boxer back then. He turned professional right after that fight and the reason he did was because he couldn't beat Mike Strange to go to the '92 Olympics. I'm kind of glad he went pro as he had more of a professional style, as he was turning into more of an exciting brawler who was so dangerous, especially when he was hurt, because his opponents would come right after him and then walk into a barrage of heavy punches... Arturo was always known for having the biggest heart in boxing, as well as probably the most exciting fighter that you would ever see."*[98]

Arturo told the Canadian Olympic Boxing Coach, Yvon Michel, that he was finished with amateur boxing. Arturo stated, *"I will never be able to beat a guy that is trying to slap like a girl when I am willing to punch like a man."* Michel remembered his response to Arturo, *"I told him, 'Arturo you are making the biggest mistake of your life if you leave the amateur ranks to pursue a professional career in America.' Boy was I wrong!"*

On January 8, 1991 at the Blue Horizon in Philadelphia, Joe knocked out Maryland's Aaron Smith, 5-4-1 (1 KO), in the 3rd round. Gatti and Smith both weighed in at 159-pounds.

Whenever Joe fought, he would take the $1,500 or $2,000 that he earned and go shopping with Arturo. The brothers loved to wear the latest fashion.

On January 27, Pat Lynch attended Superbowl XXV in Tampa, Florida. At the hotel where Lynch was staying, he met his future wife Lisette Rizzotto. Rizzotto would move to New Jersey with Lynch. Lynch would turn in his bachelor lifestyle for a slower-paced family life.

On March 25 at the Meadowlands Convention Center, Joe returned to the ring for his first 10-round fight on the Main Events-promoted Regilio Tuur-Manuel Batista undercard. Tuur was managed by Stan Hoffman and trained by New York's Hector Roca. The 10-round fight was broadcast live by Sports Channel.

Joe held a professional record of 11-2 (9 KOs). He would be facing New York's Matt Farrago 25-1-1 (11 KOs). Farrago was several inches shorter than the 5'11½" Gatti. Besides being very small for a middleweight, Farrago's trunks had "actor needs work" written on it. The 29-year-old Farrago was indeed trying to break into the acting business. Joe knocked Farrago out in the 2nd round. After the bout was over, Farrago hugged Joe. He then turned Joe towards Gatti's corner and said, *"Keep an eye on your management team. Watch your management team closely."*[99] There is no reason to believe that Farrago knew Joe's team. He was probably speaking from his own experiences. As far as Farrago's acting career was concerned, he wound up with a small part in the 1996 movie *Murdered Innocence*.

Joe's old friend Mike Tyson, fresh off of his March 18 knockout win over Donovan "Razor" Ruddock, attended the Farrago fight and gave Joe a high-five from ringside after the knockout.

Joe would become an actor of sorts himself, when he landed a bit part in Chazz Palminteri's *A Bronx Tale*. Joe portrayed himself in a fight scene that was filmed at the Armory in Jersey City. Eric Holland, who Joe beat a few fights prior, played his opponent.

On April 30, Joe returned to the Blue Horizon, where he knocked out 15-11 (6 KOs) Muhammad Shabazz in the 1st round of their scheduled 8-round main event bout. Joe weighed in at 165 for the bout, while Shabazz, of Connecticut, tipped the scales at 169.

Chapter 6
Arturo Moves to New Jersey

Joe repeatedly asked Arturo to move to Jersey City with him. There were two reasons for his request. Joe was lonely in Jersey City now that the Hiltons were gone. He also was concerned about his fatherless little brother running the streets of Montreal. Joe knew if Arturo stayed in Montreal, bad things would befall him.

Arturo packed his bags and moved to Jersey City. Panama Lewis, who was training Joe, started working with Arturo. Panama worked with the brothers on defense and head movement. Panama was impressed with Joe and Arturo's progress. He called the brothers his *"White diamonds."*

Mario Costa recalled setting up a gym on the second floor of his Ringside Lounge for the fighters. *"It was 1990. McCallum, he came here for 10 years. He trained here under Panama Lewis and Eddie Futch. Eddie would take him to the fights and Panama would train him in-between fights. Arthur loved Mike McCallum. They spent a lot of time there. Arthur would look up to McCallum... McCallum was a very smart fighter. So Arthur, you can imagine a kid, an amateur kid, being upstairs with the middleweight champ of the world."*[100]

Costa recalled that Futch didn't come to his gym regularly, though he did stop by. *"He came here a couple of times but he would corner McCallum at the fights or when McCallum had to travel for a fight. Panama had a good relationship [with Futch]. He came here for my 40th birthday."*[101]

Costa's gym atop the Ringside Lounge consisted of a floor ring with no padding. The ropes were attached to a wall with eye hooks. The floor was hardwood. There was an unused alcohol bar on the side and a heavy bag and speed bag were hung from a wall in the corner. The makeshift gym didn't last long. In 1991, Costa had to move the gym to one of his investment homes a few houses down from the Lounge. Costa explained the reason why he was forced to move the gym. *"I changed the gym because Arthur was starting to knock people out and they would hit their head on the hardwood floor. So Panama said we have to have a real ring before he kills somebody."*[102]

Arturo would fight one more amateur bout, on May 3, 1991, at P.S. 27 School in Jersey City. Arturo had trained earlier in the day with

Mike Skowronski. Joe had previously introduced Mike to Arturo and asked Mike to keep an eye on Arturo as he was new to New Jersey and spoke mostly French and Italian. Arturo referred to Mike as "Mikey Red" because Mike had red hair and Arturo couldn't pronounce Skowronski's last name.

Mike recalled that Arturo was always laughing in those days. The two friends were heading up to Jersey City's Mosquito Park to play soccer after they trained when they got a call about an amateur show. They were told that there was a 135-pound open-class kid looking for a fight. Mike stated, *"We got Arturo shoes and trunks and ran up to the show and got the fight."*[103] Mikey Red was accompanied by Arturo's brother Joe and a Ringside bouncer named Louis Ocasio.

Pete Maino, who was president of N.J. amateur boxing at the time, recalled Joe Gatti coming in all excited when he found out there was a fight available for Arturo. Maino recalled asking Joe if Arturo had any professional fights. After Joe confirmed that Arturo was still an amateur Maino advised Joe that Arturo would have to fight open class due to his vast amount of amateur experience. Arturo registered to fight and received his boxing passbook at the show, which was allowed at that time.[104]

Arturo's cornermen were his brother Joe and Mikey Red. Panama Lewis also attended the show. Arturo's opponent was coached by former Olympian Howard Davis Jr. Davis, Jr. and Lewis had a conversation about both their fighters' levels of experience before the match was made. At the time, amateur coaches would get together at the shows, look over the boxers' passbooks, which showed the amount of fights that each fighter had, and decide if they would make a match. There was no computerized method for checking on a fighter at that time. A fighter's passbook rarely was accurate. Some coaches were known to have several passbooks for their fighters to make it look as though they had less experience than they actually had. Since Arturo registered right before the fight, his passbook was brand new and had no fights in it.

Davis Jr., who was training fighters out of the Elizabeth Recreation boxing club, was concerned about the fact that Arturo was willing to fight his experienced open-class boxer. He had no way of knowing how much experience Arturo had. He also was concerned that Arturo was the brother of rising prospect Joe Gatti, and that world-class trainer Panama Lewis was with him. Joe and Panama were concerned themselves because Davis, Jr. was training Arturo's opponent. Davis, Jr. was an Olympic gold medalist in 1976. He won the outstanding boxer of the Olympic games, the Val Barker Trophy, beating out fellow gold medalists Sugar Ray Leonard and Leon and Michael Spinks.

Davis, Jr. received assurance from Panama that Arturo wasn't a big puncher. When these types of promises were made at amateur shows, they were almost never truthful. If someone told you that their fighter had no power the opposite was likely true. If a coach told you that his fighter didn't have much experience you could expect the opposite. Arturo had won international bouts for the Canadian national team in Ireland, Scotland, and Italy. This information, unknown to Davis, Jr., would have been easily discoverable in today's mobile media environment.

Arturo wound up defeating his opponent, Domingo Valdez, decisively, while displaying his vast amount of experience. Arturo was relaxed and had terrific in-and-out footwork. *Jersey Journal* reporter Wayne Witkowski commented on Arturo's performance. *"Gatti, 19-year-old younger brother of budding middleweight prospect 'Lightning' Joe Gatti, proved deadly in counter-punches and looked smooth throughout his bout. Joe Gatti worked his brother's corner for the first time. Arthur Gatti flashed a pro style as he emphasized footwork and setting up his punches rather than the typical amateur approach of scoring quickly. 'He stuck to his game plan, stick and move,' said Joe. 'I move from the outside and just touch him to make him come in and then I hit him with a hard shot,' said Arthur. Valdez tried to press the fight and landed a good right early in the third round. But Gatti slipped punches and scored counter-punching in combinations."*[105]

Arturo would hit his opponent and step away before his opponent had an opportunity to counter, just as Panama had taught him. Panama often told Arturo that he wanted him to fight like a Black fighter, because they were the fighters he would fight the most in the pros. After the bout, Howard Davis Jr. got into an argument with Lewis. He felt that Lewis had been less than truthful in regards to how much experience and punching power Arturo had.

Arturo earned the Ricky McQuade "Fighter of the Night" award for his performance. Mario Costa recalled Arturo's last amateur fight. *"He was given his trophy and he was so proud to have his first trophy in America. He looked like a little baby. Arthur came back here so happy."*[106]

Joe recalled that his brother briefly returned to Montreal. *"He goes back. I go, 'Yo, you gotta come back over here.' Because he was messing around over there. He was fooling around and I didn't like who he was hanging around with. He was hanging around with the Hiltons. He could get in trouble or get hurt. I wish I left him there. I kinda forced him to come over here because he was there by himself, and me and him, we were always together. I was over here by myself. I said, 'Come over here. You can stay with me. We are going to train over here. We chose these people and we will turn you pro.'*

"Then I called him back again. I got him here and they signed him up. They gave him $5,000 and he stayed. I told Pat Lynch, these were the exact words I said, 'Listen I want you to meet my brother, he came down one time then he left. The first time I got him here Mario paid for his ticket, and I want you to meet him. He's better than me,' cause they thought I was the greatest. I said, 'My brother is better than me.' Pat said, 'He is?' I said, 'Yeah.' So then he's like, 'We gotta see this guy.' So when they got him here they signed him right away."[107]

After Arturo returned, the East Coast Boxing group signed him to a management contract. Arturo, like his brother, was given a $5,000 signing bonus. Mario Costa described Arturo's return. *"He arrived in Jersey City with a plastic bag and some clothes and no money, a big dream, a big heart, and a big smile. The dream was so big the money didn't matter. The dream was for Joe and Arthur to be champions for their father."*[108]

Joe recalled that both he and Arturo received their nicknames from Panama Lewis. Panama gave Joe the ring name "Lightning" and Arturo the ring name "Thunder." Both names perfectly reflected the style of fighting the brothers displayed. Joe was lightning-quick while Arturo had thunderous punching power. Joe and Arturo would train with Panama each day at one o'clock. They would travel to various gyms in the metropolitan area for sparring.

Mario recalled, *"Panama, one time took Joe and Arthur to Philly to spar. They stayed there for two weeks. They went and boxed all over. The guys in Philly said, 'Oh here comes the White boys and Panama.' They got a room in a hotel and slept there for two weeks. Panama took them to different gyms in Philly."*[109]

The brothers would run each morning around Pershing Field, a park in the Jersey City "Heights," which had a dirt track inside of it. The track helped not only with leg strength and endurance but it also helped with side-to-side movement. There was broken glass and potholes all along the poorly maintained dirt track which caused the runners to constantly side-step the obstacles.

Lynch directed the East Coast Boxing group to pay Panama Lewis $500 a week to train the Gatti brothers. That amount was unheard-of for training non-champions. Costa recalled that after six months, Lynch complained that they were paying Lewis too much. Costa reminded Lynch that it was his idea to offer Lewis the $500 weekly salary.

Mikey Red described how he felt when Pat Lynch took over the Gatti's careers. *"I felt like a jealous step-son because of the way Joe and Arturo were treated by Pat. Pat would take Joe and Arturo to Ferragamo's in the city, to buy them custom suits. He really took care of them. They had access to Pat's cars, he had a Corvette."*[110] Vikki recalled, *"Pat gave the brothers action. Lent them his corvette. Took them to clubs."*[111]

Skowronski noted how often Arturo would reflect on his father. *"Arturo was always choked up when talking about his father, and he was upset that his father wasn't around to see the fighter that he had become. How proud his dad would have been, because of how tough his dad was. His father was a tough guy."*[112]

Arturo and Joe trained together, ate together, ran together, and even hung out together. They listened to Metallica and Englebert Humperdinck and they went to see Hank Williams Jr. in an outdoor concert at the PNC arts center with Mikey Red. The movies they enjoyed were low grade "C" horror movies such as *Wishmaster*. Joe and Arturo loved soccer and hockey. They were both talented athletes. They played in a charity softball game at Persian Field. They had no experience at softball and didn't play well, though they enjoyed the event.

It was easy to find trouble in the Hudson County area, especially on weekends. The streets, clubs, and bars were filled with tough guys looking to make a name for themselves. Hoboken was home to many business-type "yuppies" but it also had a government run housing project section. At one point, Hoboken was rumored to have had more bars and clubs per square mile than anywhere else in the United States.

It was in Hoboken that the two Gatti brothers found themselves faced against four tough guys looking for trouble. Joe and Arturo had enjoyed their evening in a club and were leaving. Arturo walked out first. Apparently he had an issue with someone in the bar and that person followed Arturo outside with his three friends.

When Joe walked out of the club, Arturo was already engaged in a fight with the four guys. Unaware with whom they were messing, the tough guys were soon left sprawling on the sidewalk. During the fight, Joe slipped to the ground because of the dress shoes he was wearing. He removed his shoes and fought in his socks.

Joe and Arturo jumped into Lynch's Acura Legend, which they had borrowed, and drove off. Joe left his shoes at the scene of the fight. As Joe was driving from the area, he made a wrong turn down a one way street and had to back up a little. He bumped into a car behind him. Joe turned to Arturo and said, *"What should I do?"* Arturo looked at his older brother and said, *"I don't know."* Joe got out of the car to check that neither car was damaged. He had a torn shirt and ripped socks from the altercation he had just been involved in. There were four males in the other car. The driver of the other vehicle stepped out of his car. He looked like a linebacker as he strutted towards Joe with a Clint Eastwood gait.

Joe didn't see any damage so he told the other driver, *"I'm sorry. Is your car ok? Can I leave?"* The other driver pushed Joe and said, *"You tried to run, ah?"* Joe, his adrenaline still pumping, said, *"No, I wasn't trying to run and please don't touch me."* The guy pushed Joe again. Joe repeated, *"Don't touch me. Can I just leave."* Arturo was sitting in the car watching his brother. The driver pushed Joe a third time as his three friends in the car appeared to be getting ready to exit the vehicle. Joe threw a short left hook and the driver fell to his knees. He dazedly looked up at Joe. Joe drilled a right hand down on the driver, putting him to sleep.

The other three passengers exited the car as Arturo stepped out of the Acura. Joe knocked out another passenger, who slid down the bark of a tree. Joe turned and watched as Arturo was landing shot after shot on the third passenger, but the guy wasn't moving. Joe walked over and clipped the third guy and down he went. Joe turned around and saw the last guy and yelled, *"You too!"* As Joe's punch was on its way he heard Arturo yell, *"No, no!"* Joe had mistakenly struck and dropped a bystander who was walking by with his girlfriend. The guy had stopped to watch the fight.

Joe picked the guy up and told him he was sorry, while the guy's girlfriend was cursing at Joe. Joe and Arturo hopped back into the Acura and took off. Joe later said of that evening, *"I was 8-0 with 8 knockouts. The story was, there was these two little kids knocking everybody out, and it was us [laughing]."*[113] This was just another night out for the Gatti brothers.

Wayne Witkowski covered the brothers' careers for the *Jersey*

Journal. He recalled some of the concerns with the brothers early on. *"Because both of them, as well as the Hilton brothers, who were related to them, were free spirited guys, there was always the worry between fights whether there would be problems with Joe and Arturo outside of the ring. But things always seemed under control."*[114]

Arturo was always dating someone, and they always seemed to be blondes. The two brothers ate anything, but they loved Italian food. Joe, Arturo and Mikey Red would hang out at Mario's Ringside Lounge and drink like they owned the place. They were like kings in the bar. Mario even gave Arturo a key to the lounge. Mikey Red was told wild stories from their days back in Canada. Joe was like a god in Montreal before he came down to New Jersey.

Arturo was the jokester in the gym. Mario recalled his mischievous behavior. *"In the beginning he would pull the guys' shorts down. He pulled his brother Joe's pants down, Francisco Dejesus'. They joked all the time. We'd get in an elevator and when the guys we were with were not looking, he'd pull their pants down. When he took a girl to the movies he'd put his [penis] through the [bottom of the] popcorn container for a joke. He would do all sorts of things. Always talking to my staff. He would tell them things that he wanted to do. He was a real good respectable kid."*[115]

On June 10, 1991, Main Events promotions returned to the Meadowlands Convention Center. Olympic Gold Medalist and Main Events-promoted Mark Breland was the main event. He took on Henry Anaya Jr. in a 10-round bout. Joe was the co-main event, taking on Ralph "Good Grief" Moncrief. On the undercard, pro debuting Arturo Gatti took on Trenton, N.J.'s 0-1 Jose Gonzales. Gonzales, 25 years of age, had the look of a hardened street fighter.

Arturo would later comment on his thoughts, standing across the ring from Gonzales. *"I looked across the ring and I saw him and I was like, 'Oh man,' I was scared to death. Here was a guy fresh out of the can with a ponytail and tattoos all over his body. I was a teenager. I never saw anything like him before in my life."*[116] Arturo quickly got over his fear of Gonzales. He was never in trouble in the bout. Like most pro debutants, Arturo took his time sizing up Gonzales before knocking him out in the 3rd round with a hammer-like left hook.

Costa described Arturo's pro debut. *"The first pro fight for Arthur, Tyson came to his fight. How crazy is that? He came to the [Ringside] bar. From the bar we went to Arthur's first pro fight because he knew Arthur since he was a kid. Arthur used to go to the Catskills to see the Hiltons and Mike knew him. Mike said, 'I knew him since he was a little kid.' And he did."*[117]

Arturo earned $300 for his professional debut.[118] Joe took a majority decision over Moncrief 25-14 (15 KOs) of Cleveland. The durable Moncrief made a close fight of it, as the judges' scorecards were 96-93 and 95-94 for Gatti, while the third judge had it 94-94.

Joe Chessari of the *Bergen Record* described the contest. *"Moncrief, 41, survived the rockiest of fourth rounds when Gatti, 24, was all over him in the final minute. Moncrief was in as much trouble as a fighter could be in without being knocked down. Gatti, who afterward said he wants to challenge for a national title, caught the veteran with a left-right to the chin and Moncrief went reeling into the ropes, turning his back on Gatti as the younger fighter rushed in. Gatti threw wildly as Moncrief staggered from one side of the ring to the other. Another vicious left-right combination sent Moncrief into a neutral corner, but he didn't go down. In the third round, Gatti went down, the result of a head butt. Moncrief stepped in to throw a right but instead clashed heads with his target. Gatti quickly got to his feet as the bell sounded. The early rounds featured Moncrief trying to avoid toe-to-toe exchanges while attempting to counter the often wild Gatti."*[119]

Two-time former welterweight champion, Mark Breland, won a 10-round unanimous decision over Henry Anaya. Mario Costa worked both Gatti boys' corners on the show.

Carlos Humberto "Panama" Lewis was Joe and Arturo's main trainer. He was unable to work their corners because he had received a lifetime ban from working corners by the New York State Athletic Commission in 1986. Lewis was involved in the removal of padding from Luis Resto's gloves when he fought Billy Collins Jr. at Madison Square Garden on June 16, 1983. Collins received permanent eye damage from the criminal act and was forced to retire.

Lewis was convicted of second and third degree assault, criminal possession of a weapon, and tampering with a sports contest. Collins would be dead nine months later when, under the influence of alcohol, he drove his car into a ditch. It will never be known if Collins' death was an accident or suicide.

Before Lewis' lifetime ban, he had worked with many top fighters, most notably Aaron Pryor, Mike McCallum, Livingstone Bramble, and Vito Antuofermo. During Pryor's first bout with Alexis

Arguello, after the 13th round, Lewis was overheard telling his cutman, Artie Curley, *"Give me the other bottle, the one I mixed."* Arguello would later say of Lewis, *"They ought to put him in the garbage."* Years later, Lewis admitted that the mixed bottle had crushed antihistamine tablets mixed in with the water. Using anything other than water is illegal. Whether or not something stronger was in that bottle will never be known.

Lewis and Costa were close friends. Lewis was living in one of Costa's apartments. Costa met Lewis at his Ringside Gym in Manhattan. The gym, which opened in 1982, was now closed. The Gatti brothers were staying in a small apartment approximately 100 yards east of the Ringside Lounge, on Manhattan Avenue.

The Gatti apartment was on the second floor of Costa's residence. Mario lived on the first floor. Joe and Arturo both had their own small beds with a dresser in-between. On the dresser, Arturo kept a picture of his father with a lit candle and a statue of Our Lady of Fatima that Costa had given to him. It was the same photograph that Arturo kept on the dresser of his room back home in Montreal.

Joe and Arturo, who were both religious, felt the apartment was haunted. The woman who had lived in the apartment before the brothers moved in had died there. The woman's son had been murdered and stuffed into the trunk of a car.

The brothers heard noises from under their beds, and the toilet would flush on its own. They felt that the woman's spirit haunted them because she was angry at any boy that lived while her son had died. When the brothers told Mario about the haunting, he laughed it off. The brothers discovered that the noises from under the bed came from a mouse, but they never did discover the source of the toilet flushing, which was most likely due to a leaky seal. The brothers placed crosses around the apartment to ward off the spirit.

Besides housing them, Costa also fed the Gatti brothers and their trainer Lewis. They would sign a food ticket receipt after each meal, as Joe recalled. *"Panama took his own pass and signed his own ticket. He was eating lobster [laughing]. Those people never ate lobster in their lives. He had shrimp, lobster and he signed the ticket. Panama did all that damage to Mario. We signed all our tickets, which Mario should have been paid for. If we never made no money, Mario's like this, 'You know what guys, [wiping his hands] we tried.' So anyhow we wound up sleeping over there [at Mario's]. In the beginning we were very tight. We didn't spend a lot of money because there was no money to be made. A lot of times I had to pay for my own things. They paid me for the fight. They didn't cut me. It was a thousand dollars. It was peanuts. We didn't make no money then."*[120]

Costa kept a ledger of the meal tickets used by the fighters. The three co-managers, Costa, Lynch, and Seibert, were supposed to split the meal fees when the fighters started earning "real" money.

The Ringside Bar and Grill is located in a rough-and-tumble section of Jersey City. It is on Tonnelle Avenue, which is a busy, two-way trucking route that heads south to Newark and north to North Bergen. In the early 1990s the area, which was lined with cheap motels and auto body shops, was home to street-walking prostitutes and their pimps at night. That section of Tonnelle was mostly industrialized, but the block that Ringside was on was lined with rows of two-family homes. The exterior windows of houses in the area were caked with dirt and grime from the exhausts of the thousands of trucks and cars that traversed the main corridor each day and night.

The Ringside Bar and Grill served Costa's native Portuguese cuisine. If the name of the bar didn't tell you what sport the owner preferred, the facade of the building did. The building is adorned with murals of past and present fighters, including Mike Tyson, Chuck Wepner, Jack Dempsey and later Arturo Gatti. The interior of the bar has photos of Costa's favorite fighters, as well as old boxing trophies and title belts.

On the weekdays, Costa's bar was a quiet location to have a drink and eat a good meal. Costa would sit at the bar and watch televised fights on Tuesdays while he chomped on his unlit cigar. Arturo would sit behind him at a small round table and chat with one of his girlfriends while he sipped on an orange juice.

On Friday and Saturday nights, the quiet bar was transformed into a Deejay spinning nightclub. The bar and small dance hall in the rear were packed with locals from Jersey City and Newark.

Arturo returned to action for his second pro fight on July 9, 1991 against 1-1 Luis Melendez of Allentown, Pennsylvania. Arturo weighed 127-pounds for the contest, which was held at the Blue Horizon in Philadelphia. Arturo was listed as the "swing bout" on the card, which was being televised live on USA Network's Tuesday Night Fights. A "swing bout" is a standby fight that is used to fill-in TV time in case of an early knockout. A swing bout can be a blessing or a curse. It is a blessing if the main or co-main bout ends in an early knockout, because your bout gets to be televised. It can be a curse if both the main and co-main events go the distance, because you have to wait until the main event is over and you lose the TV exposure. The "swing bout" then turns into a "walk out bout."

Another curse of a "swing bout" is that if the main bout appears as though it is going to end the fighter has to start warming up quickly. If a bout looks like it is going to be stopped and then continues for several more rounds a boxer could find himself exhausted from continuously warming up and cooling down.

Arturo was in luck because both the main and co-main events ended in early knockouts. Arturo's bout was televised live on national television. Arturo would make history at the legendary Blue Horizon when he scored the fastest knockout in the building's history. In Arturo's corner were Panama Lewis, Mario Costa, and Pat Lynch. Lewis had been suspended in New York since 1986, but he was granted a license to work corners in Pennsylvania in 1991. It was Lewis' first appearance in a corner since the Luis Resto-Billy Collins tragedy. Lewis' licensing in Pennsylvania wouldn't last long. There was public outrage after Lewis was seen working Arturo's corner on TV. He would never work a professional corner in the U.S. again. In 1997, the Professional Boxing Safety Act was passed into law, which stated, in part, that all states must recognize a suspension issued by one state.

Mario Costa recalled the Melendez fight. *"That was his second, that was the quickest knockout in Philly. They thought that he had rocks in the gloves. They said take the rocks out [laughs]. There was nothing in the gloves. He was just good."*[121]

When the bell rang for the opening round, Melendez and Gatti went right at each other. Melendez landed first, with a hard left hook that knocked Gatti off balance. Both fighters were swinging freely when Arturo landed a hard right hand on the tip of Melendez's jaw that starched Luis. Melendez fell on his side, frozen, with one leg straight out over the other and both arms in front of him locked in place. It took several seconds before his body relaxed and he rolled onto his back, where he was counted out. It was a frightening knockout. Arturo needed only 19 seconds to dispatch of his foe.

Years later Arturo recalled the bout. *"My first right put Melendez to sleep. He's still sleeping, I think."*[122] Arturo was hoisted into the air by Panama. He kissed Lewis on the cheek while Melendez lay motionless on the floor. It took several minutes before Melendez regained his feet. A commission employee confiscated Arturo's gloves in the ring, no doubt due to Lewis' shady reputation.

The Blue Horizon was a unique location because the second-floor seating basically hung over the ring, making for a very fan-friendly venue. Arturo's record was no small feat, as the Blue Horizon had held hundreds of boxing shows over the years. The building was originally constructed in 1865 as multi-story connected homes. It was converted into a ballroom in 1914.

The first boxing show held at the "Blue" was on March 1, 1938. After two shows, the building wouldn't see another boxing show until 1961, when Jimmy Toppi Sr. purchased the site. Toppi renamed the building after a song from the 1930 movie *Monte Carlo* called "Beyond the Blue Horizon." Promoters Marty Kramer, Herman Taylor, and later J. Russell Peltz would hold many shows at the location. Peltz promoted more boxing shows at the "Blue" than any other promoter in its history. Harold Johnson, Curtis Cokes, Matthew Saad Muhammad, Bernard Hopkins, Meldrick Taylor, Bennie Briscoe, and Tim Witherspoon were among those who had performed at the venue. In the boxers' dressing room on the second floor, Joe Frazier signed the bathroom door. He wrote "The best seat in the house-Joe Frazier." The "Blue" closed its doors for good in June 2010.

Living in Jersey City could be difficult. Arturo's first vehicle was a blue Jeep, purchased for him by his management team. Arturo purchased a box speaker that he had installed in the automobile. Not long after, someone broke into the Jeep and stole the speaker. Arturo was livid. Joe got a tip on who had taken the speaker. It was a neighborhood hoodlum who was a delivery boy for a local pizzeria.

Joe concocted a plan with Louis Ocasio. They ordered a pie from the pizzeria where the thief worked. Joe told Mario that he ordered a pizza pie. He told Mario that when the pizza arrived to send the delivery boy upstairs to the gym, above the Ringside Lounge. Mario had no clue what was going on.

When the delivery boy arrived, Joe paid for the pizza. Louis, who Joe described as a monster, was over 6 feet tall and weighed over 240-pounds. Louis had a pool cue in his hand, as he had just finished playing a game of pool downstairs. After he paid, Joe looked in the young man's face and said, *"Where's my brother's stuff?"* The speaker-thief immediately realized why he was there. The thief looked around and realized that there was nobody there except him, Joe, and Louis. Louis grabbed him by the arm. He answered Joe, *"What do you mean?"* Joe was more specific. *"Where's the stuff from my brother's Jeep?"* The guy didn't answer, so Louis conked him over the head with the pool cue. The delivery boy screamed, *"I didn't take it. I know who did."*

Joe continued his interrogation. *"Where's the guy with the stuff? What happened to the stuff?"* The thief was trying to stall for time as he thought of an answer or a way out of the trap. Louis conked him over the head again, not too hard, but hard enough to let him know that they meant business. Again the guy yelled out in pain.

Louis conked him over the head another five times until Joe, who was trying his best to refrain from laughing, intervened, *"Louie, stop that's enough. Stop. Stop. The guy's crying."* Joe told the guy to hand over the keys to his car. Joe went downstairs and checked the trunk of the car, but the stolen speaker wasn't there. Joe came back upstairs and demanded, *"Who took it?"* The guy gave a random name. Joe pressed him, *"Where is he?"* The guy, who was now crying, promised to get the information and come back, so Joe told Louis to let him go. Luckily for the thief, Arturo wasn't around. Joe recalled, *"He would have killed him if he was there."* Of course the thief never came back. Every time Joe would see him, he would take off running. Joe chased him all around Jersey City Heights. But the guy always got away.

On August 2, 1991, Joe and Arturo returned to action at the Quality Inn in Newark. Joe, 14-2 (11 KOs), fought the main event against Arizona's Ken Hulsey, 11-5-1 (6 KOs). Joe weighed in at 159-pounds while Hulsey came in at 159½-pounds. The show was televised live on Friday Night Fights. Arturo was paired against former amateur star Richard DeJesus, 1-0, of Puerto Rico by way of Wilmington, Delaware. In Arturo's corner were Pat Lynch, Mario Costa, and Jimmy Glenn as his chief second. Both boxers weighed in at 126½-pounds.

Arturo had several possible opponents pull out on him. The word had spread about Arturo's amateur background and his punching power. The only guy willing to fight Arturo was DeJesus. Pat Lynch was advised by Russell Peltz, the show's co-promoter along with Gabe LaConte, that Arturo was being "matched tough." Some even opined that Lynch might be better served to pull out of the fight and find a softer opponent for the young Gatti.

To get the full understanding of why Peltz would make such a match, one must learn a little bit about Peltz. He has a reputation on the East Coast for making tough competitive matches, which is probably why he has maintained such a loyal fan base. Peltz, on making tough matches, stated, *"You have to give the fans their money's worth or they won't come back."*[123]

Peltz became a boxing fan at the young age of 12. He graduated from Temple University with a degree in journalism. After a short stint as a reporter, he began promoting boxing shows on September 30, 1969, and has been at it ever since. Peltz was known for making "Philly wars" that included names such as Marvelous Marvin Hagler, Bennie Briscoe, Bobbie "Boogaloo" Watts, Eugene "Cyclone" Hart, Richie Kates and Eddie Mustafa Muhammad.

Just being on one of Russell's cards meant that you were going to be matched tough, but when Russell actually declared that the fight was going to be tough you could rest assured that you were in for a war. Peltz fashioned himself after Herman Taylor, long considered the greatest promoter in Philadelphia's fight history. Taylor promoted shows featuring such greats as Jack Dempsey, Gene Tunney, Joe Louis, Rocky Marciano, "Jersey" Joe Walcott and a slew of other greats.

Arturo knew he was fighting a seasoned amateur. This would be his opportunity to show everyone what he could do.

When the bell rang, Arturo charged across the ring and let his punches fly with reckless abandon. DeJesus appeared shocked. He was totally unprepared for Arturo's onslaught. It almost appeared as though he expected Arturo to respect his background in the sport.

Arturo immediately landed a right hand that hurt DeJesus. DeJesus stumbled back to the ropes and was standing straight up as Gatti bombed away with hooks and crosses. A hard uppercut, left hook, right hand combo found its mark and DeJesus fell over on his side, where he was counted out by referee Earl Morton. Blood was streaming out of DeJesus' apparently broken nose. After only 28 seconds of round 1, the fight was over.

Lynch described the scene. *"The fight was held on the old New York Sports Channel and even Teddy Atlas [commentator] thought we were taking a big risk."* Atlas' exact words were, *"I think Gatti's people took a risk taking this DeJesus. From what I get on him in the scouting report he fought Cecil Thompson, a very promising amateur star from Washington D.C. in a fight and he beat him."*

This time it was Mario Costa who hoisted Arturo in the air after the win. You could feel the tension in the ring as Costa and Lynch were trying to outdo each other in regards to who could get closer to Arturo. You got the sense that the triad wouldn't last. After the bout, Arturo hugged ringside photographer Tom Casino. Tom had taken Arturo and Joe's first promo shots after they arrived in Jersey City.

Main Events' Lou and Dino Duva frantically came running back to Arturo's dressing room. Lou and Dino both knew what had just occurred. They knew Arturo had the tools and determination to be a world-class fighter and possibly more.

Lynch later recalled the DeJesus bout. *"Russell Peltz is the promoter, and we have opponent after opponent fall out. Russell comes to me the night before the fight and says, 'I just want you to know that a few of the writers think that the young Gatti is gonna lose tomorrow night.' This kid Richard DeJesus has a great amateur background, the whole bit. So I went to the hotel and I told Arturo, 'We had a lot of opponents fall out, we got you in with a kid we didn't know much about, a real tough fighter,' and he stopped me and said, 'If I can't beat Richard DeJesus, I'll never be world champion. Don't worry about it.' The next day he knocked the kid out. We were not signed with Duva at the time, and in the dressing rooms in Newark you had to go up the stairs. I never saw Dino Duva hop three steps at a time to get to the dressing room. That's when I knew we had something special. It was that third pro fight."*[124]

Shortly thereafter, East Coast Boxing signed Arturo to a promotional contract with Main Events Promotions.

Main Events also wanted to sign Arturo's brother Joe. Dan Duva reached out to Peltz with an offer. Duva offered Peltz 50% of Arturo in return for 50% of Joe.[125] Main Events considered Joe a solid 10-round prospect who was a terrific ticket seller. Peltz, a shrewd judge of talent, agreed. Peltz would later say it was one of the best business decisions he ever made. He would own 50% of Arturo, promotionally, until 1998, when the percentages were amended to 65% for Main Events to 35% for Peltz. Main Events would retain the rights to direct both the brothers' careers.

Lynch and the Duvas weren't the only ones who knew they had a special fighter. Bobby Czyz was at ringside with co-promoter Gabe LaConte. After the knockout, Czyz turned to LaConte and said, *"Gabe, I think they are building up the wrong Gatti."*[126] In the main event, Joe dispatched of Hulsey in 2:32 of the 1st round.

After the bout, Arturo was bombarded with well-wishers. One of the fans who was introduced to Arturo was Donny Jerie. Donny was eating pizza in a restaurant with his friend, Eric Ortense, when Eric's father Bobby walked in and asked them if they wanted to go see Pat Lynch's boxers fight in Newark. The boys agreed to go to the show. Bobby Ortense was a close friend of Lynch's. Donny and Arturo would become close friends. Arturo would nickname Jerie "Donny

B" after a dog they used to call "B."

Donnie worked in the auto body business with his father. After Arturo became friends with Donny, he and Joe went to Donny's father's auto body shop in Bogota, N.J. to look at a corvette. While at the shop, the Gattis decided to let Jerie repaint two Harley Davidson motorcycles that they had just purchased. Arturo picked his color out from paint chips. Jerie painted the motorcycles a purple metallic color. Arturo and Joe picked up their bikes. They were happy with the paint job. Arturo drove his bike around for a few days, and friends were teasing him that the color looked pink. Arturo returned to the shop, as Donny recalled. *"He started breaking my chops, 'I don't know Donny you did such a good job on the bike, but the color, the paint. People are making fun of me.' I said, 'Look man, I got the color chip. You picked it out!' He was going crazy. It wasn't even pink, it was like a metallic purple. I remember he kept on breaking my chops for years and years about that [laughs]. Him and his brother had some bikes."*[127]

Joe and Arturo weren't the typical Italian-American boys when they arrived in New Jersey from Canada. Mikey Red described them as Italian-Montrealians. They had a style all their own. Joe was a very fancy dresser who loved designer clothing. Mikey Red recalled that Arturo got his fashion taste from his brother Joe. When Arturo started earning money, he purchased himself $100 Versace underwear.

In August, Joe was invited to the Bahamas to partake in a fundraising exhibition contest, on the 31st, with Alexis Arguello. Arguello was promoting a card for USA Network's Tuesday Night Fights and was considering a comeback. Arturo accompanied Joe and Lynch on the four-day trip. When Joe met Arguello, one of his idols, he excitedly introduced himself. Arguello looked at Joe and said, *"Tomorrow, I'm gonna show you what boxing's all about."* At first Joe was taken aback, but then he laughed at Arguello's statement. Shortly thereafter, Joe told Lynch, *"Pat, I'm gonna knock him out tomorrow."* A shocked Lynch replied, *"No, you can't do that."*[128]

Lynch and the Gatti brothers ate and drank like kings. Sean O'Grady, the former lightweight champion, was one of the ringside announcers. Joe recalled getting paid "peanuts" for the exhibition bout. Joe and Arguello wore 16-ounce sparring gloves. Joe was a full-fledged middleweight, while Arguello had last competed in the welterweight division. Arguello was 5'10" while Joe was 5'11½".

Arguello was visibly overweight and out of fighting shape.

Arguello, true to form, attacked from the opening bell. Joe peppered him with combinations throughout the round. It was clear to see which fighter was active and which was retired. Joe's punches were much sharper. Joe hadn't forgotten Arguello's comment to him, and made him pay dearly. After the 1st round, Sean O'Grady came over to Joe's corner in disbelief. He looked at Joe and said, *"Joe, what are you doing? You gotta let him work, you're gonna knock him out! It's his show!"*[129] Joe decided to pull back. He spent the remainder of the exhibition boxing and moving. The contest originally was scheduled for 5 rounds, but was reduced to 3.

After the event, Arguello hosted a volleyball game on the beach. Arturo played on the same team as Arguello. During the game, Arguello came over to Joe, eyes swollen from the punches, and apologized for his comments and his aggressive actions in the opening round. Arguello thanked Joe for fighting hard because it helped him decide against making a comeback. Arguello would eventually make the comeback in 1994, going 1-1 before retiring for good in 1995 with a record of 77-8 (62 KOs). Arguello had originally retired in 1986. He won championships in three weight divisions and never lost any of his titles in the ring.

Joe, Arturo, and Lynch chartered a fishing yacht while in the Bahamas. They caught snapper and other fish native to the area. The heat became too much for Joe, so he decided to jump off of the boat's tuna tower to cool off. Arturo followed his big brother's lead and jumped off the tower as well.

When Joe and Arturo attempted to return to the United States, they were stopped by Immigration and Customs. The brothers were stopped at the airport and refused entry into the country because their visas had expired. The brothers were questioned as to why they were visiting the United States, and where they would be staying. Immigration decided to let the brothers in, but warned them that they needed to return to Canada and straighten out their paperwork. The brothers later returned to Canada and extended their visas.

Arturo returned to the ring at the Blue Horizon on October 22 against debuting Francisco Aguiano of Philadelphia. Arturo weighed in at 127 while Aguiano tipped the scale at 124-pounds. Arturo knocked Aguiano out in the 1st round to improve to 4-0 (4 KOs).

On November 28, Thanksgiving Day, Joe and Arturo were alone for the holiday. Even though they were successful in their young careers, they hadn't earned any significant money. They went to eat at Pepe's restaurant in Newark. After they finished eating, they walked to the park to give their leftovers to the homeless. Even when the brothers did not have money, they still felt compelled to help the less fortunate.

Joe was upset that no one on the East Coast management team invited the brothers to their home for the holidays. Both brothers were barely men and they obviously had no family in the country. Joe was visibly distressed when recalling the holidays he and Arturo were forced to spend alone from 1991 to 1993.[130]

Michelle Burke was Arturo's first girlfriend in Jersey City. Her grandmother worked at Costa's White Mana. On November 29, 1991, at the Ringside Lounge, Mario Costa, Arturo, and Burke watched James "Buddy" McGirt dismantle Simon Brown to win the WBC welterweight title. McGirt trained most of his professional career in Jersey City.

Joe, 15-2 (12 KOs), was back in action on December 5, 1991. He took on 7-3 (2 KOs) Glen Odem of Sharon, Pennsylvania at the Quality Inn in Newark. Both fighters tipped the scale at 159-pounds. Joe improved to 16-2 with 13 knockouts when he stopped Odem in the 1st round.

After the Odem fight, Pat Lynch and Main Events sent Joe to Lou Duva's Houston, Texas, training camp to train with George Benton. Joe would have to wait seven months before he fought again.

Arturo joined Joe in Houston for a few weeks, as did fellow New Jersey prospect Frankie Savannah. One night, Lou Duva decided to take the boxers out to the movies. They went to see the drama *Mississippi Burning*. Joe was puzzled as to why Duva would take them to see such a movie. Meldrick Taylor and his wife joined Joe, Arturo, and Savannah. Trainer George Benton also accompanied the fighters.

On the drive to the theater, Benton was discussing how he had seen several UFOs. Joe sat listening to Benton talk, and turned to Arturo and said, *"Can you believe this guy is training us?"* At the theater, during the more serious scenes, one of the fighters busted out laughing, apparently unaware that the movie wasn't a comedy. Joe looked around at the large African-American crowd and whispered to Arturo, *"What are they trying to do by bringing us here, see if we know how to fight?"*[131]

Lynch advised Joe that they were trying to get him a match against England's Lloyd Honeyghan. Honeyghan was a former welterweight champion. Joe spent several frustrating months in the camp. Instead of preparing him for a fight, the Duvas were using Joe as a sparring partner for Olympic prospects Raul Marquez and Montell Griffin. The trainers in camp were Duva, George Benton, and Roger Bloodworth. Joe was not happy. He felt that he wasn't growing as a fighter. He called Lynch and complained about the situation. Lynch advised Joe that he would have a match for him soon. Unfortunately, Joe received a cut while sparring. This ended any hopes of a match in the near future. Joe was upset with the way he was being handled by Main Events. He decided that when his contract expired he would not re-sign with them.

Chapter 7
The Junior Middleweight Championship

On April 22, 1992, Arturo was back in the ring at the Meadowlands Arena in East Rutherford, N.J. He was on the undercard of the Steve Collins-Reggie Johnson WBA middleweight championship fight. Arturo knocked out 1-5 Antonio Gonzalez in the 1st round of the scheduled 4-round bout.

The Don King-promoted card had a large Irish-American contingent on hand to cheer on Collins in the main event. During the undercard, the crowd started booing incessantly. The cause of the heckling was the Reverend Al Sharpton, who had entered the arena. The crowd did not stop booing until Sharpton was escorted out of the arena, apparently for his own safety. Sharpton had been vocal in several racially-charged incidents, the most recent being protest marches against the acquittal of two Italian-American teens in the killing of 16-year-old African-American Yusef Hawkins, in Bensonhurst, Brooklyn.

After the crowd quieted down they erupted again, but this time in cheers. The entire arena stood in unison as though a king or a president had entered the building. Muhammad Ali was slowly making his way down an aisle to a ringside seat. After Ali was seated, a tall Caucasian male attempted to make his way past security to greet Ali but was stopped. The man looked at the security guards and said, *"Get out of my way. I fought that guy."* Ali looked over and recognized Chuck Wepner, "The Bayonne Bleeder." Ali motioned the security guards to let Wepner through. Arturo and Wepner would become good friends, as Gatti's favorite movie was *Rocky*.

Also fighting on the card was one of Main Events promotions' first stars, Rocky Lockridge. The 33-year-old Lockridge originally was from Tacoma, Washington. He cut his teeth at Ice World when the Dan Duva-led company was in its infancy. Lockridge, who was managed by Lou Duva, won two world titles in his fourteen-year career. He left Main Events in 1989. Lockridge, who recently had moved back to Washington State from New Jersey, lost a lopsided decision to contender Sharmba Mitchell. Kathy Duva told a reporter that Lockridge had fallen on hard times. She revealed that when he was living in New Jersey, Lockridge was hiding from creditors in his basement.[132]

It was the age-old story of boxing. The young hungry warrior on the rise defeats the aging former champion. Father time would never be defeated. But it was more than age that had destroyed Lockridge. He had a serious drug problem. Lockridge would return to New Jersey and wind up a homeless crack addict, living on the streets of Camden. Lockridge died on February 7, 2019 at the age of 60.

Other Main Events fighters, such as Johnny Bumphus and Christie Elliot, would meet similar fates. Bumphus, a former world champion, would become addicted to crack cocaine. He was stabbed in an altercation that led to another man being killed. Bumphus died of a heart attack on February 3, 2020 at the age of 59. Elliot wound up a homeless alcoholic. He was convicted of beating another homeless man to death over a bottle of liquor in a Clifton, N.J. homeless camp. Elliot died on April 19, 2011, also at the age of 59. In regards to Bumphus' death, Kathy Duva stated, *"Sadly, he was also the first fighter who, to my mind, made it obvious how dangerous the combination of substance abuse and extreme weight loss could be for a fighter. I believe that all of this abuse not only cut his career short, but caused Johnny to suffer through many physical problems throughout the rest of his life."*[133]

In early May 1992, 20-year-old Arturo was taken up to Bufano's gym to spar with 27-year-old former Irish featherweight prospect Bobby McCarthy. The 10-4 (5 KOs) McCarthy had lost to Jesse James Leija by knockout two years earlier. Mikey Red was on hand for the sparring session. He recalled how impressed he and Pat Lynch were when Arturo knocked McCarthy out cold with a right hand while wearing 14-ounce sparring gloves. McCarthy laid motionless on the ring floor for several minutes. Arturo injured his right hand when knocking out McCarthy.

On May 15, Arturo returned to the ring at the Trump Taj Mahal in Atlantic City. It would be the first time Arturo fought in the city that would become synonymous with his name. The 5-0 (5 KOs) 128-pound Gatti took on 2-2-1 (1 KO) 124½-pound Joe Lafontant of Washington D.C. Although he won, Arturo was taken the distance for the first time in his career in the 6-round contest.

Lynch was concerned with the way Gatti looked during the match, specifically by the fact that his knockout streak had ended. Part of the reason Arturo failed to knock Lafontant out was due to the fact that he had broken his right hand during the fight. It was the same hand that he had injured while sparring with Bobby McCarthy. Arturo later recalled that breaking his hand in the 2nd round against

LaFontant hurt so much that he felt sick in his stomach. He forced himself to block out the pain.[134]

It would be six months before Arturo would fight again. Gatti was operated on by Doctor Richard Boiardo at Meadowlands Hospital in Secaucus, N.J. Besides operating on Arturo's hand, Boiardo fused two of Gatti's ribs together. Boiardo believed that the ribs had hindered Arturo's punching. He felt that Gatti would regain the ability to hit hard and freely after the surgery.[135]

It was decided by Lynch that Joe and Arturo needed a trainer that could work with them not only in the gym but also in their corners at the fights. Up until that point, Panama Lewis had been working with Arturo and Joe in the gym, while different cornermen were patched together to work their fights. Joe described training with Panama Lewis. *"If Panama was allowed to be in my corner until today, I probably would still be fighting and would be champ. Panama had my number. I had his number. When we separated it was because he was trying to get to Tyson. My career was over when he left. I was never the same. I tried Hector Roca but I was a killer when Panama trained me."*[136]

In June 1992, Lynch, Costa and Seibert brought the brothers to Diego Rosario of Paterson, N.J. The retired Rosario was a former five-time N.J. Golden Gloves champion as an amateur. As a professional he won the N.J. bantamweight championship. Rosario had been managed by Lou Duva. Rosario maintained a close relationship with Duva as he explained. *"Lou Duva was like a father to me. He was like the godfather. He was real good to me. I think he was real good to everybody else. He would call me all the time. He'd say, 'Come on, you gotta work for me. Come, I need you to train some fighters over here.' Without even asking he would say, 'Diego I need you.' And he would pay me good money."*[137]

Rosario was the head trainer at the Lou Costello Sportsmen's Club. The gym, which opened in 1971, was named after Paterson's Louis Cristillo. Cristillo later changed his name to Costello after actress Helene Costello. He went on to perform in vaudeville and burlesque theaters as part of a two-man comedy team with Asbury Park's Bud Abbott. Abbott and Costello starred in thirty-six feature films and several TV series.

Lou Costello had been an exceptional athlete as a child, and he loved boxing. It was rumored that he fought under the name "Lou King." Lou's family started the Lou Costello Paterson Youth Foundation in his honor. Money from the foundation was used to open the boxing club. The club was originally located in a defunct fire house on Main Street in Paterson. The gym was long but narrow. The ring was very small, only about 12 feet by 12 feet, half the size of a regulation ring. If you took two steps back you were hitting the ropes.

Rosario's style when he fought was that of an inside volume puncher. Diego retired in 1994 with an 18-6-1 (13 KOs) record. Although Rosario was known as an inside fighter, as a trainer he instructed his fighters to box. At the time the Gatti brothers arrived at Lou Costello's, the gym was thriving. The gym had over forty boxers training there each night. Some of the boxers you could find there included brothers Frankie and David Toledo, Kendall Holt, Omar Sheika, Freddy Curiel, John Molnar, Scott DePompe, Arturo Nina, and on occasion, a past-his-prime Livingstone Bramble. The majority of gym members were amateurs at the time. Amateur boxer Nasser Nettles recalled when the Gatti brothers first walked into the gym. Nettles and other amateurs had to spar with Arturo. Nettles recalled, *"That guy could punch. I would go home with headaches every day."*[138]

Mike DePompe, father of junior welterweight boxer Scott DePompe, first saw the Gatti brothers fight when Joe and Arturo boxed at the Meadowlands Convention Center in 1991. He first met the brothers in person when they came to train in Paterson. He recalled, *"At the time, my son [Scott DePompe] was training at Costello's [Gym] as an amateur getting prepared for the New Jersey State Diamond Gloves. Joe and Arturo took a liking to my son and worked with him in the ring sparring and giving him advice. Joe Gatti spent a great deal of time with him and together with Diego Rosario helped pave the way to the eventual win in the finals of the N.J. Diamond Gloves Championship. Joe and Arturo were well-liked by the kids in the Costello Gym, because they always were willing to work with them no matter what level they were at.*

"Joe Gatti was an extremely talented boxer/puncher and Arturo would often say that he wished he had Joe's boxing ability. Joe was extremely proud of Arturo and never missed an opportunity to brag about him or a minute worrying about him either. After all, it was Joe Gatti that came to N.J. first, paving the way for Arturo.

"During that time we became friends. Joe liked horseback riding and Arturo did as well, and since I had my own horses, we met up with another friend of mine and we trail rode for several hours. Of course, Joe and Arturo showed the same competitive spirit on a

horse as they did in the ring, and the trail ride became somewhat like a mini-western movie of galloping and racing through the woods and trails. [This probably gave their managers nightmares of Joe and Arturo falling off the horses and getting injured].

"It was a wonderful picture for me, Joe and Arturo together laughing and joking, riding and enjoying the moments together, moments away from the boxing scene where they were free, in the freedom of the woods, trails and nature to just be brothers enjoying some R & R. This was the start of our friendship. We spent more time with Joe, as he lived close by and was able to ride more often. However, for us, Arturo never forgot the days at Costello Gym, the horseback riding, or the fact that Joe and our family spent time together."[139] Joe enjoyed horseback riding so much he would purchase two horses of his own years later.

Each gym has the main fighter, the one who is acknowledged by all other gym members as the gym's best fighter. The "king of the gym" at the time in Costello's was David Toledo. The 16-year-old Toledo was a professional boxer with a 2-0 (2 KOs) record. David had a stellar amateur career that included over a hundred bouts and several national championships. In the United States, boxers normally have to be 18 years old to turn professional. Toledo turned professional 16 days after his 16th birthday, in November of 1991. Toledo was a light puncher but he had excellent head movement, foot work, and hand speed. He could spar 8 rounds in the 12 x 12 ring without anyone laying a hand on him. As the old-timers would say, "you couldn't hit him with a handful of rice."

David's older brother, Frankie, also trained in the gym. Frankie was a half inch shorter than the 5'7" David. Although Frankie was a light puncher, he had an inside style that mirrored his trainer, Rosario. Frankie had a 10-2 (4 KOs) record as a pro when Joe and Arturo arrived. Frankie would go on to win the IBF featherweight title in 2001. Frankie and David both campaigned in the 126-pound weight class at the time. Gym members were anticipating its star, David, getting into the ring with Arturo. They would have to wait, as Arturo's hand injury from the Lafontant bout was not yet healed. Rosario explained, "Already, that was from day one. He had hand problems because he was a puncher, a good puncher."[140]

Rosario explained how the Gatti brothers took to his training methods. "They caught on to everything I taught them. As far as experience, Joe had a little more experience than Arturo. When I got Arturo, Arturo didn't move. I got Arturo to move and dance."[141]

Rosario recalled that Lynch wanted Arturo to box more, but he didn't want Arturo to stop using his power. *"I remember Pat Lynch telling me that Arturo's good. That he wants to learn how to box too, but not taking away, you can't take away the punching, you know. I was the one who got him to box. He didn't have any boxing abilities."*[142] Rosario added that it wouldn't have made sense to have Arturo running around because that would have diminished his punching power. Rosario felt that more head movement and some better footwork was all Arturo needed. Rosario would go on to lead Bruce Seldon to the WBA heavyweight title in 1995.

Finally, after a few weeks, David and Arturo sparred each other. From the first round it was apparent that Arturo was too big and too strong for David. He had little trouble trapping David in a corner, where he worked the body and head. David, although a polished combination puncher, was not proficient at fighting on the inside. After two or three sparring sessions, Rosario stopped sparring them against each other. At the time, Rosario told the gym members that he stopped sparring David and Arturo because both of them had huge egos. The sparring would get too heated because both boxers wanted to get the upper hand. Years later Rosario admitted, *"Arturo was always a little too strong."*[143]

Joe recalled when he and Arturo went for a haircut at a barber shop owned by Giuseppe Boccia on Kennedy Boulevard in Jersey City. Boccia, a native of Naples, Italy, was confident that one or both of the brothers would find success in America. As Joe recalled, *"Joe the barber was the best. We were at Joe the barber getting our hair cut and he goes, 'You guys, you two guys over here, you're beautiful Italian boys.' He said, 'Listen don't make nobody come between you guys, cause they're gonna try.' He said, 'They're gonna be jealous and try and separate you guys. Don't let it happen, if you make it, he makes it, if you make it, he makes it.'"*[144]

On July 30, Joe, 16-2 (13 KOs), had his first fight with his new trainer Rosario. The 161-pound Joe took on the 7-5 (2 KOs) 163-pound Mike Williams of North Carolina at the Waterloo Village in Stanhope N.J. Joe knocked Williams out in the 1st round of the scheduled 8-round contest. The bout was on the undercard of the Al Cole-James Warring IBF cruiserweight title fight.

In August 1992, the SCI investigation from 1985 resurfaced. N.J. Athletic Control Board Chairman Larry Hazzard was brought before the N.J. Senate permanent subcommittee on investigations. He admitted that he ignored information in the report concerning boxing manager Al Certo. The report revealed that Certo was an associate of the Genovese organized crime family and that Certo was particularly close to John DiGilio, a Genovese crime family member. The report added that DiGilio, a former middleweight boxer who was killed in 1988, controlled gambling, loansharking, extortion and waterfront racketeering activity for the Genovese family in Hudson County. The commission recommended that Certo be barred from boxing because of his *"admitted close associations with organized crime figures."*[145]

John DiGilio, or "Johnny Dee," as he was known, was a former welterweight boxer out of Bayonne who retired with a 28-10 record. He won the N.Y. Daily News Golden Gloves 126-pound sub-novice title in 1950. One of the "muscle men," or collectors for DiGilio was Jersey City light heavyweight boxer Frankie DePaula.

Larry Hazzard defended his decision to keep renewing the license of Certo, who managed WBC welterweight champion Buddy McGirt. *"We do not feel, based on a report submitted by the SCI, that we should deny Mr. Certo his right to participate in the business."*[146] Certo, a former fighter who compiled a 9-1 record, owned a tailor shop and co-owned the Italian Cove Restaurant, both in Secaucus N.J. The report added that Certo's businesses were *"mob hangouts,"* and as a promoter he regularly arranged *"mismatches"* and employed *"a number of boxers with criminal records."*[147] Certo, originally from Hoboken, felt that the report picked on him because he was Italian.

Certo commented, *"Who the hell are these guys in New Jersey to say I should be banned from boxing. Give me a reason. I happen to have been friendly with a guy who got killed [DiGilio]. He became a gangster. I became a tailor. Why should I be a gangster? This is guilt by association. I have never done anything wrong in my life. If I have done something wrong, why don't I have a record?"*[148] Certo later admitted that he was convicted of manslaughter in 1974 for *"punching someone out."*[149] He said the incident was *"personal and had nothing to do with boxing."*[150] Jack Dempsey was one of many celebrities who wrote letters to the court on Certo's behalf during the manslaughter trial. Certo added that if the politicians wanted to ban everyone with a criminal record from the boxing game, *"there would be no fight game."*[151]

N.J. Athletic Commission member Gary Shaw commented, *"It's alleged he is involved with organized crime, but it doesn't mean Al Certo is a bad person. He has not been indicted or convicted. There are no irregularities with Al Certo in boxing.* "[152]

In September, there were cries from the public and media for federal oversight of boxing. Former N.J. State Athletic Commission deputy and current president of the IBF, Robert Lee, invoked his Fifth Amendment right when asked if he received cash bribes when he was a state official in the early 1980s. It was alleged that Lee accepted a $3,000 bribe from an FBI undercover informant in 1981 to help someone gain a boxing promoter's license. Lee allegedly passed the bribe on to then commissioner "Jersey" Joe Walcott. Besides federal oversight, there were calls for a computerized registry of boxers, uniform health and safety rules, minimum licensing standards, and controls over independent boxing federations that rate fighters and sanction championship bouts.

On November 13, 1992, Main Events-promoted heavyweight champion Evander Holyfield took a terrible beating while losing his title to Riddick Bowe. Dan and Lou Duva compassionately urged Holyfield to retire. When Holyfield refused to retire, the boxer and his promoter parted ways. A year later, Holyfield would regain the title and avenge his loss to Bowe.

Joe returned to the ring on November 14, 1992 at McAfee N.J., with a lopsided 10-round decision win over 22-10-1 (10 KOs) Terry Whitaker of Chicago. Joe weighed in at 154-pounds for the contest, while the much shorter Whitaker tipped the scale at 152. Whitaker had campaigned most of his career in the junior welterweight division. Gatti dominated the fight, dropping Whitaker four times with lightning left hooks, en route to a unanimous decision victory. The show was held next to Vernon N.J. and the Mountain Creek ski resort, which was the training camp for Roy Jones Jr. at the time. The 23-year-old Jones, 19-0 (18 KOs), was in attendance at the show. He had yet to win his first world title. Pat Lynch had lobbied for Arturo to fight on the Main Events-promoted McAfee card, but his partner Ritchie Seibert had already committed Arturo to a Peltz card three days later.[153]

On November 17, 1992 at the Blue Horizon, after six months of inactivity as a result of a broken hand, and with a new trainer, Arturo finally returned to the ring. The 6-0 (5 KOs) 127-pound Arturo faced Philadelphia's King Solomon, a light-punching 129-pound boxer who sported a record of 6-1-3 (1 KO). Solomon's only loss was via decision. Again, this was a Peltz-promoted card, which meant Arturo was not going to get a "dead body." A "dead body" was a term used to describe fighters who did not have the skills or desire to win and basically fought for a paycheck. Those types of fighters were very rare on Peltz-promoted cards, even if they were to be matched against a Peltz co-promoted fighter, such as Arturo.

Pat Lynch was unsure of the Solomon match. He approached Diego Rosario about the match-up before they signed the contract. Diego recalled the conversation. *"Pat Lynch asked me if that was a good fight or no. I said, 'Arturo could punch. Arturo could box. It's up to you. You're the manager.'"*[154]

After the opening bell rang, Solomon boxed with his hands very low. His punches were wide and came from unusual angles. Fifty seconds into the 1st round, Solomon caught Arturo with a wide hook. Arturo was feinting well and using his jab. Arturo started matching Solomon's wild shots with winging shots of his own. At the 2:27 mark, Gatti telegraphed a right hand. Before the punch came forward, Solomon countered with a wide left hook that found Arturo's jaw, snapping Gatti's head back. Rosario kept screaming from ringside for Arturo to use his jab.

At the 2:40 mark, Gatti and Solomon threw right hands at the same time. Solomon's punch landed on the top of Gatti's head. Arturo's right cross missed. Arturo was standing over the painted ring canvas Budweiser logo that was wet from sweat. He had bent his right knee to get more leverage on his punch. The combination of Solomon's punch with Arturo's foot on the slippery logo caused Arturo to go down on his right knee. Referee Rudy Battle correctly ruled a knockdown and sent Solomon to a neutral corner. The timekeeper stood up and started counting. Battle picked up the count at four as the Gatti contingency who made the two-hour drive to the fight booed the knockdown call. Arturo rose to his feet and turned to the timekeeper in disbelief. The 1st round ended shortly after. Solomon returned to his corner with his arms raised.

Lynch and Percy Richardson worked the corner with Rosario. Rosario asked Gatti to move his head more, use his jab and work the body on the inside. Arturo opened the 2nd round with a solid right. Gatti worked his jab as he looked to land bombs. Solomon was busier, throwing wide combinations. The two boxers exchanged shots in the middle of the ring. Solomon scored a solid hook that triggered a moan from the crowd. Arturo landed a short right on Solomon's jaw at the 2:36 mark that dropped Solomon onto the seat of his trunks. The pro-Gatti crowd rose to their feet. After Solomon got back up, Arturo swung for the hills until the bell rang.

At the start of the 3rd, Solomon ripped hooks and a right to the body. He still held his hands dangerously low. Arturo appeared more tentative in this round. The crowd tried to motivate Arturo by chanting, *"Gatti! Gatti! Gatti!"* Arturo landed two rights to the body. Lynch yelled, *"Double up that jab, Arthur!"* The pace slowed considerably, though Solomon was busier. A little over two minutes into the 3rd, Solomon landed a crunching right hand while backing away. The blow twisted Arturo's head. Gatti responded by sticking his tongue out at Solomon. Solomon answered with a hook that nearly cut Gatti's tongue off. Arturo rushed the retreating Solomon and was caught by a hard left hook that caused the crowd to groan. Solomon grinned as Arturo, showing a solid jaw, kept stepping forward. Solomon landed another solid hook on Gatti. The round ended with both boxers staring each other down.

Lynch applied an ice bag to Arturo's neck as Rosario pleaded with Gatti to box. Both fighters traded wide blows to start the 4th round with Solomon landing the flusher shots. Arturo started circling the ring as Solomon pursued. Solomon landed another left hook on Gatti. Arturo refused to keep his right hand up. The round ended with Solomon in control.

Arturo started the 5th jabbing. He landed a solid right 43 seconds into the round. Solomon landed a flush right halfway through the stanza. Solomon landed two more rights that sent Gatti reeling off-balance. Arturo danced around the ring, regaining his footing. He landed a sharp lead hook. Solomon came back with three hooks of his own. Solomon ended the round with a crisp right hand. Arturo appeared to need a knockout going into the final round.

Arturo dug two hard body shots to start the 6th. Solomon pulled away. Gatti kept attacking behind the jab, but Solomon landed the cleaner blows. Arturo connected with a ripping left hook. Solomon took the punch well. Gatti landed another hook and right hand. He used every ounce of his weight in his punches. Arturo missed a hook. Solomon countered with a right that rocked Gatti. Both fighters threw with reckless abandon as the final bell rang. Both boxers raised their hands in victory. Arturo broke his right hand during the match.

Mario Costa was not at the fight. He was vacationing in his native Portugal. Richie Seibert was missing from the ring after the fight for the first time as well. This was most likely due to the disagreement with Lynch over putting Arturo on Peltz's card. It was obvious that Pat Lynch had become the main member of East Coast Boxing who was driving the careers' of Joe and Arturo. Lynch was growing closer to Main Events and leaning heavily on the expertise of Dan and Lou Duva.

Arturo looked frustrated that he was unable to put Solomon away. Solomon wasn't very fast, but he was a busy fighter. He was adept at pulling away after punching. Arturo's left eye was swollen from the right hands he absorbed. He made the sign of the cross as he paced around the ring awaiting the decision.

Ring announcer, Ed Derian, announced a split decision. Judge Carol Polis had Arturo winning 57-56. Judge George Hill had it 58-55 for Solomon, while judge Al Morris scored the bout 59-55 for Solomon. After the decision was read, Solomon's corner exploded in celebration. Arturo and Lynch paced around the ring with their heads down, unable to digest what had just occurred. Rosario and Richardson remained frozen in the corner.

Rosario recalled, *"It was pretty close till the end when Solomon started outboxing Arturo. You know, he outboxed him by running and pitter-pattering."*[155] Peltz recalled, *"I was telling everyone to watch this kid Gatti. Next thing I know he gets dropped. He got up and dropped Solomon later, but lost on points."*[156]

Arturo's team was stunned by the loss. Gatti cried in his dressing room. Lynch and Main Events immediately tried to secure a rematch, but as Peltz recalled, *"Solomon wanted way too much [money] for a rematch."*[157] Solomon would fight and win one more bout before retiring with an 8-1-3 (1 KO) record. Solomon would go on to become a boxing trainer.

Gatti would later admit that he hesitated too much in the fight and he didn't fight his fight. When Arturo was asked, years later, what his most painful experience was in boxing, he replied, *"Broken hands, I would think. But I would say my first professional loss. I felt that you had to be undefeated to become a world champion. But it wasn't that way."*

Before the Solomon match, for the first time in his career, Arturo studied tapes of his opponent. After losing the fight, he rarely would review tapes of an opponent. Arturo stated, *"I based myself on [Solomon's] last performance, but when he fought me he fought totally different. It's ridiculous. You can't watch a guy [on tape] and base what he's going to do against you on that performance."*[158]

Mikey Red recalled the Solomon match. *"Arturo dropped Solomon and it was called a slip. And later, Arturo slipped and it was called a knockdown. Arturo hurt or broke his right hand in the fight. His power was too big for his bone structure. The loss didn't set Arturo* back and didn't hurt him [mentally]. I was blown away. He just went on."[159]

In boxing, fighters constantly have people that whisper in their ears, telling them that their trainer, manager, or promoter is no good. The blame for the loss had to be placed on either the fighter for not executing the gameplan, the trainer for not preparing him properly, or the manager for accepting the wrong opponent. Rosario was blamed for the loss and replaced with Hector Roca of New York City. Panama Lewis recommended Roca, who was also Panamanian. Skowronski explained the change. *"Pat wanted the knockout ratio. He didn't want Arturo boxing like Diego Rosario was teaching him."*[160]

Rosario recalled being replaced. *"They blamed me for that loss because I should have said no to that fight... but because I didn't say no, they blamed me, and then Panama Lewis got them to get Hector Roca. They went to Hector Roca or else I would have been with Arturo. The reason why Arturo got beat was that Arturo lost his cool and he went back to the slugging style and this guy just outboxed him. If Arturo would've kept his boxing ability I think he would've had a chance with the kid. Yeah, he lost his cool and this guy was too slick; this guy was slick. They didn't do nothing to improve him, nothing. Arturo got there [to the top] because Arturo could punch and he could take a shot. You know, that's why Joe is a little different."*[161]

Rosario reminisced about both brothers. *"Joe was a little bit more serious. Arturo was a little bit more of a clown. I hung out with Arturo. Arturo stayed in my house for like a week when I was working with him. He didn't have a place to stay. So I let him stay over at my house. And Arturo, when you would hang out with him, he was a clown, a fun guy. And Joe, he was a clown too but a little more serious than Arturo. Arturo was a little bit more of a slugger. Joe could hit hard too, but Arturo was more of a slugger, like Rocky Marciano. Joe had power in both hands."*[162] Regarding who was the better boxer Rosario stated, *"I would have to say Joe."*[163]

Besides Rosario, Russell Peltz was blamed for matching Arturo too tough. Obviously, as the management team, East Coast Boxing reserved the right to refuse any opponent that was offered to them. Richie Seibert was blamed for pressuring Arturo to fight on the Peltz card instead of the Main Events-promoted card. This issue created an irreparable friction between Seibert and Arturo.

Blame also was placed on Mario Costa. Lynch moved the Gatti

brothers out of Costa's house in Jersey City. As Costa recalled, *"When he lost that fight [to King Solomon]. That's when they left. When Pat pulled them away. Pat tried to blame us too, for the loss. He wanted Roca to take him in some other direction or whatever. But Panama, we didn't get that fight. That Solomon fight. Pat was already trying to take them away from us. Panama and me had nothing to do with that Solomon fight. I was in Portugal when he lost that. I wasn't even here!"*[164]

Lynch moved Joe and Arturo out of the apartment owned by Costa and into an apartment on Ogden Avenue in Jersey City. The apartment building on Ogden was owned by Bobby Ortense, or "Bobby O", as he was known. Ortense knew Pat from Lynch's ticket business, Curtain Call Tickets. Joe and Arturo didn't stay on Ogden Avenue for long. The brothers also spent time at the Robert Treat Hotel in Newark. Lynch was friends with the hotel's owner.

Joe recalled the early years. *"Lynch made us stay at Mario's. He didn't want to pay for a place. Then me and my brother stayed at this apartment, one of his friends [Bobby Ortense in Jersey City]. We froze. We had to put a heater on with the gas and sleep in the same bed. That's how they took care of us. They forgot about that."*[165] Joe added, *"Lynch bought me a car once but he wanted it back. I had to sell it back because he needed the money. An Audi, an $8,000 Audi. Pat goes, 'Yo Joe, I'm in a little bit of trouble.' My brother made him a fortune. Now he's set."*[166]

The new trainer, Hector Roca, had a reputation as being a "puncher's" trainer. He focused mostly on teaching his fighters to "sit on their punches," which is transferring weight with the punches while pivoting. In order for a boxer to fight in that style, he has to sacrifice foot movement. Roca never boxed himself, as he explained in an interview. *"My brother and father boxed, but I boxed only for fun, my sport was cycling. I made two Olympics as a cyclist. So my sport is cycling. When I moved to America I see there's lots of opportunity in boxing, as a trainer, because the technique is tough."*[167]

Roca did not mettle in his fighters' personal lives. Most professional trainers differ in their approach to this subject. Although a trainer must have total control over their fighter in the gym, if a trainer becomes too involved in a fighter's personal life it can have negative consequences. For instance, if a trainer gives an opinion on a boxer's dating partner, it could blow up in his face later if the fighter falls in or out of love with the person he is dating.

Roca had trained several world-class fighters, including Buddy McGirt, Iran Barkley, Michael Olajide, Reynaldo Snipes, and Regilio Tuur. Tuur, a super featherweight from the Netherlands, would go on to win the WBO super featherweight title in 1994 and defend it successfully six times. Roca trained fighters out of Gleason's gym in Brooklyn. Arturo would now have to travel to Brooklyn for training.

In December 1992, Joe Gatti was ranked #5 by the WBA. In January 1993, the WBC rated Joe #14, while the IBF rated him #11 in the world at junior middleweight.

Arturo started dating a girl named Emily. She would be the first of several girlfriends who earned a living by dancing in "gentlemen's clubs." Donny Jerie recalled, *"Emily was nice. She was a cool girl. Every one of them didn't like what he did [partying and womanizing]. He wanted to do what he wanted to do basically. She was a little crazy you know. I'll be honest, I think every girl that Gatti dated was a little out of whack."*[168]

Joe returned to the ring on March 6, 1993 at the mecca of boxing, Madison Square Garden. Kathy Duva would later state that the Garden had electricity that you could touch and feel.[169] Joe weighed 162-pounds while his opponent, Oscar Noriega of Hackensack N.J., weighed in at 164-pounds. Noriega was listed on the show's poster as having a solid winning record. In reality he was 1-5 with 1 KO. Gatti easily dispatched of the overmatched Noriega in 2 rounds. Joe now held a record of 19-2 (15 KOs). The fight was on the undercard of the Pernell Whitaker-Buddy McGirt welterweight championship bout.

Hector Roca was still working with Regilio Tuur. Tuur was defending his European super featherweight title against Michele La Fratta on March 23, 1993 in Rotterdam, Netherlands. Arturo was secured a match on the undercard. Arturo fought Plamen Gechev 4-5 (2 KOs) of Bulgaria. Arturo easily knocked out Gechev in the 1st round to improve to 7-1 (6 KOs).

On April 1, Salvatore "Sammy the Bull" Gravano testified before a Senate subcommittee that Al Certo had ties to the Gambino crime family. Certo angrily denied the charges at the same hearing. Gravano had admitted to 19 murders. He also testified against his former boss, New York mobster John Gotti. Gravano stated that Certo was connected to the family through "made man" Joseph "Jo-Jo" Corozzo.

Gravano added, *"His [Certo's] relationship with Jo-Jo Corozzo is how we had a piece of McGirt. McGirt is a fighter, and although Certo brought him by the club once and introduced him to some people, it really wouldn't be fair for me to say that he [McGirt] is an associate of organized crime. But Certo was with us, and that gave us our interest in McGirt. Because the size of purses has gotten so big over the past 20 years, organized crime is more and more interested in getting back into it."*[170]

Certo shouted, as he countered Gravano's allegations, *"Here's a man who has admitted killing 19 people. He's the gangster here. He's the one who knows everything. I've never met this guy in my life. He's full of crap. You look at me with the dark glasses and I talk out of the side of my mouth, and you say, 'He must be a bad guy, organized crime.' Gambino, gamschmino! I've never heard of these guys."*[171]

Certo later admitted that his co-manager, Stuart "Stuey" Weiner, had introduced him to Corozzo. He said Weiner and Corozzo were childhood friends. Weiner was at the hearings as well. He invoked his Fifth Amendment rights six times when asked if he had ties to the mafia. McGirt testified that he was unaware if Certo or Weiner had ties to organized crime or that the mafia owned any part of his contract. McGirt did say that he knew Corozzo as a "friend" of Weiner's.

In the April 1993 ratings, Joe was listed #5 by the WBA, #8 by the WBC, and #10 by the IBF at middleweight. Arturo was unranked.

Arturo and Joe were back in action on April 7, in Newark N.J. It was one of the rare times that the brothers would box on the same card. Arturo fought 3-11-1 (1 KO) Curtis Mathis of Philadelphia, knocking him out in the 3rd round of the scheduled 4-round bout. Joe boxed the main event against 6-2 (5 KOs) Nate Woods of Connecticut. Joe took the 10-round bout by decision.

On May 15 in Bricktown, N.J., Arturo knocked out 13-11 (6 KOs) Clifford Hicks in 3 rounds. Joe continued his climb up the rankings. He was now ranked #3 by the WBA, #10 by the WBC, and #9 by the IBF. Arturo remained unranked.

Joe advised Lynch that he wanted to leave the Main Events/Peltz promotional team and sign with Don King promotions. Piero Santini, the owner of the La Gondola restaurant in Nutley N.J., was friends with King, and influenced Joe's decision. Santini had been involved with former WBO heavyweight champion Francesco Damiani. Santini told Joe that if he signed with King, Joe could get a title shot against Gianfranco Rosi.

King paid $25,000 to buy out Joe's contract. Joe recalls signing with King. *"I left because I wanted to fight Gianfranco Rosi and these guys, they were gonna make it happen."*[172]

Joe's decision to leave Main Events would negatively affect both his boxing career and his relationship with Arturo. Main Events had invested heavily in Joe's career. Joe held a 20-2 record with 15 KOs. He had reeled off 12 straight victories. Main Events and Lynch had carefully selected each of his opponents, which were tailor-made to advance his career. Main Events was known to take their time in molding their prospects. Joe was rated in the top ten of every major sanctioning body when he left the company. Main Events was known in boxing as more of a "mom and pop" promotional company, that treated their fighters like family, while Don King Promotions had a much larger stable of fighters and more of a business type relationship with their boxers.

While Joe may have been anxious for a title shot when he decided to leave the company, he may not have given much thought to how this move would affect his brother. Arturo, 9-1 (8 KOs), was still under contract with Main Events and Peltz Promotions. Joe's move put Arturo in a very difficult situation. Main Events would have to rethink how much they would be willing to invest in Arturo, as it was unknown how much influence Joe might have on Arturo's future career decisions. They had to be reassured that Arturo would not abandon the company as his brother had. Joe and Arturo were still living together at the time. Joe's move put Pat Lynch in a precarious situation as well, as it looked as though he had no control over the fighters that he managed. If Joe's decision to leave Main Events bothered Arturo, he never mentioned it to his friends. Main Events, to their credit, continued building Arturo's career as though the situation with Joe had never occurred.

In June 1993, Joe went back to Montreal to renew his work visa, as he was a Canadian citizen. While in Canada, Pat Lynch called him. Lynch told Joe that King wanted him to fight Terry Norris for the WBC super welterweight title. Joe initially refused to fight Norris, until he was told that King would drop him if he did not take the fight. Joe and Lynch went to King's office. King promised a Rosi fight if Joe beat Norris. Joe asked to speak to Lynch privately. In the hallway, Lynch reminded Joe that King would drop him if he refused the Norris fight. Joe asked Lynch for help in making a decision. Joe advised Lynch that he was weighing 190-pounds, and getting to 154 would be difficult in 12 weeks. Lynch felt that three months would be enough time to be fight-ready. Joe and Lynch went back into King's office and advised King that they would take the fight. Lynch didn't sign for the Norris fight. Joe signed the contract himself, with Piero as his adviser.

On June 20, 130-pound Arturo took on 132-pound Christino Suero of New York City in the 8-round co-feature at Harrah's Casino in Atlantic City. Suero's record was 1-5 (1 KO) but was listed as 4-6-2 on the Prime Network televised card. In the corner, with Hector Roca, was Mario Costa.

Gatti started the bout with a hard right to the head followed by a solid hook to the body. Arturo ripped hard double hooks to the body and head. Two more solid body punches followed. Arturo started circling the 32-year-old Suero, displaying fast footwork and boxing ability. Suero landed a hard right over Gatti's guard early in the 1st and another hard hook later in the round. Arturo finished the round with several more hard body punches.

During the 2nd round, the announcers mentioned that Arturo's brother Joe might be in line for a shot at Gianfranco Rosi's junior middleweight title. Arturo controlled the round with a stiff jab, hard right hands, and solid hooks to the body. Gatti stepped over flawlessly after he finished punching. Halfway through the 3rd, Arturo landed a hard lead right uppercut while stepping over to his left. A few seconds later, Gatti landed a hard hook to the body of the crouching Suero. The blow sent Suero down to his knees, where referee Earl Morton counted him out.

During an early July morning, after a night of partying with friends, Arturo decided he wanted to go down the Jersey shore to Seaside Heights. Arturo and a few friends hopped into his Jeep Wrangler, with the top down, and headed down the Garden State Parkway. The traffic was bumper to bumper, a normal occurrence for a Jersey weekend in the summer. Arturo grew frustrated with the traffic. He noticed the local lane side of the Parkway was moving much quicker. The only problem was, there was a grass median with a gully that was dividing the local and express lanes. Arturo drove across the median, into the gully, and back up onto the local lanes.

When Arturo and his friends arrived at Seaside Heights they walked the boardwalk before entering a local club. Arturo started doing funnel drinks. Funnel drinks utilize a plastic funnel attached to a plastic hose. The funnel is filled up with beer while the hose is curled up to prevent the beer from coming out. The drinker puts his thumb on the end of the hose and holds the funnel up over his mouth.

He then releases his thumb which causes the beer to rush down the drinker's throat at a high rate of speed.

After Arturo drank the funnel shot, he threw the beer back up, as Donny Jerie recalled, *"all over the place."*[173] Arturo's friends were laughing hysterically. When Arturo was finished puking he said, *"I'm not done yet. Give me another one."* This time Arturo handled the rush of alcohol with ease. Donny watched Arturo conquer the funnel drink and he thought to himself, *"This guy don't stop with anything in life he wants to succeed at. Whatever it may be. This kid is gonna be a world champ."*[174]

Arturo enjoyed all kinds of music, but Jerie recalled that TKA and Journey were two of Arturo's favorite groups. Arturo loved "Wheels in the Sky" and "Don't Stop Believing" by Journey. When Arturo partied, he followed the lyrics of "Don't Stop Believing." *"Working hard to get my fill, Everybody wants a thrill. Payin' anything to roll the dice, Just one more time."*[175]

On July 8, 1993, Madison Square Garden Promotions held its final boxing show at the Paramount Theater. Kevin Kelley headlined the card. The Garden still would hold boxing shows, but they would be promoted by independent promotional companies.

After the closing, the Garden's assistant matchmaker, 33-year-old Carl Moretti, was hired by Main Events as its matchmaker and vice president. Moretti had worked for the Garden since 1986 under Garden matchmaker Bob Goodman, who was Murray Goodman's son. Goodman and Moretti were preceded at the Garden by matchmaker Teddy Brenner, who Russell Peltz called *"the greatest matchmaker who ever lived."*[176] Pat Lynch would become very close to Moretti, both professionally and personally, and lean on Carl's expertise to help guide Arturo's career.

On July 30 in New York City, Arturo dispatched of Robert Scott, 1-2, in the 1st round, with a right hand and a cracking left hook.

On August 24 in Atlantic City, Arturo knocked out 0-2 Luis Guzman in the 1st round. The Main Events/ Peltz promotional team was keeping Arturo active. After the Guzman win, Arturo's record was 12-1 with 11 KOs.

To prepare for the Terry Norris fight, Joe Gatti was sent to Don King's camp in Ohio to train. Joe was dismantling his sparring partners. He was sure that word of this was getting back to Norris, as his brother Orlin was spotted at the Ohio camp. Aaron Snowell was helping Joe prepare for the Norris battle. Joe would have preferred Panama Lewis' help, but Lewis was busy training another fighter. Joe was concentrating on landing the right hand. With a few weeks remaining until the fight, Joe started bringing his weight down. When he reached 163-pounds, he started feeling drained from the weight loss. Joe struggled to complete 4 rounds of sparring with a welterweight. He spent two weeks in Texas before they moved the camp to Las Vegas. Joe was so drained from weight loss, he had trouble jogging. Joe was convinced that he would have to attack Norris at the opening bell if he was to have any chance of victory.

Although Panama Lewis spent virtually no time with Joe in camp, he accompanied Joe and his team to San Antonio, even though he couldn't work the corner. While Joe was upstairs resting in his hotel room, Panama was downstairs in the restaurant ordering lobster, shrimp cocktails, and $30 glasses of cognac. Panama charged everything to Joe's room. He lifted his glass of cognac, toasting, *"This is on Joe Gatti."*[177]

On September 10, 1993 at the Alamodome in San Antonio, Texas, "Lightning" Joe Gatti, 20-2, 15 KOs, faced "Terrible" Terry Norris, 35-3 (21 KOs), for the WBC light middleweight title. Norris was defending the title, which he won in March 1990, for the 10th time. Some of the elite fighters that Norris defeated included John Mugabi, "Sugar" Ray Leonard, Donald Curry, Meldrick Taylor, and Maurice Blocker.

According to Mikey Red, Pat Lynch felt that Joe had a very good chance of knocking off Norris. They felt that Norris could be KO'd because of his knockout loss to power-puncher Julian Jackson in 1989. But more than that, they felt that Norris was slipping due to his recent match against Troy Waters. In that bout, Waters dropped Norris before being stopped in the 3rd round of their June 19 bout. The *Newark Star Ledger* stated, *"Manager Pat Lynch decided to roll the dice and put Joe in with Terry Norris... Lynch thought that his man was ready and could catch Norris on an off night."*[178]

Joe received $135,000 for his title bout with Norris, by far the largest payday of his career. Joe was ranked #9 by the WBC. If Joe could win the bout, his earnings potential was unlimited. The Joe Gatti-Terry Norris fight was televised live on Showtime's SET pay-per-view. There were 65,000 fans in attendance, mostly to see the main event showdown between Julio Cesar Chavez and Pernell "Sweet Pea" Whitaker for the WBC welterweight title.

Arturo attended the fight. In the dressing room before Joe walked out, Arturo spoke to Joe in private. Joe recalled, *"When I fought Norris my brother was right there. He said, 'Bro you win this fight*

I'm done. I'm not fighting anymore.' I said, 'You don't need to bro, you're with me.' I guess if I would have been stronger, ah whatever."[179]

Mario Costa recalled, *"I didn't want him to fight the Norris fight. I wanted him to fight the kid [Gianfranco Rosi]. We wanted to fight Rosi, and Joe would have beat Rosi. Panama always said Joe could punch. It's just that Joe froze. I guess if Joe would have won, Pat would have been, 'I signed for the fight.' Then he blamed me and Panama. And that was one of the reasons they got Joe out of here and Arthur. He blamed me and Panama for taking that fight."*[180]

In the dressing room before the match, Joe was complaining of a headache. Aaron Snowell gave Joe an Advil.

As both fighters waited for the bell to ring, Joe had a concentrated look on his face, while Norris looked angry. Joe held a 2-inch height advantage over the 5'9½" Norris. Mario Costa and Aaron Snowell were in Gatti's corner. Joe weighed in at 153¼ while Norris tipped the scale at 153½-pounds.

When the bell rang for the 1st round, Joe threw and missed a right while Norris missed a counter hook. Joe jabbed and circled Norris. They remained in each other's range, exchanging quick blows. Joe threw two left hooks, landing one, while Norris attempted a hook of his own that missed the mark because Joe leaned away. Joe landed a lead left uppercut. Norris began applying pressure. Joe missed a one-two-hook combo as Norris continued stalking. Norris landed an overhand right around Joe's guard followed by a right to the body. Both fighters clinched.

Referee David Avalos broke the fighters. Joe threw a left jab and turned it into a left uppercut. He followed with a hook, but as he did so his right hand was very low. Norris capitalized with a short left hook that dropped Gatti at the 56-second mark. Joe rose quickly and looked to his corner for guidance as he received an 8-count.

When the action resumed Norris continued his attack. Gatti attempted jabs and hooks that were blocked. Norris pinned Joe on the ropes. He unloaded a series of powerful rights and left hooks, with the right hands in particular piercing Gatti's guard and landing flush on the jaw. The blows sent Joe down for the second time, through the bottom two ropes onto the ring apron, wincing in pain. Referee Avalos pulled Norris away and waived off the contest.

After watching the way the fight ended, Arturo turned to Panama Lewis and told him not to worry, that when his opportunity came he would not disappoint. Arturo confided in Mike Skowronski that he was disappointed that Joe didn't fight *"the Gatti way."*[181]

Back in the locker room, Joe was crying hysterically. He had sacrificed his entire life, with all the pressures put on him by his father, and he had not succeeded. He was devastated. Joe had fought one of the top pound-for-pound fighters in the world, and one of the biggest punchers in any weight class, but Joe could not be consoled with these facts. He was born and bred for this moment. No one could understand his pain. Not even his brother Arturo, who had the option of boxing in his youth. For Joe, there had been no option, he had no choice, this was his path in life. Giovanni Gatti had made that decision for him almost at birth.

Gatti's camp wasn't far off base in feeling that Norris' jaw was suspect and that he was ready to be taken. In Norris' very next fight, three months later, he was knocked out in the 4th round by Simon Brown.

Mario Costa watched Joe fall apart in the dressing room. Costa realized that this very well could be the largest purse Joe ever received in his career. Feeling terrible about Joe's loss, Costa implored Lynch and Seibert to let Joe keep his entire purse. Costa hoped that the money would in some way ease Joe's pain. He recalled, *"So Joe got paid $100,000 [after taxes]. So 33% was $30,000, ten for me, ten for Pat and ten for Richie. So they're ready to take the money. Now this was the first time that Joe made $100,000. He made no money whatsoever. We're going on the elevator upstairs and Pat and Richie were going to take their 33%. I think Joe or Arthur was there. And I said to them, 'No. I don't want it.' I said, 'You need the $10,000 Pat? I don't need the $10,000.' I said, 'I don't need the money. This is the first time the kid made $100,000. Let him keep the whole purse. I don't want $10,000. And the next time he fights, if he gets a good purse and you want to take the 33%, fine. This is the first time in his whole life he made some money. Let him take the $100,000 and go to Canada and take care of his mother.'*

"So right away they looked at me funny. Like, 'Woo, woo, what do you mean?' I said, 'That's what I mean. You need it? I don't need it. You need $10,000?' So right away they didn't like me. So we came back from Texas. Joe kept the whole check. Besides whatever Don King took for taxes. But Joe kept the $100,000. We come back. This is maybe a year, or two years later. Joe said, 'Mario remember that time you said, don't take no money, and I kept the money? Well, when we came home, Pat said he was short for his payroll, and he

borrowed the $10,000 and he never gave it back.' So he found a way to get the money from the kid."[182]

After Joe's loss to Norris, things started changing. Joe was no longer the up-and-coming prospect. In boxing, there is a certain kind of romantic aura that surrounds a rising prospect. Once the prospect falters, the dreams of fame and fortune dissipate before the gloves are removed in the ring. Mikey Red recalled the team's feeling after the Norris fight. *"After that, Arturo changed, because Joe was the rising star and fell off."*[183]

Joe later admitted that if he would have known he wasn't going to get the Rosi fight, he never would have left Main Events. When it came time for Arturo to renew his promotional contract, he would be influenced by the outcome of Joe's decision to leave Main Events. Arturo would not make the same mistake that Joe did.

Arturo was no longer the little brother on Joe's undercards. The hangers-on and groupies all started migrating towards Arturo. The sudden physical and emotional shift was difficult for both brothers to deal with. It didn't help that some were trying to create a rift between the two brothers to get closer to Arturo. Gossip was constantly being spread to separate the brothers. Additionally, Joe leaving Main Events and then losing his very first fight without the company put added strain on his relationship with Arturo. It was clear to both brothers that Joe had made a career-altering error by leaving Main Events.

Boxing photographer Tom Casino asked Joe to participate in a photo shoot at the Natilus Gym in Bayonne. Casino was a young boxing photographer. He had arrived on the boxing scene at almost the same time that Joe and Arturo did. He grew close to the brothers after taking their first publicity shots. Arturo trusted Tom. He allegedly asked Tom to be his manager. Tom didn't have the money or the connections to manage Arturo, so he declined. Tom worked out at the Natilus Gym. He became friends with a beautiful blonde girl named Victoria Ballora, or Vikki as she liked to be called. Vikki and Tom would talk while they trained.

After the shoot, Joe was given a free membership to the gym. Joe, Arturo, and Mikey Red went back to the gym for some workout classes. At one of the classes, Joe was thunderstruck by the tall, beautiful blonde Vikki. She was no easy catch. She regularly turned down offers to date. One of the gym members who tried to date Vikki was Joe and Arturo's friend, John Capone.

Vikki asked Tom about Joe. Tom told Vikki that Joe was a nice boy. He introduced Vikki to Joe. Vikki recalled the meeting. *"When I first met him and he told me he was a fighter, I was just like, 'You're a boxer? What! What do you do for a living and what's your income? Where do you work?' He's like, 'That's what I do.' I was a nurse's assistant."*[184]

Vikki continued, *"Meeting people around boxing and seeing what goes on from an outside stand point. Oh my god. I went home and I told my mother, 'Nobody sells insurance to these fighters?' I asked Joe, when I met him, 'Where do you have a bank account?' He said he shared a bank account with Pat. I said, 'What!'"*[185] Joe explained, *"Because I had no social security."*[186]

Mikey Red recalled that Joe stopped hanging out with him after he started dating Vikki. Joe would say that Vikki helped him realize that many of the people hanging around him were just using him for his money. When Joe had money, everyone came around to go party, but when he had no money, no one invited him out. They would sneak out without him.

Joe noticed that the same groupies that hung around him started gravitating towards his brother. Joe stated, *"I'd see them. They started hanging out with my brother. I said, 'Ah ok, they found another fish.'"*[187]

Joe got up the nerve to ask Vikki out. Vikki accepted. Soon the pair were inseparable. Joe's group of boxing friends became very jealous over this new girl who was grabbing Joe's attention. Joe, like Arturo with his girlfriends, was very possessive of Vikki. One day they were shopping at the Short Hills Mall. The couple were taking a break in the court area, when Joe thought that a man was staring at Vikki. Joe started staring back. Vikki said the stare down felt like it lasted for nearly twenty minutes. Finally, Joe shouted to the man, *"You, what are you looking at?"* The man walked over and Joe was all set to defend Vikki's honor when the man meekly asked, *"Are you Joe Gatti, the boxer?"* The man wasn't looking at Vikki, he was a boxing fan who was staring at Joe. Vikki turned to Joe and shook her head in disbelief.

Vikki recalled when she first met Arturo. *"You could see the love in Arturo's eyes when he saw Joe. It was scary."*[188] When the two brothers and their girlfriends went out to dinner, Arturo would follow Joe everywhere. Vikki recalled, *"If Joe went to the bathroom, Arturo would say, 'I have to go too.' Arturo emulated Joe."*[189]

Lynch sent Joe and Arturo to live with Dino Bizzario, who owned a car lot on Kennedy Boulevard. Joe was recovering from hand surgery at the time. Joe recalled, *"Dino was taking care of us and then they got afraid Dino was stealing us. Stealing us? We're just hanging out over there. You put us here! Nobody wanted to pay for us. We had nowhere to stay. And then they get afraid they're gonna steal us. I mean, I don't understand it."*[190] Joe recalled that Dino was a terrific Italian cook. Both brothers enjoyed staying with Bizzario.

Chapter 8
Arturo's First Professional Belt

On October 23, 1993, 132-pound Arturo returned to action at the Sands Casino in Atlantic City. He knocked out 133-pound 7-2 (3 KOs) Derek Francis of New York City in 1 round.

Mario Costa recalled seeing Arturo on the day after the bout. *"I walked into the diner at 1 or 2 o'clock in the afternoon and Arthur's sitting there with a girl. And he just fought Saturday night in Atlantic City. So I walk into the diner like I always do, from the house, to get a cup of coffee. I walk in and he's sitting there with a girl in the first booth with two cheeseburgers, french fries and a cheese steak. And he's like having a fillet minion meal. I said, 'Arthur, what are you doing champ?' He goes, 'Mario, let me tell you something, I had to make weight for this fight. And I had to starve myself. And the night before the fight, I was dreaming of the White Mana cheeseburgers and cheesesteaks.' He was sitting there like he was having the meal of his life. And I was like, look at this guy. Here it was so funny, it was unbelievable. He couldn't eat because he had to make weight. And he came back from Atlantic City and came right into the White Mana."*[191]

Arturo followed up the win with his fourth straight 1st round knockout. He dispatched of the 3-7 (1 KO) lefty Glenn Irizarry, in Melville, N.Y. Irizarry, of North Bay Shore N.Y., weighed in at 141, while Arturo came in at 136-pounds for the contest. Arturo now held a 14-1 (13 KOs) record as 1993 came to a close.

As 1994 arrived, many changes would befall the Gatti brothers. The momentum of their careers were rapidly moving in contrasting directions. The tension between Joe and Pat Lynch was intensifying. Lynch did not approve of Joe leaving Main Events, and he wanted to ensure that Arturo would not make the same mistake. Pat grew much closer to his rising prospect, Arturo, while distancing himself from Joe.

It was easy to see the shift in the brothers' careers simply by looking at the hangers-on or groupies. Like the music business, Hollywood, or other sports, boxing has its groupies. Joe had a cult-following lead him into the ring when he was coming up. There were always hangers-on that were ready to party with the rising star, that is, as long as the fighter was paying the way. They wanted the notoriety of being seen with him in public. As soon as Joe lost to

Norris, the groupies started flocking towards Arturo. It was as if Joe was a stock that was bottoming out, while Arturo's stock was soaring. Joe, realizing how fake these supposed friends were, started distancing himself from them. Joe tried to warn Arturo about the phonies, but Arturo, like most stars on the rise getting advice from someone on the slide, thought it was just sour grapes. It would be several more years before Arturo would begin to open his eyes.

Arturo, who had always been "Joe's little brother," was now the rising star. He enjoyed his newfound attention immensely. In the past, Joe would attract the good-looking girls because of his matinee looks and charm. There were even several times when Arturo met girls and they wound up switching to his brother instead. The competitive nature of the sport, Arturo's success inside of the ring, Arturo's growing fan base, and Pat Lynch trying to maintain control over Arturo, all helped to fuel the increased tension between the brothers. They still lived together, but they were growing apart.

Around December 21, 1993, Arturo disappeared for several days. Joe was worried, because this was out of character for his brother. A few days later, Arturo returned for his belongings. Arturo had decided to move in with his girlfriend Emily. Joe was understandably upset. He cherished his relationship with his brother, his only real family in America.

Joe was still close to his family in Canada, and they would call him for money whenever they needed some cash. Although Arturo was the hot prospect on the rise, he had yet to earn any serious money. He still was fighting only 6- and 8-round fights which paid only around $1,000 to $1,500 a match.

Some fight managers "cut" their boxer's purse as soon as they turn professional, while other managers wait until their boxers make a significant payday. "Cutting" is taking their allotted percentage. The maximum allowed by law is 33%, but that does not include expenses that the manager might incur before the fight. The trainer traditionally is entitled to 10%. The cutman usually receives 1 or 2%, unless a boxer earns only $500 or $600, then a flat fee of $50 would be charged. A boxer earning $1,000 can come home with as little as $517 after manager, trainer, and cutman percentages are deducted. He also has to pay taxes on the whole thousand, although he can deduct the fees paid out as expenses. There are some trainers/managers that even charge their boxers for the gauze to wrap their hands.

Lynch, Costa and Seibert were not that type of management team.

According to Joe, the group never cut the Gattis when they were coming up fighting 4, 6, and 8-round fights. As can be seen by looking at the records of Joe and Arturo's opponents as they were "cutting their teeth," they were getting the "right fights" as they were coming up. Arturo was matched tougher early in his career, but that was due partly to his weight class. It is much more difficult to find opponents in the lower weight classes than it is in the middle to heavier weight classes. There were simply less available fighters in the lighter weight classes, especially on the East Coast.

Even though East Coast Boxing Management was the official group directing Joe and Arturo's careers, and Mario Costa was the president of the group, it was becoming more apparent that Pat Lynch was taking the lead in making the important business decisions regarding both boxers careers. Costa believed that Lynch advised Arturo to avoid the Ringside Lounge. Costa felt that pulling Arturo away from Ringside had a negative effect on him. Costa believed that Ringside was Arturo's home base and his foundation. He felt that Arturo connected more with the working-class people that frequented the club rather than the business types who Lynch was steering Arturo towards.

Costa recalled that even after Arturo stopped being a regular visitor at the club he was still proud of his Ringside affiliation. *"Arthur told me one time that Pernell Whitaker was fucking with him in one of the camps. And Whitaker goes, 'You're a White boy.' Arthur said, 'I'm a White boy? Listen to me. Where I come from I fuck with the real Niggas, Jersey City. The real Niggas, Ringside.' So every time Pernell Whitaker used to pass here he said, 'I always wanted to come in.' And Panama said, 'Arthur got his balls and his confidence here at Ringside.' Panama used to say to Arthur when he first came here with Mike McCallum and Wali Muhammad, the light heavyweight from Newark, 'I'm gonna treat you worse than a Nigga. You're a good-looking White boy. You're not gonna fight no good-looking White boy. You're gonna fight Puerto Ricans, Spanish, and Blacks that want to knock your head off.' And that's what Panama said. 'Move your head. Don't get hit. Move your head.'*

"Arthur got to the point that when he walked over to Ringside he was the prince. He was the fucking king in the bar. And the girls, he used to sign their shirts in the beginning. He used to tell them, 'I'm gonna be the champion.' He loved that, and then they took him away from all that stuff. I took buses, two or three times, to Arturo's fights.

I took buses full of fans, and then I stopped because Pat wouldn't even look at me."[192]

On January 8, 1994, Arturo returned to the ring in Catskill, New York, against 12-3-1 (8 KOs) Leon Bostic. Both boxers weighed in at 131½-pounds for the contest, which was being televised live by Telemundo. Mikey Red recalled, *"Looking at the Leon Bostic fight, it was tougher than the King Solomon fight. They drove up to the Catskills in a snowstorm for what was to be an easy win and it turned out to be a real tough fight."*[193]

Arturo was led into the ring by Pat Lynch, Hector Roca, and his brother Joe. Arturo looked focused as both fighters awaited the opening bell. Bostic looked unsure of himself.

Arturo started strong behind his jab, and stunned Leon with a power jab less than a minute into the fight. Gatti, who was several inches taller than his foe, put together several hook-cross combos that mostly grazed Bostic. Leon was trading with Gatti, but his balance was off, and he was leaning in with his head. At the 1:11 mark, as Bostic was reaching in with a left hook to the body, Gatti caught Leon with a short left hook to the head that dropped Bostic to his hands and knees.

Bostic was up quickly. Referee Wayne Kelly waived off the count, apparently calling it a slip, but it was a clear knockdown. Arturo went straight in for the kill, but Leon was game. Bostic attempted an overhand right but was countered by Gatti's own right and was dropped again, onto the seat of his pants. This time Kelly ruled it a knockdown and gave Leon the mandatory 8-count.

Arturo attempted to finish Bostic. With 20 seconds remaining in the round, Arturo threw a hard left hook well below the waistline which sent Leon down in a heap. At the time, Gatti's head was being pushed down by Bostic, which may have contributed to the errant blow. Referee Wayne Kelly warned Arturo, *"Keep em up."* Shortly thereafter, the bell rang to end the first stanza.

Gatti began the 2nd round circling, but Bostic showed that he was game as he landed two left hooks in a row. Leon was snapping his jab. He landed a crisp lead right uppercut. Both fighters followed with wild swings, mixing it up. Arturo again timed the lunging Bostic with a right hand, but this time Leon's legs didn't buckle. Arturo ripped a double hook to the body and head. The hook to the body strayed below the belt, onto Leon's leg. Again Gatti was warned for low blows. Bostic landed a solid right to the jaw. He followed with a left hook and a head-jarring left uppercut which got

Arturo's attention. Gatti started circling away. Bostic threw bombs while Arturo was standing straight up against the ropes. Gatti was in an eerily similar position that his brother had been in against Norris, but he held on. Obviously Bostic did not have Norris' world-class power, but he was a very good puncher who was throwing hard. Arturo started backing up as the round came to a close.

Diego Rosario, who trained both brothers, explained why Arturo appeared to have the ability to take a better punch than Joe, and addressed whether it was mental or physical. *"No, that's not mental. That's physical. That's like if you're a puncher, you're a puncher. You can't put power behind somebody. There's kids that can't take a punch at all. And people say hit, hit and they can't and they look all muscled but they can't crack an egg. It's the same thing with an ability to take a punch."*[194]

The 3rd round started with Bostic stepping in with several jabs. Leon jumped in with a sizzling left hook to the jaw that turned Gatti's head. Arturo flurried back and tied Bostic up. Gatti complained about a clash of heads to Referee Kelly. Arturo landed three hard hooks to the body but Bostic was undeterred as he kept swarming in. Leon again came in with his head down. Arturo started timing him with uppercuts. Gatti was busier as Bostic started breathing heavier. Arturo landed a slightly low right, and shortly thereafter another low right to the hip/thigh area. Kelly stepped in and deducted a point for low blows. Gatti raised his arms in disgust.

After the action resumed, Arturo cornered Bostic, firing away, but Leon quickly spun out and smothered Gatti. Right before the bell rang, Arturo threw a left to the body just as Bostic was pushing him down. The blow strayed low again, this time more significantly, but Kelly declined to deduct another point. Gatti complained to Kelly about Bostic pushing his head down. After the round ended Kelly gave Leon extra time to recover.

Between rounds, Kelly went over to Arturo's corner and warned him again, *"You can't hit low or you're gonna lose the fight."* Gatti responded, *"I know that."* Roca complained to the ref about Bostic pushing Arturo's head down. In the corner, Roca told Gatti that he was trying too hard. He wanted more combinations and body punching.

The bell rang for the 4th round. Bostic struck first with a hard jab. Arturo timed a left hook that landed as Leon was pulling his head back to avoid the punch. Bostic staggered and his glove hit the canvas as he tried to balance himself. Kelly started counting, but then stopped and decided to rule the incident a slip, another knockdown that was ruled a non-knockdown. The pro-Gatti crowd moaned as Arturo raised his gloves in frustration.

Gatti appeared more relaxed, working his jab, and again, tried to time a counter right that missed. Arturo dipped under a jab and threw a hook to the body. As he did so, Bostic again pushed Gatti's head down which caused the blow to land under the belt line. Leon winced in pain as Arturo bowed to the referee in apology. Gatti was warned but no point was deducted.

Arturo landed a hard hook followed by a stiff jab. With less than 20 seconds remaining, Bostic stepped in with two hard hooks that backed Arturo to the ropes. Gatti winced as he bit down hard on his mouthpiece, but he fought back and weathered the storm. Arturo escaped the ropes, but was trapped against the ropes again on the opposite side of the ring, where Leon landed two hard right hands. As the bell rang, Bostic, although winded, lifted his legs high in celebration.

Leon came out confidently stalking in the 5th. Gatti was boxing from the outside. Both boxers were throwing solid blows. Bostic found the mark with some hooks and an overhand right. Gatti landed a solid hook to the body that strayed slightly low. He was given a soft caution to keep his punches up. Gatti landed a solid hook, followed by a right, and another hook. Arturo returned to slugging and got caught flush on the jaw with a hard right uppercut. Gatti's eyes became glassy and his knees buckled as Bostic sensed an opportunity and pressed the attack. Arturo showed he still had his wits about him as he did the Ali shuffle while his back was against the ropes. Gatti circled back out to the center of the ring, but Leon lunged in with a right cross that found its mark right before the bell rang.

Gatti's career hung in the balance. In order to move from prospect to contender, a boxer must beat this type of fighter. Arturo wasn't simply getting hit. He was getting hit with hard, head-jolting blows.

Bostic's corner cheered him on. They instructed Leon to shorten up on his punches and take his time. Bostic's corner felt that he was hurting Arturo in every round. They asked for more jabs.

Gatti came out for the 6th with a bruise under his left eye. The pace slowed. Arturo hit Leon with a combination. A hard right drove Bostic against the ropes for a moment. Arturo seemed the fresher of the two. He easily ducked Leon's ever-widening roundhouses. Roca implored Arturo to use the jab. Gatti landed a short hook and hard right uppercut. He immediately shook his right hand, which indicated that he injured it. With 25 seconds remaining, Arturo landed three left hooks in succession that wobbled Bostic. He followed with a right that floored Leon. Gatti shook his hand again, in obvious pain. Bostic fell onto all fours, but rose at the count of three. He received an 8-count while sucking air into his open mouth. Arturo tried to finish his foe, but Leon fired back, as the round ended.

Bostic started the 7th with a left hook but proceeded to hold immediately afterwards as Arturo fired back. Leon landed a hard right as Gatti tried to pull away. Arturo landed a couple of solid hooks, one of which slightly buckled Bostic's knees. Leon responded with a hook of his own. Both fighters swung wildly, missing most of their punches for the rest of the round. Roca yelled for a jab and uppercut. Gatti tried the uppercut but it missed its mark. The round appeared fairly even, with perhaps a slight edge to Arturo.

As Roca applied the enswell under Gatti's left eye, he implored Arturo to keep his hands up. Roca told Gatti that they needed the last round. Bostic's corner asked for two good power punches, one right behind the other.

The bell rang for the 8th and final round. Both boxers touched gloves. The round was mostly uneventful. Bostic attacked several times, but could not land. Gatti landed the more telling punches. After the round ended, both fighters embraced and raised their hands in victory.

The announcer read off the scores as Pat Lynch nervously paced back and forth in the ring. Judge Wynn Kintz scored the bout 75-73 for Gatti. The second judge had it 74-74, and judge Harry Papacaralambolous had it 75-74 for the winner, by majority decision, Arturo Gatti.

The fight was a judge's nightmare. Gatti scored one official knockdown, two apparent knockdowns that were ruled slips, and he had a point deducted for low blows. With all that, Arturo barely pulled out the win. If he would have lost another point for low blows, the bout would have been ruled a draw. After the win, Joe kissed his brother on the cheek. Arturo took time off after the Bostic fight to heal his injured hand.

Bostic would never fight again. Also fighting, and winning on the card, were Ivan Robinson and Tracy Harris Patterson, two fighters who would figure prominently in Arturo's career.

Joe returned to the ring on February 5, 1994 at a club show in Long

Branch, N.J. Joe's opponent was 7-8 (2 KOs) Mike Williams of North Carolina. Williams had lost three straight fights by knockout, including his first fight against Joe on July 30, 1992. The rematch ended in the same manner, when Joe knocked Williams out in the 2nd round. Joe now held a record of 21-3 (16 KOs). He still had a chance to resurrect his career with a few quality wins.

Joe's girlfriend Vikki drove a Corvette. Joe decided to surprise Vikki by getting her car painted. Dino Bizzario recommended an auto body shop in Hoboken owned by a man named Jack Nessie. Joe decided to take the car there. While Joe was waiting to talk to Nessie about the Corvette, he noticed a Porsche that was being repaired. As he admired the Porsche, the car's owner, Mike Sciarra, approached him to say hello. Sciarra owned a local strip club called the Squeeze Lounge. The strip club was located at 1820 Willow Avenue in Weehawken. It was said that the only thing that got squeezed at the Squeeze Lounge were the patrons' wallets. Joe was invited to hang out at the club. In the future, Arturo also would meet and befriend Sciarra, as a result of Sciarra's chance encounter with Joe.

On March 31, 1994, Joe was confronted with a crossroads battle. The bout took place at the Huntington Hilton in Melville N.Y. Joe's opponent was the battle-tested veteran Rafael Williams, 31-13 (19 KOs), of Queens N.Y. Williams was on a six-fight losing streak dating back to November 1990. Although Williams lost six in a row and eight out of his previous nine fights, his opposition was high quality. Some of the opponents he lost to included Livingstone Bramble, Hector Camacho, Pernell Whitaker, Buddy McGirt, Bo James and Verno Phillips. Williams was an opponent, but a higher level opponent. He was a stepping stone to world title contention.

The bout didn't turn out as Joe had hoped. Williams walked away with a close but unanimous decision. *Star Ledger* boxing columnist Chris Thorne commented on Joe's performance, stating that it was *"[a] fight he apparently didn't take seriously."*[195]

On May 6, 1994, Arturo returned to the ring at the Boardwalk Convention Center in Atlantic City. With a freshly healed right hand, Arturo took on 9-3-1 (6 KOs) Darrell Singleton of Charleston, South Carolina. Singleton had lost three in a row and was a perfect fill-in fight while Arturo's team looked for bigger and better opportunities.

To outsiders of the sport, guiding a boxers career may look easy, but the sport isn't that easy. It's a business where the management team is responsible for not only finding the right opponent that their fighter can beat, but also the right opponent that will advance their fighter's career. One also has to keep in mind that you have to choose between the opponents that are available to you and how much that opponent will cost. Just because an opponent is the "right guy" to fight doesn't mean they will accept a fight against your boxer.

Arturo blasted Singleton out in 1 round to improve his record to 16-1 (14 KOs). The 1st round knockout was the tenth 1st round knockout of Arturo's young career.

Joe and Arturo's managerial contracts with East Coast Boxing were expiring. Pat Lynch drove the brothers to the Best Buy parking lot in Secaucus, N.J. In the lot, they were both asked to sign new contracts. Mario Costa's name was not on the new document. Even though it was visibly noticeable that Costa's name was missing, no one brought the subject up. Richie Seibert's name was also missing. Lynch, who later stated that Arturo refused to sign a new contract if Seibert was involved, would take sole control over the management of the Gatti brothers.[196] Joe recalled, *"Guys amazingly and mysteriously disappeared from the contract. Mario was off the paperwork and Seibert was off the paperwork and only Pat was on it."*[197]

Costa admitted that Lynch asked him to sign Arturo to a management contract, but Costa declined the offer. At the time, Costa was content with helping out without being the manager of record. If Costa had signed Arturo, he would have been responsible for the expenses of the young boxer. It was an investment that had risks. There was no guarantee that Arturo would be successful, and even if he was, he might not earn enough for Costa to break even or make a profit. It appeared as though Costa was apprehensive about investing heavily in a fighter after the substantial financial losses he suffered while involved with Matthew Hilton.

Costa advised Lynch to sign both brothers. This would make Lynch responsible for all of the expenses, but if the brothers were successful, Pat would reap all of the rewards.

Even though Mario had told Lynch to sign the brothers, he still was shocked and hurt after he heard about the Best Buy parking lot signing. He expected the Gatti brothers to reach out to him before signing a new contract. After a while, Joe mended his relationship with Mario. Arturo, however, was lost forever. He barely came back to the Ringside Lounge. When he did, he was not the same starry-eyed young man who shared his dreams with Costa.

Joe recalled, *"Mario let us go. I was very disappointed but that was Mario. He didn't wanna get involved. Mario said, 'I'll help you get fights. I don't want no money and I don't want to put up no money.' He loves the game. He wants to be in it. He did that with Matthew. He didn't want nothing from me. He wants to be involved. He wants to be in the middle of everything. So that's how he is. But he likes to help. He'll feed you. You need a little money. I'm very disappointed because I thought Mario would have done a little more for us than he did."*[198]

On June 28, 1994 at the Meadowlands Convention Center, Arturo fought for his first professional boxing title on USA Network's "Tuesday Night Fights." Arturo was fighting on the undercard of the Main Events-promoted Buddy McGirt vs. Kevin Pompey bout. Arturo took on 25-2 (18 KOs) Pete Taliaferro of Mobile, Alabama. On February 20, Taliaferro had won the United States Boxing Association (USBA) title by defeating Bernard Taylor, 45-3-2 (22 KOs), by split decision in Biloxi, Mississippi. Gatti would be fighting in his first scheduled 12-round fight. He had been 8 rounds only once in his career.

Before the fight, Arturo was asked how he felt about being in with the vastly more experienced Taliaferro. Arturo boasted that he was ready and confident. Arturo admitted that Taliaferro had more fights under his belt, but Gatti felt that the fact that he had been fighting in New York, New Jersey, and Philadelphia gave him the advantage of having fought tougher competition. Most of Taliaferro's fights had taken place in his native Alabama. Arturo also pointed out that he had been getting terrific sparring with world champions John John Molina, Jesse James Leija, and Jake "The Snake" Rodriguez. Arturo had sparred for over a month with WBC super featherweight champion Leija, more than holding his own against Leija. Taliaferro did not agree with Arturo's assessment. He pointed out that Arturo hadn't fought any world class, top-ranked fighters.

Twelve of Taliaferro's eighteen knockouts came inside of the first 3 rounds. Like Gatti, he was a fast starter. Taliaferro weighed in at 130, while Gatti tipped the scale at 129½-pounds. Arturo had a 1/2-inch height advantage over the 5'7" Taliaferro, and a 1/2-inch reach advantage. Gatti was unranked, while Taliaferro was ranked #11 in the world by the IBF. Both of Taliaferro's losses were split decisions. He had never been stopped.

Hector Roca and Pat Lynch were in Gatti's corner. Mario Costa did not attend the match. Lynch nervously chewed gum as he stood behind Arturo as the fighters waited for the bout to start. Gatti's fans gave a loud ovation when the Jersey City transplant was announced. The crowd roundly booed the visiting Taliaferro.

When the bell rang, Arturo threw the first punch, a jab that was blocked. Gatti kept throwing the jab as a "feeler" punch. Arturo landed a hard jab that snapped Taliaferro's head back. He followed up with a lead hook-straight right combo that brought a roar from the crowd, even though both punches fell short of their mark. After a few more jabs, Gatti landed a hard straight right to the body. Taliaferro landed a crisp jab and followed with a counter right a few moments later. Arturo stepped in with two jabs. Taliaferro followed with a counter right over the jab. After another "feeler" jab Arturo noticed Taliaferro's left hand was low. He shot a cannon-like right hand that landed flush on the jaw, dropping Taliaferro to his knees.

Taliaferro rose quickly as referee Jimmy Condon gave him an 8-count. The partisan crowd exploded as Gatti waited anxiously for the referee to waive him back in to finish off his wounded prey. Gatti pressed forward and threw a grazing hook to the body. He missed wildly with an overhand right as Taliaferro retreated.

Gatti kept winging hooks and rights. Announcer Sean O'Grady, who mistakenly called Arturo "Joe," opined that Arturo needed to settle down while trying to finish his hurt opponent. After two more wild swings by Gatti, Taliaferro landed a solid uppercut and held on. The referee broke the two fighters. O'Grady cautioned that Arturo could not afford to waste punches and added that "Joe" Gatti needed to look to land on Taliaferro's chin. Announcer Al Albert corrected O'Grady on the name mix-up, but noted that the brothers did look alike.

Arturo cornered Taliaferro and landed a grazing right. Taliaferro came back with a left hook to the jaw. Gatti was unmoved. Arturo slipped to the right and launched a wicked right hand that dropped Taliaferro to his knees with 20 seconds remaining in the round. Taliaferro remained on one knee as he took the 8-count.

With 8 seconds left, the referee waived the fighters to continue. Arturo immediately landed a solid hook. After missing a right he landed a power left jab. Taliaferro took a knee. The referee waived the contest over with 4 seconds remaining in the 1st round.

The three-knockdown rule was not in effect. Taliaferro protested the stoppage. The crowd erupted as Gatti ran to a neutral corner and jumped up onto the ropes with his hands extended skyward. Pat

Lynch jumped into the ring with his arms raised. Gatti ran into the opposite neutral corner, where he again jumped up onto the ropes with his hands raised as his throng of fans went berserk. Lynch picked Arturo up from behind and carried him around the ring. An ecstatic Joe Gatti entered the ring, along with Hector Roca, Mikey Red and Main Events matchmaker Carl Moretti. Lou Duva was in attendance. He also climbed up onto the ring apron. Hector Roca raised Arturo into the air. Arturo hugged Lou Duva as the USBA championship belt was brought into the ring and strapped around his waist.

After the bout, Arturo commented on the knockout, *"They were looking for my left hook. As soon as I dropped him I knew it was over. I hit them so hard they can't recover. I was surprised he went down so quickly because I thought he could take a better shot. He had a lot of fights but a lot of them were in Alabama, while I've fought in New York, New Jersey, and Philadelphia where the fighters are a lot better. A lot of my fights end in the first round because I do my work in the gym. And it paid off right here. I'm twenty-two and have had eighteen fights. I'd like to have about twenty-five fights before I fight for a world title. I'm not in a hurry. Once I win the title, I'll keep it forever."*[199]

Pat Lynch was asked for a time frame on when Arturo might fight for a world title. Lynch had no immediate date, but did voice his interest in a possible fight against WBO junior lightweight champion, Oscar De La Hoya. De La Hoya would have been way too much for Arturo to handle at this point in his career. The only conceivable reason to match Arturo against De la Hoya would be a payday. Main Events and Lynch would wisely choose a different path to a world title fight.

Buddy McGirt, who met Arturo for the first time at the weigh-in, was in his dressing room relaxing when he learned of the quick 1st round stoppage. He later recalled, *"I met Arturo in 1994. He fought on my undercard at the Meadowlands Convention Center. I met him briefly and I said good luck. My old trainer Hector Roca was training him. I said, 'You got a good trainer there, stick with him and you'll be champion.' I was getting ready to fight Kevin Pompey. I was pretty sure his fight was going to go the distance, but Arturo knocked the motherfucker out. I was like, son of a bitch! You couldn't give me time to get warmed up!"*[200]

Even though Mario Costa did not attend the fight, Arturo visited him at the Ringside Lounge right after the Taliaferro win. Costa recalled, *"Arthur came here when he won the USBA belt. He came and brought it upstairs and he goes, 'Mario, I want to get the real one. When I make money, I'm gonna take care of you for taking care of me and my brother. So I said, 'Alright Arthur.'"*[201]

A couple of days later, Pat Lynch allegedly found out that Arturo had visited Costa. Lynch appeared concerned that Arturo had returned to Ringside. He impressed on Arturo that Ringside was not a good place for a rising boxer to hang out. Lynch allegedly told Arturo that Costa was telling everyone that Arturo was going to reimburse Costa for all the expenses he paid out. Of course, Gatti would not be able to pay Costa back with his USBA winnings. He would need to win a world title.

According to Costa, Arturo was already abusing alcohol and drugs at this time. After Costa discovered that Lynch had allegedly twisted his comments, he confronted Arturo. Costa told Arturo that he never said anything about getting reimbursed for expenses. Costa alleged that near the end of his career, Arturo started to understand that he was being manipulated. He told Mario that he and his brother should have never left him. Costa would never be reimbursed for expenses incurred while housing and feeding the Gatti brothers.

Costa recalled first meeting Arturo. *"When I first saw Arthur, he was 12 or 13. We always called him Arthur. He would come behind me and his eyes would look at me. He said, 'Please take me to America. I want to go with you. I want to go to America.' So I said, 'No, no. I'll take you but you got to wait. You're too little.' So when he came back he said he wanted Panama Lewis to train him.*

"Arthur said, 'The same thing you're doing for my brother, can you do that for me?' He's asking me like a little kid. You had to see his eyes. He was looking at me so excited. It might have been around 1985, around that time. Joe came when the Hiltons came. Joe came right away. Arthur stayed in Canada because he was little. He couldn't come. But every time I used to go up there [to Montreal] he came behind me, always chasing me.

"I went up to Montreal with Matthew every time he fought. I worked Matthew's corner. Of course me, the father, and the cutman for Don King, Al Braverman. And I'm in Matthew's corner when he beat the guy from Philadelphia when he became junior middleweight champion, Buster Drayton. That was sold out at the Molson Center. The Hiltons lived in my house at 277 Manhattan Avenue. That's why Gatti fought out of Jersey City. Arthur and Joe, they both fought out of Jersey City because of my address. Pat don't

live in Jersey City. Pat lived in Union City. Matthew stayed from 1984 to 1988. Five years in my house. And Joe too, he slept upstairs with the Hiltons. 1988, that's when Matthew lost with Robert Hines. And that's when he went back to Canada.

"And that's when Joe said, 'Please Mario.' Joe would come here a lot. Then Arthur would come with him sometimes, and he stayed upstairs, because they were all fighters. All they did was fight. Arthur ate breakfast at the Mana. He would walk up the hill and go run in Persian Field. Go to the gym at 1 o'clock. I used to take them to gyms in Newark. If we went to Newark it was Triple Threat, or Bufano's in Jersey City. Then we trained over here. I gave Joe and Arthur the Lady of Fatima candle that was in my house because when they came I went upstairs and they had a picture of their father on the dresser. All they wanted to do was fight and become champions for their father. Because their father died young and they felt they wanted to do it for their dad. So I brought them a candle upstairs of Our Lady of Fatima, a saint.

"One time I brought Our Lady of Fatima to the fights in Atlantic City and Arthur was already not himself. I could see that whole crowd around him. The way he was talking to me. The way he would glance at me. He was not the same, I could tell. Because of the way he lived. The lifestyle that he lived. He had no structure in his life. He had lost that.

"Arthur always came to Ringside. He would come and then I wouldn't see him for six months because Pat would find out that he was here. Pat's thing is like, 'Don't go there. Ringside is no good.' The most important thing is not making the money. It's making sure you're doing the right thing. People that know me know I don't want anything. I'm not better than you or anybody else or somebody that came from the hood or the projects. Pat was always that big shot. A million dollar house. A big car. I don't work like that. Those things never impressed me."[202]

Allegedly, Lynch used the meal ledger that Mario had kept as an example to show Arturo and Joe that Costa was only interested in money. Arturo was told that Mario was spreading rumors that Arturo owed Costa $30,000 for housing and feeding him for three years. Arturo was upset. He mockingly told the person who told him this to go tell Mario that he would be sending Costa a check. Mario stated that he never put a number on what Arturo owed him. He said it was Arturo himself who first mentioned paying him back for his help. Mario believes that Pat Lynch instigated the $30,000 rumor to put a wedge between him and Arturo. Donny Jerie recalled how Arturo dealt with the money owed rumor. *"Mario tried to be buddy buddy with Arturo. To try to get a taste of his money. Then Arturo turned on them all."*[203] Joe explained that if he would have made any significant money in boxing, he would have taken care of Mario. Joe stated, *"Mario paid for all the gas, travel, and food for us and the Hiltons. Mario was in the hole for thousands. He got burned so much."*[204]

Arturo returned to Montreal. He honked the horn outside of his childhood friend Christen Santos' house. When Santos opened the door he saw Arturo standing there with his arms outstretched, and his new USBA championship belt wrapped around his waist. Arturo yelled up to Christen, *"We did it!"*

In-between bouts, Pat Lynch left the Gatti brothers to their own devices, which Joe felt was a mistake. Joe recalled, *"There's nothing to do. These guys are not professional. You find things to do for the fighters. They left me one time for two weeks and they couldn't even find me. They said, 'Alright Joe, you got two weeks off and then you get back in here.' Nobody called me. They didn't know where I was for two weeks. I could have been dead."*[205]

Chapter 9
Charging to the World Title

On August 16, 1994, Arturo returned to the ring on a Peltz-promoted card at the Blue Horizon in Philadelphia, on USA Network's "Tuesday Night Fights." He defended his USBA crown against 13-5-2 (7 KOs) Richard Salazar, a southpaw from Corpus Christi, Texas. Salazar had been stopped in 3 rounds by Regilio Turr in 1992. Gatti weighed in at 129 to Salazar's 130. Arturo's previous win had moved him up to #7 on the IBF's super featherweight rankings and #12 on the WBC rankings. Hector Roca was again the chief second in the Gatti corner with Pat Lynch assisting.

Arturo controlled the opening round against the cautious Salazar. Gatti showed patience, picking his punches for the first time in his career, but he still was the aggressor, throwing and landing the harder blows to the head and body. USA Network's analyst Sean O'Grady commented that Salazar needed to wake up and start fighting.

In the 2nd round, USA's blow-by-blow commentator Al Albert commented that he could feel Arturo's punching power from ringside. O'Grady agreed that Arturo was a strong and heavy hitter. Salazar was defensive, rarely throwing punches.

Arturo easily controlled the action, methodically pounding on Salazar in the 3rd and 4th rounds, hurting Salazar in the 4th.

After the 4th ended, Roca instructed Gatti not to swing wildly. Roca also advised Arturo not to be lazy.

In the 5th, Gatti landed a hard hook-straight right combo. Commentator Sean O'Grady felt that the heavy punches that Salazar was absorbing to the body and head was sapping his strength. A poised Arturo easily won the round.

During the 6th round, Arturo slowed up a little, but still landed many solid blows. O'Grady went to the Gatti corner and questioned Roca, asking if Arturo was tiring. Roca responded that Arturo was not tired, but he was not used to hitting someone with solid punches and not knocking him out. Roca felt that Arturo needed to stop looking for the knockout and instead concentrate on landing combinations.

At the end of the round, Arturo landed hard body punches and snapped Salazar's head back with a right hand. The blows brought Arturo's brother Joe, who was sitting ringside, to his feet.

Arturo easily won the 7th. Just over two minutes into the round, Gatti hit Salazar with a sneaky-fast left hook to the body. Salazar took a step back, cringed slightly, then went down voluntarily face first. The momentary delay caused the referee to rule it a slip. Gatti was breaking Salazar down. Between rounds, Referee Frank Capuccino went to Salazar's corner, asking him if he wanted to continue, and cautioning that if he wanted to continue he needed to start fighting back.

The pounding continued. With a minute to go in the 8th, Arturo dropped Salazar to one knee with a hard left hook to the jaw. Salazar rose and weathered the storm. After the round, Cappucino tried to convince Salazar to retire, but he refused.

Arturo experienced the 9th round for the first time in his career. He was winning with ease, but Salazar refused to submit.

With 48 seconds remaining in the 10th, Salazar took a knee from a digging left hook to the liver. As referee Capuccino was administering the 8-count, Salazar's corner threw in the towel.

Joe entered the ring and kissed his younger brother. Al Albert remarked that Joe previously had appeared to be the first Gatti brother who might win a world title, but now Arturo was making leaps and bounds towards a title. Salazar had been the perfect non-threatening opponent to get Arturo the experience of 10 rounds.

On October 8, 1994, Joe returned to the ring in Vernon, N.J. against 14-9 (8 KOs) James Stokes of Mississippi. Joe trained for the fight at the Triple Threat training facility in Vernon, N.J. Hector Roca was in charge of training Joe. The training facility, which contained a ring and several punching bags, was housed in an oversized metal shed. The gym was located on the grounds of the Great Gorge ski resort. The facility was secluded. It was a perfect training camp location. Also training at the camp were Roy Jones, Jr., Ray Mercer, and Charles Murray.

Joe stated that he had finally gotten over the Terry Norris loss.[206] Joe gave credit to his girlfriend Vikki Ballora for grounding him. He spoke of continuing his career. *"I felt like it would be a shame to stop it now. I just turned twenty-seven. I still have some time."*[207] Lynch had questioned Joe's desire after the Rafael Williams fight. Lynch felt that Joe was going through the motions when he lost to Williams.[208] He now felt that Joe was taking the sport more seriously after watching Arturo climb up the rankings. Lynch also felt that Vikki was helping Joe take the sport more seriously.[209]

Joe gave credit to Arturo for inspiring his comeback. *"Watching* him win that belt put new life in me. Usually the small brother looks up to the big brother. Now I have to look up to him. This is my last shot. I've gotta do it."[210]

Stokes had lost four fights in a row and six out of his previous seven. Joe quickly dispatched of Stokes in 50 seconds of the 1st round. Describing the fight, the *Star Ledger's* Bill Bode wrote, *"Stokes initiated the action and caught Gatti with a stinging right uppercut to the side of his face. Gatti answered with a left hook counter and followed with a flurry of ten to twelve punches that had Stokes on the defensive. A right uppercut to the head put Stokes down for the count."*[211]

Reflecting on the victory, Joe said, *"I know anybody that is hit flush is going to go. I don't care who he is. I took my time like my trainer [Hector Roca] was telling me. That's what happened. He told me I could punch, and I don't have to run. I was right there for him. I'm totally different now and have my future wife here with me. I'm very serious about it."*[212] Joe spoke of how he dealt with the tall, long-reaching Stokes right hand. *"I saw it. I'm learning new things so I just took it and counter-punched. I don't ask questions. I just go out and fight."*[213]

Joe spoke of Arturo. *"We're family. Everything is working out, and I feel like a new man. No comeback or nothing. For these fights, the ten-rounders or main events, I'll fight at 153 or 154 because that's where I feel strongest."*[214] The win pushed Joe's record to 22-4 (17 KOs).

Pat Lynch was pleased with the large turnout of fans. He was hoping to get Joe back in the ring in seven weeks.[215]

On October 24, it was announced that George Benton, chief trainer for Main Events, was leaving the company. Benton, a former middleweight, and Lou Duva, had worked together for seventeen years. Benton boxed professionally from 1949 to 1970, amassing a 62-13-1 (37 KOs) record. Some of the fighters Benton worked with included Pernell Whitaker, Meldrick Taylor, and Evander Holyfield. Benton remarked on the split, *"Lou and I could have gone on forever, but all of a sudden he got greedy. When it comes out what the real deal is, you're really going to be surprised that he thought that I could be so dumb. The stuff is going to hit the fan. My lawyers are working on something now. They're going to make a proposal, and, if he doesn't agree to it, the whole mess is going to come out. He never gave me Golota. He never gave me any of his White fighters. That's the way he is."*[216]

Duva responded to Benton's allegations, *"That's bull. I won't dignify that. It's so far from the truth it's ridiculous. George is saying I only gave him Black fighters? Well where did that $5 million come from that he made? I gave him the very best fighters we had, and he did a good job with them. Who would he rather have worked with, Evander Holyfield or Andrew Golota?"*[217]

Benton was upset about another issue, that of Duva being hailed as the main trainer. *"He was no damn trainer. But I never knocked him for saying that he was."*[218] Duva wasn't the only chief second during fights that wasn't the main gym trainer of his fighters. Secaucus' Al Certo fronted Buddy McGirt while McGirt had several trainers during his career, such as Dominic Amoroso, Jimmy Dupree, and Hector Roca. Amoroso trained McGirt right up until Buddy fought the Frankie Warren rematch. Amoroso was let go by Certo. Sal Alessi recalled that the move *"broke Dominic's heart."*[219] Amoroso had also trained Gino Perez and Ramon Ranquillo for Certo. McGirt credited Amoroso for helping him become a successful professional.

Little-known Cuban Luis Sarria assisted Angelo Dundee in preparing Muhammad Ali for his fights, working mostly on conditioning. Sarria worked with Ali for all but two of his title fights, but most have never heard of him. Sarria felt that Ali was surrounded by leeches when he was champion.[220] Arturo would soon come to learn of the leeches that Sarria was speaking of, as he climbed the ladder of success.

Arturo's fan base was growing exponentially. Wayne Witkowski described the phenomenon. *"Arturo immediately drew a local fan following when he had his amateur fight late in that phase of his career in Jersey City. And as he fought professionally, that base continued to grow. Hudson County sports fans always considered themselves great fight fans, and rightly so, and they admired Arturo's 'warrior' determination. The only way you could stop him was to put him on the canvas. He had almost a super-human willpower, a refuse-to-lose mentality to bounce back in the face of defeat. Arturo was the working-class hero for the blue-collar fans. In my experiences covering him, I remember him always flashing the smile and confidence of a winner, and he always remembered those who stood by him in the beginning of his career as he became more popular."*[221]

Arturo was back in action, defending his USBA 130-pound super featherweight championship on November 22, 1994 at the Meadowlands Convention Center, against Jose Sanabria, 21-10-3

(11 KOs), of Venezuela. Sanabria would be the first current or former world champion that Arturo faced in his career. Sanabria had a wealth of world-class experience, far greater than anyone Arturo had fought. Sanabria had held the IBF 122-pound world title from May 21, 1988 until March 10, 1989, losing it on a split decision. Amongst his three successful title defenses, he had stopped former and future world champion Thierry Jacob in the 6th round. In 1991, Sanabria had lost a close 10-round split-decision to Regilio Tuur. After losing the title Sanabria had not been as successful, going 5-6-1. He had been fighting a much higher class of competition than Arturo, and had been stopped only once in his 32-fight career up to that point. Gatti had only 17 fights, 11 of which were 1st round knockouts. Al Albert of USA Network noted that Gatti had fought 53 total rounds versus Sanabria's 246 rounds over the course of a 10-year career.

Gatti was ten years younger than the 32-year-old Sanabria. Arturo was ranked #4 in the world by the IBF. Arturo wore a New Jersey Devils hockey jersey into the ring, with the number '1' and the name 'Gatti' on the back. Sitting right behind Gatti's corner was his good friend and biggest fan, Devils general manager Lou Lamoriello.

Arturo started fast, taking the 1st round, but Sanabria slipped many of Gatti's bombs. The 2nd round found both fighters settling in, though Arturo appeared to take the round with his aggression and harder, more effective punching, particularly to the body. Sanabria was relaxed and quick, landing occasional leads and clean counters. Sanabria was more defensive than the aggressive, harder-punching Gatti.

During the 3rd round, after landing several thudding body blows, Gatti rocked and wobbled Sanabria with a combination to the head, but the wily and tough veteran weathered the storm. Later in the round, Arturo was cautioned for a low blow. Gatti injured his left hand throwing a hook, but Arturo demonstrated his ability to continue fighting hard regardless of the pain.

Gatti boxed successfully in the 4th round, jabbing and moving while carefully picking his moments to attack. When he did attack, Arturo outmuscled Sanabria on the inside. Sanabria was content to counter Gatti with single shots. Both boxers fought more methodically in the 5th with Arturo sprinkling in heavy power shots.

In the 6th, both fighters opened up, exchanging punches in the middle of the ring, thrilling the crowd. Sanabria had grown more aggressive and trapped Gatti along the ropes. Arturo appeared to be hurt by a hook to the body followed by a right cross to the jaw. Gatti came back with a hook well below the belt, but Sanabria, unfazed, kept punching. As Arturo moved away, Referee Steve Smoger jumped in and warned Gatti for the low blow. Arturo's brother Joe jumped out of his seat when Smoger gave the warning. Joe might have thought Smoger was giving Arturo an 8-count as Arturo was receiving heavy punishment. The break in action actually seemed to benefit Arturo, as it briefly stopped Sanabria's momentum.

Announcer Sean O'Grady visited Arturo's corner and asked Hector Roca if he was concerned that the pace was picking up this late in the fight. Roca answered that Sanabria was a very experienced fighter. He added that Arturo needed to face experienced opponents such as Sanabria. O'Grady asked why Gatti was moving around more in this fight. Roca replied that Sanabria's experience had forced Arturo to be more mobile. Roca felt that Arturo would get Sanabria in the later rounds. As Gatti was taking punishment to the head, O'Grady asked Roca if he was going to change anything between rounds. Roca replied that Arturo just needed to fight.

Gatti spent a good portion of the round against the ropes, taking many clean, solid punches to the jaw and body, but he fought back hard, landing bombs of his own. His defense was porous, but he demonstrated the trademark toughness and calmness under fire which would make him famous.

In the 7th, Arturo came out moving and jabbing. Gatti took the momentum back, landing several combinations and a hard overhand right, as his fans fueled him on. Sanabria had taken his foot off the gas, allowing Arturo to box him more effectively.

For the first minute of the 8th Gatti was faring well, until he retreated to the ropes after getting tagged with several blows. Once again he fought back hard. Both fighters stood their ground, exchanging thunderous bombs, to the crowd's delight. Arturo spun off the ropes as the slugfest continued. Gatti decided to move and box. His left eye was starting to swell. For the first time in his career, Arturo had an opponent in front of him who didn't seem fazed by his punching power. Sanabria landed a double right.

Near the ropes again, Arturo got pounded with several hard shots that twisted his head sideways. Responding to the head-jolting blows, commentator Al Albert questioned whether Gatti was rushed into fighting someone as experienced as Sanabria. Sanabria kept advancing, firing his shots, as Arturo retreated. Gatti decided to stop and stand his ground, firing back with bombs of his own. Both boxers thrilled the crowd with their courageous back and forth exchanges. Up to that point, Sanabria had won only 2 of the 8 rounds, but he had done significant damage in both of those rounds.

During the first 40 seconds of the 9th, Sanabria punished the back-peddling Gatti with hooks and crosses, as well as jabs and uppercuts. O'Grady commented on Arturo's low left hand and how Sanabria was walking through Gatti's punches. Arturo valiantly tried to fight back and box as best he could, but his defense was virtually non-existent.

About halfway through the 9th, Sanabria pinned Arturo on the ropes again. Gatti appeared to be wilting under the assault. Yet, with his back to the ropes, Arturo showed the heart of a lion, matching each Sanabria bomb with bombs of his own.

With 20 seconds remaining in the round, both fighters threw right hands at the same time, with Sanabria's clearly hurting Gatti. Arturo winced in pain as he stepped back, covering up as best he could. Before the round ended, Gatti absorbed four more hard rights to the head and chin. Sanabria strutted back to his corner with both arms raised. The crowd was wild with delight at the action.

The ringside doctor examined Gatti and asked how he felt. *"I'm all right"* was the response. He asked Arturo if he wanted to continue. Gatti responded firmly, *"Yeah."* Referee Steve Smoger was known for giving hurt fighters every opportunity to get back into a fight. Smoger visited Arturo's corner and asked him how he was doing. While Gatti sat with his mouth open, Roca immediately answered that Arturo was *"very good."* Smoger affectionately smacked Roca on the back of his neck and walked away. Roca implored Gatti to use his jab more and work the body. He also asked Arturo to shorten up his punches and cover up more on defense.

Arturo started the 10th moving, using his stiff jab as Sanabria pursued. Gatti landed several hard body punches. Sanabria came right back with hard hooks to the body and head. Gatti kept moving and jabbing. With about a minute remaining, both boxers traded solid punches. Arturo was trying to avoid mixing it up, moving his feet and head, while picking his moments to punch. Sanabria went for the body. Gatti replied with a quick combination. Sanabria was not able to land as solidly as before on his nimble, elusive target. In frustration, Sanabria urged Gatti to stop moving, motioning both hands towards himself and then outstretching both arms to the side, taunting Arturo to stop back-peddling and fight. After the round, Sanabria raised his hands, but it was a close round. Some might credit Sanabria's aggression, while others might favor Arturo's boxing and cleanly landed punches.

The crowd started booing in the 11th, as Arturo continued to back away and box from long-range. Arturo responded with a six-punch-combination to the body and head that brought the crowd back to life. Sanabria trapped Gatti on the ropes and landed several hard hooks and crosses before Arturo held. Gary Shaw, of the New Jersey State Athletic Commission, was sitting ringside. He peered from left to right, observing the expressions on the ringside fans' faces. After moving from the ropes, Arturo stopped and landed a solid left hook. His brother Joe implored him to attack. However, Arturo clearly thought that his fleet-footed boxing was the smarter strategy. Arturo landed a combination which knocked Sanabria's mouthpiece out. Sanabria's pressure was relentless, but nevertheless, Gatti boxed well during the final minute of the 11th, demonstrating his versatility and excellent conditioning.

Between rounds, Roca asked for quick combinations and movement. Roca cautioned Arturo to keep his hands up.

Early in the 12th, Sanabria landed several solid rights. Arturo replied with a thudding left hook. Sanabria advanced and pressed Gatti into a corner. Arturo fired off several combinations, before spinning off the ropes and continuing to punch. Gatti kept moving while landing a right uppercut and left hook combo. Sanabria pressed the jabbing Gatti, landing a solid right. The ever moving Arturo suddenly stopped and landed a combination to the body and head, with a left hook causing Sanabria's mouthpiece to fly out again. The combatants exchanged blows, with Gatti's hooks and crosses landing cleaner and more solidly. Sanabria motioned Gatti to bring it on, but Arturo wisely kept moving. Arturo scored well in the final minute while punching and moving, particularly with his jab and hook. When the final 10-second tap of the canvas was heard, Sanabria raised his hands in triumph.

After the final bell, both corners lifted their fighter up as a sign of victory. Al Albert wondered whether Arturo might have lost his belt. O'Grady suggested he might have retained it.

Ring announcer Jimmy Marotta announced the unanimous decision in Gatti's favor, with scores of 116-112 and 118-110 twice. Al Albert commented that even the pro-Gatti crowd seemed surprised, not only because he won, but because he had won by such a large margin. Sean O'Grady thought that Arturo had won the fight, but by a much closer margin than the judges had it. While Sanabria had won the three most exciting and brutal rounds, Gatti had won more rounds overall. After the fight, Gatti stated, *"I tasted world class opposition. My corner told me just to keep boxing. I knew if I tried to out power him, I wasn't going to win the fight."*[222]

Arturo looked as though he had been in a war. His injured left hand blew up like a balloon. His left eye was swollen, and his nose was out of place, most likely from a Sanabria head butt.

The feeling after the bout was that Gatti was a tough kid with a lot of heart, but his technical skills were questionable. Pat Lynch later admitted that he had been leery about taking the Sanabria fight. Before the bout, several people told Lynch that it was a mistake to take the match.[223]

Ultimately though, the fight was a litmus test on Arturo, exposing both his positives and negatives. At times he was very hittable and he revealed that he could be hurt. But he also exhibited a granite chin, heart, toughness, conditioning, and versatility. He had held his ground, brawled when needed, and boxed when it favored him to do so. Defeating a former world champion with much more experience, in a tough fight, was no small accomplishment.

On the undercard of the USA Network's "Tuesday Night Fights," Philadelphia's Ivan Robinson moved his undefeated record to 16-0. Robinson struggled to earn a split decision win over Newark, N.J.'s Juan Negron.

Besides losing top trainer George Benton, Main Events was forced to replace their president, Dan Duva, due to a brain tumor. Dan became chairman while he fought his illness. His brother Dino took over as president. Dan's sister, Donna Duva-Brooks, became the organization's vice-president.

The Ring magazine's January 1995 ratings had Arturo in the #8 spot at junior lightweight. Regilio Tuur was rated #7 and Main Events-promoted John John Molina, the IBF champ, held the top spot. Arturo was ranked #8 by the WBC.

At the end of January, Lou Duva asked Pat Lynch if Arturo could fly to Texas to help John John Molina prepare for his upcoming battle with Oscar De La Hoya. Lynch and Arturo jumped at the opportunity to once again spar with Molina.[224]

Arturo traveled back to the Netherlands on March 9, 1995 with Lynch, Roca, and Regilio Tuur. Tuur was defending his WBO super featherweight title against Tony Pep. Gatti took on 0-3 Ruslan Smolenkov of Russia. The mismatch with Smolenkov would never have been approved in the United States. Arturo hurt Smolenkov with a left hook early in the 1st. He followed with a barrage of punches. A perfectly placed left hook to the body dropped Smolenkov to his knees. He was counted out with 1:12 remaining in the opening round.

Lynch and Main Events needed to be very careful who they matched Arturo with, as he was closing in on a world title shot. Arturo commented on the Smolenkov bout, *"I really wanted to knock him out. After my last two fights, I think I really needed the knockout. I didn't necessarily look for the knockout in the first round, but once I hurt him I tried to finish him like I always do."*[225]

In April, the March 1995 IBF rankings were released. Arturo was ranked #3.

On April 22, Arturo was back in action at Bally's in Atlantic City. He boxed the main event on Telemundo's "Boxeo" boxing series against Tialano Tovar, 9-8-1 (5 KOs), of Denver Colorado. Arturo walked into the ring wearing his New Jersey Devil's hockey jersey.

Gatti was easily controlling the action in the 1st round when he landed a crushing left hook that twisted Tovar's head around and sent him down. Tovar was counted out by Wayne Hedgepeth with 1:20 remaining in the opening round.

The win was Arturo's 20th against only 1 loss. Gatti now had thirteen 1st round knockouts. Pat Lynch commented that this was Arturo's most impressive knockout because it was accomplished with one punch. Lynch added that he would keep Gatti busy while they waited for Tracy Harris Patterson's team to agree to terms on a fight for Patterson's IBF belt.[226]

On May 7, Joe Gatti was back in action at the Biloxi Grand Theater in Biloxi, Mississippi. He was taking on two-time former world champion James "Buddy" McGirt. The 31-year-old McGirt had been a professional for thirteen years. McGirt was fighting with a repaired tendon that had been torn from his left rotator cuff against Pernell Whitaker in March 1993.

McGirt had always felt that he could beat Joe since he first saw Joe fight at the convention center in Secaucus in 1991. Buddy felt that if he could handle Matthew Hilton's power, he could handle Joe's punches.[227] Joe asked Hector Roca, who had trained him for the Stokes fight, to train him for the McGirt fight. Roca accepted.

Joe recalled the McGirt fight. *"I took the fight with Buddy myself. I don't know how I did it but somebody called and I said, 'I'll fight Buddy,' and we fought."*[228]

When Joe arrived at the airport with Roca, Lynch and Vikki he was stunned to find that McGirt and his team were on the same departing flight. Joe felt that scheduling both teams to be on the same flight was purposely done as a psychological ploy to disrupt his prefight focus. Although it is rare to see two opponents on the same flight it may have been incidental since both teams were leaving from Newark. If booking the fighters to be on the same flight was intentionally done to disrupt Joe's focus the move succeeded.

Joe recalled that the agreed upon weight was changed after he arrived in Biloxi. *"You give me a fight at a weight class and all of a sudden I got to drop three more pounds at the last minute cause he won't fight me and look at the picture, it was like I was on crack."* [229]

Joe recalled that the original agreed-upon weight was 164 or 165, but at the last minute it was changed to 160. Joe felt that losing the final 3 or 4-pounds weakened him immensely.[230] Joe explained that Matthew Hilton had the same problem, losing many pounds right before his bouts. Joe sighed, *"Yeah, but he (Hilton) was able to handle it."*[231] Ironically, McGirt was also experiencing weight issues, having to shed a pound right at the weigh-in.

Joe was three years younger and held a 5-inch height advantage over the 5'6½" McGirt. Buddy had held world titles at junior welterweight and welterweight, but had never fought as a full-fledged middleweight. Still, McGirt possessed a vast amount of experience, with quality wins over Frankie Warren, Rafael Williams, and Simon Brown, and two close, competitive losses to Pernell Whitaker. Joe entered the contest with a 22-4 (17 KOs) record to McGirt's 65-4-1 (44 KOs) mark. The bout was televised live on CBS. Jimmy Dupree, the former light heavyweight contender from Jersey City, trained McGirt for the Gatti fight.

Before the bout, when interviewed, McGirt spoke of his durability, as he was participating in his 70th professional bout. McGirt was asked about his two loses to Pernell Whitaker and his injured left arm. McGirt felt that his arm injury was more mental than physical, as he was scared to throw the left after the injury. McGirt added that many people felt that his career was over after the Whitaker losses, but in his heart and mind he knew that it was not.

Broadcaster Gil Clancy spoke of Joe's power, that Joe was a good puncher and an exciting fighter. Clancy added that Joe was inconsistent, because he sometimes became frustrated and tried too hard. This caused him to start winging his punches. Clancy pointed to Joe's close decision loss to Rafael Williams as an example.

Hector Roca was Joe's chief second. Pat Lynch was also in Gatti's corner. Al Certo seconded McGirt, along with Howie Albert and Certo's cutman nephew, Danny Milano. Although Jimmy Dupree had trained McGirt for the Gatti fight, Certo did not use him in the corner.

After the opening bell, Joe immediately utilized the jab on his smaller foe. McGirt started feinting punches, before landing a double hook to the body and head. Gatti caught Buddy stepping in with a cracking left hook that forced McGirt to take two steps back. Buddy landed a quick-jab straight-right combo. Gatti continued with the jab as Roca yelled for him to throw first. McGirt ended the round with a fast straight right.

Joe came out jabbing in the 2nd. He landed a short right cross as the two fighters came together. Joe landed a solid hook on the beltline. Referee Elmo Adolph warned Joe to keep his punches up. At the 1:44 mark, McGirt timed an overhand right over Gatti's jab. McGirt attempted the punch again, but fell short as Joe countered with a straight-right straight-left combo. Roca implored Gatti to step in with his jab. McGirt landed a right to the head. Joe countered with a straight right to the body. Gatti came in behind the jab and followed with a hook to the body. Joe continued to utilize his jab while McGirt was trying to time his right hand over Joe's jab.

In the 3rd, Joe was working his jab well but McGirt had no trouble getting inside his taller opponent, landing a solid left hook. McGirt followed with a double hook to the body and head. Buddy landed a hard right over Gatti's guard. McGirt was waiting for Joe to lead, to shorten the distance for his counter shots.

Joe attempted a left hook that was blocked. McGirt came back with dazzling, short combinations down the middle that seemed to frustrate Gatti. Joe received a cut over his left eye. He attempted over a dozen punches in the final minute of the 3rd, but McGirt displayed his ring craftiness by slipping and blocking them all.

After the round ended Roca implored Joe to put pressure on McGirt and to punch with both hands. Roca complained that when McGirt would stop punching so would Joe. Roca begged Joe to keep punching after McGirt stopped.

At the start of the 4th, broadcaster Gil Clancy expressed his amazement over Roca thinking that McGirt would fade if Joe kept the pressure on. Clancy also criticized Joe's head hunting instead of targeting McGirt's body, especially if Gatti wanted to wear McGirt out.

In the opening minute of the 4th, Joe landed two hard body shots. McGirt landed a sharp right-hand left-hook combo halfway through the round. With 1:20 remaining in the round, McGirt timed and barely missed an overhand counter right. McGirt landed several solid shots in the final minute. Clancy believed that if McGirt would have hit a lighter opponent with the solid shots he hit Joe with, the fight would have been over.

In the 5th, Joe threw jabs and rights but they did not appear to have any strength behind them. A minute into the round, McGirt landed a hard right hand over the top. McGirt kept throwing the overhand right. Gatti dipped to his right to avoid them but his left hand was low, exposing his jaw. McGirt, seeing this, timed the right hand again. With 1:20 remaining in the 5th, McGirt drilled a right hand into Joe's jaw, dropping him on his back.

Joe rolled over and rose to his feet six seconds later, but referee Elmo Adolph waived the fight over at the 1:44 mark. Hector Roca climbed up onto the ring apron as soon as Joe was dropped, with a towel in his hand, to stop the fight. Matchmaker Carl Moretti jumped into the ring and kissed the Main Events-promoted McGirt on the cheek while Joe sat on a stool with his head down.

Joe was devastated after the McGirt loss. He recalled Arturo talking to him about finding a way to turn his bad luck around. *"One time he told me, we were talking about our careers, and I lost a big fight. 'You gotta go with the devil, if you wanna make it. You gotta go with the devil.' And maybe Arturo, he did that. Maybe that was the difference."*[232] Joe felt that Arturo was dead serious when he made the comment.

Joe was fed up with Pat Lynch. He told Lynch that he didn't want him managing his career anymore. Lynch agreed to release him, but he reminded Joe that he was still under contract. Joe asked Lynch what it would cost for him to get out of the contract. Lynch told Joe that he would have to pay $5,000 for his expenses and lost earnings. Joe wrote Lynch a check for the $5,000. The only professional boxing link left between Arturo and Joe, Pat Lynch, had now been broken. Joe had first left Main Events, and now Pat Lynch. The same Pat Lynch who had Arturo on the verge of a title shot. Joe parting ways with Lynch would further strain his relationship with Arturo.

On July 13, 1995, Arturo was set to return to Atlantic City at Caesar's, against Toronto's Barrington Francis, 21-6-4. Gatti was ranked #1 by the IBF and #3 by the WBC. Several days before the bout, Pat Lynch was advised by Dino Duva that Arturo would receive a shot at Tracy Harris Patterson's 130-pound IBF title. Patterson had just won the title on July 9 with a 2nd round knockout victory over Eddie Hopson. Patterson's manager, Marc Roberts, had wanted a big-money match with Oscar De La Hoya, but that fight fell through.

Russell Peltz, Arturo's co-promoter, was promoting the Gatti-Francis card. The bout was broadcast live on cable's PrismTV. On paper, the Gatti-Francis match appeared to be a rather safe fight. Unfortunately for Team Gatti, the contest must be decided in the ring not on paper. There were no guarantees. A lucky punch, a severe injury or a devastating knockout loss could all put the championship bout, and future paydays, in jeopardy.

Barrington Francis, a former Canadian and WBF champion, had last fought WBC super bantamweight champion Hector Acero-Sanchez, losing a 10-round decision on October 28, 1994. Barrington weighed in at 131, while Arturo weighed 132-pounds. Although Arturo was a little over an inch taller than Barrington, Francis held nearly a 4-inch reach advantage. Arturo had sparred with Francis in Canada when he was a 15-year-old amateur. At the time, Francis was already a veteran of nine professional fights. Arturo spoke of the importance of the match. *"All I'm thinking about is winning this fight. Then after that, I should get a title shot by the end of the year. It doesn't have to be the next fight, but it has to be before the end of the year. I think I deserve that much."*[233]

Arturo, who had sparred with Hopson in the past, spoke of Tracy Patterson defeating Eddie for the IBF belt. *"I was shocked. Going into the fight, I thought Eddie would win. I never thought he'd get knocked out, especially so quick [second round]. I still don't think Patterson has the power at 130-pounds. Eddie came in real nervous. He wasn't himself. He got caught."*[234] Arturo commented on the Francis fight. *"He [Francis] likes to fight. I'll have to be smart and use my head. He's going to go all out and try to beat me. He hasn't been in the ring as much as I have. I'll be sharper."*[235]

Lynch was asked if Arturo might be looking past the Francis fight. Lynch replied that Arturo was definitely not looking past the bout. Lynch stated that Arturo watched the Patterson upset and was aware he was fighting a tough opponent. Lynch added that after the Francis fight, he and Arturo would meet with Dino Duva to discuss future plans.[236] Lynch commented on Arturo changing trainers from Diego Rosario to Hector Roca after the King Solomon fight. He believed that Rosario was a great trainer, but the change was all for the better, as Roca was doing a great job with Arturo.[237] Rosario's name had come up because on April 8, he led Bruce Seldon to a stunning victory over Tony Tucker for the vacant WBA heavyweight title.

Arturo entered the ring against Francis with his New Jersey Devils hockey jersey on. Gatti later recalled, *"I wore the jersey before every game of the Stanley Cup Finals."*[238] The Devils won the Cup in 1995 with a sweep over the Detroit Red Wings.

Arturo started the Francis fight with quick jabs and combinations. Barrington, wary of Arturo's power, was cautious and defensive. Near the end of the 1st, Francis started engaging Arturo with counter shots, although Arturo was much busier in the round.

Gatti started the 2nd stanza by circling to his left. Francis was working his jab. Two minutes in, Barrington scored a counter right over Arturo's jab. Gatti quickly came back with a counter hook. Arturo squatted low to slip a punch and Francis pushed him, causing Gatti to fall. Referee Arthur Mercante Sr. warned Barrington for pushing off. When Arturo rose to his feet his demeanor completely changed. He jumped all over Francis, pummeling him with head and body shots for over 40 seconds. Barrington was wobbly, covering up with a tight guard and moving his head as best he could, but the punches were having their effect.

After surviving the 2nd round onslaught, Francis looked fresh to start the 3rd. He was quick and active, scoring a solid right hand while also displaying crisp head movement. Barrington kept trying to reach Gatti with his right, but he threw it a little wide, which gave Arturo the extra moment he needed to step back and avoid the shots. The aggressive Francis kept stepping forward. With a minute remaining in the 3rd, Arturo opened up with hooks and crosses on the charging Francis. Arturo finished the round by snapping his jab off of Barrington's head.

Francis was competitive and tough. The Gatti team may have been nervous at this point. A world championship fight and a major payday was hanging in the balance for Gatti, Lynch, Main Events, and Peltz.

In the 4th round, Arturo landed two hard hooks and a solid right. Francis kept trying for a home-run punch. Barrington landed several solid punches. Gatti replied with a left hook. Arturo opened up with a flurry of punches, but most of them missed, though a solid hook landed. Francis displayed very sharp defensive skills. With 27 seconds remaining in the round, both fighters traded heavy blows. Arturo's title-opportunity was hanging in the balance with every bomb that Francis threw. Both fighters continued trading haymakers as the round came to a close. Peltz was delivering another war for his faithful fans. Peltz had previously stated, *"You have to give the fans their money's worth or they won't come back."*[239]

Early in the 5th, Arturo started snapping the jab more frequently. Francis utilized his reach advantage and was matching Arturo's jabs. Gatti landed some blows to the mid-section. Barrington was countering quickly and consistently, but most of his shots missed the mark. Arturo started waiting more, and when he swung his punches were wider. Arturo alternated between boxing and jabbing and standing flat-footed, trading power shots. The round ended with both fighters looking for openings.

Both boxers started the 6th trading jabs and jousting. Francis kept attacking, but his guard was low and his jaw exposed. Gatti landed hard rights and lefts to the body followed by a hook and right up top. Barrington wobbled slightly. Francis kept moving his head, slipping most of the follow-up blows. With his back against the ropes, Barrington partially blocked a left hook. He eluded two Gatti follow-up blows with his alert head movement when Arthur Mercante stunningly jumped in-between the fighters and stopped the contest at 1:23 of the 6th round. Francis had a look of utter shock, surprise, and dismay on his face.

The crowd booed the 74-year-old Mercante's decision to halt the contest. Francis clearly was not that hurt, and was effectively defending himself. The television announcers tried to justify the stoppage by saying that Francis was helpless. The TV replay shows Francis had his full senses, slipping several punches. Arturo's supporters cheered, while the rest of the crowd booed the stoppage. After the victory, Arturo put his N.J. Devils jersey back on.

Years later, Francis recalled, *"I would rather die than to win a fight the way that Gatti won over me. They wouldn't even give me a rematch. I did not even know the conspiracy about fighting for a world title against Tracy Patterson."*[240]

Although Arturo was ahead on the cards and may have stopped Francis moments or rounds later, there was no defining moment in that round, up to that point, that mandated a stoppage. Mercante clearly erred in his decision to stop the bout so quickly.

Mercante commented on his decision to stop the battle. *"You've got to consider the talent involved. Gatti is a tremendous puncher. He [Francis] took a lot of shots. He came back in spurts, but he continued to take an awful lot of head shots, jabs to the head and* body. His mouth was all bleeding, but the people couldn't see that. His eye was cut in a very vulnerable spot. What am I going to do? Let the kid get pounded until he knocks him dead? For who? That's not my style."[241]

Francis' trainer, Bill Lehman, disputed the stoppage. *"If Mercante had looked at some of Francis' fights, he wouldn't have stopped it. He came back to score a knockout in the tenth round against Richard Salazar [a year earlier]. If they were going to stop the fight, they should have stopped it in the second round."*[242]

Francis was interviewed after the battle. *"I believe that I was treated unjustly. Arturo Gatti admitted [that] after the fight. I'd like to do it [fight Gatti again] with another referee, probably Larry Hazzard."*[243]

Arturo commented on the stoppage. *"I thought the fight would go on. If it would have gone into the seventh, I would have stopped him."*[244]

Both Joe and Arturo had some down time, as neither would be back in action for two months. To pass the time they would go out "clubbing" together. One of the towns they frequented was Hoboken. One night, the brothers and Mikey Red went out for a good time. The trio spent some time in a nightclub, then decided to leave. Joe described what happened next. *"I just remember, I went outside looking for my brother. I saw a guy walking towards me with blood on his face. I said, 'Are you okay?' He grabbed me and body slammed me. I got up and knocked him out. I looked over and I saw three guys fighting my brother. I ran there and I went crazy. I was eight for eight with eight knockouts [laughs]. Seriously, it was like a movie scene. Then we ran away because of the sirens of the police and the ambulance."*[245]

Donny Jerie recalled another incident when he, Arturo, and another friend went out to Club Abyss in Sayreville. *"We were down the shore one time. We're at Club Abyss. Our friend happened to leave us so we were on our way out and this guy was being a wise guy. 'Hey Gatti you aint nothing, bla, bla, bla. You aint that tough. Give me a fight.' He kept on egging him on. And Gatti's like, 'Don't worry buddy, I'm gonna be a champ and be worth millions one day.' He kept on egging him on. And I wind up zapping this dude. I hit him on the chin. I thought if Gatti got involved with this, there's gonna be trouble. I hit him and he goes down to the ground, and Gatti was like, 'Oh, we gotta put him in a cab.' We put him in the cab and Gatti gave me money for the cab. Gatti's like, 'Here take this guy home.'*

"And we wind up going home in a cab. This is the funniest thing. [Gatti], me, and my buddy Ralph. And the [cab driver] was dropping us off and we're like, 'Dude we ain't paying for this cab bro. We're jumping this cab.' So he pulls up and we're going over to Pat's house. This is when he lived down the shore. Arturo's like, 'Bro, we gotta pay.' And we're like, 'Na bro, we ain't paying. We ain't paying dude. We're getting out of the cab.' So Gatti's like, 'Ah alright.' So we get out. We're running through the backyards. We're jumping over fences. We're trying to get to Pat's house. Gatti falls in the bushes. Me and my friend pick him up. We're looking in-between cars and we see the guy in the cab. He's looking for us. He's trying to hunt us down. Gatti gets in my car. He's got this thing on two wheels. I'm telling you, this guy's trying to track us down. He's got it on two wheels. We go from Pat's house in Marlboro down to Gatti's condo. I mean you want to talk about hilarious."[246]

On September 27, 1995 at The Roxy in Boston, Massachusetts, Joe Gatti returned to the ring against Willie Kemp. Joe took a 6-round decision over the 14-19 (8 KOs) Kemp to improve to 23-5 (17 KOs).

Joe quickly returned to the ring a month later, on October 3, in Memphis, Tennessee. The commission in Tennessee was much more relaxed than New Jersey and New York. This gave managers and promoters a location to bring their fighters for an easy win against inferior opponents that probably wouldn't have been approved in the stricter states. Joe took on the 3-26 (1 KO) Tim Bonds. Bonds was what insiders coined a "professional opponent" who came to give rounds if he could hang in the fight, or if not he would bow out quickly. Joe dispatched of Bonds in the 1st round.

On October 7, Arturo returned to the ring against Carlos Vergara of Massachusetts at the Convention Center in Atlantic City. Vergara, 16-11 (5 KOs), was carefully selected to give Arturo some work as he waited for his world title opportunity. Vergara had lost six out of his last eight fights, being stopped four times. Arturo knocked Vergara out in 57 seconds of the 1st round. Gatti ended the bout by backing Vergara into a neutral corner, then landing a left hook to the ribs and a right to the head that sent Vergara to the canvas. Referee Tony Perez counted up to five, then waived the bout off. After the match, Arturo stated, *"I've seen coffee breaks that lasted longer than that. I wouldn't have minded if it went a little longer. But I worked very hard in the gym and in the ring. I took my time looking for the good punch. But they were just straight punches."*[247] Arturo improved to 23-1 with 20 KOs, including 14 stoppages in the 1st round.

On December 1, Joe traveled across the river to Staten Island to take on 15-14-1 (4 KOs) Tim Dendy of Jackson, Tennessee. Joe took a 10-round unanimous decision over Dendy. All three judges scored the bout 97-93. Joe now held a professional record of 25-5 (18 KOs). Joe injured his right elbow in the bout, and was forced to undergo surgery. The injury would sideline him for nine months.

Chapter 10
A Dream Realized

On December 15, 1995, Arturo Gatti, 23-1, participated in his first world championship contest, against Tracy Harris Patterson, 54-3-1, the defending IBF 130-pound super featherweight champion. The bout was held at the Mecca of Boxing, New York's Madison Square Garden.

At the pre-fight press conference, Patterson's manager, Marc Roberts, bashed De La Hoya for ducking Patterson and fighting Jesse James Leija instead. Patterson, whose ring name was Caesar, was the adopted son of former heavyweight champion Floyd Patterson. Floyd was the N.Y. State Athletic Commissioner at the time, and had to act as impartial as possible during the build-up to the fight.

Lynch was nervous before the match, especially due to the fact that Arturo was fighting at Madison Square Garden for the very first time. Lynch's concerns may have been due in part to the way Joe performed when he was in front of 65,000 fans against Terry Norris. Years later, Arturo recalled Lynch's nervousness. *"I fought when I was eight years old. I fought in front of twenty thousand. It was a pro-am [professional-amateur show]. And it was a funny story because my manager [Pat Lynch] was worried when I fought for the title, 'cause there were so many people there, like over fifteen thousand. And he was, 'How are you going to handle that?' I said, 'Oh, don't worry about it. I fought in front of twenty thousand people.' And one day I showed him the picture. And he thought it was recently, like when I was in the amateurs. But I showed him the picture and I was like eight-years-old [laughs]."*

Tracy Harris Patterson turned professional on June 19, 1985 on a Lou Duva-promoted Ice World card in Totowa N.J. Seven years later, on June 23, 1992, Patterson won his first world title, defeating Thierry Jacob by 2nd round knockout, winning the WBC super-bantamweight title. After losing the title in 1994 to Hector Acero-Sanchez, Patterson won the IBF super-featherweight title on July 9, 1995, when he knocked Eddie Hopson out in the 2nd round. Patterson started boxing at age eleven. He won two N.Y. Golden Glove titles as an amateur. Patterson had more than twice the number of professional fights as Gatti, giving him a vast experience edge. He had gone 5-1-1 in world championship contests.

Patterson split with his father a few months before the Gatti fight, signing up with Triple Threats' Marc Roberts. Roberts fervently tried to secure a match with Oscar De La Hoya, who was boxing in the main event. The "Golden Boy" had only nineteen fights at the time, but he already was boxing's rising superstar, and a mega payday for anyone lucky enough to be selected as his next opponent. Top Rank's Bob Arum, De La Hoya's promoter, called Oscar, *"The emerging superstar of boxing."*[248]

A De La Hoya match would mean a huge purse for Patterson and Roberts. Patterson stood to make $375,000 against De La Hoya, but instead made only $175,000 against Gatti. Arturo brought home a career best $65,000 in the Patterson match. Arum originally agreed to the Patterson match, but later withdrew, stating De La Hoya couldn't make the 130-pound limit. De La Hoya's choosing not to fight Patterson cleared the path for Arturo's title shot, as he was the #1 ranked contender. De La Hoya wound up defending his WBO lightweight title against Leija, knocking Leija out in the 2nd round of the main event.

The Patterson fight would be Arturo's first fight on Home Box Office (HBO). Years later, Gatti explained how he prepared in the locker room for a fight. *"I'm thinking about how I'm gonna come into the ring. Physically and mentally I know I'm prepared. [I] make sure I do that in training camp. I do everything right, so [I'm] very confident. Just concentrate on how I'm going to step in the ring and what I'm going to start with."*

Arturo had never lost faith in his abilities. Not even after his early career loss. Just like the song from one of his favorite bands, Journey, "Don't Stop Believing" was Arturo's mantra.

Arturo held a 2½-inch height advantage over the 5'5" Patterson. Main Events helped secure the Patterson fight by owning the rights to three of Tracy's title defenses. Patterson had defeated Main Events-promoted Eddie Hopson for the title. Main Events, as most promoters were allowed to do at the time, had a clause that if Patterson beat Hopson, they would own the promotional rights to his next three fights.

Patterson, from New Paltz, New York, was fighting in Madison Square Garden for the first time since he won the 125-pound open class Daily News Golden Gloves title in 1985. Patterson's chief second was Tommy Parks. Arturo had Hector Roca as his chief second. Parks, a former professional boxer who fought in the welterweight division, compiled an 18-3 professional record between 1947 and 1949. Upon retiring, Parks worked with boxers such as Rubin Carter, Bobby Czyz, Livingstone Bramble, and Triple Threat fighters Charles Murray, Al Cole and Ray Mercer. Marc Roberts, Triple Threat's director, organized for Parks to work with Patterson.

Several of Arturo's Canadian friends and boxing stablemates made the trek to New York City to support their friend. Arturo's former amateur coach, Dave Campanile, made the journey down Interstate 87's New York Thruway. Walking Arturo into the ring were manager Pat Lynch, trainer Hector Roca, and friend Mikey "Red" Skowronski. Carl Moretti held the ropes open for Arturo to pass through. Former middleweight champion Jake LaMotta, "The Bronx Bull," was sitting ringside for the fight. Joe Gatti asked for a ticket to the fight. According to Joe, he was given a bleacher ticket and was not allowed access into the dressing room.

In the 1st round, both fighters felt each other out. Arturo was the busier fighter with his left jab. Patterson appeared cautious of Gatti's power. After the round, Tommy Parks advised Tracy not to worry about leading. Parks told Patterson not to bend down prior to Arturo throwing a jab. In Gatti's corner, Roca advised Arturo to throw at Tracy's shoulders. He also told Arturo to keep using his jab, keep his hands high and finish with combinations.

As round 2 began, Arturo had minor swelling under his left eye. A little over a minute into the 2nd round, Gatti caught a slightly leaning-in Patterson with a sneaky-fast right uppercut. Tracy was dropped onto the seat of his pants. He rose quickly and took the mandatory 8-count.

Later in the round, Arturo landed a solid left hook. Patterson continued reaching at the taller Gatti instead of working his way inside. After the round, Parks advised Tracy to keep his hands up and stay closer to Arturo.

Both boxers traded jabs for the first two minutes of the 3rd, with Gatti's height enabling him to land more. With 30 seconds remaining in the round, Gatti landed a hard left hook. Patterson came back with his own left hook, followed by a hard overhand right which backed Gatti up. Tracy followed up with a hard hook to the body and straight right to the head. Patterson started closing the distance.

After the 3rd round ended, Roca implored Arturo to relax and work the jab. Before the 4th round started, Roca angrily turned to the Patterson corner and yelled that they were doing something illegal.

Referee Wayne Kelly ordered Roca out of the ring. Roca was upset that Tracy's cornermen were tampering with Patterson's glove. Kelly told Roca that Patterson's cornermen merely cut a string off of the glove.

The 4th round was non-eventful as both boxers were content to box from the outside. Arturo's left eye was becoming more of an issue. Patterson's left eye also showed signs of swelling. After the round, Parks counseled his fighter to jab and keep his hands up. Parks asked for more counter punching. Roca advised Gatti not to look for the knockout, that it would come on its own. Even though Arturo clearly had a swollen left eye, cutman Percy Richardson failed to apply any cold compression to the eye.

The crowd started booing in the 5th, as Gatti was content to keep Patterson at bay with his jab. With a minute remaining in the round, Arturo opened up with a right to the body followed by a combo to the head. He followed that up with a double hook to the body and head.

After the round, Richardson again neglected to treat Arturo's swollen left eye. During the 6th round, commentator George Foreman remarked that Gatti had turned into a boxer. Arturo kept jabbing away. The crowd started booing again halfway through the round, as they wanted more action. With 30 seconds left in the round, both fighters started trading. At the 15-second mark, Arturo opened up with lefts and rights as Patterson covered up.

After the round, Roca told Gatti he was getting hit too much. Richardson, amazingly, still did not treat the swollen eye with an enswell or ice. Gatti was controlling the 7th with his jab, when halfway through the round, he attempted a right uppercut but was countered with a hard right by Patterson. With a minute remaining in the round, Arturo landed a hard right to the body. Gatti finished the round strong and appeared to be well ahead.

Patterson's adoptive father, Floyd, was sitting ringside. HBO commentator Jim Lampley noticed that Tracy was starting to become more aggressive. Lampley pondered whether Tracy had finally overcome the distraction of fighting in front of his estranged father. Lampley was talking about the well-publicized dispute between Tracy and Floyd that had been ongoing for several months, which led to Patterson signing with Marc Roberts. Patterson would later say it was a major distraction for him to fight Arturo while his father, with whom he was feuding, was sitting ringside. In-between the 7th and 8th rounds, Larry Merchant opined that Arturo had enough rounds in the bank to win the fight. Merchant felt that it was up to Patterson to start throwing punches if he wanted to retain his title.

The crowd started booing again in the 8th as Arturo continued to control the action with his jab. Gatti turned up the pace in the 9th with fast combinations. Arturo started the 10th by landing solid combinations while stepping around. Jim Lampley called Gatti's effort a masterful performance. Patterson, sensing he was far behind on the cards, stepped it up in the 10th with hard shots to the body and head. Gatti came right back with power shots of his own. The welt under Arturo's left eye broke open, blood started to flow from the wound. Both fighters stood and traded toe-to-toe as the round came to a close.

For the first time in the fight, the crowd rose to their feet in applause. Roca screamed at Gatti to avoid a slugfest. As Roca spoke, Gatti just stared ahead, as though Roca wasn't even there. In the opposite corner, Parks told Patterson that Arturo was ready to be taken.

HBO analyst Harold Letterman believed that if Gatti lost the fight the blame would rest with his corner. Letterman was referring to the terrible job that Percy Richardson was doing on Arturo's cut eye. Letterman questioned whether Gatti could see right hand punches being thrown at him with the swollen eye. Arturo would later state that his eyelids were stuck from Richardson applying too much Vaseline, which caused him to blink frequently.[249]

In the 11th round, Gatti continued moving, although he was jabbing less. Patterson landed several hard body punches. Arturo's mouth was wide open as he sucked in as much air as his lungs would allow. Tracy poured it on with a minute left in the round.

Parks encouraged Patterson before the final round, telling him that he could knock Gatti out. Roca, in the opposite corner, begged Gatti to throw only quick combinations.

Halfway through the final round, both fighters traded blows. Patterson seemed to get the better of the exchanges. Patterson caught Arturo cleanly with several hard shots to the head. Gatti fought back courageously. Both of Arturo's eyes were now swollen. Gatti threw a right-hand left-hook combo just before the final bell. He then raised his hands in victory as the bell clanged.

Arturo later revealed that he didn't see the punches coming in the final two rounds. He was very fatigued during the fight, but inside of his heart he knew that he wanted to be a world champion.[250]

Arturo sprinted to a neutral corner and jumped up onto the ropes with his hands held high. Patterson did the same, but with much less confidence of victory. The scoring was 116-111, 115-112, and 114-113, all for the winner by unanimous decision and new IBF super featherweight world champion, Arturo "Thunder" Gatti.

Arturo let out a scream of satisfaction as Pat Lynch raised him up from behind. Gatti hugged strength trainer Bob Wareing and Hector Roca. Larry Merchant predicted that boxing fans were going to see a lot more of Arturo. He added that fans would fall in love with Gatti. Joe came down from his bleacher seat to join in the celebration. He walked up to Lynch and asked if he could have the $5,000 back that he had paid Lynch to get out of his contract now that Arturo was the world champion. Joe stated that Lynch laughed at the request and walked away.

Years later, Arturo was asked to name the greatest moment of his career. *"For me it's gotta be 1995 when I won the world title against Tracy Patterson in Madison Square Garden. And it was the most incredible moment because I dreamt about it when I was eight years old."*

After the victory, Russell Peltz commented, *"He's a good boxer and, obviously, a good puncher. Arturo's got everything going for him. He's a breath of fresh air. We're looking at [Jeff] Fenech. If we can make that fight, and if Arturo wins it, which I think he can, there's no telling how far he can go. We could have him defend the title in Montreal. He could defend it in Rome, or Atlantic City, or back in the Garden, and he'd be big in all those places. I know this must sound like pie in the sky, but he can do it."*[251]

Arturo's fight with Patterson, though tough, appeared easier than his fights against Sanabria, Bostic, and Solomon. On the undercard, wildly popular boxing cult figure Eric "Butterbean" Esch, 15-0 (10 KOs), suffered his first defeat as a professional when he was knocked out by the 1-7-1 (1 KO) Mitchell Rose.

After his championship victory, Arturo went home to Montreal to celebrate Christmas, and his new title, with family and friends. Just before Arturo won the title, he had been signed by Integrated Sports International, a sports management company. ISI also had football players Steve Young and Drew Bledsoe, basketball player Hakeem Olajuwon, and boxer Oscar De La Hoya signed to their stable of athletes. James Crimmons, director of athlete services for ISI, stated that he was excited to have Arturo sign with ISI. Crimmons felt that Arturo was a terrific person. He also felt that Arturo speaking

English, French, and Italian fluently would be a marketing advantage. Crimmons felt that Arturo and Oscar De La Hoya were both intelligent, well-spoken individuals who represented themselves and boxing extremely well.[252]

Arturo commented from Montreal, *"I don't really feel like a world champion yet. People come up to me and say something about it, and that's when I think about it. But I don't feel any different than I did before I won the title. Actually, that's the way I want to feel. Being with ISI and everything is terrific, but it's a secondary thing. I appreciate everything that's being done for me, but I'm a fighter first. I've trained fifteen years to become a world champion. Now my goal is to become a great champion. The only way I know how to do that is to always remember how I got here in the first place.*

"For the Patterson fight, I trained 10 weeks. I know I'll have to train at least that long and that hard for every fight from now on. There can't be any letdowns, no slacking off. That's happened to too many other fighters. It's how champions become ex-champions. I'm not about to let that happen to me. My brother [Joe] always has been my role model. I always thought he'd be a world champion, but it hasn't worked out that way. Not yet, anyway."[253]

Arturo admitted that the Patterson fight was the first time he wasn't nervous before a fight, because he knew he was prepared. On knocking down Patterson, Arturo said that he knew he did not connect solidly, which is why he did not try to go crazy to finish Tracy. After the final bell rang, Arturo knew he was the clear winner. Even so, he asked Lynch who he thought had won. Lynch told Arturo that he was the new champion.[254]

Lynch was beside himself that some thought Patterson had won. He had watched the tape of the fight several times and there was no doubt in his mind that Arturo deserved to win. Lynch added that boxing fans finally saw what an outstanding boxer Arturo was.[255]

There was an anonymous letter that was received by the IBF that claimed Arturo had an unfair advantage because he had a steel plate in his right hand. The letter was signed, "Amateur Boxing." Arturo did have metal screws in his hand from an operation in 1991. The hand controversy was disregarded as ridiculous, as many fighters had the same operation. Arturo even downplayed the rumor by stating that he controlled the fight with his left hand, not his right.

Main Events promoter Dan Duva remarked that the significance of Arturo defeating Tracy Harris Patterson in Madison Square Garden, on HBO, could not be downplayed. Duva felt that Arturo was the complete package, that he was good-looking, charismatic, and had an exciting style. Duva believed that Arturo could be as big as Oscar De La Hoya.[256]

Chapter 11
The Rodriguez War

The 23-year-old Arturo was now the International Boxing Federation's super featherweight world champion. Christmas was more joyous than ever. Arturo returned home to Montreal for the holidays. His father's friends told him how proud Giovanni would be to know that his son was a world champion.

Arturo had no problem finding friends with whom to enjoy his newfound fame. Arturo's core group of friends included gym-mate Mikey "Red" Skowronski, John Capone, Bobby Villanova, Jimmy Cassano, Joey Perrenod and Donny Jerie. Perrenod was the step-son of Arturo and Joe's physician, Dr. Frank Rotella. Arturo purchased two Seado jet skis. One for Jimmy Cassano and one for himself. He stored them at Jack Nessie's garage in downtown Hoboken.

Arturo was young, good-looking, a boxing celebrity, and en route to becoming wealthy. He was surrounded with single friends who loved night clubs, strip clubs, and the general party scene. Mikey Red recalled that the groups' party sessions were legendary. *"We were like the cable TV show Entourage... Arturo being a good-looking kid, he did well in the clubs."*[257] It was even said that Arturo danced like Fred Astaire.[258]

Arturo appeared more comfortable in a go-go bar than at a regular club. He loved fast women and the attention they gave him. Arturo also loved fast cars, especially his corvette and later his Z3. Mikey Red often teased Arturo because Gatti was unable to drive his cars due to his license always being suspended for one reason or another.

Vikki Gatti explained why Arturo was so attracted to strip clubs. *"Well, who else is he really going to associate with? When you're taking drugs and alcohol, where do you go?"*[259] Joe added, *"Who's gonna deal with it? At nighttime you can't walk into a nice restaurant like that."*[260]

Vikki felt that Arturo was shy. It was much easier for him to frequent strip clubs where the girls approach the customers. A boxing champion was sure to garner special attention, especially since Arturo had money. Joe continued, *"Arturo went to Lookers [strip club]. Mario had to go get him. They said he put his credit card down and bought the whole bar a drink!"*[261] Vikki added, *"He was just hungry for love. Arturo in the ring was an animal. Outside, no confidence, no self-esteem. You could make him cry in two seconds. You're going to sit in dirty strip clubs with a beautiful girl at home? Your fiancé? Your wife? Your kids? Because when Arturo Gatti walks into the local strip clubs, like the Squeeze Lounge, what do they all do? They are, 'Oh my God.' And that's what he wanted. He just wanted that love."*[262]

Alcohol, prescription drugs, cocaine, and marijuana were all available for the new champion. No one in his inner circle would dare tell Arturo to scale back on the fun. Arturo was taking OxyContin, Vicodin, Percocet and other powerful painkillers. Arturo's future fiancée, Vivian Penha, later would recall that Arturo used the pills to combat the pain from his hand operations, which she believed hurt him more than any punches he received in the ring.[263]

Those in Arturo's inner circle feared being kicked out of the new champion's party clique if they spoke up. It was akin to Elvis Presley's entourage. No one dared be the one to tell him to stop. Jersey City adopted Arturo has one of their own, as he fought using the city's name as his home address. Jersey City councilman Bill Gaughan organized a ceremony giving Arturo the key to the city at city hall. Arturo was untouchable in Jersey City.

Not long after winning the title, veteran trainer Lou Duva must have sensed young Arturo's vulnerability to his newfound fame. Duva gave Arturo the book, *The Old Man and the Sea,* by Ernest Hemingway. Duva was asked if he gave that book to other fighters or just Arturo. Duva stated, *"No, just Arturo. Life can screw you up and I thought he needed that book."*[264] Arturo would later say, *"That's the only book I read. I finished it. Yeah, it was good."* Arturo enjoyed reading the book, but one has to wonder if he grasped the meaning of the story.

The Old Man and the Sea is a story about an old fisherman named Santiago, who while in his small row boat, traveled farther into the ocean than he ever had, in his quest to hook a massive blue marlin. Before long, Santiago's struggle to boat the prized fish became a life and death confrontation. The old man would have to choose between his life-long quest for this trophy fish or his actual life. Santiago made the commitment to sacrifice his life to catch his longed-for prize.

The old man suffered great physical and emotional injuries in catching the marlin. He succeeded in conquering his prize, but he then was faced with another problem. He was unable to bring the huge marlin into the small rowboat. So he tied the fish to the back of his boat and started his long journey back from the ocean to the dock. On the journey home, sharks started appearing; attacking the prized catch that he had worked so hard and sacrificed so much to capture.

It appeared that the sharks took joy in tormenting the old man by destroying his prized catch bite by bite. Each shark bite created a new stream of blood from the marlin which led to more sharks joining in on the feast. Santiago realized that his struggle to catch the prized marlin was for nothing, as the sharks slowly devoured his trophy fish.

Santiago realized that he could not stop the sharks from destroying his fish, but the sharks could not destroy his accomplishment. Santiago thought to himself, *"A man can be destroyed but not defeated."* Santiago wondered if his traveling too far out into the ocean for his catch cursed his ability to bring the prize home untarnished. He questioned himself and his quest for the great prize. *"I went out too far."*

Did Lou Duva have a premonition when he gave Arturo the book? Did Arturo understand the meaning and how it related to his winning the title; how the sharks would come around and try to devour his success? At the time, could he even understand who those sharks might be? There would soon be a stream of hangers-on that would swarm all over him because of his fame and fortune.

The turning point had begun. The title that Arturo wanted to win for his father had been accomplished, but he was not satisfied. Arturo's soul was not content. His brother Joe described what he felt were some of his brother's frustrations. *"I remember one thing. He was mad because my father thought I was going to be champion. And he became champion and my father wasn't there to see it. So a lot of it played with his mind. He needed psychiatric help. Arturo said, 'Oh, it should have been you. I wish it was you that became champion. I wish it wasn't me.' He was crying. We were in his apartment. In his condo in Weehawken. He was crying. They found him. The door was open. He was on the floor. He was naked. Black and blue. Three times they found him overdosed, and I was watching. I couldn't watch him no more. I used to follow him, but I couldn't no more. I had a job to go to. It's like I can't do it no more."*[265]

Joe recalled that he talked to Lynch about his brother's issues. Obviously, with Arturo's fragile mental state, he was unable to deal with the rush of fortune and fame. When the cheering at the fights stopped, did he feel the love for him stopped as well? Joe's wife Vikki commented, *"He was just hungry for love."*[266]

Arturo was facing additional challenges. His manager, Pat Lynch, seeing the monetary potential of his young fighter, started pressuring Arturo to avoid certain people and places. On the top of that list was Mario Costa's Ringside Lounge. Lynch complained to Costa about not wanting Arturo to hang out at the Ringside Lounge. Lynch felt it was too dangerous for a young celebrity to be in that environment. Costa was offended.

Sal Alessi recalled discussing the issue of Arturo hanging out at Ringside with Mario. *"He told me that Pat Lynch was a fucked up guy, because Pat Lynch didn't want Arturo hanging out in the bar. And I said to Mario, 'Why would you want a fighter hanging out in a bar?' And he just looked at me like I was out of my mind. You know, it was more important, he was more apt to want Arturo in the bar so that he could draw customers than this kid becoming a great fighter. And Pat didn't want him in a bar. He didn't belong in a bar."*[267]

Fighters are supposed to stay away from any location that could negatively affect their careers. Lounges, bars, nightclubs, and strip clubs were at the top of that list.

Mario spent most of his time at the Ringside Lounge because he owned it. It should be noted that Costa himself never drank or used drugs of any kind. His only vice was the unlit cigar that he would chomp on while he worked. Lynch may have been legitimately concerned about Arturo frequenting Ringside due to the bar atmosphere, but he also likely was concerned about Gatti being influenced by Costa, who was giving Arturo a different perspective on how his career was being managed.

Costa made the argument that, if Arturo was going to be fighting Puerto Rican, Mexican, and African-American opponents, he should familiarize himself with them in his lounge. Lynch told Costa that he wanted to keep Arturo away from illegal drugs and those who sold them. Although Costa would never knowingly allow drugs in his bar, it would be nearly impossible to stop Arturo from finding drugs in Jersey City if that was what he wanted.

Lynch wanted to market Arturo as a clean-cut Italian kid. He wanted Arturo to move to Middletown, N.J., where Lynch recently had purchased a home. Middletown was approximately thirty minutes south of Jersey City. The town was made up of mostly one-family homes, occupied by middle-class families. Arturo rented an apartment in Middletown. Joe was renting an apartment in Jersey City. Within a year, Joe would move into an apartment with Vikki in Bayonne.

According to Costa, Lynch started spending more time with Arturo to maintain his trust. Arturo was enjoying the single life. Lou Duva did not agree with the way Lynch was directing the young Arturo, and he expressed his thoughts to Pat on several occasions. Pat told Lou that Arturo was an adult, and he could live his life and spend his money as he wished.[268]

In a *Bergen Record* interview, Lynch admitted that whenever he tried to curb Arturo's behavior, Arturo would reply that Pat should consider him the family black sheep; every family has one. Arturo broke up with his girlfriend Emily and started dating several other dancers from "gentlemen clubs."

Arturo went up to Stan Hoffman's training camp with Mikey Red. While up at the camp they visited a nearby petting zoo. Skowronski recalled, *"Arturo was not afraid of animals. If he saw a doberman pinscher tied up to a post, he would just walk up to it and start playing with it. He had no fear of animals. There was a billy goat at a petting zoo and Arturo whistled to the billy goat and the billy goat came over. Arturo head butted the billy goat. It was one of the funniest things I ever saw Arturo do. Arturo told me he was dizzy from the head clash. I replied, 'Dude, you just head butted a billy goat!'"*[269]

On January 28, 1996 at Sun Devil Stadium in Tempe, Arizona, the Dallas Cowboys took on the Pittsburgh Steelers in Super Bowl XXX. Lynch, owning a ticket agency, had access to tickets to the game. Donny Jerie recalled, *"Pat went to many Superbowls."*[270] Arturo decided to fly out to the game with Lynch.

Four days before the game, on January 24, Arturo was arrested in Arizona for driving while under the influence of alcohol. Arturo later pled guilty to the charge. This would be the first of four times that he would be charged with drunk driving in the U.S. Arturo's brother Joe was upset that Lynch didn't monitor Arturo more closely while he was in Arizona. In the March 2004 issue of *The Ring* magazine, there was a photo of Arturo and Lynch. Arturo was wearing his new IBF championship belt and Lynch was wearing a Super Bowl XXX polo shirt.

On January 30, Main Events suffered a tragic blow. Dan Duva, the company's leader, died of complications from a brain tumor. Kathy Duva commented that Dan had been the linchpin that held Main

Events together. When he died, Kathy and the Duvas were unable to trust each other.[271] Dan's will had a "spousal trust" in order to set up administration of his business interests. His children were trusted the business, and his wife, Kathy, was installed as chairwoman of the board. Kathy enrolled in law school at Seton Hall to keep herself from having confrontations with her brother-in-law, Dino Duva. She also was busy raising her three children Nicole, Lisa, and Bryan.

In mid-February, news broke that heavyweight Tommy Morrison was infected with the HIV virus. The news sent shockwaves throughout the sport. N.J. State Athletic Commissioner Larry Hazzard wanted to implement mandatory HIV testing, on a six month basis, for all boxers. Dino Duva threw his support behind Hazzard. Joe Gatti was asked his thoughts on the subject. *"A lot of fighters are scared. They'd rather not take the test and go by how they feel. I'd rather know if I'm infected. Every fighter should talk about this issue and demand that the commission send us for the tests."*[272]

On March 23, 1996 at Madison Square Garden in New York, Arturo Gatti, 24-1 (20 KOs), defended his IBF super featherweight title for the first time. Arturo would earn $100,000 for the bout. His opponent was Wilson Rodriguez, 44-8-3 (25 KOs), of the Dominican Republic. Rodriguez had been stopped six times in his 11-year career. He was considered a "safe opponent" for Gatti, although he currently was ranked #2 in the world by the IBF. Back in 1990, Rodriguez had lost an 8-round decision to future WBO champ Jimmi Bredahl. On November 26, 1994, Rodriguez fought for the IBF super featherweight title, losing by knockout in the 10th round to John John Molina. He had won five fights since then, four by knockout.

A few days before the fight, a firestorm erupted. An unknown party had sent letters to the New York State Athletic Commission, the *Daily News*, the IBF sanctioning body, Pat Lynch, and Dino Duva stating that Arturo Gatti was fighting with a metal pin in his right hand. It must have been the same person who had sent the letter to the IBF previously. Pat Lynch denied the allegation.[273] However, the pin was put in his right hand when he had an operation, and was still there. Arturo commented that he had injured the hand against Bobby McCarthy while sparring. *"I knocked him out. That's how I hurt it."*[274] The bout went on as scheduled.

HBO televised the title bout between the 30-year-old Rodriguez and the 23-year-old Gatti. Although Rodriguez was only a 1/2-inch taller than Gatti, he held a 7-inch reach advantage over Arturo. Rodriguez's chief second was Jose Luis De la Sagra, who Rodriguez fought twice in his career. Arturo weighed 130-pounds, but hydrated back up to 142 on fight night.

The day before the Rodriguez fight, Arturo sat down with reporter Jim Lambert of the *Star Ledger*. Arturo spoke of his father. *"I think about him every time I fight. He's a big reason why I'm a fighter. I owe him a lot. When I was six, my father told his friends that I would be a world champion someday. When I went back to Montreal for Christmas I saw a lot of my father's friends. They all said, 'Hey, Giovanni always said his kid would be a champion. Can you believe it?' My father's dream was to see me become a world champion. It really bothered me that he couldn't be there to see it. But I know he was looking down proudly and I feel he gave me the strength I needed to become a world champion. My father had a big heart and was a very tough, strong, and confident person. Those are the things you need to be a world champion. I'm thankful that I have his genes."*[275]

Arturo spoke of how his brother Joe and he got started in boxing. *"My father got us both started. My brother moved to Jersey City to start a boxing career and I followed him. It was one of the best moves I've ever made in my life. I feel very good coming into this fight. He's a good defensive fighter, so I'll just try to keep the pressure on him and be the aggressor. He'll try to outbox me, so I'll have to try to slow him down. He's been knocked out five times, and I feel I have the power to make it six."*[276] It would later be discovered that Rodriguez had actually been knocked out six times prior to the Gatti fight. Arturo spoke of his recently broken right hand. *"It's fine now. Besides, it's my left hook that knocks people out anyway."*[277]

Rodriguez also was interviewed. *"I'm not afraid of his right or his left. He won't be able to reach me. Gatti will make a great champion in the future but Saturday night he'll lose his title and I will go back to the Dominican Republic with the belt."*[278]

Gatti made his way into the ring with his ever-growing entourage, to the AC/DC song "Thunderstruck." Mikey "Red" Skowronski held Arturo's championship belt over his head. Pat Lynch led his fighter into the ring, as trainer Hector Roca jogged behind. Carl Moretti followed Roca and Dino Duva. Sitting ringside were Arturo's mother and stepfather, and his best friend from Montreal, Christian Santos. Arturo's strength-and-conditioning coach, 45-year-old Bob Wareing, also was ringside. Wareing was Pernell

Whitaker's long-time strength coach. Cedric Kushner, Main Events, and Peltz Boxing co-promoted the event. There was a new face in the Gatti corner, cutman Joe Souza. Percy Richardson was replaced after his poor performance in the Patterson fight.

Gatti started the 1st round by stalking Rodriguez with his jab. Wilson scored a right hand over Arturo's jab while retreating. Rodriguez displayed good head movement while landing another right hand. Gatti did not appear as patient as he had been in the Patterson fight. He was looking to force the action. Rodriguez landed a hard left hook and right hand. Arturo's left eye already was swelling two minutes into the 1st round. HBO analyst Jim Lampley opined that Arturo was getting a boxing lesson. Larry Merchant added that Rodriguez was getting bolder and bolder as the round wore on.

Rodriguez kept scoring with jabs and rights, connecting often, while his footwork and head movement gave Gatti fits. As the bell sounded, Arturo painfully blinked both of his eyes. He then wiped his thumb over his eyebrow. After wiping his brow he looked at his glove, checking for blood. There was no blood but his left eye was closing rapidly.

In the corner, Roca instructed Gatti to stop head hunting and instead concentrate on attacking the body. He also asked Arturo to stay low, move his head, and throw more combinations. Arturo was concerned with his eye. He asked how it looked. Both Roca and Souza told him his eye was fine.

In Rodriguez's corner, Wilson was advised not to get nervous or excited. De la Sagra reminded Rodriguez that Gatti's eye was beginning to close. He asked Rodriguez to keep moving to the left.

Arturo came out fast in the 2nd with a jab and hard right to the body. Gatti cornered Rodriguez and landed a hard left hook to the body and another to the head as Wilson retreated. Rodriguez started slipping, jabbing, and stepping to his left. He kept landing on Arturo's face. Gatti's left eye was swelling up fast, and his right eye was beginning to swell as well. Analyst Roy Jones, Jr. remarked that Gatti's eye did not look good. Merchant added that Arturo was in real trouble unless he could do something dramatic.

Arturo kept blinking as he stepped forward with punches. Gatti stepped in with several hard body punches, apparently sensing that Rodriguez was bothered by them. Arturo timed a hard left hook to the body as Rodriguez stepped to his left. Lampley commented that both of Gatti's eyes were swelling with extreme rapidity. He had never seen a fighter's eyes swell up so fast. Gatti kept blasting the mid-section. Merchant commented that Gatti would need two enswells on his eyes, both of which were barely slits. As Arturo pressed forward, he was caught by a right hand-left hook-right hand combination that dropped him to the seat of his pants. Lampley and Jones, Jr. both felt that Gatti did not see the punch that dropped him because of his swollen eyes.

Arturo would later say, *"When he knocked me down, all I was thinking about was that this is my first title defense and that I had just ordered an expensive car, like the one in a James Bond movie. When my eyes started shutting, and I was down, all I thought was, 'Damn, I better get up or I'll have to cancel that order.'"*[279]

Although the knockdown only lasted moments, it felt like a lifetime to Gatti. It was a frightening moment for him. Arturo felt that the fear of losing, losing everything, while recalling all he had sacrificed to get to this point, helped him to rise and continue.[280]

Arturo rose to his feet at the count of three, jumping up and down, trying to get the blood flowing back into his legs. Gatti blinked hard in an attempt to clear his vision. He nodded he was okay to referee Wayne Kelly.

Arturo courageously stepped forward. Rodriguez rewarded him by drilling home punch after punch, landing an endless barrage. It looked as though Gatti didn't see the punches coming at all. Lampley felt that Arturo was in serious trouble, and he was. But Gatti kept pressing forward and firing back. He landed a hard hook to the body. Rodriguez scored at will, but Arturo was taking all his shots and still coming forward with hard blows of his own.

Gatti landed a hook on Rodriguez's thigh. Kelly yelled for him to keep his punches up. The round ended with both fighters staggering each other in exciting fashion. After the bell rang, Arturo walked to the wrong corner. When he turned to head back he tapped Rodriguez' glove in a sign of showmanship.

Roca begged Gatti to keep his hands up and work the body. While Roca spoke, Souza applied the enswell to Arturo's eyes. Souza dramatically warned Arturo that he didn't have much time left before the referee would stop the fight. Gatti's right eye was completely shut, and the left eye was swollen badly. Souza did the best he could, but the situation was nearly hopeless.

After the bell rang to start the 3rd, Arturo came storming out with wild bombs. He landed an overhand right that sent Rodriguez reeling. Gatti kept throwing power punches as Rodriguez did his best to defend and fire back. Jim Lampley remarked that it would take some real drama to rescue Arturo's star status. He also wondered whether the fight came too soon after the Patterson bout. Gatti landed a hard left hook. Rodriguez back-peddled again. Arturo was digging deep, firing away. One must wonder if he could hear his father's voice, *"Ah sinistra!"* The crowd was on edge from the intense combat, chanting, *"Gatti! Gatti! Gatti!"* Lampley forecasted it would take a near miracle for Arturo to knock Rodriguez out. But Arturo sure was trying.

Gatti cornered Wilson and unloaded several bombs, but Rodriguez fired right back with a fast combination. Arturo responded with crunching left hooks. Rodriguez answered with solid right hands. Lampley stated, *"This has been a time-capsule round."* Arturo took a series of blows as the round came to a close. Lampley added, *"Hard to imagine that Gatti can last much longer."* The crowd gave both boxers a standing ovation.

As Souza pressed the enswell against Arturo's severely swollen right eye, Roca begged Gatti to continue his body attack. The ring doctor tried to push his way past Souza to examine Gatti's eyes. The doctor yelled at Souza, *"Back off. I said back off!"* Souza angrily responded to the doctor. *"Don't push on me, Goddammit!"* The doctor shot back, *"I'm pushing you!"* Souza was intelligently buying time to work on the damaged eyes before they were examined.

The doctor ordered Gatti, *"Cover your left eye."* Arturo replied, *"I'm all right."* The doctor threatened to stop the fight, ordering Gatti, *"Cover your left eye or it's over."* Arturo covered his left eye, but quickly removed the glove from his eye as the doctor asked him how many fingers he was holding up, while holding up two fingers. *"I said cover it."* Gatti placed the glove back over his left eye. *"How many fingers?"* Arturo replied, *"Two."* The doctor then held up one finger. *"Now?"* Gatti answered, *"One."* Satisfied, the doctor said, *"All right,"* and exited the ring.

Arturo's right eye was nearly swollen shut. Some wondered whether Roca had helped Arturo cheat the test somehow. Sometimes trainers will whisper the numbers in Spanish or tap the fighter's leg with the correct number. However, it was possible that Arturo could see just enough through the little slit in his eye to see the fingers.

Many fighters would have packed it in at this point, admitting that their vision was hampered. Arturo was the exact opposite, trying to convince the doctor to allow him to continue. Such toughness and courage in the face of adversity would help to make Gatti the legend he would become. Arturo truly believed that he possessed the power to change the direction of a fight with one punch.

As the replay showed both fighters exchanging punch after head-jarring punch, Merchant opined, *"This is world-class stuff, folks."* Roy Jones, Jr. echoed the sentiment, *"This is World War III."*

At the start of the 4th round, Arturo primarily focused on the body. He landed a hard right to the mid-section that had Rodriguez retreating. As Wilson was backing away, he kept landing head shots, as he had throughout the fight. Gatti landed a crunching right hand over Rodriguez's jab. Arturo followed with hard body shots. Wilson countered with a head-jolting right hand up top that momentarily froze Gatti, but Arturo quickly recovered. Gatti trapped Rodriguez along the ropes and landed a flush right hand that caused Wilson to clinch. With a minute remaining in the round, Rodriguez attacked with both hands in nonstop fashion, landing cleanly with nearly every punch. Arturo's head twisted with each blow, sending him back to the ropes and clinching. After the referee separated the fighters, they went at it again. Merchant wondered, *"What is keeping these guys up?"*

With just over 30 seconds remaining in the round, Rodriguez stunned Arturo with a right hand and left hook. Arturo stumbled helplessly back into a corner as Wilson poured it on, twisting Gattis head skyward with a right uppercut followed by a series of fast, head-jarring blows. Gatti stumbled out of the corner like a zombie, retreating across the ring as Rodriguez continued swarming him with shots.

Gatti miraculously regained his composure and came back, landing a left hook, followed by a right that landed very low. Wilson tried to hold. With 10 seconds remaining in the round, Arturo wailed away as Rodriguez covered up along the ropes. Both men continued punching after the bell had rung.

As the referee separated the fighters, Arturo gave Rodriguez a look as if to say, "bring it on," as he staggered back to his corner. Rodriguez looked bewildered as he was led back to his corner by his trainer. Merchant stated, *"I don't know if this kid's gonna have his title before this night is over, but he is sure showing us some championship heart."*

Souza pressed the enswell against Gatti's bloated right eye. Arturo, in obvious pain, pulled back momentarily. The doctor again checked Gatti's vision, doing the finger test, this time covering Arturo's left eye on his own, instead of allowing Arturo to cover it. Arturo again passed. Both Merchant and Jones Jr. questioned whether Gatti could last another round at this current pace. In Rodriguez's corner, his trainer implored him to stay away from Arturo.

At the start of the 5th round, most of the crowd was on its feet. Lampley commented that it was somewhat of a small miracle that Gatti had made it this far. Arturo controlled the first minute with body blows, several low, as Rodriguez moved away. Wilson landed a few head shots then grabbed Arturo. Both Merchant and Lampley commented on Gatti's low, south-of-the-border body-punching. Arturo's fans chanted, *"Gatti! Gatti! Gatti!"* Arturo responded with a vicious left hook to the head. He followed with a hard hook to the body that clearly hurt Rodriguez, who back-tracked again. Gatti landed a right hand to the body that was very low. Wayne Kelly jumped in and took a point away from Arturo. With the knockdown and the point loss for low blows, Arturo was several points behind on two of the three judges scorecards.

After a brief respite, the referee waived the fighters to continue. Arturo pressed forward behind his jab. With Rodriguez against the ropes, Arturo ripped a hard left hook to the body that dropped Wilson to his knees.

Rodriguez slowly rose at the count of eight. Arturo resumed his attack while Wilson fought back with a flurry. Gatti fired another blow below the beltline. The bell ended another exciting, dramatic round. The fighters tapped gloves again en route to their corners.

Roca implored Arturo to keep working the body, advising Gatti that Rodriguez was about to quit. Wilson's corner told him he was winning the fight, and he was, but cautioned that he should box from a distance.

Arturo started the 6th round attacking the body with both hands. Gatti kept pressing forward as Rodriguez retreated. The swelling in Arturo's eye actually seemed to have improved. As Arturo attacked, the crowd chanted *"Gatti! Gatti! Gatti!"* Arturo, fueled on by his rabid fans, seemed to have more energy than Rodriguez, as his body punches were taking their toll.

With less than a minute remaining in the round, both boxers threw left hooks to the head simultaneously. Gatti's landed flush, dropping Rodriguez onto his back. Arturo observed Wilson as he walked to a neutral corner, checking to see if his foe would get up. Rodriguez, unable to rise, was counted out as he lay prone on the vinyl canvas.

Larry Merchant was confident that boxing fans would never forget this fight. It would be watched over and over again. Gatti's corner erupted as Pat Lynch, Joe Gatti, Mike Skowronski, Dino Duva, Lou Duva, Hector Roca, and others celebrated their fighter's victory. Arturo playfully referenced the *Rocky* movie as he yelled, *"Yo Adrian, we did it."*[281] The comparison was appropriate, for it had been a brutal war that featured a closed eye, both fighters being knocked down, and a dramatic finish. Rodriguez remained on the ring canvas for several minutes as he was attended to by ringside physicians. Arturo's mother, Ida, climbed into the ring and hugged her son.

After the match, Arturo recalled that he knew the situation was getting desperate as soon as he got dropped. He confessed that he never would have believed that Rodriguez could knock him down. Arturo didn't realize he had been dropped until he looked around and saw he was on the canvas. At that moment he thought to himself, *"Oh my God, I'm going to lose the fight."* Gatti felt that working Rodriguez's body helped to turn the tide of the fight.

Arturo believed that his punching power won the fight for him. *"People were saying, 'You have to move your head more. You have to box more.' Listen, if I would have boxed, I would have lost that fight. He would have shut both of my eyes, and that would have been it. The way I fought that fight was the only way I had to do it. That's the only reason I won, because I went out there and fought the guy. I took his heart. That's why I'm a champion today. It's not because I'm a great, talented fighter. I've got a lot of heart. I've got a lot of power. And it's gonna take more than a punch to take me out."*[282] When later watching the Rodriguez fight on tape, Gatti commented, *"I couldn't believe it when I saw it."*[283]

Arturo praised Joe Souza for Souza's work on his eyes. Arturo said that he had no problem seeing during the fight. He added that he had trouble finding a rhythm during the contest, partly due to Rodriguez's jab. Arturo knew he was hurting Rodriguez to the body. When Gatti was dropped, he quickly realized that he needed to wake up or else he would lose his title.

Rodriguez was surprised that Arturo came back. He congratulated Arturo on being a great champion, with a great heart, and a great future. In regards to the knockout blow, Rodriguez recalled that Gatti kept hitting him with left hooks to the body, so he wasn't expecting Arturo to throw a left hook to the head. He never saw it coming.[284]

Many boxing insiders, including the HBO analysts, questioned

Gatti fighting so quickly after his tough title-winning effort against Patterson. A fighter usually is given more time to heal his injuries. For Gatti to fight only three months after boxing Patterson meant he likely was sparring and getting hit on his damaged eye relatively soon after the Patterson fight in order to prepare for Rodriguez. Also, when a fighter is in a tough 12-round fight, his brain needs time to heal from the trauma. Not giving a fighter ample time to heal could shorten his career and lead to internal injuries that are not readily noticed. The counter argument is that by keeping him active, Gatti was sufficiently fight-sharp to mount the spectacular come from behind victory.

Eric Gelfand, who worked for Madison Square Garden in the public relations department, recalled Arturo's comical side. *"After the Rodriguez fight, I was walking him to the post-fight presser. Pat Lynch and Carl Moretti were behind us. His right eye was shut. We were just about to leave the Theater. He turns to me and says, 'Watch this,' and proceeds to walk into the only closed door. Pat and Carl leaped towards him, thinking he's hurt. Arturo turns toward them and just laughs."*[285]

Mikey Red recalled that everything changed after the Rodriguez fight. That's when Arturo really became a star. People started noticing him in public wherever he went. Donnie Jerie recalled Arturo getting real upset when men stared at him in clubs. He thought they were eyeballing him, looking for a fight. Jerie would try to calm Arturo down by telling him that they were probably just fans. Jerie told Arturo to just ask what they wanted. Jerie recalled, *"Nine times out of ten the guy was just staring at him because they couldn't believe that a famous boxer was in the same club as them."*[286] Some guys did want to challenge Arturo, but most incidents were settled before it got physical. Jerie did add that Arturo knocked out at least five guys that stepped to him over the years. One tap on the jaw was all it took.

Arturo later recalled his miraculous comeback against Rodriguez, *"I could barely see. That left hook saved me. It was the biggest comeback ever. That was the fight that made 'Arturo Gatti, The Warrior.' After that, it was just great fights."*[287]

Arturo sat down for an interview that was published in *Boxing Monthly* magazine. Arturo said that he felt the spiritual presence of his father in the ring with him during the Rodriguez match, and that his presence lifted him to victory. Arturo's father never boxed, but he was a passionate boxing fan. Giovanni used to take Arturo and

Joe to boxing shows at the Montreal Forum. Arturo was only eight or nine years old at the time, and would fall asleep at the shows.[288]

Arturo recalled his father's death and how shocking it was to the entire family. Giovanni was so strong that no one in the family ever thought that he could die. Arturo added how much he was bothered by the fact that Giovanni never saw him fight professionally. Arturo was sure that his father would have loved to see that his son became a world champion.[289]

Gatti recalled how he got started in boxing by following his big brother Joe to the gym. It wasn't until he was 15 years old that Arturo took the sport seriously. He spoke of how he and Joe grew up with the Hiltons. Arturo recalled sparring with Davey and Alex Hilton. Arturo felt that leaving Montreal and moving to New Jersey helped his boxing career because there were many more opportunities for a boxer in New Jersey. He believed that he would have only gotten into trouble if he had stayed in Montreal.[290]

Arturo recalled meeting Hector Roca. Gatti was training himself in Gleason's gym when he asked Roca to work with him for a week. After the week, he decided to hire Roca.[291]

Arturo felt that the Rodriguez fight proved his worth. He described what it felt like when his eye was closing. *"I could see a little bit. The swelling doesn't hurt but it's like a heartbeat, you can feel it on your face when it gets warm and I knew right away, it's my eye. The doctor kept coming to my corner and that was bothering me. I thought he was going to stop the fight. But I hope all the doctors and referees saw that fight, because you can't stop a championship fight. You're dealing with my life and you have to let it go at least six, seven, eight rounds. And I'm glad it went like that because the referees saw what type of fighter I am, so if I'm ever in a fight like that again, and hopefully I'm not, the referee won't stop the fight."*[292]

Gatti believed that the 4th round was the turning point in the Rodriguez match. When Rodriguez hurt him and he came right back, he felt that at that point, he took Rodriguez's heart. At that moment, Arturo knew that he would knock Rodriguez out.[293]

Gatti spoke of his constant hand issues. He described how the tendons that hold the bone down tore, which would cause the bone to keep popping up. Arturo confessed that when he went to Florida after breaking his hand the first time, instead of relaxing, he was jet-skiing and playing around. The hand felt good but it never healed right. After the bone fusion with a piece of bone from his hip, he had no issues with the hand.[294]

Gatti felt that he received his punching power from his father. He referenced Giovanni knocking out a mule. *"From the time I was six years old when my father had a couple of drinks in him he'd get me to shadow box in front of his friends and he'd tell them, 'See this kid, he's gonna be world champion.' They thought he was crazy, but now I've done it... My goal is to be a million dollar fighter."*[295]

Arturo spoke of Azumah Nelson. He felt that Nelson was slow and ready to be beaten. Arturo felt that he could knock Nelson out, because Nelson fought recklessly. Gatti did state that he was aware of how hard Nelson punched.[296]

Pat Lynch believed that the popular and exciting Arturo had all the tools needed to become a superstar. He also felt that Arturo was a big 130-pounder who eventually would move up to 135 or 140-pounds.[297]

Arturo started dating Laura Sosnowski. He met her at a club in Elizabeth, N.J. Donny Jerie described Sosnowski. *"Laura was very hot. To sum up them all, they were all pretty good looking, very hot. Pretty much you know, they all had that stripper background, you know."*[298]

When Joe Gatti was away, fighting Tim Bonds in Memphis, his Pontiac Grand Am was stolen from in front of his house in Bayonne. The car recently had been recovered, but it was in terrible condition. He had purchased the car from Dino Bizzario's used car lot on Kennedy Boulevard for $2,000. Joe took the car to Nessie's auto body shop in Hoboken. While he was talking to the owner about fixing up his beat-up old car, Arturo pulled up with his brand new, two-seat BMW Z3. Arturo asked Joe what he was doing there. Joe explained what had happened to his car while he was away fighting. Joe had expected his world champion brother to offer to buy him a new car. After talking for a few minutes, Arturo wished Joe luck, hopped into his Z3, and drove away.

The May ratings of *KO* magazine had Arturo ranked #2, behind Azumah Nelson. In mid-May, Arturo was relaxing in Virginia Beach when he was interviewed by Nigel Collins of *KO* magazine.

Arturo responded to concerns that he was taking too much punishment during his fights. Arturo admitted that he was concerned, especially since fighters who take that kind of punishment usually have short careers. Arturo felt that he would have to concentrate on moving his head more.[299]

Gatti was asked why his eyes appeared swollen when he entered the ring against Rodriguez. Arturo stated that his eyes were fine before the fight. He believed that his large cheekbones, coupled with his weight loss, made his cheekbones stand out even further. This, he believed, made it easier for his eyes to bruise and swell. Arturo was planning on seeing a doctor. He was hoping that he could have any excess fluid under his eyes drained.[300]

Arturo was asked if he needed time off after the Rodriguez fight. He stated that he felt fine. He didn't believe he needed a rest, because he was a hot commodity. Arturo added that although he knew that Rodriguez would be tough, he didn't expect him to be so big physically. He also was surprised at Rodriguez's reach. Gatti saw Rodriguez fight John John Molina and wasn't overly impressed. As soon as the 1st round began, Arturo knew he was in for a tough fight.[301]

Gatti was honored that his brawl with Rodriguez was being compared with brawls in which Marciano, Graziano, and LaMotta had participated. Arturo confessed that he did not realize how exciting the fight was until he watched it on tape the next day. When he watched the fight he thought, *"Oh my God!"*[302]

Arturo was asked if he felt that he had let Patterson off the hook. Gatti stated that he had prepared and paced himself for a 12-round fight. He was concerned he would run out of energy. Arturo and Roca had concentrated on speed, not punching power. Arturo assured that he would sit down more on his punches and try to land more power shots in the upcoming rematch.[303]

Gatti described what went through his mind when he traded toe-to-toe. He was confident that he could knock anyone out. Arturo explained what it was like growing up in a boxing family. Boxing was all that his father talked about. It was very important to his father that Arturo and Joe went to the gym every day. They would get in trouble if they missed the gym. Boxing was always a part of both brothers' lives. Arturo felt that it was more so for Joe than for himself. Arturo recalled that he was allowed to play soccer and hockey, but Joe was not. Giovanni never really pushed Arturo to be a fighter. He fought amateur because he liked it. Arturo recalled that when he won the Canadian title he started traveling, which led him to appreciate boxing even more. By the time he was 14 or 15 years old, he knew that he wanted to be a fighter and win the world title.[304]

Arturo realized how important his family was when he moved to New Jersey. He felt closer to his mother and siblings in Canada since he moved away. He joked that his mother needed a break from his mischievous ways.³⁰⁵

Arturo indeed grew closer to his mother after he left for New Jersey. Donny Jerie recalled, *"He would always call his mother up, 'Hey Ma, you need money? Is everything ok?' His brother Fabrizio too. He took care of that kid very well."*³⁰⁶

Gatti described training in Brooklyn. *"The first time I went to Gleason's Gym, and I looked around, I said to myself, 'If I can get out of here alive, I can be a world champion.' And I did real well; everybody was impressed. I needed some work, of course. A couple of times I had like little brawls, and I wanted to take my gloves off and fight. Guys would say, 'If you can't stand the heat, go back to Canada.' But after two years of being there, I was ruling that gym. I was the man."*³⁰⁷

Arturo reflected on his loss to King Solomon in 1992. He believed that the fight totally changed his career. Pat Lynch did not want to take the King Solomon fight. But his other manager, Richie Seibert, said it was too late, it was going to be on TV, and he'd already signed the contract. Arturo felt that taking the fight was the wrong move, especially coming back from a hand operation and a long lay-off.³⁰⁸

Gatti recalled how signing with Lou Duva's Main Events was a dream come true. He used to watch Duva on television when he was little. One time, when a young Arturo was sitting with his friend in Canada watching Lou work a bout, the friend said, *"Imagine if you go to the United States, and that's who you go with."* Arturo replied, *"Yeah, imagine."*³⁰⁹

Arturo spent extra time in training camp before fights, due to his weight issues. During the final three weeks of camp, all he ate was small portions of chicken and pasta. Arturo was asked about his struggles to make 130-pounds. Arturo felt he had a big advantage by dropping weight, because he was much bigger than his opponents when he entered the ring.³¹⁰

Gatti described how Montreal reacted to his title win. When he fought, all the bars in Montreal filled up. After Arturo won the title, he took a plane from Newark back to Montreal. When he debarked from the plane, there was a TV crew waiting for him. The passengers who had been on the plane with him were saying, *"Who was that guy?"*³¹¹

When Arturo retired, he planned on opening a tavern, with boxing memorabilia displayed throughout. Arturo basically was describing Mario Costa's Ringside Lounge.³¹²

Nigel Collins described Arturo as being intriguing, because he was on the cusp of greatness and the edge of disaster at the same time. Collins stated that this same intoxicating combination had made Arturo's previous two fights riveting spectacles.[313]

In early July, Joe Gatti sparred with William "Bo" James. Joe was helping James prepare for his IBF middleweight title try against Bernard Hopkins. Joe hit James with a hook to the ribcage that bent James over. James entered the ring against Hopkins with the injury. Hopkins stopped a fatigued and battered James in the 11th round with a hook to the same location of the ribcage.

Just 3½ months after his brutal war with Wilson Rodriguez, Arturo returned to the ring on July 11, 1996, at Madison Square Garden, against 15-5 (7 KOs) Feliciano Correa of Iowa. Arturo was originally scheduled to fight Easton, Pennsylvania's Bobby Johnson, 24-8-1 (7 KOs). Correa, a last-minute replacement, was a veteran of 182 amateur fights. The non-title bout was on the undercard of the Riddick Bowe-Andrew Golota heavyweight fight that ended with Golota being disqualified for low blows. A riot erupted in the ring between Bowe and Golota supporters after the fight ended. The fighting spread throughout the crowd. Lou Duva, who had worked Golota's corner, collapsed in the ring during the melee and had to be hidden under the ring apron before he was carried out on a stretcher. A lack of security and police presence was a contributing factor in the post-fight disruption.

Gatti's corner consisted of Roca, Souza, Lynch, and Wareing. Arturo was announced as being from Jersey City, though he recently had moved to Middletown, N.J. Arturo came into the ring with bleached-blonde hair. The Bowe-Golota bout was televised on HBO, while the Gatti fight was televised on FOX Sports. The 137-pound Arturo looked much bigger than the 136-pound Correa.

In the opening minute of the fight, Arturo landed several hard left hooks to the body. Gatti pinpointed his body punches with razor sharp precision on the overmatched Correa.

In the 2nd round, Arturo methodically worked the body. With less than a minute remaining in the round, Gatti landed a double left hook to the body and head, which dropped Correa to his knees with 32 seconds remaining in the round. Pat Lynch stood and applauded in Gatti's corner. Correa courageously rose at the count of eight and survived the round by holding and moving.

In the 3rd, Arturo continued the body attack, dropping Correa to his knees with a left hook to the liver with 1:05 remaining in the round. Correa was counted out. Arturo injured his left hand while throwing the hook. He hoped that a little rest was all that was needed to heal the injury.

Gatti was scheduled to box Tracy Harris Patterson in a rematch in only two months, on September 20 in Miami, Florida. Arturo's team had taken the Correa fight as a tune-up bout, but in a boxing contest there is always the risk of an injury or even an upset loss. The Patterson bout was now in jeopardy of being postponed due to Arturo's hand injury.

Arturo was interviewed after the Correa fight. He felt that he was a little too anxious at the start of the fight. Arturo believed that he needed the Correa contest to get ready for Patterson. Gatti admitted that sometimes he tried too hard in his fights.[314]

Hector Roca spoke fondly of Arturo. He stated that Gatti hadn't changed since he won the title. Six fights prior, Arturo had promised to buy Roca a car after he won the title. Indeed, Gatti bought Roca a new Saab after winning the belt. After the Correa fight, he gifted Roca a $5,000 ring.[315]

One of Arturo's friends, Brenda, held house-parties at her home in Secaucus, N.J. Arturo would attend the parties, which usually had plenty of pretty ladies in attendance. Brenda called her friend Steve Sandoval, who was a huge boxing fan, and told him Gatti was at her house. Steve drove to the party. Steve and Arturo hit it off immediately. After the party, Steve drove Arturo home in his Porsche. The pair partied together for two days straight.

Sandoval would often pay when he and Arturo went out. This was to show Gatti that he wasn't hanging out with him to use him for his money. Sandoval never took a photograph with Arturo, because he didn't want Gatti to think he was friends with him just because he was a celebrity. He recalled that Arturo would stay clean for a while and then go back to partying.

Joe ran into Mike Sciarra, the owner of the Squeeze Lounge gentlemen's club. He hadn't seen Mike much since they met at the auto body shop a few years earlier. Mike recognized Joe and said hello. Joe recalled the conversation. *"He came up to me and said, 'Joe, when you see your brother, remind him he owes me a $1,000 from last night.' I said to Arturo, 'Bro, what are you doing over there [at the Squeeze Lounge]? Don't go around these people, they're no good for you, alright?' He was running a tab. I said, 'What's the matter with you? This guy says you owe him $1,000. Do you?' Arturo said, 'Yeah, I gotta pay him. Don't worry.'"*[316] Arturo defended Sciarra, *"Awh, he's not going to lie to me. I said, 'Don't* *go there anymore. What's the matter with you."*[317] Not long after, the Squeeze Lounge was renovated. Joe was convinced that Arturo's frequent spending sprees at the club helped to pay for the renovations.

Donny Jerie recalled Arturo hanging out at the Squeeze Lounge. *"I think he lived there [laughing]. He spent a lot of time there. He would put a few dollars down. He wouldn't get too crazy. Then he would pick up a girl. Basically he was famous. He was a good-looking kid. He was kind. He was loving. He had a heart of gold. Sometimes Arturo would get aggravated when some of the girls swarmed him. You know, Gatti's a man. He wants to bang 'em."*[318]

The September 20, 1996 rematch between Arturo and Patterson was postponed until February 22, 1997. The match originally was scheduled to be on the Pernell Whitaker-Wilfredo Rivera undercard in Miami. In mid-August, while Gatti was preparing for the rematch, sparring in the Catskills, he re-aggravated the hand injury he suffered in the Correa bout. Arturo threw a left uppercut that landed on his sparring partner's elbow. After the impact, Arturo fell to the canvas writhing in pain. Gatti was devastated. Arturo had tried to cover up the origins of his injury, by stating he injured his hand while playing pool, before he admitted that the injury occurred during the Correa match. Pat Lynch confessed that he was to blame for Arturo's injury. It was his idea to take the tune-up fight against Correa.[319]

While Arturo was healing his hand, he flew to Miami to rest. On September 20, he attended the Main Events-promoted Whitaker-Rivera rematch at the James Knight Convention Center. Donny Jerie flew to Florida with Arturo. Jerie recalled seeing first-hand Arturo's new-found star status. *"I remember when we went to Miami. When he was supposed to fight on the Pernell Whitaker card. We all went together and sat in the front row. And everybody's coming up to him, 'Oh Gatti.' People loved him, and he liked that stuff. Sometimes he got irritated. Sometimes he just wanted to hang out with the boys. I can imagine that limelight. For any superstar to live this is a very difficult life."*[320]

Joe returned to the ring on September 26, 1996 at Medieval Times in Lyndhurst N.J., against New York's Oswaldo Bello, 6-4-2 (5 KOs). Emile Griffith, the former middleweight champion, was Joe's new trainer. Bello was considered a safe fight on paper, but three of his knockout wins, and both of his draws, came against fighters with winning records. Although Bello was a big underdog, he definitely had a puncher's chance.

During the first two rounds, Bello was looking to land his powerful right hand. Gatti's punches were wide. Joe appeared rusty from the long lay-off. In the 3rd, Bello found his mark, landing one of his trademark power shots, knocking Gatti down. Bello attempted an additional blow after Joe hit the canvas. Luckily for Bello, the foul shot missed. Joe pulled himself back up, but Bello, sensing an opportunity, landed several more hard shots, forcing referee Rudy Battle to stop the fight at the 1:47 mark of the 3rd round.

Bello and his team celebrated while the pro-Gatti crowd booed mightily. Joe was now 25-6, but more importantly, he had lost four out of his last nine fights. In the dressing room, Joe was interviewed. *"I have to do a lot of thinking. I though he [Battle] stopped it too soon."*[321] Griffith opined, *"He [Joe] is going to have to make a decision. He still can hit hard and I feel he can still do something, but I can't make the decision about his career."*[322]

Joe decided to put his energy into building a career outside of boxing. A few thousand dollars for non-televised bouts was not enough to pay the bills. Joe took up work as an elevator mechanic, and eventually was promoted to a supervisory position. Joe also drove a tractor-trailer and worked as a tow-truck operator to supplement his income.

On November 7, 1996, 35-year-old Mario Cusson committed suicide by hanging himself. Cusson was an extremely popular Canadian boxer who fought Davey Hilton twice. Their first match drew over 20,000 spectators. Cusson was having relationship problems, and he also was having problems dealing with life after boxing. Cusson's brother Serge, another boxer, ran the streets with Joe years earlier.

The Cusson family wasn't the only Canadian boxing family dealing with tragedy. Eddie "Hurricane" Melo, to whom Arturo once was compared, was murdered. Melo was attracted to the Montreal nightlife and all that came with it. He eventually migrated to the Montreal mafia and worked as a bodyguard for alleged Bonanno capo Francesco "Frank" Cotroni. On April 6, 2001, after leaving a club, the 40-year-old Melo was murdered.

Cotroni was attracted to boxing, and had invested in the Hilton brothers in the early 1980s. His grandson became a professional boxer. Cotroni's brother, Vic, allegedly was head of the Montreal mafia in the early 1980s.

Former heavyweight contender George Chuvalo also suffered

devastating family tragedies. Chuvalo's son Jesse, who had drug issues, was murdered by a gunshot to the head on February 18, 1985. After that, two of his other sons, Georgie and Stevie, died from drug overdoses. His wife Lynne, distraught by her family's curse from drugs, decided to take her own life. George Chuvalo has been an outspoken critic of illicit drugs ever since.

Chapter 12
The Patterson Rematch

On February 22, 1997, in a bout sponsored by Bally's Park Place and held at the Convention Center Ballroom in Atlantic City, Arturo Gatti and Tracy Patterson fought their rematch for the IBF super featherweight title. HBO broadcast the bout live on its "Boxing After Dark" series.

Arturo explained that he was forced to postpone the bout after his hand injury occurred. Arturo was unable to spar, punch, or even run, because his left hand was in a cast for eight weeks. Gatti was operated on by Doctor Charles Melone. Melone was a New York hand specialist who had operated on professional athletes such as Don Mattingly and Patrick Ewing. Melone did not want Arturo to do any training, not even running while his hand healed. He didn't want any sweat to get under the cast. Gatti took advantage of the opportunity to do strength conditioning on his legs and his right arm. Arturo admitted that he also used the time off to go out and party. Gatti was hoping that another win over Patterson would propel him into big-money fights in the lightweight division.[323]

Patterson felt that he had won the first fight, though he admitted that he should have thrown more punches. He stated that he didn't throw more punches because he didn't feel he needed to do so.[324] For the rematch, Patterson planned to start faster and finish stronger. The only thing on his mind was getting his title back.[325]

In the lead-up to the fight, Gatti and Patterson held a press conference at the All-Star Café in Midtown Manhattan. During the presser, Arturo admitted that he couldn't sleep at night because he was always thinking about the rematch.[326] Patterson again stated that he felt he won the first fight. He added that Gatti threw a lot of punches in the first match, but he missed many of them.[327]

Patterson kept his #1 ranking by remaining busy after the first match. He defeated Harold Warren, Joseph Figueroa and Jose Aponte, though the bout with Warren was extremely close. Patterson boasted that he took those fights because he was a warrior. He believed that staying active would help him defeat Gatti.[328]

HBO's senior vice president of programming, Lou DiBella, felt that the Gatti-Patterson rematch was a fight that had to be made.[329] DiBella believed that the match-up had all the makings of fight of the year.[330] Angel Manfredy was scheduled to box Wilson

Rodriguez on the undercard. A Gatti win would put him in line for a title fight at lightweight with the legendary, but aging, Azumah Nelson.

Roca advised Lynch that Arturo training at Gleason's gym in Brooklyn was becoming too dangerous. Roca noticed that Arturo was starting to develop bad habits training in the area. There were too many nightclubs, women, and other distractions. Lynch agreed that Arturo would have to change his training location. Since all world champions are allotted training expenses in the promotional contract, it was a no-brainer for Gatti to have a proper training camp, away from public view.

As the rumors regarding Arturo's wild partying habits spread, Lynch did his best to protect his fighters reputation by deflecting questions. Anyone who asked about the rumors, including Lou Duva, were told that there were no problems with Arturo. When they left Gleason's, Gatti's troubles followed him. The location was not the problem. The problem was within Arturo. Lynch even went as far as to assign chaperones, who acted as bodyguards for Arturo. First there was Luis Ocasio, to be followed by John Capone. Unfortunately for Lynch, Arturo easily outmaneuvered his watchdogs, and even partied with some of them as well.

Pat Lynch, in desperation, resorted to using Joe Gatti to monitor his brother. Joe was married and working, but his children were not yet born at the time. Following Arturo around was difficult for him. Lynch would call Joe in the middle of the night and ask him to go search for Arturo. Joe would find himself acting as a detective, searching after hour Manhattan clubs for his brother. John Capone would later admit that, at that time, Arturo was 35 to 45% properly prepared for his fights. Nothing more. Arturo's lifestyle would soon start showing itself during his performances.

The Gatti team decided to move their camp from Gleason's to Virginia Beach, where Pernell Whitaker had his fight camps. For strength and conditioning, Gatti worked out at Wareing's Gym under the direction of trainer Bob Wareing. For boxing, Hector Roca trained Arturo at Whitaker and Lou Duva's boxing gym.

Unfortunately, the Virginia Beach training camp was close to plenty of bars and nightclubs. This environment would lead to more trouble for Arturo in the future. Arturo spent 14 weeks training in Virginia Beach.

Accompanying Arturo to his Virginia Beach training camp was John Capone. Capone, from Jersey City, was described as being clever and streetwise. He did not have a regular job, so he was able to attend camp with Arturo. Some questioned whether Capone was the right personality for Gatti to have in camp with him. Arturo purchased Capone a new Cadillac.

Bob Wareing was the son of John Wareing, who had run a strength and fitness gym in Virginia Beach since the early seventies. Bob was a former wrestler and amateur boxer. Pernell Whitaker often praised Wareing for his strength training methods. Wareing not only directed his fighters on how to strength train, he actually trained alongside them. He would run and lift weights with his athletes. As the fighters dieted to make weight, Wareing would also eat the same low fat foods as his fighters. This type of sacrifice led to his forming a special bond with the boxers he trained.

Bob, who won the Virginia welterweight state boxing championship as an amateur, knew Pernell Whitaker since 1973 when Pernell was a 9-year-old Junior Olympic boxer. It was at a local amateur boxing show that "Pete" Whitaker received his ring name. Whitaker's supporters were chanting "Sweet Pete" during one of his fights, but a local reporter thought they were yelling "Sweet Pea" and reported the same. The ring name stuck and "Sweet Pea" Whitaker was born.

Whitaker was in camp with Arturo as he was preparing to defend his WBC welterweight title on January 24, 1997 against Diobelys Hurtado. Philadelphia's Ivan Robinson joined the camp as well. Robinson had challenged Phillip Holiday for the IBF lightweight title in December 1996, but lost a decision. Robinson only sparred Whitaker in camp; never Arturo.

Robinson recalled Virginia Beach and Arturo. *"We used to be in camp all the time... When Whitaker fought that kid in Atlantic City, that kid from Cuba [Hurtado]... It was just me, Gatti, and Pernell Whitaker. And I was wondering why me and Gatti never sparred. We always sparred Pernell Whitaker. And I came to find out later, Main Events had this promotional thing. Maybe it was a good fight to put together. Maybe somewhere down the line."*[331]

No one could foresee that the Virginia move would have devastating results on the young and impressionable Gatti. Being around the great Pernell Whitaker, how could the young Arturo not want to emulate the fighter who had previously been crowned the top fighter, pound-for-pound, by the *Ring* magazine? Whitaker looked to Arturo as a younger brother and affectionately called him "Shorty." Pernell teased Arturo, telling Gatti that he wasn't street tough because he didn't grow up in the "hood." Arturo would reply that he lived in one of the toughest sections in the United States, in Jersey City, by the Ringside Lounge. Whitaker was so curious that one day while he was in the New York Metro area, he stopped in the Ringside Lounge. Pernell told Mario Costa that he wanted to see the tough Ringside Lounge that Arturo used to brag about.

Unfortunately, Whitaker taught Arturo more than just boxing moves, as Arturo's brother Joe explained. *"I was there. Pernell Whitaker messed up and was selling the stuff [cocaine] to him. He told my brother, 'As long as you show up to work the next day you're fine. You can do what you want. You gotta get up tomorrow morning. You gotta run. You gotta go to the gym.' My brother was, 'Hey, it's fine. As long as I go to the gym and train.' So when he trained, half the time he was high... but nobody knew that [sarcastically].*"[332]

On October 17, after defeating Andrey Pestreyaev, Pernell Whitaker tested positive for cocaine. The decision was changed to a no-contest. Whitaker would test positive again in 1998 and check into a drug rehabilitation clinic.

The Gatti-Patterson rematch was held in Atlantic City. *Star Ledger* reporter Jerry Izenberg called the Atlantic City location for the fight, *"New Jersey's version of Sodom-by-the-Sea."*[333] Izenberg jokingly stated that the first Gatti-Patterson fight was so good that the rematch demanded a more glorious location then Madison Square Garden.

Several days before the match, Izenberg interviewed Arturo in his Bally's hotel room. Arturo admitted that he had been involved in too many unnecessary wars. Arturo felt that his jab had worked in the first Patterson match. His corner had cautioned him not to get suckered into a brawl during the first fight, but he couldn't resist. Although Gatti admitted that too many wars weren't healthy, he strongly believed that he would have lost his title to Wilson Rodriguez had he not stood toe-to-toe. Arturo was working on controlling his emotions during a fight, and knowing when to box or brawl. Gatti admitted that in the ring there was something inside of him that was always ready to explode.[334]

On February 19, Tracy Patterson was interviewed at the Atlantic City PAL Center while he worked out. Patterson felt that he had his best training camp ever in preparation for the rematch. Even though Patterson still believed that he had won the first match, he was aware that another close match might not go his way. Patterson planned on a convincing victory.³³⁵

Patterson, and his trainer, Tommy Parks, used the extra time from the delay in the rematch to sharpen up their strategy. Parks even went as far as to predict a knockout. Parks believed that Patterson had developed more power and consistency. Parks was confident that Patterson would stop Arturo. He also felt that a longer fight would favor Patterson.³³⁶

On February 20, *Atlantic City Press* columnist David Weinberg sat down with Arturo. Gatti talked about his recent bouts during which he was forced to brawl to be victorious.³³⁷ Pat Lynch added that Arturo had no choice but to brawl against Patterson and Rodriguez. Lynch recalled that Gatti had boxed Patterson for nine rounds, but he was forced to start slugging because he had trouble with his vision. During the Rodriguez fight, Lynch stated that Arturo brawled because the doctors said they were going to stop the fight because his eyes were nearly swollen shut.³³⁸ Lynch commented on the eye problems that Arturo had been having of late. He admitted that Arturo never had any problems with his eyes until the Patterson fight.³³⁹

Main Events president Dino Duva spoke of the rematch. He commented that several recently televised fights were not worthy of TV. Duva felt that the Gatti-Patterson rematch needed no hype or promotion. He described Tracy Patterson as a fierce competitor, a veteran who knew every trick in boxing. Duva believed that Arturo was on the verge of becoming the best junior lightweight in the world. Duva felt that Gatti needed to beat Patterson to get to that level.³⁴⁰

If Arturo defeated Patterson again, he was eyeing a mega-fight against either WBC super featherweight champ Azumah Nelson or WBO featherweight champ Naseem Hamed. A bout against WBU super featherweight champ Angel Manfredy, though not on the monetary level of Nelson or Hamed, was also being considered. Arturo would rather have gone after the money fights now, but the close scoring of the first Patterson fight had many calling for the rematch. Arturo opined, *"People who know boxing know I won the fight, but they wanted to see it again. I understand that and if that's what it takes for Arturo Gatti to get respect and those major paydays, then let's do it. There are a lot of things in my future and I'm not going to let Tracy Patterson keep me from that."*³⁴¹

Patterson was ready for the rematch. He had never looked forward to a fight more than this one.³⁴² The *Atlantic City Press* predicted that Patterson would win by 10th round knockout.

On the undercard, Indiana's Angel Manfredy got off of the canvas in the 10th round to successfully defend his WBU super featherweight title, defeating Wilson Rodriguez by unanimous 12-round decision. The judges scores were 116-111 twice and 117-110.

Patterson, 57-4-1 (40 KOs), made his way into the ring with Tommy Parks, Anthony Hamm and Percy Richardson as the mostly partisan Gatti crowd booed. Richardson, Gatti's former cutman, was now working Patterson's corner.

As Patterson's team waited in the ring, the Rocky theme song "Gonna Fly Now" started blaring throughout the Hall's speakers. Gatti was led down the aisle by his team. Arturo was coming off of the longest inactive streak of his career, 225 days, due to his broken left hand. Arturo blew up to 165-pounds during his lay-off. Larry Merchant commented on Gatti's inactivity and the fact that the operation on his left hand was the cause. Merchant felt that the layoff was a blessing in disguise, mainly because Arturo had fought two very tough fights earlier in the year. Merchant felt the rest gave Gatti a chance to refuel for the rematch.

Joe walked Arturo into the ring, along with Lynch and the entourage, which was growing ever larger. In Arturo's corner were Roca, Bob Wareing, Joe Souza, and Roger Bloodworth. Bloodworth was a Main Events assistant trainer. Although Bloodworth never boxed himself, his son fought in the amateurs and Roger would glove up fighters at the amateur shows. Dino Duva was in the ring with Arturo, as was Carl Moretti and N.J. boxing commissioner Larry Hazzard. The HBO "Boxing After Dark" televised bout was co-promoted by Main Events and Peltz Boxing. Arturo gained 15-pounds after the weigh-in. He entered the ring weighing 145-pounds.

Referee Rudy Battle gave both boxers their instructions and sent them back to their corners to await the bell. As soon as the bell rang, the pro Gatti crowd started chanting, *"Gatti!, Gatti!, Gatti!"* A little less than a minute into the 1st round, Arturo timed a right uppercut on Patterson, who was leaning in. The blow sent Patterson stumbling backwards. The crowd went wild. Gatti tried to follow up on his advantage, but most of his shots missed their mark.

Arturo was not boxing and stepping around like he had in the first match. With 37 seconds left in the 1st, Gatti missed a right and Patterson timed a hard counter right hand that landed flush on the jaw. A stunned Gatti covered up and retreated to the ropes. Arturo let loose with a left hook to the head, but as he threw, Patterson landed a perfect left hook to the liver that dropped Arturo to his knees.

As soon as Gatti went down Rudy Battle incorrectly ruled the punch a low blow, indicating no knockdown by saying *"No, no, no!"* He told Arturo, who rose after about five seconds, *"Take your time."* Arturo bent over in agony.

Battle walked over to an indignant Patterson and warned him to keep his punches up. Tracy angrily responded that the punch was legal. Gatti walked around the ring, still writhing in pain. HBO analyst Roy Jones, Jr. was shocked. He asked to see a playback of the punch because he didn't believe it was low.

Thirty-three precious seconds had elapsed before the fighters were waived back in to continue the contest. Patterson did not try to rush Gatti, for Arturo had now recovered. The round ended as Jones, Jr. pleaded to see the replay.

As the analysts reviewed the knockdown, Roy Jones, Jr. lamented that Battle had taken a knockdown, and possibly a knockout, away from Patterson. Jim Lampley agreed. Larry Merchant felt it was a borderline punch. Jones, Jr. cut him off, stating that it was a clean body shot.

In Patterson's corner, Tommy Parks instructed Tracy to be wary of the uppercut. He cautioned Patterson not to stay inside when Arturo threw the punch. Parks asked Tracy to move his upper body side to side to avoid the uppercut.

Halfway through the 2nd, Patterson landed a hard counter right hand to the body. Gatti finished the round with hard body shots and a solid left hook. Patterson was cautious about trading.

Parks asked Patterson for more jabs. In Gatti's corner, Roca instructed Arturo not to step in too far when he punched.

Gatti came out strong in the 3rd with hard body punches and hooks to the head. Gatti controlled the first two-and-a-half minutes with his activity. With 30 seconds left in the round, Patterson landed two rights to the head. Gatti responded with a hook to the leaning in Patterson, who stumbled momentarily. After the round ended, Arturo walked back to his corner smiling.

Roca asked Gatti to remain cool. He advised Arturo not to look for the knockout. He told Gatti that he had won the first three rounds. Roca asked Arturo to keep turning Patterson. He also told Gatti to keep low and keep his composure. While Roca was speaking to Arturo, Gatti was peering through the ropes towards Pernell

Whitaker, who was telling him to stand flatfooted and take Patterson out.

Arturo dominated the 4th round. Patterson seemed content to cover up and block. After the round, Whitaker, who was sitting ringside with Dino Duva, yelled out to Roca, telling him to make sure that Gatti stayed low at all times. Whitaker was taking Arturo's attention away from Roca.

After the fight, Roca would speak to Lynch and implore him to move Arturo's training camp away from Virginia Beach and Whitaker, to another location. Roca's situation was precarious. As Arturo, and by proxy Pat Lynch, continued to climb the boxing ladder, their connections expanded to include boxing's elite trainers, including some who made careers pilfering talent from other trainers. Roca's position would become increasingly untenable. It didn't matter that Arturo was winning; boxing insiders would find something negative to say about Arturo's performances.

Arturo easily outboxed Patterson in the 5th, utilizing his height and reach. After the round, Tommy Parks warned Tracy that he had lost all five rounds. He told Patterson that he could not afford to lose another round. He pleaded with Tracy to start fighting back harder. Roca instructed Gatti to keep his distance and use angles. He told Arturo that he had won the first five rounds. He asked Gatti to protect himself and stay low.

In the 6th, Gatti controlled the first half of the round with combinations and footwork. Halfway through the round, Patterson landed a flush right hand that snapped Arturo's head back. Tracy, sensing Gatti was stunned, stepped in with power shots. With less than a minute remaining in the round, Patterson closed the gap and landed a hard right hand. He followed with another hard right hand-left hook combo as Arturo covered up.

Gatti tried to step in. Patterson snapped Arturo's head back with a stiff jab. Gatti gamely fought back but Tracy finished the round strong. After the bell, Rudy Battle had to separate the two fighters as they exchanged words. Patterson butted his head against Arturo's.

At the start of the 7th, Patterson worked Gatti to the ropes, where he landed several hard body shots. Arturo spun out into the middle of the ring. With 1:20 remaining in the round, Gatti landed a left hook to the body that strayed below the belt. Battle warned Gatti to keep his punches up. Arturo yelled, *"Come on,"* to Battle in disgust, disagreeing with the warning. Arturo dominated the final minute with over a dozen hard shots. After the bell rang, Patterson stuck his tongue out at Arturo as Gatti gazed at him.

Roca implored Gatti to stay low. Roca cautioned Arturo that he was squaring up his body too much. He asked for quick combinations. Roca told Gatti that he was up seven rounds to nothing. Parks instructed Patterson to start throwing a lot of punches. He asked for more head movement. Parks reminded Tracy that the referee was not going to help him win the fight. Patterson appeared to drift off in thought as Parks spoke.

In Arturo's corner, Gatti disregarded and disrespected Roca by leaning his head through the ropes towards Pernell Whitaker to receive instructions from "Sweet Pea." Jim Lampley asked Roy Jones, Jr. if Whitaker's advice was helping or distracting Arturo. Jones, Jr. replied that Whitaker was indeed being helpful because he was a confidence builder. This may be true, but if Whitaker was giving instructions that were contrary to Roca's, the advice might only confuse Gatti as to which instruction to heed.

The 8th round began with both fighters mauling and pressing for an advantage. With 1:56 remaining in the round, Arturo threw a right uppercut that landed quite low, onto Patterson's leg, under the hip. Battle immediately separated the two fighters and took a point away from Arturo for low blows.

When the action resumed, Tracy landed a solid right hand. Gatti responded with a flush uppercut. Arturo was effectively utilizing his left arm to push Patterson's lunging head to the side. Joe was motioning for Arturo to work the body on the inside. Gatti landed a hard left hook. Arturo outworked Patterson in the final minute, although Tracy did land a few solid rights.

Arturo returned to his corner nodding his head as the crowd roared with approval. Patterson's right eye was nearly closed from the left hooks he was absorbing.

Parks continued to try and motivate his fighter. He begged Patterson to fight. He told Tracy that he would win if he started fighting. Parks felt that Arturo's power was gone. He advised Patterson that he needed a knockout to win, and the only way he could get the KO was by being aggressive.

Forty seconds into the 9th, Patterson threw and landed a right hand, but lost his balance on the wet "King of Beers" Budweiser logo in the center of the ring. As Tracy was falling Gatti threw a left hook that missed over the top. Amazingly, Rudy Battle called the slip a knockdown, his second significant blown call of the fight, both of which hurt Patterson.

Tracy rose in anger and frustration as Battle gave him an 8-count. Broadcasters Larry Merchant and Roy Jones, Jr. both correctly stated that Patterson's fall was a slip. Lampley initially thought it was a knockdown, though he changed his mind later upon seeing the replay.

Arturo boxed well in the final two minutes, as Patterson again failed to pull the trigger. Gatti smiled at Tracy as the round came to a close.

Roca instructed Arturo to use angles and keep Patterson in the middle of the ring. Roca advised Gatti not to throw six, seven, or eight-punch combinations, apparently fearing a counter punch. Instead, Roca wanted Gatti to throw one or two punches and step over.

Arturo was controlling the 10th by boxing. His fans were enjoying his performance, as they chanted, *"Gatti!, Gatti! Gatti!"* After the round, Patterson complained to Parks that he couldn't see Gatti. Arturo was stepping around to his left, which was towards Tracy's nearly closed right eye. Parks tried to convince Patterson that it wasn't the swollen eye, but maybe a foreign object that might have gotten into Tracy's eye, that was affecting his vision. Richardson applied an ice bag to Patterson's eye. Parks instructed Tracy to throw punches. Roca advised Arturo that there were only two rounds left, while Whitaker yelled to Arturo that the fight was his to win.

Gatti started the 11th with his chin tucked behind his lead left shoulder to protect him from counter punches. Arturo utilized his jab while dominating the round. After the bell sounded, Gatti raised his hands in triumph.

In Gatti's corner, Roca asked Arturo to continue boxing. Roca actually motioned Gatti to peer through the ropes and listen to Whitaker's instructions. In Patterson's corner, Tracy complained to Parks that he couldn't breathe. Parks replied that if Patterson didn't get a knockout, he would have plenty of time to breathe after the fight ended.

Arturo out boxed and out hustled Patterson in the 12th. When the final bell rang, Gatti jumped for joy as Patterson sullenly walked back to his corner. Roca, Lynch and Joe all hugged Arturo. Lynch and Joe embraced each other.

The judges' scorecards read 118-108, 117-109, and 116-110, all for Arturo. As the scoring was announced, Joe raised his brother into the air. Arturo threw his arms skyward. According to CompuBox's PunchStats, Gatti threw 1,031 punches compared to Patterson's 354,

Arturo landed 463 to Tracy's 195.

Arturo was interviewed by Larry Merchant, who asked why he had won the rematch so much more convincingly than the first contest. Arturo stated that he used his head more and boxed Patterson in the middle of the ring.

Arturo was asked if the punch in the 1st round, that caused him to take a knee, was indeed a low blow. Arturo felt that the blow was on the beltline, and admitted it took his wind a bit. Arturo was asked if the referee's call may have helped him. Arturo felt that he had won every round anyway, so it didn't matter.

Merchant asked Gatti if he would fight Manfredy, who was under contract with HBO, and who had defeated Wilson Rodriguez on the undercard. Arturo felt that he didn't need to fight Manfredy. He wanted to fight Azumah Nelson, who he believed could advance his boxing career more. If he couldn't get the fight he wanted, he would move up to 135. Arturo yelled into the camera, *"Montreal!"*

The 38-year-old Nelson, 39-3-2 and current WBC super featherweight champion, was past his prime, but still quite dangerous, coming off victories over Gabriel Ruelas and Jesse James Leija. He would be a smart business move for Arturo, as a fight with Nelson would generate much more cash for Gatti. However, the Azumah Nelson fight would never materialize, as Nelson lost his title to Genaro Hernandez a month later.

After leaving the ring, Arturo stated that he showed that he was a true champion with his performance.[343] Arturo added that he came into the fight as a champion and he felt that that made a big difference.[344]

There were those who felt that Whitaker had helped Arturo with his head movement. Lou DiBella believed that Whitaker was a positive influence on Gatti.[345] Pat Lynch and DiBella agreed that Arturo needed to continue working on his defense.[346] Russell Peltz joked that there was no rule against making an opponent miss every now and then.[347]

Patterson blamed his subpar performance on a sinus infection that caused him blurry vision over the second half of the bout. He revealed that he forgot to take his medication before the fight. Tracy stated that from the 5th round on, he couldn't see Arturo. After that, he just tried to react to what Arturo was doing. Patterson said that if Gatti had known that he couldn't see, he probably would have stopped him.[348] Gatti felt that he took Patterson's heart away in the 9th and 10th rounds.[349]

Tracy spoke of the controversial non-knockdown of Arturo in the 1st round. He stated that the referee forgot to wear his eyeglasses, because he landed a clean body shot and it should have been ruled a knockdown. Patterson added that he was not knocked down in the 9th round.[350]

Arturo commented on his former brawling style. He admitted that it wasn't very healthy to be an action fighter.[351] Dino Duva added that it was the cleanest Arturo had looked, physically, coming out of a fight in a long time.[352] Arturo took a jab at HBO because the network televised his bout on the 11 p.m. "Boxing After Dark" series instead of its championship boxing time slot of 9 p.m. Gatti stated, *"Maybe now I can get on HBO at nine o'clock."*[353]

It appeared as though Arturo soon would get his wish, as the Patterson rematch drew a 10.1 rating for a 24% audience share. The rating was an all-time high for "Boxing After Dark." Lou DiBella stated that the rating was enormous. He added that Arturo had earned a nine o'clock start.[354]

Chapter 13
Ruelas

A little over two months after defeating Patterson, on May 4, 1997 at Caesar's in Atlantic City, in a non-title bout, Arturo took on 34-year-old Coatesville, Pennsylvania native Calvin Grove, 49-8 (18 KOs). Gatti trained in Arizona with Roca and Pernell Whitaker, helping Whitaker prepare for his close, semi-controversial losing battle against Oscar De La Hoya. The 25-year-old Gatti took a 27-1 (22 KOs) record into the match. The quick but light punching Grove was a former IBF featherweight champion. Grove won the title in 1988 but lost it the same year. The bout was televised by CBS sports. Arturo weighed in at 136¼-pounds to Grove's 137.

Before the fight, Arturo spoke of growing up in Canada. *"Hockey was the biggest thing in Canada, but with our family, boxing was the main thing. You know, at night after supper we would watch TV and the next thing you know you would see gloves popping up and furniture moving. And we would glove up and just spar and go for the whole night."*

Gatti spoke of his future goals. *"Whenever they ask me to do something for kids, especially kids, I love kids. I can't wait to have my own kids someday. Anytime I can do something for somebody I love to do it. And it's fun, you know, people look at the different side of me. They don't just see a fighter, an aggressive guy. 'Cause I am in the ring but outside the ring they see who I really am. And it's fun. I like to do it. My first goal was to become a world champ and I did it. And now I see myself winning a few titles. Not only one, but a few titles would definitely make my life happy."*[355]

Arturo said that he was fighting Grove because he felt he could learn a lot from the former champion. Gatti also wanted to remain active.[356] Arturo was upset that Grove called him a shot fighter. *"That really ticked me off. I'm not usually like that, but I got upset because my career is just starting. Now I think of it as a big joke. The way I see it, he's got to use something to pump himself up and convince himself he's got something over me. I never look past anyone. I never think I'm fighting a bum. It doesn't matter if the guy I'm fighting is 0-10, I train for every fight as if it's for the championship. Calvin's very good and more experienced. And I've had trouble before with boxers. But I've trained well for this one. I want to beat him to show him I'm above him."*[357]

After wrapping up training with Whitaker, Arturo returned to Virginia Beach with Roca to complete his training. Gatti's corner remained the same as his previous bout. Grove was seconded by former middleweight contender Bobby "Boogaloo" Watts.

In the 1st round, Arturo, who was much bigger and stronger than Grove, punished Calvin with body punches and hard double hooks. Grove landed several combinations and was putting all his weight behind his punches, but they still did not appear to bother Arturo. Gatti was punching wide with his shots, apparently due to the fact that he didn't respect Grove's punching power. Watts yelled at Calvin to double his jab up, but Grove seemed more concerned with avoiding Arturo's bombs by backing away.

In the 2nd round, Grove landed a few right hands, but spent most of the round retreating from Gatti's assaults. Arturo's head movement seemed improved, and he showed flashes of Pernell Whitaker's defensive prowess by his slipping and squatting moves.

Forty seconds into the 3rd, Arturo landed a punishing hook to the body. Gatti pushed Grove around the ring like a rag doll. Whitaker yelled to Arturo from his seat, *"Bend your knees!"* With a minute remaining in the round, Gatti landed a hard straight right to the body and followed with a solid hook to the head. Unlike the Patterson fights, where Arturo was content to throw fast combinations, Gatti was putting his body weight behind his shots. Even the punches that Grove blocked were jolting his balance. Joe and Mikey Red shouted encouragement to Arturo from ringside, as Arturo's supporters chanted, *"Gatti! Gatti! Gatti!"*

Grove kept pulling away from Gatti in the 4th, as Arturo yelled, *"Come on,"* trying to entice Calvin into trading punches. Arturo cornered Grove but missed most of his attempts because he was telegraphing his wide power shots. Gatti landed several hard body punches as he pressed forward. Grove replied with a hard left hook as Arturo recklessly walked in. Calvin quickly followed with a hard straight right that stopped Gatti in his tracks. Arturo retreated as Grove tried to press his advantage. Calvin slugged away sensing an opportunity. Gatti swung and missed a left hook, following it with an inadvertent head-butt that caused Grove to stumble backwards.

Arturo charged after his hurt foe. Grove, cut under his left eye, received another head-butt while clinching. He complained to referee Brian O'Melia that the injury was caused by the Gatti head-butt.

O'Melia called time and summoned the ringside physician to

examine Grove's eye. While awaiting the doctor, Calvin's cutman jumped up onto the ring apron and applied the enswell and adrenaline to the injured eye. The doctor allowed the fight to continue. The round ended a few seconds later.

Gatti was controlling the 5th until Grove landed a hard right that staggered Arturo. He followed with five more right hand blows. Gatti came back with two rights of his own. The bout was turning into a street fight. Calvin landed a grazing left hook that opened a cut over Arturo's right eye. Gatti responded with a left hook of his own that shook Grove's entire body. Calvin sagged into the ropes. The veteran quickly recovered and survived by sliding along the ropes as the round ended.

Roca yelled at Arturo, complaining that he was trying too hard for a knockout. Cutman Joe Souza fervently worked on Arturo's right eye while Roca yelled instructions. The ring doctor examined Arturo's damaged eye.

Grove started the 6th trying to land another right to the head, while Arturo worked both hands to the body. Both fighters landed hard shots in the round. Gatti still was the aggressor. With a little over 10 seconds remaining in the round, Grove drilled Arturo with a hard right hand that sent Gatti's mouthpiece flying out.

Gatti stalked Grove in the 7th, landing a few hard rights to the body. After the 7th round ended, Grove retired in the corner, claiming he was experiencing vision problems.

Calvin claimed that he was thumbed in the 2nd round and started having double vision. He complimented Arturo on being a good puncher. Grove had advice for Gatti. *"I think he needs to improve his defense. I was able to hit him with right hands."*

Arturo stated that he was in great shape. He complimented Grove on being crafty. Gatti admitted that he was hit more times than he would have liked. Arturo expressed that he wanted to defend his 130-pound title once more before moving up to lightweight.[358]

Lynch spoke of Gatti's future. He was targeting Gabriel Ruelas as Arturo's next opponent at 130-pounds. Lynch admitted that Arturo was having trouble making the 130-pound limit.[359] Gatti needed three stitches over his right eye.

Dino Duva commented that Arturo always gives the fans their money's worth. He added that Gatti drives everybody on his team crazy with his brawls, giving everyone gray hairs. In Duva's opinion, Arturo was the most exciting fighter in the world.[360]

On June 14, 1997, Joe Gatti married his fiancé, Victoria Ballero.

Arturo was the best man. The wedding was held at Buffett Christina, on Jarry Rue, in the Saint-Leonard section of Montreal. Among the weddings attendees were Arturo's girlfriend Laura Sosnowski, Mario Costa, Pat Lynch and his wife Lisette.

Joe recalled Laura. *"She was the best out of all of them. He should have married her. Every time he got close to a girl they would take over my brother, because he would fall in love. Pat would manage to get him out. Sabotage the relationship. Arturo was paranoid when he started using cocaine. They tried to blame all that stuff that he was doing because he was paranoid. No, he was paranoid because of what he was doing, drugs. And because of what they were doing by telling him not to trust any girls. He had no trust no more."*[361] Vikki continued, *"If you had a decent woman in your life all that would stop."*[362] Joe added, *"Its only normal. You fall in love with a girl and she starts waking you up."*[363]

Arturo gave Joe and Vikki a $10,000 check as a wedding gift. At the reception, Joe serenaded his new wife with the Englebert Humperdinck song "After the Lovin," as she sat in a chair in the middle of the reception room.

Arturo had told Joe several times that he wanted a relationship with a woman like Joe had with Vikki. Some of Joe and Arturo's boxing friends from New Jersey, including Scott DePompe and his father Mike, attended the wedding. The night was not devoid of family issues. Arturo became heavily intoxicated and was using drugs. He started getting annoyed at the cameramen and photographers who were documenting the wedding. A local TV station from Montreal was capturing the event. Arturo stormed out of the wedding because he felt that the cameramen were following him around. Joe tried to explain to Arturo that the cameras were not following him. The paranoia from the drugs and alcohol he had consumed had convinced Arturo otherwise. Joe felt that Arturo also was paranoid because he believed that everyone was trying to make money off of his fame. This led Arturo to be even more suspicious of those around him. Donny Jerie recalled, *"Some people would only hang out with him so they could tell people, 'Oh, I know Gatti. He's my buddy.'"*[364]

On June 30, 1997, Arturo and his friend John Capone, who also doubled as his bodyguard, went out for a night of partying in Hudson County. They partied past midnight. At around 2:45 a.m. on July 1, Arturo was driving his BMW Z3 up the Viaduct from Hoboken into Union City. Arturo and Capone were enjoying themselves, drinking out of a bottle of Jack Daniels. A local police officer in Union City observed Gatti run a red light. The officer followed and watched Arturo run two more red lights and a stop sign. Arturo was driving south on Bergenline Avenue when the officer decided to initiate a motor vehicle stop. The officer activated his overhead lights and sirens. Gatti continued south on Bergenline, apparently trying to reach the Jersey City border, while the police vehicle followed closely behind. Arturo had been given the key to the city in Jersey City, and possibly felt that he was more likely to be let go with a warning if he reached the border. Arturo was only 15 blocks from reaching his adopted hometown.

At 12th Street and Bergenline Avenue, Arturo's vehicle got stuck behind a taxi at a traffic light. He couldn't go around the car because another vehicle was coming in the opposite direction of the two-way road. Gatti flashed his high beams and hit the horn in an attempt to get the taxi in front of him to move out of the way. Several officers descended on the scene from different angles, surrounding the car. Both Gatti and Capone were ordered out of the vehicle at gunpoint. Arturo yelled out, *"Don't shoot."* [365]

Arturo stumbled out of the Z3 and walked four steps before laying prone on the ground. When an officer stepped forward to handcuff him he had trouble placing the cuffs around Arturo's large wrists. The officers observed Capone move his hands under his seat. He was putting the cap on the bottle of Jack Daniels. Capone exited the vehicle and yelled to one of the officers, *"You are going to be fucking sorry for this mother fucker!"*[366] When Capone was told to raise his hands he replied, *"Fuck you guys. I'm not raising nothing. Hey tough guy, come and get me."*[367]

The officers placed both unknown parties under arrest. Arturo was asked for his paperwork. He said he didn't have it on him. His wallet was checked for identification. There was none, but there were over a dozen police courtesy cards from several different departments, including the New Jersey State Police.

Arturo's words were slurred, due to his intoxication. He struggled to free himself from the handcuffs. The officer, Omar Hernandez, looked at the courtesy cards and saw the name "Arturo Gatti." The officer asked Arturo if he was the boxer. Arturo's temperament immediately changed. He went from nervous and confused to cocky and arrogant. Arturo stated, *"That's right, I'm the boxer. I'm gonna fuck you up. I'm gonna shoot you in the face."*[368]

Arturo's car was towed while he and Capone were driven to police headquarters. On the drive to the police station, Arturo threatened to shoot the officers in the head. He told an officer that he was going to *"knock him out like a fucking punk."*[369] Arturo also said, *"I'm gonna get you fired."*[370] Upon arrival at the police station, Arturo attempted to head-butt an officer. When the officer tried to remove Arturo's personal items, Arturo pushed him away. Arturo took his earrings, ring, and watch off and threw them at the officer stating, *"That's more than you make in a year."*[371]

Arturo was asked for his social security number. The officers thought he was refusing to give it. In fact, Arturo, like his brother Joe, did not have a social security number.

After Arturo realized he wasn't angering the officers with his actions, he started crying. Capone and Arturo both had one arm handcuffed to a bench in the prisoner holding area. Capone tried consoling Gatti by stating, *"Arthur, Arthur,"* as he patted him on the back with his free hand.[372] Arturo responded by punching Capone several times in the face and spitting on him. Capone, still cuffed to a bench, picked Arturo up by his feet and started shaking him upside down. While Arturo was upside down he told Capone that he was going to shoot him in the head. Officers rushed in and broke up the tragicomic scene.

Capone was issued a summons and was told he was being released. Arturo was in shock. He turned to Capone with tears in his eyes, *"You're leaving me John? Don't leave me. You're supposed to protect me."*[373] Capone had his personal items returned and took off. The officers quickly capitalized on Arturo's newfound vulnerability and started teasing him. Arturo was told that he was being sent to the county jail and that he was going to see real quick just how tough he was when he arrived there. The officers joked about how the champion would react when he came face to face with gang members in the Hudson County correctional system. Arturo started crying again. One of the officers said, *"Boo Hoo. You're not such a tough guy anymore, are you?"*[374]

The Hudson County jail was overly crowded and packed with hardened criminals. Besides county prisoners, the jail also held inmates who were supposed to be housed at state facilities, but were held at the county because of overcrowding at the state prisons. Gangs such as the Bloods, MS-13s, Latin Kings, Caucasian biker gangs, and other hardcore gangs flourished in the facility.

Arturo was booked on a warrant for aggravated assault on an officer, resisting arrest, eluding, and driving while under the influence. He was walked from the holding area to a damp basement cell. The 4'x6' cells in Union City were nearly a hundred years old. The cells had a wooden plank to sleep on and a dirty, seatless toilet. Large cockroaches scavenged the cells looking for food and water. Arturo sat in the cell and cried, stating that he wished he were dead. Arturo never made it to the county jail. He was released on $10,000 bail at around 9 a.m. Before Arturo's release, his arrest already had made national headlines across the sports world.

The more serious charges of aggravated assault and eluding were downgraded from Superior Court back to municipal court in Union City on July 8. Attorney Dennis McAlevy and Pat Lynch's brother, John Lynch, also an attorney, worked on Arturo's case. McAlevy felt that Arturo's actions did not seem egregious. He pointed to the fact that no police officers were treated for injuries or sent to the hospital for medical treatment.[375]

The case was brought before municipal court Judge Joseph N. Falbo. Falbo, 80-years-old at the time, had been a municipal judge on and off since 1969, when he was first assigned the position by then Mayor William V. Musto. Falbo, a graduate of John Marshall Law School, was a veteran of World War II, serving in the United States Air Force. Falbo was a character on the bench. He would open court each day by spending nearly half an hour preaching to the always-packed courtroom about honor and duty and the love of one's country. He also would preach of the importance of fish and game licensing.

The courtroom usually was filled primarily with Central and South American immigrants, many of whom needed an interpreter when they stood before the bench. That mattered little to Falbo, as his diatribe was expected each morning as sure as the sun rose. Falbo was known as "let 'em go Joe" by the many prisoners that passed through his courtroom over the years. The moniker fit the hard-talking but soft acting judge.

Falbo was proud of Union City, which was where he was born and raised. He was even more proud of his physique. He worked out regularly and was in terrific condition for a man his age. It was a circus atmosphere on the day that Arturo arrived in Falbo's court. Pat and John Lynch, Dennis McAlevy, members of Arturo's entourage, and the media were all on hand.

Before the court proceedings started, Falbo invited Gatti to his chambers, which were in his office behind the bench. Falbo proceeded to shadowbox in front of Gatti. God only knows what Arturo was thinking. The court case was listed as The State of New

Jersey vs. Gatti and Capone. It sounded like a classic mafia trial.

When the court proceedings began, Judge Falbo veered off of his usual God and country speech. He talked about what great physical condition he was in and even flexed his biceps for any skeptics. Falbo went on to explain that he used to train in Joe Jennette's boxing gym as a kid. The judge asked if anyone else in the courtroom had any boxing experience. The courtroom and Gatti remained silent. Arturo looked clueless as to what was going on. When it was Arturo's turn to stand before the judge, all of the charges were dropped except the D.U.I. complaint. Gatti pled guilty to the drunken driving charge and apologized to the officers who arrested him. Arturo explained that he was very drunk on the evening of his arrest.

At the time of his arrest in Union City, Arturo was known to party two or three days straight without stopping. He would follow this up by crashing for 24 or more hours in a comatose state. Friends would attempt to wake him up, for fear he was dead. There are those who claim that Hector Roca and Pat Lynch were aware of Arturo's partying habits. In his book, *Le Denier Round,* author Jacques Ponthier alleged that Lynch received a phone call by a friend of Arturo's who said that Gatti appeared to be in a coma in his apartment in Jersey City. Lynch allegedly replied by telling the caller to check if Arturo's chest was rising and falling. When told that it was, he told the caller to make sure that Arturo continued breathing and hung up the phone.

Arturo's drug problems were not confined to Jersey City. When he went home to visit family in Montreal, he didn't miss the opportunity to enjoy that party scene. Arturo made sure to visit the local bars in the Little Italy section, making frequent trips to the bathroom to use his drugs. Some friends recalled that he would go through an ounce of cocaine a week. One of Arturo's close friends commented on Gatti's drug suppliers. *"Arturo didn't have one main dealer. He would buy drugs in church if that's where they were."*

Around this time, Main Events chairwoman Kathy Duva started to exert her authority on the promotional company. Friction was developing between Kathy and her brother-in-law Dino and sister-in-law Donna. Kathy had started Main Events with her husband Dan in 1978, with the help of Dan's father Lou.

Arturo, who was renting an apartment in Middletown, N.J., told Joe that he was thinking of buying a house in the town. Joe told Arturo that he and Vikki were also planning on buying a house.

Arturo had an idea that they should buy houses near each other so they could be closer to one another. Joe told Arturo that he couldn't afford to live in the area where Arturo was looking. Arturo offered to help. He said, *"Pick what you want. I'm gonna give you $50,000."*[376]

Joe and Vikki decided to buy a newly-built home in Jackson, N.J. for $350,000. They went out to dinner with Arturo and Laura to celebrate Arturo's engagement to Laura. Arturo gave Joe a $10,000 check so Joe could straighten out his bills before they purchased the house. Joe and Vikki had saved $11,000 for a home. They used the money as down payment.

The builder called Joe when the home was nearly finished. They needed to come up with the rest of the down payment. Joe called Arturo for the $50,000 he had promised, but Arturo didn't pick up the phone. Joe kept calling and calling but there was no answer. Finally the builder couldn't wait any longer and Joe lost the house and his $11,000 down payment.

Laura later told Joe and Vikki why Arturo did not answer the phone. Laura told Joe that she and Arturo went to Pat Lynch's house. Arturo told Lynch that he was going to help Joe buy a house near him. Lynch allegedly questioned why Arturo was helping Joe buy a house. He felt that Joe should be responsible for paying for his own home.[377] Laura called Vikki after Lynch had spoken to Arturo and told her there was no way that Arturo was going to give them the $50,000. Vikki believed that by keeping the two brothers separated from each other, Lynch could exert more control over Arturo. Joe recalled, *"When they separated us he didn't know how to come back."*[378] Vikki added, *"It ate Arturo alive. It ate him alive."*[379]

Joe was convinced that Lynch had compromising or potentially damaging information regarding Arturo, which was how he was able to control him. Joe did not know what that information might be. Of course, Arturo was an adult, and had final say regarding what he did or did not do with his own money. When Joe asked for his release from Main Events and Lynch, a rift was created that could never be repaired. Arturo was aware that his career was very successful and profitable and he may not have wanted to jeopardize that success by upsetting Lynch.

Joe wrote Arturo a letter, describing how hurt he was that his brother had offered to help and then let him lose his money and his house. In the letter, Joe wrote, *"How could you do this to me? We're brothers. Why did you even offer to help? We were fine and were going to get our own house. Why'd you even bring it up?"*[380] Joe left the letter in Arturo's mailbox, but wonders if he ever received it.

Donny Jerie believed that there were three issues that created friction between the brothers; jealousy, money, and women. Jerie recalled that Arturo would get upset that Joe appeared to be calling solely for the $50,000. One time, Donny was with Arturo when Joe called. Arturo turned to Jerie and said, *"He only calls me for money."*[381]

Donny recalled that Arturo was wary of others as well. Jerie was with Arturo when he borrowed Lynch's car. A Lynch family member called Arturo asking when he planned on bringing the car back. Arturo responded, *"soon."* After Gatti hung up the phone he turned to Donny and said, *"I paid for that fucking car, I'll bring it back when I'm good and ready."*[382] Jerie felt that after Arturo started making money, he was very leery of friends and family. Arturo told Donny that certain people only called him during their birthdays or Christmas, asking Gatti what he was giving them. He found it hard to believe that people loved him, especially when the phone call involved money. Arturo always had his guard up against being used.

Besides money, Donny believes that there was jealousy over Arturo's career being much more successful than Joe's. Another big issue was girlfriends. According to Donny, Joe and Arturo's girlfriends rarely got along. There always seemed to be disagreements. It appeared as though the girlfriends may have been jealous over the relationship between the two brothers. When Arturo's new girlfriends injected themselves into conversations about money and family, it made matters worse.

Another issue that led to the brothers being pulled apart was their mother Ida. She showed favoritism towards some of her children, just as Giovanni had done. This didn't sit well with Joe's wife Vikki. After trying to make it work for years, they finally had a major falling-out after Joe and Vikki had children of their own.

Arturo's lack of control when drinking also led to friction. One time, both brothers were visiting their mother. Arturo was drinking heavily. Vikki and Laura were there. Joe recalled that Arturo challenged him to a fight. *"Arturo said, 'Maybe you and me can fight. When I win a belt you can defend it with me.' Arturo was drunk and he punched the door. I picked him up and put him through the closet."*[383] Joe stated that although their disputes sometimes led to arguments, such as the closet incident, the brothers never actually swung at each other.

As friction grew between Arturo and Joe, Arturo grew closer to their younger brother Fabrizio. Arturo purchased Fabrizio anything he wanted. There were those who felt that Joe and Arturo's competitive nature placed a wedge between them. Whatever the issue was, it was noticeable by others. Piero Santini saw Joe going to work at his elevator job and he laughed as he told Joe, *"Your brother is making millions and you have to work like a dog."*[384] Joe replied, *"What do you want me to do? Tell him to support me? What do you want me to say?"*[385]

Arturo wouldn't even pay for a hotel room for his brother when he fought. Joe recalled, *"I was at one fight with Vikki, when people asked me what hotel I was staying in. I was ashamed to tell them that I was staying in a Quality Inn because I couldn't afford to stay in the casino hotels. My brother didn't comp me a room or tickets. Everyone was staying in Bally's. So I lied and said I was staying in Caesars in one of the suites. When Vikki and I were headed back to our hotel, we watched to make sure no one was watching where we were going."*[386]

As much as the brothers fought, at the flip of a switch they were friends again. Vikki recalled a time that the brothers weren't talking to each other, and Arturo saw Joe driving past his condo in Weehawken. Arturo flagged him down and invited him to hang out. As quick as the feud began, it would be over. When Vikki first met Arturo, the brothers were inseparable. Even afterwards, when they fought or didn't see each other for months, if they ran into each other, they hugged and talked as though nothing was wrong.

On October 4, 1997 at Caesar's in Atlantic City, Arturo returned to the ring, defending his IBF super featherweight title against former WBC super featherweight champion Gabriel Ruelas. The bout was on the undercard of the Lennox Lewis vs. Andrew Golota WBC heavyweight championship fight. Gatti was originally slated to be the main event, before the heavyweight bout was added. Arturo spoke of being knocked off the headline. *"It doesn't bother me that we were pushed back. It gives us great exposure. We're going to put on a great fight, and being on the same card with Lewis and Golota doesn't bother me at all. It's good for boxing."*[387] Going into the show, all of the attention was on Golota and his low-blow foul punches. Main Events' Dino Duva predicted that the Gatti-Ruelas bout could steal the HBO TVKO televised show.[388]

Arturo's camp opened at West Palm Beach, Florida. Later, the camp moved to Virginia Beach. In Florida, Gatti trained alongside the Main Events-promoted Golota. Arturo sparred NABF super featherweight champion Jesus Chavez. Chavez was fighting on the undercard against Troy Dorsey.

Arturo's behavior was becoming increasingly bizarre and uncontrollable. In the final week of September, only a week before the Ruelas match, Arturo went out on a drinking binge. Joe recalled the incident. *"They found my brother in the park before he fought Ruelas. My brother was 10-pounds overweight the week before. They found him in the park, in Virginia. That's why he cried when he won. My brother got on his knees and cried. He never thought he was going to pull it off. He went on a binge."*[389] Joe's wife Vikki added, *"They found him on a park bench passed out."*[390]

Vikki recalled the night of the Ruelas bout. *"That night we were there. And I was with his fiancé at the time, Laura. We were praying to the gods above, because we said he is not going to be able to handle this. And when Ruelas fights, he hits you like a sledge hammer. If he hits you, you're going."*[391] Vikki explained how they discovered that Arturo was passed out in a park. *"We got the phone call anytime, anything that happened to him. Joe got the phone call."*[392] Vikki recalled that it was not Pat Lynch who called Joe. *"No, Pat would never. The guy who found him called."*[393] The bar owner who found Arturo told Joe, *"Yep, we picked him up. We found him. We didn't know who he was. I brought him back to my bar."*[394]

Gabriel Ruelas, 44-3 (23 KOs), and his brother Rafael both started boxing after stumbling upon Joe Goosen's boxing gym while selling candy door-to-door. Gabriel was 12 and Rafael was 11. Goosen tried to get rid of the brothers, as he only trained professionals, but the Ruelas brothers harassed Goosen until he gave in and trained them. Both brothers would go on to become world champions. Gabriel had won the WBC super featherweight world championship title in September 1994 by winning a unanimous 12-round decision over Jesse James Leija. In a May 1995 title defense, Ruelas stopped Jimmy Garcia in the 11th round. Unfortunately, Garcia died from brain injuries he sustained in the fight. Many boxing insiders felt that since then, Ruelas had not fought with quite the same intensity that he had displayed before defeating Garcia.

Strangely enough, a month before his fight with Garcia, while promoting the fight, Ruelas visited a church in New York City with his wife. Ruelas recalled what happened next, *"Strange, but I lit a candle that day for Gerald McClellan, even though I don't even know him at all. Gerald was still in a coma after being beat up in* the ring, and it just popped in my head. I prayed for him. Who would've thought it would then happen to me?... I had gone in that ring to beat him, but no one goes with the intent to kill. I knew it was not my fault, but I keep feeling it is my fault because I was hitting him. Everyone says, 'Come on, the guy lost 30-pounds, he was weak,' but, no, I still hit him."[395]

Ruelas was born in the mountain village of Jalisco, Mexico. When he took his wife to visit his birthplace, she was shocked at the poverty. She said that Jalisco looked *"like something out of National Geographic."*[396]

Ruelas would later state that he also lost his life in the ring when Jimmy Garcia died. He lost his anger after the tragedy. He believed that anger was needed in order to be successful as a fighter. Ruelas' fighting spirit was not the same. His trainers noticed it during sparring sessions. Ruelas would back off from his sparring partners and not hit them hard.[397] Ruelas lost his title to Azumah Nelson in his very next fight, in December 1995. It had been more than two years since the Garcia fight, and nearly two years since he lost the title. Ruelas was on a three-fight win streak.

Arturo would be Ruelas' first world-class competition since losing his title to Nelson. No one was sure what type of fighter would enter the ring against Arturo.

Gatti, however, was having his own problems. Arturo began training camp weighing 170-pounds. Hector Roca would later state that Arturo was always 6 or 7-pounds overweight two days before most fights. Roca admitted that Arturo was 25-pounds overweight two weeks before the Ruelas fight.[398] Furthermore, as stated, Gatti had gone on a drinking binge, and was found completely passed out on a park bench a week before the Ruelas fight.

Donny Jerie recalled that Hector Roca had no control over Arturo whatsoever. Arturo came and went as he pleased. He didn't fear Roca or respect him at all.

Mario Costa commented, *"In the park, in Virginia Beach, a week before the fight, and they put him in the ring. You do that to a fighter? Even if that's not your son? I don't think so. I don't give a fuck if you're fighting for $10 million dollars. You're not fighting. Pat [Lynch] never did that. If he did that once for Arthur I would never speak a word against him.*[399]

"At the time, people thought that I hated Pat because of the money. I got my own money. I got my own business. All Arturo wanted to do was to be champion. But then when they got him out of here, they

went to New York to Casa Dante. In the limousines, the massage parlors. The champagne, the Pinot Grigio, all that bullshit. And the suites down in Atlantic City. I never got a suite in my life when I went to Atlantic City. Give me a regular room. I come from a totally different world than Pat.

"You see, it's not that I hate Pat. The only reason to me that he's not a good guy, is because he never cancelled a fight. I used to beg, I said, 'Pat, you know that he's not ready. You gotta call HBO and tell them the truth.' Na, he didn't want to fucking call HBO because why is he gonna cancel the fight. Lose all the money. Everything was money. And the last time I seen him I said, 'You know what Pat? You're a real piece of shit.' I told him right straight to his face. He don't give a fuck about the fighter. He don't care. It's only about the money because if he had any conscience he would've called that fight off with Ruelas.

"Pat's the manager, the brother [John Lynch] had power of attorney. How you gonna have the manager and the brother representing the fighter? What is the fighter gonna do against the manager or anybody? I have pulled kids out of fights amateur or pro with Panama. Pro guys for not doing their roadwork. You're not fighting. You got a kid that's doing coke, that goes to camp, disappears from camp. You're gonna let that guy fight? They didn't know where he was a lot of times in camp.

"Pat bought up tickets for Arturo's fights and sold them at a high price, which is why he didn't want to cancel the fights."[400]

It is not uncommon for fighters to experience setbacks while away in training camp preparing for high level fights. The pressure of being away from family and friends, the boredom of camp life while counting the days to a fight against a quality opponent, along with crash dieting can all lead to a fighter acting out of character.

On February 11, 1983, Hector Camacho was in Anchorage, Alaska, where he was supposed to be resting in his hotel room for his nationally televised fight on CBS against John Montes the following day. CBS announcer Tim Ryan recalled that they received a call from one of Camacho's handlers stating that Hector was trying to jump out of a hotel window because he was *"completely out of his mind drug wise."*[401] They somehow calmed Hector down, but they obviously were concerned with how he would perform the following day. Camacho dominated the fight against Montes, knocking him out in the first round. It was as though the previous evening had never occurred.

Don Elbaum, veteran fight promoter, manager, and matchmaker, was asked his thoughts on continuing with a bout after a fighter suffered an alcohol or drug-related episode in training camp. Elbaum felt as long as the fighter had a solid training camp, he did not believe that one or two days of partying would affect the fighters performance. Elbaum did caution, however, that if a fighter was having a poor training camp and was partying excessively, he would recommend canceling the fight for the boxers safety.

When Arturo arrived back in New Jersey from his Virginia Beach training camp, he still was dangerously overweight. Arturo actually used cocaine in front of his brother Joe. When Joe asked Arturo why he was using drugs so close to fight time, Arturo replied that snorting cocaine helped to curb his appetite for food. If Arturo was using cocaine leading up to the fight, he would have had to stop three days prior to the fight due to the prefight urine test, unless he found a way to mask the test. Mike Tyson admitted that he would cheat the urine test process by using a device called a Whizzinator.[402] Other fighters were known to put "clean" urine in a condom or drink large amounts of vinegar.

On September 30, three days before the weigh-in, Arturo was in a wetsuit sweating off the extra pounds. He worked out in a portable ring and gym set up in Convention Hall. In the stifling heat, Arturo sparred, hit the heavybag, pumped out sit-ups, and jumped rope. Arturo was forced to restrict his usual training diet even further to cut the extra pounds he was carrying. Arturo planned on moving up in weight after the fight.

During an interview, Arturo admitted that he was having a difficult time bringing his weight down. He joked that he was surprised he hadn't grown feathers with all the chicken he was forced to eat. Arturo was aware that Ruelas wanted to turn the bout into a brawl. Gatti was confident that he could win the fight by either boxing or brawling.[403]

Ruelas was motivated for the fight. He needed a challenging opponent like Arturo. Ruelas was looking forward to a war.[404] Dino Duva joked that Arturo was always in a good fight, even when shadowboxing.[405] Arturo acknowledged that fans expected a war when he fought.[406]

Ruelas was asked by reporters if the ring death of Jimmy Garcia was still haunting him. Ruelas had claimed that he saw Garcia's face during his loss to Azumah Nelson. Ruelas now stated that he was suffering from diarrhea and a fever leading up to the Nelson match.[407]

Ruelas was a 3-1 underdog. The former WBC champ was considered an overachiever in his hometown of Jalisco, Mexico. Ruelas believed that everyone thought he'd be working in a car-wash because he didn't graduate from school. Ruelas had been waiting anxiously for another opportunity at a championship.[408] The *Press of Atlantic City* predicted a Gatti victory by decision.

Hector Roca was not happy with Arturo's brawling style. He felt that Gatti made things harder on himself when he brawled. Roca believed that Arturo brawled because he was trying to please the fans, not because he needed to fight that way to win.[409]

At the weigh-in, Arturo stripped for the scale. He took off his diamond earrings, gold necklace, and gold-coin-embedded ring that his brother Joe had bought him. He left his jewelry in his bag. Arturo and Ruelas both weighed in at 130-pounds. When Arturo finished weighing-in, he looked in his bag for his jewelry, but it was gone. The jewelry never was recovered, and the thief never identified.

Joe had three gold-coin rings made. One for himself and one each for Arturo and Fabrizio. Joe hadn't given Fabrizio his ring yet because he was too young. After Arturo's ring was stolen, Joe gave him Fabrizio's ring. The gold-coin ring wasn't the only jewelry that Joe bought for Arturo. Vikki had purchased Joe a custom, hand-crafted pair of gold-and-diamond boxing gloves. When Arturo saw the gloves he said, *"I love them."* Vikki went back to Pennsylvania, where she had purchased the first pair, and had another pair made.

Arturo was led into the ring by his brother Joe, who was holding Arturo's IBF championship belt over his head. Walking next to Joe were Carl Moretti and Pat Lynch. Arturo's walk-out song was "I'll Be Missing You," by Puff Daddy. Arturo selected the song as a dedication to his good friend Russell, who recently had passed away. Walking behind Arturo were Mikey Red and John Capone. Sitting at ringside were Arturo's mother Ida and his stepfather Gerardo Di Francesco.

In an interview before the match, Arturo avowed, *"If the war is in me, I'll fight the war. I can adapt to whatever style Ruelas wants to use."*[410] In Gatti's corner were Roca, Souza, and Wareing. Gatti held a ½-inch height advantage over the 5'7" Ruelas, but their reach was equal at 68 inches. When he was reweighed on the day of the fight, Arturo had rehydrated 16-pounds to 146. Ruelas gained 15½-pounds to 145½.

Gatti started off the fight behind his jab, blocking many of Ruelas' wide swings. Halfway through the 1st round, Arturo landed his signature hook. Gabriel took the punch well and responded with a hook to the body. Both fighters scored solid head shots as Roca yelled for Gatti to attack the body first. Arturo appeared the stronger of the two, but Ruelas was a little sharper defensively.

Forty-five seconds into the 2nd round, Ruelas landed a solid uppercut. Arturo landed his own uppercut as both fighters seemed comfortable working on the inside. Gabriel seemed to be landing more, and was quicker, but Arturo's punches were more powerful. With a little over a minute remaining in the session, Gatti landed a quick, well-timed left hook that jarred Ruelas' head. Gabriel stood his ground and traded. Arturo landed a right hand-left hook combo. Both fighters traded as they moved to the center of the ring. Gabriel started giving ground as he nodded to Gatti to bring it on. Arturo trapped Ruelas against the ropes and worked the body while he looked for opportunities to land head shots. Gabriel was looking to counter. The round came to a close.

Ruelas' trainer, Joe Goosen, instructed his boxer to keep his right hand up to avoid being hit by Arturo's hook. Goosen cautioned Gabriel to avoid brawling. Goosen also counseled Ruelas not to sit on the ropes. Roca instructed Arturo to stay low.

Both fighters started the 3rd round trading on the inside. It was high quality back and forth combat. Halfway through the round, Arturo effectively utilized his jab. With a little under a minute remaining, both men landed solid left hooks. Ruelas came back with a short right to the body, a right and left hook to the head and a hook to the body that was several inches below the beltline. Referee Benjy Esteves warned Gabriel to keep his punches up. Both fighters traded power shots for the remainder of the round. Arturo's blows snapped Ruelas' head back.

Roca advised Arturo to use his jab and not punch wide. Roca also instructed Gatti not to look for the knockout. Goosen counseled Ruelas to box.

Early in the 4th, Arturo landed a solid combination, punctuated by a straight right that knocked Gabriel back. Arturo started getting a rhythm going, landing jab after jab. Ruelas landed a solid uppercut and a straight right that earned Arturo's attention. Gabriel drove Arturo to the ropes, nailing his head and body. Ruelas kept pounding away, forcing Gatti onto the ropes again, but Arturo spun his way out and turned Gabriel towards the ropes. Both fighters swung freely, with Arturo landing sharp left hooks to the body and head.

Ruelas landed flush uppercuts, but Gatti answered with power shots of his own. Gabriel turned Gatti back to the ropes and landed a flush right uppercut. Ruelas landed several body shots, and followed with a left uppercut that caught Arturo completely by surprise, buckling his knees. Gabriel poured punches in from all angles, with one straying low. Arturo stumbled back to the center of the ring. Ruelas landed a hard right uppercut. The punch seemed to wake Gatti up, as Arturo fired back with several hard blows. The crowd roared with approval as the bell sounded. Lampley exclaimed, *"What a battle!"* Compubox had Ruelas landing 44 power shots in the round.

In Arturo's corner, Roca screamed for Gatti not to brawl with Ruelas. Arturo complained that he hurt his right hand. Roca replied that he knew that Gatti injured his hand. Roca advised Arturo to use his jab and box. Roca implored Gatti not to stand in front of Ruelas. He wanted Arturo to box and move.

Both boxers started the 5th round right where they left off, with furious close quarter combat. Ruelas landed a flush hook on Arturo's jaw. He followed with uppercuts and hooks. Gabriel picked Arturo's head up with a right uppercut. Ruelas landed another uppercut that twisted Gatti's head. Ruelas kept punching, but Gatti countered with a perfectly timed left hook. Still, Ruelas kept coming, punching Gatti from one side of the ring to the other. The blood thirsty crowd roared with approval as the two gladiators performing for them gave it their all.

Arturo later recalled the moment, *"It's when I'm hurt or I'm in trouble, and when I know I'm in trouble, I see everything and I hear all the crowd. I see my trainer. I see my mom at ringside and looking at that, you know, it inspires me a lot. It kind of wakes me up."*[411]

Gatti turned Ruelas around and started bombing away with body and head shots. Arturo later explained why he disregarded Roca's advice to box. *"My life is on the line, like people got to understand that. Cause I got hit a lot, but I got to do what it takes to win the fight."*[412] The fighters continued to unload on each other. Arturo landed a ripping right uppercut. Esteves broke both fighters. Jim Lampley commented that although it was only a minute into the round, the action was vicious.

Both fighters jockeyed for position on the inside, using their legs, arms and heads. Arturo landed another head-snapping uppercut. Ruelas replied by smiling and clapping his gloves onto his chest in a gesture that indicated, "I can take it; bring it on." Gabriel landed hard left hooks and two solid uppercuts that hurt Gatti again. Arturo came right back with his own power shots. The ebb and flow continued. Arturo's left eye was swollen and bleeding. Larry Merchant commented that Ruelas looked a hair stronger than Arturo. He felt that the small edge in strength might help Ruelas weather the storm.

Gatti attacked the midsection. He followed with a hook and right cross. Just as Rafael was in the process of firing a right uppercut, Arturo landed another perfectly timed left hook that dropped Ruelas as though the floor had collapsed underneath him. His head violently slammed against the rings canvas covered floorboards. The crowd stood and cheered as Gatti jogged to a neutral corner.

Ruelas was up at the count of 8, but he stumbled back slightly to the ropes. Esteves waived the fight off at the 2:22 mark of the 5th round. Esteves recalled the stoppage. *"Gabe [Ruelas] was as tough as nails, but he was starting to connect on Arturo, and Arturo just put him on his seat. Arturo reminded me of Floyd Mayweather. Not his style, but Floyd Mayweather is the kind of fighter that you think you got him and he puts it into another gear. And Gatti was the same way. He just put it up a notch. No matter how much it took to get it back. He did that in the Ruelas fight."*[413]

Arturo fell to his knees with his gloves around his head in exhausted relief. Gatti was completely spent as his handlers raised him upright. Pernell Whitaker jumped into the ring to congratulate the champion. Arturo's mother and stepfather climbed up onto the ring apron, where they hugged the winner. Larry Merchant spoke of Arturo's amazing ability to recover. He stated that Gatti had a bottomless well of willpower that just couldn't be stopped.

Arturo later reflected on the Ruelas match. *"I remember I had so much trouble making weight for that fight. I lost like 15-pounds in two weeks for that fight. He was hurting me every time he punched me; my eardrum, my jaw. I wasn't even thinking of the [junior lightweight] title during that fight. I was just thinking, 'How the heck am I going to get through this?' I couldn't believe the way I ended it, out of nowhere. My left hook is magic."*[414]

Arturo was raised into the air by his brother Joe. Joe told Arturo that he loved him. Ruelas' corner was vehemently complaining to Commissioner Larry Hazzard, apparently upset with the stoppage. As he was announced the winner, Arturo was raised into the air again by Joe, this time with his IBF belt in his arms. Ruelas, after spending time sitting on a stool recovering, walked to the center of the ring where he hugged Arturo.

In addition to the swelling under Arturo's left eye, his mouth was cut and swollen. In the post-fight interview, Arturo admitted that he had been hurt in the 4th round, that Ruelas was very strong, and that fighting Gabe took a lot out of him.

Merchant asked Ruelas if the stoppage was too quick. Ruelas admitted that he was hurt. He agreed with the referee's decision to end the bout. Ruelas congratulated Arturo on being a great champion. Merchant went back to Gatti and pressed him in regards to an Angel Manfredy fight. Arturo said that he would only fight Manfredy if it were a winner-take-all bout.

The Gatti-Ruelas fight would be named *The Ring* magazine's "Fight of the Year" for 1997. Gatti later stated that Ruelas took a lot out of him right from the 1st round.

After the fighters exited the ring, they were interviewed again. Ruelas said that when he had Arturo hurt in the 3rd round, he momentarily froze, thinking of the Jimmy Garcia match. Ruelas knew he had Arturo in serious trouble at one point, but he claimed that he saw a flash that made him stop and lose his focus.[415]

Arturo had expected a tough fight. He absorbed many uppercuts, but he figured he was better off staying in close than fighting from the outside. Arturo admitted that he was hurt during the match. He was hurt so much that he was forced to keep his hands together.[416]

At the post-fight press conference, Ruelas was advised that Arturo had been taken to the hospital with a cauliflower ear injury which gave him equilibrium problems during the match. Ruelas sent his prayers to Arturo.[417]

Dan Goosen felt that the bout displayed the typical Arturo Gatti at his best. Arturo got hit with some great shots and had the announcers and crowd thinking the worst, but somehow, someway, he withstood it all and came back to have his hand raised in another memorable fight which ended in another KO victory.

Booking agent Johnny Bos cautioned that Arturo needed to move up in weight. He predicted that Arturo wouldn't last five more years if he kept draining himself to make 130-pounds. Bos believed that when boxers struggle to make the weight, they are already exhausted by the time they enter the ring. He felt that this caused fighters like Gatti to load up with Hail Mary punches to try to end the fight quickly. Bos opined that Arturo might be the type of fighter who gets bored boxing carefully, which is why he turned some of his fights into brawls. Bos added that Arturo couldn't quite control his emotions during contests. He believed that if Arturo did box more he might not be so popular. Bos felt that Arturo might be the most exciting boxer in the sport, because he always finds a way to win even if his eyes are swollen shut. The fact that Arturo constantly landed a punch, seemingly out of nowhere, whenever he was in serious trouble, proved that it was no accident or lucky punch.[418]

Teddy Atlas commented on Arturo's brawling style. He felt that Arturo was the kind of fighter who gave fans a lot of pleasure, but possibly at the expense of his career longevity. Atlas added that Gatti reminded him of Matthew Saad Muhammad. Saad Muhammad's career ended earlier than it should have as a result of his brawling style. Atlas stated that with every life-or-death victory, a fighter loses something. Atlas cautioned that when the Gatti type of fighter loses his ability, it happens overnight. He pointed to Saad Muhammad, who was as game and tough as they came, and then suddenly, one day, he was a shadow of himself. Atlas felt that Arturo was aware of the fact that his brawling style was damaging him physically, but it was human nature to think of the immediate rewards first.[419]

Arturo had invited Mario Costa to the Ruelas fight. Costa recalled the event. *"Arthur said to me, 'I want you to come to my dressing room.' I said, 'Arthur, I can't go to your dressing room. Everybody looks at me funny. I don't want to go there, 'cause I'm like an outsider.' 'No, I want you to come.' So now I go to the Ruelas fight and they're all looking at me funny. They didn't want me to be there. So I went to the dressing room. I went to the ring. They went to the ring. He fought and then we went back. I'm walking with him to the dressing room. That's the last time I was really close to Arthur in a fight like that. And 'cause then I saw how Pat was. How everybody was towards me. I said, 'Listen, I don't want to be bothered with these people. They are crazy. These people are not here for you. These people are up to something else.' I could sense that.*

"So I'm walking back with him to the dressing room. He's not even looking at me. I'm not looking at him. He's got the hood on and he won the fight. And I'm walking and I'm talking to him. And I'm looking forward and he's looking forward. And I said, 'Arthur what the fuck is wrong with you? Why did you stay in front of this guy and trade punches with this guy, when you know Ruelas is a puncher?' I said, 'What the fuck is your problem? Did you do your road work? Did you run? Arthur, why would you stay flat footed, punching with this guy? You see this guy was a killer.' He goes to me, 'Mario, look at my face. Is my face ok?' I said, 'Look at me.' And he turned

around and he looked. He thought that his face was distorted. That's how hard Ruelas hit him. Arthur was out. He thought his face was fucked up. He looked at me like this [picking face up] and I looked and he actually was ok. But he must have got hit so hard from Ruelas that he thought his face was fucked up. And after that, I never went to the dressing room again."[420]

When interviewed years later, Ruelas recalled, *"I was supposed to get a rematch, but it never happened for some reason... [Gatti] later said he had never been hit harder than in our fight and that was a great compliment, him saying that."*[421]

When Arturo was asked about his amazing wars, he laughed at how tough his fights were. While Gatti was participating in the fights, they didn't seem as violent as when he watched them later on TV. Pat Lynch admitted that watching Arturo fight was not easy.

Joe Gatti discussed how he felt watching his brother's dramatic wars. *"People go, 'Oh, he was in such a great fight,' and I say, 'Yeah, for you guys it's a great fight. But not for me. This is my blood.' I was there at a lot of his fights with tears."*[422] Despite all of the punishment, Arturo was not worried about permanent physical damage.[423]

Arturo displayed a carefree attitude towards the punishment he was receiving in the boxing ring. In a way, he resembled Audie Murphy. Murphy lost his mother at the age of 16. Murphy entered the military the next year, at age 17, with a forged letter from his sister claiming he was 18. Murphy displayed the same attitude that Arturo did when confronted with danger. Both men seemed to mock life-threatening danger and death. Murphy was legendary for standing in battle and taking on the enemy while bullets flew past his head, while others ran and ducked for cover. He fearlessly remained at his post, disregarding the bullets.

Although Arturo wasn't a war hero, he did display the same warrior-like attitude that Murphy did. Murphy spoke of his mother's passing. *"When she passed away, she took something of me with her. It seems I've been searching for it ever since."*[424] Is it possible that Arturo felt the same way about his deceased father?

After the Ruelas win, Arturo partied in Mario Costa's Ringside Lounge with his friend, Jayson Williams, of the New Jersey Nets basketball team. Williams had a history of cocaine and alcohol abuse. Mario Costa recalled that both men lived up to their reputations during the victory celebration. The two partied on the second floor of his club, which was closed to the public. Williams would break his leg in 1999 and never play in the NBA again. In 2002, Williams was involved in the accidental shooting death of his limousine driver, Costas Christofi. He later plead guilty to aggravated assault. He also had been found guilty of trying to cover up the incident.

Chapter 14
Manfredy

After the Ruelas win, Arturo became an overnight star. Everyone wanted to hang out with the champ. His newfound status was accompanied by the pressures that stardom brought with it. Trusting people became more difficult. Mikey Red felt that sometimes Arturo took out this stress on his close friends. He recalled that Arturo usually treated outsiders better than he did his friends. Arturo expected his friends and family to understand his open, unfiltered personality.

Donny Jerie recalled that everyone wanted to walk Arturo into the ring. John Capone was always bothering Arturo to walk into the ring with him. Jerie never walked Arturo into the ring. Donny stated that Arturo told him, *"You, you're my boy. You don't need to walk in the ring with me."* Donny continued, *"Gatti was the kind of person, when we'd hang out, he just wanted to be with his friend. In the go-go club he didn't want to be bothered taking pictures. He just wanted to be a regular dude sometimes. As he started getting bigger, fans would yell, 'Yo Gatti, yo Gatti, autograph, autograph,' and he would give autographs. Some people would start to cause trouble with him because of who he was. He was the same person as when he first started but the limelight got bigger."*[425]

Donny was an accomplished break dancer and Arturo enjoyed when he danced at the clubs. Arturo would help form a circle around Donny. Arturo was very good at dancing but not break dancing. Arturo would joke with the vertically-challenged Donny by telling him to drop his weight to 100-pounds. Arturo laughingly told Donny that he would help him become a horse jockey if he lost the weight.

Because Donny was so close to Arturo, he was able to ask him questions that no one else could. Donny wondered if Arturo was nervous before he fought. Donny recalled asking Arturo, *"I said, 'Man, I get butterflies when you're fighting. Do you get nervous?' He said, 'Come on, of course I get nervous. I get over the nervous feeling because I want to fight. I'm ready to go. After the training and everything I want to get in there.' And the best thing about it. That he said that he loved more than anything, was walking out with the music and everybody going crazy. He used to love that."*[426]

Angel Manfredy, with pressure from HBO, was selected as Arturo's next opponent. Arturo once again was caught using cocaine. This time, prior to starting his training camp for Manfredy. He was caught in Montreal by his brother-in-law, Rocco Crispo, when Crispo opened the door to a limo that Arturo was sitting in.[427]

Against Hector Roca's wishes, training camp was again set up in Virginia Beach. Arturo's personal problems continued. John Capone once again accompanied Arturo to camp.

On December 20, while supposedly in training for the Manfredy fight, Arturo was again arrested for driving while under the influence of alcohol. The arrest was only 28 days before the Manfredy fight. It was his third arrest for drinking and driving in less than two years.

Joe again questioned why Arturo's manager didn't monitor him more closely. Joe couldn't understand why people who were supposed to be chaperoning Arturo were allowing him to drive after drinking. *"Pat partied with him. He got his DWI with Pat."*[428] Joe continued, *"You and me drink, I'm a fighter. A professional athlete. Me and you drink instead of training? Instead of taking a cab, you decided on driving? Then he lost his license."*[429]

The drunk driving charge would cost him his license for several years. Arturo was ordered to attend the Virginia Alcohol Safety Action Program, also known as VASAP, as part of his conviction. Arturo failed to attend the substance abuse counseling program and a warrant was issued for his arrest. The warrant was later purged.

Joe described hanging out with Lynch. *"Well, at first we hung out after the fight. There was always a party. The best thing for Pat was not the fight, it was after the fight. You know, the victory party."*[430] Al Cole, when asked about Lynch, said that Pat was young and inexperienced when he got started in boxing. The fact that he was close in age to the fighters likely led him to feel comfortable hanging out with them.

On January 14, three days before the Manfredy fight, *Press of Atlantic City* reporter David Weinberg visited Arturo at the Atlantic City PAL. The fight was being billed "To Hell and Back." The billing mirrored the way Gatti was living his life.

Arturo no longer needed the rubber sweat suit, because the non-title fight was a weight class higher. He was now wearing black spandex and a white T-shirt. Arturo reported to his Virginia Beach training camp ten weeks prior weighing only 145-pounds. He normally would go into camp weighing 160 or more. He weighed 150 just two weeks before the Manfredy fight. That meant he actually gained 5-pounds in his first eight weeks in camp. With two days left until the weigh-in, Gatti weighed 138, 3-pounds over the contracted weight. Arturo said that he felt great both mentally and physically. Gatti added that he was not going to look for a war. He was confident that he could outbox Manfredy.[431]

Hector Roca felt that the beatings Arturo took in some of his previous fights finally made him realize that he needed to prepare properly for his fights. Roca added that being 3-pounds overweight was a lot better than twenty. Roca felt that the Manfredy training camp was the best camp Arturo ever had. He said that Gatti worked like a true professional and was in bed by 7:30 or 8 p.m. Roca confessed that for the first time he could go to sleep at 9 p.m. and not have to worry about what Arturo was doing. Hector purposely omitted Arturo's drinking episodes during camp, when interviewed, to protect his fighter's image. Roca warned Arturo that if he continued brawling the way he was, he would be lucky if he lasted two or three more fights, because his reflexes would be gone.[432]

Two days before the fight, Arturo was back in the Atlantic City PAL working out, this time with a rubber sweat suit on. Arturo again was asked about his weight. He said that mentally he had a tough time making the prior 130-pound limit. Gatti admitted that he did not diet properly and it showed in his previous performances. Arturo confessed he was completely dried out in the Ruelas fight, but he could see that Ruelas was the same way. Gatti stated that he would never enter the ring if he felt weak, and there never would be enough money offered for him to go into the ring knowing he would lose a bout.[433]

Manfredy's trainer, John Taylor, was asked if he was concerned about Arturo's usual post-scale weight gain. Taylor wasn't concerned, because the weight gain wouldn't be muscle, it would be liquid that was sitting in Gatti's stomach.[434] Manfredy also believed that Arturo's weight gain wouldn't matter, because he felt that he was bigger and stronger than Arturo.[435]

Gatti would gross $1.1 million, while Manfredy would take home $200,000. Manfredy finally was getting his shot at Arturo. Although it was a non-title bout for both champions, Angel was hopeful a win over Gatti would propel him into "big money" bouts. Manfredy was known as a tough fighter with a limited amateur background.

Angel, who was from East Chicago, Indiana, said that he had been stalking Arturo for two years because he knew that the only way he could establish himself was by beating Gatti. Manfredy submitted to all of Arturo's demands to make the fight; including the weight limit and the money. Angel stated that Arturo may be getting a million dollars, but he also was going to get a butt whipping.[436] Manfredy spoke of his 13 car accidents, one that left him with 235 stitches on his face. Angel admitted that the accidents occurred while he was going through a wild time in his life.[437]

Manfredy wished that the IBF and WBU titles that Arturo and he held would have been at stake. Angel felt that if Arturo was a true champion he would have put his belt on the line. However, Gatti was done forever with the 130-pound weight class and would relinquish his title.[438]

The British *Boxing News* magazine ran an article titled, "Angel Could Be Real Devil Against Gatti." The article alluded to the fact that Manfredy's precision punching, coupled with Arturo's recent wars, could lead to Angel being in the right place at the right time for an upset. British referee Mickey Vann worked the Manfredy-Jorge Paez fight, watching Angel stop Paez. Vann commented that Manfredy was brilliant in the fight.[439]

Manfredy's co-manager, Sam Colonna, revealed that the gameplan they were working on was speed and body shots. Colonna felt that many of the fighters that fought Gatti tried to go for his chin instead of his body. Colonna believed that Angel punched like a middleweight. He also pointed out that Manfredy, though shorter, had a longer reach.[440]

Hector Roca felt that Gatti had the edge, that Arturo could outbox or outbrawl Manfredy. Roca did caution that Angel was a fast fighter who needed to be slowed down. Roca admitted that Arturo was not fully focused for the Ruelas fight because he was 17-pounds overweight two weeks before that fight.[441]

Arturo spoke of his mindset going into the Manfredy battle. He stated that his defense was his offense. Gatti felt that he got hit much more when he tried to box as opposed to when he brawled.[442] Arturo felt that his style mirrored that of Aaron Pryor because, like Pryor, even though sometimes he got caught with punches, he kept coming forward. Arturo felt that his willpower was the biggest reason why he was winning his fights. Gatti admitted that he needed to stop making stupid decisions in his personal life, but he failed to elaborate on the statement.[443] While Arturo was being interviewed, he was wearing the large gold glove charm that Vikki had a jeweler custom make for him.

As fight night approached, Manfredy sounded confident. Angel revealed that ever since he first saw Arturo fight, he knew that Gatti was the perfect style for him. He did admit, however, that fighting Arturo would be a challenge. Manfredy believed that defeating Gatti would propel him into the elite class of boxing. He suspected that Arturo was not putting his title on the line as an insurance policy against a loss.[444]

HBO's Lou DiBella felt that Manfredy had a lot of pizzazz. DiBella believed that Angel was high on the list of up-and-coming fighters. He felt that both Gatti and Manfredy had similar styles, and both gave their all in each and every fight.[445]

At the January 16 weigh-in, Manfredy weighed 135-pounds, but Arturo was overweight. Angel's handlers refused to let Gatti slide on the few ounces. They forced him to strip naked to make the 135-pound limit. Manfredy remarked that Arturo looked much smaller than him at the weigh-in. He questioned whether Arturo could handle the pressure he would bring.[446]

Lou Duva was looking forward to the battle. He had two fighters competing on the undercard, but he would not work either corner, because he didn't want to miss the Gatti-Manfredy bout.[447]

Angel promised that the fight would not go the distance. He commented that Arturo's previous, hand-picked opponents all had hurt Gatti. He believed that he punched harder than all of Arturo's previous opponents.[448] Arturo responded by stating that he had the heart of a champion. He looked forward to getting in the ring with Manfredy, who was talking a lot.[449] Hector Roca revealed that Gatti's game plan was to alternate between boxing and in-fighting. Roca felt that Angel would try to box, which would force Arturo to *"be the tough guy."*[450]

The *Press of Atlantic City* was predicting a 9th round TKO victory for Gatti. It appeared that the winner of the bout would be in line for a match against Prince Nassem Hamed. Arturo felt that Hamed was *"nothing but a clown who is well-paid."*[451]

Gatti was 1½-inches taller than Manfredy, but Angel had a one inch reach advantage. Arturo was two years older than the 23-year-old Manfredy. After the weigh-in, Arturo was asked what weight he might hydrate up to, he responded, *"I don't want to scare nobody. I'm going to try to keep it as low as I can."*[452] Gatti only hydrated up to 146-pounds. Manfredy gained 7-pounds to 142.

Three-and-a-half weeks before the match, Angel had suffered an injury to his left ribcage. He worked through the injury because he was making a career-high purse.

Joe recalled that Arturo was partying all the time leading up to the

Manfredy match. He felt that those close to Arturo did not try hard enough to stop him from self-destructing. Joe explained that Arturo picked up his heavy partying habits in New Jersey.[453] Joe added that Arturo did not party much in Canada. *"No, he was too young. He was still young and he barely drank with me. We were never drinkers. I did as I got older, but I was never a drinker like I gotta go drink."*[454]

Lisette Lynch, Pat's wife, spoke of Arturo being an animal inside the ring, but outside the ring he was funny and had a big heart. She added that her children called him uncle Arthur, and he treated her children as though they were his own.[455] Lisette spoke of how difficult it was to watch Arturo in action. A week before the second Tracy Patterson fight, she could hardly eat. When at the fights, her friends had to hold her down in her seat.[456]

Joe spoke of his younger brother to the *Newark Star Ledger*. *"I was feeling alone because Arturo was in camp so much and I couldn't be there. Manfredy is a good fighter, but once he feels my brother's power, he'll wish he didn't take the fight. It ain't going past five rounds."*[457] Joe also spoke of Arturo earning his first million dollar purse. *"He's a superstar now, and he's almost at the top of the hill. He hasn't changed because he is well known. He's the same person he was when he was coming up. The only difference is he wears more jewelry. He'll make it to the next level because he's hungry."*[458]

Dino Duva believed that every fight Arturo partook in was risky because of the way he fought. Duva admitted that Arturo wanted to fight the toughest fights, and Manfredy was one of them. Duva added that Gatti was making $1 million for this fight because the competition was tough.[459]

Manfredy didn't believe that Arturo could pull out a miraculous comeback against him like he did against Ruelas and Wilson Rodriguez.[460] Prior to signing for the match, Angel continuously appeared at Arturo's fights and called Gatti out to fight him. Arturo got tired of hearing Manfredy's mouth, as did Arturo's friends. As Arturo explained, *"It really bothered me that my friends started saying, 'Why don't you fight this guy that keeps calling you out?'"*[461]

On January 17, 1998, the fight that HBO kept pushing for finally took place at Convention Hall in Atlantic City. Arturo "Thunder" Gatti and his team had no plans or desire to fight Angel "El Diablo" Manfredy. Manfredy was below Gatti in stature. Pat Lynch summed it up best when he said that they did not need to fight Manfredy.[462]

The all-risk, no-reward situation, took a one-hundred-eighty degree turn when HBO offered Arturo $1.1 million dollars to fight Manfredy. It was by far Arturo's largest payday to date. HBO wanted the match, and they showed it with their pocketbook.

Arturo shadow boxed in his dressing room as his brother Joe, Hector Roca, Pat Lynch, John Capone, Bob Wareing, Mike Skowronski and actor Mickey Rourke cheered him on. While Arturo was shadow boxing, he watched the monitor, which showed HBO's prefight segment.

During the segment, *Boston Globe* reporter Ron Borges spoke of Gatti's give-and-take style, and that Arturo was a flawed fighter that overcame his deficiencies during his life-and-death battles. The dramatic comebacks thrilled his fans. Borges felt that Gatti eventually would pay a high price for his brawling style. He predicted that the same crowd that was hollering Gatti's name during his wins would sit silently by when Arturo finally got knocked out.[463]

Borges used the word "flawed" twice in his description of Arturo's fighting style. One can only imagine what was going through Arturo's mind as he heard those words. It was words such as "flawed" and "C-level fighter" that seared through Gatti's psyche and tormented him throughout his career. Those words stung harder than any punch he received. Mikey Red recalled, *"It would bring Arturo down when people would say he was 'a tough guy' but that he was not an elite fighter."*[464] Arturo was still watching the monitor as it played a tape of him expressing how pleased he was, after his fights, when fans would congratulate him on being involved in the greatest fight they had ever seen. Arturo added that he had a warrior reputation to uphold.[465]

Jim Lampley asked Larry Merchant what he thought of Borges' comments on Arturo paying too high a price with his slugging style, and possibly being too exciting for his own good. Merchant admitted that he was one of the fans who loved watching Gatti fight. Merchant likened Arturo to a comet that streaks across the sky for a week. He added that the streaking comet was much more exciting than a fixed star. Merchant surmised that there was no way of knowing if Gatti would have a short career. He reminded viewers that Henry Armstrong, Carmen Basilio and Tommy Hearns all had long, great careers. Merchant called Gatti's career the *"The Perils of Arturo."* He stated that he, like millions of others, was looking forward to seeing Gatti's exciting career as it unfolded.

Manfredy entered the ring wearing his customary red devil mask. El Diablo's record going into the match was 22-2-1 (18 KOs). There were two possible reasons that Arturo's team felt confident accepting the Manfredy fight. The first was the fact that Wilson Rodriguez had dropped Manfredy in their February 1997 bout, although Manfredy won that fight rather easily on points. The second reason was Angel's performance against David Toledo in March of 1996. Although Manfredy was the aggressor in the match, landing the heavier punches, he displayed little head movement, which allowed Toledo to have a high connect rate. Angel came in with his head on several occasions during the bout, which was ruled a no-contest due to cuts Toledo received from a clash of heads. No doubt, Arturo's team felt that if Gatti could land the punches that Toledo did, he could knock Manfredy out.

Joe recalled the Toledo-Manfredy match. *"Toledo was beating him. He was faster than Manfredy, until he got cut."*[466] Vikki Gatti added, *"Toledo was ahead. So when Arturo got the fight we were like, Arturo is gonna whip him."*[467] Actually, two of the three judges had Manfredy winning by a point 48-47, while the third judge had Toledo winning 48-47 at the time the bout was stopped.

Gatti was much stronger than Toledo when they had sparred, and his team hoped this would help make for a rather easy victory. Another plus for Team Gatti was the fact that Manfredy had a limited amateur background. Arturo had a vast amount of overall experience compared to Angel. The only fighters in common between the pair were Calvin Grove and Wilson Rodriguez, whom they both beat.

Arturo made his way into the ring at Boardwalk Hall with his brother Joe, Pat Lynch, Hector Roca, Mikey "Red" Skowronski, John Capone and many others. *Rocky's* "Eye of the Tiger" blared through the speakers as he passed through the crowd of 4,267 screaming fans.

When Arturo entered the ring, he bounced around to get a feel for the canvas' softness. He then hugged his brother Joe and kissed him on the lips. In certain sections of Italy and the Mediterranean, family members kissing each other on the lips is a common cultural practice.

Main Events and Peltz Boxing co-promoted the event. Arturo came into the fight with a record of 29-1 (24 KOs). Although both Arturo and Manfredy held titles, they were both held at 130, and would not be on the line. Manfredy held the WBU junior lightweight championship, which was not considered to be one of the major belts.

Main Events' Dino Duva and Carl Moretti were in the ring with Arturo. When the ring announcer, Michael Buffer, announced Manfredy, the crowd roundly booed. As soon as Buffer finished announcing Angel the crowd converted its boos into a cheering crescendo as Buffer announced Arturo. After announcing both fighters, the contestants were called to the center of the ring by referee Wayne Hedgepeth. Arturo started to the center and then stopped, turned around, and headed back to his corner to get one more security hug from his brother Joe. The Arturo fanbase started chanting, *"Gatti!, Gatti!, Gatti!"* even before the opening bell rang.

The opening round started with both fighters trading jabs. Both boxers had their moments. With 14 seconds remaining in the 1st round, Manfredy landed a thudding right hand that opened a deep gash over Arturo's left eyelid. The cut was a terrible injury to suffer in the opening session of a 10-round fight. As blood flowed from the wound, Arturo fully understood the handicap the injury presented.

As Gatti sat on his stool after the round, he lamented, *"Mother fucker!"* Bob Wareing tried to calm Arturo down by telling him that the eye was fine. Joe Souza cleaned the area around the eye and began treating the cut. Roca warned Arturo to keep his chin down.

Arturo started the 2nd trying to take command. A little over a minute into the round, Manfredy landed another hard right hand over Arturo's left. Arturo unloaded body shots and hooks upstairs but Manfredy's tight defense blocked the blows. With 46 seconds remaining in the round, Angel dug two crisp shots to the body followed by a short right hook that pushed Arturo backwards. Manfredy ripped a left uppercut-overhand right combo as Gatti retreated to the ropes. Arturo finished the round by landing two solid body blows. He wiped his cut eyelid as he walked back to his corner.

Roca instructed Gatti to finish with his left hook. He asked for Arturo to step in-and-out and to stop standing in front of Manfredy. In Angel's corner, trainer Sam Colonna reminded Manfredy to use his one-twos and finish with hooks. Colonna also asked for more lateral movement.

As the 3rd round began, Arturo bounced around on his feet while Manfredy, as he had done the first two previous rounds, wasted no energy as he walked Arturo down. Angel had his balance set to let loose power shots at any moment. Thirty seconds in, Manfredy jarred Gatti with a right cross-left hook combo. Angel landed several more solid rights. Gatti tried to establish the jab but Angel kept slipping the punches. Arturo tried a hard left hook but Manfredy slipped his head just prior to the blow's impact. The shot barely grazed off the top of Angel's clean-shaven head.

Manfredy utilized his left arm, outstretched, to keep Gatti at bay. With 1:07 remaining, Angel and Arturo threw left hooks at the same time. Gatti's missed wide. Manfredy's landed flush, dropping Arturo onto his side. Gatti stumbled to his feet at the count of four, jumping up and down trying to recirculate blood through his legs.

Manfredy landed a variety of punches on the forward-charging Arturo. Gatti responded with several hard rights and lefts as the bell rang. Manfredy looked bewildered at Arturo's resiliency. In an act of defiance, Arturo stuck his tongue out at Angel as he walked back to his corner.

Roca reminded Gatti not to drop his hands. He also asked Arturo not to be so wild. Colonna advised Manfredy to throw right hands up the middle.

During the first minute of the 4th, Arturo dug several body shots deep into Manfredy's ribcage. Manfredy winced from the punches. Apparently, Gatti's team did not do their homework. If the broadcast team of Lampley and Merchant knew about Manfredy's damaged ribcage, why didn't Gatti's people know? If they did know, why hadn't they instructed Arturo to target the injured area earlier?

Manfredy backpedaled into the ropes and dropped his arms to his side, to protect his ribs. The pro Gatti crowd finally had something to cheer about. They erupted in emotional support for their warrior. Arturo completely controlled the round, ending the stanza with stiff jabs.

Roca told Gatti that Manfredy was ready to go. He asked Arturo to keep working the body. He also wanted Gatti to bring his gloves back to his head when he finished punching.

Arturo started the 5th on the attack. He was exposing his jaw as he brought his punches up from his hips in an attempt to maximize the power behind his shots. Both fighters traded furiously in the middle of the ring. A minute in, Manfredy started to find the range again with his right hand and hooks. Both fighters traded body shots. Angel came back up top with a crisp hook-cross combo.

With a little over a minute remaining in the round, Manfredy landed a right hand and winced. He clearly injured his hand with the punch, but he kept throwing, disregarding the pain. Arturo's left eye, though cut, was not bleeding heavily, but the eye was bothering him, as he was blinking hard and often. Gatti landed a solid hook that picked Angel's feet up off the ground. Arturo followed with five unanswered shots straight down the middle. Cedric Kushner, Manfredy's promoter, was sitting ringside. He jumped out of his seat screaming for Angel to move his head.

After the round, Roca told Gatti that he was looking good. He asked for more jabs and for Arturo to fight from a distance. In Manfredy's corner, Colonna instructed Angel to throw punches up the middle and to stay loose. John Taylor, Manfredy's assistant trainer, advised Angel that he would yell HBO when there was thirty seconds left in the round.

Gatti started the 6th round fast, landing body punches and a hard hook up top. Manfredy took the shots well. Angel came back with a hard hook to the side which sent Gatti retreating. Arturo moved to the center of the ring. Both boxers traded bombs. Gatti threw punches with wild abandon. Arturo's eye was bleeding heavily as the round ended. When the bell rang ending the session, Angel acknowledged Gatti's heart and courage by embracing him.

Roca instructed Gatti to remain active. As Souza worked on the cut, Arturo advised his corner that he was feeling pain in his eye. In Manfredy's corner, Angel was complaining about his injured right hand. Colonna told Manfredy to utilize his left hand.

Manfredy unloaded in the 7th, targeting Arturo's damaged left eye. Gatti, visibly bothered by the eye, retreated to the ropes, where Angel opened up with lefts and rights. A Gatti left hook created some room for Arturo to escape from the ropes. A little over a minute into the round, Manfredy landed a hard right hand that Gatti didn't see at all. The full blunt force of the blow made a thudding sound as it crashed against Arturo's skull. Gatti responded with a few home run shots, but they had little effect on the granite-chinned Manfredy. Angel's left cheekbone was beginning to swell. The bell rang.

Gatti winced as Souza tried to clean the gash over his eye. The doctor looked at Arturo's eye and commented that it looked worse than before. He asked Arturo if his vision was alright. Arturo nodded with his head up and down, indicating that he was ok. The doctor turned to the referee, Hedgepeth, and advised him that he would leave the decision on whether or not to stop the fight up to him. The doctor added that the referee should take into consideration that Gatti was throwing punches. HBO commentator George Foreman questioned the doctor's decision to defer to the referee. Merchant replied that only the referee could stop the fight, and the doctor was only there to instruct the referee. Merchant most likely meant the doctor was there to give a recommendation to the referee, not instruct. Harold Letterman, an HBO analyst, replied to Merchant by stating that the referee will always go along with the ringside doctor's recommendation.

At the start of the 8th, Arturo's top left eyelid was torn completely open, exposing the bone. The skin was hanging over Gatti's eye. Blood was streaming into the eye. Arturo writhed in obvious pain. Gatti was aggressive and scoring well. Almost two minutes into the round, Manfredy landed a frighteningly flush right hand. It was apparent that Arturo didn't see the punch because he hadn't even attempted to move his head. Joe recalled watching his brother absorb punches that he couldn't see. *"I'm watching this and I'm going hysterical. I can't do nothing about it."*[468] Joe, unable to watch anymore, and seeing that no one else was acting, left his seat and ran over to Arturo's corner.

Arturo's corner did not see a man who was seriously injured. They saw a warrior who would rather die than quit. They saw a gladiator with a bottomless reserve of heart and desire, who could snatch a victory from the jaws of defeat, no matter how dire the situation might be. Joe saw his baby brother, bleeding heavily, unable to defend himself from the punches being hurled at him.

Arturo somehow kept pressing forward as Manfredy retreated. Gatti sensed that Angel was weakening, both physically and mentally. The fans in attendance were transfixed on the action. They were anticipating another magical comeback unfolding before their very eyes. With 20 seconds remaining, Arturo worked Manfredy back to a corner where he landed two jabs and attempted a right hand. Manfredy dipped his head to avoid the right then brought his head back up, spearing it towards Gatti. Arturo reflexively dipped his head away to avoid a clash of heads. As he did so, the left side of his face pressed against Manfredy's left bicep. Angel's elbow bone rubbed against the exposed brow ridge bone over Gatti's eye. Hedgepeth broke the fighters. Arturo grimaced in pain as he squeezed his eye. The referee stopped the action and called the ringside doctor up to examine the injury. Gatti implored the referee, *"I'm alright."*

While the doctor was examining the eye, Joe threatened Roca, *"Hector, if you don't stop it. I'm stopping it."*[469] Roca followed

Joe's advice and tossed a towel into the ring. Doctor Domenic Coletta saw the towel fly into the ring and nervously told Arturo that his corner had ended the fight. Manfredy and his corner celebrated as Arturo threw his right arm up in disgust. He walked around the ring with his hands on his hips like a bull that wanted to get at the matador. The fight was officially recorded as a TKO victory for Manfredy when in fact it was a retirement by Gatti's corner.

Manfredy yelled out to Arturo that Gatti was a warrior. Angel embraced Arturo and whispered, "*God bless you*" into his ear. Gatti didn't respond, apparently still pondering the stoppage and what might have been. Manfredy, taking it as a slight, told Arturo, "*You know what, fuck you.*" Arturo gave Angel a searing look, then turned away, as Manfredy offered a rematch. Angel looked into the camera and advised the fans watching that he wanted Gatti's belt but he would settle for taking Arturo's soul.[470]

At the fight's end, two of the judges had Manfredy ahead, 67-65 and 68-65, while the third judge had the bout even at 66-66. Arturo appeared to be winning the 8th, so at the point of the stoppage, the fight potentially was winnable for Gatti without a knockout.

Joe's urging to have the fight stopped would put a further wedge into his relationship with Arturo. Allegedly, members of Arturo's entourage would tell Arturo that Joe was jealous of Arturo's success and wanted the fight stopped so Arturo would lose.

Arturo was not the first fighter who paralyzed his corner, the referee, and the doctor during his fights. The biggest name of course was Muhammad Ali. Ali was famous for his "rope a dope" comeback wins. For this reason, Ali was handed a terrible beating at the hands of Larry Holmes. That fight should have been stopped much sooner than it was, but Ali was the master of the comeback. No one gave thought to the internal damage that he was sustaining from the punishing blows to his brain. Most of the people watching, much like Arturo's team, had never been punched in the head in a boxing match. As a matter of fact, the only person in Arturo's entourage who had been a professional boxer, besides Joe, was Mickey Rourke. Rourke, as a guest of Arturo's, was in no position to tell the corner to stop the fight.

Manfredy was interviewed after the match. He said that when he cut Arturo in the 1st round, he knew it was a bad injury. He also knew that the referee and doctor wouldn't stop the fight in Arturo's home state. Manfredy added that his hand felt broken. He admitted that Gatti had rocked him a couple of times, but he felt he was never in serious trouble in the bout. Manfredy confessed that he had injured his ribs while sparring for the fight. When asked if he wanted to fight Gatti again, Manfredy instead called out Prince Naseem Hamed, the WBO featherweight champion.

Dr. Coletta stated that the cut was originally three centimeters long but that it had opened to five centimeters in the final two rounds. He was convinced that Gatti could only see out of one eye.[471] Arturo believed that the only reason that Manfredy won the fight was because of the cut. He was confident that he would have knocked Manfredy out if his corner hadn't thrown the towel in.[472]

Cutman Joe Souza did his best to stop the bleeding for the first 6 rounds, but starting in the 7th, the blood flowed freely into Arturo's eye. Permanent eye damage could have resulted if Arturo continued fighting.

Pat Lynch gave credit to the referee and doctor for giving Arturo every opportunity to try and win the fight. Lynch admitted that if the referee hadn't stopped the fight he would have. He obviously didn't realize that it was his own corner that had stopped the fight. Lynch didn't feel that Arturo's value would be lowered because of the loss.[473] Lynch was asked about Gatti's return. He said that he was more concerned about Arturo's health, but immediately added that he was thinking of a July or August return.[474]

Manfredy tore a ligament in his right hand. An X-ray confirmed the injury. HBO's vice president, Lou DiBella, indicated that Arturo would be given the opportunity, before Manfredy, to fight Hamed once his eye healed. The fight most fans wanted to see, however, was a Gatti-Manfredy rematch.

While Manfredy, Dino Duva, and Pat Lynch were giving interviews, Arturo was on his way to the Atlantic City Medical Center where he would receive 20 stitches to his cut left eye, 13 on the outside and 7 on the inside. Before departing, Arturo said that he wanted a rematch.[475]

Dino Duva predicted that May or June would be the earliest for a Gatti return, but added that as soon as a big fight was offered, Arturo would be back in the ring.[476]

The entourage who proudly walked Arturo into the ring for the big fight, who jockeyed their positions for maximum television exposure, were gone. They were either partying in the clubs, gambling, or heading home. Joe and Vikki rode to the hospital with Arturo and his girlfriend, Laura Sosnowski. While alone with

Arturo, they took the opportunity to try and open his eyes to the vortex that was sucking him in.

Vikki asked Arturo where all of his supposed friends were. Before he could answer, she told him they were probably back at the bar enjoying themselves. She also asked Arturo where his manager, Pat Lynch, was. She asked if he was driving in a car behind them or if he was going to meet them at the hospital. Arturo, Vikki, and Joe all sat silent for a moment. They all knew the answer to that question. No one would be coming. Lynch may have known that Joe was driving to the hospital with Arturo, and since his relationship with Joe was strained, he might have been avoiding an uncomfortable situation.

Arturo was quickly realizing the reality of professional boxing. When you're winning and paying for the party everyone is available to celebrate, but when you lose and are in need of consolation and support the entourage evaporates quicker than an ice cube on hot summer asphalt.

Vikki recalled the ride to the hospital. *"Well, after of course, his eye was hanging out. There was nobody there, just us, Arturo, and his girlfriend Laura."*[477] Joe added, *"I feel like he knew everything but he couldn't get out."*[478]

Vikki and Joe had Arturo's blood all over their clothes. They waited in the emergency room with Arturo for hours. Arturo, with a sad look in his eyes, said, *"I can't believe it. Everybody left me but you guys."*[479] Vikki recalled that it was times like this when it appeared as though the brothers would become close to each other again, but when Arturo returned home, the partying and the influence of others pulled them apart again.

At 2:30 a.m. on the night of the Manfredy loss, Mario Costa sat with Hector Roca at the Bally's coffee shop. Costa recalled the conversation. *"Hector Roca, after the Manfredy fight, everybody was blaming him. Roca said, 'Mario, how am I gonna train him if he doesn't come to the gym? We're in the camp and nobody knows where he's at. How can I train him?' So I said, 'Hector is that true?' He said, 'Yeah, he doesn't come to the gym. The manager is worse. Worse than the fighter.'"*[480]

Costa spoke with Arturo after the Manfredy fight. *"I said, 'Arthur, why would you fight him? Why would you take the fight? The guy is not above you. He's not better than you. He's just a junkyard dog. Why even take that fight? So he can make a name for himself?' Arthur said, 'Mario, I don't know why they stopped the fight. I had his heart in my hand. His heart was right here, right here in my hand. And they stopped the fight. I was gonna get him.' It hurt him so much losing that fight."*[481]

After Arturo was discharged from the hospital, Joe and Vikki drove him and Laura back to their hotel. Joe and Vikki went back to their hotel room to sleep. The next day, Sunday, Joe and Vikki called Arturo and told him they were heading home. They both had to work Monday morning. Arturo begged them to stay with him. Joe, as usual, could never say no to his little brother. Vikki recalled that Arturo looked like a lonely child. She tried to use the opportunity to finally get Arturo to realize what was happening to him. She asked him again where his supposed friends were. They were always around after a big win to share the spotlight and the money. When Arturo was celebrating a win, he spent freely. Again Arturo skirted the question.

Vikki thought that Arturo appeared as though he finally was waking up to the situation. But when he returned back north, he drowned himself in drugs, alcohol, and strip clubs. Arturo consumed cocaine, oxycodone, vicodin, and amphetamines. Mikey Red recalled, *"Early in his career, Arturo liked to be up, cocaine."*[482] After one of Arturo's cocaine-filled sex parties he called Donnie Jerie. Arturo was extremely upset. He told Jerie that an NBA basketball player tried to have sex with him.

Joe recalled that there were friends of Arturo's who would bring the pills into camp for him. *"They didn't want to help him. They fed him. They fed him all the pills. The oxycodone, because he was in pain. They didn't want him to leave the camp, so they would send Dr. Rotella's son, Joe Perrenod, to get the pills and bring them into the camp."*[483]

Dr. Frank Rotella had his practice in Jersey City and he lived in Secaucus. He was Joe's primary-care doctor, recommended by Lynch, before he became Arturo's doctor. Rotella became close to Arturo. He watched Arturo's German Shepherd when Arturo went away. He also held Arturo's WBC belt when Arturo traveled. It should be noted that no one suspected or alleged that Frank Rotella had any involvement with Arturo abusing prescription drugs.

Joey Perrenod was Dr. Rotella's step-son. Joe Gatti alleges that it was Perrenod who got Arturo addicted to the club life and the pills and coke that went along with it. Perrenod would die at the age of 37 on November 10, 2012.

Donny Jerie recalled Perrenod. *"Joe wasn't a good dude. Arturo* was tight with him and the father. I hung out with Joe too, don't get me wrong. God rest his soul. I don't want to say anything bad about him, but he was kind of a leech to be honest. I mean, he had a good father. He was the type of guy that wanted to walk out in the ring, you know. Arturo let him walk out a few times."[484] Steve Sandoval stated, "Joey [Perrenod] liked the exposure. He put on a big front or act. Joey covered up the real reason he hung out with Arturo."[485] Sandoval felt that Perrenod, and many like him, hung out with Arturo because he was famous. Another reason to hang out with Arturo was because he paid for everything. Sandoval alleges, "Joey had a big part in Arturo's death."[486] By that, Sandoval meant Perrenod allegedly played a role in Arturo getting hooked on prescription drugs.

Mario Costa commented on the drugs. "Arthur told me percs [percocet]. But I know that people said he messed with oxycodone. I didn't even know the names of these pills until this happened to him. And regarding the percs he said, 'Mario, every morning when I wake up, I have three percocets for breakfast.' I don't know if this started when he got operated on his hands and they took the bone from his hip. But he was addicted. He was addicted to the pain killers. And he took the pain killers just like drugs. And I hear that pain killers make you more paranoid than drugs. They play with your head and you get more screwed up than you would on coke. And he did everything else. He did the pain killers. He did the coke. He did the weed. He did the drinking."[487]

Sandoval believed that Arturo had low self-esteem. He recalled Arturo expressing that people looked down on him as unintelligent and "punchy." Sandoval stated that Arturo used the word "punchy" often when describing how he felt people perceived him. Sandoval believed that the reason Arturo hung out with a seedy crowd was because they would give him a great deal of attention and make him feel confident in himself. The group would attend go-go bars with Arturo and get rowdy and unruly, which made Arturo laugh. Sandoval recalled that some who hung around Arturo would embellish their accomplishments so Arturo would continue to hang out with them.

Sandoval described some of the groupies who hung out with Arturo. "When Gatti was so high that he didn't know where he was at, they didn't care for him. They wouldn't tell him to stop. They didn't care for his health."[488] Steve felt that there was always a battle taking place in Arturo's mind over whether to relax or to go crazy and party.

Sandoval explained why Arturo was depressed. *"He rarely felt that people hung with him because they truly liked him."*[489] Steve recalled that when Arturo would start one of his three-day party binges, he was usually happy, but sometimes angry, depending on his mood. Arturo would become mellow when he started coming down off of the drugs. He would let his guard down, exposing his true feelings. This was when he usually talked about his depression and suicidal thoughts. Steve recalled that Arturo never spoke of suicide when he was sober, but when he was coming down off of a high, he would open up about his depression. Once, when Arturo mentioned his suicidal thoughts to Sandoval, Steve asked Arturo how often he thought about suicide. Arturo replied, *"I think about suicide every day."*[490]

Sandoval recalled that Arturo would visit him when he wanted to use cocaine because Arturo felt safe in Steve's apartment. Arturo was always leery and paranoid that people would try to record him when he was using drugs.

Joe recalled talking to Arturo after the Manfredy fight, in Arturo's apartment. *"So I see him at the house, weeks later. I said, 'Bro what's wrong with you? I'm not in the corner, so I can't do anything. But if I was there in the corner, all they had to do was stop the fight. There would have been a rematch. Everybody wants to see the fight cause you got cut. You didn't stop. You wanted to fight. You're the fighter. Your corner is supposed to be in control, they're the boss not you. You can't fight. Your cut's this big [opens fingers to animate a three inch gash]. You're trained to fight. Your eyeballs could be hanging out. You're a warrior. You're not going to say, 'No, I can't fight.' They should stop the fight.'"*[491]

Joe understood that his brother would never quit, especially on HBO. He was shocked that Arturo's corner didn't understand this. Joe added, *"If I'm the boss, fight's over, like this [waiving hands]. We're gonna get a rematch, 'cause now people wanna see it."*[492]

Hector Roca was dismissed as Arturo's trainer. Roca had wanted Arturo's camp moved away from the distractions of Virginia Beach and Whitaker. Arturo and Lynch blamed Roca for the Manfredy loss even though Arturo had been partying up until a few days before the fight. Roca did not have the capability to command discipline from Arturo or keep him in line. Roca worked for Arturo and was in no position to make demands.

For a trainer to be truly effective, he has to do and say some very unpopular things. He also has to understand that by doing these things, he may lose his job. Roca might never have the opportunity to train another fighter like Gatti. This probably tempered his disciplining of Arturo. According to Mario Costa, Roca had voiced his displeasure regarding the actions of both Pat Lynch and Arturo. If that were accurate, then Roca's hands truly were tied. To whom could he complain?

The release of Roca sent shockwaves throughout Team Gatti. Friends of Arturo's were too frightened to speak their minds. No one dared tell Gatti that he was self-destructing, for fear of being thrown out of the inner-circle. Telling Arturo that the stoppage of the Manfredy fight was proper could also lead to banishment. The fact that Joe had pushed Roca to stop the fight had put him on thin ice with Team Gatti.

Arturo purchased a first floor, tenant-owned apartment, in the gated Gregory Commons condominiums on Gregory Avenue in Weehawken, N.J. Pat Lynch's sister, a realtor, handled the closing on the $235,000 condo. The condo was less than a mile walking distance to Arturo's favorite strip club, the Squeeze Lounge. Since Arturo was frequently on the drivers suspension list he was able to walk to his favorite club from his new home.

Mike DePompe described the change when Arturo became famous. *"Arturo continued to rise up the boxing ladder. He began to drift into a fast crowd of party goers and, as Joe once called them, 'bugs.' Although, I can clearly remember Joe and his wife constantly trying to convince Arturo to slow down a little and choose his relationships carefully, but, he had simply become addicted to the fast-paced life. This is no secret now, as the newspapers are full of comments from his closest 'real' friends that noticed the same pattern. But none worked much harder than Joe, who endured any negativity, and was not afraid of being misconstrued for his concerns about Arturo's welfare. Family usually has the hardest task when it comes to giving advice, perhaps correct advice that someone just cannot or does not want to hear. For some reason, friends are expected to just accept whatever they see, right or wrong."*[493]

With all the partying and lack of control, it appeared as though the Gatti Cinderella run had ended. Everything was unraveling. The money, the fame, the women, the drinking, the drugs, and a promotional company who had much bigger stars on their roster to concern themselves with. Joe felt that the Manfredy loss had long-lasting effects on Arturo. He didn't think his brother ever fought the same after that fight. Joe recalled, *"He was a totally different fighter after that."*[494]

Not long after the loss, Mikey Red received a phone call from Arturo, who was having trouble starting his Corvette. Mikey came over to Arturo's condo in Weehawken to try and help him move his car for the street sweeper. Mikey immediately noticed that Arturo was high on cocaine. Mikey looked under the hood. The car was starting, but the engine wouldn't turn over. While Mikey was looking to see what was wrong with the engine, he noticed Arturo was staring at him. Mikey asked Arturo what was wrong. Arturo looked at Mikey with a serious face and said, *"You stole my engine, didn't you?"*[495] Mikey was stunned. He knew Arturo was high so he couldn't laugh. He had to be cautious with his reply. Mikey asked, *"How can I steal your engine when it's in the car?"*[496] Arturo responded, *"You took my engine out and put this piece of shit engine in its place!"*[497] Mikey couldn't believe what he was hearing. It looked as though the spark plugs were loose, so Mikey tightened them. The car started and Mikey helped Arturo move the car across the street before heading home. The incident would become the butt of many jokes in the years to come. Arturo's friends would come up to Mikey and ask, *"Did you give Arturo his engine back yet?"*[498]

Arturo asked Lynch not to take the taxes out of his purse for the Manfredy fight, so he could have his first real million dollar payday.[499] Lynch did as he was told. As a result, Arturo would later pay a handsome $75,000 monthly penalty to the IRS.

Some felt that Lynch feared Arturo. Not so much physically as financially. None of Lynch's other fighters were earning anywhere near Arturo's purses. Lynch had to carefully balance managing Arturo's career, giving him advice, while also not getting overly involved with Arturo's personal life. Mike Skowronski recalled the paranoia surrounding Team Gatti. *"People around him tried to help him deal with his fame. If you tried to push him too much, he would just push you away."*[500]

Lou DiBella felt that a Gatti win over Manfredy would have assured him a fight with Naseem Hamed. Manfredy wanted a lucrative match with the Prince, who was under contract to HBO. DiBella scoffed at that match. *"I don't think Hamed is going to run to this fight so quick. I also think Hamed and Manfredy is before its time. People need to get to know Angel a little bit more. People need to see him fight a few more times... The next likelihood is a rematch with Arturo, because that's the biggest fight out there for him."*[501]

A Gatti rematch would be cheaper for HBO, as they could secure Manfredy and Arturo for much less than Hamed would command against either fighter. Unfortunately for Angel, neither a Gatti rematch nor a Hamed match would ever materialize.

After a seventeen month lay-off, Joe Gatti returned to the ring. On February 28, 1998, Joe took on Salvatore Di Salvatore. Di Salvatore, 16-4-1 (11 KOs), of Calabria, Italy, hadn't fought in twenty-two months himself. Both boxers were fighting for the International Boxing Council's light heavyweight title. The bout took place in Zofingen-Aarau, Switzerland. Joe was knocked out in the 7th round. His record fell to 25-7 (18 KOs).

Chapter 15
Robinson I & II

Arturo flew to Miami to relax while his eye healed. He recently had broken up with Laura because someone had told him that she was seeing his limo driver. Joe believes that this rumor was spread purposely so that Arturo would break up with her, because Laura was beginning to enlighten Arturo in regards to controlling his own assets. Joe also believed Laura was opening Arturo's eyes to the type of friends with whom he was surrounding himself.

Laura was deeply concerned about Arturo's health. One of his friends already had died of a drug overdose, and several more were to follow. Laura wanted him to stop his partying ways. Donny Jerie recalled Laura begging Pat Lynch to help change Arturo's lifestyle. Jerie also believed that Laura was jealous of Arturo hanging out with his friends, when in reality she may have simply been concerned for Arturo's well-being. Jerie felt that all of Arturo's girlfriends tried to control him. Jerie explained, *"Every one of Arturo's girlfriends was jealous of me. When they saw we were too close they tried to push us away. He wouldn't let that happen."*[502]

Pat Lynch was concerned about Arturo going to Miami alone after the Manfredy fight. Lynch asked Jerie to go with him. Jerie was working for his father in his auto body shop. He told Lynch he would not be able to get off work. Lynch was desperate. He didn't want Arturo alone. Lynch called Jerie's father and begged him to let his son go to Miami with Arturo. Donny's father gave in and said yes. Arturo paid for the entire trip. Lynch's fear of Arturo going to Miami for an extended period would turn out to be intuitive. Pat called Donny and said, *"Just meet Arturo at the airport. Everything is done and taken care of."*[503] Gatti pulled up in a limousine and jumped out of the car. *"Yo, what's up Donny. Come on. We're gonna have some fun."*[504]

In Miami, Arturo went out with Donny and Donny's friend Jaimie, who lived in Florida. They ran into one of Jamie's old girlfriends, Cynthia Shaw. Jamie introduced Arturo to Cynthia, who was an exotic dancer. Arturo was immediately attracted to the sexy, curvy blonde, who had no inhibitions. Before long, Jerie returned to New Jersey, and Arturo, who remained in Miami, was dating Shaw. Cynthia worked at the Solid Gold gentlemen's club in North Miami Beach. The Solid Gold club allowed fully nude lap dances, among other things.

On March 20, 1998, Arturo went out to a nightclub in South Beach called the SOBE Club, or Living Room, with Shaw. At the club, Arturo met a 51-year-old male named Michel Tsouws. Arturo and Shaw were invited back to Tsouws' apartment to party with him and Tsouws' roommate Zlatose Jerabkova.

After partying at the apartment, Arturo and Shaw decided to leave. At some point, while preparing to leave, Arturo and Shaw became separated. Arturo searched outside for Shaw for thirty minutes before returning to Tsouw's apartment. Shaw was back in the apartment when Arturo arrived. She told Gatti that she was waiting for him outside, and after he didn't show, she went back inside the apartment. Arturo didn't believe her story. He thought that Shaw had purposely stayed behind to be with Tsouws. Tsouws dismissed Arturo's accusations with a backhand waive in the air. Gatti became enraged and assaulted Tsouws in a fit of jealousy. The *Miami Herald* would later state that Arturo *"allegedly punched Tsouws in the head repeatedly."*[505]

To make matters worse, Tsouws had staples in his head from a recent surgical procedure. Tsouws bled profusely from the assault. The police were called. Arturo fled the scene with Shaw. The police arrived and searched the building, finding Arturo's blood-soaked shirt in a nearby stairwell. Arturo and Shaw were spotted at the security gate leading out of the complex. Arturo and Shaw both told police that Gatti was a professional boxer. Apparently Arturo was hoping his star-status would help him avoid an arrest. Unfortunately for Arturo, this was Miami Beach, not Jersey City. Arturo was placed under arrest.

Arturo refused to comply with the officers and was forced to the ground and handcuffed. Arturo pleaded with the officers, *"I only beat up a criminal."*[506] Arturo's struggle with the police officers led to resisting arrest being added to his assault charge. Gatti threatened the arresting officer by saying he was *"gonna get the officer, make him pay, and fuck him up."*[507] Arturo also stated that he was the *"IBF number one ranked junior lightweight champion."*[508]

Arturo demanded to know the names of the arresting officers. When one of the officers showed Arturo his name plate, Arturo told the officer that he was *"dead meat."*[509] The officer observed a cut on Arturo's left hand that was consistent with the staples on Tsouws' head. At police headquarters, Gatti asked where Shaw was. An officer advised Arturo that they had driven Shaw back to Arturo's apartment. Arturo responded by stating that he was *"a very jealous man."*[510] Gatti was released on bond with a court appearance pending.

In April's issue of *KO* magazine, Arturo's knockout over Gabriel Ruelas was named *KO*'s 1997 "Knockout of the Year" and "Fight of the Year."

On April 3, 1998, the Boxing Writers Association of America held its 73rd annual awards dinner at the Crowne Plaza Hotel in Manhattan. Over 400 guests attended the ceremony. Pat Lynch was awarded the Manager of the Year for 1997. The award was also known as the Al Buck Award. The award had been conferred annually since 1967. Some of boxing's most famous managers had received the award, including Angelo Dundee, Yank Durham, Gil Clancy, Emanuel Steward, Al Certo, and Lou Duva. Lynch was in the running for the award the year prior, along with John Davimos, Michael Moorer's manager, but no one won the award due to abstinent votes. Therefore, there was no manager of the year in 1996.

According to Newark *Star Ledger* reporter Chris Thorne, many of the guests came out to honor the recently retired Eddie Futch, who attended the event. Arturo flew up for the ceremony. He and Mikey Red were in attendance to support Lynch. After Lynch received his award, Arturo and Mikey Red walked out of the hotel and wandered around the Theater District. They walked into a bar nearby that played live music. To Mikey Red's amazement, Arturo started playing the drums on stage. After he was finished, Arturo showed his fancy footwork by taking a stab at tap dancing. Gatti returned to Miami soon after.

In mid-April, Arturo and Shaw went on a partying binge. On April 18, Arturo would have another run-in with the Miami police, once again involving Shaw. After three nights of partying with cocaine, the couple had a fight, and the police were called. Shaw alleged that Arturo forced her to stay with him and to engage in intercourse with him. Shaw added that the sexual encounters caused physical injury to her. Shaw claimed that when she resisted Arturo's advances, he struck her in the head and right ear, causing an injury to her head. Shaw added that Gatti threatened her with a golf club when she attempted to leave.[511]

The day prior, April 17, Shaw tried to escape and made it outside the apartment but Arturo grabbed her and carried her back in. Shaw stated that Arturo told her he would kill her children and her family if she called the police.⁵¹²

On April 18, Shaw pretended to call a friend, but instead called 911. When the police arrived, they found Shaw outside of the apartment crying, dressed only in a shirt. She told the police that Arturo was in the apartment armed with a golf club. Police entered the apartment and found Arturo clothed in a bath towel. Arturo was arrested for sexual assault and kidnapping. Shaw led police to the drawer where Arturo kept his cocaine. The police discovered a mirror with suspected cocaine residue on it in the drawer.⁵¹³

Shaw originally stated that Arturo assaulted her for refusing to have sex with him. Arturo was interviewed by the police. He said that he had consensual sex with Shaw about eight times, while they partied with cocaine. Arturo added that he was shocked that Shaw would claim that he forced her to have sex with him. Shaw later recanted her story. She admitted that Arturo never threatened her physically if she were to leave. She had left the apartment with Arturo to buy cocaine several times throughout the three-day ordeal. Shaw stated that Arturo would cry when she told him she was leaving. She said he told her he would hurt himself if she left. Shaw also recanted that she was forced to have sex. Shaw's new statements led to Arturo being released without charges being filed.⁵¹⁴

On April 27, the incident with Tsouws, which included threatening a police officer, was published in the *Miami Herald* newspaper. The article stated that Tsouws was not going to pursue criminal charges. Prosecuting attorney Rey Dorta said that jail didn't seem to be an option or alternative. Arturo's attorney, Jeff Weiner, believed a fair resolution would be agreed upon.⁵¹⁵ Tsouws didn't follow through with criminal charges, but he would later file a civil suit against Arturo.

The Solid Gold gentlemen's club, where Shaw worked, was alleged to have ties to organized crime. It was relayed to Arturo that he would have to pay for the lost income of Shaw missing work at the club. The club had been owned by Michael J. Peter, until he pled guilty to mail fraud. Peter previously had been charged with kidnapping and extortion.

Reputed mobster James Tortoriello Jr. and his wife and sons all worked in Peter-owned clubs. Tortoriello is the son of James "Mugsy" Tortoriello, a muscleman capo under Sam Giancana of the Chicago Outfit. Tortoriello Sr. was murdered in 1984 in Fort Lauderdale. Tortoriello Sr.'s other son, Mark Tortoriello, was murdered in Miami in 1982.

It was long rumored that a captain in the Gambino crime family was a silent partner in the ownership of the Solid Gold night club, possibly through Jeanne Williams, whose husband, James Williams, was an alleged Gambino and Lucchese crime family associate.

Arturo's brother-in-law, Rocco Crispo, of Montreal, recalled that Arturo had to pay $300,000 to make the incident *"go away."*[516] Joe Gatti recalled that the figure was closer to $250,000. Arturo's fascination with the mafia would grow, but he learned an expensive lesson during his Miami escapades.

On Wednesday, June 17, 1998, a boxing card at the Robert Treat Hotel in Newark, NJ turned ugly when boxer Jamar Carter tried to fire his manager, Tom Hockey, for failing to find him a replacement after his fight against Teddy Reid fell out. *The Star Ledger's* Chris Thorne reported on the incident. In the article James Ali Basheer, a boxing manager, stated, *"These guys [the boxers] are nothing but headaches. You help a fighter make something of himself, then he goes on and signs with somebody else. All these guys want is to go with the big managers, big trainers and big promoters and to hell with the people who gave them a chance."*[517] Thorne added, *"The managers see the kind of loyalty that Arturo Gatti has displayed with Pat Lynch and they would like to see it come their way."*[518]

Main Events had been experiencing bad luck over the last few years, with Evander Holyfield leaving the company, Andrew Golota's disqualification losses to Riddick Bowe, and Pernell Whitaker's public battles with substance abuse. Arturo, who was once considered a mid-level earner on the Main Events roster, was now an indispensable commodity.

Arturo's promotional contract with Main Events and Peltz was expiring. Top Rank's Bob Arum was allegedly interested in signing Arturo. Mario Costa recalled that Arum was so interested in signing Gatti he was offering a substantial signing bonus. Costa recalled the offer was rumored to be $1 million dollars. One of Top Rank's matchmakers at the time, Ron Katz, vaguely confirmed, *"I remember some discussions about trying to get Gatti."*[519]

Main Events offered Arturo a $75,000 Dodge Viper car as a signing bonus. Arturo was a world champion and one of the most popular fighters in the sport. He had recently been involved in the fight of the year against Ruelas, and his current promoter was offering him a car. Arturo didn't even have a driver's license, as it was suspended. Arturo, however, had just lost a brutal battle against

Manfredy and there may have been concerns that Gatti was in decline. Main Events was struggling. Their stable of fighters was aging, and their cash flow purportedly was low, or less than it had been.

Mario Costa talked to Arturo and advised him to seriously consider Top Rank's offer. Costa recalled, *"Bob Arum said he wanted to sign Arthur for a million dollars. Main Events' contract was up. So they're looking to re-sign him. They wanted to give him a car, which they did, a Viper. Arthur didn't even have a license to drive! So now, I was telling Arthur this story. So he must have went back and told Pat [Lynch] because I'm sitting in the bar and Carl Moretti calls me up cursing at me, 'What are you doing? What are you talking to Arturo for! It's not your business.' I said, 'Listen Moretti, I'm not his manager. The manager is Pat Lynch. But you guys must think that fighters are real stupid. Now you want to give him a car, for him to sign a new contract with you, Main Events, right? You got Bob Arum...' Moretti cuts me off, 'Ah Bob would never do that.' 'I don't know if he will give him a million or not, but he's offering him a million dollars to go in a different direction. What you guys are doing is no good. So maybe Bob will take care of the fighter and take him in a different direction.' And watch, cause Bob gets more close to the fighters.*

"I told Arthur this too. 'Arthur, Bob Arum will look at you. If he sees you don't go to the gym he's gonna try and help you. Because Bob is that type of promoter.' And maybe Arthur needs this, to go to the West Coast. And Bob Arum wants to take him in a different direction and give him a million dollars. So who am I, Mario Costa? I'm gonna tell Arthur which way to take? What is he stupid? What's he gonna take the car or the million dollars? He don't have to be no scientist. So they told me, 'Leave the fighter alone. It's none of your business.' I said, 'You're right. It's none of my business. But he's my friend. And I know him.' And all I did was present this up to him. I'm not the manager. Pat is the manager. Moretti said, 'Bob is full of shit. He's not going to give him nothing. Bullshit.' Now I'm waiting one day to see Moretti. Now he works for Bob Arum. He's the vice president. He's gonna tell you about all the glory. How many times they sold out Boardwalk Hall. And Pat too, 'Arturo made $15 million dollars with me.' Yeah, but he's dead. He's dead. What are you talking about? It's not about the money. It's about the human being. It's about the person. You worry about the money. The millions. Look, your kid's in trouble here.

"Like Joe Gatti said, when Lynch sold $50,000 worth of tickets for Arthur's fights, he probably doubled or tripled his money at the gate. That's cash money for his pocket. So that's his business. So of course where's he gonna get the tickets from? The promoters. If you probably look at the stats, Pat bought more tickets than anyone else for those particular fights. And he sold them for double or triple the money."[520]

Was the alleged Arum/Top Rank offer fact or fiction? If there was such an offer, Costa raised an interesting argument. Why would Arturo's manager have his fighter, who may be in decline, accept a $75,000 car instead of an alleged million dollar signing bonus. Most likely, Lynch was comfortable with Main Events and trusted them with guiding Arturo's career. Lynch, with his close relationship to Main Events, also didn't have to worry about them steering Arturo towards another manager. Some promotional companies are closely aligned to certain managers and try to steer their fighters toward those managers, and vice versa. Relationships of trust can develop.

There also was the issue that Costa raised, that Lynch was profiting from ticket sales through Main Events. If true, controlling part of the ticket sales in Atlantic City would be a windfall which could diminish if Gatti was not with the company. It's worth noting that although Arturo was a popular ticket seller, he was not yet selling out arena's and would not do so for several years. Even if Gatti decided to sign with Top Rank, it would be a smart business move to keep him fighting in Atlantic City, which was close to his fan base. It is also possible that Top Rank's offer, if any, did not actually beat the Main Events offer, or not significantly enough for Arturo to change promoters.

Joe recalled that a few years earlier the Goosen brothers had shown interest in signing him and Arturo. Joe felt that Pat Lynch didn't pursue the Goosen offer because Pat was afraid he might lose the brothers to the Goosens. The Goosen brothers usually trained, managed, and promoted most of their fighters themselves. Dan Goosen confirmed that he was interested in signing Arturo to a promotional contract.[521]

Lynch had a great deal of help selling tickets for Arturo's fights. Early on, Costa brought bus-loads of fans. Donny Jerie recalled, *"I never asked Gatti for nothing. I sold up to $20,000 of tickets for Arturo's fights. Pat would say, 'Here's some tickets. Go sell some tickets for your boy.'"*[522] In addition, Jerie always paid for his own seat.

Some promoters gave their fighters 10% of ticket sales after the fighters bout cost was paid. For example, if a fight cost $5,000 (which included both boxers purses, medicals and travel) every ticket sold over the $5,000 amount would garner the fighter 10% for each ticket sold. Large scale ticket movers, such as Arturo's friends, were also given 10% of their ticket sales by some promoters to help motivate sales. Jerie recalled that there were always people trying to get free tickets. Donny wasn't the only one who sold tickets for Arturo. Mikey Red sold hundreds of tickets to his friends in Jersey City, totaling thousands of dollars. Neither Jerie nor Skowronski were ever offered a percentage for their ticket sales.

On July 13, Arturo signed a three-year contract extension with Main Events and Peltz Promotions. His bonus was the Dodge Viper. At a press conference at the All-Star Café announcing the re-signing, Pat Lynch admitted that they had been working on the new contract for three or four months. Lynch added that it was a tribute to Arturo that Main Events felt he was good enough to re-sign.[523] Dino Duva felt that Arturo was boxing's most exciting fighter. Duva predicted that Gatti had three or four good years left in him.[524] Before the signing, Dino, now with Kathy Duva more involved in the business aspect of the company, reconstructed Main Events' 50-50 deal with Peltz promotions to a 65-35 split in favor of Main Events.

At the press conference Gatti spoke about his face-first style. *"That's the way I fight. Cuts are a part of boxing and they've been a big part of my career. I'm fine and I'm not going to change anything. I believe I would have won the [Manfredy] fight if the cut wasn't so bad."*[525] Pat Lynch added that the cut was down to the bone.[526] Arturo continued, *"That's why they shouldn't have stopped the fight. I couldn't get hurt anymore. I'm not going to change it [his style] now. I feel comfortable with it. They tell me to box more, to move my head more. But I'm in trouble a lot of the time, so I have to fight more to win. I want to fight for the title, but the number one man on my hit list is Angel Manfredy. I want him more than I want the title."*[527]

After re-signing, Arturo revealed, *"I love working with Main Events. They helped give me a lot of exposure when I was coming up and not many people around the country knew who I was. They have treated me fairly. I couldn't work for anyone else."*[528]

Arturo was currently ranked #1 by the WBC. After internal discussions between Main Events and Pat Lynch, it was agreed upon that Gatti would fight Philadelphia's Ivan Robinson. Main Events' Kathy Duva and Carl Moretti argued that Robinson was a light puncher who was past his prime. Mario Costa recalled learning of the match-up. *"I said, 'Don't take the Robinson fight!' I told Pat that. Robinson throws a thousand punches. He's a boxer. He's not a puncher. You got a puncher. You got a guy that wants to fight. This guy don't want to fight. He wants to run. Pat said, 'Na, na, it's alright. He can't hit.' He can't hit? At that time Arthur was a known fighter. Why you gonna put him with a guy who throws a hundred punches a round? Pat was like, 'It's okay.' You see a lot of time he was influenced by Main Events. It was Moretti or Kathy Duva. Whatever they said, Lynch went along with. He didn't want to make no waves. And they have the connections. They called the shots."*[529]

Arturo's title and multiple televised fights had brought him much fame and fortune. He frequented strip clubs and night clubs from New Jersey to Manhattan. He would stay out partying until dawn. Mikey Red recalled that sometimes Arturo would show up at his house at 3 or 4 in the morning, banging on the door, looking for someone to hang out with. Skowronski spoke of Arturo's training habits for the first Ivan Robinson match. *"At that time, you'd get three or four weeks of training out of him before a fight; the rest of the time he'd be out drinking. He was depressed, and he was just going through the motions."*[530] The party even extended to the golf course as Mikey Red recalled, *"When we played golf, he'd be drunk by the eighth hole."*[531]

Ivan Robinson was returning to South Jersey for the first time since he lost by 3rd round TKO to Israel Cardona at the Wildwood Convention Center. Robinson admitted that he barely trained for the Cardona fight, and had to lose 15-pounds in 8 days to make the contracted weight of 135-pounds. The loss was so devastating that Main Events dropped Ivan from their roster. Lou Duva went as far as to advise Robinson to find another profession. Ivan recalled that Duva told him that he shouldn't fight again. Robinson planned on showing Arturo the "real" Ivan Robinson.[532]

Two years prior, Robinson barely lost a controversial decision to then IBF champ Phillip Holliday. In his next fight, he was demolished by Cardona. Ivan had a strong eight-week camp preparing for Gatti. He didn't see his wife or two children for over a month. His only communication with them was through letters delivered by his manager, Eddie Woods.

Robinson felt that the difference between the Cardona fight and the

Gatti fight would be conditioning. Ivan believed that he was in the best shape of his career. For the Cardona match, he had only trained for four weeks and was about 25-pounds overweight when he began camp. Robinson called the Gatti match a crossroads fight for him.[533]

Arturo's gash from the Manfredy fight had healed. Arturo felt that the injury, which required 20 stitches, had actually improved his long-range vision. Gatti had to wait about six months before he could start sparring again. Arturo felt that the time off was good for him, because he had been in some rough fights. He felt that his body needed the rest. He was anxious to get back into the ring. Gatti admitted that the anticipation of returning to the ring had caused him to have trouble sleeping the week of the fight.[534]

During his 6-month lay-off, while in Miami, Arturo walked past a tattoo parlor. He was attracted to a tattoo design in the window. The design featured the word "Victory," with a pair of boxing gloves underneath. The gloves had blood dripping off of them. He decided to get the tattoo on the back of his neck. Arturo also had the design stitched to the back of his boxing robe for the Robinson fight.

The tattoo was now the source of great stress for Arturo. His mother was arriving on August 22, the day of his fight, to watch her son. She did not know that Arturo had acquired the tattoo. Arturo admitted that his mother hated tattoos, because all the people she saw with them on TV were bad guys. Arturo was expecting a smack in the head from his mother when she saw the tattoo.[535] While Arturo was talking to reporters at the press conference, everyone thought he was drinking soda, when in fact he was sipping wine from a cup.[536]

Pat Lynch stated that they focused on improving Arturo's defense in training camp. Lynch admitted that Arturo was the type of fighter who was willing to let you land four punches so he can land one.[537] Arturo was working on a new defensive style with his new trainer, Bob Wareing. Wareing moved from strength coach to head trainer after Hector Roca was let go. Gatti was working on staying patient and being more relaxed in the ring.[538]

Arturo had invited welterweight Freddy Curiel to his Virginia Beach training camp as a sparring partner. Curiel would later star on the second season of "The Contender" boxing reality show. Curiel's style was nearly identical to Robinson's. He was a fast, light-hitting, volume puncher. Curiel had trained alongside Arturo and Joe in 1992 at Lou Costello's gym in Paterson, under the direction of Diego Rosario. Curiel knew both brothers well.

Curiel would later comment that he had always wanted, as all fighters do, to become a world champion. However, when he arrived at Arturo's camp in Virginia Beach he saw the effects that fame and fortune had on the once fun-loving Gatti. Arturo was not the same happy-go-lucky kid that he had met years earlier. Gatti appeared stressed and depressed. Arturo had realized the dream that all fighters struggle to achieve. Curiel couldn't help but think, if this is what being a world championship fighter who fights on HBO is like, maybe he was lucky that he never won a title.

Arturo was miserable while shedding the 25-pounds needed to make the contracted weight. Curiel recalled that Gatti's punches were weak, and Curiel often was told not to spar full-force with Arturo during their sessions. It should be noted that many fighters, in the weeks prior to their fight, are often drained from the training, weight loss, and boredom of being locked down with the same sparring partners in camp. It is not uncommon for fighters to look lackluster at times during training camp.

Eddie Woods, Robinson's manager and trainer since the age of 9, told Ivan that no one expected Robinson to win. Robinson stated, *"And we kept getting calls from around the world saying it was a bad fight. I could get killed. They didn't think that I deserved to be in that fight. I trained tremendously hard thanks to Mike Stewart, who I fought later, Mike Melvin, and Anthony Thompson. Those were the three guys that I worked with for both Gatti fights, and they got me in tremendous shape. I needed the help. Prior to the fight we were just concentrating on boxing Gatti, boxing. I knew he was dangerous, I knew."*[539]

Arturo was once again using cocaine while training for the Robinson fight. A friend of Rocco Crispo's admitted that he had used the drug with Arturo the night before his match against Robinson.[540] That would contradict the mandatory drug testing that Arturo was forced to undergo on the day of his fight. Unless, of course, he had access to some type of drug masking agent that concealed the drug. Crispo, Arturo's brother-in-law, could not understand how Arturo passed his required pre- or post-fight drug tests during this time, given his frequent drug usage.[541] Normally, in New Jersey, boxers would go into a stall by themselves to urinate. Hiding clean urine in a condom, using the Whizzinator, diluting the urine sample or detoxification to flush the toxins from the body were all possible methods to mask dirty urine.

Robinson stayed in his hometown of Philadelphia to train for the

Gatti fight. Ivan knew the fight would be difficult. He praised Arturo for his tremendous heart and stamina. Robinson felt that it would be impossible to follow a game plan against Arturo. Ivan needed to avoid getting into a war with Gatti, because Arturo was the bigger puncher. He planned on utilizing his jab in the match.[542]

Bob Wareing believed that Arturo was prepared for battle. Wareing wanted Arturo to catch the jab and fall away from the right hand. He wanted Arturo to keep Ivan in front of him, to make him fight.[543]

Pat Lynch spoke of being ringside for Arturo's wars. Lynch admitted that he would be thrilled to watch Arturo if he was just a fan. But as his manager, he would rather not see a thrilling fight. Lynch was aware that this was a huge fight for Arturo because a win could get him right back into world title contention.[544]

Arturo spoke of why he cut so frequently. He felt that it had a lot to do with leaning his head in on the inside. Gatti praised Robinson for being a gentleman who doesn't shoot off his mouth. Arturo felt that he would have to stalk Ivan, who reminded him a little bit of Calvin Grove. Arturo was hoping that a victory over Robinson would put him in line for a bout with either Manfredy or Prince Naseem Hamed. Arturo wanted to shut both of the aforementioned fighters up.[545]

HBO's Lou DiBella predicted that Arturo would win and look impressive doing so. He cautioned that nothing is guaranteed in boxing. He pointed to the Manfredy war and how it may have taken a toll on Gatti physically. DiBella added that the one thing that Gatti could take away from the Manfredy loss was that he was more popular now than ever.[546]

Arturo displayed his support for Pat Lynch winning the 1997 BWAA Manager of the Year award by placing a full page ad in the Gatti-Robinson program honoring Lynch. Arturo congratulated his manager for his accomplishment.

Robinson was ready for battle. He felt that he was one of the best fighters in the lightweight division.[547] Ivan had been a gifted amateur who boxed Oscar De La Hoya three times. De La Hoya commented on how tough Robinson had fought him in the amateurs. Ivan came close to joining De La Hoya on the 1992 U.S. Olympic Team. Robinson lost two very close computer scoring decisions to Olympian Julian Wheeler at the U.S. Olympic Trials. The losses were still fresh in his mind. Ivan felt that if he would have made the team he would have won a gold medal.[548]

Robinson had an opportunity to fight De La Hoya as a professional in 1995 but was advised to turn the fight down because of the purse, which would have been a career-high $250,000, but still too low for such a high risk bout. Ivan also was forced to pass up a fight with Shane Mosley when he nicked one of his eyes in sparring.[549]

The *Press of Atlantic City* predicted a Gatti victory by 8th round TKO. Arturo was a 5-1 betting favorite. Gatti weighed in at 136-pounds, while Robinson tipped the scale at 135¾ at the Friday weigh-in. Jim Lampley described Arturo as looking *"totally dehydrated."* Gatti gained 16-pounds after the weigh-in, while Robinson added just 8¼-pounds. Robinson held a slight 1½-inch height and 2-inch reach advantage over Arturo.

On August 22, 1998, Arturo took on "Mighty" Ivan Robinson at Convention Hall in Atlantic City in front of 2,602 fans. Arturo would earn $400,000 for the match, while Robinson grossed $57,000. Robinson's purse would be his second-highest career payday to date, with his highest, $60,000, being against Phillip Holiday. Robinson, 25-2 (10 KOs), of Philadelphia, was considered a "safe fight." Robinson was not a big puncher, and he had lost two out of his last four fights. His two wins came against club fighters. Gatti's advisors remembered Robinson's split-decision struggle against Juan Negron on the Gatti-Sanabria undercard back in 1994. However, this time Robinson didn't play around in training camp. He stated that camp was brutal. Every night he went home aching.[550]

It was Ivan's loss to Philip Holiday, on December 21, 1996, that would be the most foreshadowing. In that battle, for the IBF lightweight crown, Robinson threw over 1,100 punches. Gatti's team was more focused on the fact that Robinson was not a big puncher and that he had been hit 440 times by Holiday. Panama Lewis visited Pat Lynch with his concerns over the matchup. Lynch is alleged to have told Lewis that Robinson couldn't crack an egg.[551] The relatively light-punching Robinson hadn't won a fight by knockout in over three years.

Lynch told Panama that the Robinson match was the most attractive that HBO offered. HBO usually presented several opponents to their house fighter's management and promotional team. Opponents that HBO deemed satisfactory, in order to make competitive bouts. No doubt Lynch and Main Events felt that if Arturo could land 440 punches on Robinson, Ivan wouldn't be around for the final bell. Gatti's team perhaps failed to take into consideration Arturo's taste for the nightlife. The Gatti-Robinson non-title fight was scheduled for 10 rounds.

HBO televised the Gatti-Robinson bout for their "Boxing after Dark" series. Robinson ran out to the ring to Diana Ross' "I'm Coming Out." He left his team behind him as he took off for the ring. Robinson recalled the moment. *"Thirty seconds before we ran out to the ring I had a big argument in the back of the dressing room with my manager, because my manager kept telling me what he always does, stick to the game plan, box. Do what you do best. And thirty seconds before I went, it was supposed to be a walk, but I ran out. I had told my whole team that I was going to fight him and everybody kept saying, 'No, don't do it. Don't do it.' And my last words to my manager were, 'If he is going to beat me. He is going to have to kill me. So you are going to have to call an ambulance and the hospital because I'm gonna be dead.' And I ran out and that's exactly what I did. I ran out."*[552]

Larry Merchant believed that Robinson running into the ring showed that he came to fight. The last time Merchant remembered somebody running down the runway and into the ring was Buster Douglas, at the Tokyo Dome, when he shocked the world with his stunning upset of Mike Tyson.

Arturo smiled as he made his way down the runway to the *Rocky* theme song "Gonna Fly Now." Walking Arturo out were his brother Joe, Carl Moretti, Pat Lynch, Mikey Red, John Capone, Lou Duva, and Arturo's new head trainer, Bob Wareing. Joe was smiling as he walked next to his brother, clapping his hands. After Roca's dismissal, Lou Duva moved into working Arturo's corner with Wareing. Joe Souza remained Arturo's cutman. Carl Moretti and Dino Duva were in the ring before the match, representing Main Events.

When Robinson was announced, he was roundly booed by the small but partisan Gatti crowd. Lou Duva walked Arturo to the center of the ring for the referee's pre-fight instructions.

When the bell rang for the 1st round, Robinson came charging across the ring throwing two clubbing right hands. Ivan later described why he started so fast. *"My whole thing was, run over there and get respect, and I had to do something because I was going in as a 4-1 underdog."*[553] Robinson relaxed and started flicking out fast left jabs as Arturo loaded up with heavy shots. With a minute remaining in the round, Arturo twisted Ivan's head with a left hook. Robinson came right back. Arturo's left eye already was showing signs of swelling. Arturo landed a hard right hand to the head and followed up with several more blows as Ivan was trapped along the ropes. Robinson turned Gatti around and landed solid right hand uppercuts and straight rights to the head.

Ivan and his corner had the textbook plan to beat Gatti, as the straight right and right uppercut were the two punches that were most successful by Arturo's opponents in the past. Gatti breathed heavily as he walked back to his corner after the 1st round ended. Robinson jumped and fist-pumped into the air as he walked back to his corner.

Arturo's fans chanted Gatti's name as Lou Duva jumped into the ring and applied Vaseline around Arturo's eyes. Wareing, poking his head through the ropes, implored Gatti to use his jab and go to the body. Wareing kept trying to get Gatti's attention, to no avail. Arturo looked like a bar patron who had way too much to drink as his glassy eyes wandered away.

A minute into the 2nd round, Arturo ripped hard shots to the body and head. With 30 seconds remaining in the round, Robinson stepped over to his right and landed a crunching right uppercut followed by a left hook. The crowd roared as though they were attending a Roman Coliseum battle. The difference in the fight thus far was Ivan's footwork. Gatti bore straight ahead while Robinson stepped in-and-out and side-to-side. When the bell rang ending the round, Roy Jones, Jr. questioned why Gatti's management and promotional team would put Arturo in with another boxer when he had so much trouble with Manfredy.

In Robinson's corner, Odell "Butch" Cathay spoke to his fighter. He warned Ivan not to stand in front of Gatti. Cathay asked for jabs and movement. In Arturo's corner, Wareing instructed Gatti to take his time and get into a rhythm. There was considerable cheerleading in Arturo's corner, but not much specific instructions. Without a doubt, Arturo's excessive partying, coupled with his rapid weight loss, had affected his strength, punching power, and especially his footwork.

Arturo started squinting out of his left eye in the 3rd round. Gatti landed several hard body punches early in the round as Robinson kept trying to spin around him. Ivan was effective at scoring and leaning back away from counter shots. Arturo started bleeding from under his left eye. Gatti landed another hard left hook but Robinson took it well. Arturo looked discouraged as the round ended.

Robinson's corner advised him to keep throwing right hands and uppercuts. They also told him to keep turning Gatti. In Arturo's corner, Wareing and Duva advised him to slow the pace down but to keep pressuring Robinson and make him miss. How could Arturo slow the pace down when Robinson was attacking him and setting the pace? Gatti looked spent. Arturo would later say, *"I kinda got worried a little bit 'cause my mind was telling me to do something but physically I couldn't do it. Something was missing, but I didn't know what it was."* Usually older fighters complain that they cannot pull the trigger, but Arturo wasn't old. Could it be that the ring wars, coupled with his thirst for the nightlife, were catching up with him? Robinson later said that by the 3rd round he felt very comfortable with the tone he was setting to win the fight.

During the first half of the 4th round, Robinson kept scoring and spinning Arturo. With 44 seconds remaining in the round, Arturo landed a right hand on the top of Robinson's head as Ivan tried to slip underneath. Robinson went down on all fours from the blow. He appeared more off-balance than hurt. Larry Merchant believed the blow muscled Ivan down, rather than the usual brain jolt that causes the leg muscles to collapse or stiffen. As soon as Robinson hit the ground, he waived his glove to his corner in a motion to display that he wasn't hurt. The crowd erupted in support of Gatti. Robinson rose at the count of seven.

Arturo tried to capitalize on the moment. He turned the pressure up, trying to finish Robinson off. Arturo later spoke of the knock down. *"That's when I knew the fight was changing, right there. When I hurt him. Because I really didn't throw it hard and he went down."* Gatti's legs were very far apart as he swung wide roundhouse blows. When the bell rang, both fighters, who were friends, smiled at each other.

Wareing screamed at Arturo to listen to him. He wanted Gatti to take his time and not go wild looking for a knockout. Robinson's corner told him to keep throwing down the middle.

The 5th round started with both fighters landing well. Arturo was throwing more combination punches instead of loading up. Robinson landed several flush right crosses on Arturo's temple, reminiscent of the Manfredy fight. Both fighters landed solid blows to end the round. Robinson's corner told him that he could make the fight easy if he kept spinning Arturo after he punched.

For the first two minutes of the 6th round, Arturo stalked Robinson, as Ivan appeared to take a break. With a little under a minute remaining in the round, Robinson stunned Gatti with hooks and crosses. After taking a dozen hard shots, Arturo reached out and uncharacteristically grabbed Robinson. The bloody gash under

Gatti's left eye was even more prominent. Referee, Earl Morton, broke the fighters.

Robinson continued the onslaught. Jim Lampley spoke of how the action reminded him of the Gatti-Ruelas battle. Just as Lampley spoke, Arturo jolted Ivan with a perfectly timed right hand. Robinson wobbled back to the ropes, clearly hurt. A desperate Gatti tried to finish Robinson off. Arturo punched his injured prey from pillar to post. Merchant asked, *"Can you believe this guy?"* Jim Lampley added, *"Unbelievable!"*

Joe Gatti stood up, cheering his brother on. Larry Merchant kept repeating that he couldn't believe Arturo was making another historic comeback. The crowd rose to their feet.

After the round ended, Robinson's corner told him not to worry about knocking Gatti out. They told him to use his quickness to box and move. Arturo grimaced in pain as Souza applied pressure to his left eye with the enswell.

Gatti stalked Robinson to start the 7th. With a little over a minute remaining in the round, Ivan landed several hook-cross combos on the inside. Arturo came back, digging a left hook to the body. Robinson landed several solid blows to end the round.

Wareing asked Arturo to use the jab to get inside. He told Gatti that he knew Arturo was tired. Wareing repeatedly asked Arturo if he was okay but Gatti didn't respond. It was surprising that no ring doctor was inspecting Arturo, especially with his closing left eye and the amount of punishment he was taking.

At the start of the 8th, Jim Lampley suggested that the Gatti legend might be taking a step towards extinction. The pace slowed as Gatti stalked. Robinson was trying to box from the outside but was forced into exchanges by Arturo's constant pressure. Arturo landed a solid left hook at the end of the round.

Arturo was fighting well in the 9th, until Robinson landed a thudding left hook with 1:14 remaining in the round. The blow sent Arturo reeling backwards. Robinson landed ten more flush shots. A wobbly Arturo tried unsuccessfully to slip the punches while his hands were at his side. It wasn't just the fact that Gatti was being hit so often, but that he was hit so solidly, and that his head snapped back the way it did, that was so shocking. But Arturo somehow collected himself and found the inner strength to press forward with a vicious assault that had Robinson retreating. As the round came to a close, Larry Merchant stated that people continuously asked him what was in Gatti's future. Merchant opined that a rematch with

Robinson may be in Gatti's future.

Robinson's corner advised him not to look for the knockout, just to win the fight. Ivan's corner also told him that he needed to win the last round.

Robinson controlled the first minute of the 10th round with crisp combinations. Arturo came back with hard hooks and crosses followed by a straight combination. Ivan landed a right cross on Arturo's left eye that made Gatti wince. Robinson kept throwing and throwing, rarely missing. Arturo gallantly fired back, desperately trying to keep pace with Ivan's onslaught.

With 48 seconds remaining in the final round, Arturo unleashed a left hook that crashed against Robinson's temple. Ivan was out on his feet as he fell back into the ropes. He tried to hold on but Arturo refused to let him, as he pounded away. Gatti later admitted that he knew he would have trouble finishing Robinson off because he was exhausted.

Ivan slipped several punches then smiled as he came back with a jab and right hand. Robinson was buckled again by a left hook moments before the final bell rang to end this unforgettable battle.

Ring announcer Mark Vero advised the crowd that there was a split-decision. Judge Ed Leahy scored the bout 96-93 for Gatti. Judge Melvina Lathan scored the bout 98-93 for Robinson. The final judge, Steve Weisfeld, scored the bout 96-94 for Robinson.

In the post-fight interview, Robinson revealed that he would grant Arturo a rematch. Larry Merchant asked Ivan why he jumped on Gatti at the opening bell. Robinson replied that he knew Arturo was a slow starter, but that Gatti would come on in the later rounds. Ivan added that he wasn't a knockout puncher so he needed to build up points early in the fight. He admitted that he was hurt in the 10th round, and at other times, but weathered the storm.

Robinson later said he wanted the rematch because he didn't want his win questioned because of Arturo's cut eye. A rematch would also garner Robinson a much larger payday. Ivan confessed that he didn't even remember the 10th round.[554]

Gatti also wanted a rematch. Arturo complimented Robinson on giving him a tough fight. Merchant asked Arturo if he was surprised at how hard Robinson came at him in the opening rounds. Gatti was not surprised. He felt that Robinson was trying to intimidate him by rushing at him.

While both boxers were being interviewed in the ring, Pat Lynch stood behind his fighter. He looked despondent, like someone who had just been told that his stock dropped by 50%. The only silver lining was that there was a rematch clause in the contract.

Judge Melvina Lathan felt the fight was exceptional. She said that she didn't think she breathed for the whole 10 rounds.[555] The *Press of Atlantic City* scored the bout 97-95 for Gatti. HBO's Harold Lederman had it 95-94 for Robinson. Main Events president Dino Duva was proud to have promoted such an exciting match. Duva added that people left the arena shaking their heads in disbelief.[556]

Pat Lynch reflected on Arturo's lack of defense. He revealed that Arturo had worked all through training camp on keeping his hands up, moving his head, and slipping punches. Lynch added that once Gatti is hit a few times the macho-man in him comes out.[557] Lynch spoke of why they made a change in trainers. Arturo wasn't as comfortable as he needed to be, so they made the switch from Hector Roca to Bob Wareing.[558]

Lynch's wife, Lisette, was due to have a baby in two weeks. When asked if she almost gave birth during the fight, she confessed that she was very close to doing just that.[559] Lou DiBella, HBO's executive vice president, revealed that negotiations were already underway for a Gatti-Robinson rematch. If Gatti was to lose the rematch, DiBella recommended that Arturo should retire. DiBella revealed that HBO wanted Gatti to come back, because even in losing, he still was the most exciting fighter in boxing.[560]

The Robinson-Gatti bout was voted "Fight of the Year" and "Upset of the Year" by *The Ring* magazine. Newark *Star Ledger* reporter Chris Thorne later opined that boxing may have witnessed the last of Arturo Gatti in the Robinson fight.[561]

Joe Gatti recalled how Arturo's entourage partied and then went home. His brother was left alone again after another loss. Arturo told Joe and Vikki that they were always the only ones who remained with him after a loss. Vikki recalled being in an elevator with Joe, Arturo, and Laura after the fight. *"We were in the elevator and we're going upstairs and I said, 'Come on babe. We're gonna go.' And what did Arturo say? He was like a puppy, 'Are you gonna stay with me?' I said, 'No, we're going home. It's like everyone else Arturo, they leave you.' Pat went home. So Arturo goes, 'I want you guys to stay with us for the weekend.' And you know, I was just being angry. You're paying these people and they didn't even come to see you. They're partying. They went home. Party's over. We both had jobs. We took off work and we stayed the whole weekend with him."*[562] Joe added, *"And you know that every time I went there I had to pay my own room. Pat never gave me a room. Pat's the one who made us become estranged. That's what he did. But people don't know that.*"563

Joe recalled that whenever he and Arturo went out from 1996 to 2000 Arturo never had any cash on him. He was always asking Joe for money. Joe didn't have much, so when Arturo asked him for $300, Joe would only take out $100. He would tell Arturo that the ATM would only give him $100. Joe recalled that he worked a whole week to make $300. Joe laughed, *"Are you kidding me. Everybody he goes out with, he's paying. Me, when he goes out with me, I'm paying [laughing]. I don't understand; every time I go out with him I have to pay for everything."*564

Mikey Red recalled that Arturo had an American Express card with a $20,000 monthly limit that always seemed to be maxed out before the end of each month. Once, when Arturo and Mikey were out eating lunch, Arturo turned to Mikey, who was making only around $40,000 a year, and said, *"Hey, are you gonna pay for lunch once in a while?"* Mikey was stunned.565 Pat Lynch may have set the monthly limit on the American Express card at $20,000 to prevent Arturo from spending all his money.

After it was announced that Arturo would box Robinson again, Ivan stated that he must be crazy to give Gatti a rematch because Arturo had sent him into orbit and back a couple of times during the match. Robinson admitted that he had nothing to gain from a rematch. If he beat Gatti again it would only prove that Arturo was washed-up, but if Ivan lost then his first win would be looked at as a fluke.566 However, Robinson did have one thing to gain from the rematch, he would make a career-high $400,000.

Arturo admitted that he wasn't himself in the first match. He blamed the 8-month layoff. He promised he would be ready for the rematch.567 Robinson, because he had won, wanted the rematch to take place in Philadelphia, not New Jersey. Obviously, ticket sales would dictate the location.

Former editor of *The Ring* magazine, Nigel Collins, felt that the Gatti-Robinson match was extraordinary because there was so much ebb and flow during the contest. He added that when the underdog turns in such a great performance, it adds a lot, because it isn't expected. Collins likened the match to a horse race that went to the wire.568

On October 1, 1998, at the Robert Treat Hotel in Newark, N.J, Joe Gatti took on 9-11-1 (3 KOs) Kelvin Prather of Albany N.Y. Prather had trained under Kevin Rooney and utilized Cus D'Amato's peek-a-boo style. The show's promoter, Gabe LaConte, of First Round Promotions, was thrilled to have the popular ticket-seller on his card. LaConte felt that having Joe on the card would bring a lot of excitement to the show.[569]

Joe had an entirely new team as he prepared to campaign in the light heavyweight division. Joe signed a three-fight promotional deal with LaConte and a new management deal with Piero Santini. His new trainer was Jose Rosario of Newark. Joe knocked Prather out in the 2nd round of their scheduled 6-round bout. Joe's record improved to 26-7 with 19 knockouts.

On October 4, the *Bergen Record* newspaper reported that eyewitnesses had observed a free-spending Arturo Gatti at the Jersey shore shortly after he signed for the rematch with Ivan Robinson.[570]

In October, the Gattis' brother-in-law, Davey Hilton, Jr., was in Miami training for his November 27 battle against Stephane Ouellet. The 35-1-2 (24 KOs) middleweight Hilton was closing in on a title opportunity. Ouellet, of Jonquiere, Quebec, was 25-1 with 16 KOs. Hilton's wife and two daughters were staying with him at the Colony Hotel in Miami Beach. Hilton returned to Canada for a pre-fight press conference.

It was during that time that Davey Hilton's daughters told their mother, Joe and Arturo's sister Anna-Maria, that their father had been sexually assaulting them. It was any parents worst nightmare. Anna-Maria's daughters, Jeannie and Anne-Marie, confided to their mother that their father had been assaulting them for five years. Jeannie was 15 and Anne-Marie was 13 years old.

As would be expected, both the Gatti and Hilton families were in shock. Joe and Arturo were furious when they learned about the abuse of their nieces. Arturo wanted to exact his own revenge before the courts did, but he eventually calmed down and let the legal process take its course.

Arturo and Donny Jerie went back down to Miami in October. Gatti relaxed while also spending time with his sister and her children. Gatti and Donny were shopping for shirts in Miami when Jerie spotted Angel Manfredy. Donny recalled, *"I said, 'Oh shit, Angel Manfredy.' And they saw each other and exchanged pleasantries, saying 'good fight.' When we walked away Arturo said, 'Damn, I should have told that dude let's get a rematch on.'"*[571]

While back in Miami, Arturo received a large stab wound on his shoulder blade, courtesy of his wild relationship with Cynthia Shaw.[572] Arturo got into a fight with another man over Shaw and was lucky he was only stabbed in the shoulder. Gatti was intoxicated at the time and didn't even know he had been cut until his back became soaked with blood. Mikey Red recalled Arturo saying, *"I would never do this stuff if my father was alive."*[573] Lynch later reflected on the Miami incidents, stating that they were tough times for Team Gatti.[574] The Miami police were growing tired of dealing with Arturo's escapades. They strongly advised Gatti to consider returning to New Jersey.

In early November, Arturo was interviewed while in training camp. He promised to give a better effort in the Robinson rematch.[575]

On December 12, 1998, Arturo Gatti and Ivan Robinson met for the second time. The original date of the rematch was scheduled for November 24 at Foxwoods in Connecticut, but Arturo needed more time to heal his injured eye. He also needed time to heal the knife wound he received to his shoulder blade. While Arturo was mending his wounds, Robinson was offered a shot at the WBC lightweight title held by Cesar Bazan. Ivan turned down the world title shot, opting instead for the more lucrative rematch with Gatti.

The HBO televised rematch was held at the Trump Taj Mahal, Mark Etess Arena. In an interview before the rematch, Arturo confessed that he was only 50% prepared for the first fight. He promised that he would be 110% ready this time. Robinson took offense to the quote by replying that Gatti's statement was a cop-out.

Team Gatti again changed trainers for the Robinson rematch. Arturo would use another Lou Duva-affiliated trainer, Ronnie Shields. Shields was a former junior welterweight boxer from Texas. Shields had previously worked with Pernell Whitaker. Shields spoke of taking over as Arturo's trainer, and how he wouldn't change much of Arturo's style, offensively. Shields felt that Arturo needed to work more on tightening up his defense. Pat Lynch and Arturo would change trainers six times during Gatti's career.

On December 11, it was announced that N.J. Nets center, Jayson Williams, a good friend of Arturo's, would carry the spit bucket into the ring for Arturo's rematch against Ivan Robinson. Lou Duva joked that he would pay Williams $30, plus a tip, if he didn't commit a turnover and drop the bucket on the way to the ring.[576]

Arturo revealed his frustration over the first Robinson match. *"I watched the tape over and over and a lot went through my mind. Sometimes you want to kick yourself in the butt afterward and that's how I felt. I probably took him a little too lightly the first time and I was also coming back from a long [eight-month] layoff, so I wasn't in great shape. And when you're not in great shape, you get hit a lot. It's going to be different this time. This time, everything is right. I'm treating this as if it was a championship fight and it's going to show on Saturday night. People are going to see what they should have seen from me in the first fight. I knew I was in trouble in the first round. I was the one getting punched instead of the other way around and I knew something was wrong. But it was my own fault. There was no one else to blame but me. That fight was a wake-up call."*[577]

Oscar De La Hoya, who fought and beat Ivan Robinson three times in the amateurs, wasn't surprised with Robinson's performance in the first fight. He knew Robinson would beat Gatti. Everyone in De La Hoya's camp thought Gatti would knock Robinson out, but Oscar knew Robinson had a big heart. De La Hoya described his three amateur fights with Robinson as wars. Oscar felt that Robinson could have beaten Gatti more easily if he had boxed in-and-out, but Robinson had a bad habit of letting the crowd dictate the way he fights. If the crowd was cheering for Gatti, he'd try to make the crowd cheer for him. That could be dangerous. De La Hoya predicted another Robinson win.[578]

Arturo made several changes for the Robinson rematch. He changed his training camp from Virginia Beach to Vero Beach, Florida, where he trained at the House of Champions Boxing Club. Lou Duva recalled, *"I had a lot of fun with Arturo in Florida. I loved Gatti. He's a good kid."*[579] Both Duva and Gatti were big pasta lovers. Unfortunately, Duva lost his pasta pal when fight-time neared and Arturo's dieting increased.

Arturo planned on changing his fighting style, putting more focus on boxing, instead of standing toe-to-toe. Arturo had made that promise in the past. He knew that a third straight loss would be devastating. *"If it doesn't end my career, it will certainly set me back. I lose this one and everyone will be saying, 'Arturo who?' I need to win this fight, not so much for other people as for myself. After what happened last time, I want to be able to walk out of the ring with my head up."*[580]

Ronnie Shields wanted Arturo to show more angles and head movement. Shields was impressed with Gatti in camp. He said that

Arturo was one of the easiest fighters he ever worked with.[581] Shields promised a different Arturo in this fight. He said that Arturo would not stand straight-up. Gatti would be throwing more combinations and moving his head more. Shields promised that Arturo would be a better fighter physically and mentally. Arturo had tried to knock Robinson out in the first fight. He threw all power shots, and didn't try to set up his power shots. Shields expected Ivan to come out fast again, but this time Arturo would be ready.[582]

Robinson's manager, Eddie Woods, gave his boxer an added incentive to win. Woods promised to donate $5,000 from his cut of Robinson's purse to Ivan's children, Ivan Jr. and Chantel, if Robinson threw more than 1,200 punches in the bout. Robinson, the consummate Philly fighter, attended the same high school as two-time world champion Meldrick Taylor. Woods stated that Ivan threw 900 punches in the first match, but promised he would throw 1,200 this time.[583]

Gatti-Robinson II, and the co-main event, Fernando Vargas-Yory Boy Campas, were blacked-out in Atlantic City. Dino Duva convinced HBO to black-out the televised fights because rival casinos were planning on showing the bouts to their preferred customers at their casinos, which would negatively affect ticket sales. Vargas, 14-0 (14 KOs), also a Main Events-promoted boxer, was fighting Campas, 72-2 (62 KOs), for Yory Boy's IBF junior middleweight title.

Robinson reflected on the first bout. He admitted that he studied the tape of the first fight every day. Ivan felt he had the Lord on his side because of the way he recovered from being hurt in several rounds. Robinson planned on defeating Arturo again. He was hoping another victory would put him in line to make a million dollars against Naseem Hamed or Shane Mosley. Ivan was expecting Gatti to try to come out fast and knock him out.[584]

Robinson had been released by Main Events after his 3rd round TKO loss to Israel Cardona on July 1, 1997. Even though Dino and Lou Duva were impressed with Robinson's victory over Arturo, there were still many critics who thought Ivan's victory was a fluke. The criticism annoyed the Philly fighter.[585] Ivan's trainer, Odell Cathay, was confident that his fighter would use his hand speed to make the rematch easier than the first bout.[586]

Arturo spoke of his position going into the rematch. *"It's a 'Catch-22' situation for me. I'm sure I can outbox him, but it might be better for me to get into a slugfest because then I can knock him out early.*

But I know the longer it goes, the easier it will get for me. I was out of shape the first time and he was on my level. People have counted me out before, but I've always come back. I'm the one who will decide when my career is over. The only way it will be over [tonight] is if Ivan brings a shotgun into the ring."[587]

Arturo was excited that he was featured in a new video game. He jokingly stated that he hoped that the manufacturer did not make him look like Rocky. Gatti reminisced about playing video games against the Mike Tyson character when he was growing up. Now the kids Arturo grew up with in Montreal could play against him in a video game. Gatti conceded that his fans needed a win.

Arturo had lost 30-pounds in 7 weeks leading up to the first Robinson fight. He had ballooned up to 170 after the Manfredy loss. This time Gatti took the weight off gradually. He was only 7-pounds overweight a month before the fight. Arturo promised to put pressure on Robinson right away. Gatti felt he was at his best when he was desperate during fights. Arturo admitted that although he practiced head movement, slipping punches and working on defense all through camp, when he entered the ring to fight he usually abandoned his defense. He added that when fans see him fight they are never disappointed.[588]

Pat Lynch spoke of the first Robinson match. He felt that Arturo left his fight in the gym. He had never seen Arturo holding on during a fight. Lynch was convinced that Gatti was back to being his old self. Lynch could not overstate the importance of Arturo needing to win the Robinson rematch.[589] Arturo felt that he fought best when he was in a desperate situation. Even though he stated this, Gatti still said he would try to avoid putting himself in such situations. He disregarded the naysayers in boxing who were worried he was absorbing way too much punishment.

Arturo would earn $650,000, while Robinson earned a career-high $400,000 for the rematch. Robinson was listed as a 6-5 betting favorite. The *Press of Atlantic City* predicted a late-round knockout victory for Arturo. Gatti weighed in at 135, while Robinson tipped the scales at 133¾. Robinson gained 12¼-pounds after the weigh-in, while Arturo gained 15-pounds. Arturo kept repeating that Robinson was going to meet a 100 % Gatti this time.

A reported 4,396 fans turned out for the rematch at the Trump Taj Mahal Casino Resort. Arturo walked into the ring first. Joe had his arm draped around his brother as Pat Lynch, Ronnie Shields, and John Capone followed. The speakers blared the *Rocky III* theme song "Eye of the Tiger." Arturo entered the bout with a record of 29-3 (24 KOs), while Robinson entered with a 26-2 (10 KOs) mark. In Arturo's corner with Shields were Lou Duva and Joe Souza. Bob Wareing was gone. Wareing was bitter at being removed as head coach. Arturo wanted Wareing to remain his strength coach for the Robinson rematch, but Wareing declined the offer.

Arturo started the 1st round jabbing and moving his head effectively. Halfway through the round, as Arturo leaned his head forward to avoid punches, Robinson ripped several angle punches upwards, flush on Arturo's face. Although Arturo had changed trainers several times, he still was slipping his head up-and-down instead of side-to-side. Arturo landed several hard shots as the crowd chanted his name. Ivan came back with a flurry. Gatti tried to slip and block the shots but his hands were at his side, which led to many of Robinson's blows landing.

After the round ended, Ivan's corner advised him to stay off the ropes. Shields asked Arturo to throw uppercuts and step around Robinson.

At the start of the 2nd round, Arturo's hands were very low. Robinson made him pay with a left hook. A minute in, Arturo threw a crisp jab followed by a right cross around Robinson's guard. Robinson answered with a solid uppercut as Gatti again put his head straight down. Arturo started displaying more head movement, but he still got caught with a left hook because his hands were low. Arturo started bleeding from a cut in the corner of his left eye. Both boxers traded blows at the end of the round, but Robinson's punches appeared to have more snap on them.

Referee Benjy Esteves recalled the match, *"During the Robinson match I was really amazed with how much respect they had for each other. They were talking to each other throughout the whole fight, but no trash talking. You know, 'Good shot, nice move, I love you.' And when the bell rang, you know, it was like I couldn't believe it. Cause these guys were having a conversation like they were at the dinner table. I was shocked cause they were so cordial to each other while they were punching each other out."*[590]

Robinson's cornermen implored him to keep his right hand up off of his chest. In Arturo's corner, Shields instructed Gatti to move to his right. He also asked Arturo to throw uppercuts on the inside. Shields was visibly frustrated with the way Arturo was performing.

Arturo started the 3rd round strong, as he landed several hard body shots. In the second half of the round, Robinson opened up on Gatti with power blows.

It was clear to see that Arturo had lost the strength and speed needed to score a one-punch knockout. Either it was the move up in weight, or his partying, or a combination of the two, that led to Arturo losing his crunching power. He still punched hard, but not hard enough to end the fight with one punch.

Arturo was hurt with a hook to the body. He stumbled around the ring as Robinson unloaded on him. At the bell, Arturo was hurt again with a frighteningly flush right hand. Robinson landed 59 out of 100 punches in the round.

Souza went straight to work on Arturo's damaged eye as Shields shouted instructions. Shields wanted Arturo to stay low and step around Robinson after he finished punching.

Both fighters slowed up considerably in the 4th. Arturo started the round digging several hard body punches. Gatti appeared to try to use his head to spear at Robinson. Ivan pushed Arturo's head down. Gatti responded by throwing a left hand very low, into Robinson's groin. Ivan grimaced in pain.

Esteves separated the two and halted the action to allow Robinson time to recover. When the action resumed, Ivan landed a thudding left hook as the round came to a close.

Shields told Arturo that he wasn't moving his head. Both corners asked for more jabs. Robinson's corner told Ivan that Arturo was desperate. Robinson was told to retaliate with his own low blow if he was hit low again.

During the first minute of the 5th, Arturo trapped Robinson along the ropes, but again Robinson took the punches well. HBO's announcers started contemplating Arturo's future if he were to lose the fight. Both boxers had their moments in the round.

Both fighters looked tired to start the 6th. A little over a minute into the round, Arturo landed two more low blows. Esteves warned him again. Robinson landed crisp blows on the inside, as Arturo again tried to use his head to push Robinson off of him. Arturo's vision appeared to be affecting him, as he missed many more shots than he had in the first fight. A sharp Robinson right hand had Arturo holding on as the round came to a close.

Larry Merchant voiced his surprise that both fighters still knew where their corners were. Shields instructed Arturo to stay low. Shields also wanted uppercuts and body punches when Gatti was on the inside. Shields told Arturo that he was standing up too straight. The HBO broadcasters displayed their surprise that Duva was entering the ring in-between rounds, and not allowing Joe Souza to enter the ring, as he would be in a better position to treat Gatti's cut eye.

In the 7th, Robinson landed a tremendous number of head shots. Arturo was extremely lucky that Ivan was not a knockout puncher. Arturo landed a right hand on Robinson's thigh but Esteves did not intervene. Both fighters landed hard shots as the crowd responded with "oohs" and "aahs." Robinson finished the round landing several hard rights to the head. Arturo properly slipped away from the rights but his chin was not tucked against his shoulder. This lapse in defense allowed Robinson's punches to land anyway. Merchant opined that Arturo was taking a terrible beating. Lampley added that no matter how much the fans adored Arturo, it could not be entertaining for them to watch him taking a beating like this.

Arturo stumbled drunkenly back to his corner. He sat on the stool and his head dropped downward. Shields threatened to stop the fight unless Arturo started using head movement. Arturo absorbed 77 punches during the round and hundreds more during the fight thus far.

In Robinson's corner, Butch Cathay advised Ivan that he was way behind. As Cathay spoke, Ivan sat on his stool with his mouth wide open in disbelief. Robinson gazed at his trainer with a look that appeared to say "Are you crazy?" There was hardly a spectator in the building who thought that he was behind in the fight. Obviously, Cathay was trying to motivate Robinson to finish strong and possibly stop Arturo.

Arturo came out hard in the 8th, as he swarmed Robinson. Gatti landed a left hook that strayed very low. Referee Esteves stepped in and took a point away from Arturo. Gatti finished the round strong, pounding Ivan's body over the final minute. The round may have been Arturo's best of the fight. Unfortunately for him, the point deduction nullified the solid round.

Shields applauded Arturo's performance and asked for more uppercuts and body punches. In Robinson's corner, Cathay complained that Ivan was letting Arturo outwork him on the inside. Robinson argued that Arturo was landing low blows on him.

Gatti tore into Robinson in the 9th. Ivan quickly spun Arturo around and landed clean head shots. Both fighters traded bombs. Arturo landed a thumping right hand flush on Robinson's jaw. Ivan seemed unfazed. Arturo pounded on Robinson along the ropes. Esteves broke the two fighters, mid action, to have Arturo's eye examined. He led Gatti to his corner, over Arturo's protest. Gatti knew he had Robinson in trouble and wanted to continue his assault. Arturo pulled his arm away from Esteves as the referee tried to lead him to the ringside doctor, to have his eye examined. The eye was bleeding, but Arturo's eye had been in much worse condition in many previous fights.

A shocked Larry Merchant asked what was going on. Merchant did not see any change in the cut. Lampley agreed. Gatti was infuriated. He felt he had Robinson in trouble with the body assault. Arturo's eye looked the same as it had for several rounds. Esteves is a top notch referee whose motives are unquestionable. However, it could be argued that he should have waited for a lull in the action before having the eye checked.

When Esteves called the fighters back into action, Robinson had the bounce back in his legs. With 30 seconds left in the round, Arturo landed another low blow. Esteves motioned as though he was going to intervene, but suddenly changed his mind. Lampley couldn't believe that a second point wasn't being deducted.

After the round, Robinson's corner told him to retaliate with his own low blows when Gatti hit him below the belt. In Arturo's corner, Shields told him that he needed a knockout to win.

Both fighters tapped gloves and heads in a show of mutual respect as the bell rang for the 10th and final round. Arturo came out like a fighter needing a knockout to win. Robinson fought like a fighter who was way ahead on the cards. In the back of Ivan's mind, he may have remembered how close he came to being knocked out in the 10th round in the first fight. Halfway through the round, Arturo lunged at Ivan and both fighters fell to the floor in exhaustion. Arturo finished the round stronger than Robinson, as Ivan appeared to fight safety-first. Both fighters raised their hands as the final bell rang.

Dino Duva and Carl Moretti made their way into the ring, clearly disappointed in the outcome. Judges George Colon and Joseph Pasquale both scored the bout 95-94, while Jean Williams scored the bout 97-92, all in favor of the winner, Ivan Robinson. If Arturo hadn't lost the point for a low blow, the fight would have been judged a draw. In reality, Esteves could have justifiably taken several more points from Arturo.

Regarding the point he took from Gatti in the 8th round, Esteves recalled, *"I took a point away from Arturo Gatti. I could've taken more because he threw a lot of low blows, but I didn't want to become a part of the match. Hey, I just wanted to let the guys work it out. If I didn't take the point deduction it may have been a draw. I have no control over that, but I am just glad that the right guy won."*[591]

Robinson landed 98 more punches than Gatti. Larry Merchant asked Ivan if this bout was easier than the first one. Robinson revealed that Arturo fought much harder than in the first fight. Ivan admitted that he couldn't hit Arturo as much in the head because Gatti was moving too much. He credited Shields with doing a great job on Arturo's head movement. Robinson confessed that Arturo was a terrific body puncher, but added that several shots were below the belt.

Arturo stated that he had tried his best. Gatti credited Robinson with being a great boxer and a terrific defensive fighter. Merchant asked Arturo if he would continue fighting or retire. Gatti said that he would continue fighting, but he was contemplating moving up in weight to 140-pounds.[592]

Robinson was headed to Mexico to celebrate his fourth wedding anniversary. He was not interested in a third bout, unless the money was right.[593]

Lou DiBella felt that this wasn't the end for Arturo Gatti. He added that you don't end a career when your last three fights are all fights of the year. DiBella assured that Arturo would be back.[594]

In confidence, a member of the Gatti team revealed, *"I honestly do not know how Arturo was able to engage in those three matches in 1998. With the life he lived at the time. It is a virtual miracle."*[595] Before he left for the Atlantic City Medical Center, Arturo reflected on his third straight loss. *"I did my best. I trained really hard for this fight. But I got away from my game plan and I started too late again. I can't take anything away from Ivan, though. He's a great boxer and a great defensive fighter. I had a hard time connecting my punches on him."*[596] When Arturo arrived at the Atlantic City Medical Center's emergency room, the admitting nurse, upon seeing him, shouted, *"Not you again!"*[597]

Dino Duva was concerned for Arturo's health. Duva stated that in the past, even though Arturo would be taking punches, he kept waiting for that one punch that would turn the fight around. But this time, for the first time, Dino started feeling terrible watching Gatti get hit. He could barely watch as Arturo absorbed punch after punch. During the last couple of rounds, Duva felt sick to his stomach watching Gatti get hit by Robinson.

Arturo told Duva that he still felt like he had more to give in boxing. Gatti told Dino that he needed one more fight to get back on track. Duva believed in him, but Dino wanted to take the safe route. He didn't want Arturo in another high-risk fight right now. Duva wanted to take Gatti to Montreal for a homecoming against a beatable opponent. Dino could use the match to gauge how much Arturo had left in his fight career. Duva thought now might be a good time to go to Canada to build Arturo's career back up.[598]

Robinson commented on Arturo's lack of defense. Ivan didn't think Arturo could last another year taking the type of shots that he was taking. Robinson recalled being in a clinch at one point, around the 6th round, and Arturo said to him, *"You're a champion, man. I love you."* Robinson was thinking, *"I'm beating you up. Why you saying that?"*[599]

Veteran fight manager and promoter, Mike Acri, stated, *"All those constant beatings, plus the way he has to beat his body to make weight at 135, I'd be asking myself how he's going to be in five years if I had him. I understand the TV aspect of it. He makes great fights. But Arturo needs to be looked at closely for his own safety now. I'm not saying he shouldn't fight again, but he needs to take some time off and take a real, long look at things. He's been in a half dozen tough fights. Matthew Saad Muhammad and he should be brothers. Every fight was a war for both of them. Wars lead to casualties. You got to remember that Arturo is the kind of guy who will fight until he's dead."*[600]

Booking agent Johnny Bos didn't think that Arturo would be a world champion again. Bos recommended that Gatti's handlers should lower his level of competition until a big fight comes along. Bos added that he heard a rumor that Arturo was going to move up to 140 to fight Julio Cesar Chavez. Bos believed that Chavez would kill Gatti.[601]

Arturo was well aware that he was on the precipice, as far as his career was concerned. Gatti revealed, *"I don't like to be a great loser. I'm tired of the Rocky stuff. I want to fight for a while. People tell me I'm a good lookin' kid, but I know if I'm not careful I'll lose those looks."*[602]

Mario Costa spoke to Pat Lynch after the Robinson losses. *"I used to say to Pat, 'You can't do this. Every time he loses it is like somebody is stabbing him in the back with a knife.' But they didn't understand that. It hurts me because all Lynch cares about is 'nine times Arthur sold out the Convention Center.' Every time Pat brought him down to Atlantic City to fight, he was bringing him closer to his death.*"[603]

Chapter 16
Gamache

Joe Gatti was the first brother to box in 1999. He returned to the ring at Zofingen-Aarau, Switzerland, on January 2, where he took on 17-9-3 (11 KOs) Allen Smith of Creston, Iowa. The 12-round bout was for the International Boxing Council's Intercontinental light heavyweight title.

When Joe and Vikki arrived in Switzerland, they were shocked to find a large media presence waiting for them as they exited the plane. Joe thought the photographers were there for someone else, but they were there for him. There was a limousine waiting to drive them to their hotel room. Joe's boss, Robert Merlo Sr., accompanied Joe to the fight.

Like most boxers, Joe was on edge before his fights. He had the same jealous streak that Arturo displayed. On the day of the fight, Joe was enjoying lunch and a glass of wine with his wife and his boss at a local mall. There were four men sitting across from Joe's table. The men, who were eating, kept looking over in Joe's direction. Although the men probably were fans, Joe thought they were staring at his wife. Joe shared his thoughts with his wife. Vikki thought Joe was crazy, but she jokingly said, *"They are looking at me. I'm beautiful."*[604] Vikki's comment sent Joe over the edge. He stormed over to the table where the men were seated and slammed his hand down on the table. He said, *"What are you looking at?"*[605] He realized that the men did not understand what he was saying. He asked them what language they spoke. When they said Italian, Joe spoke in their language. Joe told the men, *"I'm going back to my table and you better not look up. Stare at your food and eat!"*[606]

Vikki wanted to crawl under the table. To make matters worse, another Italian man walked over to the table and praised Joe in his handling of the situation. That's the last thing Vikki wanted to hear. She told the man, *"Don't egg him on."*[607] Joe's boss Merlo knew of his jealous streak. He played a joke on Joe the night prior. He called Joe's hotel room and when Joe answered he disguised his voice and said, *"Poopie, is he sleeping yet?"*[608] This was done to make Joe think Vikki was preparing to meet someone when Joe fell asleep.

The Gatti-Smith bout was preceded by a beautiful display of lights, with accompanying smoke machines. Al Certo, and his nephew Danny Milano, worked Joe's corner. Joe dispatched of Smith in the

3rd round to win the IBC Intercontinental title. Joe used the purse from the fight to buy his first home in Paramus, N.J.

Arturo took some time off to heal up after the second Robinson fight. Arturo and Donny Jerie planned another trip to Miami. Jerie recalled the night before they left. *"Around 10 p.m. Gatti said let's go to a club. We had to catch a flight to Florida at 11 a.m. We went into the city and I was like, 'We got to get that flight. We better get outta here. Let's go.' We all got in the car and Gatti got in the car and we went back to the house. And then we went to watch a little TV. Arturo liked to watch his DVDs when he fought. He had every one of them."*[609] Jerie recalled that Arturo would get excited when he watched tapes of his fights. He would wince and say, *"Ah man, Ooh,"*[610] as he watched himself getting hit. After they were finished watching the tapes they went to Lynch's house. Lynch saw how intoxicated everyone was and said, *"You guys are crazy."*[611] Jerie recalled, *"We were all banged up when we got on the plane."*[612]

Donny recalled how Arturo accessed money while in Miami. *"Pat controlled the money. Every once in a while he would FEDEX money to Arturo when he called. Three or four times he sent money."*[613] Donny spent eight days in Miami with Arturo. He remembered Arturo saying to him, *"Donny this trip's on me. Whatever you want."*[614]

While in Miami, Arturo went out with world championship wrestling's Missie Hyatt. She was nine years older than Arturo. Jerie recalled that Hyatt was trying to control Gatti, and *"Arturo sent her on her way."*[615]

Arturo and Donny stayed in the most expensive room in the Casa Grande Suite Hotel in South Beach. Donny recalled that they left for Miami with no luggage. They had to go shopping for clothes. Donny recalled shopping with Arturo in Miami. *"Whatever I wanted, Calvin Klein suits, shirts, cause we didn't go there with anything."*[616]

In March 1999 a small controversy erupted. The *London Sunday Mirror* reported that 43 phone calls between Ivan Robinson and boxing judge Eugenia Williams occurred in the weeks before the second Gatti fight. Williams had the widest score in the bout, 97-92. She gave two more rounds to Robinson than did the other two judges. Robinson downplayed the calls by stating that he clearly defeated Gatti. He admitted that he had spoken to Williams via phone and that he and Williams had been friends since he boxed in the amateurs. Robinson knew Williams' son and daughter. Robinson admitted that it would be improper for him to be too close to Williams, because she was a judge.

Pat Lynch commented on the controversial phone calls. He called for an investigation. Lynch felt that if Williams was a friend of Robinson's, she, as a professional, should have bowed out of working the fight.[617] Lynch added that he would not protest the decision, as it was unanimous. If the phone calls weren't suspicious enough, Williams had filed for bankruptcy in January, stating that she had $20 in the bank. Williams, who earned a $37,000 yearly salary in Atlantic City, made two deposits into her bank account totaling $8,465 in the months following the second Gatti-Robinson match.[618]

Williams was under great scrutiny around this time, owing to her 115-113 score in Evander Holyfield's favor against Lennox Lewis in a highly controversial draw on March 13, a fight in which virtually everyone except two of the three judges thought Lewis clearly won.

Previously active as a judge, Williams did not judge again for a year-and-a-half following Holyfield vs. Lewis I, but as of mid-September 2000, she was back judging again in New Jersey.

Joe Gatti was concentrating on work and paying his bills. Of course, if a good payday was offered he would return to the gym.

In the spring of 1999, Joe and Vikki stopped in a deli in Lyndhurst, NJ to buy some sandwiches. While the couple were on line, Joe was carelessly looking around when his eyes locked on someone familiar-looking. He couldn't believe what he was seeing. The pizza delivery guy who allegedly took Arturo's car speaker eight years earlier was on line in the deli. Joe had told Vikki about the stolen speaker incident, but she had forgotten the story.

As Joe was staring, the man recognized him. Joe recalled, *"It's like he saw a ghost. I know he knows who I am. But I pretended that I didn't recognize him."*[619] Joe walked past the guy and swept his arm behind him, causing him to barrel into the potato chip stand like a stuntman would in a slapstick movie. Bags of chips went flying all over. Vikki was shocked. She turned to Joe and asked, *"Did you mean to do that? Joe, do you know that guy?"*[620]

Joe turned to Vikki and whispered, *"That's the guy! That's the guy who took Arturo's stuff."*[621] Joe apologized to the Deli owner and offered to pay for anything that was damaged. Joe then walked outside to where the man had stumbled. The man's girlfriend was right behind him. The man was yelling at Joe, *"I'm gonna sue* *you."*⁶²² Joe had waited eight long years and ran many city blocks in Jersey City for this moment. Joe replied, *"I know, I know all about it. You're gonna sue me. I'm gonna rip your head open. Let's go [Joe took a fighting stance].'"*⁶²³ The alleged thief squared off and said, *"Let's go."*⁶²⁴

As Joe prepared to exact his revenge, a man standing by the curb pleaded with Joe, *"No sir. It's not worth it. It's not worth it. Leave it alone. Leave him, it's not worth it."*⁶²⁵ While Joe was contemplating his next move, the guy's girlfriend started yelling at Vikki. Vikki yelled at Joe to get in the car. Joe thought it over and said, *"I guess it's not worth it."*⁶²⁶ Joe then turned to the man and said, *"You're lucky."*⁶²⁷ Joe hopped into his car with Vikki and drove off. Eight years had passed and Arturo was a millionaire, but Joe still felt that he had to confront the guy who took his little brother's property.⁶²⁸

On April 17, 1999, Angel Manfredy completely dominated Ivan Robinson in a one-sided fight.

In mid-May, it was announced that Arturo would return to the ring against Erie, Pennsylvania's Reyes Munoz. Gatti started his camp in Lake Tahoe, Nevada because his trainer, Ronnie Shields, was there working with heavyweight contender David Tua. By June, Arturo was back in camp in Virginia Beach. He and Bob Wareing had gotten past the ill feelings of Wareing's dismissal as head coach. Wareing was Arturo's strength coach again.

KO magazine's Nigel Collins interviewed Arturo after he arrived back at his Virginia Beach training camp. Gatti told Collins that after his second loss to Robinson, he went back to Montreal to visit with his mother. Arturo told Collins that he met up with friends from high school and went out chasing girls. Arturo was asked about getting stopped by the police while driving in Montreal. Arturo stated that it was nothing like the New Jersey incident. Arturo was out with friends partying and was the only person remotely capable of driving when he was stopped.⁶²⁹

Arturo was selected the "Most Exciting" and "Most Courageous" boxer in the world by *The Ring* magazine. He admitted that he was not happy with his performances in 1998. He felt that moving up in weight would help bring him success in the ring.⁶³⁰

Arturo was asked if his body needed extra time to heal from the brutal fights he had participated in. Gatti answered by stating that he did not consider his fight with Manfredy a loss, because of the way the bout ended. Arturo felt that he had won the first Robinson match.

He believed that Robinson beat him more with his intelligence than with his talent.[631]

The second fight against Robinson would have been ruled a draw if Arturo hadn't been penalized a point for low blows. Arturo was asked if he thought the point deduction was appropriate. Gatti admitted that some of his blows were indeed below the belt line. He felt that the second fight would have ended much differently if he would have been awarded the first match.[632]

Arturo was asked about his habit of starting slowly in his bouts. He felt that being forced to lose weight was draining his body. Gatti was optimistic that moving up to 140-pounds would give him an advantage.[633]

Collins asked Arturo if he was interested in fighting for the IBF lightweight title vacated by Shane Mosley. Gatti replied that he would be, especially if Manfredy won the title. Arturo wanted to give Angel a beating. Gatti felt that regardless of whether or not he fought Manfredy for a title, he couldn't wait to run into Angel again, because Manfredy kept talking about Gatti. Angel's mouth obviously was getting on Arturo's nerves. Gatti added that Manfredy needed to keep talking about him, because without Arturo, Angel was irrelevant.[634]

Arturo was asked why he couldn't knock Robinson out. Gatti confessed that Ivan was a very smart fighter who gave him few opportunities to hit him solidly. Arturo revealed that he told Lynch that he wanted to fight brawlers, not boxers that he had to chase around the ring. In regards to whether he was losing his power, Gatti boldly declared, *"Everybody who fights me knows that if I crack 'em right, they're going to sleep."*[635]

Arturo advised Collins that Bob Wareing returned as his strength and conditioning coach. Gatti felt much stronger when he trained with Wareing. Arturo stated that he wanted to fight three more years and win two more world titles. Arturo was asked if he ever thought about being seriously injured in the ring. Gatti revealed that if he felt he would be seriously hurt he would quit boxing. Arturo admitted that his mother asked him to retire, but he wouldn't, because boxing was his life. He enjoyed the excitement and the money.[636]

Collins asked Arturo if he was saving money from his fights. Gatti confided that Lynch was entrusted with saving his money. Arturo felt that his best paydays were still ahead of him.[637]

Collins commented that Arturo lived his life outside of the ring with the same reckless abandon that he employed during his fights.

Collins pointed to Gatti's DWI arrests and the street fight that left a knife scar on Arturo's back. Collins likened Arturo to a 27-year-old teenager rather than a thug. Collins felt that Gatti was a fun-loving guy who sometimes allowed his exuberance for life to overtake his common sense.[638]

By August, Arturo had moved his training camp to Vero Beach, Florida, where he was sparring with New Jersey prospect John Molnar and Texas' Juan Lazcano. Molnar was co-managed by Pat Lynch and Peter Finn.

Arturo and Lynch flew to David Tua's fight against Gary Bell on July 17, at Caesars Tahoe in Stateline, Nevada. When Arturo walked into the Circus Maximus showroom, fans started screaming his name. Before long, the entire audience started chanting, "Gatti, Gatti!" Fans were lining up in the aisles for autographs and pictures with Arturo. Gatti turned to Lynch and said, *"Can you believe this?"*[639] Arturo was shocked that he had so many fans.

Lynch felt that the eight-month layoff would help Arturo get his confidence back. Lynch pointed to the fact that Arturo's three loses could have easily been wins. Lynch added that Arturo's next opponent, Reyes Munoz, seemed to be durable and aggressive. Arturo commented, *"I've heard people say he's a good opponent for me because of his style."*[640]

Arturo returned to the ring on August 14, 1999, against the 21-3 (9 KOs) Reyes Munoz. The bout was held at Foxwoods Resorts in Mashantucket, Connecticut. Munoz had only defeated three boxers with winning records in his career. Munoz would receive $35,000 for his efforts, by far the largest purse of his career. Arturo's friend, Jayson Williams, of the N.J. Nets, attended the match.

Arturo was desperate for a win. Carl Moretti and Main Events tried to make sure that he would get a victory. Arturo's bout was on the undercard of the Stevie Johnston-Angel Manfredy WBC lightweight championship bout. Johnston would win the fight by decision, retaining his title. Both the Johnston-Manfredy and Gatti-Munoz fights were televised on HBO's "Boxing after Dark" series.

Arturo was interviewed a week before the Munoz battle. *"I'm doing good with my training and I'd just like to say to my fans and to the people back in Jersey City that I want to thank them for supporting me and I'll be back. I'm very confident. I'm working very hard for this fight. I'll be in shape and I'll be ready. This one is important because I am coming off those three losses in a row."*[641]

Arturo was moving up to the junior welterweight division for the first time.

Munoz worked by day creating concrete barriers in an Erie, Pennsylvania factory. Many boxing insiders considered the bout a complete mismatch. Working Arturo's corner for the Munoz fight were Lou Duva, Ronnie Shields, and Joe Souza.

As soon as the bell rang starting the bout, one could immediately see the difference in talent. Arturo was taller, quicker, faster on his feet, and of course stronger. Near the end of the 1st round, Reyes attempted to duck a Gatti right hand but Arturo landed the punch on the back of Munoz's head. As Reyes was falling backwards, Arturo followed up with a left hook on Munoz's shoulder. Reyes dropped to the floorboards.

He pulled himself up as Referee Eddie Cotton counted. Cotton peered into Munoz's cloudy eyes. Munoz's left eye was closed and his pupil was severely dilated. As Cotton reached the count of eight, Reyes stumbled around the ring as though he were dancing the Jitterbug. Cotton waived the bout over. Munoz was led back to his corner where he was directed to sit on a stool.

HBO announcer Jim Lampley mockingly said that the Gatti-Munoz affair was good matchmaking. Ringside physician Anthony Alessi ordered a stretcher into the ring after examining Reyes. Munoz's wife and mother cried at ringside as he was wheeled out of the building on a stretcher.

Reyes spent several days in the hospital. The knockout was so vicious that Munoz's professional boxing license was permanently suspended in the United States. Doctor Alessi felt that Reyes suffered post-traumatic left third cranial nerve palsy.[642] HBO Boxing's vice president of programing, Lou DiBella, admitted that although the Gatti-Munoz match looked good on paper with their win-loss records, Munoz had no shot of defeating Gatti.[643]

The *New York Times* reported that Arturo was so shaken by Munoz's injury that he skipped the post-fight news conference. It also may have been that Arturo was embarrassed by the mismatch. Reyes nearly lost consciousness en route to the hospital. Arturo visited Munoz in the hospital and refused to leave until doctors assured him that Reyes was not in serious danger.

After Arturo was assured that Munoz would be okay he went out partying with Mikey Red and Donny Jerie. Skowronski recalled, *"When Arturo fought in Connecticut and knocked out Reyes Munoz we had a lot of fun afterwards. I was so drunk, I pissed in the phone booth at Mohegan Sun and Arturo was so nervous he thought that I was going to go to jail for life."*[644] Jerie added, *"We were shot. Arturo was pissed because he was embarrassed [with the mismatch]."*[645]

Critics displayed their disgust with the obvious mismatch. Lou DiBella took the brunt of the criticism. Pat Lynch defended DiBella by stating that they had turned down easier opponents, such as Mike Capiello of Boston. Lynch added that he was surprised when he saw that Munoz looked intimidated prior to the start of the bout. Arturo wasn't happy with the match. He had hoped to get into a rhythm and get a good workout in.[646]

In August 1999, Arturo invited Joe to go with him to Martell's Tiki Bar in Point Pleasant. When Joe told Vikki about the invite, she immediately realized that the two brothers going to the summer beach bar was a bad idea. Vikki accompanied Joe. Arturo's fiancé Laura also went. Arturo started drinking heavily. Joe also had a few drinks.

It wasn't long before the two beautiful blondes were garnering looks from other male patrons in the bar. The intoxicated Arturo noticed this and started arguing with his fiancé. He could not contain his jealousy. Vikki called Arturo the little Gremlin. Just like the Gremlin would change from nice to bad with a meal after midnight, Arturo was the same way. His mood would change if he was drinking or using drugs. Laura became fed up and started walking out of the bar. Vikki got up and followed Laura out. Four guys in the bar followed Laura and Vikki outside to ask them to come back inside, not knowing that the two guys they left behind were their fiancé and husband. They also had no idea that the two brothers were professional fighters. Joe tried to calm Arturo down before they got up to leave, not knowing that men were following their women.

When the girls reached the parking lot one of the men asked Laura and Vikki if they wanted to go back inside for a drink. He told the two girls that they need not worry about Arturo and Joe, who he must have thought the girls just met in the bar. The men asked Laura and Vikki what they were going to do for the remainder of the night. Vikki nervously advised the men that they were talking to the wrong two women. She told them to go back inside the bar, that there were numerous women for them to talk to in there.

Joe and Arturo reached the parking lot. Joe, realizing that the men were flirting with Laura and Vikki, walked up to the leader of the group and asked him if he had a problem. Arturo, though drunk, was closely watching Joe. He had witnessed this same scene many times in Montreal where his brother would knock out several tough guys with ease. Joe again asked if the men had a problem, but this time Joe prepared to start swinging. One of the men realized that Joe was way too confident and was standing like a boxer. The man reached into his back pocket and pulled out a wallet. He opened the wallet and showed Joe a police badge. He stated he was concerned for the two women. Vikki knew that this was not true, but she was glad the situation ended without anyone getting hurt.[647]

Main Events was struggling. Many of their top fighters were losing, aging, or leaving the organization. Thirty-five-year-old Pernell Whitaker had lost two fights in a row and was nearing the end of his career. Meldrick Taylor and Evander Holyfield left the organization several years earlier. Kathy Duva had suspended Dino Duva in May, in part due to Dino allegedly giving a $25,000 bribe to International Boxing Federation president Robert W. Lee Sr. In May 1998, Lee solicited the $25,000 from Dino to move junior middleweight Fernando Vargas up in the rankings. After Dino agreed, Lee and several others in his organization moved Vargas from #5 to #1 in the world. Dino allegedly paid Lee the bribe money in December of the same year. Dino would later cooperate with federal authorities in their investigation of Lee.

In December, Kathy Duva fired Donna Duva-Brooks. She discovered that Donna was helping her brother, Dino, and her father, Lou, organize a new promotional company called Duva Boxing. Kathy replaced Dino with longtime N.J. State Athletic Control Board employee Gary Shaw. Shaw took over as Chief of Operations. The IBF president, Lee, would later be convicted on six charges, including tax evasion and money laundering.

Many of Main Events' fighters were unhappy and threatening to leave the company. The company was in its darkest hour and on the verge of collapse. Kathy later admitted that the only reason she didn't give up the company was because doing so would have meant letting go of her husband Dan.[648]

In the same month, Dino and Donna filed a lawsuit in State Superior Court against Main Events and Kathy Duva for their dismissal from the organization. The lawsuit would eventually be settled out of court in the spring, at the behest of family patriarch Lou Duva. Kathy would bring a much different management style to the company than her deceased husband did. Dan was known as "The Bull," for his loud and autocratic style. Kathy was more quiet and calculating.

On November 20, Stephan Johnson was struck in the head twice in the 10th round of his Atlantic City bout against Paul Vaden for the USBA light middleweight title. Johnson was knocked unconscious and remained in a coma for fifteen days. Johnson had also lost consciousness in a bout on April 14, 1999, in Toronto, against Fitz Vanderpool, when he collapsed in the 11th round. Johnson had won two bouts after the Vanderpool loss.

Larry Hazzard's executive assistant, Rhonda Utley-Herring, said that Johnson's CT scan prior to the bout showed no abnormalities. Hazzard added that Johnson had gone through, and passed, the standard prefight testing.[649] On December 5, Stephan Johnson died.

New Jersey had some of the strictest medical examination requirements in the country. They required boxers to undergo an EKG, a CT scan, an HIV test, an eye exam, as well as a prefight and postfight physical. The tests cost the boxer, or more accurately, the manager or promoter, $600. The average 4-round boxer made only around $600 or $700 for a match. There were even some promoters that would pay fighters with tickets, though this practice later would be banned by the commission.

Besides taking heat from lawmakers and the public in regards to boxer safety, Hazzard was taking heat from boxing trainers, managers, and promoters for the astronomical prices of medical tests. Al Certo, who survived the state investigation, said he lost $6,000 on two shows that he promoted in the summer. Each show attracted around 400 spectators. The costs of boxer purses, physicals, insurance, and commission fees were destroying small-time boxing shows.[650]

Certo complained that he could not afford to run club shows any longer. Gabe LaConte echoed that sentiment. He ran two club shows in 1999 and they both lost money. Certo and LaConte laid the blame at the feet of the boxing commission. At LaConte's last show, at the Robert Treat in Newark, 20 state officials were on hand. He was forced to pay $3,102 for the officials. LaConte said that the fee is the same that casinos pay for large-scale TV shows. LaConte stated that he lost $2,500 on his last show. Some states charged half the fees that New Jersey did. Local fight manager Lou Romano lamented the fact that physicals in New Jersey cost between $500 and $600 no matter if it was a 4-rounder or a 10-rounder.[651]

Hazzard countered that the taxpayers of New Jersey were not interested in footing the bill for boxer physicals. Hazzard seemed unconcerned with the club show promoters' complaints. Hazzard felt that if the club show promoters worked with each other it would help alleviate some of the issues that they were complaining about.[652]

Some promoters felt that Hazzard was purposely trying to sabotage the club show scene. The number of club shows drastically dropped under Hazzard's reign as commissioner.

Few people came out publicly against Hazzard because they did not want to be subject to his wrath. Gabe LaConte felt that Hazzard ran the commission like a boot camp. Certo opined that Hazzard wanted to rule with an iron hand. Certo felt that Hazzard thought he still was a schoolteacher, treating the promoters like he would his students. Certo added that Hazzard only fought as an amateur boxer and knew nothing about fighters trying to make a living in the sport.[653]

Hazzard did have his supporters, even if they were swayed by the fact that he ran boxing in the state. Lou Duva stated that Hazzard was one of the best in the business. Duva added that Hazzard had been a good amateur boxer, a good referee, and that he knew boxing from A to Z.[654]

Hazzard's background was impressive. Born in Newark, he won three N.J Golden Glove titles as an amateur. He worked as an amateur and professional referee, working 35 championship fights. Hazzard earned a master's degree in school administration from Montclair State University. He was employed as a junior high school principal prior to being appointed state boxing commissioner. Hazzard earned $84,500 from the position in 1999.

Hazzard criticized the local promoters by pointing to the fact that most of the fights they put on were mismatches. Hazzard felt this led to a poor turn-out for local shows.[655] Hazzard did not take into consideration that the local promoters were trying to protect their ticket sellers with the matchmaking. The fans of these boxers didn't care how they won, just that they won. It is the popular fighters that help to keep the club shows afloat. Hazzard had no qualms about suspending fighters that he felt did not give a good effort. In his first year as commissioner, Hazzard suspended 35 boxers that promoters used to "pad" their prospects' records. The 35 represented 9% of the licensed boxers in the state. Hazzard called the 35 suspended boxers his turkey list.[656]

On December 15, Arturo's team announced that Hector Roca was returning as head trainer. Gatti's merry-go-round of trainers was continuing. They also announced that Arturo would be back in action on February 26 at Madison Square Garden, against former two-time champion Joey Gamache. The fight would be on the Oscar De La Hoya vs. Derrell Coley undercard. Pat Lynch revealed that the Gamache fight was a match that HBO wanted. He added that it would be a competitive fight.[657]

Arturo originally had plans for an additional fight before the end of 1999, but he sprained his hand in training, which ended those thoughts. Lynch revealed that Arturo would start his conditioning for the Gamache fight in mid-December.[658]

Arturo's training camp for the Gamache fight was changed from the usual location of Virginia Beach to the Fernwood Resorts in the Pocono's region of Bushkill, Pennsylvania. For sparring, Gatti's team brought in Leonard Dorin, a Romanian, and Fathi Missaoui, a Tunisian, both of whom resided and fought out of Canada. Arturo also was sparring with New Jersey's John Molnar.

Lynch acknowledged that Arturo would have to get used to having his training camp in cold weather, because all of his previous camps had been at warm weather locations.[659] Lynch commented on bringing back Hector Roca as head trainer. He stated that Ronnie Shields was a good trainer but Arturo wanted to work with Roca again. Lynch added that Gatti felt that he never really lost a fight training under Hector, because the Manfredy fight ended from a cut. Lynch wanted Arturo to be comfortable and work hard in camp. If that meant changing trainers, so be it.[660] Allegedly, Arturo had asked Shields to work with him again, but Shields, apparently frustrated that Arturo didn't listen during the fights, told Gatti that Roca was probably a better fit for him.[661]

Vikki commented on the change of training camp locations. *"I wanna say the only time he fought 100% is the camp that me and Joe went to with him, when he fought Joey Gamache. He was 100% and he almost killed the kid in the ring. He was clean cause he couldn't get away, cause we were there."*[662] Joe drove over an hour every Friday night, after work, to spend the weekend helping Arturo prepare for Gamache. Joe was paid $2,500 for his efforts. Vikki also spent the weekends with her husband and brother-in-law.

Working Gamache's corner was Diego Rosario. Diego had trained both Joe and Arturo in 1992. Diego still worked with Joe on occasion.

Arturo's training camp was in full swing by the first week of February, as he added Agapito Sanchez and Sterling Gethers as sparring partners. Lynch felt that Arturo was boxing and moving much more in camp than he had during his previous few camps.[663] Arturo added, *"I want to box three or four times this year, so I've got to give up the wars if I'm going to do that. I'm going to box more. I did it when I faced Tracy at the Garden when I won the title."*[664]

The week before the Gatti-Gamache match, *Jersey Journal* reporter Wayne Witkowski visited Arturo's camp. Hector Roca was asked about reuniting with Arturo. Roca said that he loved Arturo and never talked about the past with him.[665] Arturo's final sparring session was 7 hard rounds of action against John Molnar and Agapito Sanchez. Arturo was supposed to spar 10 rounds, but Gatti looked so sharp that Roca cut the session short.

Arturo commented on the camp. *"I like it here. I just want to get out of here and get in the ring. It's been nine weeks [of training camp]. I actually feel faster, I don't know why. I'm happy to be back with Hector. Maybe we should never have separated. He knows me real good as a fighter. I feel really confident. There's something about him that brings it out of me."*[666] Witkowski mentioned that a Gatti win might bring about a match with either Billy Irwin or the winner of the WBU super lightweight title match between Shea Neary and Micky Ward. Pat Lynch shot down rumors of a possible rematch with Manfredy.[667]

Arturo spoke of his future should he defeat Gamache. *"A lot of good things for me could come out of this fight. It's a big event, like fighting for a world title, and my people expect a big fight from me. I appreciate their patience and being there for me in New Jersey and New York and the whole world. It's having the fire back. Some people probably think I still have it and I do. It wasn't in me the last few fights. I can't wait to put on the 8-ounce gloves and see my performance."*[668]

Witkowski felt that Arturo looked very sharp in sparring and appeared to have rediscovered his boxing ability. Roca helped Gatti go back to his old style of feinting the body, feinting his feet, throwing combinations, and not looking for the one-punch knockout. Roca wanted Gatti to think he was a fighter, not a bully.[669]

Gamache felt that Arturo's skills were declining. Joey believed that there were many who were questioning what both he and Gatti had left in their careers. Gamache was confident that he had more of a future than Arturo because he lived a cleaner life outside of the ring. Joey felt that speed and versatility were the keys to victory.[670]

Arturo and Pat Lynch, with help from Mikey Red and Donny Jerie, sold nearly all of the 700 tickets they were allotted. Lou DiBella called the Gatti-Gamache match traditional old-fashioned New York boxing.[671]

Hector Roca felt that Arturo looked better than the last time they worked together. Roca commented on Arturo's fights after he was let go. Roca revealed that he couldn't watch Arturo on TV because of the way he fought. Roca felt that Gatti was more mature now. He also felt that Arturo was hungry, angry, and very upset because Gamache didn't respect him.[672]

Arturo was asked if he had any butterflies. *"I have them right now. I have to be more cautious. I can't change my boxing style. But I'm faster now and more explosive. And I won't go into the ring bloated like I did the last few fights. I'm leaner now. I'll stay at this weight, but if there is a world title shot at 135-pounds, I'll go for that."*[673]

Gamache had previously held both the WBA super featherweight and lightweight titles. Joey was on a ten-fight win streak dating back to 1996, when he was knocked out by Julio Cesar Chavez. Gamache, of Lewiston, Maine, was guided by the matchmaking prowess of Johnny Bos. Bos had also guided Tracy Patterson's career. Bos, an eccentric individual, was an honors student in the art of matchmaking and giving his fighter "the edge" needed to be successful.

On paper the match looked like a good one. Gamache was a seasoned veteran with good footwork and ring smarts. The 33-year-old Gamache held a record of 55-3 with 30 KOs. Two of Joey's three career losses were by spectacular knockout fashion. He was flattened on his back by Tony Lopez and Orzubek Nazarov, both in WBA title bouts.

Bos originally wanted the contract weight for the bout to be between 145 to 147-pounds.[674] Gamache's previous two bouts had been against middleweights Jerry Smith and Craig Houk. Main Events would not agree to a higher weight. Either Gamache would take the match at 141 or Main Events would find another opponent.

Ironically, Gamache wound up having no trouble making the weight, but rather it was Arturo who was suffering. At their final press conference in Manhattan, Gamache tormented Arturo by eating a chicken cesar salad with an ice cream sandwich for dessert. Arturo, still overweight, sat nearby looking emaciated. As Gamache was leaving, he teased Arturo, asking him if he wanted a bite of his delicious ice cream sandwich.

The fireworks would begin at the weigh-in on February 25. Earlier in the day, Gamache checked his weight on the official scale. He weighed in at only 137. When his manager, Johnny Bos, brought this information to officials, they checked the scale with a 100-pound weight. The scale read 97-pounds. Was the scale's calibration off by accident? Johnny Bos didn't think so. Arturo had spent the day in a plastic suit jumping rope, spitting, riding exercise machines and sitting in a steam room. It was rumored he still was 1½-pounds overweight after a day of torture.

The official weigh-in took place at 4:30 p.m. on the sixth floor at Madison Square Garden. The N.Y. State Athletic Commission's director of boxing, Bob Duffy, a former police officer and former president of New York's Metro amateur boxing program, was mysteriously missing during the weigh-in. Duffy had conducted hundreds of weigh-ins for the commission, as its director of boxing. In his place, conducting the weigh-in, was executive director Tony Russo. Russo did not have much experience at the scales. Assisting Russo was boxing commissioner Melville Southard. Russo had told Duffy that he wanted to perform the weigh-ins. Duffy felt slighted and did not appear at the weigh-ins, which were videotaped. De La Hoya and Coley were the first on the scales. Coley's team complained that Oscar jumped off of the scale while the needle was still bouncing up and down.

After Coley weighed in, Arturo stepped onto the scale. The videotape clearly showed the needle of the scale striking the top of the beam, which indicated that Arturo was heavier than the 141-pounds that the scale was set at. Russo can then be seen readjusting the counter-weight to a heavier position than 141. Commissioner Southard was looking on as this occurred. The needle was still hitting the top beam. Gatti was asked to raise his arms and take a deep breath. The needle fluctuated, and before the needle settled, his weight was called out as 141. Arturo quickly stepped off of the scale and began rehydrating.

Gamache's team, which consisted of Johnny Bos and trainers Jimmy Glenn and Diego Rosario, immediately screamed foul and demanded that Gatti be re-weighed. Their requests were shot down, as Russo could be heard saying, *"Shut the fuck up, stop stirring up shit."* Russo even went as far as to call Bos an alcoholic. Gamache weighed in at 140¼-pounds. Bos demanded that Arturo be re-weighed. Gatti stood nearby, ignoring Bos, drinking fluids with the same satisfied look that Gamache had displayed at the press conference while he was eating ice cream. To be fair to Arturo, once the commission declares that a fighter has made weight, a fighter can drink and eat all he wants. Pat Lynch later stated that he would never allow a fighter to go to a weigh-in seven or eight or even 3-pounds overweight.[675]

It was announced that Arturo had sold $190,000 worth of tickets for the fight.

Arturo admitted that Gamache had much more experience than he himself had. Gatti added that Gamache had fought Chavez when Chavez was still in his prime. Arturo felt that having Hector Roca back helped him to be more physically and mentally prepared than he had been for his previous three fights.[676] Gamache felt that he had the edge in the matchup.[677]

On February 26, 2000, Arturo continued his climb back up the rankings against the former two-time world champion, Joey Gamache. A few hours before the bout, both fighters were re-weighed. Gatti weighed 160-pounds, while Gamache tipped the scales at 146. Gatti added 19-pounds in 24 hours. The weight gain, over 13% of his body weight, only added to the controversy that Arturo was overweight during the weigh-in.

Arturo's purse was $300,000, compared to the $75,000 that Gamache would take home. Arturo held a 1½-inch height advantage over the 5'6" Gamache. Arturo also held a 1-inch reach and a 6-year age advantage over the 33-year-old Maine native. During the pre-fight introductions, HBO analyst Larry Merchant commented on Gatti's penchant for punishment. Merchant stated that Arturo ate punches like most people ate french fries.

Scott DePompe recalled how composed Arturo was before the fight. *"Arturo forgot his mouthpiece for the Gamache fight. He told several people to chew gum and he stuffed it in an amateur mouthpiece that had been boiled, and used it. He never sweated anything."*[678]

Gamache made his way into the ring for the 10-round non-title bout. Walking him into the ring were his manager-adviser Johnny Bos and his trainers Jimmy Glenn and Diego Rosario.

Arturo was walked to the ring by Hector Roca, Pat Lynch, Joe Souza, and his brother Joe. Jon Bon Jovi's "Living on a Prayer" blared through the Madison Square Garden speakers. When Gamache was standing in the ring facing Gatti, one of the last things he remembers saying to himself was, *"This guy looks big."*[679] Gamache turned to Bos and asked if it was Arturo he was fighting or his middleweight brother Joe.

The bout opened with both fighters trading jabs. Gamache landed a short left hook 30 seconds into the round. Arturo fired a wide right hand and left hook but both punches missed. Joey slipped to his left to avoid a jab but his right glove was slow to follow, creating a gap between his jaw and his glove. Arturo quickly capitalized on the opening with a sharp right hand. Gatti followed with a left hook around the guard of his smaller foe. Gamache again leaned to his left, trying to avoid another jab. This time his right glove was on his chest, exposing the entire right side of his face. Arturo landed another flush right hand that dropped Joey onto his side.

Gamache was up at the count of five as Arturo celebrated with his hands raised in a neutral corner. Gatti came right at Joey and was caught with two solid left hooks. Arturo dipped and landed a crunching left hook to the body, followed by another to the head that deposited Gamache onto the canvas again.

Joey was up at the count of four, but his legs were unsteady. Arturo came pouring in again, but his chin was exposed. Gamache landed several flush hooks on the free-swinging Arturo. Gatti came back, using his entire body to level a left hook that landed flush. Arturo looked to see if the blow had starched Gamache but Joey remained standing. Arturo slipped to the floor while loading up with a punch. Several seconds later the bell rang. While referee Benjy Esteves was separating the fighters, Arturo landed another hook that stunned Gamache. Joey walked to a neutral corner before realizing where his corner was.

Bos complained of the punch after the bell to Tony Russo. He asked for five minutes for his fighter to recover. His plea's fell on deaf ears.

In Gamache's corner, Jimmy Glenn asked Joey how he was feeling. Gamache replied that he was good. Glenn then asked Joey if he knew where he was. Gamache replied that he was in a hell of a fight. A commission inspector repeated the question and Joey replied that he was in a Gatti fight. In Arturo's corner, Hector Roca advised Gatti to set up his punches, use his jab, and keep his composure.

Thirty seconds into the 2nd round, Arturo landed another stinging left hook which sent Gamache reeling. Arturo attempted a hook that missed but a follow up right landed flush. Arturo took a half step back and then came in with a sizzling uppercut, hook, cross combo. All three punches landed solidly, flattening Gamache.

Esteves waived the fight off immediately as Gamache was dropped like a felled tree. He laid motionless on the canvas. Arturo, Lynch, and Joe Gatti celebrated on the opposite side of the ring while Gamache looked as stiff as a corpse would at a funeral wake. Lynch shouted to the HBO announcers that Team Gatti was back.

Gamache attempted to sit up several times, each time falling back down. Joey would later state that the knockout would cause him a decade of headaches and memory loss, which would force him to take pain killers. Gamache added that he experienced numerous suicidal thoughts from the career-ending incident.

Arturo looked deeply disturbed after the violent Munoz knockout, but he didn't look particularly fazed after this knockout. Maybe he remembered Gamache teasing him with the ice cream at the final press conference.

The emergency medical personnel wanted to carry Gamache out on a stretcher, but Joey demanded that he be allowed to walk back to his dressing room. Arturo went to Gamache's room and offered apologies for the brutal knockout, but Joey told Arturo that he did what he was supposed to do as a fighter. Gamache would spend the night at St. Vincent's hospital experiencing terrible headaches and vomiting. The official time of the stoppage was 41 seconds of the 2nd round.

Jim Lampley spoke of the rumors of a possible Gatti-Chavez fight in the future.

Larry Merchant interviewed the winner, asking Arturo about his back-to-back frightening knockout victories. Arturo admitted that the Munoz knockout was scary but Gamache appeared all right. Merchant then asked how Arturo accomplished such a quick knockout. Gatti said that he had trained very hard for the fight. Merchant asked Arturo about the obvious size difference between he and Gamache. Arturo side-stepped the question by stating that as soon as the fight began he realized that he was much stronger than Gamache.

Arturo would later comment on the weight issue. *"We both do the same thing. I don't care if the guy is 20-pounds more the next day, as long as he made weight the day before. I feel bad; I hope [Gamache's] well. I don't wish that on anybody, getting hurt in the ring. But it was a fair thing. I weighed in at 140, and whatever happened, happened. And gaining so much weight doesn't help you all the time. It can make you slower... You can become sluggish. You're not used to carrying that much weight."*[680]

Arturo was asked who he would prefer to fight next. He immediately answered Kostya Tszyu at 140, without giving the question much thought. Arturo was again asked about his weight gain. With a smile he said that he felt good, not bloated and that he felt quick, even though he gained "a good" 19-pounds.

On March 8, it was announced that the N.Y. State Athletic Commission was turning over all of their records on the Gatti-Gamache fight to the district attorney for review of any criminal violations.

On March 11, Joey Gamache announced that he was retiring from boxing. Gamache revealed that doctors had told him that he was very lucky not to have suffered severe brain damage from the knockout. Gamache felt that he was lucky to be alive. Gamache's father, Joe Sr., stated that it was a criminal tragedy. He believed that Arturo failed to meet the contracted weight.[681]

On March 16, at the Downtown Athletic Club in Manhattan, attorney Paul Callan announced that he would be suing the New York State Athletic Commission for $5 million dollars on behalf of Joey Gamache, who he claimed suffered a permanent traumatic brain injury from the knockout. Gamache laid the blame squarely on the shoulders of the commission and not Arturo.[682] The boxing commissions in New York and Nevada kicked around the idea of changing the day-before weigh-ins to same-day weigh-ins. The idea was briefly adopted by New York.

After the Gamache fight, Arturo went back to his hard partying. Joe recalled Laura trying to change Arturo's dangerous partying habits. Laura approached Pat Lynch about the situation. Joe recalled, *"Laura argued with Pat to control Arturo because she couldn't."*[683] Not long after, Arturo broke up with Laura. She may have crossed the line when she went to complain to Lynch.

Donny Jerie recalled that after Arturo and Laura broke up, Arturo ran into her in a club. *"Arturo stops in a club in New York. He sees Laura there dancing with some guy. This is after they broke up. Arturo tries to get Laura to dance with him. He's drunk. The guy that Laura's with says, 'Hey buddy, what are you doing?' Arturo said, 'Do you know who the fuck I am?' The guy opened up his jacket and showed Arturo a gun. Arturo backed away."*[684]

At one point, Joe was driving past Arturo's Gregory Commons condo and decided to stop in to say hello. When Joe walked up to the door of the first-floor condo he noticed the front door was open. He entered the apartment and found his brother passed out on the floor. His skin was black and blue. He appeared to be overdosed. Joe helped bring Arturo back to consciousness.

After the incident, Joe stopped by frequently to make sure his brother was ok. Their relationship improved. Whenever Joe was assigned to work in Hoboken for the elevator repair company, he would call Arturo and they would meet for lunch.

Arturo met Vivian Penha. Penha, of Brazilian descent, stated that she met Arturo while she was in a North Jersey restaurant with some friends. A friend had invited Vivian to see Gatti fight in Atlantic City against Angel Manfredy and Ivan Robinson, so she knew of Arturo before they met. Arturo was impressed with Vivian's knowledge of his career. The pair had been inseparable since meeting.[685]

Penha would later discuss Arturo's partying lifestyle and how hard it was to deal with at first. Vivian described Gatti as an extreme person. Either he was really good or he was really bad. Penha added that when Arturo was good, he was the greatest person in the world. Vivian felt that Arturo struggled because he had achieved fame and fortune at an early age. The fact that most of his family was in Canada led to him being lonely at times. Penha revealed that she told Gatti many times that he needed to open his eyes and get himself together.[686]

Arturo spoke of meeting Penha and how she brought him back down to earth.[687] Gatti credited Vivian with helping him to drop some of his party friends and live a cleaner life.[688] Arturo was madly in love with Vivian. Photographs of the couple were featured in both *The Ring* and *KO* magazines. Arturo stated that by dropping certain friends he was able to avoid drugs and alcohol.

When Arturo first started dating Vivian, he called Joe in a state of excitement. *"You have to see her. She's just like Vikki."*[689] When Joe met Penha he thought to himself, *"Oh my God, my brother's blind already."*[690] Donny Jerie had a different view of Vivian. *"I wish he was still with her because he would still be alive. They had their differences but I'll tell you right now, she still loves him. I know that. She didn't want him to party at all."*[691] Before long, Arturo invested in a clothing line that Vivian started.

Arturo believed in the spirit world. When he was high and spoke of spiritual things, those around him were careful not to laugh. If he felt you didn't believe, or made fun of him, he would get angry very quickly. Vikki felt that Vivian exploited Arturo's belief in sorcery. Vikki recalled that Penha would put things in the freezer, in the tradition of conjures or hoodoo. Putting a symbolic item, such as a photo, in the freezer, symbolized freezing that person's words or activities. It could even mean freezing that person out of your life. Vivian would tell Arturo, *"Your head's going to fall off."*[692] Arturo believed in these types of spiritual paradigms.

Penha would play mind games on Arturo by telling him that she was placing a spell on him. Arturo was truly frightened of these things. Joe and Vikki did not get along with Vivian. They felt that Penha was threatened by Joe's relationship with Arturo.

Arturo would experience the same problems with Penha that he experienced in all of his relationships. Arturo was very possessive, even borderline paranoid in his relationships. Vivian would soon move into Arturo's condo at Gregory Commons in Weehawken. Later, the couple would move into a home in Mahwah. Vivian would jog with Arturo when he was conditioning himself in-between training camps, but she mostly stayed behind when Arturo went away to camp in Vero Beach.

Joe and Vikki would stop by and visit Arturo when he lived with Vivian in Weehawken. Arturo would take out a Ouija board when they came over. Vikki had no idea where Arturo even found the game. During one visit, Arturo took the Ouija board out and asked a question. The planchette moved by itself. Arturo's eyes opened wide and he jumped up out of his chair and ran into the kitchen. Vikki wanted to laugh but she refrained. She was amazed at how a tough, champion boxer was afraid of a board game. Joe believed that Arturo received his spiritual fascination from his mother, who would pay psychics to tell her the future.

Joe recalled that Arturo would frequently tell him, *"You walk at night, you walk with death."*[693] What did Arturo mean? Did he literally mean not to walk in the evening? It sounds more like he was making a spiritual statement. In the Bible there are many quotes which tell the reader to walk in the light, meaning to walk with God. The Bible consistently equates Jesus with light and life, and Satan with darkness and death. What exactly was Arturo trying to communicate to his brother? How aware was Arturo of the meaning of his words? Arturo was knowledgeable in religion as well as witchcraft.

Not long after, Joe decided to buy a Harley Davidson motorcycle in Rochelle Park, NJ. Joe and Vikki were driving in their car with Arturo when Joe mentioned to Arturo that he was thinking of buying a motorcycle. As soon as Joe opened his mouth Vikki cringed. She knew that Arturo had a history of promising to help his brother verbally, only to renege on his promises later. When Arturo heard

Joe say he was buying a bike he said, *"No, no, no, Joe please, I'll buy the motorcycle for you. I'm building one already in Canada. You remember all the hottest motorcycles that we always wanted? I'm having one of those custom built and I'll have one made for you too."*[694] Vikki jumped in, *"No, no, no, no, Arturo. Thank you but we want a stock bike, a custom bike would be too much trouble."*[695] Arturo broke down and started crying, *"I know what I did to you guys with the house. Vikki please, please, let me do this."*[696] Vikki stated, *"No, no, no Arturo. That's ok."*[697] After the house incident, Joe made a pact with Vikki that they would never trust Arturo when he offered help because of the money they lost in the house venture.

Finally Vikki gave in because Arturo wouldn't take no for an answer. Arturo called Joe a few weeks later, asking Joe if he was going to go to Canada because his bike was ready to be picked up. Arturo needed to pay the balance on his bike. Arturo gave Joe a blank check to pay off his bike. He told Joe to add $5,000 for the down payment to start work on Joe's bike. Arturo said, *"It's ready. Go pick up my bike and put the $5,000 down on your bike."*[698] Joe and Vikki drove the eight-hour drive up to Montreal on a Friday night in Joe's Dodge Ram. He rented a trailer that he attached by a hitch to use to transport Arturo's bike back to New Jersey.

Joe and Vikki arrived at the bike shop and told the owner that they were there to pick up Arturo Gatti's bike. The owner pointed to a corner and said, *"Well, there it is."*[699] Vikki and Joe turned to look at the bike. They were shocked at what they saw. The bike was up on a lift with no tires on it. The owner said, *"I told your brother to come down. He has to sit on the bike. I have to customize the seat."*[700] Vikki turned to Joe and said, *"Yeah, that's our gremlin."*[701]

Joe told the shop owner that he wanted a custom bike made for himself and he gave the specifications. The owner said, *"No problem."*[702] Joe took out the check that Arturo had given him and told the shop owner, *"I'm going to give you $5,000."*[703] The owner asked, *"Is that $5,000 American or Canadian?"*[704] Vikki motioned to Joe to say American but Joe said, *"Nah, Canadian."*[705] If Joe would have said American that would have been equal to about $7,500 in Canadian dollars. Joe was confident that Arturo wouldn't back out on his promise again. When Joe called Arturo and told him his bike wasn't ready, Arturo said, *"Well that's what the guy told me."*[706]

About a month later, the shop owner called Joe for another payment. Joe called Arturo. The bike cost $58,000 total, Canadian.

Arturo, who had promised to pay for the bike, didn't give Joe another penny. Joe believed that Vivian told Arturo not to pay for the bike. Mario Costa felt it was Pat Lynch that got into Arturo's head and made him back out on his promise. Joe had to finish paying for the motorcycle, $38,000 U.S., on credit cards. Even after Arturo reneged on paying for the bike, he asked Joe to bring his bike home when Joe went up to make a second payment on his bike. Joe agreed to bring his brother's bike home.

Joe and Vikki picked up Arturo's bike and were heading back to the U.S. At the border, the Canadian Border Patrol asked for the registration or title to the motorcycle. Joe did not have either one. The border patrol confiscated the bike. Joe started crying. He told Vikki that they would never see the bike again. It would get chopped up. Vikki asked to speak to the head of the border patrol. He promised that he would hold the bike until they came back with the proper paperwork. Joe and Vikki drove eight hours back to New Jersey to pick the title up from Arturo. The following Saturday they drove back up with the title, picked the bike up and brought it down to New Jersey.

While Arturo was away at camp, Joe kept an eye on his apartment. Joe was taking Arturo's mail into the house when he noticed a letter from the IRS. Arturo owed $75,000. When Joe asked Arturo why he owed the money, Arturo replied, *"I owe the taxes. I have to pay my penalties. I didn't pay my taxes."*[707]

Joe went to Lynch and demanded to know why no one paid his brother's taxes. Joe recalled the conversation. *"'How come my brother didn't pay his taxes? I thought you were the manager?' Pat said, 'Well, you know your brother.' I said, 'No, I don't know my brother. You are his manager. Are you scared he's going to get rid of you? How are you going to give him that money, to do what he wanted with it? Now he owes money.' He had to pay $75,000 every month until he paid his principle."*[708] Joe gave Lynch advice, *"Hire an accountant to make a deal."*[709]

Vikki spoke of the IRS fiasco. *"Yes they [IRS] gave him a payment plan. I would have died."*[710] Joe continued, *"It all escalated. It was just no good. It was just falling apart. And meanwhile, Arturo's going up and down. I asked [Arturo] who he was fighting. I asked him to put me on the show. I said, 'Bro put me on the card, so I can come back. I need a good show to come back on. This was before I made my last comeback. [Arturo replied,] 'I don't know if Pat's going to do that.' I said, 'Bro, what do you mean Pat? You're the boss. Without you there's no Pat. Come on, what's wrong with you?' I'm yelling and he looked at me. He didn't know what to say. I said, 'Forget it. I thought you were my brother.'"*[711]

Vikki interjected, *"Pat had him so brainwashed."*[712] Joe continued, *"First Arturo asked, 'Would you fight on my undercard?' I said, 'Are you kidding me? You're the champ. What do you mean do I mind. Of course I'll fight on your card. I'm proud you're the champ.' So then he goes, 'I don't know if Pat's gonna let it happen.'"*[713] Arturo apparently thought Joe would be ashamed to fight on his undercard because Joe was the star, main event attraction, when Arturo was still an amateur. Another road-block that would have made it nearly impossible for the brothers to fight on the same card was the fact that Arturo fought under the Main Events promotional banner, and Joe had left the company on bad terms.

The one incident that may have overshadowed everything else was the issue of a forged check while Joe was watching Arturo's condo in Weehawken. Several friends of Arturo's recalled that they had heard that Joe wrote himself a $20,000 check, with Arturo's checkbook, without permission. They recalled that Arturo was more hurt by his brother's behavior than he was angry about the money. They added that Arturo never fully got over the incident. Joe denied ever cashing a check of Arturo's.

Joe commented that he never cashed a check without Arturo's approval. He said that when he was cleaning and doing laundry for Arturo in his apartment in Weehawken, on one of the many times Arturo was away in camp, a box of blank checks came in the mail. Joe recalled that he gave the box to one of Arturo's friends to give to him. He assumed that it was this person who forged the check. Either way, the relationship and trust between the brothers was severely fractured, if not shattered.

Pat Lynch handled Arturo's finances. When he noticed that the forged check had been cashed, he brought it to Arturo's attention. Arturo was told, and more importantly he believed, that Joe had forged the check. Arturo went down to speak to Mario Costa about the incident. Arturo told Mario that he was disappointed in his brother. Mario looked Arturo in the eyes and said, *"Are you kidding me. That's your brother. You should give him anything he wants."*[714]

Arturo was now a millionaire, but only he and a select few were reaping the rewards. Not his brother who brought him to America, nor Mario, who had spent thousands housing and feeding both brothers. Arturo offered Costa no compensation for his expenses and thus would garner no sympathy from him. Still, Joe and Mario supported Arturo because they loved and cared for him, but they expected Arturo to be as loyal to them as they were to him.

It didn't matter to Arturo that they had helped him attain fame and fortune. He was so wrapped up in the whirlwind of success that he expected them to be as blindly obedient to him as the rest of his entourage were. Joe and Mario would never be able to do that. They spoke bluntly to Arturo when he was partying too much or when he was spending too much money on phony friends and relationships. Arturo didn't want people like that around him. He wanted people that acquiesced to his wild lifestyle.

Arturo was slated to be back in action on April 29, on the Lennox Lewis-Michael Grant undercard at Madison Square Garden. Gatti's team was experiencing problems finding Arturo an opponent. Lynch was asked about the opponent status on April 3. He hoped to have an opponent locked in by the end of the week.[715] Some of the possible opponents mentioned were Gary Kirkland, Homer Gibbons, and Wilfredo Negron. Lynch was asked about the New York State Athletic Commission's investigation into the scale issue for the Gamache fight. Lynch stated that he hadn't heard anything since the investigation was opened.[716]

On April 13, it was announced that Arturo would fight Homer Gibbons, 40-7 (30 KOs), of Georgia, in a 10-round bout. Lynch was relieved that an opponent had been found. Lynch wanted Arturo to fight four times before the end of the year, with the final fight for a world title in October.[717] After Gibbons was selected it was discovered that he was under suspension in New York after suffering a damaged vertebrae in a fight several years prior. Carl Moretti still tried to get the bout approved. Lynch admitted that Gibbons had the style that Team Gatti preferred. He was a straight forward, tough opponent.[718]

On April 20, Team Gatti received more bad news. The fight with Homer Gibbons was off again. The N.Y. Commission would not approve Gibbons without additional testing to prove that his vertebrae was healthy. Moretti stated that a possible opponent for Arturo might be Vivian Harris because he was known to stay in shape and always be in the gym. Moretti had only eight days to the weigh-in. He needed an opponent who would not only make the weight, but also one who had the proper medical tests completed. Moretti felt that it was sometimes easier to find a last-minute opponent because it was an opportunity for someone to fight a name fighter like Arturo Gatti for a decent payday. Moretti cautioned that if Gatti knocked his opponent out, some would say it was because the opponent took the fight on short notice. Moretti was not concerned with the critics, he was more concerned with keeping Arturo active, in shape, and making money.[719]

Gatti's opponent, when they found one, would receive $20,000 to $25,000 for the match. Lynch felt that Arturo needed to fight a tough, competitive opponent. Lynch added that whomever Gatti fought, Arturo would be criticized. If he knocked his opponent out quickly the fight would be called a mismatch. If the bout went a few rounds, Gatti would be condemned for not displaying the power to stop his opponent. In Lynch's eyes, it was a no-win situation.[720]

Arturo was asked if he was concerned that he did not know who his opponent would be at such a late stage in his camp. *"It doesn't matter to me who the opponent is because I always prepare the same. As long as he's in great shape. I just want to fight someone legit and not hear any excuses. And I don't want to hurt anyone."*[721]

The New York State Athletic Commission decided to change the weigh-in to the same day as the fight to avoid the controversy of the Gamache bout. Gatti's camp didn't believe it would be a problem as Arturo had fought in Pennsylvania four times early in his career. Pennsylvania has same-day weigh-ins. The last time that Gatti fought in Pennsylvania, however, was six years prior.

Arturo was asked about the Gamache weigh-in controversy and the fact that the upcoming fight's weigh-in was changed to the same day of the fight. *"Everybody asks about my weight because of that fight but it [the same day weigh-in] doesn't matter. It's just stupid they have to do that. Because of me, they'll ruin it for other fighters."*[722] Lynch commented that he would have liked to have had the weigh-in the day before, because fighters often dehydrate to make weight. The longer a fighter has to replenish himself, the safer it is for the fighter. Lynch pointed to the fact that Arturo gained 16-pounds after he weighed-in for the Ivan Robinson fight, but the weight gain was not an issue because Gatti lost that fight.[723]

On April 24, it was announced that an opponent for Arturo had finally been found. Arturo's opponent would be Indiana native Eric Jakubowski, 20-6 (4 KOs).

On Wednesday, April 26, at the final press conference, a disruption occurred. Sean Daughtry, a New York welterweight with a 16-3 record, stood up and demanded justice. Daughtry claimed that he had been promised a match with Arturo. Daughtry took off work from his job as a stockbroker to make his claim at the press conference.

The promoter, Panos Eliades, promised to look into the matter at a later time. Arturo waited, along with everyone else, for Lennox Lewis to arrive to start the conference. Lewis arrived over an hour and forty minutes late.

Arturo was forced to leave the conference early because his federal boxing I.D. was expired. He had to drive to Trenton N.J., an hour and a half away, to renew it before 4 p.m.

Daughtry revealed that he was contacted by Gatti's team three weeks prior, to fight Arturo. He said that he trained hard the last three weeks in Gleason's Gym to make sure that he was at the proper weight for the match. Daughtry added that Jakubowski had fought his own brother twice.[724] It was indeed a fact that Jakubowski lost to his brother Marty Jakubowski, by knockout, in 1993. Daughtry said that he rushed to get his pre-fight blood test completed on Tuesday, April 25.

Carl Moretti commented on the mix-up. He admitted that Daughtry was a back-up in case Jakubowski was not approved by the commission. Lynch stated that Daughtry was only considered after the Gibbons match fell through. Lynch added that it was discovered that Daughtry had had an operation on his eye. Main Events was concerned that the medical issue with his eye could have prevented him from being cleared to fight. Even if he were cleared, Team Gatti worried that if Daughtry's eye was further damaged during the fight it would be a publicity nightmare.[725]

Daughtry admitted he had previously had an eye injury that was surgically repaired. He felt that the real reason he was being turned down was because Arturo's trainer, Hector Roca, knew Daughtry from Gleason's Gym and felt he was too tough of an opponent.

On the morning of the fight, the boxers were weighed in. Jakubowski weighed 145. Arturo weighed 149-pounds, 2-pounds above the welterweight limit. Some were worried that Arturo would be affected mentally by his previous two fights, during which both of his opponents were taken to the hospital.

During the HBO/TVKO pay-per-view broadcast, announcer Jim Lampley revealed that Arturo took several months off to rejuvenate his body after his three straight losses. That couldn't be further from the truth. Arturo wasn't resting his body. He was putting it through the same abuse that he received in the ring. The only difference was that instead of punches causing the damage it was drugs and alcohol that were delivering the damaging blows.

Lampley spoke of how Arturo's previous two fights were brutal mismatches, and how Jakubowski, who hadn't fought in over a year, took this fight on one-week notice. Arturo was walked to the ring by Lynch, Roca, his brother Joe, and cutman Joe Souza.

Before heading to the ring, TVKO representatives asked Arturo to step on a scale that they had placed outside of his dressing room. Arturo refused to be re-weighed. He stated that his promoter and manager advised him against doing so.

On the telecast, Arturo revealed that his sister Pina (Giuseppina) was married earlier in the day. He apologized for not being able to attend the wedding, but congratulated her.[726]

From the opening bell, Arturo pressed the overmatched Jakubowski with body shots. Eric landed a few left hooks while he was against the ropes. Amazingly, Jakubowski scored with ease when he threw. Arturo's head was stationary and his hands were held slightly below his ears, exposing his temple. Arturo continued to dig piercing shots to the midsection which caused Jakubowski to drop his guard to protect his abdomen. With 35 seconds remaining in the round, Arturo took advantage of the drop in Eric's guard by timing a lead right that landed flush on the jawbone. Arturo opened up. The crowd oohed and aahed as though they were watching a fireworks display. With 25 seconds remaining in the round, Gatti landed a perfectly placed left hook on Jakubowski's exposed jaw that dropped Eric onto the seat of his pants.

As Jakubowski rose to his feet, some of the fans jokingly yelled for him to stay down for his own well-being. Arturo landed another solid right hand as the round came to a close.

Jakubowski's corner told him to stick to boxing. In Arturo's corner, Roca advised Gatti to bounce around and cut off the ring. He told Arturo not to press too hard. Roca predicted that the overmatched and outgunned Jakuboswki would get knocked out in the next round.

Thirty seconds into the 2nd round, Arturo landed a right uppercut. He missed a left uppercut that was blocked and followed with a right to the head that split Jakubowski's guard and dropped him onto his backside.

Eric rose at the count of eight but stumbled sideways. Referee Wayne Kelly had seen enough and waived the fight over at the 40-second mark of the 2nd round.

After the match, Larry Merchant asked Arturo how he felt fighting in the welterweight division. Arturo felt that his punching power was harder, but his legs felt kind of slow. Jakubowski was asked his thoughts after the match. He complimented Arturo on being a hard puncher. He added that Gatti's body punches in the 1st round took everything out of him.[727]

Arturo was further interviewed after the bout. *"This is great; 147 is good for me. I feel comfortable. I like to fight at 147, definitely. I would love to fight Oscar De La Hoya at the end of the year. I think he's a great fighter; the best in the world. I am a 100% boxer and want to fight the best in the world. I think I should jump up [in weight]. I needed these fights when I came back [from three straight losses]. I needed them for myself. You know my manager schedules my fights. I will fight anyone my manager brings and I think it is time for us to step up. They [welterweights] punch a little harder. I was kind of slow tonight."*[728]

Arturo was approached by Wayne McCullough after the fight. McCullough asked Arturo if Gatti remembered him from their amateur match in Ireland. Arturo replied, *"I couldn't forget you!"*[729]

On May 12, 2000, Lou DiBella left HBO after 11 years at the company. DiBella walked away from a $600,000 yearly salary with a guaranteed $300,000 annual bonus. He started his own promotional company, DiBella Entertainment. Before departing, DiBella secured 15 television dates from the cable company. Bernard Hopkins was the first fighter that DiBella brought on board.

On May 26, 2000, the United States Congress passed the Muhammad Ali Boxing Reform Act. The law was enacted in response to widespread abuse of boxers through exploitation, conflicts of interest, rigged matches, and rigged rankings. The law ordered that all boxers must receive their purses prior to managers and trainers taking their "cut." The law also required promoters to advise the boxer how much television stations were paying the promoter for the boxer to perform on the network. Of course, it didn't take long for promoters to find loopholes around this new law.

On June 1, 2000, Arturo's wish for a De La Hoya match came true. It was agreed that De La Hoya would meet Arturo on September 9, as long as Oscar defeated Shane Mosley on June 17. Pat Lynch acknowledged that everything, including the money, was agreed upon. The only remaining issues were the number of tickets and hotel rooms that each fighter would receive.[730]

Lynch and Gatti would be flying to California on June 15 to be ringside at the Staples Center for the Mosely match. De La Hoya was taking home $8 million for the Mosley fight. Lynch and Gatti hoped to be in line for that type of payday soon.

On June 17, Oscar De La Hoya lost a close split-decision to Shane Mosley. The Gatti vs. De La Hoya match was now in jeopardy, as De La Hoya might seek a rematch with Mosley. Lynch commented on the disappointing turn of events by stating that Arturo was happy for Shane, but he was bummed out because the De La Hoya match might not happen.[731] Rumors were spreading that De La Hoya was going to fight a Mosley rematch on September 9.

On August 9, Lynch and Gatti decided not to sit around and wait for De La Hoya. They took an offer from InterBox and Yvon Michel for Arturo to fight in Montreal against undefeated Joe Hutchinson, 18-0-2 (8 KOs), of Indiana. Davey Hilton was originally scheduled to fight the main event against Eric Lucas but Lucas pulled out with an eye injury that he had suffered while sparring. The promoter scrambled to find another opponent for Hilton. The show was in peril of cancellation from the potential loss of the popular Hilton.

There would be a major distraction for this fight. For the first time since the child abuse of his nieces was made public, Arturo would come face-to-face with his brother-in-law, Davey Hilton. The show needed the fan-favorite Hilton on the card. A replacement was found in Stephan Ouellet, a boxer that Hilton had fought and beaten twice previously. Hilton, 39-1 (26 KOs) was awaiting trial for his child abuse charges.

Arturo's hometown of Montreal was in a frenzy over their prodigal son's return. Lynch stated that 2,300 people lined up just to see Gatti work out. There was a huge billboard on the side of the Molson Centre with a picture of Arturo on it that read, "Gatti-Mania 2000."[732]

Arturo, who was ranked #4 by both the WBA and WBC at junior-welterweight, did not have his normal training camp before the fight. Everything seemed rushed. Roca complained that he did not have the proper time to prepare for the left-handed Hutchinson. When Arturo arrived in Canada, he took off with his girlfriend Vivian. InterBox supplied Gatti with a limousine and bodyguards. The bodyguards may have been to protect Davey Hilton from Arturo as much as they were to protect Gatti from the public. The week of the fight was hectic, as old friends and boxing fans vied for Arturo's time and attention.

Joe and Vikki drove up to the fight. They made the poor decision of taking Arturo's ex-girlfriend Laura with them. Joe and Vikki felt that Laura was the best girl for Arturo. They were trying to get Arturo to leave Vivian and go back with Laura, but their plan backfired. Joe and Vikki, obviously unaware that Arturo had brought Vivian with him, took Laura to Ida's house. Arturo walked into his mother's home with Vivian and was shocked to find that Laura was there. Arturo was very upset with Joe for getting involved in his personal relationships.

Arturo and his brother Joe had a relationship like most other siblings. They fought, and later they forgave each other. When the brothers did fight, the tension usually boiled over to the rest of the family. One time when the brothers were fighting, Ida removed all of the photos of Joe from her walls to show her support for Arturo. Arturo himself thought this act unnecessary and asked his mother to hang Joe's pictures back up. Ida's preference for Arturo over Joe may have been due to a combination of Giovanni's favoritism of Joe as a child, coupled with Arturo's monetary success as a boxer, or she may have simply bonded more with Arturo as he was younger than Joe. One thing was certain, Arturo had the finances to provide for his siblings and his mother and Joe did not.

On September 7, at 4 p.m., the weigh-in was to take place at the Casino de Montreal, which was the largest casino in Canada. The weigh-in was postponed until 4:45 because Arturo could not be located. When Arturo finally arrived both Hector Roca and Lou Duva smelled alcohol on his breath.[733] If he had indeed been drinking, it didn't affect Arturo's weight for he weighed in at 146.7. Hutchinson weighed in at 141.6.

That night, Arturo stayed out with friends until 5 a.m.[734] His girlfriend Vivian was sent to spend the night with Ida. Arturo was enjoying the attention he commanded.

On Friday, September 8, at the Molson Center, 18,150 fans showed up for the return of their hero, Arturo "Thunder" Gatti. Arturo would enjoy several small victories that evening. First, he was the headliner, not Hilton; second, Davey wound up losing a decision to Ouellet; and third, Hilton would have his entire purse confiscated on behalf of Arturo's sister, Anna-Maria.

In a repeat of the Gamache fight, Arturo's team forgot his mouthpiece at the hotel. His brother Joe scrambled to find and boil an amateur mouthpiece in the dressing room.

The Canadian boxing community, Yvon Michel, and InterBox promotions, all had been trying to get Arturo to box in Canada for the longest time. This would be the first time that Arturo would enter a boxing ring in Canada since he was an amateur, ten years prior. Arturo would earn $600,000 for the fight, which would be televised live on ESPN. Lynch described Hutchinson as a sound defensive fighter who threw a lot of punches.[735]

Arturo was interviewed by ESPN's Bob Papa before the bout. Gatti admitted that it felt great to be so enormously popular in Canada. Arturo felt that he had earned the admiration of his fans by the grueling wars in which he had participated.[736] Hutchinson was asked how he planned on defeating Gatti. Hutchinson said he would box and jab, keep his hands up, move laterally and never stand in front of Arturo. Gatti responded to Hutchinson's game plan by stating that he would stalk Hutchinson and set him up for his signature left hook.[737]

Arturo planned on stepping to his left and keeping his left lead foot outside of the lefty Hutchinson's lead right foot. This would put Arturo in a better position to land his jabs and straight rights while avoiding Hutchinson's straight left. Hutchinson planned on "catching and countering" Arturo's punches while stepping outside to his right, or Gatti's left.

Arturo made his way to the ring behind Queens, New York heavyweight Vinnie Maddalone, Lou Duva, and Pat Lynch. Walking behind Arturo were Hector Roca and Joe Souza. Even though Duva had started a new promotional company with his son Dino and daughter Donna, he still was welcome in Arturo's corner. Arturo's brother Joe held the ropes open for his brother to slip under. The 28-year-old Arturo held a ½-inch height advantage over the 30-year-old Hutchinson, who was 5'7" tall. Surprisingly, Gatti announced his address as being Jersey City instead of his native Montreal, which would have led to an even greater explosion of applause from the partisan crowd. The crowd did give a rousing applause regardless.

Bob Papa announced that Hutchinson had six weeks of preparation for the bout.

Hutchinson started the fight landing lead right jabs, straight lefts, and lefts to the body. Gatti found it easy to land hooks to the body and head. Halfway through the 1st round, Arturo landed a flush right hand. He looked for a reaction, but Hutchinson took the punch well. Arturo landed blistering hooks to the body and head, but Hutchinson came right back with a solid straight left. With 30 seconds remaining, Gatti dipped inside to his right and landed a crunching right uppercut. Again, Hutchinson took the punch well.

Arturo opened the 2nd round with another crisp straight right lead. Hutchinson was landing cleanly as he bounced in and out. Gatti was very flat-footed in the round. Halfway through the round, Hutchinson's confidence grew as he stopped and landed several combinations to the head.

In-between Hutchinson's assault, both fighters' heads clashed. Arturo squinted in pain as a cut opened over his left eye. Arturo retreated as Hutchinson, sensing an opportunity, pressed forward. Hutchinson opened up on Gatti while Arturo covered up along the ropes. Arturo, uncharacteristically but intelligently, reached out and grabbed his opponent. The referee, Michael Griffin, stopped the action with 15 seconds remaining to have a ringside physician look at the cut.

As Doctor Miller made his way up the ring stairs, Lou Duva followed him. The experienced Duva told Miller that if he stopped the fight he would set off a riot. As the doctor was looking at the cut, Duva, in violation of the rules, was treating it. If the cut was ruled from a punch, and the fight was stopped, Arturo would lose the match. The gash was almost two inches long, between the eyebrows. Both the doctor and the referee allowed the fight to continue. Duva wasn't the only member of Gatti's team lobbying for the fight to continue. Russell Peltz, Gatti's co-promoter, who was working as an on-site coordinator for ESPN, was ringside begging the chief boxing inspector to allow the fight to continue.[738] The round ended with Gatti landing two punches after the bell.

The referee incorrectly ruled the cut to be from a punch. To be fair, in real time, it was difficult to see the head-butt.

The 3rd round started with Gatti pressing forward. Arturo loaded up with uppercuts that missed, while he breathed heavily through his open mouth. It was visibly apparent that he was not prepared for this type of battle. Halfway through the round, Hutchinson landed a solid hook to the body while leaning in. After the punch landed, both boxers heads clashed directly over Arturo's cut. Arturo, disgusted, raised his glove towards the referee and stated, *"Come on, man!"*

The referee called time and took Arturo to a neutral corner, partly to calm him down and partly to have the doctor look at the cut again. A new cut opened over Arturo's right eye from the clash of heads. The doctor allowed the fight to continue.

Arturo appeared to be losing his composure. Gatti came rushing in throwing body punches. He followed with several intentional spears of his forehead into Hutchinson's face. The referee stopped the action and warned Gatti for the fouls.

When the action resumed, Arturo ripped several hard punches to the midsection. The referee broke the fighters and warned Arturo for punching low, although the punches appeared clean. After the fighters came back together, Hutchinson finished the round landing several solid straight lefts.

In the 4th round, some of Arturo's punches were missing by wide margins of a foot or more. Gatti opened up with hooks and crosses, but to Hutchinson's credit he blocked most of them. Arturo landed a right to the beltline. Hutchinson complained that the blow was low. The referee called time to warn Arturo. When the action resumed, Arturo tore punches into Hutchinson's midsection. One of Arturo's punches was clearly low this time. The referee called time again but not before Arturo landed a hard right to the head. The referee took a point away from Arturo for the low blow.

Even though Gatti appeared to be winning all of the rounds with his activity, he was struggling. Both fighters landed clean punches as the round came to a close. Again, Arturo landed a punch after the bell.

As round 5 started, Arturo was punching very wide, but he was, to his credit, committed to working the body. With a little more than a minute remaining in the round, Hutchinson landed hooks and crosses directly onto Arturo's gashes, causing blood to spray out of the wounds. Arturo appeared to be crying blood as the crimson liquid dripped down under his eyes. The round came to a close with both fighters landing cleanly. Arturo's punches had no snap or sharpness to them. He was "pushing" his punches, and looked more like a club fighter instead of the world-class fighter that he was. But he still had his world-class heart and toughness.

ESPN's Teddy Atlas had Arturo ahead 48-47, while Bob Papa had the bout 47-47 through five rounds.

In the 6th, Arturo threw what appeared to be a medium speed left hook counter that dropped Hutchinson onto the seat of his pants. It looked as though Hutchinson blocked the punch, but the power of the blow sent him to the floor. Either way, a punch was thrown and Hutchinson went down. Gatti was credited with a knockdown.

Arturo followed with several well placed punches to the body and head. Gatti loaded up with a left hook that missed badly. The errant blow caused Arturo to spin around, lose his balance, and fall to the floor. When Gatti regained his feet Hutchinson responded with a few short straight punches, but there wasn't much power behind them.

The referee stopped the action again as Arturo's left eye was gushing blood. The doctor quickly checked the eye and allowed the fight to continue. If the bout was to be stopped for the right eye cut, which was now under control, the fight would go to the scorecards. If the bout, however, was stopped for the left eye cut, Hutchinson would win by TKO.

Arturo opened up the 7th with a barrage of wide punches that were mostly blocked. Gatti landed another low blow halfway through the round and was warned by the referee. Arturo was still the busier of the two boxers and had been for most of the bout. Hutchinson landed several good shots near the end of the round but Arturo refused to let him steal the round. He roared back with volleys of his own.

The 8th was dominated by Hutchinson, as Gatti stopped punching. Near the halfway mark, a point was deducted from Hutchinson for coming in with his head. When the fighting resumed, Arturo opened up with more roundhouse punches that were blocked by Hutchinson's high guard.

Atlas had the bout 76-74 for Gatti, while Papa had it 75-74 for Arturo through eight rounds.

Both fighters looked tired and sloppy in the 9th. Halfway through the round, Hutchinson threw a left uppercut, but picked his chin up in the process. Arturo countered with a thunderous left hook, his best punch of the night. Both boxers finished the round sloppily, looking like novices with wild, winging punches.

Arturo was the busier fighter in the 10th, although most of his shots were wide of their mark. The crowd cheered as the final bell brought an end to the action.

Atlas scored the fight 95-93 and Papa scored the bout 94-93, both for Arturo. Gatti's mother, Ida, and his girlfriend, Vivian, entered the ring. Ida was clearly upset with her son's mangled face.

Arturo was announced the winner and was raised up by his brother Joe while his brother Fabrizio pumped his fists into the air. The three judges scored the bout 100-92, 99-92, and 98-93, all for Arturo. The Montreal crowd cheered their hometown hero. Pat Lynch looked visibly dejected at the performance.

Arturo would receive five stitches on his left eye in the dressing room and another fifteen when he returned to New Jersey.

Vivian videotaped Arturo in the dressing room with a camcorder. Arturo became annoyed and asked her to shut the camera off.[739]

Joe Gatti recalled the Hutchinson fight. *"Hutchinson cut him up to pieces. I had to put him in the shower. They told him to lie down. He was about to pass out. He probably would have went into a coma. He's like this [sleeping]. Hector goes, 'Lie down.' I said, 'No, no. Get up.' I put him in a cold shower to wake him up. Because it looked like he was passing out. I got him in the shower and I put cold water on him."*[740]

Joe was correct. After a tough battle a boxer should never be allowed to lie down and sleep. It is best to keep him awake and alert to monitor him.

Arturo would later comment on how he landed punches on Hutchinson through his bloody eyes. *"I'd been boxing so long, I knew he had to be out there somewhere. Anyway, I'm at my best when I see red."*[741]

Arturo believed that Hutchinson's gloves were tampered with, but there was no evidence offered to prove that. Doctor Miller later admitted that he was put in a very difficult position in regards to deciding whether or not to stop the fight.[742]

Arturo had his dressing room cleared out. He didn't want his supporters to see him in this state. Arturo, indeed, nearly passed out as he was helped into the shower by his brother Joe. Cold water was thrust upon him. Hector Roca screamed at Arturo to stay awake as he placed an ice bag on his head. Vivian would later recall that this was the worst condition that she ever saw Arturo in after a fight, and she was on hand for all of the Ward battles.[743] Arturo at first refused hospitalization, but later was driven to the hospital by Vivian after they first returned to their hotel room.

Rumors started circulating of a possible match-up between Arturo and Shane Mosley. The Mosley-Gatti fight would never materialize. Pat Lynch would later state that he wasn't very interested in fighting Mosley because of his hand speed.[744] It was rumored that De La Hoya was going to retire. He was working on a new career as a singer. His music CD would be nominated for a Grammy as best Latin pop album of 2000.

Chapter 17
The Golden Boy

Arturo's poor outing against Hutchinson made it appear that a bout against Oscar De La Hoya would be a complete mismatch. It didn't appear to be a fight that the public would be hungry to see, nor one that would generate much excitement.

On November 4, Pat Lynch sat ringside at the Shane Mosley-Antonio Diaz fight at Madison Square Garden. Mosley dismantled Diaz in 6 rounds. A possible Mosley-Gatti fight was discussed for HBO on February 24, 2001. Team Gatti was also offered an ESPN bout against Kostya Tszyu on December 15, 2000 in Montreal, by promoter Cedric Kushner. Arturo would not be able to consider the Tszyu fight, as he was still recovering from the two cuts he suffered during the Hutchinson battle. Lynch and Main Events wanted to avoid the Mosley match. They were trying to avoid fast-handed boxers at all costs.

In November 2000, *Sports Illustrated* published an article on Arturo called, "He's Bloody Good." In the article, Arturo admitted that he loved to bleed. He added that fans who sat ringside for his fights needed umbrellas to avoid getting splashed with his blood.[745] Arturo was asked if he preferred to fight either Kostya Tszyu or Shane Mosley. He replied that it didn't matter much to him who he fought because blood was blood. Arturo joked that he was a calm person, when he slept.[746] The bout Gatti really wanted, though, was De La Hoya. That was the money match. Unfortunately, De La Hoya was embroiled in a legal battle with Top Rank and HBO.[747]

Mikey Red recalled the De La Hoya matchup. *"Arturo begged Main Events for the De La Hoya fight. Pat wasn't for it, but it was such a lucrative fight. Arturo wanted to fight the best. That's what he told me. He was taking the fight because he wanted to test himself against the best because I think he was on a roll up until that point."*[748]

Pat Lynch didn't think the De La Hoya match would ever happen. Either Arturo and Oscar were in different weight classes, or some other obstacle surfaced. Gatti made Lynch promise him that if it ever were possible to make the match, Lynch would make it. Arturo desperately wanted to fight De La Hoya before he retired. Lynch was afraid that time would run out on their careers before the fight could be made.[749]

A breakthrough in negotiations finally occurred. Arturo was offered $1.2 million to fight De La Hoya. Vikki and Joe visited Arturo in his apartment in Gregory Commons in Weehawken. Joe told Arturo not to settle for $1.2 million because Arturo was the most exciting fighter in boxing. Joe told Arturo, *"You got to get rid of Pat. You're not making the money you're supposed to be making. You don't need a manager. Look at Roy Jones."*[750] Arturo allegedly replied, *"No, you don't understand. I feel like a caged lion. I tried to get out but I can't. I'm stuck."*[751]

On November 30, it was announced that a contract had been signed, sealing a De La Hoya vs. Arturo Gatti bout. Arturo and Pat Lynch boarded De La Hoya's private jet to sign the contract. Unbeknownst to Arturo, Floyd Mayweather Jr. was on the plane. For nearly the entire flight, Mayweather ridiculed and badgered Gatti. Arturo was extremely upset about Mayweather being on the plane.

The fight would be held on March 24, 2001. The location wasn't set, but it was rumored that it would be held in Las Vegas. It was announced that Arturo would earn a career-high $1.8 million for the bout. The matchup was viewed as a going-away gift from HBO for Arturo's memorable battles on the network. Gatti single-handedly made HBO's "Boxing After Dark" series a household name.

Newark Star Ledger's boxing beat reporter, Chris Thorne, felt that neither De La Hoya nor Mosley were good matches for Gatti. Thorne did state, however, that even though De La Hoya was too big for Arturo, at least Gatti had a chance to make the fight interesting in the early rounds.[752]

Lynch revealed that discussions for the bout intensified while he was out in Las Vegas for the Lennox Lewis-David Tua match. Obvious stumbling blocks were De La Hoya's contract dispute with Top Rank and the recent suspension of Bob Arum's promotional license in New Jersey. Arum was suspended after revelations at the trial of IBF president Bob Lee alleged that Arum had made payoffs to Lee in return for his fighters gaining improved rankings.

The official promoter of the fight would be Univision. De La Hoya was represented at the negotiations by a Univision attorney. Lynch stated that both De La Hoya and Gatti were so popular it wouldn't matter where the bout was held. Lynch felt that boat-loads of fans would attend regardless of the location.[753]

Arturo's poor performance against Hutchinson may have been the catalyst for Lynch and Main Events' decision to make the De La

Hoya match. His obvious deterioration may have led to panic that his career was nearing its end. This could be his last opportunity to make a seven-figure payday. It made no sense to risk Arturo losing in a six-figure bout when they could make close to $2 million against De La Hoya. Mikey Red recalled the De La Hoya matchup. *"At the time, the De La Hoya fight was called an HBO gift to Arturo. Here's your reward. At the time it was his biggest payday."*[754]

The four-division champion, De La Hoya, 32-2 (26 KOs), had lost two out of his last three fights. His losses, however, were to elite fighters Felix Trinidad and Shane Mosley. Oscar would look at this fight as a tune-up for bigger and better things. The agreed-upon contract weight was 147-pounds.

In December, the WBA welterweight rankings placed Arturo at #3 and De La Hoya at #2, with the championship slot vacant. Oscar's mother's death inspired him to become an Olympian and dedicate his life to bettering himself. In a way, Arturo and Oscar were similar. Their careers were both inspired by the death of a parent.

On December 15, 2000 at the Molson Center in Montreal, Davey Hilton became the WBC super middleweight champion. He defeated Dingaan Thobela by split-decision to take the title.

On January 12, 2001 a federal court ruling voided Oscar De La Hoya's contract with Top Rank. Oscar immediately announced that he would be promoted by Jerry Perenchio, the owner of Univision.

On February 7 at a press conference, De La Hoya formally announced his return to the ring. Oscar stated that he never really retired. He had taken a little vacation to regroup and relax physically and mentally.[755] De La Hoya added that while he was working on music he would often think about returning to the boxing ring. Oscar announced he would be fighting Arturo Gatti in a 12-round bout on March 24, at the MGM Grand in Las Vegas.

The only stumbling block was HBO's television contract with De La Hoya. The contract had several fights remaining. Oscar planned to honor the remainder of the contract. De La Hoya announced that he was changing trainers for the first time in his career. He replaced his long-time amateur and professional trainer, Roberto Alcazar, with Floyd Mayweather Sr. De La Hoya believed that Alcazar took him as far as he could.

Joe Gatti was the first brother to enter the ring in 2001. He followed his brother's footsteps and fought on an Interbox promoted card at the Molson Center in Montreal on March 2. Joe took on Vancouver's Roberto Dellapena, 7-3-1 (5 KOs). Joe would be fighting in Montreal for the first time since June 1989. The boxing bug never left Joe, as he stated, *"Sometimes you don't get the fights you expected. You get depressed because you don't get the breaks. But boxing never left me. I've missed everything, the excitement, the weigh-in, and the rush you get as you're going into the ring. I'm flattered [InterBox] has given me a chance. It's a little weird to see how the people are reacting, but it's like I never left."*[756]

In 1999, Yvon Michel called Joe to try and match him up against Eric Lucas, but Joe wasn't interested in fighting in Montreal until Arturo broke the ice and fought there first. Joe had ballooned up to 195-pounds while he was inactive. It took him three months to get down to 168.

Michel coached Joe when he fought on the Canadian national team as an amateur. Michel believed that fans in Montreal would like Joe because of his charisma and style. Michel admitted that Joe was not as aggressive as Arturo, but he felt that Joe was more calculated, more cerebral and was flamboyant in the ring.[757] A win by Joe could result in a multi-fight deal. Joe was even considering moving his family back to Montreal if all worked out as planned. Joe commented, *"Some fighters mature at 28, but I didn't. For me, it happened at 32, 33. I've never felt this good or looked this good. I didn't feel flat in the gym and I won't in the ring."*[758]

Joe easily outboxed Dellapena, shutting him out on all three judge's scorecards. Joe improved to 28-7 with 22 knockouts. Michel was looking to match Joe up against some of the other leading super middleweights in Canada. They included Eric Lucas, Stephane Ouellet, and WBC champ Davey Hilton.

Arturo's promotional contract with Main Events was coming to an end. Several individuals approached Arturo with offers from other promotional companies. Arturo turned all of the offers down. Pat Lynch proudly recalled Arturo's answer, whenever he was presented with an offer. Arturo would always answer, *"Call Pat."*[759]

The Gatti-De La Hoya match was televised on tape delay by HBO sports. Before the bout, Arturo was asked if he was concerned about getting cut during the match. *"It is something I have to deal with. If it happens, I can deal with it. It does not scare me. I am used to it. I'm going to show the world I'm not just a bleeder. I think I'll be stronger in the later rounds. I'm a tough fighter. He thinks it is going to be an easy fight for him because I get cut. That's all right with me. It's better that way. I do not see them taking me seriously, but that doesn't matter. It's all about being inside the ring."*[760] Arturo stated that he was only cut once in his career by a punch, in the Manfredy fight. He added that all of his other cuts were caused by head butts and elbows.

De La Hoya praised his new trainer, Floyd Mayweather Sr. He said that if he had Mayweather earlier in his career, he would still be undefeated and champion.[761] Oscar planned on moving up in weight after the Gatti fight and capturing championships at 154 and 160-pounds.

Arturo commented on De La Hoya's new trainer by stating that Mayweather wasn't God. Gatti also questioned how many new things De La Hoya could learn at this stage of his career. Arturo felt that Mayweather Sr. would be a motivator for De La Hoya, and nothing more.[762]

De La Hoya, a 30-1 betting favorite, was so confident in victory he had already planned his next fight after Gatti. He planned on returning to the ring on June 9 to face Javier Castillejo for Castillejo's WBC super welterweight title. It was now being reported that De La Hoya would earn $5 million, while Arturo would earn $1.3 million, still by far Gatti's largest payday.

When asked, Arturo revealed that he gave no thought to being such a huge underdog. Gatti felt that De La Hoya was not taking him seriously.[763] Pat Lynch added that De La Hoya's camp was banking on Arturo's soft skin and aggressive style to make the fight easy for Oscar.[764]

Arturo had been in training at Vero Beach, Florida with Hector Roca since a week before Christmas. As of February 3 his weight was 158, only 11-pounds over the contracted weight. Not the twenty or so pounds over that he usually was.

Buddy McGirt stumbled upon Arturo's training camp in Vero Beach by accident while Gatti was in training for De La Hoya. McGirt was driving in a car with his daughter when he noticed a boxing gym sign. He decided to stop in and check the gym out. When McGirt walked into the gym, Arturo told Hector Roca to make Buddy leave. Gatti thought that McGirt may have been sent to spy for De La Hoya. Hector told Arturo that Buddy was living in Vero Beach. Gatti didn't believe that McGirt lived in town. He reiterated his feelings that McGirt was spying on him. A week later, Arturo saw McGirt shopping in town and he asked Buddy why he was in Vero Beach. McGirt told Gatti that he had just moved into town. Arturo said, *"Oh shit. I thought you were a spy."* Both Gatti and McGirt shared a laugh over the incident. McGirt was working for Don King, training fighters at the time.

When McGirt fought Simon Brown in November 1991, he trained at a hotel in Fort Pierce, which is just south of Vero Beach. After the Simon Brown fight, Lou Duva asked McGirt's manager, Al Certo, where they had trained for the Brown fight. When Certo told Duva they had trained in Fort Pierce, Duva took all of his fighters, including Pernell Whitaker, to train at the warm-weather location. When the hotel was closed down, they moved the training camp to the next town over, Vero Beach.[765]

While Arturo was in camp, Joe and Vikki kept an eye on his condo in Weehawken. Joe and Vikki recalled a strange occurrence on one visit. Vikki was cleaning Arturo's floors when she felt something on her back. She told Joe that she wanted to leave because there were too many people bothering her in the condo. But Joe and Vikki were alone. Vikki asked Joe to look at her back. She felt that something was on her back. Joe pulled up Vikki's shirt and was shocked at what he saw. Vikki's back was covered with scratches and gouges.

Both Joe and Vikki felt that there was an evil presence in the condo. They left the apartment and drove home. They were unsettled by the incident. Before leaving, the couple counted Arturo's windows and doors. Joe and Arturo's mother had a method for warding off evil spirits. She would place salt and garlic on the window sills and doors. Joe and Vikki returned to the apartment the next day and treated the apartment. Joe explained, *"The bad spirits, by the time they count the salt the light comes out and they gotta leave. They can't stay in there. I can't even talk, I get chills."*[766] The next time Joe and Vikki returned to the apartment they felt that the evil spirits had departed. They also felt that Arturo's personality had improved when he returned.

Another time, before Arturo left for camp, and before the salt and garlic treatment, Joe and Vikki stopped by to visit. On the drive over they called Arturo and told him they were coming. Arturo told them he would be home. When Joe and Vikki arrived at the apartment Arturo didn't answer the door. They didn't have the key so they kept banging on the door. They feared that Arturo might have been in trouble inside the apartment.

Joe called the local police. The police arrived and gained entry into the apartment. No one was inside. After the officers left, Joe and Vikki checked the apartment again. They went through a back door and it slammed behind them. They noticed that a handkerchief was in-between a door and the door jamb. They watched as the handkerchief got pulled through the jamb and disappeared. They opened the door thinking that Arturo was playing a joke. There was no one behind the door and the handkerchief was gone.

Hector Roca was confident in Arturo's chances of victory. Roca felt that fans figured Arturo had no chance of defeating De La Hoya. Hector confessed that Arturo usually trained three weeks for a fight, but this time he had been training in isolation for three months. Gatti was eating and training right. Roca reminded the non-believers that Arturo could box. Hector felt that De La Hoya's style was perfect for Arturo. Roca added that Oscar doesn't punch hard when he is moving around the ring. Hector's game plan was to put pressure on De La Hoya, to get inside of his reach. Roca was confident that Gatti would hurt Oscar. In regards to Arturo's soft skin, Hector felt that Arturo losing weight in the past softened his skin too much. This time Arturo would be fighting heavier, so Roca believed his skin would be tougher to cut.[767]

Ivan Robinson had fought both fighters- De La Hoya three times in the amateurs and Gatti twice in the pros. He wasn't convinced of a De La Hoya blowout. Robinson felt that De La Hoya should win, but he cautioned that if Gatti could get close enough he was capable of knocking De La Hoya out.[768]

On Friday, February 23, Gatti's camp received terrible news. Arturo's long-time strength and conditioning coach Bob Wareing passed away from a brain aneurysm in the morning. He was only 48 years old. Lynch had spoken to Wareing just one day before he died. Arturo, who was in Vero Beach, walked to the ocean, sat down and cried uncontrollably. Arturo was devastated. He was extremely close to Wareing. Lynch felt that Arturo would not have completed the Tracy Patterson fights if Wareing hadn't worked with him. Arturo needed every ounce of strength he had to keep Patterson from defeating him.[769]

Arturo spoke of Wareing. *"I think about him all the time. He always taught me to go to the end. I have a funny feeling that he'll be there with me telling me, 'Don't worry about it [the fight].' I haven't stopped thinking about him. If this fight was in Atlantic City, I would have the crowd on my side. I know Oscar is the man in Vegas and that has made me work harder. I'm gonna move my head more. I'm well prepared for this fight. Hector and I have worked extra hard for this fight. Oscar is the type of fighter who is going to give me more time to think in the ring. I have a lot of pride in my heart. I don't give up and that's what the crowd likes."*[770]

If Wareing's death wasn't enough of a distraction, Arturo was being asked about his brother-in-law, Davey Hilton, who had recently been convicted of abusing his daughters. Arturo called Hilton a sexual predator. Arturo added that Hilton deserved to spend the rest of his life in prison.[771] When Davey found out about Arturo's comments he called Le Journal of Montreal from the Riviere-des-Praires prison and stated, *"I hope Oscar De La Hoya puts him [Arturo] in a coma."*[772]

On March 16, 2001 in Quebec, Canada, Davey Hilton Jr. was convicted of sexually abusing his two daughters in nine sexually related counts. In May, he would be sentenced to 7 years incarceration. Aggravating sentencing factors were the girls' young ages, the number of abusive incidents over a prolonged period of time, and the fact that Hilton Jr. in 1992 had been sentenced, along with his brother Matthew, to jail for the robbery of a Dunkin' Donuts.[773] His mother Jean Hilton was quoted as saying, *"His only guilt is having a problem with alcohol."*

Upon hearing of the conviction, Arturo stated, *"I would have been floored if the judge had acquitted him. Davey is a dangerous sexual predator and the justice system has to keep him out of society to protect other potential victims... A murder can be committed in legitimate defense, but sexual assault on a 12-year-old child is unforgivable."*[774]

Hilton denied that he was guilty, *"I'm innocent. If I was guilty, I would have agreed to plead guilty and did two years in jail."*[775] Hilton would be stripped of his WBC super middleweight title by Jose Sulaiman after his sentencing. He would remain in prison until June 20, 2006, when he was paroled.

Mikey Red recalled that everyone on Team Gatti walked around on eggshells all the time. Anything that was said might be perceived the wrong way. This could mean lifetime expulsion from the Gatti team. Skowronski always considered himself a personal friend of Arturo and Joe's. Mikey was given $5,000 once for helping Arturo in training camp, but aside from that, he was not on the payroll. Skowronski often would leave his job, at his own expense, to spend time with Arturo as he prepared for his fights.

While they were preparing for De La Hoya, someone approached Mikey and asked him what his involvement with Arturo was. Mikey innocently said that he was *"on Arturo's team."* This quote got back to Pat Lynch. He confronted Skowronski about the quote. Mikey didn't know what to say. He didn't think he had said anything wrong. Lynch felt that Mikey Red was indicating that he was on Arturo's management team. Mikey told Lynch that he never meant his comment to be taken that way. Skowronski felt that Lynch was distant with him after the incident. Mikey was made to feel uncomfortable after this confrontation, but he refused to abandon Arturo. He remained close to his friend.[776]

Arturo did not invite Joe to the De La Hoya fight. Joe flew out to Las Vegas alone, at his own expense, to support his brother. He rented a cheap hotel room. When Joe arrived in Vegas, Arturo told him that he didn't know that Joe wanted to come to the fight. Arturo apologized and gave Joe a ringside ticket. This would be the only time that Arturo would fight in Las Vegas.

At the weigh-in, billed "Return of a Hero," De La Hoya towered over Gatti. At 5'11", De La Hoya was a full 3½-inches taller than Arturo. Phil Woolever, of *Boxing Digest*, said that De La Hoya made Gatti look like a little boy.[777]

By the day of the match, the odds had dropped from 30-1 to 8-1. The wagering was so heavy on Arturo that some of the big casinos stopped taking bets. Joe's ringside seat was on the opposite side of Arturo's corner, by De La Hoya. Joe's sister Mirella, and her husband Rocco, were sitting by Arturo's side of the ring. Approximately 10,000 fans passed through the turnstiles for the HBO-televised event.

Arturo made his way to the ring, led by Roca and Lynch. Following Arturo were his brother Joe, Mikey Red, and Arturo's best friend from Montreal, Christian Santos. Alabama 3's "Woke Up This Morning," the theme song to the HBO hit series *The Sopranos*, blared through the MGM Grand speakers. Using the New Jersey-based cable series theme song as his entrance only further solidified his roots as a Jersey boy. Arturo couldn't bring De La Hoya to New Jersey, so he brought New Jersey to De La Hoya.

Prior to the fighters being called to the center of the ring, Carl Moretti was visibly nervous. He kept peering into Arturo's eyes, trying to gauge how he was handling the biggest moment of his career and life. Listed as working Arturo's corner were Roca, Lynch, and Joe Souza. In reality, Lynch was not in the corner, Joe Rivera was. Rivera was a cutman from Paterson, NJ. That meant Arturo had two cutmen in his corner.

Arturo started the match aggressively, stepping forward behind his jab. Near the halfway point of the 1st round, De La Hoya landed a hard right hand to the body. Moments later he landed a flush right to Gatti's head. With 1:25 remaining in the round Arturo stepped in with a left hook. Oscar tried to step back but Arturo caught him on the jaw. Gatti landed a solid jab and followed with a roundhouse right-cross moments later. Arturo was displaying crisp head movement. With 25 seconds left in the round, De La Hoya opened up with a flurry, driving Arturo to the ropes. A crunching left hook dropped Gatti to his knees. Arturo looked as though he was praying as he knelt on the canvas.

Referee Jay Nady took up the count. Arturo was up at the count of seven. De La Hoya went right back to work, unloading hooks and crosses, until the bell rang. Gatti suffered a cut under his right eye from one of De La Hoya's hooks.

Roca begged Arturo not to wait and not to stand up too straight. He also cautioned Gatti not to look for one shot. Roca wanted Souza to trade places with him inside of the ring, so Souza could better treat the cut. Roca yelled at Souza to hurry up and enter the ring to work on the cut. In De La Hoya's corner, Mayweather Sr. advised Oscar to throw the right hand and left hook. He also asked for the jab. Mayweather told De La Hoya that Gatti was afraid of his right hand.

At the start of round 2, Arturo came out throwing bombs while De La Hoya tried to put combinations together. Arturo threw a right uppercut that was blocked. De La Hoya landed several stiff jabs and followed with four hook-cross combinations around Arturo's guard. Oscar's height gave him the ability to throw hooks and crosses from the outside while being safely outside of Gatti's reach. De La Hoya was committed to throwing the jab to the body, which was bringing Arturo's hands down.

Oscar landed two hard body shots followed by a crunching right hand to the head. You could hear the thudding power in De La Hoya's punches. Every time Arturo worked his way inside, Oscar would use his left shoulder to push him off. De La Hoya looked relaxed as he calmly made Arturo miss nearly every punch he threw. Oscar dug two more hard body shots as blood poured from under Arturo's right eye. De La Hoya punctuated the round with vicious hooks to the body and head.

Roca implored Arturo to move his head and work the body more. As Roca spoke, Arturo tilted his head to the side to look around Roca at De La Hoya, possibly to see if Oscar was tiring.

Arturo kept trying to hit the lottery. He swung bombs as the 3rd round began. Gatti jumped in with a right hand and left hook. The blows landed cleanly but De La Hoya was unfazed. The fighters clinched. When the referee ordered them to break, Arturo threw a hard right cross. The blow barely got Oscar's attention but it did get the referee's, as Arturo was warned not to hit on the break.

De La Hoya landed a long-range straight right a minute into the round. Oscar kept digging hard body shots. De La Hoya later recalled that after he landed one of his drilling body punches Arturo responded by saying, *"Oh man, that hurt!"* But Gatti kept coming forward. Arturo was squinting with his right eye. Oscar was warned for pushing off with his left shoulder. With 19 seconds remaining in the round referee Jay Nady called time. He led Arturo to a neutral corner and called the ring doctor up. The doctor inspected the cut and allowed the fight to continue. Gatti later stated that when he was hurt during a fight, the ring would feel smaller and smaller. And the smaller the ring became, the tougher the fight became.

As the fighters came together, De La Hoya landed a solid right hand-left hook combo. Off balance, Arturo came back with a left hook of his own. Oscar drilled a right uppercut home as the round ended. Arturo was taking the type of methodical beating that was much more dangerous than a one punch knockout.

The ring doctor came to Arturo's corner. Souza and Roca quickly advised the doctor that Arturo was okay. Mayweather cautioned De La Hoya to stop getting into exchanges with Gatti. He told Oscar to box and move his hands. Blood trickled from De La Hoya's nostril as he listened to Mayweather. Up until this point, Oscar had landed 131 punches to Arturo's 65.

Arturo came out winging to start the 4th. Nady again warned Oscar about using the shoulder to push off. Gatti landed a solid left hook but it seemed to have little effect. With a minute left in the round, De La Hoya opened up again, punching down on Arturo like a carpenter would a hammer to a nail. Arturo kept trying. He landed a hard hook with 30 seconds remaining in the round. Oscar came back with a straight right. Arturo's body punches had no effect at all, as they never penetrated De La Hoya's guard.

Arturo kept throwing and Oscar kept blocking. While he was parrying the blows, De La Hoya was looking for openings. Oscar unloaded a left hook-straight right combo. He followed with the same combination again. The crowd was chanting, *"Gatti, Gatti!"* for the underdog. De La Hoya continued to pick his shots. Oscar landed two more hard body shots followed by a hook-cross combo up top. De La Hoya finished the round with six heavy shots that were capped off with a hook to the body. The blow to the midsection hurt Arturo and had him reeling backwards. Every punch that Oscar threw had deadly intentions.

After the round ended, the doctor asked Arturo if he felt alright. Gatti responded, *"Yeah."* Mayweather told Oscar to keep throwing the left hooks and right hands. Cutman Al Gavin told De La Hoya that Arturo didn't have much left.

Arturo started the 5th coming forward. De La Hoya landed two straight rights, but they did not land cleanly. Blood started trickling from the outside corner of Oscar's left eye. De La Hoya landed two left hooks followed by three digging shots to the body. He drove Arturo into the ropes with seventeen straight punches. De La Hoya hammered Gatti with a left hook. As the fighters clinched, Roca threw the towel in. It was a mercy stoppage. Arturo was visibly upset with Roca. When Gatti was examined by the doctor, post-fight, he said that he felt fine. He proved it by doing several jumping jacks while smiling.

CompuBox punch stats had De La Hoya landing 192 of 308 punches while Arturo landed 87 of 308. After the bout, De La Hoya stated that he needed to improve on his boxing. Larry Merchant asked Oscar if Arturo was tougher than expected. De La Hoya admitted that Gatti was tough and could take a punch.

Arturo was asked if he thought the stoppage was appropriate. Gatti said that he could have continued, but admitted that he also could have gotten hurt. Arturo added that he respected Hector Roca's decision to stop the bout. Arturo praised De La Hoya's defensive prowess because he rarely was able to hit Oscar flush with any punches. De La Hoya was faster than Gatti expected. Oscar praised Arturo at the post-fight press conference, calling him a strong warrior. Arturo expressed, *"I fought my heart out, but that's all you can do. I could have kept going but I respect my corner's judgment."* [778] Hector Roca added, *"If I didn't stop it he could have gotten killed because he wouldn't have stopped it."*[779]

Joe questioned the stoppage of the fight by Roca. *"They were in a clinch when they stopped it. Watch the fight and you tell me if that's supposed to be stopped."*[780] Joe's sister, Mirella, heard someone yell to Roca, *"Stop it now."* Joe felt that the fight was stopped prematurely to satisfy the betting odds that the fight would not go further than 5 rounds.

After defeating Gatti, De La Hoya announced that he was going to put boxing first again, and would save his singing aspirations for when he retired.[781] De La Hoya gave his performance against Arturo a 'C' grade.

Arturo responded to Valley Hospital, where he received sixteen stitches to his face. He did not attend the post-fight press conference. Gary Shaw predicted that Arturo might return to the ring in September, in Canada.

Arturo did not take the De La Hoya loss well. He became depressed. Gatti was aware of the rumors that HBO had given him the De La Hoya match as a parting gift, a going-away payday. Mikey Red felt that Arturo's depression came mostly from self-doubt. Gatti prided himself on being a winning prizefighter. It would bring Arturo down when people would say he was "a tough guy" but not an elite fighter. He would get upset when he heard that people were saying that he was a shot fighter. He wanted to be known as more than just a blood-and-guts warrior. Arturo was reading the boxing magazines and newspapers that were saying he was shot. Skowronski told Arturo, *"You're not shot. Reinvent yourself and get back down to 140."*[782]

Steve Sandoval recalled that Arturo came to his apartment at 179 Bleeker Street in Jersey City a few days after the fight. Arturo nearly kicked Sandoval's apartment door in at 5:30 in the morning. Arturo was standing there with tears in his eyes. He asked for a beer, sat on Steve's sofa, and started crying. Through his sobs, Arturo stated, *"Steve, I need a new trainer. Hector made a $400,000 bet that the fight would be stopped in the fifth round."*[783] Arturo told Steve that someone in his camp informed him that Roca bet against him because Hector believed that Gatti was finished. Arturo told Steve that he had proof of the betrayal, though he never showed the proof.

Sandoval recalled that Arturo fell into a deep depression after the De La Hoya loss. Arturo brought up his suicidal thoughts during several conversations with Steve. Sandoval recalled, *"When Arturo was sober he didn't want to talk about real things in life. When he had a little buzz he was all about laughing. He could be an aggressive drunk. When coming down from a buzz, when he was with someone he was comfortable with, he would talk."*[784] Steve recalled that Arturo loved Pat Lynch. He told Steve that he never opened up to Pat about his personal issues. Steve recalled Arturo sharing his feelings. *"He grabbed a Budweiser and said, 'People think I'm stupid but I'm not stupid.' Arturo had low self-esteem. He was insecure and felt that people brought him to parties just to be around a star."*[785]

Several people close to Arturo also felt he was betrayed. Where did this information come from? Were people, including Arturo, using Roca as a scapegoat for the loss? Were people around Arturo feeding this information to him so he would fire Roca? This would open up the lucrative head trainer position to someone else. If there was any evidence that the bout was rigged, an investigation would most likely have taken place. No evidence was ever produced to back the claim that the stoppage was rigged.

The betrayal story is very hard to believe. A large sum of money like that would have been very difficult to transfer without being traceable. Where would Hector even get the $400,000 from? Roca was lucky if he made $300,000 total in his nine years with Arturo. Hector was allotted, at most, 10% of Arturo's purses. Arturo never forgave Roca for stopping the De La Hoya fight. Gatti felt as though Hector had betrayed him. When a fighter is told something and believes it to be true, evidence doesn't matter.

Sandoval was friends with Buddy McGirt. Buddy would usually call him in the morning to talk. McGirt called Steve at 6:45 a.m. while Arturo was partying in Sandoval's apartment. Steve told Buddy that Arturo was with him and he was looking for a new trainer. Gatti was in the bathroom vomiting when McGirt called. When Arturo came out of the bathroom Steve put him on the phone with McGirt and the two talked. Arturo recalled running into McGirt while he was training in Vero Beach. Sandoval claimed that McGirt offered to compensate him if Steve could help persuade Arturo to hire McGirt as his trainer. Sandoval alleged that Buddy offered him 10% of his trainers cut if he could help broker an agreement. Steve told Arturo and Buddy not to forget him if they came to a successful arrangement with each other.

Arturo visited Mario Costa not long after the De La Hoya match. Costa commented, *"Pat knew everything that was going on with Arthur. With the drugs and the liquor. Everything. The pain killers after he got operated on his hand. Arthur said, 'Mario, they took a bone out of my hip. When it rains I get pain.' When they took bone chips from his hip, every time it rained, he had that pain. The pain was going through his whole body. Arthur said, 'Sometimes I remember, sometimes I don't remember. I forget. I don't know what I did.' He said, 'My eyes, I can't see. My hands, I look like a cripple.' His hands were all messed up. He said, 'I feel like an old man. They're using me. They're using me.' That's what he kept saying. 'They're using me and I'm broke.'*

"Because at that time, I don't think he had a [TV] contract. And he

said that HBO, this is his exact words, he was not a prejudiced guy, but he was talking street. He said, 'They're treating me worse than a Nigga. Actually they finally gave him a contract near the end of his career because I think he threatened them, that he was going to leave. They gave him a six-fight contract at the end. And then I went to Pat and said, 'Hey listen, he's being used. He doesn't have a contract.' And Pat goes, 'Mario,' and this is Pat's quote, 'Mario, he's not an 'A' fighter, he's a 'B' fighter.' That's his exact words in his office. I said, 'Did you tell him that? Did HBO tell him that?' This was right after the De La Hoya fight. Cause Arthur told me here [at Ringside] that he felt he was being used. And he was broke.

"So I went to Pat and I told him Arthur wanted to get help. And I was happy. I went to Pat. I said, 'He wants to get help. You got to take him to a psychiatrist, a psychologist, something. He wants to get help.' Arthur said, 'I have a thousand things, a million things in my head, and I want to talk to somebody.' I told him, 'Arthur, you keep telling me you have all these problems. I'm not a professional. You have to go talk to somebody who can help you.' Arthur goes, 'Yes, I want to.' And I went to Pat and I told him. Pat's answer to that, he would say, 'Well, he had a problem with a girl.' I don't know who the girl was at the time because he had problems with all his girls. Most of them were all go-go girls and in the go-go bars. And Pat said, 'He had a problem, but he's okay now.' I said, 'Listen, he said to me he wants to go see a psychiatrist. So because he said he wants to go, he should take the opportunity and talk to somebody. I don't care who you take him to, but just try to get him some help and go to a rehab.'

"Arthur told me, 'Mario, I want you to tell everybody. I want you to tell everybody what they did to me. They used me worse than a Nigga.' And I would go see Pat Lynch and tell him, 'He's gonna kill himself.' Pat Lynch always had excuses, 'Oh, he had a fight with his girlfriend.' He played it out like it was nothing. He said, 'The problem with Arturo is he's a 'B' fighter, he's not an 'A' fighter.' They used him because he could bring the crowds, bring the money."[786]

Arturo took home around $800,000 for the De La Hoya match. When Arturo received the check from Lynch, he squinted at the check and said, *"What is this?"* Lynch replied, *"That's your cut."* He told Arturo that he took his cut out, which was why it was only $800,000.[787] Joe recalled that Lynch had power of attorney over both him and his brother. He added that Lynch controlled both of their bank accounts because they weren't citizens. When Arturo asked for money, Pat would take it right out of the account he controlled for Arturo. It may have been that Lynch was controlling Arturo's money so he didn't waste it all on partying and strip clubs.

Costa recalled the De La Hoya fight. *"Arthur had a couple of million dollars in the bank. He always made excuses about money, so I thought he was lying to me. When he was crying, this was after the De La Hoya fight. Arthur got $1.2 million and he came home with $800,000 and then right after he came home he came by me. That's when he told me he was broke. He was so upset with that fight that he made me call Panama [Lewis] at around 4:30 or 5 in the morning. And the only thing he wanted to ask him is, 'Do you think I still got it?' "*[788]

On April 30, 2001, Pat Lynch announced that Arturo would return to the ring on July 10, on an ESPN card in Montreal. The card would be promoted by InterBox. Arturo was scheduled to box at 144-pounds. After the July bout, Pat Lynch planned on having Gatti return to the ring in October. Lynch was eyeing Kostya Tszyu or Hector Camacho Jr. as possible October opponents. Arturo was still upset about the De La Hoya stoppage. Gatti had watched the tape of the fight and believed that the stoppage was premature. Lynch had a long talk with Arturo and tried to convince him that Roca's stoppage was the right decision.[789] Lynch may or may not have gotten Arturo to agree with the stoppage, but Arturo never would work with Roca again.

Boxing, perennially on the verge of collapse, was experiencing another downturn. It was so bad that *Newark Star Ledger* reporter Chris Thorne stated that three years prior, people were calling Atlantic City the boxing capital of the world. Today, you might need two sea gulls and a piece of bread to see a great fight in Atlantic City.[790] In 1998, New Jersey hosted 36 professional boxing shows. In the following two years, they hosted only 16 shows a year. Nevada hosted nearly four times the amount of shows that New Jersey did.

Again, New Jersey boxing sages were complaining about the expensive and stringent medical testing, one of the toughest in the nation. Commissioner Larry Hazzard called the testing life-saving, while others said it was killing the sport. Another problem was Atlantic City's Convention Center. The Hall was undergoing a $90 million renovation that was still six months from completion. The project began in 1999. Hazzard predicted that when the state-of-the-art renovations were complete, the Hall would host 10 to 15 boxing shows a year.[791] In the past, the Hall had played host to Mike Tyson, Roy Jones, Jr. and Lennox Lewis. In June 1988, 22,000 fans turned out to watch Mike Tyson annihilate Michael Spinks at the Hall.

Local promoters felt that Hazzard was catering to large-scale promotional companies while dismissing the club-show, grass-root promoters. The club-show promoters were the ones who helped to build the fan-following and give the local boxers the wins they needed to jump to the next level. They were a necessary ingredient that apparently was being overlooked. Boxing has always been known to live and die by the way of big-name attractions. It was the fighters that carried the sport and not the other way around. The same can be said for most sports, but in boxing, where only two fighters enter the ring, personas are magnified.

Atlantic City was feeling the pressure of new boxing venues such as Connecticut's Mohegan Sun Casino. There was also a new Gulf Coast Casino in Mississippi that was drawing major fights. Lou Duva recalled that in the 1980s, and even during most of the 1990s, Atlantic City was the place to be for boxing. Many boxers from throughout the world fought in the Jersey-shore town.[792] Nevada's boxing commissioner, Marc Ratner, felt it was cyclical. He predicted that Atlantic City would get the big fights again when the Convention Center was finished. Ratner pointed to the fact that Nevada had a lull period a few years prior and then bounced back. Ratner felt that the same thing would happen in New Jersey.[793]

Hazzard believed that the completion of the new Hall would bring big-time boxing back to New Jersey. Hazzard felt that the return of the big fights would help generate more club shows.[794] There were many who believed it was the opposite that was true.

Ken Condon, president of Bally's Park Place, was convinced that boxing would return at a high level. He blamed the down cycle on the lack of exciting heavyweights. Condon was trying to keep boxing alive through small ballroom shows in Atlantic City.[795] Another problem with New Jersey boxing was the lack of big-time promoters such as Bob Arum, Don King, and Cedric Kushner. The IBF scandal led to Arum and Kushner making a deal with casino regulators, that they would not promote in New Jersey. Don King was staying away, due partly to the scandal, and partly to the fact that he was doing well promoting at other locations such as Las Vegas and New York's Madison Square Garden.

Al Certo and Gabe LaConte were still angry with the way Hazzard was running boxing in the state. Certo felt that promoters were afraid of running shows in New Jersey because of the expenses. He laid the blame squarely on Hazzard's shoulders.[796]

LaConte, who ran First Round Promotions, added that club shows were almost extinct in New Jersey. LaConte avowed to never run another show in the state as long as Hazzard was the commissioner. LaConte felt that instead of cleaning boxing up, as Hazzard proudly boasted he had, he actually chased boxing out of the state.[797] Lou Duva felt differently. He saw opportunities with the completion of the Convention Center nearing. Duva did want medical testing procedures to be revised though. He felt that Hazzard needed to let local hospitals administer the medical tests to help alleviate the hardship of having the fighters travel several hours for testing in south Jersey.[798]

Hazzard stood fast to his beliefs, as he felt that the local promoters weren't interested in the welfare of the fighters. He believed that they were more concerned about themselves and their own profits. Hazzard reiterated that it was his mission to assure that when fighters enter the ring there is a reasonable assurance that the boxers are healthy. Hazzard stated that if anyone could show him a better way of accomplishing that feat, he would gladly incorporate it into the process.[799]

Chapter 18
The Battle for Montreal & Millet

On June 25, it was announced that Arturo would not be fighting on the July 10 card in Montreal. Instead, his brother Joe would take his spot on the ESPN2 show. Joe originally was slated to fight Stephane Ouellet. Alex Hilton stepped in as Ouellet's replacement with three weeks to fight time. It would be the first and only time that a Hilton fought a Gatti. The bout was billed as the "Battle for Montreal."

Working Joe's corner were Diego Rosario and Nelson "Pepe" Cuevas. Notably absent from Hilton's corner was his father, Davey Hilton Sr. Joe had a 1½-inch height advantage over the 5'10" Hilton. As Alex Hilton was being announced, commentators Max Kellerman and Mario Diaz spoke of his six-year lay-off from boxing, from 1985 to 1991. The lay-off was due in part to his battle with alcohol addiction as well as legal issues.

Hilton started the bout aggressively, while Joe looked to counter. A minute into the 1st round, Joe landed two sharp left hooks. Halfway through the stanza, Joe landed another solid hook. Hilton was targeting the body with straight rights. Joe started establishing the jab in the final minute of the round.

Joe kept peppering the jab in the 2nd, while Hilton was committed to the body, though he rarely got close enough to be effective. Halfway through the round, Joe feigned a jab and turned it into a lead left uppercut that scored. Hilton attempted to duck the jab but dipped straight into the uppercut. Joe controlled the round by boxing in-and-out.

Joe continued to control the 3rd with his jab as Hilton looked tentative. Joe landed a solid left hook with 40 seconds remaining in the round. The crowd started booing Alex's inactivity.

Halfway through the 4th, Joe timed a right uppercut that landed flush. Joe started putting a straight right behind his jab. It took Hilton two-and-a-half minutes to land a punch.

Thirty seconds into the 5th, Joe landed a piercing lead left hook to the body. Up until this point, Hilton had landed only four punches throughout the entire bout. Halfway through the round, Joe landed another solid hook. He followed with a hook that missed, but he immediately came back with a straight right as Alex tried to lean away. The blow dropped Hilton onto his side.

Alex rose to his feet at the count of seven. Joe looked ringside to where Arturo was shouting instructions to him. Joe wasted no time rushing in with a right to the body. He came back with another right followed by a left hook to the head that dropped Hilton again. The referee waived the fight over without a count. The fans exploded in applause as Arturo jumped into the ring to hug his brother.

When the brothers returned to the U.S. Arturo flew to Vero Beach to relax while his body was healing from the De La Hoya fight.

Buddy McGirt, besides training boxers for Don King, was also training his amateur son, James McGirt Jr. In 1999, McGirt fell on hard financial times. He had spent most of the money he earned in his career and he was looking to start over as a trainer. Before McGirt moved to Florida, sheriff's officers had responded to his home on Long Island, with guns drawn, to repossess his car. The worst part of the incident for McGirt was the disappointing look in his daughter's eyes. McGirt's move to Vero Beach was an opportunity to start over.

Arturo was jumping rope in a local gym, just to stay in condition, when McGirt strolled in. Arturo broke the ice and started a conversation with Buddy. Neither one had followed up on the telephone conversation that Sandoval had put together in March. Arturo asked if McGirt was training anyone at the moment. Buddy responded that he wasn't. Gatti asked McGirt if he would be interested in training him. McGirt told Gatti that he would work with Arturo for two weeks to see how the chemistry was between them.[800] Two days later the Gatti-McGirt era began when Arturo told Lynch to call McGirt and tell him that he was hired. McGirt later commented that *"the rest was history."*[801] Arturo was in need of a trainer and McGirt was in need of a second chance in boxing.

Lynch wasn't sure if Arturo should continue his boxing career after the De La Hoya loss. He asked McGirt for Buddy's opinion on whether or not Gatti should continue boxing. McGirt felt that there was nothing wrong with Arturo. He just needed to go back to using his boxing skills.[802]

On July 13, 2001, Massachusetts' Micky Ward decisioned Emanuel Augustus in what *The Ring* magazine would later vote as 2001's "Fight of the Year." Ward, 36-10 (27 KOs), outworked the 24-17-4 Augustus. Both boxers threw a combined 2,000 punches during the contest.

On July 25, Pat Lynch announced that Arturo would return to the ring in October, possibly against Micky Ward. Lynch asked Arturo if he wanted to fight Ward. After looking at a tape of Ward, Arturo answered, *"No problem."* When asked about a possible Ward-Gatti bout, Lynch revealed that HBO wanted the matchup. He added that negotiations were underway, and if the money was right, the fight would be made.[803]

On July 28, Arturo held an engagement party. He was planning a September 2002 marriage to his new fiancé, Vivian Penha. The party was attended by many family and friends. Arturo became extremely intoxicated at the party. In front of his guests Arturo walked up to Pat Lynch, grabbed him and started shaking him. As Arturo held Lynch he said, *"All you do is fucking rob me. I know you're robbing me."* After the two were separated, Lynch left the party.[804]

When De La Hoya fought Mosley, Oscar earned $15 million while Mosley earned $4.5 million. Undoubtedly, Arturo and his entourage were aware of this. If Gatti's anger was directed at his De La Hoya purse he could not be faulted for feeling he was being undersold. Although Arturo was fighting a superstar it was not considered a superfight because De La Hoya was a much physically bigger fighter who had success against a much higher level of opposition than Gatti had. The most obvious evidence that points to the fight being of a lesser market value than De La Hoya vs. Mosley was the fact that Oscar earned $10 million less for the Arturo fight than he did for the Mosley bout. Before long, Gatti and Lynch worked out their differences.

On November 17, Arturo was offered a match with Jesse James Leija for January 5, 2002. Lynch and Gatti turned down the HBO-telecasted opportunity because they would have had barely six weeks to train for the bout. Gatti, who was still seeking a match with Kostya Tszyu, felt that he needed eight to ten weeks to prepare. The fact that he gained so much weight in-between fights was a major factor in his decision to turn down Leija. Another factor was Arturo's lacerated eyebrow. Gatti was originally scheduled to return to the ring in October but the eye injury had prevented him from doing so. Ward's camp grew tired of waiting for Gatti and they wound up signing to fight Leija. In mid-November, Arturo went to camp with his new trainer, Buddy McGirt. Mikey Red accompanied Arturo to Florida.

On December 3, Joe and Vikki Gatti gave birth to their first child, daughter Versace Victoria. She was named after Giovanni "Gianni" Versace, the internationally renowned Italian fashion designer and owner of the Gianni Versace International Fashion House. Versace was originally from Reggio Calabria, Italy.

On December 12, Pat Lynch announced that Arturo would return to the ring on January 26, 2002. His opponent would be former IBF junior welterweight champion Terronn Millett, 26-2-1 (19 KOs), of Colorado. Millett had won four straight bouts since losing his title to Zab Judah by 4th round knockout on August 5, 2000. Millett's resume included a decision win over Freddie Pendleton and a TKO victory over Vince Phillips. The fight would be held at the Madison Square Garden Theater on the Shane Mosley-Vernon Forrest undercard.

Arturo hired a new strength and conditioning coach. Taking over for the deceased Bob Wareing was Teddy Cruz. Cruz was friends with Mikey Red. He asked Mikey to introduce him to Arturo to see if he could take over as Gatti's strength coach. The two hit it off immediately. When Cruz started working with Arturo he appeared to take over John Capone's position as hangout partner in camp.

Cruz recalled, *"When we first met, I trained him in N.Y. Sports Club in West Caldwell, and we clicked right away. He was like, 'Would you be willing to go on the road with me?' I said, 'Yeah, you're Arturo Gatti. You're one of my favorite fighters. Of course. I'm doing personal training. So the money has to kinda take over from what I'm making here from my clients.' He said, 'That's no problem.' We came up with a number. We made an agreement. And we went down to Vero Beach."*[805]

Arturo was not the first fighter with whom Cruz had worked. Cruz had worked with Arturo's brother Joe. He had also worked with Kendall Holt, Frankie Toledo, David Toledo, Scott DePompe, Jameel McCline, and Michael Grant. Many of the fighters Cruz worked with were from the Lou Duva camp after he split with Main Events.

Cruz was raised in Jersey City. His brothers all trained at Bufano's boxing gym. Cruz explained why he went to Bufano's gym in 1983. *"I was 13. I wasn't interested too much in a career. I was just worried about learning how to fight so I wouldn't get into trouble."*[806] Cruz recalled Bufano's gym. *"Old School. Legend. They don't have gym's like that anymore. That's history. That's what I think about Bufano's. One of the original gyms of the 1950s. One of those classic stereotypical gyms. The real gyms."*[807] Of Dominic Bufano, Cruz recalled, *"Dominic was old traditional, old school, old timer. Seeing him and talking to him was just a privilege. Me being privileged to be there for $20 a month at the time, it was* *good."*[808]

As a child, Cruz was more interested in breakdancing than boxing. He would dance for money, on a piece of cardboard, at the Hudson Mall in Jersey City. Cruz got involved with strength conditioning of boxers through his cousin, Diego Rosario. At the time Rosario was training Joe Gatti and the Toledo brothers.

Arturo, Cruz, and McGirt were just getting a feel for each other while training for the Millett fight. As Cruz recalled, *"For Millett it was just pretty much, it was a starter fight. So we were just trying to get him tuned to us. To Buddy as well as myself, with the strength and conditioning. All three of us were kinda comin' in fresh at the time. We were just trying to get ourselves and our chemistry working right."*[809]

Cruz would work with Arturo for the remainder of his career, mostly on weight training, strength and conditioning, and dieting. Cruz recalled that Arturo would never quit during his strength and conditioning drills no matter how tough they were or how weak he was from losing weight. Arturo would say to Cruz, *"What are you going to do to me? You're going to kill me."*[810] After complaining, Arturo always completed his exercises. He never cheated himself when it came to his training with Cruz. Mikey Red was always in Arturo's dressing room and walked him out to the ring, but up until this point, he had never worked Gatti's corner. Mikey would work Arturo's corner for the first time in the Millett fight.

Arturo's eye was apparently healed sufficiently enough to resume his career, but Pat Lynch was still concerned about the eye. Gatti dropped back down to 140 for the Millett bout. Arturo felt much more comfortable fighting at 140 because he believed his punches had more pop on them at junior welterweight. Lynch felt that Millett's style was nothing fancy, but they were still cautious because he was very dangerous early in a fight. He was a strong fighter with a good left hook, but one of the reasons he was selected was because he stood right in front of his opponents.[811]

Arturo was spending the fourth Christmas of his 11-year career in training camp. Gatti spent the holiday with Buddy McGirt. McGirt and Arturo passed the time by playing dominoes together. Buddy had spent many Christmases in camp at Bufano's Gym in Jersey City, so he knew how Gatti felt.[812] Arturo would have preferred to spend the holidays with his family, especially his brother Joe who recently gave birth to his daughter Versace, but Arturo was a professional who understood the sacrifices that were necessary to be successful.

Arturo was still upset over the stoppage of the De La Hoya fight. *"I felt Hector shouldn't have stopped the fight. That iced the cake [on our relationship] because Hector always told me that he never stopped a fight... A lot of fights before that, like the one with Wilson Rodriguez, should have been stopped, but not that one. Not the biggest fight of my career. It upset me. After fighting Oscar, I realized that for the first time in my life I was not the stronger fighter in the ring. After that, I decided that 140 was my weight."*[813]

Arturo spoke of fighting Millett. *"It's a good style. He doesn't move too much but stands there and likes to trade... I'm using my jab and the basics of boxing now. I have good hand speed that I never used. People are going to see my performance, one of the best performances I'll have had. It'll get me a lot of recognition."*[814] Arturo brought New Jersey welterweight Freddy Curiel into camp as a sparring partner.

McGirt was training both Gatti and another warrior, Johnny Tapia. Buddy felt that Gatti and Tapia were tied in the toughness category. McGirt believed that Arturo had gotten away from using his jab and his combinations. He was only focused on throwing the left hook. McGirt added that Arturo was too fixated on not getting cut, but not focused enough on upper body movement. McGirt praised Arturo for being a good student, although he did mention that Gatti went through mood swings. McGirt expressed his appreciation for Arturo and Lynch giving him the opportunity to train Gatti.[815] Steve Sandoval felt that he was partially responsible for bringing Arturo and McGirt together. He was upset that he wasn't compensated or acknowledged for his efforts.

On January 5, Arturo was in his rented home in Vero Beach watching Jesse James Leija box Micky Ward on HBO's "Boxing After Dark." Mikey Red watched the bout with Arturo. Leija and Ward were both nearing the ends of their careers. Leija was 35 years old and Ward was 36. The winner was rumored to be in line for a fight with Arturo. Lou DiBella pushed for the Leija-Ward match, even though they were not the well-connected big names that HBO usually broadcasted. Ward had stated publicly that if he lost, he would retire. He did not want to go back to being an ESPN-level fighter.

While watching the fight, Arturo turned to Skowronski and said, *"Fuck, I wish they would give me one of these guys to fight."*[816] The Leija-Ward bout ended in a technical decision for Leija, when the bout was stopped after the 5th round ended. Leija was leading on two of the three scorecards at the time of the stoppage. Leija had suffered a cut in the 1st round. Referee Laurence Cole ruled that the cut was the result of a head butt. A replay showed that the cut was the result of a Ward left hook. Thus, Ward should have won by TKO. There were those who felt that Leija could have continued, but his corner facilitated the stoppage after the 5th round because Ward was starting to come on strong.

Ward's corner erupted in protest over the stoppage, but Cole refused to listen. Even Leija said the bout should've been ruled a no-contest. Ward's record fell to 37-11 after the loss. Ward filed a protest with the boxing commission, but his protest was dismissed. In the main event, Leonard Dorin retained his WBA lightweight title with a disputed split-decision win over Raul Horacio Balbi.

On January 10, 2002, long-time Jersey City boxing gym owner Dominic Bufano died at the age of 93.

On January 14, reports came out of Vero Beach that Arturo was having trouble losing weight. The bout with Millett was only fourteen days away. Lynch tried to calm the rumors by stating that everything was fine.[817] Gatti had been sparring with John Molnar and Scott DePompe for two weeks.

DePompe later recalled that he always kept his right hand high because he was cognizant of Arturo's famed left hook. In one of their sparring sessions, Arturo threw a hard left hook that was caught by DePompe's high guard. When DePompe took his glove off he noticed that his thumb's finger nail had been broken off by Arturo's punch, and this was with 16-ounce gloves! DePompe also recalled that Arturo was a great prankster in the gym, pulling his sparring partners' shorts down. After Arturo finished his prank, the fast-talking Gatti would sheepishly state, *"So sorry."*[818] DePompe recalled that Arturo was very generous, always asking if his sparring partners needed anything, such as sneakers.

On January 23, Arturo arrived in Manhattan looking, as *Jersey Journal* reporter Wayne Witkowski described, *"tan and trim."*[819] The 5,000 seat Theater at Madison Square Garden was sold out for the show. Arturo commented on fighting at The Theater again. *"This is my house. Some of the greatest moments of my life were in the Garden and I'm looking forward to Saturday night. This is a tough fight for me coming back, but I'm ready for it. I'm glad I sacrificed myself to go back to 140 because there are a lot of openings there for me and it's just a stepping stone Saturday night. I've been with hard hitters already and that's the only thing he can do with me. He comes forward and is a simple fighter and all the guys who did that I knocked out, so I'm not worried about that at all, although he has faced some great opponents."*[820]

Pat Lynch revealed that Arturo was very comfortable at 140. Lynch added that Gatti went into camp in shape, which was a big plus. Arturo was able to concentrate on a game plan for the fight rather than being focused on losing weight.[821]

Arturo mentioned several possible opponents should he get past Millett. They were Jesse James Leija, Micky Ward, and Kostya Tszyu. Main Events CEO Gary Shaw believed that a Gatti win would put Arturo in the hunt for a world title.[822]

McGirt felt that the key to defeating Terron was taking control of the fight early and attacking the body. Arturo praised his new trainer for helping him to utilize his right hand more. Gatti also commended McGirt for helping him to think more in the ring instead of just throwing punches.[823]

Arturo held a ½-inch reach and ½-inch height advantage over the 5'7" Millett. Gatti entered the ring to the *Rocky* theme-song "Eye Of The Tiger." Larry Merchant commented that although Arturo was called "Thunder," his power had been muffled with his rise in weight. Jim Lampley added that Arturo was enjoying some major-league high living. Lampley cautioned that Gatti should focus more on his career.

Arturo's corner consisted of Buddy McGirt, Mikey Red, and Joe Souza. Arturo started the bout on his toes. He landed a hard hook to the body and followed with a straight right to the head. Gatti landed another hard right and displayed fancy footwork as he stepped around Millett. Arturo unloaded two vicious body shots. The flatfooted Millett was clearly having problems with Arturo's movement. Gatti landed another hard right and hook before the bell rang. McGirt advised Arturo to keep circling to his right. In Terronn's corner, his trainer and father, Marvin Millett, chided him for being too tight.

In the 2nd round, Arturo's height was playing a huge factor as he landed with ease from the outside. The muscular Millett's reach appeared restricted from his stocky build. Gatti stopped to trade and was caught by a wild right hand. Arturo recomposed himself and started utilizing the jab. Gatti set his feet to punch and was caught with another hard right cross. He came back with a right of his own. Arturo opened up to the body and finished with a thunderous hook upstairs that stopped Millett in his tracks. Another body shot and left hook had Terronn retreating to the ropes where Gatti continued his attack. Millett fought his way off of the ropes. Arturo finished the round with two more violent hooks. After the round ended, Arturo asked McGirt if he was cut, but he was only feeling sweat dripping down his forehead. McGirt replied, *"He has to hit you to cut you."*[824]

Both fighters loaded up in the 3rd. Millett landed a hard right hand halfway through the round. Gatti landed several shots from long range. Arturo made Terronn miss three punches, which brought an ovation from his ringside supporters. With 40 seconds remaining in the round, Gatti landed a huge left hook that had Millett walking on stilts. Terronn stumbled forward. Arturo could have planted a *coup de grace* uppercut on Millett but opted to step back and let him fall face first into the canvas.

Terronn courageously rose to his feet at the count of eight. Referee Jimmy Santa allowed the fight to continue. Arturo landed another hook before the bell rang. The ringside doctor was called up to look at Millett. Terronn was allowed to continue.

In the 4th round, Arturo loaded up with uppercut-hook-straight right combos on his stationary foe. Gatti pumped a few jabs home and followed with a cannonlike right hand which twisted Millett's jaw. Arturo double-pumped a jab and followed with a thunderous straight right that Terronn never saw. Millet was dropped onto his side.

Amazingly, the referee allowed the slaughter to continue. Santa asked Millett if he knew where he was. Terronn responded, *"Madison Square Garden."* Millett was dropped with another hook and the one-sided affair was finally waived off.

Millett didn't expect Arturo to be as strong and as fast as he was. Gatti was busier than Terronn expected. Millett confessed that Arturo hit him with a really good body shot. He admitted that he started feeling woozy coming out for the 4th round.[825]

CompuBox stats had Arturo landing 129 of 279 while Millett landed 64 of 212. Merchant asked Gatti how he finally managed to avoid getting cut. Arturo praised McGirt for having him box instead of brawl. Gatti was proud of winning without getting hurt. Arturo revealed that Buddy taught him to be calm in the ring. To be calm and think with his head and strike when there were openings. Not punch just because he had been hit. Arturo felt that he was much more relaxed in his dressing room before the match because McGirt was calm. Gatti believed that this helped him to remain calm and focused after the fight started.

Arturo was more comfortable fighting at 140-pounds again. Gatti felt that he had more power at junior welterweight. Arturo wanted to fight either Jesse James Leija or Micky Ward. Arturo believed that the Millett win revived his career. Gatti hugged Mikey Red, Pat Lynch, Buddy McGirt, and Joe Souza. Souza joked that he was insulted that Arturo didn't get cut during the fight.

After knocking out Millett, Arturo proclaimed, *"I always knew I had to go back to being a boxer-puncher again. As I got older, I realized I had to go back to what I used to do. I'm considered a veteran now, and to keep on going in this business, I had to go back. I didn't try at all to knock Millett out. Instead, I used my speed. I'm done with that brawling style; I don't need to brawl for people to like my performances."*[826]

Arturo thanked McGirt for reviving his boxing style and bringing back his hand-speed. Gatti lambasted those who felt that a great boxer, like Buddy, could not be a great trainer. Arturo felt that his past performances were akin to the Flintstones cartoons. McGirt ingrained into Gatti's head that standing in front of his opponent and trading was the worst thing he could do. Buddy advised Arturo that he would never regain a title by brawling.[827]

McGirt felt that Arturo had the talent to adjust his style. He believed it was just a matter of getting Gatti's tools out of the toolbox and sharpening them up. Buddy surmised that Arturo could still score a knockout without getting beat up. McGirt told Arturo that he wanted Gatti to be able to remember where he put his money after he retired. Buddy added that the rumor that Arturo was hard to work with in camp was untrue.[828]

Arturo was hopeful that his new habits would prolong his career. *"My lifestyle has totally changed. In three or four years, I've changed a lot. I've had some rough years. I wasn't doing the right things outside the ring. Vivian fixed me up to the max. She saw things that I didn't see. There was a bad environment around me. At first, though, I wasn't willing to listen to her. But being around her, I decided that she was right. I'm eating right and living right. I don't drink anymore. Before, in-between fights, I didn't know what a gym looked like. Now I want to work on staying in shape all of the time. I want to fight for a couple of years, win a world title, make some money, and then retire. I want to be happy, and have some kids, and be grateful about my boxing career. I want to be able to tell my kids what went on with my career. Living the lifestyle I lived, I blew a lot of money. But this is the best I've felt in a while.*"⁸²⁹

Pat Lynch favored Arturo's boxing over brawling. He felt that this was the best that Gatti had looked since the Patterson battles. Lynch added that Arturo fighting for the crowd was great, but Gatti needed to start winning if he wanted to become a champion again. Lynch had been concerned for Arturo's health during his savage ring battles. He hoped that Arturo would stick to boxing. Lynch praised Gatti for never losing focus while in training. Arturo never missed a workout. He even trained on Christmas Day.⁸³⁰

HBO's Larry Merchant had called the Millett fight a crossroads battle for Gatti. He added that Arturo had attained a reputation for being a great loser. Merchant felt that Gatti had the right opponent in front of him in Millett. He gave credit to Gatti for becoming an effective boxer-puncher, and more importantly, for protecting his eyes.⁸³¹

Gatti, who was unrated before the match, was hoping the win would move him back into a top-ten slot, as Millett was ranked in the top-ten by all the major sanctioning bodies.

Millett's manager, Kurt Emhoff, originally thought that Arturo was a good match for his fighter. He felt that Gatti was a busted-up, one-punch fighter. He thought the match-up was pretty even until he discovered that McGirt was training Gatti. McGirt previously had trained Emhoff's fighter Levon Easley. McGirt turned Easly from a brawler into a boxer. Emhoff confessed that they were preparing for a brawling, face-first Arturo; not the boxing and moving Gatti that showed up.⁸³²

On March 1, 2002, Joe Gatti returned to the ring at Foxwoods in Connecticut. His opponent was 21-11-1 (14 KOs) Tim Shocks. Joe paid for his mother Ida to fly down to attend his fight against Shocks. Ida normally avoided flying. Joe knocked Shocks out in the 4th round for his fifth straight win. Joe's record was now 30-7 with 22 KOs. Shocks went the distance with Vinnie Pazienza over 10-rounds in September 2001. Joe lobbied hard for a Pazienza match, but he believed that Pazienza wanted no part of him.

Chapter 19
Ward I

On March 9, 2002, it was announced that an Arturo Gatti-Micky Ward match was close to being made. Ward was offered $350,000, with an extra $25,000 for training expenses. The bout would take place on May 18. HBO was paying Main Events $1 million, with another $500,000 site fee if the bout were to be held in Canada. Ward's people were pushing for the bout to be held at Foxwoods, which was closer to Ward's hometown and fan base. Ward's management team was holding out for $500,000.

Russell Peltz felt that a Gatti-Ward match was the right fight for both boxers. He stated that if Gatti or Ward passed on the match, they'd be foolish. Peltz believed that HBO understood the value of the fight.[833] It was rumored that Ward was offered the Gatti fight because some at HBO felt badly about the way his battle against Leija ended.

On March 21, it was announced that a deal had been finalized which would bring Arturo and Micky Ward into the ring together. The bout would take place on May 18 at Mohegan Sun in Connecticut. The fight would be broadcast live on HBO's "Boxing After Dark" series. Montreal nearly won the opportunity to hold the bout, but Mohegan Sun outbid them in the end.

Arturo's recent win over Millett propelled him in the rankings. He was now ranked #3 at junior welterweight by the IBF and WBC, and #9 by the WBA. Ward was ranked #7 by the IBF. Gatti immediately began training for the bout in Vero Beach.

Micky Ward had been wanting a fight with Arturo for over a year. Ward was ecstatic that the fight had finally been made. He planned on coming out fighting from the opening bell. Ward felt that he needed to stay close to Gatti, to stay inside of his power. Ward didn't want to be on the end of Arturo's punches, but under them.[834]

On March 25, Ward's people were furious over an e-mail they received from Carl Moretti. In the e-mail, Ward was advised that he would receive no rooms, no meal vouchers, and no tickets for the fight. Those items were standard for a fight of this level. It was only a month prior that Main Events complained that Don King shortchanged them for tickets and credentials during the Lennox Lewis-Hasim Rahman match.

Lou DiBella, Ward's adviser, and Sal LoNano, Ward's manager, both believed Gatti's people were trying to kill the match. Ward agreed to fight Gatti for $435,000. Arturo would earn $1 million. DiBella felt that Main Events was treating Ward like he was a 4-round fighter. Ward's camp advised Main Events that if they refused to give Ward the standard perks for a main event fighter, the bout would be called off. DiBella believed that Main Events never really wanted the Ward match. He felt it was a bait-and-switch move.[835] DiBella threatened that if Main Events didn't give Ward an additional $25,000 to cover the costs of the rooms, meals, and tickets, the bout would be cancelled.

In mid-April, while Arturo and McGirt were in training, Buddy received a surprise visit. Angel Manfredy stopped by the gym and asked McGirt to train him. Buddy asked Gatti to do him a favor and let him train Manfredy so he could earn a few extra dollars. Arturo told McGirt that he didn't care if Buddy trained Manfredy. Soon after, Manfredy started training with McGirt. Everything was fine for about a week, until Manfredy walked into a restaurant and started flirting with a waitress. He bragged to the waitress that he was a boxer. The waitress told him that she knew Arturo Gatti. Manfredy told her that he beat the shit out of Arturo and knocked him out. The waitress told Gatti what Manfredy said about him. Arturo was furious. When he went to the gym the next day, Arturo asked McGirt what time Manfredy trained. Buddy told Gatti that Manfredy trained at 2 p.m. McGirt didn't give any thought to Arturo's question.

At 2 p.m., Gatti walked into the gym with a bucket of fried chicken. He handed McGirt the bucket and said, *"Here coach, go put this in your car."*[836] McGirt was walking to the parking lot with the bucket when he realized, *"Wait a minute, I didn't ask for no fuckin' chicken."*[837] McGirt realized that Arturo was up to something. He walked back into the gym. When he entered, he observed Gatti in Manfredy's face. Arturo was screaming at Manfredy, *"Listen you son of a bitch. The only reason you're in this fuckin' town is because of me. This is my fuckin' town. If you want pussy from a broad, you don't tell the fuckin' broad that you kicked my ass or knocked me out. I'll kick your fuckin' ass right here."*[838] Manfredy denied that he made the statements. Arturo cut Manfredy off by telling him, *"You're full of shit."* McGirt took Arturo outside the gym to cool him off. Arturo told McGirt, *"Coach, I don't mind if that guy wants a broad. That's up to him. He don't have to tell the broad he kicked my ass or knocked me out or I'll kick his fuckin' ass. He's only here because of me. He can continue to train; just don't talk shit about me in town.*"[839]

On May 11, Ward and Gatti were interviewed regarding their upcoming match. Arturo was confident that he was going to beat Ward. He wasn't worried at all. He stated that Ward was a tough fighter that he respected. Gatti felt that he had the tools needed to make it an easy fight for himself. He added that if fans were looking for a brawl they might wind up surprised at the outcome.[840]

Ward was shocked by Arturo's bold statements. Micky challenged Gatti to try and outbox him and beat him up. Ward added that it would be easier for Gatti to say he was going to beat him up than actually accomplishing it. Micky felt that neither he nor Gatti were great fighters, but they both were tough and gave the fans their money's worth. Ward was proud to be known as a warrior. To Micky, being a warrior meant that he never quit, that he gave it his all in every fight. Ward cautioned that there was a heavy price to be paid for being a warrior and it was unknown what physical damage he and Gatti may have suffered from their previous battles.[841]

The winner of the Gatti-Ward match would most likely get a shot against 140-pound undisputed champion, Kostya Tszyu. The loser would fall to ESPN status, and for either one, that probably would mean the end of their career. *Boston Globe* columnist Ron Borges joked that Gatti's boxing tools included an enswell; a quip on how his eyes swelled during matches. Borges added that Gatti's game plans during his matches hadn't surprised anyone but his plastic surgeon; a jest on Gatti's reputation of being cut during fights.

Ward announced that he would be wearing specially designed trunks featuring the "Lowell Spinners" logo on them. The Spinners were a minor league baseball team affiliated with the Boston Red Sox organization. The Spinners were selling replicas of Ward's trunks to help raise money for the "Kids in Disabilities Sports." Spinners general manager Shawn Smith said that Ward was the type of boxer in the ring, and outside of the ring, with whom the Spinners loved to be associated. Like Ward, the Spinners were from Lowell, Massachusetts.[842] Ward also would wear a Spinners baseball jersey into the ring with the number 38 on the back. The number 38 would represent his career victory total should he defeat Gatti.

On May 17, after the weigh-in, Ward gave his final comments. He reflected on his career and how he had accomplished a great deal more than people thought he ever would. Three years prior, boxing writers were saying his career was finished. He came a long way back from fighting in a hotel ballroom in Lowell, but he knew that if he didn't win this fight he wouldn't receive another major payday offer again. Ward announced that if he didn't win, he probably would have a going-away fight in Lowell then retire. If he won, Ward planned on fighting one or two more matches before retiring. Ward knew he had to get close enough not to be on the end of Gatti's punches. He planned on going all-out in the match. He realized that there were no more tomorrows for him. He wanted to go out with a bang.[843]

Buddy McGirt was confident that Arturo would be victorious right up until the weigh-in. That was when he entered the hotel lobby and a Ward fan yelled to him, *"Hey Buddy, this is Arturo."* The fan then acted as though he took a hook to the body and fell to the ground wincing in pain saying, *"Oww, it hurts!"* The act would be an ominous premonition. McGirt had felt the fight was *"in the bag"* until he ran into the Ward fan in the lobby.

6,254 fans turned out to watch Ward and Gatti battle at the Mohegan Sun arena on "Boxing After Dark." Arturo shadow boxed in his dressing room while McGirt, John Capone, and his brother Fabrizio looked on. Before the battle even began, HBO analyst Jim Lampley was calling it a classic. Larry Merchant commented that the only title that mattered to both Gatti and Ward was the warrior title. Merchant added that the only belts that meant anything to both fighters were the ones they would be landing on each other.

Working Arturo's corner were McGirt, Mikey Red, and Joe Souza. As the fighters were announced, it was readily apparent that it was a pro-Ward crowd. Ward was applauded, while Arturo was booed. Working Ward's corner were his brother Dicky Eklund, cutman Al Gavin, and manager Sal LoNano.

Ward started the bout as the aggressor. Halfway through the 1st round he was cut by a sharp Gatti hook. Arturo was easily slipping Ward's punches while landing crisp combinations. A plodding Ward was following Gatti around the ring and paying the price for not punching his way inside. With 33 seconds remaining in the round Ward slammed his gloves together in a sign of frustration. He was repeatedly getting beat to the punch by the in-and-out moving Gatti. Arturo's hand speed and movement easily won him the round.

In Ward's corner, Dicky Eklund told Micky that he needed to move his head, while Al Gavin worked on the cut.

In the 2nd, Arturo continued to set the pace with his jab. His hand speed and movement were the difference thus far. Arturo easily beat Ward to the punch. Micky applied more pressure but Arturo carried the round, punctuating it with quick shots to the body and head. At the end of the round referee Frank Cappuccino warned Gatti to keep his punches up, although Arturo's body punches all appeared to be on or above the beltline.

McGirt cautioned Gatti to keep his hands up in close, to turn Ward, and use his hand speed. Eklund asked for head movement and double jabs. Eklund also told Micky to keep his right hand high to block Arturo's hooks.

Thirty seconds into the 3rd, Arturo landed a crunching left hook around Ward's guard that jolted Micky's head. Ward switched to a left-handed stance a minute into the round. Halfway through the round the change in stance started paying off. Micky found a home for the left to the body. Arturo's movement slowed considerably, most likely due to Ward's hooks to the liver. Gatti's guard dropped as Micky's close-quarter hooks dug under Arturo's ribcage. Ward switched back to a right-handed stance. Arturo came thundering back, using his offense to combat Ward's pressure. The close round came to an end. Fifty-three power shots were landed in the round, 30 by Gatti and 23 by Ward.

McGirt advised Gatti to avoid taking body shots from Ward by moving to his left on the inside. Arturo tried to look away as he had done to Roca, but McGirt ordered him to stay focused and listen to instructions.

A little over a minute into the 4th, Ward timed a perfect right hand that twisted Arturo's head. Gatti immediately grabbed Ward to clear his head. With 1:25 remaining in the round, Gatti landed eleven hard shots, threading Ward's high guard with combinations down the middle. One of Arturo's hooks landed low, onto Ward's hip. Gatti was listening to McGirt, as he turned to his left whenever he and Ward were close. Both fighters traded bombs. With 25 seconds remaining, Arturo landed a left to the midsection that was below the beltline. The shot sent Micky sprawling to the canvas. Arturo tried to argue that the shot was legal.

Referee Frank Cappuccino quickly took a point away from Gatti. As Ward was recuperating Arturo went to touch gloves with him. Cappuccino pulled Arturo away. Cappuccino and Gatti started arguing about the errant blow. Arturo argued that it was accidental.

Arturo started the 5th by winging 22 unanswered shots. Ward kept advancing as the crowd booed a borderline Gatti body punch. Micky was getting the better of the inside work. Both fighters loaded up, toe-to-toe, throwing caution to the wind. Head movement was non-existent. A small cut opened on the corner of Arturo's right eye from a Ward left hook. Gatti landed 11 straight shots, driving a bloody Ward to the ropes. Micky came back with 17 shots of his own, punctuated by a thudding uppercut and left hook. The bell saved Gatti from further punishment. The pro-Ward crowd exploded. Micky pounded his chest as the round ended. Ninety-eight punches were landed by both boxers in the round. Both corners felt their fighter had a good round.

In the corner, McGirt screamed for Arturo to *"turn out"* when he was finished punching, to avoid getting hit. Gatti looked at McGirt with a dejected face and confessed that he had to stand and fight with Ward because his legs were gone. Arturo told McGirt, *"Coach, I'm tired. I gotta stand there with him and slow him up some."* McGirt responded, *"Okay, just don't get hit with that body shot."*[844] McGirt appreciated Arturo's honesty, which helped him to adjust his strategy going forward.

Round 6 started with the crowd on its feet. Gatti boxed, while Ward applied pressure. The pace slowed as the punches of both boxers had less steam on them. Arturo summoned the energy to box and move. Gatti ended the round by punching Ward to the ropes. Arturo appeared to have the edge in the round.

Arturo came out boxing in the 7th, Gatti dominated the round, as Ward appeared to take the round off. Near the end of the round, Micky switched to a lefty stance again. In Ward's corner, Eklund chided Micky to bang the shit out of Arturo and stop being a punching bag. Eklund threatened to stop the fight if Ward didn't start fighting harder.

Micky started the 8th switching back and forth from orthodox to lefty and back again. Emanuel Steward was amazed that Arturo had the legs to box at his age, with the wars he had been through. Larry Merchant credited Pat Lynch for rebuilding Arturo's career with mid-level opponents. Arturo appeared to get the better of the first two minutes. Ward came on in the final minute, trapping Arturo along the ropes with chopping blows. Micky landed a short right that stunned Gatti. Ward pounded away as Arturo covered up. The crowd rose to their feet as the bell ended the session.

Eklund whispered into Ward's ear that he nearly had Gatti out. McGirt told Arturo that he was taking too many shots on the inside. He asked Gatti to throw his right hand to the body. He pleaded with Arturo to give him six good minutes. He asked Gatti to do it for Jerry. The Jerry that McGirt was using to motivate Arturo was 70-

year-old Jerry Hagin. Hagin used to live in New York. He worked at LaGuardia Airport before retiring to Vero Beach. Hagin, along with 65-year-old Ken Boissy and 85-year-old Anthony "Gus" Domenico, from Vero Beach, would sit in the gym and watch Arturo train every day. The retirees also would drive up from Florida to attend Arturo's fights.

Fifteen seconds into the 9th, Ward ripped a hook to the head and came back down with a devastating hook to the body. The blow dropped Gatti to his knees in excruciating pain. Cappuccino picked up the count. Arturo barely made it to his feet as Cappuccino reached the count of nine. Zab Judah, who was sitting ringside, jumped up out of his seat in amazement. Ward swarmed Arturo, pummeling him around the ring.

Arturo appeared out on his feet. Buddy was up on the ring apron with a towel in his hand, preparing to stop the fight. Mikey Red pulled McGirt back down. Buddy turned to Mikey and said, *"If you're going to let it go, you'd better wake him up."*[845] Mikey told McGirt that if they stopped the fight, Arturo would never speak to them again.

With 1:50 remaining in the round, Arturo came thundering back. Gatti trapped Ward along the ropes. The action was intense. The HBO cameramen were grinning with satisfaction. They witnessed hundreds of rounds first-hand, but it was obvious from their expressions that this round was special. Ward came on again as he switched to southpaw. He was teeing off on Arturo's motionless head. Ward later revealed that he thought he had Gatti nearly knocked out, but he just kept coming back.[846] Both fighters dug deep from a seemingly endless reserve of energy. With 30 seconds remaining in the round Ward connected with another right that forced Arturo to hold. Both boxers traded as the round came to a close. Emanuel Steward called the 9th round *"the round of the century."*[847]

Mikey Red dumped a whole bucket of ice down Arturo's pants. Mikey described it, *"Like a shower in the corner.*[848] *I got a bucket of ice, pulled open his trunks, and poured it on his balls. And it woke him up. He won the 10th round."*[849] McGirt recalled that Arturo's lower lip was shivering and he had tears in his eyes. McGirt asked Arturo if he wanted him to stop the fight. Gatti replied that his side was killing him, but he was going to go back out and box. McGirt warned Gatti to listen to him. He told Arturo that he was not going to let him continue taking this type of punishment. Arturo promised

McGirt that he was going to box in the 10th round.

Arturo was deliberately biting down on his lip. As Mikey Red explained, *"It was a trick he learned from Dale Earnhardt Jr. When NASCAR drivers are falling asleep, they bite their lip."*[850] Gatti met Earnhardt through a Budweiser promotion they had both participated in. In Ward's corner, Al Gavin told Micky that Gatti was done. Arturo stood up and started bouncing on his toes. McGirt was amazed at Gatti's courage.

The bell rang to start the 10th. Ward started walking to the center of the ring. He noticed Gatti was still standing in his corner with McGirt in front of him. He thought McGirt had retired his fighter. Ward relaxed and started celebrating, raising his arms. The crowd roared as Jim Lampley announced that the fight had been stopped. McGirt and Gatti hadn't heard the seconds out warning or the bell ring. When Arturo walked out of his corner, Lampley retracted his comment. Cappuccino yelled that the fight wasn't over, that it was the last round. He ordered the fighters to go back to their corners.

The timekeeper never stopped the clock, so the round began with thirty seconds elapsed. Larry Merchant commented that it was good news for Gatti. At one point, Ward looked like a statue as Arturo unloaded on him. Ironically, it was Ward who would benefit from the shortened round. Both fighters tee'd off on each other. Merchant stated that he was humbled at watching the punishment both men were absorbing. Both fighters stood and threw punches for ten straight seconds. The bell rang ending the historic battle.

Jim Lampley called the bout a candidate not only for fight of the year, but fight of the century, a throwback to the 1950s. In the final round, Gatti threw 99 punches and landed 50. Unofficial HBO scorer Harold Lederman had it a draw at 94-94. Larry Merchant had it for Gatti by a couple of points.

When ring announcer Mark Berio announced that there was a majority decision, Ward looked dejected and disgusted. Arturo had a concentrated look about him, staring out into the crowd from a neutral corner. After reading Frank Lombardi's 94-94 score, Berio continued that Judge Richard Flaherty scored the bout 94-93, and Judge Steve Weisfeld saw it 95-93, for the winner by majority decision, "Irish" Micky Ward. Arturo raised his hand in victory just before Berio announced the winner, while Ward had his head buried in a towel. When Berio yelled "Irish," Ward tightened his face in a thankful gesture as he raised his hands. Arturo turned in a semi-circle, not knowing how to react.

Arturo had landed 350 of 779 punches to Ward's 268 of 550. McGirt felt that Arturo abandoned his game plan. He added that Gatti had too much heart for his own good. Arturo thought he won the 10th round because he believed that Ward punched himself out. Gatti felt that the fight was close and could have gone either way. Ward said Arturo was like granite. He thought he was close to stopping Gatti, but Arturo kept coming.[851] Ward added that his hands and elbows were hurting him. He felt that the fight was close and could've gone either way. Ward welcomed a rematch.[852] Ward was prouder of the way Arturo turned his life around than he was about the way Gatti performed in the ring. Arturo called himself the comeback boy.

Arturo stated that even though he hit Ward with good shots, Micky kept getting stronger every round. Gatti felt that Ward's defense was impressive for a fighter that didn't move a lot. Arturo said that he would love to get a rematch if possible.[853] Arturo and Ward both ended up at Backus Hospital after the bout. Ward's right hand was put in a cast.

Arturo's team complained about the scoring. More specifically, they complained about judge Richard Flaherty's scorecard. Flaherty, of Massachusetts, scored the 9th round 10-7 in favor of Ward. Both of the other judges scored the round 10-8. If Flaherty, who was from Ward's home state, would have scored the round 10-8, the fight would have been ruled a draw. In the 9th round, besides knocking Arturo down, Ward landed 60 of 82 power shots.

Ward didn't pay attention to the scoring controversy. He was proud that he and Gatti put on such a great fight. In the middle rounds, he felt that his body shots slowed Arturo down. Ward felt that if he kept putting pressure on Arturo he would eventually break him down. Ward admitted that he was pretty banged up and so was Gatti. Ward was pleased that the fans got what they expected.[854]

Ward admitted that when he thought Gatti had retired before the start of the 10th round he jumped up off of his stool and was thinking, *"Oh, thank God, it's over."* It was impossible for Ward to try and get up again, psychologically, after he thought the fight was over. He just couldn't get going again. Ward admitted that he gave the 10th round away. Ward praised Gatti for being the toughest guy, with the biggest heart, of anybody he had ever fought.[855]

The fight was instantly being called a classic. HBO's vice-president, Xavier James, said it was probably the most exciting fight he had ever attended. James added that the fight not only lived up to expectations, it actually surpassed them. Pat Lynch called the fight unbelievable. Lynch added that he was totally in awe of the 9th round. He was shocked that Arturo could summon up the energy to even come out for the 10th round after all he had been through.

Lou DiBella was amazed at both fighters' efforts. He was astounded that Gatti survived the 9th round. DiBella thought the fight was like a *Rocky* movie. He had never seen so many people standing, cheering, and grimacing at the same time. It was as though the fans were feeling the fighters' pain.

Boxing fans, HBO, and both fighters' camps clamored for a rematch. As Arturo was being taken to Backus Hospital, he told Lynch to go to the post fight press conference and ask Ward for a rematch. When Lynch finished with the news conference, he went to the hospital. He saw Arturo in a hospital bed with an IV in his arm. Arturo was receiving stitches. As soon as Arturo noticed Lynch in the room, he asked about the only thing that was on his mind; if Lynch had secured a rematch.

Lou DiBella put the match into perspective by calling the fight the Carmen Basilio-Tony DeMarco fight of this generation. He called the bout beautiful in its brutality, as well as in the commitment both men made to excellence. He praised both boxers for giving every ounce that they had. DiBella felt that both fighters left absolutely everything in the ring.[856]

In June 2002, Lou Duva, who had just turned 80 years old, had hopes of turning his new company, Duva Boxing, into a company that rivaled or surpassed his former company, Main Events. His children, Dino and Donna, were helping Lou to re-establish himself in the business. Lou believed that his new company was ready to turn the corner and go from the 4-round class to contendership. Duva had told his kids that to be a champion, you have to get off of the floor and fight back. Duva felt that boxing was on a downslide, but that the sport would come back. He felt that one popular up-and-coming boxer was all that was needed to help his new company succeed. Duva believed that New Jersey was the perfect place for him to make his comeback.[857] Duva recently added the WBA's #1 heavyweight contender, Kirk Johnson, to his stable.

Lou's son Dino admitted that they had to start from scratch. The ongoing litigation with Kathy and Main Events took a huge emotional and financial toll on the family. He added that starting from scratch with no fighters was not easy. After two years he was hoping the company would start turning a profit. Dino felt that the state of boxing in New Jersey couldn't get any worse. Dino was confident that there still was interest in boxing, and the future of the sport had great potential.[858]

While Boardwalk Hall in Atlantic City reopened in October 2001, it had not yet held a boxing show, although it did host the Miss America Pageant. Al Certo felt that boxing was in a sad state in New Jersey. Certo commented that it was the worst that he had ever seen as far as promoting boxing in the state was concerned.[859] Certo commented on Lou Duva's aspirations to work on reviving boxing in New Jersey. Certo thought that the 80-year-old Duva was out of his mind.[860] Main Events chief executive, Gary Shaw, thought that boxing was dead in New Jersey. Shaw stated that Main Events was probably the busiest promoter in the United States right now, with a New Jersey-based company, and they were doing very few fights in New Jersey. He blamed the casinos for not bringing in fights. Shaw added that boxing was very much alive everywhere else but New Jersey.[861]

On July 29, 2002, Steve Farhood sat down for an interview with Arturo at Gleason's Gym in Brooklyn, N.Y. Gatti's fiancé, Vivian Penha, accompanied Arturo to the interview. Arturo told Farhood that if he had to choose, he would rather be the most exciting fighter over being junior welterweight champion.[862]

Arturo revealed that he was going to marry Vivian and he planned on buying a nice house. Arturo was asked if it bothered him that fighters like Roy Jones, Jr. were getting paid millions by HBO to fight nobodies. *"Yes it does bother me. The first thing I do when I see guys on TV, I ask my manager, 'How much are these guys making?' It kills me. I have to deal with going to the gym or the health club and listening to people say, 'You see how much those guys got paid last night? You better get double for your next fight.' It's easy to say I do deserve it, but the network [HBO] doesn't see it that way."*[863]

Farhood asked Arturo if he ever thought about the dangers of boxing and if he ever contemplated retirement. Gatti admitted that after some fights, people he trusted told him he should retire. Arturo felt that he was smart enough to know when to retire. Instead of thinking about retirement, Gatti was thinking about ways to improve his performances. Arturo revealed that Pat Lynch questioned him all the time on when he planned to retire. Gatti told Lynch that he would retire when he was unable to perform as he usually did, because he did not want to embarrass himself in public.[864]

Arturo was asked about getting cut during fights. He felt his weight gain in-between fights had a lot to do with his soft skin. He felt that his skin stretched when he gained weight. The skin would soften and hang when he lost weight, which he felt led to him being more susceptible to being cut. Arturo admitted that his weight concerns forced him to carry a scale around, even when he got on a plane.

Arturo revealed that Vivian worried about him receiving brain damage from boxing. Gatti said that he was not going to stop boxing at 30 years old just because he had a few rough fights. Arturo added that there were some fighters who never fought the way he did and they still got hurt, and some even died.[865]

Arturo described how crazy the old Arturo was. He admitted that after fights he would go out with his friends and get really drunk. Gatti confessed that he trained and fought hard, but after the fight was over, he thought it was party time. He revealed that he lived like a rock star, not an athlete.[866] Arturo believed that his weight was easier to maintain, and he felt stronger, without alcohol.

Arturo disclosed that he changed his wild lifestyle after Vivian came into his life and helped him to see what he was doing to himself. Gatti admitted that he thought the good times would last forever. He confessed that he was so wild, he didn't know how he was still alive. Arturo felt thankful to God for making it through the past 10 years with all the battles he endured in the ring.[867]

Arturo admitted that the only reason he brawled with Ward was because he got tired. Gatti stated that Ward was the strongest fighter he had ever fought in the ring. Arturo confessed that Ward hurt him to the body in the 2nd round.[868]

Arturo described what it felt like to get hit with Ward's hook to the body. *"It's like, you can't do nothing. You can take a punch to the head and shake it off. The body, the pain just gets worse and worse. In the ninth round, I didn't want to go down. But I had to take a count to survive the round. He hit me hardest in the second round, and then in the third and fourth and fifth."*[869]

Arturo ranked his fight against Ward as his most exciting. He felt that his toughest opponent was Ruelas, because Gabriel was capable of hurting him at any moment. Arturo recalled that Ruelas hurt him with an uppercut in the 2nd round of their fight. Arturo felt that something inside of him enabled him to fight while hurt. He also felt that his punching power, and the ability to end a fight with one punch, gave him incentive to fight even when he was being beaten.

Arturo recalled the Wilson Rodriguez match and thinking that

Rodriguez didn't punch hard, until he was hit and dropped. Arturo had just ordered a BMW Z3. When he went down, he was thinking that he might not have the money to pay for the car if he didn't get up and win.[870]

Arturo confessed that the Angel Manfredy fight was the loss that bothered him the most. He still couldn't understand how he was allowed to fight from the 1st to the 8th round with the cut, but when he was coming back the fight was stopped. Gatti blamed his corner for stopping the fight. He felt that if the cut was so severe, the match should have been stopped in the 1st round. As much as Gatti wanted to fight Manfredy again, he didn't want to give Angel another big payday. Arturo finished the interview by saying that it bothered him that he wasn't getting paid the purses that he felt he deserved.[871]

Chapter 20
Ward II

A rematch between Gatti and Ward was a given. The two locations that were vying for the fight were Bally's in Atlantic City and Foxwood's in Connecticut. On August 12, Main Events announced the rematch would take place on November 23 at Boardwalk Hall in Atlantic City. Arturo and his fiancée, Vivian Penha, were planning a September wedding. The wedding would have to be postponed, as Arturo would begin his training camp in September. It was rumored that both fighters would receive approximately $1.25 million each for the rematch. The winner was again rumored to be in line for a match against Kostya Tszyu.

Joe Gatti received a call from New York matchmaker Johnny Bos, offering Joe a shot at the IBF super middleweight title held by Sven Ottke. Yvon Michel tried to talk Joe out of taking the match. Michel wanted to continue building Joe's career back up with lower-level opponents. Over Michel's objections, Joe accepted the Ottke fight. He would receive $45,000 plus an additional $10,000 for advertising the "Golden Palace" on his back via a temporary tattoo. Joe traveled to Leipzig, Germany for the August 24, 2002 match. Accompanying him were his wife Vikki and 8-month-old daughter Versace. Also accompanying Joe were his trainer Diego Rosario and cutman Nelson "Pepe" Cuevas.

Teddy Cruz was Joe's strength and conditioning coach for the Ottke camp. Cruz had worked with Joe prior to Arturo. Joe felt that Cruz had abandoned him when Teddy left Joe for the more lucrative job of training Arturo. Cruz recalled the friction. *"Joe was upset when I started working with Arturo. It was during the time when that incident happened in Germany. That's when I was working with him. I was working with him before, but Joe was very tough to work with, because he was more likely, too quick to snap. It was harder to work with him as far as his temperament. Arturo was just easy going. Well, I think Arturo's overshadowing of Joe might have led to a little jealousy or envy there. Joe was the one who was supposed to be the man. And Arturo turned out to be the man. Why would you be jealous that I'm training your brother? It makes no sense to me. Joe called me up one time because I was in Vegas with Scott DePompe and he said, 'Oh, I hope you're not coming back to work with my brother.' I'm like, 'Joe I'm independent. I'm not under any contract to work with anyone. This is my livelihood. You can't tell me not to make money.' And then we squashed the beef because he started coming around by Arturo to watch him train."*[872]

Joe started the Ottke bout landing a solid left hook. He controlled the first two-and-a-half minutes with his jab. With 30 seconds remaining in the round Sven opened up with combinations but most of the punches were blocked. Joe appeared to get the better of the stanza as he outworked Ottke.

Joe started the 2nd by jabbing and moving. Ottke landed a few solid combinations a minute into the round. Joe was hooking off the jab with success. He landed a triple hook, up and down, while Ottke came back with straight combinations. Joe slipped a right and dug a hard hook to the body. The bell rang. Gatti appeared to have another round in the bank.

Joe came out jabbing and moving again in the 3rd. Rosario yelled at him to stick to boxing. A minute into the round, Gatti landed a lead right that staggered Ottke. Joe continued to hook off the jab. He jabbed to the body and came back up with a straight right. Joe landed two solid straight rights to the body that had Ottke retreating.

After the round ended, Rosario advised Joe, *"Keep the boxing. Keep the moving. You're showing me the jab. Don't show me that jab because he's gonna counter with the right hand. Throw that jab fast. Beautiful. Beautiful. Good jab. This is yours."*

Joe backed Ottke up with jabs and hooks to the body to start the 4th. Sven didn't seem to have a game plan. He was running around the ring as Joe poured in jabs and hooks. Ottke came spearing in with his head, in frustration, as the round ended.

Ottke started the 5th more aggressively, landing a straight right. Joe landed a solid left just as Rosario yelled, *"That's the way."* Sven was lunging in with his head trying to get close. Joe kept snapping one-twos but for some reason he stopped stepping in behind his punches. Halfway through the round Ottke landed a thudding hook over Joe's low right hand. Sven, sensing a momentum change, started becoming the aggressor. The flow of the bout was changing in Ottke's favor. The round ended without any decisive edge. If the bout was in America, Joe could be up four rounds to one, but this was Germany. Ottke had received many questionable decisions in Germany.

The crowd was urging Ottke on to start the 6th. Joe seemed to be tiring. He was backing up more and sucking air through his mouth. Ottke landed a solid right while he had Joe trapped along the ropes.

Gatti boxed well during the next minute. Rosario yelled to Joe, *"When you hit him with the jab, give me the body shot."* Sven landed a right over Joe's guard. Joe came back with a combination. Ottke leaned in with his head again, causing both fighters' heads to crash against each other. The referee cautioned both boxers.

As the 7th began, Rosario called for the double hook. Ottke landed two hard right hands flush on Joe's jaw. Gatti stopped moving his head. Joe landed a straight right which caused Ottke to back away. Joe began chasing Ottke around the ring. He opened up with six punches as Ottke kept on the move. Joe landed two sizzling hooks. It appeared as though Joe was regaining the momentum when Ottke landed a sharp right hand that opened a nasty cut over Joe's left eye. The eye immediately started swelling as blood poured from the gash into his eye. Joe finished the round jabbing and hooking.

Rosario reminded Joe that he was doing good when he was boxing. He told Joe to relax. Joe complained that the blood dripping into his eye was affecting his vision. Rosario told Joe to stick to boxing.

The pro-Ottke crowd sensed a change in momentum with the cut. They started clapping, urging their fighter on.

In the 8th, Joe landed a solid hook. He kept pumping the right hand as Ottke patiently waiting for an opportunity to throw his right over Joe's jab. Sven was alternating between lunging in and circling the ring. Ottke smashed a right hand directly into Joe's injured eye. Sven appeared as though he was confident that he was ahead in the fight as he calmly picked his shots while circling the ring.

In the 9th, Joe landed what appeared to be a legal hook to the body but was warned that it was low. Joe continuously tapped his own head with his left glove and then dropped it down to his chest. Ottke, noticing the habit, stepped in with a perfectly timed straight right that dropped Joe.

Gatti was up at the count of three. He moved around, trying to clear his head but his hands were dangerously low. Ottke stalked Joe as he was looking to time another right hand. With less than 30 seconds remaining in the round, Ottke put all his weight behind a right that slammed into Gatti's jaw. Joe collapsed onto his back. He struggled to his feet at the count of nine, but the referee had seen enough and called a halt to the bout.

After the bout was stopped, Joe was taken to the emergency room for evaluation. It was discovered that he had suffered a fractured skull during the fight.

Arturo was called and was given the bad news about his brother.

Donny Jerie never recalled Arturo speaking with concern over his brother's head injury. Joe was forced to remain in Germany for several days as a precautionary measure. The doctors felt that Joe's brain needed more time to heal before being exposed to the pressure of flying at high altitudes. Diego Rosario remained in Germany with Gatti.

Joe recalled the Ottke fight. *"Diego Rosario felt so bad. And I was so sure that this was my title. Johnny Bos, he got the fight and Yvon Michel said, 'No, why don't you wait.' You know what's the problem with me? All these comebacks, I was working. I couldn't leave my job. I was tired of working and training.*

"This guy Ottke had small hands and they were all scarred up. This guy's not a puncher. That's why I took the fight. He was 35 years old. I was 35. I saw him fight. They robbed people. They never came out of Germany. I figured I'd knock this guy out because he could be knocked out.

"Vikki goes, 'Don't go.' 'Let me just take this fight, alright? I know I can win this fight.' And you know what happened? I pulled a calf. I had to swim. I couldn't run. I was sparring like this [limping]. But then it got better. So I did everything by swimming. I swam at Diego's house. He had a swimming pool.

"So we're in the dressing room, and now what I didn't like is, they was like, 'Let's get the gloves ready. Let's wrap the hands.' The cutman, Pepe, he goes in Ottke's dressing room. He comes back. The Ottke guys are here. He's like, 'Those guys don't know what they're doing.' I asked, 'What's the matter?' He goes, 'They didn't know how to wrap hands. When they wrapped the hands, they stopped here [At the top, before the knuckles, not under them].' So me, not even thinking, I'm a fighter, my mind's on the fight. Diego too, was like a little bambino, a little in la-la land. He's not like that [doesn't think like a cheater]. He did everything straight. He's too good of a guy. So in the end, I put two and two together. He stopped the wraps here [above the knuckles]. That's why Ottke's hands were mangled.

"They fractured my skull. This guy was hurting me. I was like, 'Diego, this guy is hurting me!' I'm not stunned. It's like in a street fight. You feel the bone, I mean its abnormal. I keep going. I'm trying to beat this guy. I'm trying to knock this guy out because it's the only way I won't get hurt. So the only reason he caught me that time is because the blood, he cut my eye.

"I was four days in the hospital. Diego felt bad. He felt bad because he said he should have been on top of it. I said, 'It's not your fault.' I was too fast. He wasn't hitting me too much, and I was hurting him. I was winning the fight. Then in the dressing room they told me to leave it alone. They came to see me in the hospital. They said, 'You got a beautiful family. Don't talk to the TV no more, leave it alone. Go home nice and safe.' Somebody from Ottke's team. So I got scared. I thought it was his pisan from Germany. So I didn't talk to the TV no more. I told them, 'If he fought fair and square and he didn't cheat, tell him to give me a rematch in the United States.'"[873]

Diego Rosario commented on the glove situation. *"I think that somehow they took some of the padding out of the gloves and what Joe was feeling was Ottke's knuckles. If he would've told me during the fight, I would've had the referee go and check the gloves. But he told me this after the fight. It was too late."*[874] No evidence of glove tampering was ever produced to substantiate the tampering allegations. Joe Gatti would never box again.

On the same day as Joe's fight, Bally's president Ken Condon stated that Gatti-Ward II was a great fight for Atlantic City. Condon really wanted to bring the fight to the shore town because it was one of those fights that was not just for high rollers. It was also for working class people. It was a fight that every boxing fan dreamt about.[875]

The event would be the second boxing show held at the Hall since it underwent a $90 million, 4-year renovation. Evander Holyfield defeated Hasim Rahman to re-christen the Hall on June 1. Carl Moretti admitted that the site fees were about even between Foxwoods and Boardwalk Hall. The big difference was that Boardwalk Hall could hold 10,000 fans, while the Foxwoods Theater only had seating for 4,100. Moretti felt that a fight of this magnitude deserved to be seen by a large crowd.[876] Mohegan Sun declined to bid on the rematch because of a prior commitment to an Andrea Bocelli concert.

Pat Lynch was thrilled that the rematch was being held in Atlantic City. He phoned Arturo as soon as he heard the news. Arturo was just as excited as Lynch. They considered Atlantic City their home.[877]

On September 4, at McSorley's Old Ale House in New York, Arturo and Ward held a press conference promoting their rematch. The pair then went up to Boston, where they spoke to the media at Somerville's Good Times Billiards. Micky commented on the venue change. He reminded reporters that it would only be Gatti and him in the ring on fight night. Ward added that he had fought on the road against Jesse James Leija in San Antonio and Shea Neary in London.[878]

Gary Shaw decided to leave Main Events and start his own company, Gary Shaw Promotions. Kathy Duva was suddenly thrust into taking over the day-to-day operations of the company. Some of Main Events' top boxers, Lennox Lewis, Zab Judah, and Jeff Lacy also decided to leave the company.

On November 14, the City of Lowell honored their favorite son, Micky Ward. They held a pep rally at John F. Kennedy Plaza, outside of City Hall, to show support for their hero.

Arturo had been known for his wild lifestyle before and after his fights. He believed that he had matured, due largely in part to his fiancée, Vivian Penha. Arturo recalled, *"Before, when I was young, my plan was to shower and go out after the fight. I didn't even want to get stitched up. I was a wild man. No more running around until 5 in the morning. I met a beautiful girl. I got back on earth when I met her. Sometimes I watch my fights on tape and I can't believe it's me. I'm not the richest fighter out there, but I should have been the way I fight. I fight with my heart. I'm probably one of the greatest warriors who ever lived."*[879]

Lou DiBella stated that he had never worked with a warrior-like boxer such as Gatti. DiBella was in awe of Arturo's fight-of-the-year, time-capsule, highlight-reel battles. DiBella recalled how when Arturo got beaten to a pulp by De La Hoya, Gatti's only concern was if he could keep the limousine that drove him to the hospital for the remainder of the evening.[880]

DiBella's assistant, Dave Itskowitch, recalled meeting Gatti for the first time in Atlantic City, at an after-fight party. Arturo walked into the party holding a towel to the cut above his eye. He shook Itskowitch's hand while he was still bleeding. Gatti was dressed to the nines, ready for a night on the town. Itskowitch thought to himself, *"Wow, this guy is not human."*[881]

Pat Lynch confessed that while he was watching Gatti-Ward I, he was slowly sagging into his arena chair to cover his face. Later, when Lynch watched the fight on tape, he found he was sagging into his chair at home. Lynch added that when Arturo gets hurt and mad, he goes into a macho rage. Lynch questioned how many more beatings Gatti would be able to take, and how many more of Arturo's beatings he would be able to watch.[882]

Steve Farhood felt that Gatti-Ward I was a savage rumble that justified the American Medical Association's efforts to abolish boxing.[883] Larry Merchant likened Gatti-Ward I to skydiving without a parachute.[884] Max Kellerman was so moved by the first Gatti-Ward match that he and Teddy Atlas spoke of the need for a rematch on their "Friday Night Fights" telecast.[885]

McGirt was planning on having Arturo box in the rematch.[886] Buddy worked on preparing Arturo's legs. He also had Gatti work on staying low, which would take away Ward's left hook to the body.[887] McGirt recalled a sparring session Arturo had with Freddie Cadena early in camp. When Gatti started brawling, McGirt called time and ended the round. Buddy used the technique to keep Arturo focused on boxing.[888] Kurt Emhoff wasn't totally convinced Arturo would box the entire match. Emhoff believed that once Ward hit Gatti in the face, all the boxing strategy would go out the window.[889]

On November 20, at Champs sporting goods in Times Square, Gatti and Ward held a press conference to promote their much anticipated rematch. Main Events billed the fight "Once in a Lifetime, Again." Arturo, who was wearing a black sweat suit, revealed that he had been using weight-lifting and swimming to supplement his boxing workouts. Gatti added that he was only 15-pounds overweight at most. Arturo confessed to a reporter that after a loss, sometimes he would sit alone and cry. It must have been extremely difficult for a warrior like Arturo to unveil his emotional fragility in this fashion. Although Arturo was conveying that he hated losing, it also appears that he was trying to reveal something much deeper. Gatti regretted standing in front of Ward in the first match. He didn't understand why he sometimes stood and traded when he knew it wasn't in his best interest to do so.[890]

Arturo predicted that he would defeat Ward by decision. Gatti didn't think he would knock out Ward because he felt that Micky was like his twin. Gatti-Ward I was being replayed on overhead monitors while the fighters were being interviewed. Arturo refused to look at the monitors. The fight was too fresh in his mind. Arturo admitted, *"It bothered me. I had a few tears. It makes me come back stronger and harder."*[891]

Ward must have thought he was dreaming. He turned professional in 1985, at the age of 19. In 1990 he lost to Harold Brazier for the IBF Inter-Continental light welterweight title. He would lose three more fights in a row, to young prospects, before contemplating retirement in 1991. Micky left boxing for 2 years and 8 months. He survived by working as a corrections officer and road paver. In 1994, he felt the itch to give boxing one more try. He reeled off nine straight wins before losing by 3rd round TKO to Vince Phillips for the IBF light welterweight title.

Ward had thought his career was over a few years prior. He wanted to come back because he knew he had something left. Micky didn't want to look back and wonder what would have happened if he had given himself another chance. Coming back turned out to be the best move he ever made.

At 37 years old, Ward knew his boxing career was winding down. Micky was aware that Arturo was going to try and box in the rematch. Ward planned on chasing Gatti down and staying on top of him.[892]

Ward supplemented his boxing regimen by spending time bulking up in the weight room. He jogged and sprinted up a hill in Lowell called Fort Hill.

The contract weight was changed from 140 to 142 because both fighters were having trouble making the weight.

Ward recalled that it was not too long ago, on December 30, 1995, that he was making $500 to fight a 4-round match in a dog park in Revere, Massachusetts.[893] Micky's brother and trainer, Dicky Eklund, revealed that Ward went into the first match with a ruptured left bicep, which affected his left hook. Eklund assured that Micky's arm was fully healed for the rematch. Eklund confessed that he had to have new, thicker punch mitts made from Everlast, because Ward was punching so hard. Eklund felt that Micky needed to knock Gatti out. He didn't believe that they would win a judges decision in Atlantic City.[894]

Arturo stepped on the scale smiling, wearing his blue Versace briefs and white socks. His smile quickly evaporated when Larry Hazzard announced his weight as 143. Team Gatti panicked. Any weight overage would come from his purse in the form of a fine. Arturo took off his socks and his underwear. Boxing commission employees held up a sheet to shield him from the press. The scale beam bounced, then settled at 142. Arturo's smile returned. Ward weighed in at 142. McGirt was shocked at Arturo's weight. He said that Gatti had weighed 141 in the morning, albeit on a different scale.[895]

Ward was earning $1.5 million for the rematch, while Arturo was taking home $1.2 million.

Ward was ranked #3 in the world by the IBF, while Gatti was ranked #4. Micky was thrilled to be fighting Arturo again. Arturo refused to be re-weighed on the day of the fight by HBO. He had not allowed himself to be re-weighed on the day of a fight since his bout against Joey Gamache.

Micky knew how lucky he was to be in this position at 37 years old with 11 losses. It was no secret that McGirt planned on having Arturo box Ward. Micky didn't believe that Arturo would stick to the boxing game plan. Ward was grateful that he was earning a career high purse.[896]

Arturo was confident and focused. *"I'm physically and mentally ready to box all night. I know what I have to do to win and I'm ready to do it. Everyone's looking for a brawl. They may be surprised. I'm coming to fight. I'm ready for anything. He knows I'm coming to fight to the end. It's all up to me how we fight this fight."*[897] Arturo added, *"I love boxing so much. Every time I go in the ring it's the most comfortable place in the world. This fight's going to be fun."*[898] McGirt wanted Arturo to avoid Ward's body attack, especially the hook to the liver.[899]

Ward gave a hint as to his own game plan. He spoke of the importance of knowing distance when body punching to avoid counters. Micky added that he would have to throw the body punches in combinations. He was ready to pay the price to get in position to throw his body punches because he knew how effective those punches were.[900] Ward understood that the fans expected another war.

Before the match, HBO showed highlights from round nine of the first fight in black and white. The network was trying to make the fight appear as though it was from the Gillette "Cavalcade of Sports" boxing series of the 1950s. Jim Lampley reminded viewers that Gatti and Ward were not the most talented fighters in the sport. Larry Merchant stated that Gatti and Ward struck both the courage and nostalgia nerves in boxing fans. Merchant added that both Gatti and Ward had the complexion and the connection to fight a vanilla thrilla.

Ward was re-weighed on fight night. He had only gained 4-pounds, to 146. Arturo's weight probably was in the neighborhood of 160. Arturo made his way towards the ring first, with Mikey Red, Lynch, Joe Souza, and McGirt. Also walking out with the team was "Fast" Freddie Cadena, Arturo's sparring partner and a Lynch co-managed fighter.

Arturo was wearing a Port Authority baseball hat with a matching patch on his trunks. He was accompanied by two Port Authority Police Officers. Arturo wore the Port Authority Police patch on his boxing trunks in honor of the 37 officers who lost their lives during the tragedy of September 11, 2001. Michael Nestor, the Director of Investigations at Port Authority, had asked Arturo to honor the fallen officers by wearing the patch. Nestor stated, *"I only had to ask him once and he agreed to honor the memory of the fallen officers of the Port Authority."*[901]

Arturo walked out to AC/DC's "Thunderstruck." Ward walked out to Whitesnake's "Here I Go Again," as Dicky Eklund, Sal LoNano, and cutman Al Gavin followed behind. Arturo hugged Ward in the ring.

Before the fight started, Arturo turned to Mikey Red and said, *"Man what did you do to wake me up after that 9th round [of the first fight]?"*[902] Mikey told Arturo that he poured ice down his trunks. Gatti told Mikey to have the ice ready.

12,238 fans walked through the turnstiles, breaking the record for a non-heavyweight main event at Boardwalk Hall. The previous non-heavyweight mark of 12,134 was held by Hector Camacho and Vinnie Pazienza for their bout in 1990.

Gatti dominated the 1st round with boxing and footwork. Ward switched to a southpaw stance near the end of the round, no doubt as a sign of frustration. After the round, Eklund told Ward to keep his hands up. He also told Ward that Arturo was beating him to the punch. McGirt advised Gatti not to get caught while pulling out. He asked Arturo to stay low, which gave Ward less of a target to the body.

Ward came out aggressively in the 2nd, tagging Arturo with a left hook. Micky held Gatti's left arm and reeled off four straight left uppercuts. Arturo came back with a flurry. Gatti appeared to be the busier fighter but Ward was picking up the pace as the round ended.

Eklund asked for jabs. McGirt warned Gatti that Ward was looking to land overhand rights. Buddy told Arturo to keep working the body and to double up on the jab.

Ward landed a solid left hook to open the 3rd. Arturo came back with a right hand. At the 2:18 mark, Micky jumped in and was caught by a Gatti right cross that slid off his shoulder and landed behind his left ear. The blow knocked Ward's equilibrium off. He stumbled into a corner-cushion face-first, sinking down as though he was going down an escalator.

As Earl Morton picked up the count Ward was trying to recirculate the blood in his legs by hopping up and down. Arturo went in for the kill as Ward, with his arms outstretched, tried to fend him off. Micky was able to force a clinch. After they were separated, Ward pounded his own abdominal muscles to convey to Arturo to bring it on. Gatti did, tagging Ward and rocking him again.

With 1:10 remaining in the round, Arturo opened his arms as a show of mercy, as if to say, "How many more punches do I have to hit this guy with before the referee will stop this?" He looked at Morton while he gave his animated plea. With a minute left in the round, Ward came alive. Arturo retreated under the heavy barrage of punches. It was difficult to decipher who the crowd was cheering for, as the chants were evenly mixed for both athletes. The bell rang ending the 3rd.

The doctor visited Ward's corner as Arturo screamed at Mikey Red, *"Ice, ice, fucking ice!"* Mikey cautioned Arturo that it was too soon in the fight to pour ice down his trunks. Arturo kept repeating to get him ice. He wanted the ice dumped down his trunks to wake him up. McGirt advised Gatti to use the jab and go to the body. He also told Arturo to use his right hand over the top.

The 4th started with Gatti in control. Ward switched to southpaw and caught Arturo with a straight left. A cut opened over Gatti's left eye. Arturo controlled the round, but Ward had his moments. During the round, McGirt decided it was time for the ice treatment.

After the round ended, McGirt told Gatti to suck it up. Buddy then dumped ice down Arturo's trunks. Eklund motivated his brother by saying that Ward took Gatti's best shots and now it was his turn to retaliate.

Gatti bounced on his toes to start the 5th. He was landing crisp jabs. Arturo's handspeed and volume was the difference in the round. Arturo was in a rhythm as he made Ward miss many shots with his head movement.

Gatti ripped hard body shots to start the 6th. Ward switched to southpaw again to try and change the momentum. When Micky tried to work the body, Arturo would bend low, taking away Ward's target. Gatti controlled the round and pumped his fist in the air as the bell rang. Arturo complained to McGirt that he was having trouble breathing through his nose.

Gatti dominated the 7th. With 30 seconds remaining, Arturo ripped a solid right uppercut followed by a straight left. When the bell rang, Ward stumbled back to his corner. Arturo stopped and watched

Micky for a few seconds, hoping that Ward had had enough. Micky would continue. Eklund, upset with Ward's performance, threatened to stop the fight. Ward quickly said that he was good. Eklund smacked him and told him to wake up.

Arturo was controlling the 8th until Ward landed a left hook that sent him stumbling. Gatti countered Ward's left with a right hand that stunned Micky. McGirt screamed from the corner for body punches and Arturo pounded them home. Ward looked dejected after the bell rang.

McGirt continued to advise Arturo to stay low. He warned that Ward was desperate. Eklund urged Micky to throw the left hook to the body and head. Again he threatened to stop the fight if Micky didn't improve his performance.

Ward was having one of his most successful rounds in the 9th until Arturo unleashed an avalanche of shots with less than a minute left.

The crowd cheered as the 10th and final round began. After the pair touched gloves, Ward kissed Gatti on the check. Not long after, Ward was sending punches to the same spot. With 1:30 remaining in the round, Arturo unloaded sixteen straight punches. The action was back-and-forth. As the final bell rang, Kathy Duva stood and clapped while Lou DiBella stood stunned. Both fighters embraced. Referee Earl Morton later called the scene an *"emotionally telling moment."*

All three judges had Arturo winning handily, by scores of 98-91 twice and 98-90. After Michael Buffer finished announcing the scores he said that it looked as though there would need to be a third bout. CompuBox Punchstats had Arturo landing 276 of 792 punches while Ward landed 180 of 626.

Arturo stated, *"It's one to one, and I wouldn't mind a third. I boxed the way I was supposed to in this fight. I didn't lose my energy like I did in the first fight.*[903] *We worked on staying low and it was hard for him to land good body shots."*[904] Gatti gave credit to bending at the waist for helping him to be more successful. *"We worked on that in practice, staying low and then coming up to hit the body. Ward stands there with his hands up like two pillows in front of his face and I have to pick my shots."*[905] Ward admitted that Gatti fought a great fight. He said that when he got caught behind the ear it threw his equilibrium off.[906]

Micky described how he felt after being dropped. He joked that he thought he was on the boardwalk. He recalled that while he was hurt, Arturo threw a jab and then lined him up for a right hand that caught him flush on the button. The punch woke Ward up. He wasn't stunned anymore. Arturo had dazed Ward and woke him back up all in the same sequence. Dicky Eklund admitted that he almost threw the towel in because Micky appeared as drunk as a skunk. Lou DiBella praised Ward. He said that Micky's balls were bigger than basketballs.[907]

Arturo praised McGirt for being the greatest trainer in the world. Gatti wanted to fight a third, tie-breaking match.[908] Arturo commented on the punch that dropped Ward. *"It was the greatest right hand I have ever thrown in my life. Everybody knows about my left hook, including Micky Ward, so I had to work on my right. Buddy told me I would be able to hurt him with my right. He's just unbelievable. He has the heart of a lion. I am going to become a world champion again. That's personal for me."*[909] Arturo added, *"I knew he was hurt. He was never the same after that shot."*[910] Dicky Eklund felt that a third fight with Gatti, if it happened, would be Ward's last.

After the fight Dr. Stephen Margles, who examined Ward, expressed his amazement over Micky being able to finish the fight with his damaged equilibrium. Margles stated that Ward must have felt like he was coming off of an amusement ride, dizzy and staggering around like a drunk.[911] Micky told Margles that he saw three or four Gattis during the final seven rounds.

Ward somehow managed to throw 88 punches in the final round, and at one point had Gatti holding on. Arturo felt the shot to Micky's ear was a game changer. *"He was never the same after that shot but I knew he'd fight back. I don't know how he stayed up, but I wasn't surprised he wouldn't go down."*[912]

Arturo credited his weight management for his performance. *"This camp, I came in only 10-pounds over my fighting weight, and that allowed us to work in camp on lifting weights with my legs, so my legs were very strong. I think I'm going to stick to boxing, and I'm only going to get better."*[913]

Arturo had made a promise to Lynch before the fight. While in his dressing room, Arturo promised Lynch that he would be healthy enough after the fight ended to attend the post-fight press conference. Gatti kept his promise. At the press conference, Kathy Duva jokingly congratulated Arturo for making the post-fight presser for the first time in his career instead of heading to a local hospital. Duva later recalled that Arturo was sitting at the press conference with his hand swollen to three times its normal size. Gatti gave Kathy a goofy grin and told her he would get the hand looked at the following day.[914]

Ward was taken to the Atlantic City Medical Center's emergency room. Arturo would follow, but not before attending the presser, eating Chinese food, and playing the slot machines.

Kery Davis of HBO Sports was interested in making a rubber match if both teams wanted a third fight.[915] Lynch used the opportunity to prod HBO for a new deal, as Arturo's contract with them had expired. Lynch wanted to stay with HBO. As leverage, he expressed that Showtime might entice Arturo to sign with them to make a match with Kostya Tszyu.[916]

Ward's adviser, Lou DiBella, was pushing for a third match with Arturo. He stated that Micky didn't want his career to end with a loss. He added that Ward deserved a chance to ride off into the sunset, in glory, as a winner.[917]

Both boxers had taken tremendous punishment in their two battles. If anyone needed a reminder of just how dangerous the sport of boxing was, they need look no further than Gerald McClellan. The "G-Man" was one of boxing's most feared punchers. He was in line for a fight with Roy Jones, Jr. when he met Nigel Benn on February 25, 1995. During the brutal back-and-forth battle, in the 10th round, McClellan surprisingly and uncharacteristically took a knee and was counted out. He was taken by ambulance to a hospital and induced into a coma to save his life. Gerald had suffered a blood clot to his brain during the fight. McClellan would lose his eyesight and suffer serious brain damage. McClellan's two sisters have been giving the fighter round-the-clock care since his tragic injury.

Photographer Tom Casino helped raise money for McClellan by donating bats used as props for a *Ring* magazine cover photo. Casino had Gatti and Ward face-off against each other with the bats in Gleason's Gym in Brooklyn, N.Y. The bat auction raised $1,525 for McClellan's trust fund.

Gatti-Ward II registered a national rating of 8.6, an 18% increase over their first bout, which rated 7.3. That meant that over 2.7 million homes watched the second match. HBO Sports president, Ross Greenberg, stated that Gatti and Ward were a fight fan's delight.[918]

On December 6, Arturo volunteered to help promote a fundraising event for the Make-a-Wish foundation and F.I.S.T. [Fighters Initiative for Support and Training]. Arturo signed gloves to be auctioned at the event. F.I.S.T. was an organization founded by

Gerry Cooney to help retired fighters who fell on hard times. The show was held at the Jersey City Armory. Gatti worked the corner of Cooney's exhibition opponent Paul Dunleavy.

Dunleavy had trained at Bufano's as a youth. Paul held annual fundraising amateur boxing shows for Project Grandma through his Local 164 electricians union. Boxing celebrities such as Bobby Czyz, Vito Antuofermo, Mark Medal, Riddick Bowe, Frankie Toledo, and Ray Mercer would attend the events to help with the fundraising. Paul fondly recalled Joe Gatti volunteering his time when he was asked to attend the fundraising event, *"I would invite Joe [Gatti] and put him on the poster for the event. He would come, sign autographs, and spend time talking to our guests. He was inspirational in getting people to come for a meet and greet, which helped us raise the money for breast cancer research at Hackensack Hospital. We raised over $10,000 that year."*[919]

Chapter 21
Ward III

On January 8, 2003, the IBF's December rankings were released. Arturo was ranked #3 at 140-pounds. Pat Lynch and Main Events' attorney, Pat English, went to the office of Linda Torres, an attorney for the IBF, to appeal Arturo's ranking.

English had been working for Main Events since 1982, when founder Dan Duva hired him to litigate a lawsuit against the WBA. English was successful in the 1982 lawsuit which involved Main Events' #1 ranked 154-pounder Tony Ayala receiving a title shot. Ayala never fought for the title due to an injury and later sexual assault conviction. English also successfully litigated a case against the IBF on behalf of Main Events' fighter Michael Moorer. English mostly handled contracts and litigation for the company.

The IBF's rating committee and its championship chairman, Joe Dwyer, attended the meeting. Arturo's recent victory over Micky Ward in November was not sanctioned as a title elimination bout, but Lynch nonetheless disputed the #3 ranking. Dwyer had approached Team Gatti prior to Gatti-Ward II, asking if they wanted to fight Ward in a 12-round title elimination bout. Lynch, Main Events, and Ward's team all turned down the offer. Neither side wanted a 12-round fight. Even though they turned down the elimination bout, Lynch and Main Events felt that Arturo deserved to be ranked number #1 based on merit.[920]

The rating's committee agreed with Lynch and voted to move Arturo to the #1 spot in February. The ratings change set off a firestorm, as Sharmba Mitchell and Emanuel Augustus both felt that they deserved the number one ranking.

On February 7, Augustus lost to Omar Weis, knocking him out of the #4 spot in the IBF. The next day, the IBF's monthly rankings were made public. Arturo had been elevated to the #1 spot. Many believed that Arturo's victory over Ward did not warrant the move up in the rankings. *Boston Globe* columnist Ron Borges called for the IBF to be shut down.

Ward and Arturo had twice declined to fight for the IBF's number one ranking. They did not want to pay the sanctioning fees, which usually are 3% of each fighter's gross purse. They also wanted to avoid having to make the required 140-pound limit or fight 12 rounds, all IBF requirements. The IBF rankings committee previously had announced that the number one spot would remain vacant until the winner of the Sharmba Mitchell-Carlos Vilches bout was determined. The winner of that bout would now be ranked #2 behind Gatti. Arturo jumped over the pair to take the #1 spot. The IBF ordered Gatti to fight Mitchell to end the feuding over who should be the top contender. That didn't mean that the two would fight, however.

The handlers of the IBF, WBA, and WBC Champion, Kostya Tsyzu, offered Arturo $1,375,000 for a match. Gatti's promoter, Main Events, turned down the offer. Kathy Duva didn't believe the offer was fair. She still was weighing her options in regards to Arturo's future.[921] Duva and Main Events were mulling over a third match between Gatti and Ward, which could bring in even more money than a championship bout. Gatti had a much better chance of defeating Ward again than he did the power-punching Tsyzu.

IBF president Marian Muhammad defended her company's ranking of Gatti. She stated that Arturo fought the best fighter available in the division when he fought Ward. If it weren't for the 12 rounds and the sanctioning fee, Gatti would have gone to #1 anyway. Muhammad added that she did not make the decision to move Gatti to number #1. That decision was made by the ratings committee.[922]

In mid-March, Lynch and Kathy Duva had an enviable problem. They had a choice of either Kostya Tszyu, Sharmba Mitchell, or a third match with Micky Ward. Their fighter, by way of his exciting, action-packed style, coupled with the way he packed Boardwalk Hall, was a lucrative commodity. Arturo was considered one of boxing's biggest draws. This fact put Main Events in the driver's seat in regards to purse negotiations with Tszyu, Mitchell, or Ward.

Main Events' matchmaker Carl Moretti felt that Arturo had many options.[923] Ward's manager Sal LoNano wanted a third Gatti match to settle the score. He was not happy, however, with Main Events' offer of a 75-25 split in favor of Gatti.[924] It was obvious that Main Events and HBO wanted a third Gatti-Ward match. That was the fight the public wanted as well. The stalling point was how the money would be split up.

Moretti announced that Arturo would be fighting in June on HBO. He hoped that the opponent would be Micky Ward, but if it wasn't, they would find someone else to fight.[925] Moretti's comments were meant to put pressure on Ward's team. Gatti's camp leaked that they were considering a rematch with Angel Manfredy if the negotiations with Micky Ward's camp continued to stall. Arturo did not want to give Manfredy another payday. He still was incensed at the comments that Manfredy made after their first bout. Main Events and Lynch didn't want a Manfredy fight either, because the chances of losing were much greater. The leak appeared to be a leverage move to force Ward's people to accept Main Events' terms.

Kathy Duva and Carl Moretti started looking at other options besides Ward. Lynch told Arturo that they were looking at possibly fighting someone else. Gatti cut Lynch off and demanded that he call Kathy Duva and tell her that he was going to fight Ward and no one else. Arturo felt strongly that Ward deserved another payday.[926]

Kathy Duva revealed that Gatti wanted to help Ward out financially by giving him a third fight. That was a priority for Arturo. Duva admitted that, in the end, Gatti made the final decision on who he fought.[927] Kathy Duva appeared somewhat uncomfortable when talking about the contract dispute issue. Main Events was trying to force Ward to take less money, so the company could pocket more. Arturo would have no part of that.

DiBella was pushing for a third Gatti-Ward fight. He felt the second fight would have had a different outcome if Ward's equilibrium had not been injured. As a result, Ward was fighting more to survive than to win after the injury. DiBella believed that the evenly-matched fighters would make another great fight.[928]

Pat Lynch had invested in a hot prospect from Paterson. His name was "Fast" Freddie Cadena. Lynch co-managed Cadena along with Henry Cortes. Cadena was promoted by Main Events and was used in several of Arturo's training camps. On April 4, 2003, at the Fernwood Poconos Resort in Bushkill, PA, Cadena, 15-0, stepped into the ring against 9-1 (5 KOs) Jesse Feliciano. The fight became a give-and-take slugfest. During the 6th round, Cadena took several hard shots and was dropped. Cadena rose to his feet. The normally lenient Steve Smoger uncharacteristically waived the fight over.

Cadena walked back to his corner and sat down on his stool. As he was being examined by the ringside physician, Cadena fell off of the stool and suffered a seizure. The incident occurred live on national television. On the way to the hospital, Cadena suffered a second seizure. It later was discovered that Cadena's strength coach had put Cadena on a nut and distilled water diet in the weeks leading up to the fight. Some speculated that the diet, coupled with dehydration and the punches he received, may have contributed to the seizures.

Cadena was rushed to the Pocono's Medical Center, and from there he was taken to St. Luke's Hospital. He was admitted into the intensive care unit. Pennsylvania's boxing commission suspended Cadena's boxing license indefinitely. Cadena would fully recover but never fight again.

On April 5, Team Gatti and Team Ward finally came to an agreement. On April 7, the deal for Gatti-Ward III was announced publicly, although contracts had yet to be signed. It was reported by the *Boston Globe* that Ward was prepared to walk away from a third fight. Micky received $375,000 for the first bout and $1.5 million for the second bout. He was upset that Main Events was offering him only 25 percent, or $800,000, for the third fight. Gatti's team wanted a 75-25 split, while Ward's team wanted a 50-50 split.

Ward was particularly incensed because after he defeated Arturo in the first fight he agreed to a nearly 50-50 split in the second match. Micky gave Arturo a rematch instead of fighting for the title. Now he felt he was being undercut for a third bout. Main Events reportedly received $3.2 million for the third bout, $2.2 million from HBO and $1 million from Bally's for the site fee to host the event. Those numbers did not include the live gate, which would bring in over $1.7 million. Carl Moretti felt that Ward was overestimating his worth to the promotion, while underestimating how much of the $4.9 million had to go to Gatti and everyone else involved in staging the event.[929]

Ward agreed to a contract that would give him in excess of $1 million for the third bout, a substantial improvement from Main Events originally offer. Arturo would receive $1.7 million. That still would leave Main Events with $2.2 million before other expenses were paid out. After the announcement, Ward revealed that win or lose, he would retire after the bout. He added that this was the only fight that he wanted.[930]

Ward, his manager Sal LoNano, and his adviser, Lou DiBella, had been negotiating for months for a third bout with Arturo. Ward would be responsible for paying his manager, cutman, trainer, and advisers. He also would be responsible for his training camp expenses. Ward felt that he was worth at least a third of what the fight was worth.

Ward was upset with the negotiations. Micky felt that Gatti's team double-crossed him. He thought that a fair deal would have been a 50-50 or 60-40 split. Ward commented that his fans purchased as many tickets as Gatti's fans did. Micky believed that Main Events was tough with negotiations because Lou DiBella was his advisor.

Ward felt that they would have given him an extra $250,000 if he cut DiBella out. Micky would not sever his ties with DiBella for extra money. Ward revealed that if the fight fell through, and he was forced to go back to paving streets, he was fine with that. He questioned why Gatti's team was being so greedy.[931] Sources revealed that Main Events raised Ward's purse to a guaranteed $1,075,000, plus 25 percent of the net gate for Micky's final career bout.

Kathy Duva remained silent on the issue, but Carl Moretti defended Main Events. He said that Ward's team had a funny way of calculating. He added that their numbers were all wrong. Moretti stated that Micky's team failed to take into account the expenses and Gatti's purse. In an attempt to blame Ward's own camp, Moretti added that if Micky's team were more concerned with what Ward was getting paid instead of what they were taking out of his cut, there wouldn't be any issues.[932]

The bottom line was that neither Ward nor Gatti wanted to fight anyone else. They both felt that a third match against each other gave them more money than they would receive from a title shot. More importantly, they felt it was a fight they both could win.

LoNano, who owned a taxi company, said that he was fair with Main Events after Ward beat Gatti, but Main Events wanted to tear Team Ward apart when they obtained the upper hand. He added that Main Events had a problem with DiBella, but Ward shouldn't have to pay for that. LoNano was told that if Team Ward dumped DiBella, they would get paid more. LoNano felt that Ward got screwed in the first fight, but was fair to Team Gatti in the rematch when Ward had the leverage.[933]

DiBella commented on the controversy surrounding his involvement with Ward. He announced that he didn't have a contract with Ward. He had a handshake deal. DiBella added that he had two handshake deals, one with Bernard Hopkins, who screwed him over, and one with Ward, who was a stand-up guy. DiBella felt that Main Events bullied them and treated them unfairly during negotiations.[934]

On April 7, Main Events announced that Gatti-Ward III would take place on June 7 at Boardwalk Hall. Bally's president Ken Condon was ecstatic that they had landed the rubber match.[935] Arturo already was in Vero Beach preparing for whomever he would be fighting. His hand was almost fully healed. McGirt planned to have him start sparring in early April. Arturo stated, *"I have a tremendous amount of respect for Micky. Our first two fights were memorable for boxing fans, and I don't think our third fight will be any different."*[936]

On April 19, Ward confirmed that this would be his final boxing match. He planned on redeeming himself and then walking away from boxing.[937]

On April 25, Gatti and Ward planned to break training camp to attend the Boxing Writers Association of America's annual awards dinner at the Marriot Marquis Hotel in New York. A press conference to promote their fight was scheduled at the hotel before the dinner. Ward attended the presser, but Arturo never showed. Ward exited the hotel visibly upset. Gatti's team advised the press on hand that Arturo missed his flight from Florida to New York.

Arturo did attend the award ceremony later that evening. At the event, author Thomas Hauser ran into Gatti. Hauser recalled, *"I was at the annual Boxing Writers Association of America dinner at a hotel in midtown Manhattan when Gatti and Micky Ward were co-honored for participating in the 2002 Fight of the Year. Midway through the dinner, I left my seat to go to the men's room. When I got there, an intimidating young man was blocking the entrance. 'You can't go in there,' he said. 'Why can't I go in there?' 'It's in use. You'll have to go to another floor.' 'What do you mean, it's in use? There are a dozen urinals and toilets in there.' At that point, Arturo staggers out of the men's room, dead drunk, accompanied by a woman who looked very much like a dancer at a not-very-exclusive adult club. 'Blow job,' Arturo announced when he saw me. And he pointed to his fly. Which was still unzipped"*[938]

Buddy McGirt sat down for an interview with *KO* magazine. He was asked if Arturo had any unusual quirks. Buddy acknowledged that Arturo was different from other fighters he had trained. McGirt added that instead of pointing with his finger, Gatti would lift his head and poke his lips out to get Buddy's attention when he wanted to quietly point something out, such as letting McGirt know when he didn't want certain people in the gym that he didn't recognize. McGirt recalled Arturo having him kick out a boxing manager who was watching him jump rope after Gatti discovered that the manager was from Connecticut, which was too close to Ward's Massachusetts for Gatti's liking.[939]

On May 10, it was announced that fewer than 500 tickets remained for the third Gatti-Ward match. The public certainly had not tired of their bouts. Ward felt that the fans and the boxing writers all believed that Gatti would win.[940]

Joe Gatti began training Kinnelon, N.J. junior welterweight Scott DePompe. When Arturo discovered that Joe was training DePompe, he called Scott and said, *"I heard my brother's training you. Is he doing a good job?"* DePompe confirmed that Joe was indeed training him. Arturo joked, *"Well if I don't want Joe to train you, he won't."*

On June 5, both Arturo and Ward appeared at the final pre-fight press conference. Gatti revealed that he had been in training camp for three months before he started sparring. He was lifting weights and running. His main goal was to get in shape, gain some weight with muscle, and then go back down to his fighting weight. Arturo felt that the key to victory was speed.[941]

Ward admitted that he needed to use his jab more and move his head. Micky realized that he couldn't just walk straight in and take unnecessary punches, which would let Gatti build up a lead.[942] Ward added that he was going to use his mind in the ring.[943]

McGirt knew that when Arturo bent low, Ward was going to try and push him down. McGirt had prepared Arturo for Ward leaning on him and throwing uppercuts. Gatti had practiced spinning and stepping over to combat Ward's pushing down on him.[944]

While training in the dimly lit World Gym in Tewksbury, Massachusetts, Ward shared his thoughts on what the third match, which HBO billed "The Final Chapter," might bring. Ward stated that he gave his all while training in the gym and he was ready to accept the outcome, whatever it may be. Ward reiterated that although this would be his final fight, he still planned on coming out victorious.[945]

Arturo expected Ward to give his best because it was his final fight.[946] Gatti planned to utilize a strategy that trainer McGirt formulated for the second bout. He mixed boxing and angles on offense, with a crouching style to defend against Ward's body attack. It was rumored that Ward was going to try and box in his final fight.

On June 5, two days before the fight, Carl Moretti received a phone call on his cell phone that had him hysterical with laughter. Someone called him looking for tickets to the upcoming rubber match. The fan was prepared to pay $350 apiece for 30 ringside seats. Moretti told him that the only way he was going to see the fight that close was if he pulled a chair up in front of his TV.[947]

Ticket brokers were getting up to three times the face value for tickets; scalpers even more. Boardwalk Hall workers were trying to squeeze an extra 100 seats onto the floor. Part of the reason for the terrific sales was the affordability of the tickets. 3,000 tickets were priced at only $50 each, and the ringside seats sold for only $350. Obviously, that was if you were lucky enough to get the tickets before the scalpers did. New Jersey law did not restrict the amount of money a broker could charge for internet sales. Any other type of resale had a 50% mark-up limit. With ticket demands what they were, ticket brokers could have easily doubled the $1.7 million face value of the tickets sold.

Ken Condon could not remember a fight that created this much excitement. Condon initially thought that interest might tone down a bit for the third fight, but it was gaining momentum by the minute. The demand was so high they actually were trying to find places in the arena to add even more seats. Never in Condon's wildest imagination did he expect this.[948]

N.J. boxing commissioner Larry Hazzard felt that the fight sold out because boxing fans appreciated blue-collar fighters who earned their pay. Hazzard stated that Ward was a throw-back to the old-time fighters and Gatti was one of the greatest fighters he had ever seen.[949] Arturo was listed as a 7-2 betting favorite.

The attendance for Gatti-Ward III was 12,643. Another 3 million tuned in at home. The gate broke the Convention Center record of the highest attended, non-heavyweight fight, Gatti-Ward II, by 405 tickets. The total take at the gate exceeded $1.7 million, which also broke the record for Gatti-Ward II by $100,000. The Hall was packed with stars, such as former San Francisco Giant legend Willie Mays, former Philadelphia 76ers' Julius Erving, heavyweight champion Lennox Lewis, N.Y. Giant Michael Strahan, Washington Wizard Charles Oakley, and Philadelphia Flyer Rick Tocchet. And of course, actor Chuck Zito, who was hired by Arturo as a fight-week bodyguard. Zito starred in HBO's prison drama "Oz." A group of Philadelphia Eagle players wanted to attend, but there were no tickets left.[950]

Both boxers summed up what they brought to the table when they fought. Arturo boasted that if he cracked an opponent, the opponent would go to sleep.[951] Ward surmised that he was like a paving machine that only goes back and forth, never side to side. Gatti said it best after their second match when he admitted, *"I used to wonder what would happen if I fought my twin. Now I know."*[952]

Scott DePompe won his first bout with Joe as his trainer on the Gatti-Ward III undercard. DePompe won a unanimous decision over

Arthur Medina.

Ward made his way out for the bout first with his team of Eklund, LoNano, and Gavin. Arturo came out with Chuck Zito, Lynch, McGirt, Souza, and Mikey Red.

Arturo started the 1st round boxing. Ward landed a flush right hand 30 seconds into the stanza. Gatti appeared to have the edge in the round with his boxing and hand speed.

McGirt was happy with Arturo's performance, but cautioned Gatti to watch Ward's right hand counters over the jab. McGirt advised Arturo that Micky would try to hook to the body off of the right lead. McGirt asked Gatti to keep working fast jabs followed by rights to the body. Eklund advised Ward to stop following Arturo around and to throw more punches, especially right hands.

At the start of the 2nd, Ward landed a solid right. The pro-Gatti crowd started chanting for their man. Arturo responded with a double hook to the body and head. Gatti was successfully utilizing his jab and mixing in body punches. Ward looked tentative. Micky tried to force his way inside but Arturo boxed and moved well. By the end of the round, Ward's face was bruised and his nose was bleeding. Larry Merchant joked that watching Arturo and Ward box was like watching Rottweilers at a dog show.

McGirt asked Arturo to concentrate on jabs and body punches. Gatti came out with flurries in the 3rd. Arturo had success mixing his punches to the body and head, driving Ward to the ropes. Ward looked slow and old as he missed widely. Arturo landed a punch that perforated Ward's eardrum. Ward would experience balance problems for the rest of the fight due to his equilibrium being offset.

In the corner, after round 3, McGirt praised Gatti's performance and asked him to keep feinting to the body. McGirt warned Arturo to watch for the counter hook. He told Gatti to dip low, underneath Micky's punches. Ward's corner was quiet. Micky looked dejected and frustrated. Eklund offered no advice.

Thirty seconds into the 4th, Arturo threw a right to the body that crashed into Ward's hip. The extensor tendon attached over Gatti's middle knuckle ruptured from the impact. Arturo later recalled landing the punch, *"I was hurt, but I told myself if I don't keep throwing my right hand, Micky would know it."*[953] Arturo retreated. Ward took advantage and pressed forward with shots. Merchant and Lampley thought it was a hook to the body by Ward that hurt Arturo. Gatti started pumping jab after jab. Arturo tried his first right to the body at the 1:30 mark. He grimaced in pain. Ward kept throwing to the body and head. He sensed an opportunity. Arturo came back with lefts and tried another right but immediately dropped the glove in pain after landing the punch. Ward delivered a right hand bomb with 30 seconds remaining. Arturo threw ten straight left hooks and a right uppercut. Ward came back. When the bell rang ending the round, Gatti went to a neutral corner by accident.

McGirt would later reveal that Arturo originally injured his hand in training camp. After the injury, Arturo used cushioning from a bicycle seat to protect his hand while training.

Mikey Red and McGirt were on opposite sides of Arturo than they usually were. Arturo would come back to the corner and Buddy would talk to him first, then during the final few seconds Skowronski would say something to Buddy. Skowronski recalled, *"I was on Arturo's right side. He came back to the corner and he went out of his way to lean away from me to Buddy's right ear. He must have said, 'I broke my hand' or 'my hand is gonna go,' or he knew that something was wrong with his hand. And then I said to Buddy when he went out, 'Buddy what'd he say?' And he was like, 'Nothing, nothing, nothing. He's ok. He's ok.' And when he threw the right hand I saw it in his face. I was shaking Buddy, 'You lied to me! You lied to me!' We were wrestling down in the corner. And Buddy was like, 'No, he's alright.' Arturo broke his hand before and I always asked him after that how he was able to fight through it and Arturo said, 'I just wait for it to go numb. I know eventually it's gonna go numb.' Imagine that mentality of waiting for it to go numb so that he could use it again. That's the kind of guy that he was."*[954]

Mikey Red hadn't heard what the millions of viewers at home had heard, courtesy of McGirt's microphone. Arturo had indeed leaned on McGirt's chest and moaned, *"My hand's broke. My hand."* McGirt asked Arturo what he wanted to do. McGirt repeated the question. Arturo replied, *"I gotta keep going."* McGirt advised Arturo to work jabs and hooks and to keep moving.

Arturo came out for the 5th moving and even threw a few half-speed rights. Gatti crashed a right hand around Ward's guard into his left eyebrow bone. The blow tore open a gash that started dripping blood. It appeared as though Micky was fighting to Gatti's level. When Arturo threw half strength, so did Ward. When Arturo threw hard, Micky followed. Ward woke up with 25 seconds remaining. He landed three hard rights and two solid hooks.

Eklund chided Ward for letting a one-handed fighter beat him while Gavin was treating the one-inch gash over Micky's left eye. McGirt told Arturo to use his legs and to box smart.

Arturo was controlling the 6th round with jabs and hooks. He sprinkled in an occasional right hand. Ward switched to southpaw two minutes into the round but turned right back.

With 6 seconds remaining, Ward landed a flush left hook followed by a chopping right that sat Arturo down onto the canvas. Gatti used the ropes to regain his feet. Referee Earl Morton gave an 8-count as the bell rang. McGirt again advised Arturo to watch for the right hand and move to his right more. Eklund asked Ward for more pressure.

Both fighters fought hard to start the 7th. The knockdown had made the match closer on the cards. Forty seconds into the round, Ward landed a right that stunned Gatti. Micky tried to finish Arturo, but Gatti came firing back. Halfway through the round, Arturo landed a thunderous hook. Ward came back with a right. Both fighters tagged each other over and over during the final minute. Emanuel Steward stood and applauded with those in attendance.

The 8th started with the crowd on their feet cheering. The pace slowed in the round but both fighters kept throwing. Arturo's volume appeared to be the difference in the round. McGirt asked for jabs and movement. Ward's corner was more subdued. Eklund optimistically told the tired Micky that he would get a second wind. Eklund asked Ward to keep his hands in close.

Arturo again outworked Ward in the 9th. In the corner, McGirt asked Gatti to use his legs, box, move his hands, and avoid a slugfest. When Michael Buffer announced that it was the 10th and final round, both boxers smiled and embraced.

Arturo threw flurry after flurry. Ward landed a solid hook and right hand halfway through the round. With 25 seconds remaining, the capacity crowd rose to their feet in applause. Both boxers responded by standing toe-to-toe in the center of the ring. With 10 seconds left both boxers stopped fighting and glanced at each other in a show of mutual respect. After deep breaths they gave the fans one final flurry as Emanuel Steward gasped *"Oh, my god!"*

As the final bell rang, both fighters hugged. Pat Lynch and Carl Moretti joined the fighters. Arturo looked into the camera and spoke to his little brother Fabrizio, who was back in Canada, telling Fabby that he loved him. Ward returned to his corner complaining that his hands were killing him.[955]

After the bout, HBO announced that they had signed Arturo to a three-fight deal. Ward was amazed at Arturo's comeback abilities. He likened Gatti to Jason, the villain in *Friday the 13th* because every time Ward hurt Gatti, he came back.[956]

Michael Buffer announced the decision as fireworks erupted. Judges Joe Pasquale and George Hill scored the bout 96-93, while Luis Rivera scored the bout 97-92, all for Gatti. After the decision was read Vivian Penha jumped into the ring and hugged Arturo. Ward shared a bottle of water with Gatti in the center of the ring, in a show of friendship and respect. Arturo said he knew that Ward came to fight the best fight of his life. Gatti believed that anybody else would've quit. Arturo added that Ward hurt him in the 3rd and 4th rounds. Ward admitted that he was stunned when his equilibrium was thrown off by a Gatti punch.

Arturo spoke of how his hand went numb after he injured it. Arturo felt that the injury changed the fight. Gatti stated that it was important for him to tell McGirt about the injury so Buddy could come up with a game plan to win. Arturo knew that if he didn't throw the right hand Ward would figure out that he had injured it.

Ward revealed that he knew Gatti hurt his hand as soon as he threw the punch. Ward could see it in Arturo's face. Gatti stopped throwing the right with power. While being interviewed in front of Gatti and Lynch, Ward said that Arturo's ring name should be Jason, from *Friday the 13th*, not Thunder. The remark caused Gatti and Lynch to break out in laughter.

Referee Earl Morton said of Arturo, *"That 'never quit, never say die' attitude. I understand that. The will to sustain pain. The will to win."*[957]

In the ring after the match, Vivian Penha spoke of what a great relationship Arturo had with Buddy. That relationship would be severely tested in the not too distant future.

Arturo landed 349 of 845 punches to Ward's 128 of 639 as per CompuBox. Ward acknowledged that he was fine with the decision. Arturo added, *"I knew he was coming to fight. He was a great champion. There were two warriors in the ring tonight.*[958] *These three battles, we definitely made a mark on boxing."*[959]

Lou DiBella commented that it was a great night for boxing. If every boxer fought like Gatti and Ward, it would bring boxing back to the mainstream.[960] Both fighters were taken to the Atlantic City Medical Center for fractured hands and lacerations over their eyes.

After the fight, Arturo and Lynch were walking in the hotel lobby. Gatti was surrounded by friends and fans. Arturo, who was still bleeding from a cut over his eye, decided it was a good time to have some fun. Pat Lynch held a door open for Arturo and Gatti banged his hand against the door, acting like his face had been slammed into it. Arturo let out a fake scream and pointed to his bleeding face. Lynch glanced at Arturo's loyal fans, worried that they might think that he had banged Arturo's head into the door. Lynch turned to Gatti and asked if Arturo was trying to get him killed.[961] Arturo the prankster responded with a wide smile.

There would be no post-fight press conference as both fighters were taken to the hospital. In the emergency room, Arturo and Vivian sat silently as the heart monitor machine beeped. Arturo broke the silence by telling his fiancée that he wished he were better at golf.[962] Arturo broke out in laughter as Vivian responded that she wished he were better at golf too.[963] Arturo's lip was swollen and discolored.

An emergency-room doctor walked in and told Arturo that there was someone behind the privacy curtain that he might want to see. The doctor pulled back the curtain. Lying in the bed behind the curtain was Micky Ward. Arturo asked Ward how he was doing. Both boxers laughed and gave each other high fives. Arturo received three stitches above his left eye, while Ward received seven stitches to his left eye. Both boxers had their swollen right hands X-rayed.

Ward had a huge red lump on his forehead. A knuckle on his right hand was black and blue. Micky had four heart monitors attached to his chest. Both fighters had cut eyes, bloody noses, and swollen, bruised faces.

Arturo revealed that every time he hurt Ward, Micky hit him harder. Arturo was glad that he didn't have to fight Ward anymore.[964] Ward commented on ending his career in the emergency room by stating, *"Some retirement party."*[965]

The *Press of Atlantic City* stated that both boxers had purplish knuckles that were the size of golf balls. Ward's nose was more crooked than before the match, and he had dried blood caked in his nostrils. Gatti's cheeks were swollen and his lip was split.[966]

Ward mentioned to the doctor that he had been seeing double since being hit in the temple in the 3rd round. He was taken for a precautionary CAT scan. Arturo lay wrapped in a blanket a few feet away. He was waiting to have his broken hand put in a cast.

Ward was cleared to leave the hospital around 2 a.m. He was glad that he would never have to visit the emergency room after a fight again.[967] Ward walked over to Arturo wearing only socks. His boxing shoes were nowhere to be found. They had been stolen, probably by a souvenir seeker. Arturo was still on a gurney. Ward leaned down and hugged him. Micky told Gatti that he loved him and would see him on the golf course.[968] Arturo replied that he loved Ward too.[969] Both boxers smiled at each other. Ward took his pain killers and X-rays and walked out of the hospital into a waiting limo that Arturo had arranged for him.

Arturo was released at 2:45 a.m. He took the hospital robe off and slipped on his blue sweat suit and sandals. His arm was in a cast and sling. He had an ice bag in one hand and pain pills in the other. As Arturo walked out, he confessed that in a few more fights he wouldn't be doing this anymore either.[970]

As Arturo was entering his limousine with Vivian, he revealed that he felt a huge weight was lifted off of his shoulders. He was glad that Ward was able to make some money. Gatti felt that Ward deserved it. Arturo added that they both should have made more money for the trilogy.[971]

The day after the battle, McGirt commented that both fighters fought like champions. Buddy added that it is sad that today's champions do not fight like Ward and Gatti did. McGirt felt that both boxers should have received championship belts for their performances.[972]

Steve Acunto, president of the American Association for the Improvement of Boxing, believed that Pier 6 brawls, like the ones Ward and Gatti partook in, were detrimental to fighters. Acunto felt that there was no reason to brawl like that except to please the crowd.[973] Lennox Lewis, who sat ringside, commented that there wasn't a single word that could define the trilogy. Lewis felt that blood, guts, pride, and compassion described the matches.[974]

Gatti-Ward III was viewed by more than 3 million homes. It was the highest rated boxing match, up to that date, for HBO in 2003. The first match was seen by nearly 2.4 million homes. The second match was viewed by 2.996 million homes.

N.J. Attorney General Peter Harvey, his wife, and two friends were on hand for the bout. He would later come under fire for accepting free passes from Main Events to attend the show. Harvey eventually would be forced to pay for the price of the seats. He also was fined $1,500 by a state ethics commission.

Larry Merchant reflected on the Gatti-Ward battles by stating that these types of impactful trilogies were very rare today. Merchant believed that both fighters would be honored, and invited to dinners, to relive the battles for years to come.[975] Max Kellerman felt the trilogy would define the boxing era.[976]

Ward, who earned $2.3 million in his final four fights, planned on returning to his street-paving job, not because he had to, but because he enjoyed the work.[977] Ward's biggest payday in his 15-year career, before the Gatti fights, was $30,000.

Main Events and Lynch were now contemplating a match with either junior welterweight champ Kostya Tszyu, or lightweight champions Leonard Dorin or Paul Spadafora. Dorin and Spadafora would have to move up in weight if a match were to be made. Arturo commented on Tszyu. *"The big problem with Kostya Tszyu is he's going to want everything. He forgets that Arturo Gatti brings everything to the table; he brings only the titles. Kostya Tszyu can't draw flies, so you'll really have to understand that it'll have to be 50-50 or there ain't going to be no fight."*[978] Another stumbling block was the fact that Arturo was under contract to HBO, while Tszyu was contractually committed to Showtime.

The most important issue, though, was Arturo's right hand. The hand, broken in his prior two fights, needed to heal properly before any future fight could be considered. Lynch reassured that they would take as long as needed, be it six months to a year, to make sure Arturo's hand was 100% healed.[979]

On June 19, Arturo went to New York City and had his hand operated on by Dr. Charles Melone. Dr. Melone confirmed that Arturo had torn a tendon above his right middle knuckle. The surgery was a success. The tendon on the knuckle was completely repaired. A small bone near the pinky finger was also fused.[980] The hand would take nearly six months to heal. Junior welterweights Ricky Hatton and Vivian Harris were added to the list of Arturo's possible future opponents.

After the surgery, Arturo went on a partying tear. Early one morning, while Steve Sandoval was sleeping in his Jersey City apartment, he heard banging on his front door. He opened the door, half asleep, to find a drunk Arturo laughing with a male friend. Arturo walked into the apartment and sat down. He started explaining to Steve how he and his friend had just stolen a delivery truck that was left running in the street. Arturo giggled as he told Sandoval how he was making "donuts" with the truck. After Arturo finished his story, Steve looked him in the eyes and asked, *"Are you crazy?"*[981]

Seeing that Sandoval wasn't amused, Arturo changed his disposition. Steve explained to Arturo that he was a celebrity and it would be an embarrassment if he were caught in a stolen delivery truck. Apparently Arturo's thirst for excitement was insatiable.

Three weeks after the Ward bout *KO* magazine's editor-in-chief, Nigel Collins, interviewed Arturo in Pat Lynch's ticket broker office in Secaucus, N.J. Also on hand were Arturo's fiancée, Vivian Penha, and photographer Tom Casino. Collins was a huge Gatti fan.[982]

During the interview, Arturo spoke of the hand operation that Dr. Melone had performed. He had broken his fourth metacarpus and injured the tendon on his knuckle. Gatti said that the tendon had been bothering him for 10 years. Dr. Melone took bone from Arturo's hip to fuse the hairline crack.

Arturo admitted that he had a metal plate in his hand since 1995. It was the same metal plate that an anonymous letter-writer complained about, and that his team denied, before the Tracy Patterson bouts. The plate had to be removed by Melone, so admitting it now was a non-issue. His bone had grown around the plate, making removal difficult. Vivian was sitting beside Arturo after the surgery, and she witnessed when he woke up crying in pain. Gatti explained that his right hand bones were all fused together from the four operations. He joked that there was nothing left to break. The cast was scheduled to be removed on August 15.

Arturo admitted that after he hurt his hand in the third Ward fight it took him a round or two to start throwing the hand again. Collins asked Arturo if he ever thought about the fact that if he didn't get dropped in the first Ward fight, there wouldn't have been a second or third bout. Arturo confessed that he was very depressed after he lost the first Ward fight. Gatti now felt that the loss was a blessing because of all the money that he and Ward made from the trilogy.[983]

Arturo admitted that since the Ward battles, he was recognized everywhere. Gatti enjoyed when fans approached him to talk about the fights. Arturo felt good knowing that people appreciated his sacrifices.[984] Arturo confessed that he entered his matches planning to box but something always seemed to happen, such as a cut or a hand injury, that forced him to brawl. Arturo admitted that he gets anxious when he is injured, because he is afraid that the referee will stop the fight. Gatti felt he deserved induction into the Hall of Fame for the great battles he fought.[985]

Collins asked Arturo if there were any fighters that Gatti truly disliked. Arturo answered politically that there were, but he did not want to mention their names to give them publicity.[986] Collins took a guess on who one of those fighters might be; Angel Manfredy.

Arturo admitted that Manfredy was the type of boxer that he would definitely love to fight again, but he would not give Manfredy the opportunity to make a payday. Gatti knew that everyone wanted to fight him to make money. Arturo wanted to fight boxers who could make *him* more money.[987] Arturo told Collins that he wanted to become champion of the world again. He felt that becoming champion again was especially important due to the fact that people were saying his career was over after the De La Hoya loss.

Gatti believed that his transformation from brawler to boxer was due to his hard work and dedication to the sport. Arturo felt he connected with McGirt because he knew that Buddy was a world champion fighter himself. This made it easy for Gatti to heed McGirt's advice. Arturo was amazed at Buddy's knowledge of boxing. Gatti brushed aside the notion of some in the sport, that great boxers could not make great trainers. Arturo felt that he too could become a great trainer after he retired.[988]

Collins asked Arturo about Vivian's comment on his split personality. She said that when Arturo was good he was very good, but when he was bad he was very bad. This was similar to Vikki's statement that Arturo was like a gizmo/gremlin, soft and cuddly, but who could transform into a monster on a moment's notice. Arturo felt that his relationship with Vivian was uplifting. He praised Vivian for believing in him and standing by him through the rough times. Arturo also credited Vivian with helping him to wake up and see that he was heading down the wrong path in life.[989]

Arturo admitted that although many people asked him to change his wild ways, including Lynch, he didn't listen until Vivian asked him to slow down. In the past, he didn't care to change because he was young and having a good time. Arturo added that he never before had access to the huge amount of money he now possessed and he was just having a good time.[990]

Arturo never contemplated retiring after the De La Hoya loss, but he learned that he did not belong in the welterweight division. Gatti still believed that the fight should not have been stopped. Arturo confessed that he had some crazy things going through his mind in regards to the stoppage, but he wouldn't mention them. Gatti was obviously talking about his belief that the De La Hoya bout was stopped to fulfill a side bet. The De La Hoya fight taught Arturo that his punching power did not have the same impact on welterweights as it did on smaller opponents.[991]

Arturo commented on the three-fight TV deal with HBO he recently signed. Gatti felt that he should have been offered the contract ten years prior, although he admitted that he would be making about the same purses with the contract as he had made without the agreement.[992]

Arturo wanted to fight Kostya Tszyu next. He believed that Tszyu was avoiding him. Arturo felt that the fight might not happen because of an issue with the purse split. Gatti felt that Tszyu needed him more than he needed Tszyu.[993] Arturo admitted that if it were up to him he would fight Tszyu or Floyd Mayweather, Jr. because he wanted to fight the best in the division and make the most money he could. Arturo planned on fighting until 2006 or 2007, after which he would retire.

One of Gatti's favorite parts of fight night was the walk to the ring. The walk infused Arturo with excitement and adrenaline. Gatti's favorite feeling, though, came from the joy of knocking an opponent out who was trying to do the same to him. Knowing that he would not get in trouble for the act made it all the more fun. Arturo anticipated that he would miss being a fighter when he retired because being a boxer illustrated who he was. He was trying to avoid thinking about the day when he would have to retire.[994] Arturo was proud to be a professional athlete and he respected his sport.

Gatti planned on opening an Italian restaurant in New Jersey after he retired. He felt it would be successful after fans learned that they could meet him at the business. Arturo planned on having Vivian help him with the restaurant.[995]

Gatti also wanted to train a few fighters when he retired. Arturo praised his amateur trainer, Dave Campanile, for taking care of him after his father passed away when he was only 15 years old. Gatti believed that Campanile being there for him was the reason he became a successful boxer. Campanile took care of him emotionally and financially after his father died. Arturo wanted to be able to help young kids the same way he was helped. Gatti praised boxing for keeping kids out of trouble and teaching them respect.[996]

Arturo spoke of golf and bragged how he shot in the high 80s. Golf helped him to relax. He had played golf nearly every day during the three Ward camps. Gatti believed that having an older brother fueled his competitive nature. *"All my life me and my brother, Joe, have been together and we competed. It helped me in the sport. That's probably why I never give up. I think that way in everything I do, and if I can't do it, I'll keep trying as hard as I can."*[997]

On August 15, Arturo drove up to Mohegan Sun with Vivian. The couple enjoyed a night of fun with Micky Ward and his fiancée, Charlene Fleming, at Micky's retirement party.

In September 2003, Arturo, who now was living in Mahwah, N.J., announced he would return to training on November 1. Gatti had a busy week, attending many events in New York.

On September 24, Arturo received an award from the Port Authority of N.Y. and N.J. The award was given for his continued support of that organization in the aftermath of 9/11, during which time the department lost many employees.

On September 25, Arturo and Ward held an autograph signing event at Foot Locker in Times Square. The line for autographs was around the block.

On September 26, Arturo was a guest of honor at the Italian-American Night at the Waldorf-Astoria in New York.

On October 2, Arturo was honored at the Seventh Annual Italian Heritage Day in Howard Beach, N.Y.

Part 2

"A man is not made for defeat. A man can be destroyed, but not defeated."

Ernest Hemingway
The Old Man & The Sea

Gatti family portrait before Arturo's birth, approx. 1970. Top L to R Ida & Giovanni Gatti. Bottom L to R Anna-Maria, Giuseppina, Joe & Mirella Gatti. (Photo courtesy of Joe Gatti)

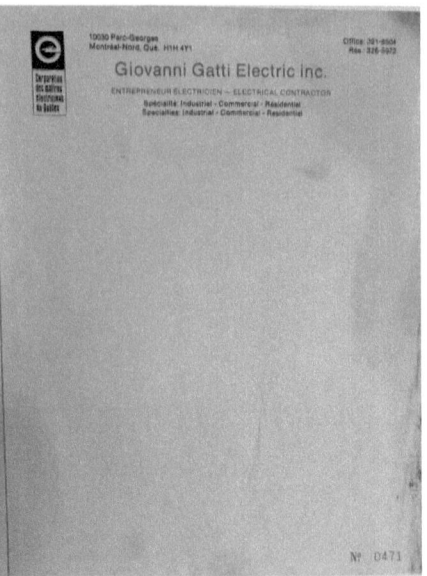

Blank work order for Giovanni Gatti Electric contractor. (courtesy Joe Gatti)

Arturo & Joe Gatti square off as youngsters approx. 1977. (Photo courtesy of Joe Gatti)

Arturo & Joe Gatti play fighting at home in Montreal approx. 1978. (Photo courtesy of Joe Gatti)

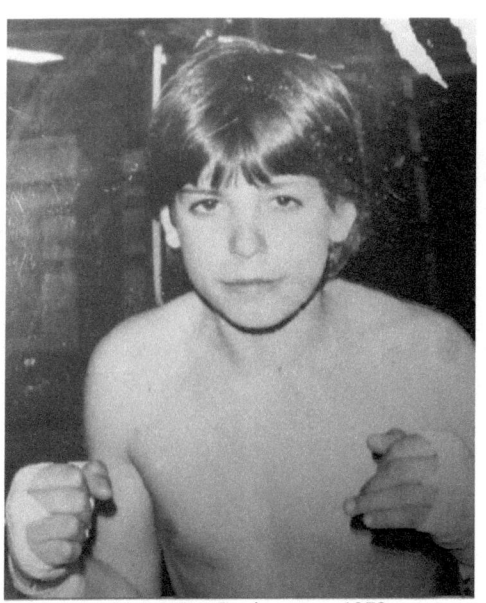
A young Joe Gatti approx. 1978.
(Photo courtesy of Joe Gatti)

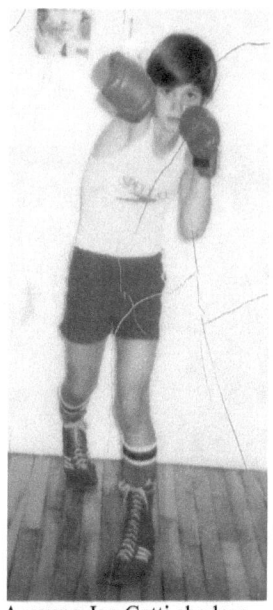
A young Joe Gatti shadow boxing in Montreal.
(Photo courtesy of Joe Gatti)

Eric Huard, left, squares off against Arturo Gatti approx. 1980.
The pair would fight two times.
(Photo courtesy of Eric Huard)

A young Arturo Gatti approx. 1980.
(photo courtesy Joe Gatti)

Joe Gatti proudly displays an amateur boxing award approx.1982.
(Photo courtesy of Joe Gatti)

A young Arturo Gatti approx. 1981.
(Photo courtesy of Joe Gatti)

A young Arturo Gatti as he partakes in an amateur boxing contest approx. 1988.

17-year-old Wayne McCullough hitting 16-year-old Arturo Gatti with a jab during their amateur bout in Ireland in June of 1988.

Mario Costa's home at 277 Manhattan Avenue in Jersey City where the Hilton's and later Joe & Arturo Gatti would stay when they first came from Canada.
(Photo by Joe Botti)

The Ringside Lounge in Jersey City. (Photo by Joe Botti)

Second Floor at Ringside Lounge where makeshift gym was located in 1991.
(Photo by Joe Botti)

Mario Costa shows the eye hooks that were used for the ropes of the make shift ring above the Ringside Lounge. (Photo by Joe Botti)

The table at the Ringside Lounge where a young Arturo would sit and watch the fights with Mario Costa. (Photo by Joe Botti)

Mario Costa holding Arturo Gatti's trophy from his final amateur bout, which is prominently displayed at the Ringside Lounge. (Photo by Joe Botti)

Arturo & Joe Gatti at the Ringside Lounge 1991. (Photo courtesy of Joe Gatti)

Joe & Arturo Gatti have fun in Jersey City 1991.
(Photo courtesy of Joe Gatti)

Arturo Gatti wearing a Lightning Joe Gatti team jacket 1991.
(Photo courtesy of Joe Gatti)

Arturo Gatti, Mike Tyson, Joe Gatti & Panama Lewis in Jersey City 1991.
(Photo courtesy of Joe Gatti)

Joe & Arturo Gatti at the Jersey Shore approx. 1991.
(Photo courtesy of Joe Gatti)

Arturo Gatti's professional debut against Jose Gonzales 6/10/1991.
(photo by Joe Botti)

Richie Seibert, Arturo Gatti & Pat Lynch celebrate Gatti's
19 second knockout over Luis Melendez 9/7/1991.

Pat Lynch, Chazz Palminteri & Joe Gatti
on the set of *A Bronx Tale* 1992.
(Photo courtesy of Joe Gatti)

Pat Lynch & Joe Gatti on the set of *A Bronx Tale* 1992.
(Photo courtesy of Joe Gatti)

Arturo after sparring in preparation for his June 28, 1994 battle against Pete Taliaferro. Standing to Arturo's right are Jake "The Snake" Rodriguez and Mikey "Red" Skowronski. (Photo courtesy of Mike Skowronski)

Arturo Gatti & Donny Jerie two days after the first Patterson fight 12/17/1995. (photo courtesy of Donny Jerie)

Arturo & Joe Gatti after Arturo defeated Gabriel Ruelas 10/5/1997. (Photo courtesy of Joe Gatti)

Laura Sosnowski, Arturo Gatti, Joe Gatti & Vikki Gatti after Arturo defeated Gabriel Ruelas 10/5/1997. (Photo courtesy of Joe Gatti)

John Capone & Arturo Gatti 8/31/1997.
(Photo courtesy of Mike Skowronski)

Joe Gatti & his mother Ida approx. 1997
(Photo courtesy Joe Gatti)

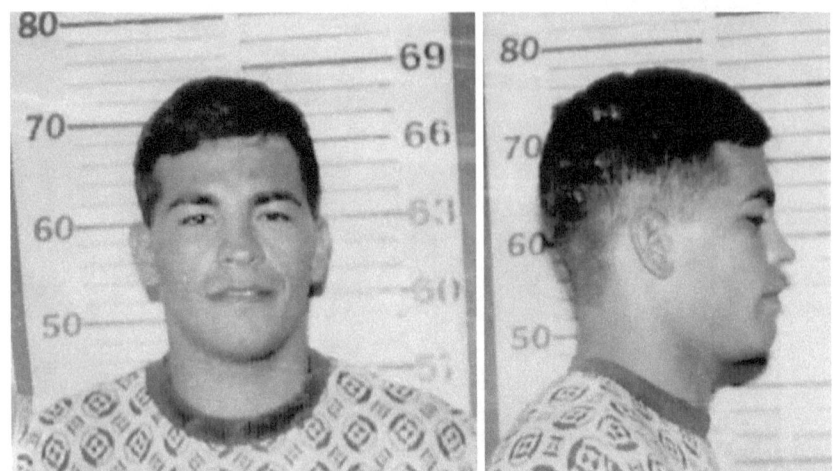

Arturo's booking photo after arrest for DWI in Union City, NJ 7/1/1997.

Jail cell in Union City NJ where Arturo was held for DWI on 7/1/1997.

Mario Costa & Arturo Gatti.
(Photo courtesy of Mario Costa)

Arturo Gatti, Step father Gerardo di Francesco & Joe Gatti after
the Angel Manfredy fight 1/18/1998. (Photo courtesy of Joe Gatti)

Joe & Vikki Gatti 2/26/1998. (Photo courtesy of Joe Gatti)

Joe Gatti between rounds during his IBC Intercontinental light heavyweight title fight against Allen Smith in Zofingen-Aarau, Switzerland on 1/2/1999. Al Certo was chief second while Danny Milano was cutman.(Photo courtesy of Joe Gatti)

Vikki & Joe Gatti after Joe won the IBC Intercontinental light heavyweight title by knocking out Allen Smith in Zofingen-Aarau, Switzerland on 1/2/1999. (Photo courtesy of Joe Gatti)

Joe, Arturo & Vikki Gatti at the Fernwood resort, East Stroudsburg, PA, training camp for the Joey Gamache match January 2000. (Photo courtesy of Joe Gatti)

Fernwood resort training camp, East Stroudsburg PA, for the Joey Gamache match January 2000. Left to right standing Joey Perrenod, Mike Skowronski, Hector Roca, Arturo Gatti & Ray Ruiz. Squatting Frank Baker.
(photo courtesy Mike Skowronski)

Mike Skowronski, Arturo Gatti & Vivian Penha at Jenkinson's boardwalk bar in Point Pleasant NJ June 2001. (Photo courtesy of Mike Skowronski)

Mike Skowronski, Arturo & Jaime (last name unknown) clown around on the beach at Point Pleasant NJ June 2001. (Photo courtesy of Mike Skowronski)

Mike Skowronski & Arturo Gatti clown around on the beach at Point Pleasant NJ June 2001. (Photo courtesy of Mike Skowronski)

Arturo Gatti at the beach at Point Pleasant NJ June 2001.
(Photo courtesy of Mike Skowronski)

John Capone, Arturo Gatti & Mikey Red Skowronski.
(Photo courtesy of Mike Skowronski)

Joe Scheurer, Mikey "Red" Skowronski, Arturo Gatti & Bobby Ortense Sr. enjoy a round of golf. (Photo courtesy of Mike Skowronski)

Billy Infante, Mikey Red Skorwonski & Arturo Gatti.
(Photo courtesy of Mike Skowronski)

Mike Skowronski, Dario Barzan, Mark DeVincentis, Teddy Cruz & Arturo Gatti
in Dominican Republic for DeVincentis' bachelor party approx. 2005.
(Photo courtesy of Mike Skowronski)

Arturo Gatti, Nick Delaportas, Donny Jerie & Wayne Chrebet approx. 2006.
(photo courtesy Donny Jerie)

Arturo Gatti & Teddy Cruz.
(photo courtesy Teddy Cruz)

Teddy Cruz, Mike Skowronski & Arturo Gatti enjoy a game of golf. (courtesy of Mike Skowronski)

Arturo Gatti's signed WBC championship belt that he gifted to Donnie Jerie. (Photo courtesy of Donnie Jerie)

Arturo Gatti bobblehead given away to fans in September 2006 at an Atlantic City Surfs minor league baseball game.

Arturo connects with a left hook while Jesse James Leija attempts to avoid the shot during their 1/29/2005 fight in Atlantic City.
(Photo courtesy of Sugar Ray Bailey)

Arturo walks to a neutral corner after knocking down Jesse James Leija during their Atlantic City bout on 1/29/2005.
(Photo courtesy of Sugar Ray Bailey)

Arturo lands a right uppercut on Thomas Damgaard during their 6/1/2006 fight in Atlantic City. (Photo courtesy of Sugar Ray Bailey)

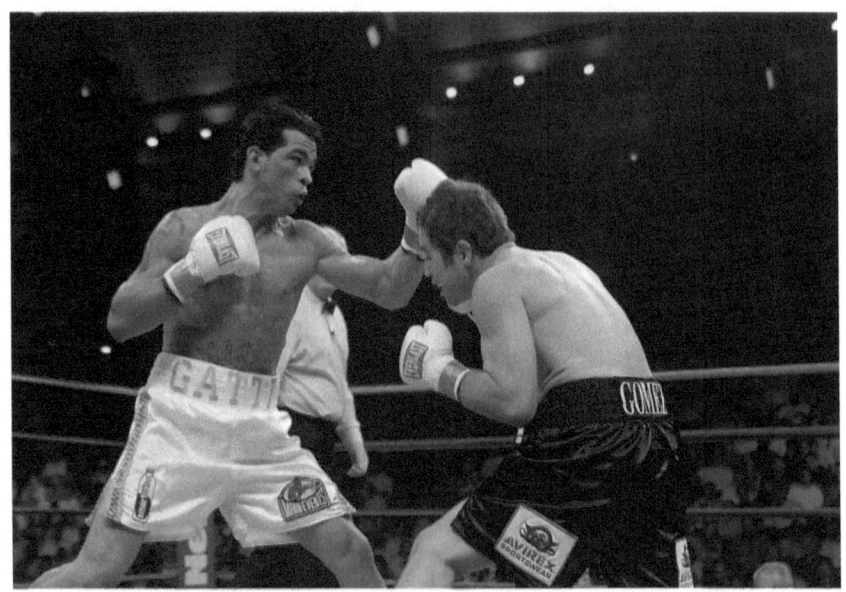

Arturo and Alfonso Gomez trade blows during their 7/14/2007 bout at Boardwalk Hall in Atlantic City. (Photo courtesy of Sugar Ray Bailey)

Micky Ward, Travis Hartman & Arturo Gatti in training at Sultan Ibragamov's Gym in Pompano Beach Florida in June 2007. Gatti was in training for Alfonso Gomez. (photo courtesy of Travis Hartman)

Micky Ward working the pads with Arturo Gatti at Sultan Ibragamov's Gym in Pompano Beach Florida in June 2007. (photo courtesy of Travis Hartman)

Arturo Gatti hitting the speed bag under the watchful eye of Micky Ward at Sultan Ibragamov's Gym in Pompano Beach Florida in June 2007. (photo courtesy of Travis Hartman)

Arturo Gatti hitting the punching bag in training at Sultan Ibragamov's Gym in Pompano Beach Florida in June 2007. (photo courtesy of Travis Hartman)

Arturo Gatti jumping rope under the watchful eye of Micky Ward at Sultan Ibragamov's Gym in Pompano Beach Florida in June 2007. (photo courtesy of Travis Hartman)

Joe Gatti with lightweight Danny McDermott. McDermott was a sparring partner in several Arturo Gatti training camps.
(photo courtesy of Danny McDermott)

The Squeeze Lounge 1820 Willow Avenue, Weehawken, NJ.
(photo by Joe Botti)

Mural of Arturo Gatti outside of the Ringside Lounge in Jersey City.
(Photo by Joe Botti)

Arturo Gatti and author's sister Donna Botti-Vacarro taken 4/11/2008 at a professional boxing show at Tropicana Casino, Atlantic City. It would be the final time that Arturo appeared in Atlantic City. (Photo by Joe Botti)

Staircase & kitchen area of condo where Arturo Gatti was discovered on the floor in the Porto de Galinhas Resort in Brazil.

Joe Gatti & Mike Tyson at NJ Boxing Hall of Fame ceremony 11/14/2013.
(Photo courtesy of Stanley Janousek)

Standing L to R Henry Hascup, Aaron Davis & Joe Gatti. Seated is Mike Tyson at the NJ Boxing Hall of Fame ceremony 11/14/2013.
(Photo courtesy of Stanley Janousek)

Standing L to R Henry Hascup, Mike Tyson, Joe Gatti, Mario Costa & Aaron Davis at Joe Gatti's induction into the NJ Boxing Hall of Fame 11/14/2013.
(Photo courtesy of Stanley Janousek)

Alla cara memoria di
Arturo Gatti
1972 -2009

Non piangete se vi ho lasciato nel dolore.

Io continuerò ad amarvi al di là della vita.

L'amore è l'anima, e l'anima non muore.

La famiglia ringrazia.

Memorial prayer card for Arturo Gatti.

Tribute to Arturo Gatti held at Bally's Atlantic City during boxing show held by Main Events.

Proposed statue for Atlantic City in honor of Arturo "Thunder" Gatti. Artist rendering by Angelo Martinez. (Courtesy of Danny McDermott)

Chapter 22
A Second Title

On October 8, 2003, the Mexican-based WBC stripped Kostya Tszyu for failing to defend his title for two years. Tszyu still held the IBF and WBA titles.

On October 12, Pat Lynch announced that Arturo would return to the ring on January 24, 2004. His opponent would be Gianluca Branca, the #1 ranked WBC junior welterweight. Gatti, ranked #2, and Branca, would be fighting for the now vacant WBC title. The bout would take place at Atlantic City's Boardwalk Hall. Arturo commented that he would have loved to have fought Tszyu and taken all of his belts. He planned on winning and holding the title for a long time.[998]

On November 8, Russell Peltz, whose co-promotional deal with Gatti ended just prior to the Ward trilogy, offered Arturo $1 million to face the winner of the Ivan Robinson-Michael Stewart fight. *Star Ledger* reporter Franklin McNeil predicted that it would take a lot more than a million dollars to get Gatti in the ring against either of those two fighters. Gatti would earn at least that much on January 24 when he faced Branca. McNeil felt that a victory over Branca surely would land Gatti a multi-million dollar payday against high profile opponents such as Kostya Tszyu, Sharmba Mitchell, Zab Judah, or Floyd Mayweather Jr.[999]

On November 11, Arturo promoted his upcoming bout with Branca at the Il Cortile restaurant, which is located on Mulberry Street in New York City's Little Italy section. Arturo expressed his excitement about his upcoming title opportunity. He thanked Main Events, Buddy McGirt, and Branco for helping to make the fight possible. Arturo's joy soon turned to pain. He thanked Vivian Penha, and as he did so, he broke down and was unable to finish his statement. Gatti sat down in obvious emotional pain. Penha did not attend the press conference as Arturo and his fiancée had split up. Arturo refused to reveal why the couple had parted ways, but he thanked her for helping to resurrect his career. As Arturo's eyes filled with tears he confessed that the issue was too painful to discuss.[1000] Pat Lynch, and his wife Lisette, led the distraught boxer to a bathroom so he could regain his composure. It was obvious that Arturo was still in love with Vivian.

New York Times reporter Tim Smith felt that Vivian had pulled

Arturo out of a self-destructive spiral of excessive drinking and partying. Gatti voiced his obvious displeasure at being underappreciated and underpaid by HBO Sports. Arturo blamed Kery Davis, the HBO boxing czar. Davis did not attend the press conference, but instead sent his second-in-command, Xavier James. Arturo felt that his popularity and tough matches should have made him a wealthy man by now. Gatti stated, *"I should be living in a mansion. I haven't made as much money as I should have, as I could have, as much as I deserve. I've stopped worrying about fighting for money, I'm fighting for history now."*[1001] Arturo voiced his displeasure over watching other boxers collect bigger paychecks while drawing much lower ratings.

Arturo confessed that it hurt that he was not counted among the pound-for-pound best in boxing. Instead, some fans looked at him as the best pound-for-pound punch-eater. Branco's Italian accent reminded Arturo of his father. Gatti told reporters that he planned on visiting his father's grave in Italy after the fight.

Donny Jerie recalled that Arturo spoke often about wanting to go to Italy to visit his father's grave site. Arturo wanted to bury his IBF championship belt with Giovanni. Jerie sadly said, that as far as he knew, Arturo never did get around to visiting his father.

Arturo displayed his humorous side at the press conference. He made fun of his face-first style. *"The only problem that I have is that when I hear the phone, I put my hands up. But that's ok. I hang around a lot of retired fighters, and I've seen some fucked-up fucks. So I'm ok."*[1002]

Arturo departed the press conference with Buddy McGirt, who tried his best to console Gatti. After four years together, Vivian had left him. Buddy tried to cheer Arturo up by telling him how much he had to be thankful for, especially his successful boxing career. None of that mattered to Arturo. He lost the one person who seemed able to, if not completely control him, at least temper down his wild lifestyle. Buddy questioned how much Vivian loved Arturo, but he would never mention this to Gatti, as he knew how much Arturo loved her.

Micky Ward was embroiled in a legal dispute over the rights to a story on his life. A settlement had finally been reached. Under the agreement, Ward's percentages were increased. Longtime manager Sal LoNano and promoter Lou DiBella were added to the project as technical advisers. Actor Mark Wahlberg was cast to play Ward. Donnie Wahlberg was originally cast to play Dicky Eklund. Matt

Damon and Brad Pitt were later considered for the part before Christian Bale was awarded the role. DiBella felt that the Ward story had the potential to be a great film.[1003]

The Ring magazine's November 2003 ratings had Arturo ranked #2 in the junior welterweight division. Kostya Tszyu was champion, Sharmba Mitchell was ranked #1, and Zab Judah ranked #3.

The Ring magazine spoke of the ten fights they wanted to see in 2004. On the list was a Gatti-Hatton matchup. The magazine felt that the fight would be akin to Gatti-Ward IV. They predicted a Gatti victory if the fight were to happen, but they felt the chances of the pair meeting were slim. This was due to Arturo being under contractual obligation to HBO while Hatton was inked by Showtime.

Arturo was aware of the fact that he was not on anyone's top-ten pound-for-pound list. Yet he also knew that he was one of the most exciting fighters in the sport. Arturo dawned the cover of *KO* magazine for the first time on the Winter 2003 issue.

Arturo wasn't the only one who noticed the lack of appreciation for his warrior style. In a letter to *KO* magazine, Bayonne, N.J.'s Josh Garnett was thrilled to see his favorite fighter, Gatti, on the cover of the Winter 2003 issue. Garnett questioned why it took *KO* so long to put Arturo on the cover. Garnett added that Gatti deserved the honor much more than Roy Jones, Jr., who had been on numerous covers.[1004]

In a *KO* magazine article, Don Stradley wrote of several boxers who should retire. Among the boxers mentioned were Oscar De La Hoya, Shane Mosley, Kostya Tszyu, Bernard Hopkins, and Arturo Gatti. Of Gatti, Stradley stated that retiring after beating Ward twice in a row would be a sweet way of saying farewell, but Stradley felt that Gatti's management team could smell the HBO money. Stradley questioned whether the money was worth the health risks Arturo was taking by continuing his career.[1005]

The Ring's David Mayo wrote an article on Arturo titled, "Looking Into The Future Of A Man Who Shouldn't Have One!" In the article Arturo spoke of how he almost partied himself out of boxing. Gatti wanted to be regarded as one of the best pound-for-pound boxers in the world, and to do that, he knew that he would have to change his fighting style. That meant the blood-and-guts Arturo was finished.[1006]

Arturo felt that winning the WBC belt would give him a great deal of leverage against either Kostya Tszyu or Floyd Mayweather Jr.

Gatti felt that Mayweather would be a better pay-per-view draw than Tszyu.[1007] Mayweather believed that a Gatti showdown would definitely be worthy of pay-per-view. Mayweather felt it was a fight the public wanted to see. Floyd cautioned that Arturo might not want to see the outcome of a fight with him. Mayweather predicted that Gatti would be put on his face with ease because he was slow, easy to hit, and cut prone.[1008]

McGirt responded to Mayweather's statements by asserting that Arturo might go out on his face one day, but it wouldn't be from Mayweather. McGirt felt that Floyd was a good fighter who had beaten everyone that was put in front of him, but McGirt believed that Arturo had too much offense for Mayweather. Arturo added that Floyd had a big mouth just like his father Floyd Sr.[1009]

In the first week of December 2003, Paterson, N.J. super middleweight Omar Sheika arrived in Gatti's camp. Sheika, a friend of Arturo's for ten years, hired Buddy McGirt as his new trainer. He hoped that some of Arturo's new magic would rub off on him. Sheika was impressed with how McGirt turned Arturo from a face-first brawler into a defensive-minded boxer. When Sheika arrived at Gatti's camp, Omar was running three miles a day. This was the same roadwork program he had used for all of his bouts. Arturo advised Sheika that they would be running five miles on weekdays and twelve miles on Saturdays.

Arturo was ranked #5 by the WBA and IBF and #2 by the WBC at junior welterweight in their December rankings. *The Ring* magazine honored the Arturo Gatti-Micky Ward III match as its "Fight of the Year" for 2003.

Micky Ward arrived in camp for four days at the request of Arturo, to help motivate Gatti's training. Arturo and Ward had remained good friends after their third battle. They spoke regularly to each other by phone. Ward took up residence at Arturo's Vero Beach rental home. Arturo and Ward were spotted by fans eating in a steakhouse restaurant in West Palm Beach. Arturo recalled the fans' reactions to seeing him eating with Ward. *"The people were amazed. They couldn't believe that two fighters that fought like they were trying to kill each other are friends, smiling, having a good time, and that we were able to forget about what we went through."*[1010] Ward worked out with Arturo. After training they played golf, watched movies, and shopped. Arturo felt that Ward understood him more than anyone else.[1011]

Chris Jones, of *Esquire* magazine, joined the former-foes-turned-friends at a game of golf. The night before the golf game, Arturo went with Ward and Jones to a local Italian restaurant. While at dinner, Ward and Arturo traded stories of their three wars. They pointed out areas on their bodies where they received injuries from each other. Arturo picked up his shirt and revealed a cyst under his ribcage. He jokingly pointed at the cyst and said that he called it the Micky Ward lump.[1012] The cyst was courtesy of a Ward body punch from their first battle.

On January 15, Arturo spoke of his upcoming Branco bout in a conference call. Gatti was excited to be fighting someone other than Ward.[1013] Branco's #1 ranking came into question. Although he had an undefeated record of 32-0-1, he had been inactive for fourteen months, and his last bout was only a 6-round decision win over Michel Raynaud, who held a paltry 8-10-1 record.

On January 20, Arturo discussed fighting Branco. Gatti revealed that he did not know much about Branco except that he was a stand-up European fighter with a good jab.[1014] Arturo rarely watched tapes of his opponents; he left that to his trainer McGirt. Carl Moretti announced that 8,500 tickets had been sold for the fight thus far. Lou DiBella likened the Gatti mystique to that of a Grateful Dead concert.[1015] HBO Sports senior vice president Kery Davis added that Gatti represented everything that was great about boxing.[1016]

On January 21, while training at Marciano's Gym in Jersey City, just three days before the fight, Arturo injured his right hand again.[1017] Arturo discussed the injury with Lynch and they both decided to go ahead with the fight as planned.

Micky Ward attended Arturo's final press conference in New York. After the presser, Ward drove in a limousine with Arturo to Atlantic City. Gatti asked Micky to lead him into the ring. Arturo felt that the crowd would erupt when they saw Ward walk him out. It fired up Gatti to have Ward at the fight with him.[1018]

The official fight program spoke of how close Lynch and Arturo were. How they were like family. In fact, several of Arturo's fight programs spoke of their closeness while displaying a photo of Lynch and Gatti together. In the program's article, Lynch spoke of how he wished that Gatti would be more disciplined. Lynch added that it hurt him to see Arturo take the punishment he was absorbing in the ring.[1019]

Arturo loved the blood and excitement of boxing. He credited McGirt for helping him to perfect his right hand. He also attributed McGirt with helping him to keep his composure in the ring.[1020]

Arturo had spent 12 weeks in Vero Beach lifting weights, running and sparring. Arturo did not swim for this camp, because the water was too cold.[1021]

On fight night, undercover police were out on the boardwalk in full force looking for scalpers and counterfeiters. The sting operation yielded counterfeit tickets and T-shirts, eight arrests, and nearly $7,000 in cash. The sting was organized after the rise of counterfeit tickets for a December show.

Arturo's brother Joe would attend the Branco fight, but not working his brother's corner. Joe was still training 25-4 (10 KOs) Scott DePompe. McGirt's son, James McGirt Jr., would also be fighting on the card, having his professional debut. Both fighters would win their bouts.

McGirt had been training Omar Sheika in Vero Beach for his rematch against Scott Pemberton on January 23. McGirt was planning on driving three-and-a-half hours up to Connecticut, work the Sheika bout, and return the same night to work Arturo's bout against Branco the following day. McGirt had signed a contract with Main Events to work exclusively with their fighters, however, Sheika was not a Main Events fighter. Carl Moretti enforced the contract and blocked McGirt from leaving Arturo on the day of his weigh-in to work Sheika's bout.

Sheika and Arturo were close friends. They both had crowd-pleasing, give-and-take styles. Sheika recalled how popular Arturo was in Florida. *"He trained hard for the WBC championship. Florida, they loved him. It was hard for him to train. Everybody wanted to take him out to party. He never took things [in life] seriously."*[1022]

When studying tapes of Gatti, Branco watched only Arturo's losses to Robinson, Manfredy, and De La Hoya. Branco wanted to learn how, and why, those fighters beat Gatti.[1023] Branco's older brother, Sylvio, the WBA light heavyweight champion at the time, spoke of his brother's desire to fight on the inside. Sylvio felt that if his brother used his intelligence and moved around, he would give Gatti a difficult fight.[1024]

The 31-year-old Gatti and the 33-year-old Branco both weighed in at the junior welterweight limit of 140-pounds. Arturo held a 1½-inch height advantage over the 5'6" Branco.

11,237 fans braved the bitter cold to watch Arturo attempt to win the WBC light welterweight title. The fact that Gatti could sell that many tickets against a virtually unknown fighter in the United States was amazing. HBO executive Xavier James jokingly said that Arturo might put 12,000 fans in the seats if *he* were Gatti's opponent.[1025]

Arturo warmed up in his dressing room while Micky Ward sat nearby. Branco made his way to the ring first. Arturo made his way out with Chuck Zito, Dale Earnhardt Jr., Ward, Lynch, McGirt, Mikey Red, and Joe Souza. Arturo came out to AC/DC's "Thunderstruck."

Arturo was wearing white trunks with blue trim while Branco wore the colors of Italy. Branco looked just as big, physically, as Gatti. When Arturo entered the ring he peered at Branco, then turned towards Lynch and remarked that he was happy it wasn't Micky Ward standing across the ring.

Branco started the 1st round by scoring several rights and hooks. Arturo banged the body hard. At the end of the round Gatti had Gianluca trapped on the ropes. McGirt told Arturo that he was doing well. He asked Gatti to move his head more and watch Branco's counter rights over his jab. In Gianluca's corner, his trainer, Francesco Cherchi, asked him to stand and fight and use his strength.

The 2nd round was back-and-forth until Arturo unloaded several hard hooks at the end of the round. McGirt asked Arturo to step to his right to avoid the right hand counters.

Arturo controlled the 3rd by boxing and stepping in and out. Branco spent a substantial amount of time with his back against the ropes.

Arturo's right cheekbone started to swell in the 4th. Gatti landed several hard hooks to the body. Branco landed some single shots but Arturo appeared to win the round with his boxing. Cherchi was happy with Gianluca's performance in the round. He asked Branco to be more aggressive.

Thirty seconds into the 5th, Arturo landed a hard right to Branco's hip. He grimaced in pain. The injury, which he had suffered in his last day of sparring, had resurfaced. Nevertheless, Gatti utilized the jab and right hand, as he outworked Branco. McGirt asked Arturo to move more and not look for the knockout. Gianluca's corner asked for more jabs.

In the 6th, both boxers jabbed often, with Gatti being slightly busier. McGirt asked Arturo to move to the right more. Cherchi asked Branco to back Gatti up.

Forty seconds into the 7th round, Arturo landed another right on Branco's hip. Once again he grimaced in pain. Halfway through the round, Gianluca snapped Gatti's head back with a right. With 30 seconds remaining, Branco landed another right followed by a hook and several more rights. Arturo's left eye was rapidly closing. Souza applied the enswell to Arturo's eye, while McGirt implored Gatti to box.

The 8th was close, but Arturo landed more jabs, and ended the round with a crunching left hook. He looked back at Branco to gauge the blow's effect. As he did so, Gianluca stuck his tongue out at Gatti.

Arturo was hardly using his damaged right hand. When he did, he didn't put much strength behind it. A right by Branco two minutes into the 9th stunned Arturo. Gianluca followed with three more hard rights. Gatti ended the round with a right hand of his own.

Arturo was out-boxing Branco in the 10th, although he was reluctant to put power behind the right. With 37 seconds remaining in the round, Arturo missed a right that Gianluca slipped. Branco tried to counter with a hook, but his right hand was low. Gatti beat Gianluca to the punch with a thunderous left hook of his own that dropped Branco onto his back.

Gianluca was up at the count of four. Referee Rudy Battle gave him a standing eight count. Arturo landed a right uppercut before the round ended. He went back to his corner with his arms raised as the crowd erupted.

Branco's left eye started swelling in the 11th. The round was close until Gianluca landed three crunching rights and a hook at the end of the round. McGirt screamed for Arturo to box. Cherchi told Branco that Gatti was spent.

Halfway through the 12th, Arturo landed two solid hooks. The second hook snapped Gianluca's head back. Arturo took the twelfth by outworking Branco.

Judges Anek Hontongkem and Tommy Kaczmarek scored the bout 116-111 while Guido Cavallieri of Italy scored the bout 115-112. After Michael Buffer announced the scores he stated that they were, *"all for the winner, and now the WBC super lightweight champion of the world, from Jersey City, New Jersey..."* As Buffer spoke Arturo climbed up onto the ropes in a neutral corner and raised his hands to his loyal supporters. CompuBox had Arturo landing 230 punches out of 838 attempts to Branco's 168 of 646.

Arturo admitted that he felt a little sluggish. He didn't understand why, since he had trained so hard for the fight. Gatti felt that he won the bout with his heart and his boxing skills.

Arturo stated that the right uppercut to the body was one of his favorite punches, and he would continue to throw it even though he frequently damaged the hand on his opponents' hip bones. Gatti was feeling comfortable during the fight up until the moment he hurt his hand. Arturo felt that after he dropped Branco with the left hook, he couldn't finish him because of the injured hand. After he was knocked down, Branco felt he could not win the fight.[1026] Carl Moretti opined that Arturo's right hand hurt, his left eye was swollen, and they had a packed house, so it must be a Gatti fight.[1027]

Arturo felt that the left hook that dropped Branco in the 10th round turned the fight around, because Gianluca was coming on.[1028] Gatti won by utilizing a safe boxing style, but his fans and the press longed for the old Arturo. Beat writer Jim Brady expressed that fans didn't flock to Gatti's fights to see him box; they wanted blood and excitement.[1029]

After the fight ended, Arturo's mother, Ida, and her husband, Gerardo di Francesco, congratulated their new champion. Ida hugged and kissed Arturo in the ring. She drove down from Montreal for all of Arturo's fights. Arturo would give his mother money to play the slot machines when she arrived from Canada.

Leonard Dorin was rumored as a possible future opponent for Arturo. That matchup would have to wait until Gatti's hand healed. Arturo headed to the Atlantic City Medical Center, but returned to enjoy the after-party celebration. The bruised and battered Arturo appeared more like the loser than the winner. Arturo spent the entire week in Atlantic City, not wanting the championship celebration to end. He was a world champion again.

McGirt confessed that he knew in advance that Arturo would have hand problems during the fight. The problem was magnified by the fact that he wore Reyes gloves. Reyes gloves were considered "punchers gloves," but they also had a reputation of causing more hand injuries.[1030] Main Events had Arturo's next bout scheduled already. Arturo would face Leonard Dorin in Montreal in July or August.

In early February, Arturo received good news from New York hand specialist Dr. Charles Melone. Arturo did not have a broken hand. He suffered a sprained tendon, which would be healed in several weeks. The good news paved the way for Arturo to return to the ring in July against Dorin. Dorin, who was co-promoted by Lou DiBella and Montreal's InterBox, stalled the negotiations until early May. Dorin finally agreed to terms after Main Events threatened to find another opponent.[1031] Dorin was selected mostly because of his similarities to Ward. Dorin was not known to move his head, and he was not a big puncher. He was a boxer who came straight ahead, which would play right into Gatti's strengths. Still, many questioned the Dorin match when Arturo had huge paydays awaiting him against Mayweather or Spadafora.

Arturo had recently sold his home in Mahwah, N.J. after his break-up with Vivian Penha. He was renting a hotel room in Secaucus, NJ.

Several weeks after the Branco victory, Arturo purchased a condominium for $950,000 in Hoboken's Tea Building at 1500 Washington Street. The building was once home to a Lipton Tea factory. Arturo had his name, "Gatti," and a pair of boxing gloves, inlaid into the hardwood floor of his new home. The artwork was beautiful and expensive. Arturo still missed Vivian. Spending money and partying was not healing the emptiness he felt in his heart.

Joe laughed when he recalled Arturo bragging about the $20,000 home stereo system that filled a wall of his condo. Joe was impressed and asked to hear the system. Arturo picked up the remote, stared at it for a few seconds, turned to Joe and said, *"I don't know how it works."*[1032] Joe recalled that Arturo's front door looked like a garage door; oversized. When Joe asked Arturo what happened to the door, Arturo said that he purchased the wrong door.

Arturo visited Mario Costa at his Ringside Lounge. He told Mario that when he died he wanted to throw a curse on the world of boxing.[1033] Gatti was disenchanted with the business of boxing, and he could find no peace in his personal life. Arturo was growing more leery of those around him. He increasingly felt that people were using him for his money and star status.

Arturo would spend more time in strip clubs, trying to feed his desire for love. Many strippers look at their customers as walking ATM machines with little or no self-esteem. One would think that most dancers extracted the money from their customers with their looks and their twerking gyrations, but that rarely is the case. The number-one money-making asset the stripper has is her mouth. For a stripper to be successful, she has to be a saleswoman. She has to make the customer believe that she truly likes him and that he has an excellent chance to take her home, or at least get a phone number. At the end of the night, customers will spend hundreds of dollars and not even know the dancer's real first name. Another tool for the successful stripper is giving her undivided attention to the customer.

The customer wants to be able to vent his personal frustrations to someone who appears empathetic.

Why do men frequent strip clubs? There are those who go out in a group for a fun night with friends, and then there are those who attend the clubs alone. Most would think that men who are obsessed with strippers are sexual deviants. Sometimes this is true. But there are, however, those men that have deeper emotional needs, such as the need for attention and control.

In the strip club environment, the man feels as though he is in total control of the women through his finances. The more cash he flashes the more control he can gain. There also is the issue of attention. Every man who walks into a strip club immediately feels the eyes of the women glancing at him and smiling. This creates the satisfying feeling that he is wanted. There is no feeling-out process or courting in a strip club. The women will come to the man. Most men are starving for attention and admiration. They need to be wanted and desired.

What some men do not realize is that the dancers are not giving them attention because of their looks or their personality. This is a business, and the dancer's job is to extract as much money from the customers as possible. Arturo was important in the club, whether he won a fight or lost. Whether he had two black eyes and twenty stitches over his eye brow or not. Unlike most men that frequented the clubs, Arturo did have the means to pay for what he wanted. On many occasions he spent in excess of $10,000 in a single night. That would include hours in private champagne rooms, and even paying to take the girls out of the club for a night of promiscuity.

Another reason to attend the strip clubs is for the straight entertainment value. While you are occupied with the dancers, you are not thinking about life's other issues. For Arturo, that would mean he could get his mind off of the magazine articles that didn't mention him in their pound-for-pound rankings. Or the articles that listed Arturo as a 'B' or 'C' level fighter. In the strip club arena, Arturo was like the boxing promoter or the fans. He controlled the action. It was the women who were up on the stage performing for his satisfaction, and his money, just as he performed for the promoters and fight fans.

There is a dangerous byproduct of frequenting strip clubs. Alcohol and drug abuse is prevalent in the environment. Just spending several hours in a strip club meant that you were most likely drinking heavily. Some who spend all night in the clubs use chemical substances to help them stay awake and functional for all those hours.

Most occasional customers of strip clubs know that it is a game, but the regular, hardcore visitors, have a somewhat distorted view. They actually believe that the workers, and in some cases the management or owners, are their friends. They cannot come to the realization that their only asset is their wallet. Some men enjoy the fact that after the evening is over, there are no strings attached, while others feel the pain of realizing that the flirting was all a facade. In this fast-moving environment, Arturo found many of his lovers and relationships.

Francisco Bojado asked Buddy McGirt to work with him for his upcoming bout with Andre Eason on Arturo's undercard. Gatti welcomed the Main Events promoted Bojado into his camp.

Floyd Mayweather Jr. and Paul Spadafora were scheduled to meet on May 8 on HBO, in an elimination bout to determine who would be next in line to fight Arturo. The bout was cancelled when the New York boxing commission refused to license Spadafora. Spadafora was awaiting trial for allegedly shooting his girlfriend on October 26, 2003. Mayweather's opponent would be changed to DeMarcus Corley. The date and location of the bout were also changed to May 22 in Atlantic City.

At a press conference for the bout with Corley, Mayweather seemed more interested in discussing Arturo and how he felt that Gatti was ducking him. Lynch stated that Gatti would have no problem fighting Mayweather if the money was right. Lynch believed that a Gatti-Mayweather match would be worthy of pay-per-view.[1034]

Mayweather's promoter, Bob Arum of Top Rank, spoke of a possible Gatti-Mayweather pay-per-view matchup. Arum felt the fight was worthy of pay-per-view.[1035] Mayweather would first have to get past Demarcus Corley.

The Ring magazine's David Mayo commented on what he believed astonished many in boxing; Arturo Gatti's sustainability. After Gatti lost the second Robinson fight it would have been ludicrous to foresee that six years later Arturo would be a world champion again.[1036]

On May 22, 2004 in Atlantic City, Floyd Mayweather, Jr. moved up from lightweight to junior welterweight and soundly defeated DeMarcus Corley in a WBC junior welterweight elimination bout. Only 6,103 fans came out to watch the Grand Rapids, Michigan native. The poor turnout would put Arturo in the driver's seat of any possible match-up negotiations, as Arturo had much more drawing power. Mayweather, who was now Arturo's mandatory challenger, taunted Gatti after he won the Corley bout by proclaiming that Arturo was scared of him.[1037]

Scott DePompe, who was still training under Joe Gatti, fought on the Mayweather undercard. DePompe was stopped in the 4th round of a rematch against Arthur Medina. DePompe would retire after the bout.

On May 25, Arturo finally responded to the verbal blows being hurled at him by Mayweather. Gatti held a press conference at rapper Jay Z's 40/40 club in Manhattan. The 40/40 club was a location that Arturo frequented when he wasn't in training. Arturo questioned why Mayweather would state that he was afraid of Floyd. Arturo felt that it was Mayweather who was afraid to fight *him*.[1038] Gatti planned on fighting Spadafora in the fall, after the Dorin match, and Mayweather after that.

Arturo turned his attention to Dorin, who he felt would be an easy opponent because he had no punching power. McGirt added that Dorin had better bring his track shoes if he planned on hitting Arturo.[1039]

While McGirt and Gatti were in training camp in Vero Beach, Pat Lynch called McGirt and told him that he had the perfect sparring partner for Arturo. A boxer who fought just like Dorin. The boxer was from Canada. Lynch asked McGirt not to let Gatti know where the sparring partner was from, as Dorin was Canadian. The first few days with the new sparring partner went fine until Arturo discovered the fighter was from Canada. While McGirt was wrapping his hands, Arturo asked, *"Coach, can I ask you a question?"* McGirt nodded yes. Gatti continued, *"Will you be honest with me?"* McGirt answered, *"Of course."* Arturo asked, *"Who the fuck is the rocket scientist that sent this Canadian kid for me to spar with, knowing that Dorin's from Canada?"* McGirt broke out laughing. Gatti asked McGirt if he knew that the boxer was Canadian. McGirt replied that he did know. Arturo again asked, *"Who is the rocket scientist?"* McGirt asked Gatti to take a guess. Arturo didn't even think. He answered, *"Fuckin' Pat."*[1040]

McGirt told Gatti that the Canadian was giving him good sparring, but Arturo's mind was made up. Gatti stated, *"Yeah, well he's going home today. 'Cause I'm going to knock this mother fucker out."* When the pair sparred, Arturo knocked the Canadian down with a three punch combination. When the Canadian got up, Gatti took the gloves off and was preparing to go bare knuckles. McGirt called Lynch and told him he needed to get the sparring partner out of camp quickly before Arturo killed him.[1041]

McGirt recalled that Arturo had a great work ethic and never missed training. He liked to train at 10 or 11 a.m. so he could go play golf. Arturo would spar under any circumstances. He didn't care if his hand hurt. Gatti would get angry if McGirt felt he needed a rest and cancelled a sparring session.[1042]

Arturo occasionally hung out with McGirt's son, who also was a boxer. They went to strip clubs together. One night, Arturo and McGirt's son went to a strip club in West Palm Beach for dinner. McGirt Sr. asked a friend named Milo, who was a police officer, to go with them to make sure they didn't drink or get into any trouble. In the club, the owner approached Milo and asked how his father was doing. Milo was befuddled. Before long, other patrons approached Milo, telling him that they loved watching his father fight. Milo went along with it because he thought he had been mistaken for another one of McGirt's sons. Everyone in the club was buying him drinks. At the end of the night, as they were leaving, the owner asked for Milo's autograph. Milo asked why the owner would want his autograph. Arturo couldn't contain himself any longer. He told Milo that he had told everyone in the club that Milo was Sugar Ray Leonard's son.[1043]

Mayweather released a statement in which he said that if he were to fight Gatti, it would have to be in Las Vegas. Carl Moretti thought the statement was comical. Moretti was confident that if the fight did happen, it would be held either in Atlantic City or Madison Square Garden, as neither fighter was a big draw in Las Vegas.[1044]

Joe Gatti sold his home in Paramus and moved to the desirable Smoke Rise section of Kinnelon, N.J. Joe used the profit from selling his Paramus home, along with some of the money he earned from his fight with Sven Ottke, to purchase the 3,263 square foot home for $875,000.

In July, *Sports Illustrated* published an article on Arturo's brawling style. In the article, Micky Ward call Arturo "Jason," because he considered Gatti unstoppable, like the serial killer in *Friday the 13th*.[1045] Fighters of yesteryear commented on Arturo's tough-guy style. Jake LaMotta remarked that Gatti reminded him of himself, taking a lot of head shots. Tony DeMarco commented that Arturo was a gutsy action fighter. Dwight Qawi added that Gatti slugged it out as though he was in a barroom.[1046] Arturo himself joked that people only recognized his face when it was beat up. Pat Lynch added that Gatti got caught up in the hype from all of his come-from-behind knockouts.[1047]

On July 21, Arturo was interviewed by Thomas Gerbasi of maxboxing.com. During the interview, Arturo joked that when the phone rang he thought it was the bell in the gym and he would start shadow boxing. Arturo spoke of the trials he went through after his loss to De La Hoya and how he never doubted himself or thought of quitting the sport.[1048]

On July 22, Gatti and Dorin held their final press conference. Senior vice president at HBO Sports, Kery Davis, commented that Arturo was the era's most exciting television fighter.[1049] Dorin's co-promoter, Lou DiBella, added that Gatti was a star.[1050] Dorin had battled to a hard-fought entertaining draw with Paul Spadafora on May 17, 2003 on HBO's "Boxing After Dark."

On July 21, event officials announced that 10,000 of the over 12,000 tickets available for the Dorin fight were sold. Most of the tickets still available were upper deck $50 seats, which meant that most of the higher priced tickets were gone. The $350 ringside seats were gone within minutes of going on sale in early June. Choice seats were selling for double and triple their face value.

Ken Condon of Bally's, who had the right of first refusal for all of Gatti's fights, commented on the rapid ticket sales. Condon believed that Arturo developed a tremendous following because he was the most exciting boxer in the sport and he also had a personality that caused people to flock to him.[1051]

Carl Moretti felt that Atlantic City had been thirsting to have big fights on a regular basis like Las Vegas. Arturo was consistently bringing those big fights to the Jersey Shore. Moretti spoke of how easy it was to sell tickets for the Gatti fights. The fans didn't even care who he was fighting.[1052]

On Thursday, July 22, Arturo strutted through Bally's lobby wearing white pants, leather sandals, a tan pullover shirt, designer sunglasses, and an eggshell beret. Buddy McGirt pointed at Arturo and joked that he looked like Miami Vice star Don Johnson.[1053]

All joking aside, Arturo was focused for this fight. He was aware that it was a championship match and a huge opportunity for Dorin. McGirt was confident in his fighter. He believed that Arturo had learned that he could box and still be exciting without standing toe-to-toe all the time.[1054]

On July 23, with one day remaining until the weigh-in, Arturo was weighing 145, 5-pounds over the contracted weight. McGirt was pleased with Arturo's 12-week training camp in Vero Beach, which included sparring, weight lifting, running, and even a little swimming.

Leonard Dorin was ready to battle Arturo and his vocal fans. The bout was originally scheduled for Montreal but Ken Condon fought to have Boardwalk Hall host the event. Arturo stated, *"Atlantic City has always treated me well, so why should I fight somewhere else? Why should I go to Montreal and have the crowd be split 50-50 or 60-40 for him? The crowd can have a big impact on the outcome of a fight. I'm sure he'll have a few fans pulling for him here, but most of them will be rooting for me."*[1055]

McGirt wasn't taking the 34-year-old 5'4" Dorin lightly. The undefeated Dorin, 22-0-1, a former WBA lightweight champion, was an aggressive boxer who liked to wear opponents down. Arturo was asked if he was worried he would suffer another hand injury. Arturo laughed and said he wouldn't hurt his hand again because Dorin was too short to hit on the hip.[1056]

Arturo weighed-in at 139¼ compared to Dorin's 139-pounds. Gatti was scheduled to take home $1.8 million, while Dorin was set to earn $550,000. The *Atlantic City Press* predicted a Gatti decision victory. Main Events' prospects, Francisco Bojado and Calvin Brock, were scheduled to be featured on the undercard. Bojado would face Jesse James Leija.

Arturo was aware that Dorin's only chance was to lure him into a brawl. Gatti's game plan was to box from the outside and come underneath with uppercuts. Brawling would not be effective, because Dorin was a smaller opponent.[1057] Dorin doubted that Arturo would stick to a boxing game plan. He felt that Gatti would try to mix it up and look for a knockout.[1058]

Carl Moretti didn't believe that Arturo would stick to his game plan of boxing either. He questioned whether the slugfest would start in the 2nd or the 5th round. Pat Lynch and his wife Lisette were contemplating bringing two of their older children, Alexandra, 11, and Kyle, 10, to see the man the children knew as "Uncle Arthur" fight. Arturo was godfather to Lynch's 5-year-old daughter Cameron. Lynch spoke of watching Arturo in action, and how the wars seemed to last forever. When Gatti boxed, however, the fights seemed to go by quickly.[1059] Lynch envisioned Gatti defeating Dorin, then Spadafora, and then capping his career with a pay-per-view showdown against Floyd Mayweather Jr. Lynch added that Arturo told him he wouldn't retire even if he were offered $10 million to do so. He was enjoying his second championship that much.

When Arturo finally did retire, he planned on working with fighters. He wanted to manage boxers, just like Lynch.[1060] Carl Moretti believed that Lynch had Arturo's best interests at heart. Lynch invested Gatti's money in preparation for his retirement. Moretti felt that Lynch and Gatti's relationship was refreshing, because loyalty was a rare thing in boxing.[1061]

On July 24, 2004, Arturo returned to Boardwalk Hall to take on Leonard Dorin, a Romanian fighter by way of Montreal. 11,863 fans were on hand. Dorin was a two-time Olympic bronze medalist who waited until he was 28 years old to turn professional. Working Dorin's corner were French-Canadians Stephan LaRouche and Pierre Bouchard. LaRouche once trained Arturo when Gatti fought for the Canadian national team. Bouchard fought alongside Arturo on the same team. LaRouche felt that Dorin was being underestimated. He pointed to Dorin's draw with undefeated Spadafora as evidence that his fighter was more than one-dimensional.[1062] When Arturo ran into his former trainer and teammate in a Bally's hallway, he greeted them both with kindness, like long-lost brothers. Arturo, a true professional, did not take their working with his opponent personally.

Dorin would give up 3½-inches in height and 7-inches in reach to Arturo. Dorin was ready to box or brawl.[1063] He pointed out the fact that he was an underdog going into most of his matches, but he always came out victorious.[1064] Pat Lynch thought it would be a tough fight because Dorin was more of a 140-pounder than a lightweight.[1065]

Before the Dorin fight, HBO telecast the Jesse James Leija-Francisco Bojado bout. Buddy McGirt worked Bojado's corner, while Joe Souza worked cuts for Leija. Main Events received a shock when Bojado, a boxer they were grooming to be Arturo's box-office replacement, lost to the 38-year-old Leija by 10-round split decision.

Micky Ward walked Arturo into the ring for the second straight fight. Before leaving the dressing room, McGirt was concerned. Buddy felt that Arturo wasn't his usual self as he was wrapping Gatti's hands. Arturo was very cranky. The tension in the room was so thick you could cut it with a knife. McGirt felt he needed to break the tension before they left the dressing room.[1066] Arturo was irritated that someone he didn't know was in his dressing room. The unwanted person kept talking about a fishing trip, while Gatti was trying to focus on his fight. Arturo gave his lip curling gesture to McGirt, that meant he wanted Buddy to get rid of the annoying visitor. There was no time to kick the guy out, and even if McGirt did, it would have only intensified the situation. Instead, McGirt had another idea after he finished wrapping Arturo's hands. McGirt broke the tension by telling Gatti that he really wanted to sleep with Hillary Clinton. The comment set off a tension breaking explosion of laughter in the room. Arturo loosened up and was ready for his walk out to the ring.[1067]

Before the Gatti-Dorin match began, ring announcer Michael Buffer recognized some of the celebrities who were in attendance. The crowd cheered for Willie Mays, Sammy Sosa, Dick Butkus, and Shaquille O'Neal, but the loudest applause was for *Soprano's* star Tony Sirico, who played Paulie Walnuts on the HBO hit show.

Arturo made his way to the ring with Ward, Chuck Zito, Lynch, Mikey Red, Joe Souza, Joey Perrenod, and McGirt. Strength trainer Teddy Cruz carried Arturo's WBC belt into the ring.

Arturo opened the fight by working his jab. He threw and landed several right uppercuts in the opening minute. Gatti finished the round with a flurry of combinations. Stephan Larouche advised Dorin to bring a right hand over Arturo's jab. McGirt told Arturo to stay loose and find a rhythm. Buddy intuitively cautioned Gatti to watch the right hand over his jab. McGirt also asked Arturo to disregard the head and target the body off of his jab.

In the 2nd, Arturo displayed his defensive prowess, as he made Dorin miss dozens of shots. Gatti worked solid blows to the body. Leonard came back with two hooks to the head. With a minute remaining in the round, Dorin threw a hook to the body that crashed into Arturo's right elbow. Gatti immediately looked down at his arm with concern. He later recalled that his elbow locked after getting hit with the blow.

Arturo peppered Dorin to the head with combinations. Leonard kept his guard high and tight to block the shots. Arturo ripped a left hook, like a guided missile, under Dorin's elbow into his liver. Leonard collapsed to his knees in agony. Dorin remained on the canvas, where he was counted out by referee Randy Neumann with 5 seconds left in the 2nd round.

Kathy Duva joined Lynch, McGirt, Micky Ward, Mikey Red,

Chuck Zito, and Joey Perrenod in the ring to celebrate the victory. Arturo looked into the camera and said, *"Vivian, I love you. That was for you."* His ex-fiancée, Vivian Penha, did not attend the fight. Arturo's mother Ida, and his step-father Gerardo, joined the celebration in the ring.

Larry Merchant asked Arturo if he had ever knocked anyone out with a body punch. Arturo replied that he had done so a few times. Gatti added that he had worked extensively on body punching in training, because Dorin held his hands up high, which exposed his body.

Arturo was asked if he felt that he was ready to fight the elite boxers in the division. With Pat Lynch looking over his shoulder, Arturo avowed that he never turned down an opponent. He boasted that he was ready to fight anyone. Gatti added that if he were to face elite opposition, he expected an increase in his paycheck.

CompuBox had Arturo landing 22 of 126 punches to Dorin's 16 of 76. Arturo praised his strength coach, Teddy Cruz, for increasing his speed and power through weight lifting. Gatti felt he was ready for Mayweather.[1068] Arturo felt it was time to test Floyd's chin and heart.[1069] Gatti believed that Mayweather was crazy for stating that Arturo Gatti was a chicken.[1070]

Dorin, who suffered his first defeat as a pro, admitted that the hook he was hit with was very good. It was the first time in his career that he went down from a body punch.[1071] Ringside physician, Dr. Kenneth Remsen, speculated that Dorin might have suffered a broken rib from the knockout punch. Dr. Remsen added that Dorin's diaphragm spasmed and he was having trouble breathing.[1072] Dorin was taken to the Atlantic City Medical Center for evaluation.

Dorin was headed to the hospital, but Arturo happily was not. *"I was determined not to go to the hospital this time. I even brought a [designer] suit here with me, so I could wear it to the post-fight press conference. I can't remember the last time I was able to be at one of those. I hear all that warrior stuff a lot. It's flattering, but I also want to be recognized as one of the best 140-pound fighters in the world."*[1073]

Arturo was able to fully enjoy the post-fight press conference and after-party, a rarity for him. Arturo quickly shed his jacket and tie for a more comfortable maroon-and-gray sweat suit with "Team Gatti" emblazoned on the back. He enjoyed the time conversing with his many fans and signing autographs before retiring to his Caesars Palace suite.

Arturo's team was now setting their sights on either Floyd Mayweather Jr., Kostya Tszyu, or Paul Spadafora. Mayweather was now the #1 contender for Gatti's belt. When Arturo was asked who he wanted to fight next his reply was, *"Mayweather, of course."*[1074] Ken Condon wanted Gatti's next fight to take place in Atlantic City, and he was willing to do whatever was necessary to make that happen. Condon felt that Arturo belonged in Atlantic City.[1075]

Gatti's newfound boxing style amazed both fans and reporters alike. Jerry Izenberg, of the *Star Ledger*, facetiously asked who had kidnapped the brawling Arturo Gatti and replaced him with the boxer.[1076] The day after the bout, rumors started swirling regarding who would become Arturo's next opponent. Spadafora's legal troubles, the fact that many boxing sages believed that Spadafora lost his fight against Dorin, coupled with the fact that his quick boxing style might present problems for Arturo, put him at the bottom of the list. Jesse James Leija's decision victory over Bojado made him the front-runner. Leija was considered a much easier opponent than Mayweather. A bout against Leija would give Gatti a chance at another relatively safe payday before the Mayweather showdown. Still, Leija was a former world champion, with victories over Azumah Nelson, Ivan Robinson, and Micky Ward.

Chapter 23
Battling Depression & Leija

In August 2004, Arturo had surgery on his nose. He hoped to be healed up and ready to start preparations for his next title defense by mid-November. Arturo was a champion again. But after the bright lights dimmed, and the crowds stopped cheering, the emptiness returned. One night, Arturo stopped by Mario Costa's lounge. He had a look of pure desperation and he appeared to be under the influence. Arturo confided in Mario that he did not want to live anymore.

Was it losing Vivian, or were the pressures of training and not letting his friends and fans down becoming too much to bear? To make matters worse, Arturo continued his obsession with all-night parties and fast women. Gatti was also upset about his purses. He felt that he was being undersold, compared to other top boxing stars. Also, Arturo, like Ward, was suffering from vision problems. He was forced to deal with daily aches and pains from all the trauma and operations his body had endured.

Costa talked Arturo into getting professional help, but Mario couldn't help but wonder why Arturo hadn't gone to Lynch with his feelings. Typically, it was when Arturo was using drugs that he spoke of his depression. Costa recalled a conversation with Arturo. *"Arthur wasn't happy. He would always tell me to hug him, give him a hug. 'Nobody loves me.'"*[1077]

Costa reluctantly agreed to go speak to Lynch about Arturo's depression as long as Arturo agreed to seek help. Costa buried his pride and went to Lynch's office in Secaucus, NJ, to plead for Gatti's health. When Costa recommended professional help, he alleged that Lynch quickly brushed the thought aside. Lynch allegedly told Costa not to worry, that Arturo would be himself in a few days. Lynch added that Arturo was just having women troubles. Costa was unable to hold back his anger. He shouted profanities as he stormed out of Lynch's ticket agency.

Arturo's depression may have been brought on by Chronic Traumatic Encephalopathy, or CTE. The condition gets progressively worse over time, and can lead to mental and physical disabilities. Researchers have found a link between CTE and blows to the head. Those at highest risk to contract CTE include boxers, football players, hockey players, and combat veterans due to their proximity to loud explosive devices that can jar the brain.

Symptoms of CTE include depression, paranoia, aggression, apathy, irritability, agitation, impulsiveness, poor concentration, memory problems, confusion, as well as other symptoms. Avoiding alcohol and drugs is part of the recommended treatment. The only irrefutable way to diagnose the illness is to examine the patient's brain after death. It was clear in 2004, and possibly years earlier, that Arturo was suffering from some type of brain trauma or mental health issue.

Traumatic Brain Injury, or TBI, is the medical term for when the brain is injured by force, such as a direct hit to the head. TBI can lead to many problems with thinking, memory, and reasoning. Sight, hearing, touch, and taste can be affected, as well as the ability to communicate, express or understand. TBI can cause depression, drastic mood swings, irritability, anger, paranoia, confusion, frustration, apathy, anxiety, aggression, disinhibition, emotional outbursts, and social inappropriateness. Another health issue that can stem from TBI is insomnia. TBI also triggers inappropriate sexual activity and drug and alcohol abuse. TBI patients can be helped with psychotherapy and medication. Concussion is the most minor and common type of TBI. The four most prevalent types of diseases associated with TBI are Alzheimer's, Parkinson's, Post-traumatic Dementia, and Dementia Pugilistica.

Arturo was exhibiting some of these symptoms. Many of those close to Arturo thought these symptoms were brought on solely by drug and alcohol abuse and his possessiveness of women, rather than being the possible by-product of brain trauma.

Dementia pugilistica primarily affects boxers after their careers have ended. Symptoms usually begin 6 to 40 years after the start of a boxing career, which includes amateur bouts. On average, symptoms begin after 16 years. There are those who show signs of the disease while they are still actively engaged in their boxing career. A trained neuropsychologist can assess a patient's need for rehabilitation. Rehabilitation is critical in the treatment and recovery from TBI. The number one way to avoid TBI is by avoiding trauma to the head, which obviously is unavoidable in boxing.

A major symptom of TBI is depression. Depression can be more than just feeling sad. It can lead to difficulty sleeping, poor concentration, feelings of guilt or worthlessness, and suicidal thoughts. Some experience these symptoms right after the head trauma, while for others it can take years. Some signs of depression include losing interest in family and friends and increased usage of alcohol and drugs.

Some drug and alcohol users utilize the substances to reduce feelings of depression. Although initially they may feel euphoria, the high is usually followed by a crash. The crash includes anxiety, depression, and a magnified feeling of suicidal thoughts, especially in those who already had these feelings. Long term substance abuse among those with suicidal thoughts is more likely to lead to an actual suicide attempt.

Substance abusers are more likely to commit suicide out of impulsive anger and feelings of abandonment or isolation rather than from hopelessness. Most suicides, over 90%, occur with individuals who were not treated for their depression.

Professional contact sports, such as football, ice hockey, boxing, and even soccer can lead to acquired brain disease due to repeated hits to the head, which contributes to depression and suicide. Football players Junior Seau, Frank Gifford, Ken Stabler, Kenny McKinley, Ray Easterling, and Dave Duerson are some of the bigger names who have suffered from depression and insomnia from dementia. Over 1,500 former NFL players sued the NFL because they alleged that the league ignored evidence that repeated blows to the head triggered chronic traumatic encephalopathy, or CTE.

The severity of brain pathology in boxers is correlated over a lifetime. Unlike a single blow or knockout, CTE is the result of repeated milder head trauma. Muhammad Ali is the most famous example of a boxer who most likely acquired Parkinson's disease as a result of repeated brain trauma over the course of a lengthy career. Countless others have suffered from Pugilistica Dementia, otherwise known as "Punch Drunkenness."

Some studies have revealed that athletes, such as boxers and football players, who take hits to the front of their heads, are more likely to experience depression and suicidal thoughts earlier in their lives. It is believed that trauma to the front part of the brain can affect mood and impulsiveness.

Athletes who committed suicide included Rick Rypien and Derek Boogaard of the NHL, and football players Junior Seau, Jovan Belcher, Andre Waters, and Kenny McKinley. Boxers who committed suicide included Freddie Mills, Billy Papke, Randy Turpin, Alexis Arguello, Gabriel Hernandez, Edwin Valero, and Kid McCoy.

Athletes, especially boxers, because of their tough-guy personas, historically have been expected to shrug off personal and medical issues such as depression, for fear it could be perceived as a weakness, which could be exploited by their opponents in the form of pre-fight hype and ridicule.

Boxers are conditioned, from the day they enter the gym, to absorb pain and discomfort without complaining. Amateur boxers who complain of headaches or hand pain often are labeled as "weak." Boxers that "forget" their mouthpieces when going to the gym are looked down upon as too scared to spar. Most boxers are conditioned from the day they have their first amateur fight to say they are "okay" when asked how they are feeling by their coach, the referee, or the ringside doctor. Answering any other way could cause the bout to be stopped, and word would quickly spread that the boxer "quit." This gym-and-locker-room culture causes boxers to refuse or deny seeking help when they feel depression or anxiety as it would be perceived as being a weakness. This would lead an athlete to be reluctant to confide in their coach or manager about issues that are affecting them, to avoid the negative consequences and stigmatization that comes along with it. A boxer with a broken hand or a broken jaw is given medical attention and rehabilitation. How many times do we hear of active boxers who are treated for mental illnesses, such as depression? It's extremely rare.

Coaches and trainers are on the front line, and would be the first to notice the signs of mental illness or brain injuries. The problem with professional trainers is they are employed by the boxer. If the trainer does or says anything that might affect the fighter's earning potential, the trainer would risk being released. The manager also is in a position where his investment would suffer if he exposed any potential emotional or mental illness regarding his boxer.

Professional boxers normally are under an enormous amount of stress. Be it a tough opponent, weight loss issues, or minor injuries, the pressure is on, not only to win but to look good doing so. The fact that they are facing increasingly tougher opposition as they rise up the rankings is also a source of continued stress. These issues, coupled with constant head trauma in training and during fights, can easily lead to mental or physical injuries and emotional breakdowns. When a boxer's head is struck, the brain collides with the skull causing brain tissue bruising and tearing of blood vessels. The trauma may also stretch or injure the nerve cells that link the brain together. Boxers are expected to be gladiator type warriors. They are expected to be tough, impenetrable, and resilient.

Some athletes will mask their illness by indulging in drugs or alcohol, or engaging in gambling activities. Domestic issues, such as abuse or promiscuous behavior, may also be used in an attempt to satisfy the emptiness they are feeling.

High paid athletes aren't expected to have problems or personal issues. Their six- or seven-figure paydays are expected to offset any personal problems. But as we see all too often with celebrities, they usually deal with more pressure than the average person. A successful boxer, who is making good money, cannot normally confide in other boxers in the gym, as again, opening up to those around them would be perceived as a sign of weakness.

Brain injuries that cause CTE or TBI can go undetected even with today's modern brain scanning technology. Paranoia has been linked to a chemical imbalance in the brain. It can be caused by stress, heredity, a traumatic life event, or a brain injury. Paranoia can also be caused by drug abuse, especially cocaine.

Joe Gatti thought Arturo's paranoia was brought on by cocaine. Paranoia leads to feelings of distrust, persecution, or suspicion. Paranoia is a type of delusion in which a person feels as though they are being singled out in a negative way.

Losing a loved one, especially separation from a parent, can also lead to short- or long-term psychological trauma. Even though a brain injury can silently and invisibly build over time, progressive brain deterioration usually exposes itself in a sudden, rapid fashion. Symptoms can include a sudden loss of memory, tremors, or other physical issues.

Arturo wasn't the first boxer to turn to drugs and alcohol to combat his mental and physical issues. Joe Louis suffered from paranoia schizophrenia. At the time, many felt the disease was triggered by cocaine abuse. Now it is apparent that head trauma was most likely responsible. It is unknown why some boxers, such as Jake LaMotta, Tony Zale, and Rocky Graziano, known for taking severe punishment, avoided brain disorders, while others who received much less damage fell victim to such disorders.

Some famous boxers who dealt with deterioration from brain disorders included Emile Griffith, Jimmy Ellis, Jimmy Young, Floyd Patterson, Bobby Chacon, Wilfredo Benitez, Jerry Quarry, Mike Quarry, Willie Pep, Meldrick Taylor, Donald Curry, Billy Conn, "Sugar" Ray Robinson, Joe Frazier, Freddie Roach, and most famously Muhammad Ali.

There are several famous boxers who have stepped forward in

recent years to speak about their depression and drug addiction issues. Ricky Hatton battled alcohol abuse, depression, and suicidal tendencies for years. He finally received counseling for his issues. Hatton felt that it was difficult for him to seek help because he was a world champion boxer and a macho man by nature.[1078]

Oscar De La Hoya had considered taking his own life. He also battled cocaine and alcohol abuse. De La Hoya recalled that using drugs and alcohol took him to a place where he felt safe and where nobody could say anything to him. It took him to a place where he could reach out and touch his mother, who passed away when he was young.[1079] Did Arturo feel the same way about reaching out to his father? De La Hoya admitted that he didn't have the courage to commit suicide. Many around Arturo felt that he would never take the "easy way out," but most who actually contemplate suicide feel that it takes courage to go through with the act.

De La Hoya felt that he had been unfaithful to his wife because he was filling the void of maybe not feeling loved to a certain point. It was filling the void of not feeling safe.[1080] De La Hoya and Gatti may have both used sex to fill the void of a deceased parent's love, attention, and approval, all things that they craved.

De La Hoya, like Hatton, received treatment for his issues. He felt that he needed treatment to keep his demons in check. De La Hoya called his battle with addiction the biggest fight of his life. He confessed that it would be easier to fight Manny Pacquiao, Floyd Mayweather, and Fernando Vargas all at once.[1081]

The euphoria of victory is a feeling that many athletes try to recapture after the event has ended. Sugar Ray Leonard admitted that nothing could satisfy him outside the ring. Nothing could compare with becoming a world champion, having your hand raised in that moment of glory, with thousands of people cheering you on.[1082] Leonard recalled how much safer and calmer he felt making a comeback in the ring after retiring. How it was easier for him to control his life and addictions while training for a fight. Leonard cautioned that an athlete must accept the fact that nothing in retirement will give him the glory or satisfaction that he receives while competing.[1083]

Arturo had been in a structured boxing environment since the age of 7. Bill Cole, a sports psychologist, felt that an athlete's "tunnel vision and regimented life" is part of the reason why top-level sportsmen and women struggle more with retirement than those in other walks of life. Cole believed that this compartmentalized existence, as much as it served athletes in their rise and sustenance as a prolific athlete, can feel stifling, yet secure, and to give it up suddenly can make an athlete feel quite lost. Cole felt that athletes suffer from depression after retiring from sports because they aren't sure where to apply that focus.[1084]

Mike Tyson recalled how he dealt with his issues. Even though he possessed incredible discipline when it came to boxing, he didn't have the tools to stop his slide into addiction. Tyson felt that it was extremely difficult to develop a sober and moral consciousness without a good support system. When he was in the prime of his career, Tyson admitted that he had a lousy support system. He was surrounded by greedy vultures who were putting their hands in his pockets, using his status for their own self-aggrandizement.[1085] Arturo had been dealing with many, if not all of the issues mentioned above. These issues were now magnified by Arturo losing his fiancé Vivian.

On September 9, 2004, Muhammad Ali went before the United States Congress and asked that they create a U.S. Boxing Commission to oversee the sport. Ali felt that boxers needed protection from promoters who exploited and injured them. Ali's testimony was read by his wife Lonnie, as he was unable to speak clearly due to his Parkinson's disease. Ali believed that reform measures were unlikely to succeed unless a U.S. Boxing Commission was created with authority to oversee the sport. Ali added that boxing still attracted a disproportionate number of unsavory elements that preyed upon the hopes and dreams of young athletes.[1086]

Ali had been grossly exploited. He filed a lawsuit against Don King for $1.2 million that was owed him for his match against Larry Holmes. King allegedly persuaded Ali to accept $50,000 in cash with the stipulation that he drop his lawsuit.[1087]

On September 10, the *Boston Globe* announced that Micky Ward would undergo surgery on both of his eyes, to try and correct blurred peripheral vision and headaches that he suffered during his final bout with Arturo. On September 17, Ward had the surgery.

On September 18, Arturo attended the Hopkins-De La Hoya match in Las Vegas. He ran into *N.Y. Daily News* reporter Tim Smith. After De La Hoya was knocked out from a hook to the body, Smith asked Gatti how he got up from Ward's body shot. Arturo answered with a laugh, *"Because I'm crazy."*[1088]

On October 18, Arturo's nieces spoke publicly about the abuse they suffered at the hands of their father, Davey Hilton Jr. Besides allegedly beating his wife, Anna-Maria, and his children, Anne-Marie and Jeannie, Hilton committed other atrocious crimes on the young girls. Jeannie confessed that she lost her childhood when she was penetrated by her father. She felt that she died at that point.[1089] The daughters vividly described how their father would switch between beating them and forcing them to perform oral and vaginal intercourse. Anne-Marie added that her father was a piece of human trash, a criminal of the worst kind.[1090]

On October 20, Main Events announced that Jesse James Leija had signed an agreement to fight Arturo on January 29, in Atlantic City.

Main Events announced a deal with ESPN that would have them showcasing monthly shows for a year on the network. Main Events, who at one time had as many stars as any major boxing promotional company, now had only three major draws; Gatti, Fernando Vargas, and Juan Diaz.

On October 27, Arturo traveled to Il Cortile restaurant in Little Italy for the 15th annual Benefit of the Retired Boxers Foundation, Inc. The non-profit organization helped retired boxers adjust to life outside of the ring. Others attending the event included Paul Malignaggi, Vito Antoufermo, Vinnie Maddalone, and HBO's Chuck Zito.

On November 11, Bernard Fernandez interviewed Arturo and asked about Davey Hilton. Arturo avoided any negative comments. He stated, *"I watched Davey with respect during my ascent. He was Davey Hilton! He was THE boxer! I trained with him, I put the gloves on with him. His father led me for a time."* Hilton Sr. schooled Joe and Arturo on proper dieting and weight loss techniques. Joe idolized Davey Hilton Jr. and ran the streets with him as a kid. They would get into fist fights with 8, 9, or 10 boys at a time. It didn't matter if knives or guns were pulled; Joe and Davey feared no one. *The Ring* magazine's December ratings had Arturo ranked #1 behind Kostya Tszyu at 140-pounds.

On January 21, it was announced that Arturo's cutman, Joe Souza, would be working Leija's corner in the Gatti bout. Souza, who along with Leija was from San Antonio, had been working with Jesse since he was a child. Souza had actually trained Leija's father. He did not feel comfortable abandoning Jesse. Arturo publicly stated that he fully understood Souza's decision. Gatti added that he wouldn't need a cutman because he planned on boxing.[1091] Privately, Arturo was angry and felt betrayed. North Jersey's Danny Milano took over the cutman duties for Gatti. Leija felt the change was a psychological advantage for him.[1092]

On January 22 at the American Airlines Arena in Miami, Florida, Floyd Mayweather defeated Henry Bruseles by 8th round TKO. The Mayweather-Bruseles fight drew only 4,000 fans. This lack of fan support would give Main Events and Gatti leverage at the negotiation table when it came time for their bout. Arturo was fully aware of the fact that there would be no Mayweather bout if he did not defeat Leija. Leija was fully aware that he was selected because Main Events expected Arturo to defeat him. Arturo would enjoy almost the same height and reach advantage over Jesse that he had against Dorin.

Lester Bedford, Leija's manager, spoke at the press conference. He reminded reporters that his fighter fought Shane Mosley, Kostya Tszyu, and Oscar De La Hoya. He also reminded those in attendance that Leija defeated Ivan Robinson and Micky Ward. The Golden Boy-promoted Leija also defeated the great Azumah Nelson twice. Arturo appeared bothered by Bedford's rantings and stated, *"Cut it off. I've got places to go."*[1093]

Bedford felt that Arturo was upset because he was struggling to make the contracted weight. Leija's trainer, Ronnie Shields, who left Gatti after working with him for a few fights, thought that Arturo was looking past this bout. He also felt that Arturo didn't want this fight, but instead wanted to go straight to a bout against Mayweather. What Shields did not speak of was the fact that Leija had injured his ribs in sparring and had not sparred in his final four weeks of camp.

HBO's Kery Davis revealed that Leija had been asking for a Gatti fight for six years. Leija recalled it was longer than that. Bedford believed that Gatti's second championship run was orchestrated by Main Events and HBO. He felt Arturo had been given carefully selected opponents who were older and fighting above their prime weight classes. Bedford felt that Gatti had been fed soft opponents, while Leija had to beat seven top contenders to get a chance to fight for a title.[1094]

Arturo wasn't taking the 38-year-old Leija lightly. He knew that Jesse had a reputation for upsetting opponents who didn't take him seriously.[1095] Arturo talked of changing his training habits. He called himself his own worst enemy. He admitted that he played around too much. He blamed his wild lifestyle for forcing him to dig his way out of major holes to win fights.[1096] Arturo was looking forward to fighting Mayweather if he could get past Leija.

Arturo was taking home $2 million for the fight, while Leija was receiving a career high $700,000. On January 28, Leija got his last pre-fight jabs in. He stated that Gatti's strengths were also his weaknesses. Arturo's warrior mentality, the way he'll let you hit him so he can hit you, could work against him.[1097] Pat Lynch said Team Gatti was not looking past the dangerous veteran Leija.[1098] Arturo spoke of his love of fighting in Atlantic City, where he won his last four bouts. *"I love it here. If I could fight here for the rest of my life, I would."*[1099]

The Gatti-Leija fight on January 29, 2005 was a sellout. Arturo was impressed with his fan support. He felt that his fans did not come out solely to root for him. The fans also knew that they would get their money's worth at a Gatti fight. Arturo also was aware that his matches brought a windfall for all of Atlantic City's casinos and their employees. Gatti felt he was more of an entertainer than a boxer. He believed that Leija would go for broke because he was desperate and knew that a loss probably would end his career. Arturo felt that a desperate Leija would benefit him during the fight.[1100]

At the post weigh-in news conference, Arturo angrily announced that Joe Souza would never work his corner again. He would later recant his statement and say, *"Maybe."* Probably the best move for Souza would have been to sit the fight out. This would not have angered anyone, nor would it have hurt his future earnings potential as a cutman.

On the day of the fight, Arturo was told that Leija planned on being aggressive. Gatti felt that an aggressive Leija would play right into his strength, which was his power. Leija revealed that his game plan was to outwork Arturo while protecting himself from Gatti's power shots.[1101]

Arturo had a 2½-inch height advantage over the 5'5" Leija. Both fighters weighed in at 140-pounds. 12,599 fans packed Boardwalk Hall to see the bout. Arturo was led to the ring by the same team, minus Joey Perrenod. Gatti displayed his "Warrior" abdominal tattoo for the first time.

Arturo appeared to have the edge after the 1st round, punctuated by two right uppercuts. McGirt asked Arturo to step to his right. He also asked Gatti to feint his jab before actually throwing the punch, to throw Leija's timing off. Shields advised Leija to counter Gatti's uppercut with an uppercut of his own.

Arturo carried the 2nd round by boxing. He landed several hard rights. Leija sprinkled in a few overhand rights. McGirt asked for the double jab and more body shots. Shields asked Leija for more body punches and head movement.

Both boxers traded several hard right hands in the 3rd. Arturo jabbed and used his reach to dominate the second half of the round. McGirt advised Arturo to time Leija's right to the body with a counter hook. Shields asked Jesse to step around, feint, throw a flurry and step around again. Leija had an exhausted look that appeared to say, *"Are you talking to me?"*

Arturo easily took the 4th. Leija was attempting "Hail Mary" overhand rights. After the round, McGirt advised Arturo to watch Leija's looping right hands. McGirt asked Arturo to back Leija up. Shields told Leija that he needed to get close and hurt Arturo.

Gatti threw several jabs to start the 5th. As Leija was slipping to his right to avoid a jab, Arturo slammed a straight right against Jesse's exposed jaw, sending him sprawling to the canvas. The crowd roared with approval. Jim Lampley exclaimed, *"What a right hand!"* Leija barely beat the count, rising at the count of nine. Gatti came bombing in to finish the fight. Arturo connected with a head jarring left hook. Gatti followed with several chopping rights that sent Leija stumbling into the ropes. Arturo connected with a left hook high on top of Leija's head that dropped Jesse again. Leija was counted out as his left knee remained on the canvas.

Lynch, Zito, McGirt, Kathy Duva, Micky Ward, and Mikey Red all jumped into the ring. Ida Gatti stepped up onto the ring apron to hug her son. Arturo landed 128 of 322 punches to Leija's 56 of 215. Gatti stated that he and McGirt had worked hard on the jab in Vero Beach.

Arturo added, *"We spent a lot of time in training camp working on the left. I knew I needed my jab to win. Once I started landing the right hand, I knew that was it.*[1102] *I won the fight and didn't have to go to the hospital. That's a big plus for me.*[1103] *I expected the right hand to be the difference. I want to fight [Mayweather] and I hope he solves his legal problems. But we're not going to wait around forever, because I want to fight. But I want to fight him because he is the best pound-for-pound fighter in the world."*[1104]

Arturo landed an amazing average of 45 jabs per round. Leija tried to get him to brawl, but Gatti didn't take the bait.[1105] For the second straight fight, Arturo was not headed to the hospital. Instead, once again, it was his opponent who was taken to the emergency room.

Leija was transported to the hospital to be evaluated for a rib and elbow injury.

Mikey Red recalled Gatti's Atlantic City magic. *"Arturo was contagious at Atlantic City. He surrounded himself with people from Jersey City. Arturo had a different fan base from his brother Joe. Arturo's fights were events, get-togethers. The after-parties were just as fun as the fights. Arturo would hang out after the fight, win, lose, or draw. He was the peoples' champ. The parties would last late into the night because Arturo would arrive around 1 or 2 a.m., [usually] after he got back from the emergency room. People would ask why they were hanging out until 5 or 6 in the morning and Arturo's friends would reply, 'Arturo doesn't get back until 2:30 in the morning. The party doesn't start until 3.'"*[1106]

All the rumors were pointing to a Gatti-Mayweather showdown on June 11, but there were no guarantees. Arturo went out of his way to let the press know who the draw was. *"[Mayweather's] not the one that's going to sell the tickets.*[1107] *I don't understand why he didn't show up to court. That's the most important thing, to take care of legal problems before getting in the ring."*[1108]

The legal troubles Arturo was referring to stemmed from Mayweather failing to appear for a trial in which he was charged with assaulting a bouncer at a bar. The failure to appear led to an arrest warrant being issued. Mayweather also was facing a hearing in Las Vegas in July for a domestic violence complaint. Main Events and Lynch were concerned that if Mayweather was to be sentenced to jail time for any of his issues, it might be the death-blow to the multimillion-dollar bout. Carl Moretti reiterated that Mayweather needed to clear up his legal issues if the pay-per-view date was to be secured.[1109]

Moretti warned that if Mayweather's troubles were not corrected, Main Events would seek another opponent. Although Moretti acted nonchalantly publicly, inside, the butterflies were swirling. A Mayweather fight would bring in millions for Main Events. Everyone on Team Gatti believed that this would be the biggest, and maybe last, mega-fight of Arturo's career. Some of Arturo's inner circle were so impressed with his victory over Leija that they even had the cockiness to talk beyond a fight with Mayweather, mentioning potential mega-fights against Kostya Tszyu and Miguel Cotto.

Boxing writer Eric Raskin questioned the Mayweather match for Arturo. He felt that Gatti was assured to be inducted into boxing's

Hall of Fame without a Mayweather win. Raskin believed that Arturo felt that he needed the Mayweather bout to be worthy of the Hall. Raskin questioned the match, not from a sporting standpoint, but from a business standpoint.[1110] Raskin added that Arturo could easily fight less risky foes at $2 million a pop. If Gatti were to fight two or three times a year for two or three years he could pocket $10 to $12 million dollars. That was, of course, as long as he continued to pack Boardwalk Hall.

Arturo wanted the bout because he wanted to fight the best pound-for-pound fighter in the sport. He felt he had the heart, will, and desire to win the bout.[1111] But did he have the skills? There were not many who believed he did. It was both his management and promotional teams' responsibility to make the best financial decisions for Arturo, while considering his physical well-being. Main Events enjoyed great financial success in Arturo's non-title bouts. Now that Gatti was a champion, the financial gain would be even more lucrative.

Carl Moretti revealed that Main Events had an alternative should Mayweather be unavailable. Mexican Jose Luis Castillo was being considered as an option.[1112]

Chapter 24
Buildup to a Superfight

On February 7, 2005, Floyd Mayweather Jr. pleaded no-contest to the charge of misdemeanor assault and battery in connection with a barroom fight that left a bouncer injured. Mayweather allegedly kicked the bouncer after the bar employee had been knocked down with a bottle by another person. Mayweather was fined and ordered to perform community service, but he received no jail time. The bouncer sued Mayweather and an out-of-court settlement was reached. The conclusion of the court case paved the way for the Gatti-Mayweather bout. Gatti's camp was hopeful that Mayweather's personal distractions would spill over into his ring performance.

On February 14, Valentine's Day, Vikki Gatti gave birth to her second child, Gianni, who was named after Giovanni Versace. Joe explained why he and Vikki named their children after the fashion designer. *"He was such a talented and vibrant man. Full of life and he loved his family. We were addicted to all his designs. His name was so powerful and represented so many beautiful things. There was no question when my wife got pregnant, she would name our first child Versace and our second Gianni. Unfortunately, we never got to meet him."*[1113]

On March 4, it was reported by Main Events that the Gatti-Mayweather bout appeared to be off again. Arturo planned on defending his WBC super lightweight title on June 11 against a different opponent. Main Events was advised by Top Rank, Mayweather's promoter, that Floyd had failed to sign the contract by the 5 p.m. deadline. Mayweather blamed Gatti for the delay and promised to make him pay, once he got Arturo into the ring.

Arturo released a statement upon hearing the news. *"I kept waiting and waiting and extending the deadline, but it still never came. I don't have time [to keep waiting]. He screwed this fight up. Maybe after June 11 he'll have [himself] together and we can try and sit down again, because I want this fight. But I'll find someone else for June 11. It's [Mayweather's] fault the fight isn't happening. He's killed the whole promotion."*[1114]

The leading contenders being mentioned to replace Mayweather were England's Junior Witter, 32-1-2 (19 KOs) and Puerto Rico's Miguel Cotto 23-0 (19 KOs). Top Rank was not interested in a Gatti match for Cotto. They stated that they wanted Cotto to add a few more fights before considering a Gatti match, most likely because they understood that Cotto needed to build his resume and name recognition before a fight with Gatti would make financial sense.

On March 7, Main Events officially cancelled the Gatti-Mayweather bout. WBC president Jose Sulaiman stepped in and threatened to put the Gatti-Mayweather bout out to a purse bid. This forced Main Events and Top Rank to either strike a deal or possibly lose the promotional rights to the fight.

On March 10, it was announced that the Mayweather-Gatti match was on again for June 25. Arturo was relieved. Gatti was anxious to get back into the gym. He promised to punish Mayweather.[1115] The deal was ironed out by representatives of Gatti, Mayweather, Ken Condon of Bally's, HBO, and the N.J. State Athletic Control Board.

Arturo went into training immediately in Vero Beach. He loved the area so much, he planned on building a home in nearby Jupiter, Florida. At the start of camp Arturo weighed 168-pounds. Mayweather started his camp weighing 145.

The HBO pay-per-view bout would take place at Boardwalk Hall in Atlantic City. Kathy Duva acknowledged that all the parties involved with making the fight happen were very cooperative in rearranging the date and site, especially Bally's and Ken Condon.[1116] Duva wanted to give Arturo some extra time to prepare. She also wanted to assure that the fight would take place in Atlantic City. Arturo would earn $3.5 million, while Mayweather would earn $3.15 million.

Kathy Duva talked to Gatti before making the match, to assure that he wanted the Mayweather bout. She told him bluntly that he could continue to sell out Boardwalk Hall against anyone, or he could attempt to make boxing history by beating Mayweather. Duva knew what Arturo's answer would be.

Nearly every boxing expert was calling the fight a mismatch. Lou DiBella felt that Arturo had no chance of defeating Mayweather. Duva possibly saw the fight as an opportunity to make one last big payday with her aging meal ticket.

Mayweather was upset with his purse. He partly blamed his promoter Top Rank and its president, Bob Arum. Mayweather felt it was Arum's fault that he was getting paid less than Gatti.[1117] Arum replied to Mayweather's statement by explaining that in order to become a pay-per-view attraction a fighter needs to have a core audience and expand on it first. Arum added that it was much more difficult to find a core audience for African-American fighters than it was for Hispanic fighters.[1118]

On March 23, Floyd and Arturo were scheduled to attend a press conference at the Copacabana in New York City to promote their upcoming match. Gatti was a no-show. Mayweather repeatedly stated that Arturo had been ducking him ever since he was announced as the #1 contender to Arturo's title. Floyd had vacated his lightweight title and moved up to junior welterweight in December 2003. Mayweather was angry that Arturo frequently mentioned Floyd's legal problems during contract negotiations. Floyd picked up Arturo's name card and started smacking it in front of the press.

Mayweather believed that Arturo tried to use Floyd's legal troubles to avoid a fight with him. Floyd predicted that he might knock Arturo out in 3 rounds. Mayweather felt that he was both faster and stronger than Gatti. Floyd announced that there were already six ways to defeat Arturo, and he would show a seventh way on June 25. Mayweather named a heavybag in his gym Arturo Gatti because he felt that Gatti was like a heavybag that stood still and received punishment.[1119] Floyd added that he was an A-plus fighter while Arturo was a C-minus fighter.[1120] Mayweather felt that Arturo was afraid of him.

Arturo, who now lived in Hoboken, didn't attend the press conference because he purportedly had an upset stomach and a 102-degree fever, possibly from the flu. Gatti said he sought medical treatment for his illness. Mayweather believed that Gatti was suffering from *"Floyd-itis."*[1121] Gatti's team told the media that Arturo would be well enough to give his own press conference the following day.

Mayweather was installed as a 3-1 favorite when the fight was announced. Bob Arum felt that the fight would be competitive. He may not have actually believed that, but he needed to sell the show.[1122] Floyd's uncle, Roger, didn't agree with Arum's assessment, and he let it be known for 20 minutes at the press conference. He believed that his nephew was going to give Arturo an *"ultimate, deluxe whupping."*[1123]

The next day, March 24, as Mayweather was flying back to Las Vegas, Arturo held his own press conference. Arturo held the presser at Gallagher's steakhouse in New York. Gatti praised Mayweather for being a great fighter.[1124] Arturo was asked about Mayweather's behavior the day prior. Gatti was glad he wasn't there because he might have done and said some things that were out of character for him. Arturo commented that big mouths must run in the Mayweather family; big mouths and glass jaws. Gatti called Floyd classless. Arturo wasn't bothered by Mayweather's disrespect. He promised to earn Floyd's respect on June 25.[1125] Gatti did not take any of Mayweather's trash talking personally. Arturo added that he would punish Mayweather for beating up women.[1126]

Larry Hazzard compared the Gatti-Mayweather buildup to that of Tyson-Spinks in 1988. Bally's Ken Condon was thrilled that the mega-fight was coming to Atlantic City. Condon felt that the fight would draw many non-boxing fans and celebrities into town, which would help Atlantic City's image.[1127]

With Arturo's drawing-power, he could have fought anybody for $1 million, but he had been hounding Main Events for a year to get him a mega-fight against either Kostya Tszyu or Mayweather. Buddy McGirt felt that although Gatti could sell out arenas fighting anyone, he wanted more. Arturo believed that in order to be the best he had to beat the best. Gatti had asked McGirt who he felt was the best fighter out there to fight. When McGirt stated Mayweather, Arturo said, *"Give me him."*[1128]

Arturo was featured in *The Ring* magazine's "All-Star Report Card." He was given an A-minus for Talent, B-plus for achievements, A-plus for marketability, A-plus for his support system, and A-minus for his growth potential.

On the weekend of April 9, tickets went on sale for the Mayweather-Gatti match. Within thirty hours, every ticket, ranging from $100 to $1,000, had been sold. Mayweather wanted and needed what Arturo possessed; drawing power. Mayweather predicted that after the Gatti fight, any arena that he fought in would sell out.[1129]

A few weeks before departing for training camp, Arturo met Erika Rivera at a New York club. Within weeks, Arturo proposed and Erika accepted. Arturo contracted a small plane to carry the message "Will You Marry Me" across the Hudson River, while he stood with Erika looking out of the picture window of his Hoboken condo. The night before Arturo departed for Vero Beach to begin his training, he went out for one last night of fun with his friends. Arturo and his friends visited a Secaucus, N.J. strip club called AJ's.

Several weeks before the Mayweather match, Arturo had what appeared to be a breakdown in Vero Beach. He told those around him that he wanted to cancel the fight. McGirt felt that Mayweather had gotten into Arturo's head.[1130] The pressure of training and losing weight, the comments about Arturo being a C-level fighter, Mayweather being a top pound-for-pound fighter, and boxing experts commenting that Mayweather would win easily, all led to an avalanche of emotions for Arturo. If that weren't enough, Arturo was being told that some of his own friends were whispering that he was going to be defeated. Of course, these comments made their way back to Arturo. The psychological effects were affecting his training.

John Rivera, Erika's father, became aware of Arturo's fragile mental state in training camp. He tried to discuss the issue with Pat Lynch. Lynch wasn't interested in discussing the subject with Rivera. John went down to Vero Beach to visit with Arturo, to try and cheer him up. Arturo cried hysterically to Rivera. Gatti told Rivera that he wanted to leave camp and cancel the fight. Rivera felt that Arturo was having a nervous breakdown. Arturo was experiencing severe mood swings and frequently missed training sessions.[1131]

Gatti was interviewed by Ted Kemp of *Razor* magazine. Arturo looked into Kemp's eyes and stated, *"When I walk into the ring, I'm ready to die in the ring. I don't care."*[1132] Arturo talked about his excessive partying when he won his first title, and how it was a blessing that he was able to rebound from his hard-living lifestyle.[1133] Arturo spoke of McGirt's influence on his career. Gatti credited McGirt for helping him to relax in the ring and control the pace of the fight by using his talents. He felt that McGirt brought out the best in him.[1134]

Star Ledger reporter Robin Gaby Fisher visited Arturo in his $6,000-a-month rental home in Vero Beach during training. Fisher discovered that Arturo's meals consisted of egg whites and bottles of carrot juice. Arturo also had jars of Gerber's strained-apples and bananas. Of course, even these meals were rationed. Arturo entertained himself by reading the *National Enquirer* or watching the Cosby Show. He spent time talking about the 33-foot Four Winns Vista cabin cruiser boat that he recently had purchased for $200,000. The 2002 model year boat was docked on the Hudson River. Gatti would later trade the boat for diamonds. Arturo also recently helped his mother purchase a home in Montreal.

Not long after arriving in Vero Beach, Arturo started rummaging through boxing magazines looking for pictures of Mayweather. He ripped out the photos of his opponent and plastered them all over his rented house, as well as in McGirt's gym. It was a tradition Arturo started five fights prior, with all of the bouts ending in victory. Arturo put his opponents' photos next to his passport when he traveled, so he didn't lose them. Arturo recalled that it would be embarrassing at the airports when he handed over his ID to security and there were photos of his opponents inside the passport.[1135]

Another way Arturo motivated himself was by looking in the bathroom mirror. He focused on the scars that he permanently wore courtesy of Micky Ward, Ivan Robinson, and Angel Manfredy. Gatti had a digital scale on the floor to regularly check his weight. The photos and the scale reminded him of his two most dangerous opponents, Floyd and food. Arturo took the Mayweather bout because he wanted to be recognized as the best. He felt that being looked at as the best fighter was the only thing missing in his career.[1136]

Arturo's training camp for Mayweather was sealed off from the public. Anytime a stranger walked into the gym, Arturo motioned for McGirt to check them out immediately. Mike Skowronski, who was in camp with Arturo, stated, *"He's always thinking someone's got an angle. Sometimes he's too street smart."*[1137] If McGirt shrugged that he didn't know a person who walked in, Arturo would have the visitor removed. McGirt recalled telling a visitor to go get lunch and come back when Gatti was finished. The visitor asked why he had to leave, noting that he was a neighbor of former New York Jets quarterback, Joe Namath. McGirt looked the man squarely in the eyes and told him that Arturo didn't care if he lived with Joe Namath. He still had to leave.[1138]

Gatti's training day in Vero Beach started at 8:30 a.m., when he spent an hour with McGirt in the gym. Arturo was driven to the gym in his white, leased Cadillac, by his strength trainer Teddy Cruz. Cruz handled Arturo's diet and prepared him for his non-boxing-related workouts. After spending an hour with McGirt, Arturo returned home for a salad, some carrot juice and a nap. Two hours later, Cruz and Gatti began a strength and conditioning routine. Arturo's strength training included the Stairmaster, swimming, the crossover treadmill, push-ups and crunches. For dinner, Arturo enjoyed grilled chicken breast and a salad. After digesting his food, he took a five-mile run. Cruz also handled special duties, such as recovering Arturo's diamond stud earring when it accidentally fell into the bathroom sink drain.

Arturo started his camp at the end of March. His training increased gradually. Cruz was in charge of bringing Arturo's weight down from 165 to the contracted weight of 140. Cruz helped reduce Gatti's weight by reducing his food portions by half. He then removed dressing from Arturo's salads. Gatti wore a rubber, surfing type wet suit, over which he wore spandex shorts and a long sleeve shirt. Arturo consumed approximately fifteen bottles of water a day. Cruz would help Gatti keep his mind off of boxing by watching low budget "B" horror movies with him.

Arturo liked to break up the monotony of training camp. When Gatti sparred, Buddy wanted him to throw fifty jabs a round. Arturo told Buddy that he would make a bet. If he did throw fifty jabs a round, he wanted Mikey Red and Buddy to box. Arturo won the bet. The next day, Arturo told Mikey to bring his sparring equipment to the gym. Arturo, Buddy, and Teddy Cruz were laughing hysterically. Arturo made Mikey box McGirt with the media in the gym. Buddy hit Skowronski with a right hand and Mikey told him, *"That's a little harder than I expected."* Buddy replied, *"Let's put on a show."*[1139]

Gatti revealed that he now knew how to separate the groupies, that started befriending him after he became successful, from his real friends. Arturo believed that his real friends wouldn't be able to sleep the night before his fight, because they knew that he wouldn't be able to sleep. Gatti was aware that many people didn't believe that he could beat Mayweather, but he was confident that his real friends knew he could win.[1140]

Instead of hitting the strip clubs, Arturo now was hitting the golf clubs. After Gatti completed his morning boxing workouts, he occupied his spare time by playing golf at the Sand Ridge Golf Club in Vero Beach. Sitting beside his two world championship belts in his rented home was his white Pig brand golf bag. His brother Fabrizio gave Arturo the bag as a Christmas gift in 2004. The bag had Arturo "Thunder" Gatti embroidered on the front. Also on the bag was an exact replica of Arturo's neck tattoo, a pair of boxing gloves, and the word "Victory."

Arturo explained why he suffered through a three-fight losing streak. *"I was going too crazy between fights. Just having a good time, going wild. Look at the way I fight, I can't be normal."*[1141] Donny Jerie described Arturo's behavior in-between fights. *"We'd be drinking in the car, going 100 miles per hour into New York City. Arturo Gatti knew how to live."*[1142] Carl Moretti commented on

Arturo's legendary party habits by stating that he played as hard as he fought. Moretti felt that Arturo didn't get enough of a release from winning a fight. Gatti would find his release after the fight, with months of drinking and womanizing.[1143]

When Arturo started losing weight, his personality often changed from jovial to cantankerous. Little things would make Arturo's temper flare, such as Mikey Red playfully swinging a golf club in Arturo's rental home. On another occasion, Arturo's younger brother Fabrizio was playing dominoes with his usually happy brother when Fabby discovered that the weight loss had affected Arturo's temper. Arturo started screaming at Fabrizio over a dominoes move that Fabby had made. Fabrizio decided to take a walk to let Arturo cool down.[1144]

When Arturo went out to eat or shop during camp, especially in the final weeks, when the weight was coming off, Teddy Cruz was forced to be a buffer between Arturo and the public. Gatti would be quick to snap if someone approached him the wrong way. This was especially so if Arturo was trying to relax while eating out. Arturo had a special built-in radar system. He knew when someone was going to annoy him by approaching him for a photo or an autograph.

Arturo would tell Cruz to make up a story and Teddy would spring into action. Cruz would fabricate a reason why Arturo was unable to speak or pose for a photo. Arturo usually didn't mind giving autographs or posing for pictures, but sometimes his mood would swing during training camp because of the weight loss. Occasionally, when Arturo was in this type of mood, he would go out with Cruz. Cruz recalled, *"Sometimes there were some moments that it was the wrong time, you know, the right timing for the wrong person to show up. And I would be like, 'Oh man.' I would see it coming too [laughs]. And I would start to laugh. So [Arturo] would laugh. I was kinda like the buffer for him."*[1145]

McGirt had picked up on warning signs to tell Arturo's daily mood even before he entered the gym. When Arturo pulled up to the gym, if his car window was up and the air conditioner was on, he was usually in a good mood. But if the window was down and his arm was hanging out of the window, he was probably not in a good mood. Sleepless nights often produced an open window arrival.

Gatti had a personable side in training camp. Skowronski recalled Arturo giving a delivery man a piece of furniture after the delivery man mentioned how much he admired the piece. Skowronski recalled Arturo immediately calling to donate money when he heard about the Indian Ocean Tsunami in December 2004.

With three weeks to go to fight time, Arturo was struggling to make the contracted weight. After training, Gatti could be seen roaming the aisles of a local supermarket in Vero Beach with Teddy Cruz. Arturo would stop and stare at cookies and other forbidden food. He would inhale the aromas, the only taste of the treats he could afford to take. Gatti would end the torture by heading to the fruit and vegetable section, where he could actually buy something. Arturo grabbed a few green apples, while Cruz picked up fresh corn, orange juice, and a few compact steaks.

Arturo was looking to gain his normal 15 or 20-pounds after the weigh-in, putting him at around 155 or 160 at fight time. Mayweather started his camp at 145 and wasn't expected to be much heavier when the bell rang. Teddy Cruz and McGirt were concentrating on speed. They wanted to make Arturo as fast as possible. By the time the Mayweather fight was made, Arturo, Cruz, and McGirt were like family.

Mayweather wasn't concerned about Arturo gaining weight after the weigh-in. Floyd was sparring against middleweights to get ready for Gatti. Mayweather knew what it was like to struggle to make weight, and he could tell that Arturo was suffering. Floyd felt that Gatti lacked discipline.[1146]

With two weeks remaining until fight time, Arturo and Buddy were busy making last minute preparations at McGirt's Vero Beach gym. McGirt's gym was located on Route 1, in a pair of converted storage units, across the street from dilapidated homes. The only air conditioning the gym received was supplied by whatever breeze was available when the storage units doors were opened. Arturo was so paranoid of potential spies that he preferred the stifling heat of a closed storage unit to that of a breeze from an opened door.

Arturo would step outside of the oven-like storage unit and have conditioning coach Teddy Cruz cool him down by pouring water over his bleached-blonde, curly hair. When Arturo struck the bag, he most likely reminded McGirt of Matthew Hilton from years earlier in Bufano's Gym in Jersey City. With every blow Arturo landed, perspiration sprayed from his sweat drenched head and poured from the edges of his rubber sweat suit, splattering to the ground.

McGirt sat nearby, holding a cup of Dunkin' Donuts coffee, watching, as Dominick Amoroso used to watch him, so many years prior. McGirt shouted out instructions while wiping Arturo's sweat from the floor mat with a towel. McGirt did this to prevent Arturo from slipping on the mat. McGirt, wearing a tank top and flip-flops, was sweating nearly as much as Arturo from the South Florida humidity. Arturo trained early in the day when the temperature was around 75°, well before the temperature reached 88° or higher. When the hour-and-a-half workout concluded, Arturo shook hands with McGirt and headed back to his rental home. McGirt stepped into his air-conditioned black Ford Expedition and lit a full-sized cigar. The Ford was a gift from Arturo to McGirt for helping Gatti to regain the world championship. McGirt's day was far from over; he waited for his next fighter, light heavyweight Antonio Tarver, to arrive.

Arturo spoke of his favorite place to fight. *"Atlantic City has always been a special place to me because of the way people receive me. They are always so nice to me and it's been that way since the beginning. I really enjoy Atlantic City, the whole atmosphere. I honestly don't see myself ever fighting anywhere else again. I know that may hurt some people's feelings, but that's the way it is. Atlantic City has always been good to me. They deserve to see something special and I'm going to try to give it to them Saturday night."*[1147]

McGirt admitted that Arturo did more sparring for this fight than usual, but Buddy made sure Gatti took some time off during camp. McGirt recalled when he first agreed to train Arturo, he had heard rumors that Gatti didn't train hard. Buddy saw immediately that Arturo was a gym rat. Right after they first met, after the De La Hoya loss, McGirt sat Arturo down and gave him a choice. Buddy told Arturo he could either leave the gym after sparring and go play golf or he could leave the gym and go home and ice his face. Arturo chose golf. McGirt advised Gatti that he would have to learn to fight the right way again. By "right way," McGirt meant boxing and head movement instead of brawling.[1148]

Ten days before the fight, a bombshell was dropped at John Lynch's law office. Steve Sandoval, who was friends with both Arturo and McGirt, was threatening to publish a tell-all book. Sandoval was threatening to expose the partying escapades of Gatti. Steve felt slighted by McGirt. He claimed that Buddy had offered him 10% of the trainer earnings if Sandoval could bring Arturo to McGirt. Steve felt that the 6:45 a.m. phone call from McGirt, while Arturo was in his apartment, was the catalyst in bringing McGirt and Gatti together. The manuscript was loaded with dates and names of drugs that Arturo had purchased. The document also included allegations that portrayed McGirt in a negative light.

It was rumored that Lynch may have initially suppressed the threatened publicity with money, but Sandoval denied ever receiving or asking for any money from Lynch. Arturo tried to quell the situation by meeting with Sandoval. After Steve explained that he felt slighted by McGirt and that he was down on his luck and had no money, Arturo wrote Sandoval a check for $800 to help pay his rent. However, before long, Sandoval was threatening to release his information again. This time, Arturo was in no mood to talk. When he returned from Florida, he paid several visits to Sandoval's apartment near Bleeker Street in Jersey City. Joey Perrenod accompanied Arturo on one of the visits. Steve refused to open the door and instead spoke to Arturo from his apartment window. Gatti angrily told Sandoval to come out of the house to settle the issue like men. Sandoval intelligently declined the invitation.

Sandoval said that he waited patiently for five years for some type of compensation for bringing McGirt and Gatti together. Sandoval felt that he was being left out, while McGirt and Gatti were involved in multi-million-dollar fights. Sandoval pointed out that when Arturo and McGirt came together, it opened up more lucrative opportunities for McGirt to train other top fighters, such as Antonio Tarver and Fernando Vargas. Sandoval just wanted the percentage he alleged was promised him by McGirt.

Sandoval wrote his manuscript with the help of a Hoboken teacher. He dropped copies of the manuscript off at John Lynch's office, Al Certo's business, and Don King's New York office. According to Sandoval, he was upset because he had helped McGirt when Buddy was down, but now that Sandoval was going through hard times, McGirt was not returning the favor.

Sandoval never received a reply from King, McGirt, Certo, or Lynch. Steve recalled that less than a week after he delivered his packages an article was written by Robin Gaby Fisher that was printed in the *Star Ledger*. The article stated that Arturo had run into McGirt while vacationing in Florida. It was this chance encounter, the article said, that was the catalyst for McGirt becoming Arturo's trainer. Sandoval felt that the Gatti camp strategically released the story on how Arturo and McGirt met in order to silence him. Sandoval's journal never was released to the press.

On June 18, Atlantic City was already experiencing the media and fight fans filtering in. Ken Condon felt that Arturo was so popular, he was sort of like an icon.[1149]

Mikey Red sat down for several hours with reporter Robin Gaby

Fisher. Mikey was pleased that his friend Arturo had put his wild partying days behind him. Mikey thought it was okay to talk about Arturo's crazy years in the late 1990s. Mikey told Fisher that Arturo drank wine out of a paper cup after the weigh-in for the Ivan Robinson rematch. Mikey also told Fisher how Arturo and he would be drunk by the eighth hole when they were playing golf. Skowronski mentioned how Arturo would come to his house at 3 or 4 in the morning to ask him to hang out and party.

The story was printed on June 19, 2005, only 6 days prior to the fight. Pat Lynch was livid. He was angry with Skowronski for shedding details on Arturo's personal life. He almost removed Mikey from Arturo's corner for the Mayweather match. There wasn't much difference between Skowronski's comments and Lynch saying that Arturo partied like a rock star, but of course Mikey's statements were more detailed and specific. Arturo, who normally wouldn't care about such things, was very upset with Mikey. Mikey Red recalled that it always seemed like there was in-fighting on the team.

On HBO, Jim Lampley interviewed both fighters live, with just one week remaining until fight time. Mayweather was in Las Vegas and Arturo was in New York City. Mayweather attacked Arturo immediately, calling him a 'C-plus' fighter and a paper champion because Arturo won the title that Kostya Tszyu had vacated. Mayweather added that Gatti and his people were hypocrites for talking about Floyd's personal life while disregarding Arturo's alcohol related incidents. Mayweather promised to punish Arturo for talking about his personal life. Arturo denied ever talking about Floyd's personal life, which was untrue. Gatti had spoken of Mayweather's domestic violence incidents on more than one occasion.

On June 20, the *Bergen Record's* Adrian Wojnarowski planned to meet Team Gatti at the City Bistro on 14th Street in Hoboken, N.J. When the reporter arrived, Pat Lynch and Carl Moretti were seated in the restaurant, but Arturo was nowhere to be found. The manager and matchmaker worked their cell phones trying to get Arturo's location. Gatti had spent the day shopping at Canal Street in New York City. While they awaited Arturo's arrival, Lynch phoned McGirt and asked if he was worried about the fight. McGirt replied that he was worried about the beating Arturo would give to Mayweather. McGirt's response caused Lynch and Moretti to laugh. Gatti finally arrived, wearing his trademark dark sunglasses with a black shirt. He wore his favorite necklace, a diamond-studded, white gold necklace with a cross medallion. Arturo seemed to take pleasure in watching Lynch and Moretti nervously await his arrival. Arturo motioned towards them and joked, *"They're nervous, aren't they?"*[1150]

Gatti was disgusted that he was an underdog, especially when he heard a popular boxing commentator repeat the line that Arturo was tough and had heart, but he wasn't one of the pound-for-pound best. Arturo stated, *"All I heard him say on TV about me is, 'We know that he's not going to quit on the stool like Mike Tyson.' Come on, I would've thought that he would come out with something better. That's upsetting to hear shit like that. That makes me fucking crazy. I'm going to give him a hell of a fight. What have I been doing for the past 14-15 years as a pro boxer? I'm Arturo Gatti, the brawler. I'm Arturo Gatti, the big heart. I'm Arturo Gatti, who comes back. I'm Arturo Gatti, one of the greatest fighters of my era."*[1151]

While the three sat and talked Dallas Cowboys football coach, Bill Parcells, called Moretti for tickets. Parcells was a huge Gatti fan. He sometimes showed Gatti-Ward fight films to his players in the locker room, to help motivate them.

Arturo turned his attention to Mayweather and said that Floyd was the kind of guy that has always looked down on him in boxing. Arturo felt that Mayweather was trying to build up confidence in himself with his antics, when in fact he really feared Gatti.[1152]

Arturo wasn't the only one upset with Mayweather's insults towards him. Micky Ward was also offended. Ward did not blame Arturo for being angry. Ward pointed to the fact that he and Gatti fought three times, almost killed each other, and didn't say one bad word to each other. Ward commented that he would probably be happier than Arturo if Gatti pulled off the upset.[1153]

Atlantic City executive director of Conventions and Visitors Authority, Jeffrey Vasser, felt the fight would be huge. Vasser expected hotels and restaurants to be jam packed.[1154] Arturo's fights brought tremendous profits for every casino in Atlantic City.

Normally it would be easy for Ken Condon to find his "high-rollers" desirable seats. For this match, even he was having trouble finding $1,000 ringside seats. A deal was struck where some of the heavy gamblers at Bally's and Caesar's would have access to an exclusive, closed-circuit showing of the fight at both casinos. Condon was asked how much the casinos might rake in from the event. Condon refused to give a casino drop number but he did say he was expecting a very successful weekend.[1155]

This fight would be the first pay-per-view main event for both boxers who were both under contract with HBO. The ticket prices for the fight were more than double what they were for Arturo's previous bouts. Top Rank and Main Events were hoping on half-a-million pay-per-view buys. The price to buy the event at home was $44.95. The promoters were staring at a possible $22 million in pay-per-view sales.

Carl Moretti summed it up best when he described Arturo's popularity. Moretti said that Gatti appealed to sports fans in North Jersey, New York, Connecticut, South Jersey, and Delaware. Moretti felt that Arturo was almost like a boxing franchise to them, another team for which to root. Moretti added that an Arturo Gatti fight was a guaranteed fun evening, whether he won or lost, you never left a Gatti fight feeling unsatisfied.[1156]

During fight week, Arturo was added to the Boardwalk's Hall of Fame, alongside Cher and Rod Stewart. Arturo's dressing room, number 107, also would be dedicated in his honor, with a brass plaque outside of the room which read, "Arturo 'Thunder' Gatti Dressing Room." Ken Condon revealed that Atlantic City had no intentions of letting Gatti fight anywhere else.[1157]

Seventy-year-old Joe Souza was back in Arturo's corner. Souza used a mixture of Avitene and Vaseline to treat Arturo's cuts. Ringside physician Domenic Coletta felt that Souza was one of the best cutmen in the business.[1158]

Larry Hazzard explained why he chose referee Earl Morton, who worked Gatti's second match with Ivan Robinson and Arturo's last two bouts against Ward, to referee the Mayweather fight. Hazzard picked Morton for his agility. He also based his choice on how well Morton handled both Gatti-Ward fights. Hazzard felt Morton would not be influenced by the large partisan Gatti crowd.[1159]

Pre-fight name calling is a part of boxing and is mostly used to sell tickets. However, the insults that both of these fighters slung at each other were personal and real. Mayweather was angry that Arturo put off fighting him to box Leija and Dorin. He also was upset with Gatti's statements about him abusing women.

Mayweather commented on the "Thunder against Lightning" billing. Floyd reminded everyone that thunder makes a lot of noise, but lightning is what strikes. Mayweather complained that Gatti was given all the advantages possible, such as the fight being held in

Atlantic City instead of Las Vegas or New York.[1160]

Pat Lynch didn't agree with Mayweather's turf statement. Lynch felt that Floyd was hated so much that Arturo would have had the crowd on his side wherever they fought, including if they fought in Mayweather's boyhood hometown of Grand Rapids, Michigan.[1161]

Floyd made negative comments about both Arturo and Micky Ward, which angered Arturo. Gatti admitted that Mayweather had talent, but added that he and Ward had more heart and guts than Floyd. Arturo promised to spank Mayweather like a little child.[1162]

With less than a week remaining until the Gatti-Mayweather showdown, the fighters had not been in the same room once since the contracts were signed. A press conference scheduled on June 22 at the Copacabana Club in Manhattan would be no different. Arturo was scheduled to speak to the press at 11 a.m. Mayweather would get his turn at 1:30 p.m. This would give Arturo plenty of time to avoid Mayweather. Arturo explained why the separate press conferences were necessary. *"I'm afraid I'm going to back-hand him... composure is the most important thing for me right now... He's trying to intimidate me. That [stuff] don't work with me."*[1163] Arturo added that Mayweather's verbal assaults didn't bother him. He felt the outbursts were good for pay-per-view sales.[1164]

Gatti's camp arrived at the press conference at 11 a.m., with the exception of Arturo and Teddy Cruz. Waiting with Arturo's camp were over a hundred reporters and television crews from around the world. Gatti's camp was growing more nervous by the minute. The last thing they wanted was for the fighters to bump into each other outside. Main Events' CEO Kathy Duva was especially bothered. She knew that the hatred between the two boxers was real, not hype. She described Floyd and Arturo's dislike of each other as "bad blood."[1165]

Outside of the club, Main Events' Donald Tremblay explained that Arturo was late because he was a fighter, and fighters have no conception of time, or they just don't care.[1166] Pat Lynch had his cell phone to his ear trying to get an arrival time on his boxer as he nervously paced up and down the sidewalk. Lynch shut off his phone and turned back towards the Copa. He shouted to a reporter that Gatti was two blocks away, on 36th street.[1167]

At 12:15, over an hour after his press conference was supposed to begin, Arturo pulled up in a white stretch limousine. Teddy Cruz accompanied him.

Arturo's face looked drawn-in by his weight loss. Eating nothing but chicken and lettuce for weeks would make anyone edgy. He was bothered by the fact that his mother wanted to take a bus from Montreal instead of flying. Every little thing annoyed Arturo at this point. He disliked television interviews. McGirt disclosed that Gatti just wanted to fight.[1168] As McGirt spoke, Arturo, wearing dark sunglasses, slipped in through a side door. After speaking to a Japanese television reporter, he took his seat at the podium. Everyone else took their seats as well, as the main speaker had arrived. The promoters spoke first, Kathy Duva and Top Rank's Bob Arum.

Around 12:30 p.m., an hour before his scheduled press conference, Mayweather burst through the banquet hall doors with his entourage. Floyd bounced past the podium shouting that he was number one, while raising his index finger for those who may not have heard him. Mayweather then turned to Gatti and shouted that Arturo was a bum. He told Gatti to leave the press conference because he was taking over.[1169] All of the media attention turned to Mayweather as he strutted around the room. He stepped up to the podium and raised his shirt so all in attendance could see his chiseled abdomen. Arturo was sitting less than five feet away.

Mayweather turned to Arturo and said that Gatti was killing himself to make weight. He added that Arturo was wearing sunglasses to hide his sunken cheekbones.[1170] Arturo didn't respond. Floyd continued by stating that Arturo was a flat-footed, wide-swinging, punch-drunk fighter with six losses. He added that Gatti had received plastic surgery to repair his damaged face. Mayweather then turned his attention to McGirt. He said that if Buddy had been boxing during his era, he would have beaten McGirt and Gatti on the same night.[1171] Mayweather made no apologies for calling Arturo a bum and a C-level fighter.[1172]

Floyd mockingly complained that if he was HBO's pride and joy, why didn't they force the match to be held at a neutral location instead of on Arturo's home turf. Mayweather declared that he would not only beat Gatti, he would talk to him while he was beating him. Floyd added that he would talk to the reporters and announcers at ringside while beating Arturo. And in-between rounds, Mayweather said he would borrow Gatti's cell phone so he could talk to a real live Arturo Gatti fan while he beat him.[1173]

Mayweather disrespectfully reached over his promoter Bob Arum, grabbed the Mayweather-name placard, and placed it on the podium to signify that this was his press conference. This would be

Mayweather's final contracted bout for Arum. Floyd sat down and immediately jumped up again in a ball of nervous energy. He ran over to the buffet table, taunting Arturo, just as Gamache and Johnny Bos had with an ice cream cone in 2000. As Mayweather reached for the food, he proclaimed that he was going to eat because he was hungry, and already had made weight three weeks prior.[1174]

Arturo turned to Kathy Duva, who was sitting next to him, and berated her. *"How could you let this happen to me?"*[1175] Lynch, who was on Arturo's opposite side, tried to calm Gatti down. He whispered to Arturo, telling him not to let Mayweather get to him. Finally, someone in Gatti's camp decided to take action. McGirt leaned over towards Arturo and asked him if he wanted to leave. The "Thunder" returned and Arturo shot back, *"I want to say my piece and leave."*[1176]

Arturo ignored the still-shouting Mayweather as he made his way to the podium. Gatti smiled and thanked everyone for attending the presser. He thanked God, his family, the media, Lynch, and McGirt. Then Arturo turned his attention to Mayweather. Silence fell over the crowd as he spoke. *"And Mayweather, I'm knocking you the fuck out on Saturday night."*[1177] After finishing the statement, Arturo walked off the podium and out of the presser, with Lynch and McGirt following behind. Just before he entered the limo, Arturo turned back to a woman who had been inside and apologized for his foul language.[1178]

Floyd definitely was the villain for this match, and he appeared to embrace the role. Bob Arum explained that Floyd was not like De La Hoya. Oscar would have everyone believing that this was the toughest fight of his career, but Mayweather did not use that approach.[1179]

Mayweather's longtime manager and adviser, Leonard Ellerbee, felt that people didn't understand the real Floyd. Ellerbee stated that the real Floyd Mayweather spends time with his kids, is involved with the Ronald McDonald Foundation and Toys for Tots, and takes money out of his own pocket to fund youth sports organizations in Grand Rapids, Michigan.[1180]

Mayweather indeed had another side. He was a passionate father who swam with his children after workouts. He handed out turkeys to needy families on Thanksgiving Day. Floyd even helped a down-and-out stranger a few months prior. While he was walking on the Las Vegas strip, Floyd came upon a man who recently had been released from jail. The man, who had worked at a car wash, was in need of employment. Mayweather gave the man a job.

In prefight buildup, Mayweather admitted that he loved going to strip clubs. That was one of the few things he and Gatti had in common.

In Atlantic City, the hotel rooms were sold out. The workers at the hotels and casinos were looking forward to a financially successful weekend. Door captain Robert Beck, who worked at Bally's Park Place Hotel Casino since 1981, remarked that Gatti drew more people to Atlantic City than anyone.[1181]

Star Ledger reporter Jerry Izenberg sat in on one of Gatti and McGirt's final training sessions at Marciano's Gym in Jersey City. McGirt forced Gatti to repeat moves over and over until they were second nature to him. McGirt explained that he had Arturo repeat the moves to make sure that his body reacted naturally.[1182]

McGirt recalled watching a young Arturo fight on TV years prior, and how impressed he was with Gatti's boxing ability. McGirt believed that Arturo started getting into wars to please the crowd.[1183] McGirt added that it was the ability to ignore the crowd and stick to a game plan that separated the contenders from the champions. McGirt recalled that he fought in wars like Gatti until he met Frankie Warren and Warren matched his pressure. That's when McGirt began to understand that he needed to find another way to win.

McGirt described how he forced Arturo to box in training camp. Buddy would stop the sparring whenever Gatti started to brawl, and he would remind him to box. He would continue to do this until Arturo understood that the sparring session would never end unless he listened. McGirt added that fighters hate when you stop their sparring to force them to listen. It is embarrassing to the fighter, especially if people are in the gym watching.[1184] McGirt's former trainer, Dominick Amoroso, now 85 years old, stopped by Marciano's to watch his former fighter work as a trainer.

On June 22, Mayweather was interviewed in New York City. He boasted that he was on the same level as Sugar Ray Leonard, but questioned if Gatti was on the same level as Roberto Duran.[1185] Mayweather was proud of his boxing heritage, which included his father Floyd Sr. and his uncles, Roger and Jeff. Arturo was nearly a 4-1 underdog less than a week before the match. When Arturo arrived in Atlantic City, one of the first things he did was unpack the wrinkled photos of Mayweather he had plastered throughout his home in Vero Beach. He taped them to the walls of his suite at Caesars Palace.

Chapter 25
Mayweather

New Jersey boxing commissioner Larry Hazzard felt that the Gatti-Mayweather match was the biggest boxing attraction in New Jersey since Mike Tyson fought Michael Spinks in 1988. Jerry Izenberg of the *Newark Star Ledger* wrote that it wasn't only the fighters, managers, promoters and networks who would be cashing in on the fight, the pit bosses and casino presidents would be salivating at the anticipated post-fight money drop. Izenberg called the event a head waiter's promise, a croupier's bonus, and a bartender's bonanza.[1186]

Arturo's ex-girlfriend, Vivian Penha, described Arturo as a great guy with a big heart when he wasn't training, but as mean as a grizzly bear when he was in camp. Bert Sugar described Arturo as a sweetheart, a wonderful guy. But once he enters the ring, he is all business. The ring is his office.[1187]

Two days before the fight, Mayweather spoke of choosing to be a boxer instead of a brawler. Mayweather felt that Gatti was being called superhuman because he got his brains beat in. Floyd reiterated that taking punishment was not cool. He believed that he could go 15 years in the business without being bruised or cut. Mayweather predicted that the crowd would go wild when Arturo swung and missed, but they would be silent after he dropped Gatti.[1188]

On June 24, 2005, the day before the fight, both fighters weighed in separately at Caesars. At 5 p.m., Arturo stripped to his briefs and weighed in at 140-pounds. After commissioner Larry Hazzard read off the weight, Arturo flexed to the assembled crowd as his fans cheered. He grabbed a bottle of water and walked out of the room.

Five minutes later, Mayweather entered the room from the opposite side. His supporters cheered. Floyd stripped to his briefs and socks. When he stepped onto the scale Hazzard shouted out *"139."* Mayweather flexed, kissed his bicep, and predicted victory.

The separate weigh-in was unheard of for a club show, let alone a mega-fight. The fighters refused to pose for the traditional face-off. At that point, Mayweather was a 3½ to 1 betting favorite.

After the weigh-in, Arturo finally was able to eat the food that for twelve weeks he could only dream about. Dishes such as chicken parmesan, rigatoni, pancakes, key lime pie, and chocolate sundaes. Arturo wasn't only thinking of food; he was thinking of the upcoming battle. *"I can't wait to step into my house. My second house. I was watching a fight the other night and the only thing HBO could say about me was that he won't quit on his stool and that I'm an exciting fighter. Everyone seems to think I have nothing more than a puncher's shot at this. That's why I can't wait for this fight. After this, a lot of people are going to owe me an apology. A lot of people.*"[1189]

Mayweather was ranked #2 in boxing pound-for-pound. He was asked if he was concerned about the pro-Gatti crowd and the influence they might have on the judges. Mayweather avowed that the judges wouldn't matter because the fight would not go the distance. Floyd added that although he felt Arturo was a built-up club fighter who would be on the canvas Saturday night, he knew that Gatti would be a winner Monday morning when he deposited his check into the bank.[1190]

After the weigh-in, Ken Condon was amazed at the electric atmosphere. He described it as overwhelming.[1191] Both of the fighters' trainers had strategies that they hoped their boxers would execute. McGirt felt that forcing Mayweather to make adjustments from his normal counter-punching style would lead him into making mistakes.[1192]

Floyd's trainer and uncle, Roger Mayweather, had his own thoughts. He felt that Gatti was nothing more than a human punching bag. Roger didn't see the need for a strategy for Arturo, because of Gatti's porous defense.[1193]

Emanuel Steward, the famed coach of the Kronk Gym in Detroit, which rolled out champions almost as often as Ford and GM rolled out cars, spoke of Arturo's chances as a puncher. Stewart pointed out Marciano's defeat of the speedy Walcott and how Marciano only defeated Walcott because he pressed the fight. Steward felt that Gatti only had a puncher's chance, that and his heart.[1194] Steward, like most boxing fans, was turned off by Mayweather's cockiness. He stated, *"If there really is a God up above, Mayweather will lose."*[1195]

Both Arturo and Mayweather had been dealing with hand injuries throughout their careers. Four years prior to their match, Mayweather hired 75-year-old Rafael Garcia to wrap his hands. Garcia had worked with the great Roberto Duran. Mayweather, who previously had wrapped himself, suffered from weak tendons in his hands. Garcia revealed that Mayweather had been wrapping his hands too tightly, cutting off the circulation. Garcia's method of wrapping hands took over 30 minutes. Garcia added that his wrapping technique gave Mayweather the protection and confidence he needed to utilize his power along with his speed.[1196]

Arturo had broken his hands four times in his career; his right hand three times and his left hand once. Arturo's hands were covered with scar tissue from the operations he was forced to endure. Arturo had undergone an increasingly popular operation for boxers, where bone tissue was taken from the pelvis and fused to the shattered bones in his hand. Small screws held the transplant in place. Gatti's team believed that the operation had extended Arturo's career. Pat Lynch recalled that doctors would say that Arturo punched too hard for his own bone structure. If not for the fusions, his career likely would have been over.[1197]

Dr. Charles Melone, who operated on Arturo's hand, was confident that Gatti's hand had healed like a rock.[1198] Melone had operated on Don Mattingly, Patrick Ewing, and Stephon Marbury, as well as approximately 200 boxers. In June 2004, Melone convinced the New York State Athletic Commission to reform their hand-wrapping policy to allowed fighters to use an unlimited amount of gauze and tape, so long as the hand could fit into the glove.

Roger Mayweather disagreed with New York allowing unlimited use of gauze. He felt that the extra gauze would be like a pair of brass knuckles over the hand.[1199] Mayweather was speaking of how the gauze gets wet from sweat, which causes it to become extremely heavy and compact.

In New Jersey, where the Gatti-Mayweather bout was being held, a fighter cannot use tape across his knuckles. Commissioner Larry Hazzard said he would entertain studying a change if it would protect the boxers' hands.

Micky Ward had a bone fusion operation. He felt that his hand was definitely stronger, with the only downside being that cold weather would cause pain and throbbing in the hand. Ward commented that a boxer fighting with a bad hand was like a cop going out into the street without his duty belt.[1200]

Although Floyd was a very talented boxer, his personality led to many wanting to see him lose. Mayweather had the same cocky attitude that Hector Camacho displayed years prior. Floyd felt that he was not cocky, but confident. Mayweather proclaimed that he was not trying to be the next Sugar Ray Leonard or Muhammad Ali. He was trying to be the first Floyd Mayweather Jr.[1201]

Arturo spent the final few days before the match in Atlantic City. On the day of the fight, Arturo ate steak and eggs for breakfast at a local diner. Later he went shopping an hour away from Atlantic City. McGirt was worried. He would have rather have had Arturo rest his legs, but at least Arturo's mind was off of the fight. When Arturo returned, he spent the remainder of the day and night in his hotel room, suite 803, in Caesars Palace. Ivano Scarpa, Joe Gatti's former manager from Montreal, spent time with Arturo in his hotel room.

Joe and Arturo weren't on good terms. On the day of the fight, Joe, like Arturo, went shopping at a mall with Vikki. Being a former fighter and having his brother fighting in such an epic and dangerous match wore heavily on Joe. He couldn't stop thinking about his brother. Finally, he broke down and threw aside his pride. He took out his cell phone and dialed Arturo's number.

He started sweating as the phone rang, unsure if Arturo would pick up, and if he did what type of response he would get. Arturo answered, and he was receptive. Joe wished his brother luck. There was silence, and then Arturo asked, *"Are you coming?"* Joe, never knowing how to say no to his little brother, replied, *"Yes, I am. You got a ticket for me?"* Arturo assured Joe that he would get him in.[1202]

Joe turned to Vikki, who was listening to the conversation. She had that, *"Oh, no you're not,"* look on her face. Joe motioned with a sad puppy-dog look to get Vikki's approval. Vikki gave in. Joe rushed his wife and two daughters into the car and raced home to drop them off. It was nearly 6 o'clock. Atlantic City was three hours away. He frantically agonized about how he could get to the show on time.

Joe called a wealthy Canadian friend who was in Atlantic City for the fight. He had a personal jet. That idea fell through. Joe got a ride to Newark and took the train to Philadelphia. The train ride was 2½-hours. When he exited the train at 8:30 p.m., he took a one-hour taxi ride from Philadelphia to Atlantic City. The cab driver wanted $300 for the ride, but Joe talked him into accepting $250.

The tension was high in Arturo's hotel room as departure time neared. McGirt was already waiting at Convention Hall. Arturo looked at the clock and told his team, *"Let's go."* At 9:45 p.m., they exited the hotel room and took an elevator to the lobby. Arturo was wearing a grey sweat suit and a blue knit cap. When they reached the lobby, they exited the elevator. As Arturo got off, he stopped and held the elevator for a woman in a wheel chair. The team then continued through the Caesars Palace lobby. Arturo was in the center of the pack. Men offered shouts of encouragement, while women screamed at the site of the legendary boxer. The group made their way to a white stretch limousine that was parked outside the lobby. A bellhop, standing next to the limo with tears in his eyes, hugged Arturo and encouraged him to be victorious. Arturo thanked the man and promised that he would win.[1203]

Arturo's closest team members were allowed to climb into Gatti's limo for the short drive to Boardwalk Hall. Gatti sat next to the door and peered out of the blackened window, lost in his own thoughts. The limousine pulled into the underground garage. The driver announced to the security guard that Gatti was in the limo. The security guard gave words of encouragement as he let the limo pass. Television cameras captured Arturo's arrival. Gatti exited the car and headed for the dressing room, which recently had been officially named "The Arturo Gatti Dressing Room."[1204]

An undercard match was taking place in the hall. When the overhead monitor inside the arena displayed Arturo's arrival, the crowd roared its approval. The familiar chant of "Gatti! Gatti! Gatti!" exploded throughout the hall. Arturo walked through the tunnel of the arena to his dressing room, where trainer Buddy McGirt was waiting. McGirt embraced Gatti with the type of hug that two soldiers would give to each other after a month together in a foxhole.

The *Star Ledger's* Robin Gaby Fisher was in the dressing room with Gatti. She closely observed the mood in the room. Gatti's team put their pre-fight faces on. The tension was hanging thick in the air. Arturo sensed the anxiety behind his entourage's forced smiles. Pat Lynch's voice quivered as he spoke. Teddy Cruz anxiously chewed on a wad of gum. Mikey "Red" Skowronski was yawning and gazing down at his shoes. Gatti broke the silence by telling Skowronski, *"Hey Mike, make sure you stay up for me."*[1205] Everyone released their tension with a laugh before they settled back into nervous silence.

Arturo's green WBC belt was laying on a table in the room. An official from the WBC walked in to confirm that Arturo had brought the belt. McGirt pointed to the belt and told the official that he brought the belt with him and Gatti would be taking the belt back home when the fight was over.[1206]

Joe finally arrived at the Convention Center around 10 p.m. He told security at the door that his brother was Arturo. He explained that his brother had asked him to come and support him. Security would not let him in. Joe was told that he was not on the guest list. Frantic, Joe called Ivano Scarpa for help. Scarpa called Pat Lynch. Lynch told Scarpa that he would see what he could do about getting Joe in.

Scarpa called Lynch a second time to get Joe in. Lynch didn't pick up his phone.[1207] Finally, Lynch's wife Lisette picked up the phone. When Ivano told her the story, she replied, *"Pat doesn't have any tickets."*[1208] Scarpa called Joe and told him that Lynch was not going to help him get in. Joe gave up.

A boxing commission doctor stepped into Arturo's dressing room to examine him. Arturo was asked how he felt. He responded that he felt fine. Micky Ward walked into the room. Arturo was pleased to see his old foe. Arturo alternated between jumping jacks and shadow boxing as he tried to contain his energy. Each boxer was assigned their own state inspector to watch the wrapping of hands. When McGirt finished the wrap, the official inspected the gauze and signed the wraps with a marker to prevent any additional tampering with the gauze.

Arturo pushed his gauze covered hands into the tight interior of the eight-ounce gloves while McGirt held the wrist ends of each glove. McGirt pulled the laces tight and taped the wrist area of each glove with athletic tape. The state inspector then covered the athletic tape with duct tape to prevent the athletic tape from coming loose during the fight. McGirt warmed up Arturo on the mitts. The padwork helped to break in the new gloves. Arturo suddenly noticed that the door to his dressing room had been ajar since his arrival. A television technician had been peering into his room. Arturo annoyingly asked, *"Is that a new fucking thing?"* Gatti's team did not appear to understand his question. They were focused on the upcoming fight. Some in the room looked as though they were watching the clock, waiting to bring a condemned man to the lethal injection room. Arturo turned to Lynch and clarified his question, *"The door. It's open. Is that a new thing?"* Lynch quickly closed the door.

A boxer preparing for battle notices every little thing out of place. Word came into Arturo's dressing room that the last bout before his, Vivian Harris versus Carlos Maussa, had ended. Maussa upset Harris by 7th round knockout, winning the WBA light welterweight title. Team Gatti was hoping that this would be the night of the upsets. It was time for last-minute preparations. Arturo put his robe on. His cornermen placed their matching white with blue-trim satin jackets on. "Team Gatti" was written boldly across the back. Although the team members were on edge, as they were massive underdogs, there was a small reservoir of hope in them. A compressed optimism that was intensely hoping to bust out in celebration, should Gatti pull off an upset win.

Arturo was sweating profusely from his warm-up. McGirt was also sweating from the pad work. Lynch was perspiring, but his sweat was from nerves. At 11 o'clock, an HBO producer advised "Team Gatti" that they would need to be ready to depart their dressing room in eight minutes. Arturo paced around the room. The same pacing that a boxer does in-between rounds in the gym. The same pacing that the trainer and boxer do in the ring right before a fight starts. McGirt knew what Arturo was experiencing. He had been in the same position many times. Buddy grabbed Arturo and pulled him close. They went over the game plan that was months in the making. Buddy asked Arturo to stay cool and find a rhythm.[1209] Arturo made the sign of the cross as the clock read 11:05 p.m.

Arturo took a rinse from a water bottle and spit it out onto the dressing room rug. He realized what he had done and said, *"Oh, excuse me."*[1210] McGirt crossed himself as Arturo's team started to clap and offer words of encouragement. Arturo stated, *"It's finally here, huh? One more time to the office."*[1211]

12,675 fans were packed into Boardwalk Hall, like sardines, to watch "Thunder and Lightning - The Storm is Coming." After the event's billing had been made public, Arturo commented, *"There is only one lightning and that is my brother."*[1212] Joe never did get inside the arena. He would receive round-by-round results of the fight from Vikki, via cell phone.

Boardwalk Hall was filled with celebrities, such as Denzel Washington, P. Diddy, Jay-Z, Beyonce, Tom Brady, Allen Iverson, Jalen Rose, Chris Webber, and Donald Trump. Arturo's mother, Ida, attended the fight with Gerardo and Fabrizio. Some of Gatti's friends from Vero Beach, 70-year-old Jerry Hagin, 65-year-old Ken Boissy, and 85-year-old Anthony "Gus" Domenico, made the 17-hour drive north for the fight. From the opposite direction, friends and family drove down from as far away as Montreal. Scalpers were out on the boardwalk selling the few remaining available tickets.

Mayweather held a slight height and reach advantage over Arturo. Floyd made his way into the ring to Queen's "Another One Bites The Dust." He was carried in on a purple and red, gold-fringed Sedia gestatoria, or ceremonial throne. Six men dressed in Roman battle uniforms carried the fighter onto the arena floor. The pro-Gatti crowd roundly booed Mayweather's entrance. The intensity was building as Mayweather stepped into the ring.

Fireworks erupted from floor props as Gatti made his entrance. The first blast seemed to startle Arturo. The crowd roared out his name in unison, "Gatti! Gatti! Gatti!" Fans were wearing "Blood, Guts, Glory," T-shirts. One fan held a sign up that read, *"Gas $40. Hotel $200. Gambling losses $300. Watching Gatti KO Pretty Boy Floyd- Priceless."*[1213] Arturo's fans ranged from twenty-somethings to senior citizens, to women wearing evening gowns and high heels. Arturo led his team out as Teddy Cruz followed behind, holding Gatti's WBC belt high over his head. AC/DC's "Thunderstruck" blared from the hall speakers. Lynch, McGirt, Zito, Souza, Ward, and Mikey Red followed closely behind. Arturo entered the ring.

The hall roundly booed Michael Buffer's introduction of Mayweather while Arturo received tremendous applause. Referee Earl Morton gave his pre-fight instructions. Arturo stared at the floor while Mayweather gazed at Arturo. Kathy Duva sat in her usual ringside, TV-side seat. Bob Arum sat two seats away. In-between the pair was Carl Moretti.

Arturo began the fight by shooting his jab. Mayweather leaned back, avoiding the shots. For some strange reason, Arturo was holding his left hand at his waist. Mayweather displayed his tremendous speed advantage by ripping blazing hooks and straight rights. Arturo's left eye immediately began to swell. Gatti made Mayweather miss several punches.

With 26 seconds remaining, Arturo ducked a Mayweather left hook and bent low. Mayweather pushed Arturo's head down with his left forearm. Morton ordered both boxers to *"Stop punching!"* As he did so, Mayweather, while still holding Gatti's head down with his left forearm, unleashed a right uppercut. He quickly followed with a left hook. Both punches landed cleanly. Gatti looked at Morton, waiting for him to intercede on the foul. Morton took no action, but slightly shook his head. Gatti had complied with Morton's order to stop punching, but Mayweather ignored the referee and used the moment to take an unfair advantage over Arturo. Even if Morton had not ordered them to stop punching, the pushing down with the forearm while throwing an uppercut was a foul in and of itself. Morton should have stopped the action and at the very least he should have issued a warning to Mayweather.

If that wasn't bad enough, as Gatti turned and stared at Morton in disbelief, Mayweather jumped in and hit Gatti with another left hook, causing Arturo to fall into the ropes. The ropes had prevented Gatti from hitting the floor, so Morton ruled the stumble a knockdown and started counting. Morton looked completely intimidated by Mayweather and the moment. The incident was a terrible injustice to Gatti, one from which he would not recover.

As Morton picked up the count, Arturo pushed the referee in frustration. Arturo shook his head to clear the cobwebs out. After the referee wiped Arturo's gloves, Gatti looked at Morton and blurted, *"That's fucking bullshit."* And it was. The incident displayed the worst of boxing. A tentative referee and an unsportsmanlike boxer. Roy Jones, Jr. opined that a boxer must protect himself at all times. This is true. But a boxer must also listen to a referee's commands and must be penalized or warned when he ignores those commands. At the minimum, Gatti should have been afforded five minutes to recuperate, and not be charged with a knockdown.

Arturo needed to be perfect in the fight. Now he was hurt. After the bell rang ending the 1st round, Arturo continued to argue with Morton. Jim Lampley commented that it was not a great round for the referee. That was a gross understatement.

McGirt tried to calm Arturo down by reminding him to stick to the game plan and keep stepping to the right. McGirt cautioned Gatti not to stand in front of Mayweather too long. In Mayweather's corner, his uncle Roger told Floyd to bang the body and head. After reviewing the video Jim Lampley felt that Mayweather did nothing wrong, even though the video clearly showed Mayweather pushing down on Gatti's neck while throwing an uppercut. They failed to replay the audio which would have confirmed that Morton ordered both boxers to stop punching. Larry Merchant felt the referee should have stepped in.

Mayweather proved to be much faster than Arturo in the 2nd round. Floyd was taking advantage of Arturo's low guard with sizzling left hooks and rights. Both of Gatti's eyes started closing. Although Morton failed to act in the 1st, he ridiculously warned Gatti for having an open glove in the 2nd round.

After the round ended, McGirt told Arturo that he was standing up too straight. Roger Mayweather advised Floyd to keep checking Gatti with a lead left hook and to follow with a right hand. HBO's Harold Lederman scored the 2nd a 10-8 round for Mayweather. Although Floyd had won the round, there was nothing to justify the 10-8 scoring. The only commentator who wasn't drinking the Floyd Kool-Aid was Merchant, who disagreed with Lederman.

Morton warned Arturo for a low blow early in the 3rd. Merchant felt that Morton's inexperience in championship fights, only five, may have led to the disaster in the 1st round. Mayweather was now dissecting Gatti with fast, crisp blows. Morton warned Mayweather for punching low.

With 35 seconds remaining in the round, the crowd chanted Gatti's name in an effort to motivate their hero. After the round ended, Roger Mayweather asked for hard shots to the head and body. McGirt asked for more head movement as Gatti downed nearly an entire bottle of water.

During the 4th, Harold Lederman incorrectly stated that Mayweather had every right to punch Gatti in the 1st round because the referee did not say stop. He couldn't be more wrong. Morton clearly said, *"Stop punching."* Maybe there was a problem with Lederman's headset. The audio of Morton was crisp and clear. Lederman amazingly said that Morton had warned Mayweather for holding behind the head in the 1st. Morton did not issue a warning to Floyd. It almost appeared as though Lederman was trying to cover up for Mayweather's foul and Morton's error. While the commentators were speaking, Mayweather was carving Arturo up. Roy Jones, Jr. remarked that Arturo was *"taking a heavy tattooing."* Kathy Duva was blinking incessantly, apparently in sync with every punch that crashed against Arturo's head. As Gatti absorbed punch after punch, Pat Lynch, sitting ringside as he always did, couldn't bear to watch any longer. Mayweather was just too fast.[1214] Lynch stood up and walked towards the ring.

After the round ended, McGirt warned Arturo that he was looking for one punch. Gatti appeared as though he understood that his chances of victory were slim to none. McGirt pleaded with Arturo to tell him what was wrong, and why he was not doing anything they had worked on. Arturo replied that he didn't know why. McGirt told Arturo that he didn't like what he was seeing and he was going to stop the fight.[1215] Arturo begged for one more round. McGirt gave him two.

Forty seconds into the 5th, Arturo gave his fans a glimmer of hope when he scored with two hard body shots. With nearly a minute gone, the exact same incident that occurred in the 1st round took place again. Mayweather pushed Arturo's head down, this time with the right forearm after missing a right hand. Morton yelled *"stop"* and jumped between the two fighters, forcing Mayweather to step back. Morton warned Floyd for holding Arturo's head down. Mayweather landed fourteen clean head shots in the final two minutes of the round.

After the round ended, McGirt advised Gatti that he was trying too hard to knock Mayweather out. Roger Mayweather asked Floyd to throw more right hooks.

During the 6th, McGirt left his ringside chair and positioned his chin on the canvas to take a close look at Arturo. It is a moment that all trainers loathe, when they must change from observing the opponent for flaws to concentrating on their own fighter's ability to continue. McGirt sensed that things were going wrong after Arturo received the eight-count in the first round. Gatti was never the same after that. All the strategy they had worked on in the gym went right out the window. Arturo started loading up on shots, which was the worst thing you could do against Mayweather.[1216]

Some of Arturo's fans grimaced and turned away while others wept openly. The sight of their hero taking such a terrible beating was too much for their eyes to bear. Bernard Hopkins likened the fight to a Volkswagen racing a Ferrari.

Near the halfway point of the 6th, Mayweather unloaded his entire arsenal on Gatti. Floyd was so fast, his punches had already landed before Arturo attempted to slip them. A body shot to the kidney hurt Gatti. Arturo's head jerked violently with every landing blow. Mayweather's quickness made Gatti look as though he was moving in slow motion. Arturo was getting pummeled. He tried to throw back but his punches had nothing on them. McGirt began walking up the stairs with a towel in his hand to end the slaughter. Mikey Red stopped him. As Mikey was pulling McGirt back down by his pants he said, *"Buddy, Arturo will never speak to us again if you stop this fight."*[1217]

Mayweather kept scoring, blasting Arturo's head from side to side. Arturo bravely, and maybe foolishly, finished out the round. Hazzard had gone over to Arturo's corner during the round and advised McGirt that if Buddy didn't stop the fight, Hazzard would.

At the end of the 6th, McGirt advised Arturo that he was going to stop the fight. McGirt used Arturo's damaged eyes as an excuse. Arturo quickly begged for one more round. Buddy repeated that he was stopping the fight. Arturo finally acceded. He told McGirt that he trusted his decision.[1218]

McGirt knew his fighter's gas tank was empty and ended the slaughter. A coach must be hard on his fighter in the gym and ignore their humanity, but when the gloves change from sixteen ounces to eight, a trainer must be able to put his competitiveness aside and focus on his fighter's safety. Arturo would later agree with the stoppage. *"Buddy made the right call by stopping it. I was getting* hit with too many punches."[1219] Arturo was out-landed 115-10 in power shots.

Mayweather walked to the center of the ring and fell to his knees crying, *"God is great."* As Floyd's hand was raised in victory, most of Boardwalk Hall's 12,675 spectators stood silent, while some clapped lightly. Debris from Arturo's loyal fans flew into the ring. When Arturo ducked under the ropes to depart the ring, his loyal fans roared for their warrior. They would not abandon their hero.

After the stoppage, Mayweather opined that he was glad they stopped the fight when they did. He added that he did not hate Arturo. He only made his prefight comments to hype the fight. Floyd praised Gatti for giving it his all. He called Arturo a great champion.[1220]

After Michael Buffer announced the time, Mayweather was raised up wearing his new WBC championship belt. Floyd landed 168 of 295 punches to Arturo's 41 of 245. Mayweather landed 57% of his punches in the one-sided contest, while Arturo landed only 17%.

Floyd was shown the 1st round knockdown on a teleprompter, without audio. Floyd described the incident by stating that you are supposed to protect yourself at all times. Merchant cut Mayweather off and showed him that Arturo was looking at the referee. Floyd repeated that you should protect yourself at all times. Mayweather added that he didn't mean to fight dirty.

Merchant turned to Arturo and asked him to describe the 1st round incident. Arturo classily tried to bypass the foul question by saying that he had head hunted too much. Merchant revisited the question by asking Arturo if he ignored boxing's unwritten rule of protecting yourself at all times. Arturo replied that it was his mistake if he didn't protect himself. Arturo was shown the replay, again without audio. He admitted that he thought the referee was going to break them apart because Mayweather was holding his head down. Arturo added that when he lifted his head to look at the referee, Floyd hit him.

Mike Skowronski recalled the Mayweather fight. *"Buddy had him in shape to box. The system had been working up until that fight. And even in the 1st round Arturo was doing well. It's when he gets hit with that stupid [sucker punch] in the clinch. Getting dropped by that stupid hook on the break when Earl Morton was separating them. He just wasn't the same after that. If you go back and look at that fight, he is just not the same guy after that break."*[1221]

McGirt felt that the knockdown messed up his game plan.[1222]

When Arturo came back to the corner after the 1st round, he was too concerned about making up the two-point deficit from the knockdown, instead of sticking to the game plan of working the body and breaking Mayweather down.

Mayweather described how Arturo was tipping off his punches. When Gatti was going to throw a regular jab, he just flicked it out, with his right hand by his chin. But if he was going to throw a right hand behind the jab, he cocked the right back. This habit allowed Mayweather to time his rolls and counters. Floyd stated that after God and his family, staying undefeated was the most important thing in his life. *Ring* magazine reporter David Mayo expressed that Gatti had a puncher's chance but no chance to land a punch. Emanuel Steward felt that Floyd was probably the closest thing to an unbeatable fighter.[1223]

Arturo somberly walked back to his dressing room. Everyone in his entourage whispered, as though at a funeral wake. A commission doctor walked into his dressing room to check on him. Arturo's family walked in, led by his mother Ida. In the dressing room, Gatti exploded on two of his friends, Mike Moffa and Ivano Scarpa. Both had driven down from Montreal for the fight. Arturo had received information days before the fight that Moffa was telling friends in Montreal that Arturo would be slaughtered.[1224] Moffa's prediction did not mean he was not rooting for his friend, but Arturo was in no mood to be empathetic. Arturo went to the post-fight press conference, though no one would have faulted him if he didn't. Arturo commented, *"There's no shame in losing to the best fighter in the world."*

Arturo was asked what happened in the fight. *"He was too quick. He was much quicker than I thought. My corner kept telling me to stop head-hunting.*[1225] *He was hard to hit and quicker than I thought he'd be. Everybody told me he had fast hands, but he's very fast with the upper body [too]."*[1226]

Mayweather had promised to punish Gatti in the fight and mocked Arturo's skills, but after the fight was stopped, he showed respect for his foe by calling Arturo a great champion. He reiterated that he made his disparaging comments to sell the fight.[1227]

After Mayweather celebrated in the ring, he went back to his dressing room, changed into a gray suit and came back out to sign a few autographs. Arturo changed into a T-shirt and shorts and put on a powder-blue ski cap. He looked around for his M-frame Oakley sunglasses, but he couldn't find them.

Arturo had worn the sunglasses all week long, claiming to need them to combat the bright media lights. Now he needed them to hide the damage sustained from Mayweather's fists. Carl Moretti probably felt it was Murphy's Law when he said that it figured that the one time Arturo needed the sunglasses he lost them.[1228] Arturo walked out of his dressing room into the hallway. He ran into Kathy Duva and told her that he was sorry he did not perform better. Duva told Gatti not to apologize to her or anyone else, because he did his best.[1229]

After the presser, Gatti asked that his mother be driven back to her hotel room. Arturo decided to walk back to his hotel. He walked along the oceanfront boardwalk with friends, as well as a police escort. A crowd started to gather and walk with him. His fans did not abandon him. They shouted words of encouragement. They told him they loved him and that he would win the next one. They reached out to touch the man who they vicariously lived through on so many Atlantic City nights. *"Gatti! Gatti! Gatti!"* echoed across the air, trailing off into the Atlantic Ocean, just as Arturo's chances of victory had. Arturo thanked everyone. He needed this fresh, salt infused ocean-air walk, to clear his punch-clogged head. He was invigorated by his fans. They gave him a much needed adrenaline boost. This was, and always would be, Gatti's town, and Boardwalk Hall always would be, as Larry Hazzard stated, win or lose, the house that Gatti built.[1230]

After the fight ended, Joe went to Arturo's hotel room. Everyone was partying like Arturo had won. Few cared that he lost and took a terrible beating in the process; it was all about the party. Joe recalled, *"They didn't give a shit what happened. It was always a big party after the fight."*[1231] When Joe entered Arturo's room his sister Anna yelled at him to leave. Other guests joined her. Joe ignored them and went to the bedroom to see his brother. Arturo's girlfriend Erika was in the bedroom with Arturo. Arturo was using cocaine to numb both the physical and emotional pain he had endured. Joe asked Arturo if he was okay. Arturo was bruised and battered and visibly upset. Arturo replied, *"You always come when I lose."* Arturo didn't understand that Joe came to the fights that he felt were the most dangerous for his brother. He didn't come expecting Arturo to lose. It sounded as though Arturo felt that Joe wanted him to lose, wanted him to fail.

Joe was stunned. He answered, *"Bro, are you kidding me? How am I supposed to know you would lose? I came here because I was* worried. This was not the fight you were supposed to fight."[1232] Erika turned to Arturo and said, *"Don't talk like that [to your brother]. That's not nice."* Joe told Arturo, *"Bro, call me if you need anything."*[1233] Joe left. As he passed the partyers in the hotel room, they continued to hurl insults at him.

As Joe exited the room he ran into Pat Lynch in the hallway. Lynch was just leaving his hotel room, which was adjacent to Arturo's. Joe and Lynch met eye to eye. Lynch was preparing to give Joe an excuse about why he couldn't get him into the arena when Joe cut him off, *"Bro, don't even think about it."*[1234] Lynch turned around and went back into his hotel room and closed the door. Joe luckily got a ride back north with one of Arturo's fans.

The live gate brought in $5 million, exceeding Gatti-Ward III's attendance by 32 people. In addition to the live gate, 340,000 homes paid $44.95 each to watch the contest, bringing in an additional $15.3 million. Excluding the site fee, the total take was $20.3 million. After Arturo and Mayweather were paid, there would be at least another $15.7 million left over for the cable provider and promoters to divide amongst themselves. After all the bills were paid, HBO, Main Events, and Top Rank would profit handsomely.

Mario Costa commented, *"The Mayweather fight, he had no business being in that fight. They're lucky he didn't kill himself afterwards. Every time he lost a fight it was like a knife in the back; it killed him. Then they would get him another fight to build him up."*[1235] Omar Sheika commented that the only thing that he ever saw that stressed Arturo was losing a fight. Otherwise, he was a happy guy that loved life.

The fight had just ended, but Main Events already was planning Arturo's next bout. Main Events planned on moving Arturo back up to the 147-pound weight class, the division that they recently had said was too heavy for him. The game plan was one or two victories at 147, and then another title shot. Kathy Duva remarked that fans shouldn't be surprised if the 33-year-old Gatti was back in action by January.[1236]

HBO's senior vice president of sports, Mark Taffet, was thrilled with the successful pay-per-view numbers, especially in the New York and New Jersey areas.[1237] The Mayweather-Gatti bout, pay-per-view debuts for both fighters, drew more pay-per-view buys than Roy Jones Jr., Oscar De La Hoya, and Lennox Lewis did in their pay-per-view debuts.

Even though he had just taken a terrible beating from Mayweather,

Gatti agreed to help launch an anti-gun-violence public service campaign. Many professional sports teams and leagues didn't bother to return calls for help with the ad campaign. The main theme was to show kids that "Guns are for Punks." Main Events PR man, Donald Trembley, stated that Arturo gladly signed up for the campaign.[1238] Arturo went to a gym, his face still bruised from Mayweather's punches, and staring into a video camera with his fists up, stated, *"This is Arturo Gatti and I got a question for you: If you're so tough, why do you need a gun?"*[1239]

On Monday, June 27, Mike Skowronski and Danny McDermott stopped by Pat Lynch's office in Secaucus. They were told that Arturo was in the office. On the ride over, Skowronski and McDermott prepared to sit with a grieving Gatti. When they entered the office they carefully approached the bruised and battered Arturo and quietly asked him how he was feeling. Arturo surprised both friends by telling them he was feeling great. He told them, with a broad smile, that he had just come back from depositing his check in the bank. If Arturo was devastated by the loss, he hid it well from his friends.

Arturo flew down to Vero Beach to recuperate. He went out to dinner with McGirt and his wife Gina. Gatti thanked Buddy for helping to revive his career. Arturo sang Karaoke songs by Englebert Humperdinck. Arturo's brother Joe loved Humperdinck songs, and Arturo followed suit. Buddy was amazed at how good Arturo sang the song "Quando, Quando, Quando." McGirt was hysterical with laughter as Arturo emotionally performed the song.[1240] It was one of the most memorable and funny moments that Arturo and Buddy shared. With a laugh, McGirt said that Arturo should have auditioned for American Idol.

Arturo, Teddy Cruz, Mikey Red and a few other friends flew down to the Dominican Republic because a friend of Arturo's, Mark DeVincentis, was getting engaged. The group went horseback riding. Arturo chartered a 45-foot fishing boat with a 25-foot tuna tower. The charter boat took the group over an area to fish, but Arturo and his friends had no interest in fishing. The group was too interested in partying. After a while, Arturo got bored and climbed to the top of the tuna tower. Mikey Red followed behind. Once at the top, Arturo told Skowronski to jump. Sharks were known to be in the area. Mikey refused, so Arturo pushed him in. Arturo laughed and then jumped in himself.

Cruz recalled the day. *"Arturo is jumping off of this big fishing* boat. It's about 45 feet long. He's jumping off of the top deck into the waters of the Caribbean. And we were like, 'Hey, there's sharks there!' I was like, 'Are you crazy. What are you doing?'"[1241]

Friends couldn't understand why Arturo was so wild and uncontrollable in-between fights. Teddy Cruz felt that Arturo acted this way because he was locked in a training camp for several months at a time. Cruz remarked, *"If you're working a normal 9 to 5 and you go to a strip club once a week, you multiply that by three months, you've gone 12 times. Arturo's in camp for three months. So when he comes out he's like a little kid going to a candy store. The first thing he does is, 'Let's go to McDonalds.' Cause he's tired of all the diet food. 'Let's go to a strip club.' It seems excessive 'cause while other people are working it's his time off."*[1242]

Arturo truly loved to eat between fights. Two of his favorite restaurants were Jules and Casa Dante, both Italian and both located in Jersey City. Jules was located on Franklin Street in the Heights section and Casa Dante was located on Newark Avenue in the Journal Square section. It was difficult for Arturo to find friends to hang out with during weekdays when he wasn't in camp, because most people worked. The ones who didn't have jobs were usually more likely to get Arturo into trouble. Cruz recalled having heart-to-hearts with Arturo about his wild behavior. *"I would ask him, 'Bro, why do you go crazy?' And he would be like, 'Bro, I'm being as good as I could be. I'm in camp and I'm sparring. I'm losing weight. And on top of that I'm dieting. And I've been training hard. Of course I wanna mess around with some women. I'm not married. It's not a regular job that I have. These are the things that I go crazy about because I've been neglected from it.' That's how he used to tell me."*[1243]

Cruz believed that Arturo was misunderstood because he was so transparent. He would say whatever came to his mind. Cruz recalled, *"He was an honest person and honesty sometimes has no filter. And where I would be a little bit more diplomatic in situations, I might find the right words to say, he would just say it as it came out. Like I say, he had no filter. And you know, he was a little rough on the edges when it came to stuff like that. But you need to know the side that people didn't see. Sometimes we could be driving around after a workout or maybe after golf or something. He would ask me, 'What are the guys doing?' And I'd say, some of the guys are training, or this guy just landed in the hospital. He'd say, 'Let's go to the hospital. Let's go buy a gift bag or a gift basket. Let's take it* to the hospital and surprise whoever that somebody was that was sick.' He would do stuff like that. But those things nobody hears about.

"We would go to church and when the offering was passed, people were barely putting in a dollar. Arturo would put hundred dollar bills in the basket. Where I would put a five or a twenty. He was always doing things for charity. One time it was a bunch of old timers that used to come and see him train at the gym in Vero Beach. One of them [Anthony "Gus" Domenico] fell and broke his neck. After our workout, Arturo showered. 'Come on, I want to go see Gus. Let's go see Gus. He's in the hospital. Take me over there.' We went over there. He made that old timer so happy that Arturo Gatti went to visit him."[1244]

Cruz recalled that Arturo would stop in a sports store and buy boxes of T-shirts for little league baseball teams that had no sponsors. He just handed them out to the kids and watched their faces light up. Arturo made sure he did these good deeds quietly, without any media attention. Cruz added, *"Those are the things that he would do that nobody knows about."*[1245]

Arturo would drive by a hospital and impulsively decide to stop and walk in, to say hi to the patients. He would think nothing of going to a mall and buying clothes for someone. Cruz recalled Arturo going over someone's house and noticing that the person's furniture was falling apart. Arturo would secretly order a sofa or bedroom set for them. He would tell people to call him and let him know what they needed. Arturo did things, as Cruz explained, *"Low key, but just from the heart. That's why nobody knows about it. But I know. I was there. I used to go pick stuff out with him. That's why I say a lot of people just saw a dark side of him, but I saw the light. The good side of him."*[1246]

Arturo and Cruz would have their disagreements, but they would always settle their problems. Arturo would playfully pull Cruz's pant legs to change the mood when things were tense in training camp. Arturo wasn't afraid to admit when he was wrong.

Donny Jerie recalled going into Arturo's condo in Hoboken and seeing photographs of smiling children. Jerie asked Arturo who the children were. Arturo told Donny that he donated money to an organization, possibly Operation Smile, that helps children with facial deformities, such as cleft lips and cleft palates. One in ten of those children die in the first year of life. The survivors are often unable to speak, eat or even smile. In some countries, these children are rejected by society. The parents of the children are often unable to pay for the surgeries necessary to correct the abnormalities. Arturo was very proud of helping these children. While looking at the photographs he told Jerie, *"These are my kids."*[1247] Arturo never told Jerie how much he donated to the organization, but Jerie surmised the amount to be in the thousands.

Arturo would regularly give money away to the homeless to buy food. One night when Arturo was visiting a nightclub in Montreal he heard someone say *"Arturo Gatti!"* in a French-Canadian accent. It was extremely cold and the person was homeless. Arturo asked the man how he knew him. The man told Arturo that he saw him fight on TV when he owned one. Arturo reached into his pocket and gave the man hundreds of dollars. The homeless man was stunned. Arturo asked the man not to use the money to drink because he had bled for the cash. The man would later acknowledge that Arturo saved his life. Over a year later he ran into Arturo in Montreal. He told Arturo that he used the money to buy a suit and clean himself up. He was able to start his life over again. Arturo cried while he listened to the man's story. Arturo hugged the man before he departed.[1248] Donny Jerie recalled, *"[Arturo] would hand out money to people on the streets, hundreds of dollars."*[1249]

One night, Arturo went to the "Crow Bar" in New York City. Gatti passed approximately twenty homeless people as he walked into the club. He left a friend in the bar at 3 o'clock in the morning and stepped outside. The friend thought Arturo was going to talk to a woman. Arturo actually walked down the block and bought every homeless person four or five hotdogs each.[1250]

Chapter 26
Damgaard

In early August 2005, Main Events pondered matching Arturo against the 43-year-old Julio Cesar Chavez, but reconsidered when Arturo refused the fight. Chavez would fight in September, and retire after losing to Grover Wiley. Publicly, Carl Moretti expressed that Main Events had no interest in pursuing Chavez for Arturo.[1251]

On September 22, 2005, Atlantic City's Leavander Johnson died from injuries he sustained in the boxing ring on September 17 in Las Vegas. Johnson was defending his IBF lightweight title against Jesus Chavez when the tragedy occurred.

The bout was stopped in the 11th round, when Johnson was hit with over ten unanswered punches. Leavander, who never went down in the match, collapsed in his dressing room and was quickly taken to a hospital by the ringside ambulance. Johnson was induced into a coma and surgery was performed to relieve pressure from a blood clot on his brain. The surgery was commenced within an hour of his dressing-room collapse. Leavander's father, Bill, was his trainer and cornerman during the bout. Johnson left behind four children. Chavez promised to donate a portion of his title defense purses to a fund being set-up for Johnson's children.

It took Johnson sixteen years of professional boxing to win the championship. In an eerie premonition, before his fateful fight, the 35-year-old Johnson expressed that he was willing to die in the ring.

Ring Doctor Domenick Coletta commented on the tragedy by saying that getting injured fighters to a hospital as quickly as possible was the key to saving lives. Coletta added that it was imperative for all fight venues to have an ambulance and emergency medical personnel on site.[1252]

There were those who were calling for professional boxers to be required to wear headgear, like the amateurs. Coletta reiterated that headgear would do nothing to prevent brain injuries. All headgear does is protect fighters from getting cut or suffering facial damage.[1253]

In the early morning hours of September 24, 2005, Arturo was rushed to Christ Hospital. He suffered from an overdose. Cocaine was found in his system, as well as other drugs. Several people close to Arturo felt that he had tried to take his own life.

Danny McDermott was in Palo Alto, Pennsylvania, preparing for a fight that evening against Eric Burke. While McDermott was resting in his hotel room with his trainer Mikey "Red" Skowronski, Mikey received a phone call that Arturo had attempted suicide.[1254] Allegedly Arturo had called Pat Lynch the night prior and told him "goodbye." Mario Costa explained the incident. *"I was told that Arthur called Pat and said, 'Tell my family, tell my mother, that I said I love them. Tell my family that I love them and goodbye.' And he hung up the phone. Pat called Mike Sciarra, who went over to Arturo's apartment. He found Arturo unconscious and drove him to Christ Hospital."*[1255]

A week later, Gatti's next fight was announced against Thomas Damgaard. The overdose was successfully concealed from the media. No one would fault Gatti's team for protecting their fighter's image, but why wasn't Arturo sent to a psychologist to help him combat his depression? Or to a rehab to combat his drug use? If he was offered help, ultimately the decision to seek that help would fall on Arturo. According to Costa, Lynch tried to downplay the overdose by saying that Arturo had a bad reaction to antibiotics. Gatti's team was doing their best to protect their fighter's image and earning capabilities.

The official hospital report stated that there were traces of several prescription drugs in Arturo's system as well as cocaine. Blood testing at the hospital showed that Arturo had traces of a sleeping pill, Ambien, in his system. The medication was used to treat insomnia. Also found in his system were traces of alcohol and tobacco. Costa recalled, *"Pat Lynch with all that money. He couldn't send Arthur to a rehab or a psychiatrist? Or try to get him help? This is what I have against him. He didn't try."*[1256]

Joey Perrenod, in an interview he had with Jacques Ponthier, confirmed that Arturo's hospital visit was indeed an overdose. Perrenod had been partying with Gatti during the binge that led to his overdose.

Perrenod, who is now deceased himself from an overdose, commented that Pat Lynch chose to ignore Arturo's personal problems and depression.[1257] Joe Gatti found it hard to believe that Arturo hung out with the crowd that he did. Joe recalled working in Harlem on elevators one day when Arturo called him. *"Arturo called and said, 'I'm coming down to see you.' I thought Arturo was going to surprise me, that he bought himself a new car or something. Arturo showed up with a beat up car with Joey Perrenod in it. I was stunned, 'Bro, what are you doing in this car?' Arturo said, 'It's not* mine, it's his.' Perrenod was driving."[1258]

Costa commented on the overdose. "*I have a copy of the document from Christ Hospital in Jersey City, September 26, 2005 [when Arturo was released]. Overdose. When I got the call from Christ Hospital, they told me that Gatti had been found unresponsive at home and that he had no heartbeat. They said he expired. Then they brought him back to fight in Atlantic City three months later in January 2006 [to face Thomas Damgaard for the vacant IBA welterweight title]. I called the N.J. Commission, Main Events, HBO. I said I was John O'Brien, a friend of Arthur's. Arthur had a serious problem. He tried to kill himself. How could you let him fight? They said they couldn't get the records from the hospital. Then I went to Pat Lynch. 'How can you do this? How can you let him fight?' Pat said he just took some antibiotics and he's okay. They covered it up. This is why he's dead. They never tried to help him. It was always about the money, about the next fight. It was about the greed. I found the truth when I got the hospital records myself, after he died in Brazil. It was an overdose and the report said that Arthur needed psychiatric consultation. And they never got the help for Arthur. For years I thought he would die in the ring. His brother Joe would call me at 5 p.m. on the day of his fights, 'They're gonna kill my brother.' Joe would drive to Atlantic City the day of the fight at the last minute. He said, 'I told Arthur you can't fight like this. You're not even 60 percent.' Arthur said, 'I'm not even 50 percent.'*"[1259]

Costa recalled that he spoke to Lynch soon after the hospitalization. "*I said, 'Pat, he's gonna kill himself.' Pat said, 'No, no, no, no.' Arthur had a gun but no bullets. Arthur said, 'Every time I overdose Mario, I come back.' So he figured if he blew his head off, he put the gun like this, he showed me like this [Costa put his finger in his mouth like it was a gun]. When he put it in his mouth I thought the finger was going to come out of his neck. And he actually said to me, 'I'm going to blow my head off so I can't come back. Because I'm too strong. I'm too strong. I always come back.' He thought because he was an athlete that overdosing won't kill him. He wanted to die but he kept coming back. Arthur said, 'I keep coming back.' He told me he wanted to die.*"[1260]

Skowronski believes that Arturo did not try to kill himself. If Arturo was partying and had to get up early the next day he would take sleeping pills. Mikey felt that Arturo took the pills specifically to sleep and not to commit suicide. Mikey recalled that early in

Arturo's career he liked to be up, on cocaine. Later in his career Arturo was in a more mellow state, taking pills and smoking marijuana more frequently, starting in 2002. Skowronski added, *"When Arturo O.D'd in Christ Hospital it was not from cocaine. Arturo had trouble sleeping for years. He would go out on binges for two or three days and then crash and sleep all day. I remember Arturo coming to my house and crashing for two days. Sleeping 17 or 18 hours straight. Someone got Arturo started on downers and valium. Arturo drank Jack Daniels and Coke and beer."*[1261]

When Arturo went out partying, it was for several days at a time. The first night out, Arturo was in a great mood. The second night out, he was ok. By the third night, you didn't know what to expect. His personality, like that of a Gizmo or a Gremlin, would change from happy to angry instantaneously. If Arturo was in a good mood he would pick up other friends' bar tabs, which sometimes ran as high as five or six hundred dollars.

Arturo was not known to fraternize with many fighters while he was not in training. Mikey Red recalled, *"The only fighters Arturo was close to were Mike Tyson, Pernell Whitaker, and the Hilton brothers. Arturo changed after he won the title, because people recognized him everywhere he went. Also, he went from making a little bit of money to a lot. He could do anything he wanted to do."*[1262]

Mikey recalled that people around Arturo tried to help him deal with his fame, *"If you tried to push him too much [to help him] he would just push you away."*[1263]

Arturo flew to Canada the week after overdosing, to announce that he was an investor in a real estate venture in Saint-Leonard. Arturo was in partnership with his childhood friend, Tony Rizzo, who was a builder. Rizzo had attended several of Arturo's professional fights. The name of the company was called the "Gatti-Rizzo Group." Rizzo was the president, Arturo was the vice president. Arturo gifted two condominiums to his family, one to his younger brother Fabrizio and one to his sister Giuseppina. Arturo took a penthouse apartment for himself.

Main Events announced that an agreement had been reached for a bout between Arturo and Thomas Damgaard of Denmark. The bout would be Arturo's nineteenth appearance on HBO. Damgaard was a left-handed boxer with a 36-0 (27 KOs) record. The bout was scheduled for January 28, 2006 at Boardwalk Hall. The fight would be Arturo's first at welterweight since he lost to Oscar De La Hoya on March 24, 2001. Damgaard would be fighting outside of Denmark for the first time in his career. Damgaard had been battling injuries that forced him to cancel several fights over the previous few years. Gatti spoke of returning to the welterweight division. *"I'll definitely win a title at 147. I'll be champion three times."*[1264]

On October 20, Main Events announced that they would start running club shows in North Jersey. They were trying to replicate the legendary Ice World cards they had held in Totowa during the promotional company's early years. The company had attempted television shows, without success, in Pat Lynch's former hometown of Union City, at the Park Theater, as well as in Secaucus and Elizabeth. The financial licensing allowance from TV did not stop the company from falling short of breaking even. Fan bases for club shows had been severely curtailed when TV started airing fights in the 1950s, and it never truly recovered. Without TV, the only way to break even on a show was to focus on local boxers who were popular ticket sellers. Main Events' prospects were not from the area, and therefore would not draw a large crowd in North Jersey.

The first show was scheduled for November 30 at Schuetzen Park in North Bergen and was billed "Back to the Future." Schuetzen Park was located on the border of Union City and was a short five-minute drive north of Jersey City. New York City was only fifteen minutes away, via the Lincoln Tunnel. The Main Events show featured company prospects Jason Litzau of Minnesota and Joel Julio of Florida. Carl Moretti, who lived in North Arlington, a fifteen-minute drive west, was hoping the undercard of local fighters would help the show break even.

Moretti was hoping to revive the great history of boxing in Hudson County.[1265] Some of the famous boxers from the area that Moretti was speaking of included North Bergen's Jimmy Braddock, Union City's Joe Jennette and Guttenberg's Gus Lesnevich. The local's on the card included Bobby Rooney Jr., whose father ran the Bayonne PAL boxing club for many years. Rooney Sr., a former Chuck Wepner sparring partner, had trained "Nino" Gonzalez over twenty years prior. Other locals on the card were Danny McDermott, Henry Crawford and Wayne Johnsen. Arturo attended the press conference announcing the event. He commented, *"It's important that people see the hard work and dedication that goes into the sport. Kids are training and fighting in gyms all over the area and this will show them that they can have a chance, too."*[1266]

For Main Events CEO Kathy Duva, trying to formulate a plan to maintain a club fighting venue, in-between the larger shows headlined by her stars Fernando Vargas and Gatti, was critical for developing her young prospects. The Schuetzen Park hall had a seating capacity of around 800. Without television, the promoter would have to rely on ticket sales to pay for the expenses, which included fighter purses, medical tests, travel expenses, state fees, and lodging. Moretti was hoping to simulate the fan base that Russell Peltz had built at the Blue Horizon in Philadelphia. Announcing that boxing celebrities, such as Arturo, would be in attendance would hopefully boost ticket sales.

On October 27, Arturo and Micky Ward got together to help raise money for the "Bear Necessities Pediatric Cancer Foundation" in Chicago. The pair signed autographs and took pictures with fans who attended the fundraising boxing show at the Chicago Athletic Association.[1267] Arturo was ranked #7 at junior welterweight in *The Ring* magazine's rankings.

Since Arturo's recent loss to Mayweather there was some concern over his marketability in Atlantic City. Main Events was hoping that at least 10,000 fans would come out to support their hero's return. Moretti felt that Arturo's fans would continue to support him after the Mayweather loss. Moretti added that the ticket prices would be very reasonable.[1268]

The Main Events-promoted card at Schuetzen Park was a mixed success. Joel Julio and Jason Litzau both won their bouts, but the local attractions did not fare as well. Of the four locals on the card, two lost and one drew, with only one local boxer winning. The card was Main Events' first club show in two years. The show was a sellout. Kathy Duva promised to hold another show on February 10, 2006. Moretti admitted that they lost a little bit of money, but they expected as much. He felt that the fights were entertaining and the fans had a great time.[1269]

Arturo attended the November 30 card at Schuetzen Park and was visibly drunk at the show. He began shouting that he was ready to get in the ring and fight. After the event, Arturo headed back down to Vero Beach to begin training for Damgaard.

On December 15, the New Jersey Athletic Control Board announced that they had informed Arturo and his management team that Gatti would have to undergo stricter medical testing in addition to the regularly required tests by the board. The recent death of Leveander Johnson had everyone in the sport on edge. Boxing was once again under the microscope.

The board required every boxer to undergo an eye exam, heart exam (EKG), brain exam (EEG), and blood work to check for HIV and Hepatitis B & C infections. Arturo was ordered to undergo a magnetic resonance imaging test (MRI) on his brain along with a complete neurological exam. Normally a boxer is required to take the MRI test once every three years, unless he is knocked out. Retirement of a boxer in-between rounds, such as Arturo was subjected to against Mayweather, as opposed to being counted out during a round, would normally not qualify for the MRI test. Arturo was not due to take the MRI for another year. However, the punishment that Arturo received from Mayweather worried many at the board, and prompted the mandating of the additional exams.

The N.J. State Athletic Commission wrote Arturo a letter regarding the additional testing requirements. *"[The NJACB is] very proud of our worldwide reputation for sincerely caring about protecting the health and safety of the athletes whom we regulate... You have been involved in many exciting contests throughout your professional career. You have been victorious in all but a few bouts, but your body has paid a tremendous toll for you to have claimed those victories."*[1270]

The board requested that Gatti have Dr. Barry Jordan of the New York State Athletic Commission perform the tests. Arturo refused to have Jordan examine him, and instead had the tests conducted in Florida, where he was training for Damgaard. There were rumors circulating that Arturo had friends who were doctors who would give him favorable test results, which might not be accurate. No evidence was ever brought forth to confirm those rumors. It would be difficult to believe that a medical doctor would put his license on the line to help a prizefighter, but celebrities were known to influence their physicians.

N.J. boxing commissioner Larry Hazzard commented on the additional tests ordered by stating that he was concerned about Arturo, just as he was with all combative sporting contestants. He added that no one in any combative sport has been more of a warrior in his professional career than Arturo. Hazzard wanted to ensure that Gatti would be safe to compete again and would be medically healthy when he chose to retire.[1271] New Jersey's Athletic Control Board had been known to order additional testing due to fighters being knocked out, losing several fights in a row, or advanced age.

Pat Lynch was surprised by the letter, but remarked that Arturo would have no problem taking the extra tests. Lynch admitted that the 33-year-old Gatti had been in many wars in his career, and it was better to be safe than sorry. Lynch added that if anything preventable were ever to happen to Arturo in the ring, he would never forgive himself.[1272]

The commission had required Arturo to have a neurological exam after his third bout with Micky Ward. Most in the sport believed that Arturo's handlers, Main Events and Lynch, wouldn't knowingly put their fighter's health in jeopardy. Mario Costa and Joe Gatti felt differently. They knew that Arturo was being sent into the ring after he had visited a North Jersey hospital for an overdose. They also knew that Arturo was sent into the ring less than two weeks after being found on a park bench, passed out, in Virginia Beach.

Arturo had been out-landed by a 168 to 41 margin against Mayweather, with Floyd landing 115 power punches in the eighteen minutes that the fight lasted. That is an enormous amount of head trauma to absorb in such a short period of time. The brain, like any other part of the body, needs time to recuperate from trauma. No one really knew the damage that Arturo may have suffered in all of his ring wars. It was common knowledge that EEGs and MRIs could not detect most forms of brain damage.

Although internal injuries were hard to detect, external effects were not. Arturo's speech had slowed, and he seemed to take more time to process information before he spoke. His facial structure had changed. He went from being a smiling, clean cut boy, to looking more like Vito Antuofermo. Antuofermo, like Gatti, was involved in many ring wars and it showed on his face. Arturo's eyelids were drooping at the corners where punches had smashed into the brow bone. Scar tissue took the place of the brow's hair where punches had sliced open gashes. Arturo's nose was developing a smashed in pancaked appearance and his lips were more spread out, giving a jokeresque aspect to them.

In boxing, the internal effects of many ring wars do not necessarily appear gradually. One day to the next, or more accurately, one punch to the next, a fighter's health can be changed forever. Once the signs of brain damage appear, they are irreversible.

Dr. Domenic Coletta, a N.J. athletic control board physician, ordered Arturo to undergo an ophthalmological dilation exam after the Mayweather fight. He advised Hazzard to suspend Arturo's license pending the eye exam results. When Hazzard advised Coletta of Gatti's upcoming match, Coletta ordered the additional MRI and complete neurological exam.

Joe Gatti recalled his brother's health problems. *"Arturo was blind in one eye for the longest time. Mario called Hazzard and said, 'This guy is gonna die in the ring. You guys need to stop him.' Hazzard said, 'Yeah, we'll look into it.' But Arturo makes too much money [for everyone]."*[1273]

If Arturo were to defeat Damgaard, two of the names being mentioned for his follow up match were junior welterweight Ricky Hatton 40-0 (30 KOs) and welterweight Miguel Cotto 25-0 (21 KOs).

After Arturo's announcement that he was returning to the ring against Damgaard, he spoke with close friend Rich Hansen. Arturo asked Hansen if he should continue fighting. Hansen advised Gatti to retire. It wasn't only because of his age and the vicious battles he had been in. Hansen had noticed that Arturo was showing physical effects from the blows to his head. When Arturo told him he would indeed fight again, Hansen asked why. Arturo replied that he wanted more money.[1274]

Before the Damgaard match, Mario Costa called N.J. boxing commissioner Larry Hazzard claiming to be someone named John O'Brien, to conceal his identity. He warned Hazzard that Arturo had been taken to the hospital in late September for an overdose. He also advised Hazzard of Arturo's vision issues and emotional problems. Costa's phone call may have triggered the additional medical tests that Arturo was ordered to complete. Arturo passed all of his medical tests which required the N.J. State Athletic Commission to allow him to continue competing. Evander Holyfield had his own boxing license suspended in New York and New Jersey. Holyfield argued that his license should be reinstated because if Arturo, who was hit in the head much more, could be licensed, then he should be licensed as well.

Arturo's personal life was in shambles again. Gatti was very jealous and possessive when it came to his dating relationships. He was fighting regularly with his current girlfriend Erika. He suspected her of cheating on him with one of his good friends. He also accused her of seeing one of her ex-boyfriends. His paranoia and rage were uncontrollable. He never trusted any of his girlfriends. His brother Joe believed that Arturo's paranoia was fueled by his drug use. Arturo even drove to Erika's ex-boyfriend's home to confront him about his suspicions.

Arturo threatened the young man with his Irish mafia connections. Arturo, through an Irish boxing friend, had indeed reached out to members of the "Westies" gang. While in Florida, Arturo allegedly tried to put a contract hit out on the ex-boyfriend. The ex-boyfriend was harassed to the point that he feared for his life. A friend of the ex-boyfriend happened to be an FBI agent. The agent responded to Pat Lynch's ticket agency in Secaucus, off the record, and told Lynch to warn Arturo that if he did not stop with his threatening behavior he would be deported back to Canada. Arturo was still a Canadian citizen.[1275]

Donny Jerie recalled that most of Arturo's dating relationships ended the same way. *"With every girlfriend, he's with them, they fall in love, they get crazy because of who he is. He's a good looking kid. And then he breaks up with them and breaks their heart. Fortunately, with every woman's heart he broke [before Amanda], nothing happened."*[1276]

Arturo had started speaking to Vivian Penha again before the Mayweather match. She even went to Vero Beach to visit him during his training for the Mayweather bout. There seemed to be a possibility that Vivian and Arturo might get back together. Arturo told Vivian that he did not love Erika and that he was planning on leaving her soon. They spoke of trying to give their relationship another try. That would all end on Vivian's birthday. Arturo called Vivian. She thought he was calling to wish her a happy birthday, but that was not the case. Arturo had a somber tone as he struggled to explain the situation. Arturo advised Vivian that Erika was pregnant. The hope of Vivian and Arturo getting back together was delivered a fatal blow. Vivian cried hysterically. She demanded to know how Arturo could do this while they were talking about getting back together. She asked how he could get Erika pregnant when he was talking about leaving her.[1277]

Carlos Baldomir shocked the boxing world when he defeated Zab Judah for the WBC welterweight title on January 7, 2006. The upset cancelled the proposed match-up of Judah and Mayweather, which was scheduled for April 8 in Las Vegas. Before having the green belt wrapped around his waist, Baldomir called out Mayweather. The problem with a possible Mayweather-Baldomir match-up was that Baldomir was largely unknown, and would be risky for pay-per-view. Baldomir's promoter, Sycuan Ringside Promotions, was also considering Corey Spinks or Arturo Gatti as possible opponents.

Arturo's phone rang off the hook in Vero Beach after Baldomir's win. Many felt that Baldomir had the perfect style for Arturo. He was small, slow, and not a big puncher. Gatti needed to defeat

Damgaard to make the Baldomir fight a possibility. Arturo called Moretti to have him pursue a match with Baldomir. Gatti had never seen Baldomir fight, but he wanted a shot at a third world title. The flood of phone calls assured him that Baldomir was the "right guy." Arturo even offered to give Baldomir money from his own purse to make the match happen.

Arturo stated, *"It would be a great opportunity for me to fight Carlos Baldomir. It would be great to fight at 147 for the WBC title I lost at 140. It also would be great for [Baldomir] to fight me instead of Mayweather. It's ridiculous for him to fight Mayweather. He'd have a better chance against me. And he'd make more money."*[1278]

Baldomir's style was similar to Arturo's. They both were flat-footed punchers. Sycuan's vice president of public relations, Mike Marley, felt that Baldomir-Gatti would be Gatti-Ward all over again. Stylistically, Marley saw Gatti as the best match out there for Baldomir.[1279]

Promoters of both Mayweather and Gatti lobbied HBO in an effort to secure a match with Carlos Baldomir. On January 17, both Main Event's Carl Moretti and Top Rank's Bob Arum met with HBO boxing executives, trying to sell a matchup with their boxer's against Baldomir. Arum tried to sell an April 8 doubleheader pay-per-view event, pitting Baldomir against Mayweather and Judah against WBO welterweight champion Antonio Margarito, with the winners to face each other on a later date. Moretti tried to sell Gatti against Baldomir in May or June on HBO. Of course, that was assuming that Arturo would defeat Damgaard.

Baldomir was hoping to make much more than the $100,000 he earned defeating Judah for the title. Arum felt that Baldomir's promoter was demanding far too much and needed to come back down to earth in regards to what Baldomir was worth.[1280]

By January 19, nearly 10,000 tickets had been sold for the Gatti-Damgaard match. Arturo had sold out his last six fights at Boardwalk Hall. He was in jeopardy of that streak ending if the remaining tickets weren't purchased. On January 25, Carl Moretti publicly announced that Arturo had passed the medical tests the State Athletic Commission required him to take.[1281] Rumors were spreading that Arturo appeared to be the front runner in the Baldomir sweepstakes, should he defeat Damgaard.

Larry Hazzard expressed that Arturo knew only one style, to give and take. Hazzard added that Gatti was the poster child for extra testing. After Arturo passed his battery of tests, Hazzard declared that whatever was going to happen would happen in the ring.[1282]

The concerns for Arturo's health and well-being were growing in the boxing community. The warning signs of sticking around the game too long were all too visible. Besides Gerald McClellan, who was home-bound with major brain injuries, there were many other stars such as Donald Curry, Meldrick Taylor, Muhammad Ali, Joe Frazier, Ken Norton, Jerry Quarry, Floyd Patterson, Wilfredo Benitez and Freddie Roach, who all suffered from health problems that stemmed from punches to the head. Arturo's team would have to look no further than his brother Joe, who suffered a fractured skull against Sven Ottke. There were countless other, less famous boxers, who suffered from debilitating injuries. There were, however, exceptions, such as Jake LaMotta, who was known for his ability to take severe punishment in fights. LaMotta retained fine mental health well into his nineties.

The *Bergen Record* commented on the sincerity of those close to Gatti, and if they really wanted him to retire. *"The people around Gatti are sincere when they say they'll know when to tell him to quit, but he's a meal ticket for a lot of people, from long-time manager Pat Lynch to Main Events, which has been his promoter since he turned pro 14 years ago."*[1283] The article went on to question why Gatti was matched with Damgaard, a tough, full-sized welterweight, in his first fight at 147 since De La Hoya. *"Why would Main Events put Gatti in with an experienced welterweight in his first fight in the weight class?"*[1284]

Arturo was now an established superstar in the sport. Besides having Micky Ward in his dressing room, Arturo was also good friends with N.Y. Jet Wayne Chrebet and race car driver Dale Earnhardt. On November 4, Chrebet suffered the sixth concussion of his NFL career. He announced that he would retire because of the injuries. Would Arturo follow his good friend's decision and retire himself? It didn't appear so. Earnhardt was a huge boxing fan. He invited Arturo and Micky Ward to the Daytona 500 in 2005, and he put a new engine in Arturo's 1972 Corvette Stingray. Earnhardt had walked Arturo out of his dressing room for the Branco fight.

On January 25, 2006, a press conference was held at Mickey Mantle's restaurant in midtown Manhattan. Arturo arrived at the presser wearing a black overcoat and a black skull cap. Arturo seemed upbeat as he was smiling and shaking hands. He even sat at the bar, sipping a diet coke. This would have been unheard of when

Arturo campaigned in the lighter weight classes. After the reporters were finished with their questions, Arturo played a new boxing video game by EA Sports called "Fight Night Round 3." The PlayStation game featured Arturo and Micky Ward on the game case cover. Both fighters were featured in the game.

Arturo seemed content that he had taken and passed the extra medical tests. *"I was actually happy and excited to know everything was OK. I was pretty sure everything was going to turn out well, but you never know what can be happening in your brain. Losing that fight to Mayweather was hard to accept. It was like someone broke my heart. But that wasn't the real Arturo Gatti in the ring that night. I know people are starting to doubt me again, but I'm going to show them I still have what it takes."*[1285]

Mario Costa commented on the extra tests Arturo was forced to endure. *"One day I told Hazzard straight up how Arthur put the phone close to his face to see it. And then the next fight he had, in the paper it said that Hazzard gave him a very strict medical and I knew it came from me. I said to Hazzard that they keep using him. But I don't know how Arthur passed the tests, because to me, he couldn't see in the last fights. Sometimes he throws the punches like a foot away from the guy. And somebody told me he used to touch the guy with his hand to see and then throw. He would try to touch him with the left and then throw the right. But you see him throwing punches and he's far away from the kid. He couldn't really see and I told Hazzard, 'Listen, something is going to happen.' And Joe always said, 'Mario, they're gonna kill my brother.' The day of a fight, sometimes an hour, sometimes two or three hours before, Joe would go to Atlantic City, because his mind would go crazy. Because he thought that they were going to kill him. He was going to die in the ring. And I thought that the way he lived, and the way that he was not getting help, that he was going to die in the ring. I really did. Then everybody would have went, 'Oh my god! What happened!' Then a week later it would have come out that his life was really bad."*[1286]

At the press conference, Arturo weighed 152-pounds, only 5-pounds over the contracted weight. Arturo had weighed 152 a few days prior to the Mayweather bout, but needed to drop 12-pounds for that match. Pat Lynch felt the change in weight class would help, because Arturo had to work out three times in a steam room on the day before the Mayweather fight. Gatti even ate macaroni the night before the Damgaard weigh-in, which would have been unheard of this close to a fight at 140.[1287] Arturo spoke of his weight. *"I'm 152-pounds right now. When I was 5-pounds away from 140, I kind of felt like I was hallucinating."*[1288]

HBO sports senior vice president Kery Davis declared that Arturo was the best television fighter in boxing because of Gatti's charisma, heart, and talent.[1289]

Arturo publicly admitted that he had a tough time dealing with the Mayweather loss. He finally stopped thinking about the defeat when he headed into camp for the Damgaard match. Arturo recalled, *"I had a really hard time dealing with how I lost to Mayweather. We worked so hard for the fight. I just wanted to give it 150 percent that night. I couldn't do it, but I'm glad Buddy stopped that fight that night, because here I am today. I'm going to win this fight and my career's going to boom again.*[1290] *I'm definitely going to win that title, the IBA, even if it's not recognized. Once it's around my waist, it's going to start being recognized."*[1291]

Damgaard, a southpaw who hadn't fought anyone of Arturo's caliber, did not attend the press conference because he was finishing up his medical testing and license application in Trenton. Arturo spoke of his game plan for Damgaard. *"I can brawl with him, or I can box. We'll see what works for me. A victory is guaranteed."*[1292]

Hudson County basketball coach Bob Hurley, a loyal Gatti fan, spoke of what Arturo meant to the area that overlooks the Hudson River and New York City. Hurley felt that Gatti was one of the most beloved sports figures in the history of Hudson County.[1293] Arturo regularly attended Hurley's fundraising golf outings to help support the Jersey City coaching legend.

Pete Maino, a boxing trainer from Bufano's recalled, *"[Arturo] always had himself introduced from Jersey City, NJ, and me being from Jersey City, I was always so friggin' proud of that and I always respected him for that."*[1294] Gatti proudly announced his residence as Jersey City throughout his professional career.

The day before the Damgaard fight, the *Jersey Journal* printed an article describing Arturo's relationship with Jersey City physician Dr. Frank Rotella. Pat Lynch had asked Rotella to be Joe Gatti's physician when Joe was managed by Lynch. Rotella was a former All-State athlete for Dickinson High School in Jersey City. When Arturo turned professional, he asked Rotella to be his physician as well. Rotella had been with Arturo since his professional debut.

The article spoke of Arturo's close friendship with Rotella's stepson, Joey Perrenod. Perrenod was an assistant coach for St. Peter's

Prep freshman football team in Jersey City. Gatti would often be spotted on the sidelines supporting Perrenod and the team. Arturo donated a large screen television to help the team study game films. Gatti often spent time at Perrenod's home in Secaucus.

Arturo had to wait until the weigh-in to see Damgaard in person for the first time. The only other time he saw Thomas was by video tape. Arturo broke his own rule and reviewed three of Damgaard's fights.

On January 26, Damgaard spoke to the press. He boasted that Arturo would have no trouble finding him during the match because he would be coming right at Gatti. Unlike the Mayweather fight, when Arturo was a 4-1 underdog, Gatti was now a 4-1 favorite. Damgaard had a long amateur career before turning professional. He did not turn pro until 1998 at the age of 26.

Arturo was not taking the Dane fighter lightly. *"I can't [look past Damgaard] because I lost my last fight, and I didn't look good at all in my last fight. He's going to stand in front of me. And if you look at my career, most of the guys who stand in front of me, I knocked them out."*[1295] Gatti was ready for Damgaard to enter his "Thunderdome." In the December 2005 ratings, Arturo was ranked #7 by *The Ring* magazine at 140.

Although Arturo never met Damgaard in person, Micky Ward knew Thomas well. In 1999, Ward flew to Denmark to give Damgaard three weeks of sparring for his bout against Khalid Rahilou. Damgaard remarked that Rahilou was the toughest fighter he had ever faced. He knocked out Rahilou in the 4th round. Damgaard credited Ward with helping him prepare for the win. If anyone was in a position to give Arturo tips on Damgaard it was Ward. Ward felt that Arturo was going to have his hands full, but he was confident that Gatti would win. Ward advised Arturo to avoid toe-to-toe confrontations with Damgaard and stick to boxing. Another reason Arturo would be better served to box was because he had injured his ribs in training. He kept the injury a secret. Damgaard held victories over former lightweight champions Greg Haugen and Phillip Holiday, though both were well past their primes when Damgaard defeated them.

Damgaard had around 100 fans who made the trip from Denmark to see him fight. The remainder of the 11,000 plus in attendance would be roaring for Arturo. Gatti fed off the crowds energy. *"I hear the cheers when I need to hear them. It feels good to know my fans are still behind me."*[1296] Damgaard's trainer, Paul Duvill, admitted that Thomas was not a very technical fighter, but he was strong and powerful. Duvill planned on making the fight very tough for Gatti.[1297]

On January 26, there were only 1,500 tickets remaining for the fight. A day later only 1,200 were left. Carl Moretti felt that Arturo not only needed to win, but he needed to look impressive doing so in order to drum up support for a Baldomir fight.[1298]

Arturo felt that moving up to 147 would benefit him. *"People may not realize it, but that extra 7-pounds is a very big deal to me. I didn't have to work out three times a day this week in order to make 140. I have a smile on my face before a weigh-in for the first time in four or five years. It means the world to me that I look good in this fight. I plan on doing this for a few more years and I plan on becoming a world champion again. This is just the beginning."*[1299]

Arturo may have been less overworked from his move up in weight, but the move up also meant that his opponents would be bigger. When Gatti's cornermen first saw Damgaard in person, they were visibly shocked at how much bigger he looked than Arturo. Damgaard, and his trainer Duvill, planned on utilizing his size, and what they believed was a strength and stamina advantage. Duvill felt that Gatti was getting old and had been badly damaged both physically and psychologically during the Mayweather fight.[1300] The *Press of Atlantic City* predicted an Arturo victory.

Both boxers weighed in at the 147 mark. Damgaard held a 1-inch height advantage, though Arturo held a reach advantage of nearly 3-inches. This fight would mark the twelfth time in his career that Arturo would be boxing at Boardwalk Hall. The Hall was commissioned to be built in 1926 by Atlantic City political boss Enoch "Nucky" Johnson. Johnson built the hall to bring year-round conventions to the normally seasonal shore town. Under Johnson's rule, the city was a haven for alcohol, bootlegging, prostitution, and gambling during the prohibition era. The building was completed in 1929 and boasted a 137-foot-high barrel vault ceiling. In 2010, HBO aired a series on Johnson's rein over Atlantic City called "Boardwalk Empire," with the fictional Enoch "Nucky" Thompson's character based on the life of Johnson. At the time it was built, the Hall, previously called the Atlantic City Convention Hall, had the world's largest clear span space. Lou DiBella commented that Gatti was to Atlantic City what Oscar De La Hoya was to Las Vegas.[1301]

11,568 fans turned out for the Gatti-Damgaard match, the seventh straight time Arturo exceeded the 11,000 mark. Arturo had not lost his Atlantic City magic. An Arturo Gatti fight was not a boxing match, it was an event. Damgaard's small but vocal group of supporters sat in the bleacher section. Boxing was one of the few events where you could find a woman with an evening gown along with a man wearing a Rolex watch, sitting next to someone wearing blue jeans and sneakers. The Hall, which was nearly empty when the first preliminary bouts were in the ring, was filling up fast as the co-main event wound down. No one of status would be caught in their seat for the opening bouts; that definitely was not in vogue. The concession stands that were lined with fans buying food and beer suddenly became abandoned as the main event neared.

Fabrizio sat in Arturo's dressing room and watched as his brother warmed up. Arturo made his way out to the ring flanked by Joey Perrenod and Chuck Zito. Working Arturo's corner were McGirt, Joe Souza and Teddy Cruz. Mikey Red, who was noticeably absent, was told that Arturo wanted to give Cruz a chance to work his corner. Skowronski's previous comments to the media, coupled with his quarrel with McGirt over retiring Arturo during the Mayweather battle, may have played a part in his removal.

Both fighters touched gloves and the bout began. It was nearly a minute into the fight before the lefty Damgaard threw his first punch. Arturo dominated the 1st round, but still felt the need to switch to southpaw with 30 seconds remaining. He switched back a few seconds later.

After the round ended, Duvill told his fighter that he was performing well. McGirt told Arturo to aim his punches for Damgaard's shoulder when throwing the hook. He explained that Damgaard would pull back which would expose the jaw for Gatti.

Arturo took the 2nd round with body punches and combinations to the head. Damgaard's face was almost as red as his gloves. After the round ended, McGirt asked Arturo to keep his left hand outstretched, so Damgaard would not be able to shoot his right jab over Arturo's left.

Arturo started the 3rd in a southpaw stance, landing a straight left to the body. Damgaard had his best round with aggression and punch volume, but Arturo landed the more telling blows.

Arturo dominated the beginning of the 4th until he injured his right hand after landing a straight right on Damgaard's forehead. Gatti shook the hand immediately after making impact. Arturo's offense slowed after the injury. Damgaard used the opportunity to crank up his offense. It appeared as though the Danish fighter was well on his way to stealing the round when Arturo rocked him at the bell with a right cross.

McGirt asked Arturo to ignore the crowd and go back to boxing in-and-out and spinning around Damgaard. Damgaard forced the action in the 5th, though Gatti was landing the heavier shots. Arturo switched back to southpaw with 30 seconds remaining in the round. Gatti finished the round strong.

Arturo effectively fought the first minute of the 6th from a southpaw stance. Pernell Whitaker, who was sitting by Damgaard's corner, left his seat and walked to Arturo's corner to shout instructions to Gatti. Arturo took the 6th. McGirt asked for more head movement. Duvill asked Damgaard to throw more punches.

In the 7th, Arturo landed a right hand high on Damgaard's head. He started shaking his glove again. Damgaard began bleeding from the center of his forehead. With 20 seconds remaining, Arturo switched to southpaw and rocked Damgaard with a straight left.

Damgaard was the busier fighter in the 8th as Arturo appeared to tire. Gatti's punching power was evident as each punch that connected shook the Dane. After the round ended, Arturo finally told McGirt that he had hurt his right hand. Duvill asked Damgaard to throw more body punches.

Both fighters stood toe-to-toe to start the 9th. Uncharacteristically, Arturo was the first to pull away. Gatti switched to southpaw again with a minute remaining and loaded up with two straight lefts.

In the 10th, Arturo switched back and forth, from conventional to southpaw. After landing a right, he bent over in pain from his injured hand. Regardless, Gatti dominated the round with power shots from both stances. After the round ended, Duvill asked Damgaard if he wanted to continue. Thomas answered in the affirmative. McGirt told Arturo to keep Damgaard in front of him and to keep spinning the Dane.

In the 11th, Damgaard held Arturo behind the head with his right and ripped several left uppercuts. Referee Lindsey Page stopped the action and quickly deducted a point for the foul. Arturo pounded Damgaard. With 10 seconds remaining in the round, Arturo landed a left hook-right hand combo that buckled Damgaard's knees. Arturo stepped back as Damgaard stumbled forward. Page jumped in and stopped the bout at 2 minutes and 54 seconds of the 11th round.

Arturo whispered into Lynch and Kathy Duva's ears, telling them that he had broken his hand again. Arturo's mother jumped into the ring. She hugged and kissed her son. Arturo landed 328 of 853 punches to 320 of 908 for Damgaard. Arturo had the edge in power shots, 275 to 196. Damgaard did out-jab Arturo 124 to 53. Gatti's punches were much more powerful throughout the contest. Arturo was well ahead on the scorecards at the time of the stoppage 100-90, 99-91 and 98-92, respectively.

Gatti administered a merciless beating. He admitted that he had hurt his hand in the 4th round. He turned to southpaw because the lefty stance was working and he was landing right upper-cuts.[1302] Damgaard confessed that he thought Gatti was shot after the Mayweather loss, but he was wrong.[1303] Gatti called out Carlos Baldomir.[1304]

After the match, Arturo admitted that if he would have lost to Damgaard he would have retired.[1305] Arturo spoke of fighting with bruised ribs. *"I was going to win that fight, no matter what. A few bruises here and there wouldn't stop me from winning a fight.*[1306] *I didn't tell anyone about my ribs because I wasn't going to pull out of the fight. I'm not that type of fighter.*[1307] *This is the beginning of a new career for me. I want to win more titles."*[1308]

Carl Moretti felt that Arturo looked very good against a quality opponent. Moretti added that a Baldomir-Gatti fight would be a real treat for fight fans, as both boxers were made for television.[1309]

McGirt brought a box of cigars with him to Atlantic City. If Arturo would have looked bad in the fight, McGirt would have broken out two cigars and shared one with his fighter as a sign that it was time to hang up the gloves.[1310] McGirt was impressed enough with Arturo's victory to only take one cigar from his box, for himself, to the post-fight party at Morton's Steakhouse in Caesars.

Christine Staatsburg, a manager at Morton's, recalled that the Gatti after-party was a high-energy bash. Staatsburg added that it became pretty intense because there was a lot of money being thrown at the door by people trying to get in that didn't have invitations.[1311] Besides Arturo and McGirt, the after party included Micky Ward, Dale Earnhardt Jr., Michael Buffer, Chuck Zito, and Wayne Chrebet. Those spectators not connected enough to get into Morton's flooded the casinos, restaurants, bars, and nightclubs.

Ken Condon revealed that the fight was only one part of the weekend's festivities. After the fight, fans gambled and partied at casino lounges and nightclubs, such as House of Blues and Mia. Condon added that fight-week gave fans the opportunity to party with the celebrities that attended the fight.[1312]

Boardwalk Hall's assistant general manager, Greg Tesone, felt that the electric atmosphere of a big-time boxing match was different from concerts or other sporting events. The anticipation of the fight led to spectators seeming more jacked up than during any other type of event.[1313] Kathy Duva added that no matter how many times she had been to a Gatti fight at Boardwalk Hall, the hair on the back of her neck would stand up when she walked in. Dale Earnhardt added that Boardwalk Hall, when full with fans, was electric.[1314]

Rodney Jerkins, a Grammy-award-winning singer, likened a Gatti fight to a night at the Grammy's. Jerkins felt that the energy and excitement of watching the fight in person, rather than on TV, is what made the night special.[1315]

In February, Arturo entered *The Ring* magazine's 147-pound ratings at #6. Ivan Goldman of *The Ring* magazine was concerned that Arturo didn't move his head or feet during the Damgaard fight. Goldman felt that Gatti reminded him of Muhammad Ali when Ali was in the final stages of his career, because Gatti relied on his ability to take punches in order to land his own shots. Of a possible Baldomir match, Goldman predicted that if Gatti didn't knock Carlos out in the first few rounds, he would get beat up, regardless of who won.[1316]

Immediately after the Damgaard match, Gatti revealed that negotiations were already underway for a Baldomir fight. Arturo would have to see a doctor first to make sure his right hand was okay. It was possible that he would need minor surgery to correct the ligament tear near his center knuckle, which was rubbing against his nerve. Arturo spoke of his hand injuries. *"Sometimes I think hurting my hand helps me out, because I start boxing, using my head more. I enjoy [brawling], but it's not going to extend my career."*[1317] McGirt revealed that Gatti was under a lot of pressure to perform at a high level after the Mayweather bout. McGirt was confident that the Damgaard win helped to silence the critics who felt that Arturo should retire.[1318]

Arturo spoke of his future. *"I plan on having a few more years in boxing. I'm not done with this game yet. I had one bad night against the best fighter in the world. But that's in the past. What's in the future for me is another world championship. I don't question Baldomir's abilities. I don't care why he couldn't make a deal with Mayweather, although I can understand it after everything we went through with making the fight. It's just a matter of timing and money with me and Baldomir. We both want this fight, and I believe it's going to get done."*[1319]

Gatti wanted a Baldomir match. The bout was being worked on, with Atlantic City the proposed location. A possible Gatti vs. Judah match was also being proposed. The match would pit two local boxers. Judah, originally from New York, now lived in New Jersey. The match appeared to be a toss-up on paper, with Judah having better hand speed and boxing ability, though not at Mayweather's level, while Arturo had the edge in punching power, heart, and ability to take a punch. The bout would sell very well in Atlantic City.

On February 9, Arturo underwent surgery to repair a torn ligament in his right hand. Dr. Charles Melone performed the surgery, reattaching a ligament near Arturo's middle knuckle.

Main Events had a devastating year in 2005, with several of their top fighters losing career-altering bouts. Besides Arturo and Fernando Vargas's careers declining, Kermit Cintron, Vivian Harris, and Rocky Juarez all lost major bouts which reduced the potential for the company's future earnings. Vargas and Shane Mosley were set to battle each other on February 25 in a pay-per-view match in Las Vegas. Main Events was hoping for a Vargas win to generate interest in a De La Hoya rematch.

Main Events needed Gatti and Vargas to keep winning to give them time to build up prospects such as Juan Diaz, 28-0 (14 KOs), Rocky Juarez, 25-1 (18 KOs), and Joel Julio 26-0 (23 KOs) on their undercards. Obviously, Main Events needed their prospects to remain successful for their investments to pay off.

Carl Moretti commented that although it was important for Main Events that Gatti defeated Damgaard, he felt that the company would have survived if he lost. Moretti added that winning created opportunities, which benefited Main Events.[1320] Main Events was still negotiating a Gatti-Baldomir match. Baldomir wanted $2 million to fight Mayweather. Top Rank declined to pay that amount. Floyd instead took on Zab Judah on April 8. Baldomir wanted $1.8 million to fight Gatti or Hatton.

On February 21, 2006, Joey Gamache filed a federal lawsuit against Arturo Gatti through his lawyer, Keith Sullivan. In the lawsuit, Gamache claimed that he received permanent brain damage as a result of a breach of contract, specifically by Arturo being overweight during the weigh-in. He added that Arturo's weight was "falsely represented."

Chapter 27
Baldomir

On March 10, 2006, Arturo attended a Main Events card at Schuetzen Park in North Bergen. The company was hoping to construct a fan base in order to build up their newly signed prospects. If the company broke even on the show it would be considered a success, because they were getting their fighters wins, which hopefully would turn into future television contracts.

Kathy Duva had grown into one of the sport's most powerful promoters. She convinced NBC and ESPN executives to once again take a chance on boxing. Steve Farhood called Kathy the most powerful woman in the game. Don King, with whom she once went toe-to-toe, called her an excellent promoter.[1321] King once had refused to give Duva credentials for a show that Main Events was co-promoting with King. The 5'7" Duva went right at the 6'4" King, forcing him to give in to her demands.

Main Events carried a smaller roster than their competitors, King and Bob Arum. Kathy felt that she worked more effectively with a small stable of fighters.[1322] Kathy relied on Carl Moretti to discover new prospective talent. In an interview with the Newark *Star Ledger* in April, Kathy declined to reveal her company's finances. Main Events had earned over half of New Jersey's annual boxing revenues, due largely to Arturo's success in Atlantic City.

Kathy credited her success from knowing how to market her boxers. Duva felt it was imperative to know which arena to put the fighter in, how to price the tickets, and how to pick the right opponent who was credible.[1323] Besides running Main Events, Kathy was still a mother. Her daughter Nicole was in law school, her daughter Lisa was studying in Russia, and her son Bryan was at home. Kathy tried to maintain a healthy family life. She occasionally flew to Iceland, halfway from Russia, to meet Lisa. Even after the Duvas split up into two separate companies, Dino and Lou had nothing but praise for how Kathy was running her company. HBO's senior vice president of sports and pay-per-view, Mark Taffet, remarked that while some business people operate with a machete, Kathy operated with a stiletto, extremely effectively.[1324]

Many of Duva's former fighters had positive things to say about the company, such as Pernell Whitaker, who expressed that Main Events stood behind their fighters with no nonsense and no foolishness.[1325] Prospect Jason Litzau reiterated that Main Events definitely looked out for their fighters.[1326]

Giovanni Lorenzo fought the main event on the Schuetzen Park card. The Mikey Red trained Wayne Johnsen fought on the undercard. Arturo, wearing a cast on his right hand, drank heavily at the show. He became combative with some of his friends, including Mikey Red. Sometime during the evening, Arturo started shouting that he was ready to climb into the ring. He banged his cast against a wall, breaking the plaster cast off. Those in close proximity to Arturo, who watched the act, were in shock. Fortunately for Arturo, he didn't damage his hand any further.

Nettles Nasser pulled Arturo out of the main ballroom after a crowd gathered around him. He led Gatti to a back room and closed the door. Arturo looked up at Nassar and said, *"Do I have strings? Do I look like a puppet to you?"*[1327] Arturo was referring to the way that Nasser was pulling him around.

On March 15, 2006, it was officially announced that Arturo would fight Carlos Baldomir on July 22 at Boardwalk Hall, for Baldomir's WBC welterweight title. Carl Moretti felt that the Baldomir match would be akin to Gatti-Ward IV.[1328]

Baldomir accepted $1 million for the Gatti bout, while Arturo would take home $1.5 million plus training expenses. Tickets went on sale on April 1. By April 12 over 9,000 tickets had been sold. Only 3,000 of the upper level tickets remained. Baldomir, who was from Santa Fe, the same town as the great champion Carlos Monzon, didn't seem fazed by fighting Arturo in Atlantic City. Baldomir had previously fought as an opponent in Denmark, South Africa, Germany, and Italy.

Baldomir was 35 years old when he faced Judah. He had not lost a fight since 1998. He was being called the Cinderella Man because of the way his career rebounded. Before he became champion, he sold vacuums, door to door, to pay bills. He earned $100,000 winning the title from Judah. When Carl Moretti called Baldomir to offer him Arturo, Baldomir's camp was thrilled. Arturo offered probably the most money for them with a much lower risk than if they fought Mayweather, Mosley, or Antonio Margarito.

Arturo's rib injury was healed, and he had successful minor surgery on his right hand. Baldomir's face-first style had earned him the nickname "Leather Face." There were those who questioned the validity of Arturo's welterweight title opportunity after beating an unknown in Thomas Damgaard. Many felt that Mayweather and

Antonio Margarito were more deserving of a title opportunity. Showtime's Al Bernstein surmised that Gatti would always get title fights because he was exciting, popular, and marketable.[1329]

Most boxing experts felt that Gatti would win the Baldomir fight. Arturo was an 8-5 betting favorite. Some were even looking past Baldomir. Veteran fight promoter Don Elbaum questioned why Main Events would pick a fast fighter like Mayweather ever again, when Gatti could fill arenas fighting less threatening opponents. Elbaum believed that Gatti versus Hatton would draw 100,000 fans in Europe.[1330]

Baldomir did not speak English. Through an interpreter, when asked his thoughts about fighting on Arturo's home turf, he said it made no difference to him.[1331] Baldomir reminded reporters that he fought as an opponent in England with 15,000 fans cheering against him. Baldomir felt that Gatti was slower than Judah and easier to hit.[1332]

Arturo was taking Baldomir seriously, as Carlos had beaten Zab Judah in a major upset. Gatti felt that Judah didn't have his heart or punch.[1333] The HBO-broadcasted event would be Arturo's twentieth on the cable channel. Only three boxers had exceeded that number; Oscar De La Hoya, Roy Jones, Jr., and Lennox Lewis.

Arturo wanted to shake his reputation of being a give-and-take brawler. *"I'm tired of being called a warrior, the human highlight film, and all that stuff. I'm going to be the welterweight champion of the world."*[1334] Gatti was banking on Baldomir's lack of power. Carlos only had 12 knockouts in his 42 wins. Baldomir also lacked movement. Gatti believed that styles made fights, and Baldomir's style was tailor-made for him.[1335] Larry Hazzard spoke of how Arturo had kept world-class boxing alive in the Garden State. Hazzard acknowledged that New Jersey owed its existence as a big-time boxing venture in recent years to Arturo Gatti. Hazzard added that boxing in New Jersey was pretty much a one-man show the past several years.[1336]

On March 30, there were only 2,000 tickets unsold for the Baldomir fight. Bob Arum was predicting a Gatti victory, and was working on a Gatti-Cotto matchup. Cotto was having trouble making the 140-pound limit and was planning on moving up to 147. Arum felt that a possible Cotto-Gatti match would be huge in Atlantic City, even bigger than Gatti-Mayweather was. Arum had even reserved Boardwalk Hall on December 2, and HBO's pay-per-view had set aside the date for a possible Cotto-Gatti match.

If Arturo won the Baldomir bout, there was concern regarding whether he would have enough time to train for a Cotto matchup. Gatti usually needed three months to shed the weight, and that was not taking into consideration any possible hand injuries or cuts.

On March 31, 2006 at St. Mary's Hospital in Hoboken, N.J., Arturo's first child was born. She was named Sofia Bella Gatti. Arturo was enamored with his daughter. He was as proud as any father could be. Many around Gatti had hoped that becoming a father would ground him and put an end to his wild lifestyle.

Joe went to the hospital and visited his newborn niece. Joe recalled that Erika and Arturo were not on good terms when Sofia was born. Joe and Vikki drove to the hospital with their daughter Versace. Arturo waited behind a glass window and tried to scare Versace as she walked in. It was the first time the pair met and they hit it off immediately. Joe and Arturo had seen little of each other in the five years since Versace's birth.

Erika would later claim that Arturo was a father in monetary terms only. She wound up moving out of his condominium a few months after Sofia's birth. She revealed that she could no longer deal with Arturo's paranoia and constant accusations of her being unfaithful.[1337]

On April 12, with twelve weeks until the fight, Arturo was weighing 168-pounds, well over the 147-pound weight limit. Baldomir was presented the prestigious *Ring* magazine 147-pound title belt by editor Nigel Collins. Gatti left for Vero Beach to begin training for Baldomir on April 25, less than a month after the birth of his daughter.

Arturo was finally opening his eyes to the entourage that hung around him. In an interview with the *Atlantic City Press*, Arturo stated, *"I made a lot of money in my career and there are a bunch of leeches that have emerged to try living off of my sweat. This will never happen again."*[1338]

McGirt knew all too well of the dangers that came with fame and fortune. In 1997, Buddy's life was at a crossroads. The millions he earned in the ring were gone. His utilities were shut off and all of his home's appliances were sold off for cash. His money was spent on bad investments as well as down-and-out family and friends. All of his cars were sold. McGirt even pawned his diamond-jeweled WBC championship ring.

The stress of his spiraling life had caused McGirt to lose over 20-pounds in a few short months. Buddy recalled that people would stare at him when he walked down the street. Half the people thought he had AIDS, while the other half thought he was addicted to crack cocaine. McGirt avoided going to the doctor out of fear of what might be found.[1339] Buddy finally sought medical testing. It was revealed that his weight loss was the result of a hyperactive thyroid and an irregular heartbeat.

In September 1997, McGirt received a phone call from promoter Murad Muhammad offering Buddy an opportunity to work as a cornerman for two undercard bouts in Atlantic City. McGirt recalled that he didn't even have a car to drive, but he did have an old motorcycle. He hopped on the bike with a pair of jumper cables wrapped around his neck and drove the motorcycle from Long Island to Atlantic City. On the drive down, McGirt prayed that he wouldn't run out of gas because he only had $4 in his pocket. An ATM machine had confiscated his bank card.[1340]

McGirt earned $500 for his corner work. Buddy went to a specialist and had his thyroid and heartbeat corrected. Fast-forward to 2006. Buddy was no longer in need of money. He was now training Antonio Tarver and Arturo Gatti. Both fighters were earning millions per fight and McGirt was pocketing his trainer's cut. Besides his earnings, McGirt received a surprise gift from Arturo after Gatti defeated Gianluca Branco. Arturo purchased McGirt a brand new Ford SUV for Buddy's 40th birthday. Arturo also surprised McGirt by purchasing him a replica WBC championship ring. Arturo commented, *"Buddy's like my big brother. I can tell him anything. And it's a mutual respect. He takes care of me and I'm good to him."*[1341]

As of 2006, McGirt still had the motorcycle that he used for that 100-mile drive to Atlantic City. He kept it as a reminder of why he needed to safeguard his money. Looking at the bike kept him grounded and reminded him of where he had been and what it took to get to where he was. Buddy purchased a three bedroom home in Vero Beach in 2004. He also owned a burgundy Cadillac to go along with his SUV.[1342]

Arturo was doting over his newborn daughter Sofia Bella. Arturo stated, *"It feels great to be a father and to have a family. That gives me something more to fight for. Before, I used to fight for myself. Now, I'll be fighting for my family. I'm getting tired of being known only as a warrior. Maybe after I beat Baldomir I'll finally be recognized as an elite fighter, because that's what I am. I know this guy is supposed to be very tough, but being tough isn't enough, especially when you're fighting Arturo Gatti.*"[1343]

Teddy Cruz explained the weight troubles that Arturo had gone through in the past. *"He restricted his body for so long through so many years that now you're going to see the real potential that Arturo's body has. During the training to get ready for 140 it was a nightmare. He feels a lot better physically, mentally stronger."*[1344]

Arturo spoke of his weight issues. *"It was a big problem because I wasn't feeling good. I didn't look good. Everyone was worried around me and I could feel like a sense or a vibration, not a good one. I'm eating grilled chicken tonight. It's pretty much what I eat every night. I'm surprised I don't have feathers on me. My strength's increased so much since I've been with Teddy. I punch real harder now than I ever did. And it definitely shows more explosive. I couldn't swim for shit. I'd swim out to half of the pool and start panicking and now I can swim 20 laps, 30 laps nonstop. It's the same thing like sprinting except you're working the upper body."*[1345]

Arturo spoke of the days when he partied and didn't take training seriously. *"Motivation wise with my old trainer it wasn't there anymore. I didn't feel like doing nothing. I used to play and train at the same time. You can't do that. No athlete can do that."*[1346] When Arturo was a young boy his father used to tell him that he could either live like a fighter or a rock star, but he couldn't do both.

Arturo's training camp was horrendous. He fought with Erika by phone all the time. Arturo's paranoia had no boundaries. He even accused McGirt of trying to sleep with Erika. Arturo, who a month earlier had called McGirt his big brother, was now saying McGirt betrayed him.

Arturo started his camp with eight weeks of conditioning and weight loss. He spent the final four weeks sparring and getting in boxing shape. Arturo planned on offsetting the size difference with Baldomir by lifting weights to build up his strength.

Evan Rothman of *New Jersey Monthly* sat down with Arturo before he went away to training camp for Baldomir. Arturo was asked why he liked to live in Hoboken. Gatti felt that Hoboken was a convenient place for him because it was close to New York City. Arturo added that everything in Hoboken is within walking distance, and the people were very nice. He loved New Jersey and couldn't picture himself living anywhere else.[1347]

Arturo explained why he continued to fight after losing to Mayweather. He knew he wasn't finished after the loss. He felt he had to move up in weight because he wasn't physically comfortable at 140 anymore.[1348]

Arturo was confident that he would defeat Baldomir. He assumed that his next opponent would be Miguel Cotto. Arturo spoke of the 84-unit high-rise investment that he was working on in Canada. Once he secured several more investments to bring in additional revenue, he probably was going to retire from boxing. He added that he loved boxing and was making a lot of money, so he saw no need to retire as long as he was being successful.[1349]

Arturo spoke of his golf game. He played mostly down in Florida, while in training camp. Although it was expensive, he was thinking about joining the Liberty National Golf Club in Jersey City. Arturo commented on how he wanted fans to remember him after retirement. *"That I was the baddest motherfucker that ever stepped into the ring! [Laughs]."*[1350]

Arturo felt that he definitely was Hall of Fame material.[1351] He commented on letting his child box. *"[Sofia's] beautiful and has brought so much joy into my life. My kids are not going to be fighters. If I have a little boy, I can't stop him, and I'd love for him to know how to fight, to protect himself. But career-wise, I don't know... Daddy's gonna pay his way through life, so I doubt he's gonna want to fight."*[1352]

Arturo spoke of boxing's negative reputation. *"When I walk into a public place, a bar, whatever, people say, 'That's Arturo Gatti, the boxer,' and I know right away that there's negativity because I'm a fighter. We have a bad reputation because of some of the things that go on inside and outside the ring. That's got to stop. Everybody wants a piece of the fighters. If the government got involved, there would be better rules, and the fighters would be taken care of. I was very fortunate in that regard. I've been with my manager, Patrick Lynch, and my promoter, Main Events, for a long time now, and we're all making good money, and we're all enjoying it."*[1353]

On July 9, Arturo had something besides boxing to cheer about. His family's native country, Italy, defeated France by a score of 5-3, in two overtimes, for the FIFA World Cup. On Newark's Bloomfield Avenue, the celebration erupted. Singing, dancing, fireworks, and Italian flags waived throughout every Italian community. Joe Gatti joined the celebration in Newark. Joe stated, *"This is like my world championship. Like everybody's prayers answered."*[1354] Joe's daughter, Versace, accompanied her father to Newark. When Italy scored the winning goal, Joe threw his daughter up in the air in celebration. The moment was captured by a *Star*

Ledger reporter. The photograph made the front page of the newspaper.

During training camp, in early July, Arturo responded to the gym with the car window open. Erika had flown to Vero Beach to visit. The thick, heavy heat of the Florida summer that was blowing into the car was nothing compared to the heat that was building up inside of Gatti. It was only 8:30 in the morning when Arturo exited the car. Instead of preparing to train, Gatti confronted McGirt. He interrogated Buddy on his whereabouts the night before. When McGirt told Arturo that he was home with his wife, Arturo exploded and called him a liar. Gatti accused McGirt of being with Erika the night before, until two in the morning.

McGirt was shocked. Either someone was feeding this rumor to Arturo or he was simply delusional with jealousy. Buddy told Arturo that he was crazy. He told Gatti that his wife Gina would never let him leave the house at that time. McGirt advised Arturo that he could no longer deal with his paranoia and was quitting as trainer. Arturo was surprised that Buddy would quit and forfeit his trainer's cut for the Baldomir bout. After word spread of the dispute, McGirt received several phone calls from Gatti's team asking him to reconsider. Buddy told everyone he would only return if Arturo apologized to him. Gatti came back to the gym and did just that. The final three weeks of training camp went surprisingly well, considering the circumstances.

With the exception of the McGirt incident, Arturo was much easier to get along with now that he wasn't forced to diet as severely as he had in the past. Arturo described the move up in weight. *"I feel great. I can't tell you how much of a difference that 7-pounds makes. Boxing is fun again. It's fun to train and it's fun to eat without having to worry so much about my weight."*[1355] Arturo was now able to add whole grain bread and pasta to his normal diet of fruit, vegetables, and lean meats. Gatti no longer had to spend hours on a treadmill while wearing a sweat suit.[1356]

Arturo could focus on sparring and hitting the punching and speed bags. He added plyometric exercises to his training regimen. The most important thing that Arturo added, of course, was the ability to eat the foods he loved, such as steaks, pork chops, and turkey burgers.[1357]

The Ring magazine's July ratings had Arturo ranked #8 at welterweight. Baldomir was the champion and Floyd Mayweather was rated #1. By July 19, all the tickets for Gatti-Baldomir had been sold. Ken Condon commented that the demand for the fight was just incredible. He was trying to figure out ways to add more seats.[1358] Moretti called the boardwalk a scalper's paradise.[1359]

Arturo always had been bothered by the "blood and guts" and "warrior" labels. He felt that those descriptions downplayed his talent. He was tired of being known only as a warrior. He hoped that after he defeated Baldomir he would finally be recognized as an elite fighter.[1360]

The Atlantic City Surf's minor-league baseball team announced that they would be having an Arturo Gatti bobblehead doll giveaway on September 22, as part of fan appreciation weekend. The first 1,000 fans who attended the game, at Bernie Robbin's Stadium, would receive a collector's bobblehead.

On July 20, the *Bergen Record* printed an article on Arturo's relationship with his manager, Pat Lynch. The article spoke of the rarity in boxing of a fighter remaining with the same manager and promotional company for his entire career. The article called the Gatti team, *"A rock of stability."*[1361]

At the final news conference, before his match with Baldomir, Arturo gave Lynch all the credit for his success. Arturo avowed, *"I am who I am today because of Pat's help."*[1362] Arturo admitted that he was not perfect and had made mistakes in his life. Gatti walked into the press conference wearing his diamond-studded crucifix, a matching watch, and a diamond earring.

Arturo and Lynch were very close. Gatti was the usher at Pat's wedding in 1991, and he was the godfather of Lynch's son. Lynch was planning for Arturo's life after boxing. He felt that although Arturo's retirement would be sad, as long as Gatti walked away healthy and wealthy, Lynch would be happy.[1363] Arturo, though, was not planning on retiring. He felt good physically and was not ready to talk of retirement just yet.[1364]

At the press conference, Arturo smiled, turned to Baldomir, and said, *"You won the title in New York and you will lose it in New Jersey."*[1365] Arturo realized that his career was winding down. He wanted to seal his legacy by adding another world title to his resume. Gatti believed that if he could win a third world title, he finally would get the credit he deserved. A win over Baldomir, he felt, should definitely make him Hall of Fame worthy.[1366]

Baldomir was more reserved, wearing a black t-shirt that read "WBC Championship." Baldomir spoke no English. Through an interpreter he said that although Gatti is a superstar, he is slower and has taken too many punches.[1367]

According to Gatti, he wasn't fighting for the money. He wanted to win the welterweight world title.[1368] Arturo was hoping that winning his third title, in three different weight divisions, would finally silence the critics who felt he was not an elite or "A"-level fighter. With a win, Arturo would join an exclusive list of active fighters to accomplish that task; including James Toney, Floyd Mayweather Jr., Oscar De La Hoya, Roy Jones, Jr., and Manny Pacquiao.

This would be the first time that an Arturo Gatti fight was completely sold out prior to fight night. Pat Lynch, a ticket agent, couldn't get his hands on any more tickets. Main Events reasonably priced their tickets, which helped to move them more quickly. Tickets were priced at $50, $100, $150, and $250, with ringside seats selling for $400.

Kathy Duva commented on the ticket pricing strategy and how some people felt that it was better to sell fewer seats at a higher price. Duva felt there was a greater financial reward in pricing the tickets lower and having a full arena than it was to price the tickets higher and have a half-full arena.[1369]

Main Events co-promoted the Shane Mosley-Fernando Vargas match on July 15 at the MGM Grand Garden Arena in Las Vegas. The Main Events-promoted Vargas lost to the Golden Boy-promoted Mosley for the second time, being knocked out in the 6th round. Tickets for that event sold very slowly. The ticket prices for the Vargas fight were double what they were for the Gatti-Baldomir match. Part of the arena had to be curtained off to give the appearance that the arena was full. Only 9,722 fans attended the Vargas match. Sources revealed that as many as 25% percent of those tickets were given away. The ticket prices for the Vargas match were set by Golden Boy Promotions and MGM Grand.

Arturo's career had more lives than a cat. Many boxing experts had considered his career over after his defeats to Manfredy, Robinson, De La Hoya, and Mayweather. Mike Skowronski recalled an Ivan Robinson fan shouting to him at the end of the rematch, *"Your boy had a good run. But everybody gets old. It's over."*[1370] That was in 1998, eight years prior. Pat Lynch had his own thoughts on the man who Micky Ward called Jason from *Friday the 13th*. Lynch felt that Gatti was at his best when he was being counted out by people.[1371]

Scott Woodworth, a promoter for Baldomir, complained to Hazzard about Wayne Hedgepeth's selection as referee for the match. Woodworth, and others at Sycuan Ringside Promotions, felt that Hedgepeth wasn't experienced enough to handle a fight of this magnitude. They also complained that Hedgepeth had only refereed two 12-round and four 10-round bouts in the prior eight years. Hazzard responded that if Woodworth and Baldomir did not agree with his referee selection, they could pack their bags and go back to California. Hedgepeth, 53 years old, had been refereeing for eighteen years.

Hedgepeth had been the referee for Arturo's fight against Angel Manfredy. Baldomir's manager, Javier Zapata, did not think that Hedgepeth was a poor referee, but he was concerned that he had only refereed one other title fight prior to this one.[1372]

Sycuan had first protested the judges that were selected for the bout. Two of the judges, Tom Kaczmarek and John Stewart, were from New Jersey, and one, Hubert Minn Jr., was from Hawaii. They wanted a New Jersey judge replaced with one from Argentina.

Sean Gibbons, matchmaker for Baldomir's promoter, was worried that Gatti's fans would be so loud, it would be possible for Arturo to miss punches, and with the screaming fans, the judges might actually think Gatti was landing shots.[1373] Hazzard refused to entertain changing the referee or the judges. He pointed to the fact that they all had impeccable credentials and none of them had ever been involved in any controversial decisions.[1374]

The small group of supporters who would be cheering Baldomir on included his wife and four children. Baldomir was a part-time boxer and part-time feather duster salesman. The feather dusters were used to clean chimneys. Baldomir sold the cleaning equipment with his father Juan Carlos.

Baldomir worked with veteran trainer Amilcar Beusa, who had trained middleweight champion Carlos Monzon. Since Beusa became head trainer Baldomir went on a tear, going 18-0-2 over an eight-year stretch.

In one of his final interviews prior to the fight, Arturo clarified that he, not Main Events, selected all of his opponents. Gatti added that after he defeated Baldomir, he wanted his next fight to be against Miguel Cotto.

At the weigh-in, Arturo was much smaller than his opponent. Most boxing insiders felt that Baldomir was a much higher level fighter than Damgaard was. Carl Moretti admitted that the fight was going to be difficult. Arturo would have to outbox Baldomir and find a way to keep the Argentine of off him for as long as possible.[1375]

In the dressing room, Arturo laid down to relax. In the room with Arturo was Pat Lynch, Teddy Cruz, Buddy McGirt, and Mikey Red. On the undercard was Paterson's Henry Crawford, a 10-0-1 welterweight. Crawford was trained by Nasser Nettles, with McGirt and Skowronski assisting. Crawford was the third bout on the seven-bout card. Crawford was warming up in a separate dressing room with Nasser. McGirt, Skowronski, and Cruz were getting ready to go assist with Crawford's bout when Arturo erupted, *"What! Are you going to leave me alone here? What am I?"*[1376] Skowronski turned around and remained in the room with Arturo. Besides feeling pissed that his team was leaving him to work a 6-rounder, Arturo may have been thinking that his team felt that his career was nearing its end, and they needed a new prospect to get behind.

Arturo's brother Joe attended the Baldomir fight. When he saw Arturo take his shirt off, Joe was shocked by how muscular Arturo looked. Arturo had been working more with weights. Joe felt that Arturo may have bulked up to give himself a better chance against the bigger Baldomir.

12,765 fans packed Boardwalk Hall for the Gatti-Baldomir bout. The number was a non-heavyweight record turnout for the Hall, surpassing Gatti-Mayweather by 88 spectators. Arturo walked to the ring to "Thunderstruck" while being flanked by Pat Lynch and Chuck Zito.

Baldomir trotted down the runway past Anna-Maria, Ida, and Arturo's step-father Gerardo. All three looked solemnly at the champion as he hopped by them, while one of his team members waived an Argentinian flag.

Arturo looked old as Michael Buffer announced him. He had long sideburns and his hair was dyed dark brown. Gatti had a stressed, concerned look on his face, almost as though he was unsure of his own capabilities. The bouncy confidence that he had displayed before all of his previous battles had evaporated. Arturo turned towards his manager as Buffer announced that he was from Jersey City, NJ. Lynch gave Arturo a confident eye wink as Buffer announced, *"the former junior lightweight world champion, the former light welterweight world champion and current IBA champion of the world!!!!"* As Buffer was speaking Arturo put his head down. The stressed look slowly transformed into a confident smile as Buffer listed Gatti's accomplishments. Arturo bobbed his head up and down in agreement. He made a sign of the cross. Gatti then raised his eyes and panned the sold out arena, admiring his throng of adoring fans, while feeding off their energy. He raised his arms skyward as the crowd stood and cheered. When Buffer announced Baldomir an avalanche of boos rained down from every corner of the Hall. Working Arturo's corner were McGirt, Joe Souza and Teddy Cruz.

In the opening round Arturo appeared the quicker of the two combatants. The size difference between the two men was obvious. Baldomir's gloves appeared smaller than Arturo's because his upper body was so much bigger than Gatti's. Two minutes into the round, Gatti and Baldomir's heads clashed. Neither fighter was cut from the butt. Baldomir was committed to the straight right and left hook, as he threw and landed both punches often. Arturo landed a crunching left hook near the end of the round but Baldomir, unfazed, took the punch as though it were a jab. Round one was fairly even.

McGirt warned Arturo not to get into a slugfest with Baldomir. In Baldomir's corner, Jose Lemos advised Carlos to move his head and stay relaxed.

Baldomir appeared stronger in the 2nd round, landing stiff right hands. Even Carlos' jabs were snapping Arturo's head back. Gatti's left eye started to swell. After the round ended, Buddy asked Arturo to keep his legs closer together for mobility. He also asked for hooks to the body and more movement to the right. Lemos was pleased with Baldomir's performance. Carl Moretti nervously massaged his throat with his hand as he watched McGirt counsel Arturo.

A minute into the 3rd, Gatti landed a solid right that drove Baldomir backwards. Carlos smiled and came right back at Gatti. Baldomir was walking through Arturo's punches and even taunted him by banging his gloves on his own abdomen, asking Gatti to bring it on. The two boxers stood toe-to-toe during the final ten seconds, with Baldomir clearly landing the more telling blows. After the round ended, McGirt pleaded with Arturo to ignore the crowd and box.

Gatti backed Baldomir up for most of the 4th, though the damage inflicted was equal. Arturo kept pressing forward, trying to turn the momentum in his favor. With 19 seconds remaining in the round Arturo landed a thunderous right hand flush on Baldomir's jaw. Carlos, undaunted, fired right back. Arturo looked perplexed at Baldomir's ability to absorb his power shots. Blood started streaming from the cheekbone under Arturo's right eye.

Lemos told Baldomir that they had Gatti right where they wanted him, bleeding and brawling. McGirt asked Arturo for combinations and head feints.

Arturo boxed during the first minute of the 5th. Halfway through the round a Baldomir right stunned Gatti. Carlos swarmed Arturo with chopping blows. Gatti was forced back to the ropes. He threw hooks to the body and head with all his might, just as his father had taught him. *"Sinistro!"* Baldomir was undeterred. He kept pressing forward with shots of his own.

Baldomir had connected with double the power shots of Arturo up to this point. A distressed Carl Moretti stood, took a deep breath, and yelled *"come on!!"* to Gatti in an attempt to motivate Arturo. Moretti was clearly disturbed at what he was witnessing. Baldomir crashed dozens of flush power shots onto Arturo's head. After the 5th ended, McGirt implored Gatti to stop absorbing so many right hands.

Forty-five seconds into the 6th, Baldomir unloaded a power hook to the body. Arturo caught the blow with his elbow and winced in pain. He looked at his arm to check if it was okay. Hedgepeth, thinking the Baldomir punch was low, broke the fighters and warned Carlos to keep his punches up. Gatti switched to southpaw then switched back to orthodox, winging shots at Baldomir. Carlos was grinding Arturo down with his hammer like blows.

McGirt, in an attempt to motivate Gatti, told him that he was fighting much better. Baldomir dominated the 7th with straight rights. Arturo attempted to pick his shots and move, but he had no answer for Baldomir's sustained onslaught of power shots.

Arturo found success in the 8th by punching and moving, but he just couldn't hurt Baldomir. Gatti slipped many shots, but rarely countered cleanly. The pro-Gatti crowd had little to cheer. Arturo hit the canvas twice in the round. Both falls were correctly ruled slips.

McGirt pleaded with Arturo to keep feinting and moving in-and-out. Lemos advised Baldomir to aim for the liver. Arturo bombed away in the 9th, trying to land something that would turn the tide. Gatti missed a wide hook and was winding up with a right when Baldomir countered with a short right of his own that buckled Arturo's knees. Carlos drove Gatti to the ropes with a flurry of punches.

Baldomir connected with punch after punch on Arturo's jaw. Gatti's mouthpiece came flying out. Arturo tried to open up, but every time he did, Baldomir countered with a crushing blow. Pernell Whitaker screamed for Gatti to fight harder. Russell Peltz jumped out of his seat, anticipating the end of the bout. Several young Arturo fans could be seen yelling, *"No, No, No!"* as the blows rained down on their hero. Arturo loaded up with a hook, hoping for another miraculous comeback, but as he did so he exposed his jaw. Baldomir countered with a hook of his own that dropped Gatti to his knees with 34 seconds remaining in the round. Arturo was up at the count of six.

Baldomir, sensing the end was near, stormed right back in with a flurry of combinations that drove Arturo onto his back with 12 seconds remaining in the round. Hedgepeth had seen enough. He waived the fight over. He pulled Arturo's mouthpiece out while Gatti was still on his back. Baldomir's corner exploded in celebration.

Baldomir landed 267 out of 562 punches to Arturo's 161 of 445. Gatti appeared to have injured his right hand in the 5th round. Arturo didn't think the hand was broken. Gatti landed 36% of his punches compared to Carlos' 48%. Arturo landed only 116 power blows compared to Baldomir's 226. Arturo commented that he had never fought anyone as physically strong as Baldomir. He added that every round Carlos seemed to get stronger, while he grew weaker.

Before Michael Buffer announced the official time of the stoppage he asked for a round of applause for *"the champion who has given us so many thrills here in Atlantic City and around the world, Arturo Gatti."* It appeared as though Buffer made the statement in anticipation of this being the final fight of Gatti's career. Arturo would not commit to retiring. He said that he just wanted to rest. Larry Merchant repeatedly asked Arturo if he was going to retire, almost hinting at Gatti to hang up the gloves. Arturo replied that he would think about it. Baldomir wasted no time in calling out Floyd Mayweather, Jr.

Mario Costa had said that when Arturo lost, it was like someone stuck a knife in his back. And that was when Gatti lost while he was still standing. This was different. Arturo, the warrior, was forced to surrender on his back in front of the very people who idolized him. He couldn't get out of the arena quick enough. His fairytale career appeared to finally end via an unceremonious knockout defeat.

Gatti announced that he would contemplate retiring, but no one believed that he would. He had one fight remaining on his HBO contract. His home was the squared circle. Leaving the ring after a victory was all he could wish for now. Veteran boxing beat writer Jack Obermayer said it best. *"Should Gatti retire? I would say yes. Why continue in rather meaningless fights? Maybe one more to go out a winner."*[1377] Everyone close to Arturo knew how important that was to him. He desperately needed to go out on top.

Arturo was known to briefly attend post-fight press conferences, if he attended them at all. He either had an emergency room to visit or a party to attend. This night, his appearance was short because he was stunned and devastated. Everyone had told him that this would be an easy victory. He practically could smell the leather of the championship belt that was going to be wrapped around his waist. It was not to be.

The *Bergen Record* opined regarding Arturo's future, *"Before he becomes a name opponent for rising fighters to beat on their way up, Gatti needs to take stock of his life. At 34, he has a young family to think of. If he wants to enjoy his daughter growing up, he needs to hang up his gloves before he's another casualty of a brutal sport... Fortunately, Gatti, unlike many boxers, has people around him who care for him. Although Gatti has always had a fondness for a fast-paced lifestyle, Pat Lynch, who's as much his friend as his manager, had Gatti invest in real estate in his native Canada."*[1378]

HBO Sports' Kery Davis announced that the network would follow Arturo's lead as far as retirement was concerned. Davis added that they would throw a party for Gatti if he decided to retire.[1379] There would be no retirement, and no party; not with one fight remaining on his HBO contract.

In boxing, as in life, winners are only praised when they are winning. Many in Arturo's entourage had scattered to the wind. Out on the boardwalk a severely inebriated male was lying on his back. As the police attempted to stand him up, he flopped back down to the ground. One of Gatti's fans, who was passing the scene, shouted, *"Hey, Arturo Gatti, get up!"*[1380]

In one night, all of Arturo's heroic battles had been erased from memory. He now was being compared to a homeless drunkard. After earning over $16 million in his career, it appeared time to hang the gloves up.

Main Events middleweight prospect, 25-year-old Giovanni Lorenzo, stopped Byron Mackie on the undercard to improve to 21-0 with 13 KOs. The Dominican Lorenzo was being groomed to be the next big draw in Atlantic City.

Ken Condon felt that it would be a setback if Gatti retired, because Arturo had carried boxing in Atlantic City for several years. Condon added that he could not thank Gatti enough for what he did for Atlantic City. If Arturo ever decided to fight again, Condon said his door would always be open.[1381]

Arturo didn't let the loss interfere with his after party. He went out drinking and eating with his new girlfriend, bartender Carrie Kauffman. He ate at The Palm restaurant in the Tropicana hotel. After eating, Arturo was spotted at the 32 Degree Luxe Lounge with Micky Ward. He was buying bottle after bottle of Cristal Champagne. The bottles cost hundreds of dollars each.[1382]

Arturo ran into McGirt at the bar in Bally's. Buddy was waiting for his paycheck. The boxer and trainer embraced. Arturo thanked Buddy for helping to revive his career. Arturo had already decided that they would never work together again. Their five-year fairytale run was over. It ended like any other relationship that lacked trust and loyalty. It didn't matter whether Arturo's accusations were real or imagined. Arturo was convinced that McGirt had betrayed him. Of course, a win might have smoothed things over, but the loss only magnified the tensions.

Buddy was leaving the hotel at 5:30 in the morning when he heard Arturo calling his name. Arturo had been partying all night. Gatti asked McGirt to have a drink with him before Buddy left. McGirt politely declined, but Arturo insisted. Buddy gave in and shared a drink with Arturo. The pair avoided the issues that had led to Arturo's distrust of him. It was not the place or time. Their relationship had run its course. McGirt would later state that Arturo was paranoid with everyone, not just him.

Buddy headed to the airport and back to Vero Beach. McGirt tried having friends inside the business talk to Arturo. He even reached out to Pat Lynch himself, in an effort to mend the ill feelings. Buddy wanted to continue coaching Arturo. Lynch appreciated all that McGirt had done for Team Gatti, but he was not in a position to dictate who Arturo's trainer would be. Lynch bluntly told McGirt that Gatti was the boss. Arturo made the decision on who his trainer would be. When Lynch was asked by reporters to comment on the split, he diplomatically stated that he did not know what had caused the break-up between Arturo and Buddy.

Besides his trainer, Arturo ultimately made the final decision on who he fought as well. Mikey Red recalled Arturo asking him his opinion whenever an opponent was presented to Gatti by Lynch or Main Events. Skowronski felt that Lynch was annoyed that Arturo was not always satisfied with Lynch's and Moretti's choice of an opponent. He felt that Lynch was even more irritated that Arturo sought Mikey Red's opinion on prospective opponents.

Arturo wasn't the only one on a slide. McGirt's golden touch as a trainer was taking a heavy hook to the jaw. Besides Gatti's demise, McGirt fighters Lamont Brewster, Antonio Tarver, and Joel Julio all lost major fights under Buddy's guidance in 2006.

Chapter 28
Gomez & Retirement

A few weeks after his loss to Baldomir, Arturo was hired for a photo shoot by the Everlast boxing equipment company. Arturo was photographed wearing equipment for their fall catalog. The session was held at the World Boxing and Fitness Center in Jersey City. Arturo arrived for the photo shoot with his German Shepherd, Rex. After the session was complete, Arturo sat down for an interview.

Gatti was asked how he was feeling. He admitted that it had been especially hard for him to watch boxing on TV. If he had won the Baldomir fight, everything would be different. He would be walking around as world champion again.[1383]

Arturo put to bed any rumors of retirement. He was lifting weights to get bigger and stronger so he would be able to compete against welterweights. Instead of going on a party binge, Gatti was back in the gym a week after the Baldomir fight.[1384]

Arturo would not be seeking a rematch with Baldomir, but he felt that he still could win another world title. He stressed that he was not going to walk away from boxing as a loser. He wanted to fight Miguel Cotto, because Cotto had been hurt at 140-pounds. Gatti felt that he too could hurt Cotto.[1385]

Arturo commented on his tribute website page, where fans were saying that he had "more heart than anyone ever." His fan support encouraged him to continue fighting.[1386]

Regarding his connection to the North Jersey fight fan and his success in drawing crowds to Atlantic City, Arturo felt that fans supported him because he was a hard-working overachiever. Although he was blessed with power, he admitted that he had average hand speed and size for a fighter.[1387]

Arturo spoke of the always present danger of suffering permanent physical damage in the ring. *"I look at it this way: I believe in heaven and I know my dad looks out for me. He passed away when I was a kid, but I know he's there. I know that he would be so proud of me for what I've accomplished and I know he's behind me in the ring."*[1388]

Gatti felt that being a boxer made him an easy target for girls looking to take advantage of him. He also had to deal with tough guys in bars wanting to fight with him to make a name for themselves. Arturo admitted he enjoyed fighting in bars when he was younger, but he now realized it was a no-win situation. If he knocked someone out in the street he would get sued.[1389]

Arturo wanted to be a role model for his daughter. He wanted her to be proud that she was Arturo Gatti's offspring. One of the reasons Gatti was not retiring was because he wanted to use the money from his next fight to invest in his construction project in Montreal. He was proud to be bringing jobs to Canada, though he added that he never would want to live in Montreal full-time.[1390]

Arturo spoke of what Boardwalk Hall meant to him. He planned on returning to the Hall often, for the rest of his life. He planned on taking his daughter there to explain to her what her father had accomplished in the building. Gatti felt fortunate to have a place to return to like Boardwalk Hall. He stated that not many soldiers could go back to the battlefield and be able to say that this was where they fought their wars.[1391]

On August 6, an article was published concerning the current misfortunes of Main Events. Arturo's loss and possible retirement, coupled with Fernando Vargas' loss a week prior, had devastated the company. Vargas, who earned $3.4 million, was knocked out easily by Mosley. Many in boxing felt he was finished as a contender and should retire. Adding to the bad breaks, two of the company's costly investments, heavyweight Calvin Brock and WBA lightweight champion Juan Diaz, now were free agents, as their contracts with Main Events had expired.

Carl Moretti commented that Main Events' success or failure was not dependent on one or two fighters. Main Events wanted to continue working with Brock and Diaz if the price to re-sign them was realistic.[1392] Moretti added that the situation was magnified because two of their top earners had lost back-to-back fights. He admitted that Main Events already had been planning for when Gatti and Vargas would retire.[1393]

With the Baldomir loss, Gatti's projected match with Cotto was off the table. Another Main Events investment, Rocky Juarez, lost fairly easily to Marco Antonio Barrera in their championship rematch on September 16. Joel Julio's loss in a bid for a world title turned the company's slide into an avalanche.

Kathy Duva knew that Vargas and Gatti's careers would come to a close one day, but she admitted that she didn't expect it to happen all at once.[1394] Both losses were broadcast on HBO. Main Events needed the lucrative financial benefits, from licensing fees and purses, that they received from their boxers fighting on premium cable channels and pay-per-view. The funds were needed to help pay the salaries of their employees, provide extra money for signing bonuses of new prospects, and fund local club shows to build the records of their prospects, both on their own shows, as well as small-time-promoter-run shows.

The biggest loss from not having a marquee name on a premium cable channel was losing the opportunity for their rising prospects, such as featherweight Jason Litzau, 19-0 (17 KOs), and bantamweight Raul Martinez, 15-0 (11 KOs), to have the exposure of fighting on the big-fight undercards that might eventually turn into a main event slot on the networks.

Arturo and Erika wound up in court in September over child support and visitation rights. Erika allowed Arturo to visit Sofia as often as he liked, but he rarely did. Erika and Arturo fought constantly whenever they spoke. Erika claimed that Arturo threatened to take Sofia to Canada against her wishes. Erika also alleged that when Arturo was taken to Christ Hospital two years prior, it was because Arturo had attempted to commit suicide.

Arturo's friend Chuck Zito recalled that Arturo made sure that Sofia wanted for nothing. Zito alleged that Erika was addicted to money.[1395] Pat Lynch's brother John, an attorney, claimed that Erika was focused solely on Arturo's boxing fortune and was out to get as much money as she could. John Lynch added that the child support battle was nasty. The legal proceeding left a bitter taste in Arturo's mouth. It only confirmed his belief that everyone was trying to use him for his money.[1396]

Arturo allegedly spent $700,000 in legal fees during the court battle with Erika over Sofia. Erika's only connection to Arturo's family during the ordeal was through Arturo's brother Joe. Erika would bring Sofia to Joe's house, and Sofia would play with Joe's daughters Gianni and Versace. Joe would tell Sofia stories about himself and Arturo, when they were young kids growing up in Montreal. Joe was still working as an elevator mechanic foreman. He earned extra income as a part-time flatbed tow truck operator.

On September 18, WBA lightweight champion Juan Diaz, who Main Events invested heavily in for six years, announced that he would not be re-signing with Main Events. Diaz signed with rival promotional company Don King Productions.

Main Events did re-sign Calvin Brock. The *Bergen Record* believed that the company had *"overpaid"* in re-signing the prospect.[1397] Soon after, Main Events secured a title match for Brock with Wladimir Klitschko. The company had promoted three heavyweight champions in the past: Evander Holyfield, Michael Moorer, and Lennox Lewis. Main Events was well aware of the benefits they would gain if Brock pulled off the upset. Carl Moretti acknowledged that it would take three Rocky Juarezes or Juan Diazes to equal Calvin Brock becoming heavyweight champion. Moretti was speaking of the leverage and money-making capability associated with owning the rights to the heavyweight champion.[1398]

Kathy Duva commented on the ups and downs of the boxing business, and how Main Events survived down cycles in the past. She recalled when Vinny Pazienza fought Greg Haugen for the lightweight title in 1987. Dan Duva told Kathy if Pazienza were to lose, Main Events would be forced to go out of business. Pazienza won the fight. Kathy assured that Main Events was still a strong company, even with the current bad breaks they were experiencing.[1399]

Main Events had indeed experienced many ebb and flow moments in its existence. A little over a year after the Pazienza-Haugen match, the company would experience its second round of world champions, after Johnny Bumphus, Rocky Lockridge, and Bobby Czyz, when Meldrick Taylor, Pernell Whitaker, and Evander Holyfield won titles. The three superstars had put Main Events on par with Don King Promotions and Top Rank.

Kathy Duva explained that having a heavyweight champion would change everything overnight. When Holyfield won the heavyweight title, her family's lives changed dramatically. She was hoping for a repeat when Brock fought Klitschko on November 11.[1400] Duva was lucky to get the Klitschko match when negotiations for a Shannon Briggs-Klitschko fight fell apart.

Main Events tried to make a match with Brock and Wladimir's brother, Vitali, but Brock backed out of that match because he felt he wasn't ready for that big of a step up. Unfortunately for Duva and Main Events, Brock was unable to pull off the upset. He was knocked out by Wladimir in 7 rounds.

Dan Rafael commented that even though boxing fans were bloodthirsty, no one wanted to see a fighter such as Arturo get seriously hurt.[1401] In "The Final Word" section of World Boxing's winter 2006 issue, reader Nick Strother reiterated Rafael's thoughts when he expressed that it was heartbreaking watching Arturo get beat up by Baldomir. Like most fans, he hoped that Arturo would retire for good.[1402]

Pat Lynch was asked his thoughts on Arturo's future, as he had one more bout remaining on his HBO contract. Lynch said that although he would be happy if Gatti retired, he admitted that they were looking for a fight for the spring or early summer of 2007. Lynch added that Arturo wanted to retire with a win, and he supported Gatti's decision. Lynch was looking at Atlantic City, New York, or Montreal as possible locations for Arturo's next match.[1403]

Joe Gatti sold his home in Kinnelon and moved to Wycoff, N.J. His relationship with his brother continued to be strained.

On November 29, it was confirmed that Arturo would fight again in the summer of 2007. Ken Condon pondered whether anyone could replace Arturo's drawing power in Atlantic City. He understood that East Coast fight fans were desperate for a boxer to support.[1404]

Carl Moretti spoke of plans to bring the 34-year-old Arturo back to Atlantic City. He believed the best fight for Gatti would be against Miguel Cotto. He added that Arturo did not want to retire after a lopsided loss.[1405]

Top Rank's Bob Arum was hoping that his fighter, Miguel Cotto, would fill the Atlantic City void left by Arturo's looming retirement. Arum pointed to the fact that Cotto was an all-action, exciting fighter who had a solid fan base.[1406]

Who Arturo's trainer would be for his next bout was still up in the air. The only thing known for sure was that McGirt would not be his trainer. Arturo's longtime friend, Mikey "Red" Skowronski, lobbied hard for the assignment. Arturo told Skowronski that he would consider hiring him as trainer. Al Certo, Buddy McGirt's old trainer/manager, was considered to be the front-runner for the job.

Arturo was still reeling from his legal dispute with Erika Rivera. He entertained himself by frequenting the Squeeze Lounge gentlemen's club in Weehawken, N.J. Arturo was attracted to the club because he did not need a car to get there. Arturo could walk from his condo or take a quick cab ride. The Squeeze Lounge had a bar that was approximately 15 feet wide by 30 feet long. There were two dancing poles and 20-foot-high ceilings. The club, with its dark colored walls, had an impersonal, commercial feel to it. When you entered, two bouncers greeted you at the door. Eight to ten girls, some attractive, but most average looking, took turns dancing and making their rounds collecting tips. The club had a depressing atmosphere. One could sympathize with Arturo, under the influence of drugs and alcohol, spending his nights searching for companionship at the club.

How could being the "celebrity" matter in such a dreary place? The patrons didn't respect the dancers and the dancers didn't respect the patrons. The dancers looked at the customers as though they were ATM machines. All a girl needed to do was use her charm to get the customer's attention and the ATM password was hers.

It was possible that Arturo looked at the girls much like boxing looked at him. An entertainer up on a stage that was being controlled by the money and the excitement. Instead of a pole and a stage, his tools were gloves and a ring. It was the same flesh peddling, but one was stripping, while the other was fighting. When Arturo was up on his stage, in the ring, did he feel as though he was the clown that was described in Journey's hit "Faithfully," when they sang, *"Circus life, under the big top world, we all need the clowns to make us smile."*[1407]

Before Arturo started hanging out at the Squeeze, he frequented many other strip clubs in the North Jersey and New York City area. Arturo hung out at Scores in New York, Lookers in Elizabeth, Satin Dolls [known as Bada Bing on the Sopranos show] in Lodi, and AJ's in Secaucus. There were months when Arturo visited AJ's almost on a daily basis in the late 1990s.

Arturo spent most of his time in the private lounge areas which were lined with sofas and chairs. The expensive champagne would flow whenever Arturo arrived. An hour or so in a private room with a dancer would run Arturo a thousand dollars or more. Arturo would pay for his friends to indulge in the entertainment. The Squeeze had a private upstairs lounge. Arturo would take many a dancer up to the room, paying hundreds of dollars at a clip.

One of Arturo's friends observed Gatti's credit card statement and saw that Arturo had spent over $30,000 at Lookers. Arturo's brother Joe wasn't surprised, as Arturo loved his Dom Perignon. Some of Arturo's friends surmised that he spent over $750,000 at the Squeeze Lounge in his lifetime. Arturo would have been better off buying his own strip club. When Arturo walked into the Squeeze, it was like the club had hit the jackpot. Arturo's brother Joe recalled that Arturo once spent $40,000 in a week at the Booby Trap strip club in Pompano Beach, Florida. Arturo became so wild in the Booby Trap, the owner of the club was forced to call Joe and plead, *"We need your brother outta here."*[1408]

Some of Arturo's friends felt that Gatti was attracted to the "fast girls" because they were the only ones who would tolerate his crazy lifestyle. Joe felt that Arturo was trying to fill a gap left by a lack of real love from his family. Chuck Zito, a bodyguard for superstars who had met Arturo at Scores in New York City, felt that Arturo was attracted to the club life because he could satisfy himself sexually without any effort. Some claimed that the repeated blows to his head had destroyed Arturo's moral compass.[1409]

Arturo became friends with Zito and hired him to be his bodyguard on the weekend of his Atlantic City fights. Zito walked Gatti into the ring. Arturo was very superstitious on fight weekend. He ate in the same places and was surrounded by the same friends. Zito was one of the rare newcomers who was allowed into his inner circle. It hurt Joe that his brother never offered him a fight week bodyguard assignment as Joe could have used the money that the assignment generated. When Arturo retired, he told a close friend that he felt guilty that he did not hire Joe to be part of his fight week security team.

Arturo walked into the Squeeze Lounge in late 2006 with his German Shepherd Hex. Although dogs normally were not allowed into the club, the general manager made an exception because Arturo was a celebrity.[1410] Amanda Rodrigues allegedly was one of the girls dancing in the club. It should be noted that Amanda has consistently denied ever working in the club, and insisted that such claims were false. According to the club's manager, Amanda was working in the club and she asked why a customer was allowed to bring a dog into the business. The manager told her that Arturo was a world champion boxer, the owner's close friend, and he was permitted to bring his dog into the club. Although Amanda maintains that she never was employed at the Squeeze Lounge, several club employees claimed that this is where Amanda met Arturo.

In the Squeeze Lounge, the girls would work in groups of three. They would rotate dancing on the stage in bikini's. After the girls rotated off of the stage they would make their rounds, enticing patrons to buy them drinks and tip them heavily. It was all part of their money-making routine.

When Arturo walked in with his dog, Amanda allegedly reacted to Hex by telling a barmaid, *"Look at that dog. He's humongous."*[1411] Amanda was 5'2" tall, with a petite build. She had a belly-button piercing and a powerful yet seductive manner.

Amanda had come to the United States from Brazil in 2000 with her mother, Rosie Barbosa. Amanda was only 14 years old when she entered the country. Barbosa, when interviewed, recalled that her daughter had attended Hillside High School and Union County Community College, studying business. According to Barbosa, Amanda also worked at a Toyota dealership, a Nextel store, and a clothing shop. Barbosa did not believe that her daughter ever had worked in a Gentlemen's club.[1412]

Not long after, Arturo called his friend Omar Sheika, a super middleweight contender, and asked him if he wanted to go to the Squeeze Lounge. Sheika and Arturo often went out together. Sheika picked up Arturo and they drove to the Squeeze. Sheika stated, *"I was there when Arturo hooked up with Amanda."*[1413] Sheika allegedly recalled Amanda dancing on the stage for him and Arturo. Barmaid Nehomy Prosperi also purportedly recalled Amanda dancing in the club.

Arturo and Amanda would later state that they met in the park in Hoboken, while walking their dogs. However, Amanda lived 15 miles away, in Elizabeth, N.J. Why would she drive 15 miles to walk her dog? Nevertheless, Amanda stated that she was walking her small dog, Bella, and Arturo was walking Hex when they met. She recalled that the two dogs met and fell in love with each other. She added that Arturo took her phone number and they went out that same day, after which they became boyfriend and girlfriend.[1414]

Amanda not only denied that she had ever worked at the Squeeze Lounge, she was confident that there was no documented proof that she had ever worked there. Even when a photo surfaced of her on the stage in a bikini, she said that she was only dancing for someone's private birthday party. Amanda challenged the club's owner to show proof that she had ever worked at the club. No documents were ever produced.[1415] A source stated that some of the girls who danced at the club did not have the required bar card license. A club that employed dancers without a bar card would not be able to officially list the unlicensed girls as employees. The club risked being fined if it were discovered that they had unlicensed girls dancing on stage. If Amanda was working without a bar card she could be confident that there would be no record of her ever being employed at the club.

Not long after Arturo and Amanda met, the jealousy started. Arturo still frequented the Squeeze Lounge, which became a source of arguments between the couple. Most women would disagree with their man hanging out in exotic strip clubs, but for Amanda the situation was magnified. Arturo not only had an affection for the clubs, many of his relationships had evolved from girls he had met in the clubs. Within weeks of meeting, Amanda and Arturo were a couple. Soon thereafter, Amanda allegedly quit her purported job at the club. A dancer at the Squeeze named Jessica recalled that Arturo would often tip the dancers with $100 bills. After Gatti started dating Amanda, she advised the other girls working in the club that Arturo was off limits.[1416]

Arturo would call Omar Sheika when he wanted to go party. The pair would go out drinking, hopping from one exotic club to another. One night at around 4 a.m., Sheika told Arturo that he was calling it a night. Arturo begged him to go to New York with him, but Sheika refused. At 8 a.m., Sheika was fast asleep when his cell phone started ringing. He saw the name Arturo Gatti and figured Arturo was calling him to ask if he wanted to go eat breakfast. When Sheika answered the phone, he could hear music blasting in the background. Arturo told Sheika that he was in Scores Gentlemen's club in New York, playing cards. He asked Sheika to come over and hang out. Sheika replied, *"What are you crazy?"*[1417] Arturo partied like he trained, hard. Scores would secretly stay open after hours for celebrities. Sheika recalled observing NBA stars, such as Dennis Rodman, at the club. Actors, including stars from the *Soprano's* series, also frequented the club.

Not long after the pair became a couple, Amanda allegedly forbade Arturo from going back to the Squeeze Lounge. Arturo would still sneak into the club on occasion. Once, when Amanda found out that Arturo had been to the club, she went to the Squeeze to confirm the rumor. When she was advised that Arturo had spent time in the club, she asked if any of the girls had given him lap dances. Jessica admitted that she had, because it was her job. Amanda confronted Arturo about his visit to the club, which resulted in a heated argument. Arturo stopped going to the club.[1418]

Both Amanda and Arturo were described as jealous and possessive. Amanda's mother Rosie blamed alcohol for most of the couple's troubles. She revealed that, although she loved Arturo like a son, when he drank he lost control of himself.[1419]

On January 3, 2007, Pat Lynch was contacted by a representative of the New York Jets. The football team had an important game coming up against the New England Patriots, the AFC Wild Card game at Gillette Stadium in Foxboro, Massachusetts. Jets head coach Eric Mangini, a huge boxing fan, wanted Arturo to give a motivational speech to his players. Arturo had planned to fly up to

Canada to visit family, but he rearranged his plans to speak to the team.

On Saturday, January 6, a day before the game, Arturo flew up with retired Jet Wayne Chrebet to speak to the team at their hotel in Providence, Rhode Island. The Jets offered Arturo sideline passes to the game, but he preferred to sit in a private luxury box seat with Chrebet. Mangini played the video of Gatti-Ward II to the team before Arturo spoke. The speech did not lead to a victory, however, as the Jets lost 37-16.

On January 4, 2007, Main Events was hit with another devastating loss; this one not in the ring. Carl Moretti, who less than a year prior had avowed that Main Events was not in trouble with their recent string of losses, announced he was leaving the company. Moretti joined Main Events' metropolitan area rival, DiBella Entertainment. Moretti commented that Lou DiBella's monetary offer was too lucrative to turn down.[1420] DiBella had a much larger stable of fighters than Main Events, led by middleweight champion Jermain Taylor. DiBella also had a close relationship to his former employer, HBO.

Kathy Duva had relied heavily on Moretti's experience in all of her boxing decisions, since his hire in 1993. Prior to working for Main Events, Moretti had worked seven years for Madison Square Garden as a publicist and matchmaker before they closed their boxing department. When Gary Shaw left Main Events in 2002 to start his own company, Moretti was promoted from matchmaker to vice-president of operations. To try and change the company's bad luck, Kathy decided to move its headquarters from Bloomfield back to its original location of Totowa, N.J.

On January 22, Main Events announced that it was re-signing 44-year-old Evander Holyfield. Donald Tremblay, of Main Events, stated that Holyfield's recent victory over Fres Oquendo convinced Kathy Duva that Holyfield still could be an impact in the heavyweight division. Holyfield had been suspended indefinitely by the New York State Athletic Commission in November 2004, following a one-sided loss to Larry Donald. He appealed the suspension after passing several medical exams. The suspension was changed from a medical restriction to an administrative constraint. Many insiders looked at the signing as a desperate move by a failing company. Holyfield had won just four of his previous eleven fights, dating back to 1998.

Arturo was giving hints that he might want to try MMA fighting after he retired from boxing. He was spotted at an MMA event at the Tropicana in Atlantic City, in January. Arturo was sitting ringside along with Ray Mercer and adult film star Jenna Jameson. Mercer would try his hand at MMA. Arturo spoke with Felix Martinez, the promoter for Cage Fury Fighting Championships, several times to discuss the possibility. Arturo would eventually decide against MMA fighting.

In February, Kathy Duva, Pat Lynch, and HBO sports president Ross Greenburg met to discuss possible opponents for Arturo's July 14 bout. Greenburg was appreciative for all Arturo did to bring HBO's "Boxing after Dark" series the recognition it received. But Greenburg was a businessman, and the network refused to allow Arturo to box a pushover.

On February 7, it was officially announced that Arturo would return to the ring on July 14 against an undetermined fighter. It also was confirmed that his longtime trainer, Buddy McGirt, would not be in his corner. Secaucus, N.J.'s Al Certo was still rumored to be the front-runner for the trainer position. Main Events and HBO were in negotiations with Caesars-Atlantic City to host the event. One of the possible opponents being mentioned was former multiple division champion Diego Corrales.

On April 24, Arturo purchased a brand new, five bedroom, four-and-a-half bath, 4,262 square foot home for $1,250,000. The home was located on a cul-de-sac in the upscale Morganville section of Marlboro, N.J. Donny Jerie recalled a print that Arturo hung on the wall in his Morganville home. The quote, by Albert Einstein, read, *"You never fail until you stop trying."* Donny felt that the quote accurately reflected Arturo's hard work ethic in training camp. Shortly thereafter, Amanda moved into the Morganville home with Arturo.

On July 25, Kathy Duva announced that Main Events was hiring J. Russell Peltz as a consultant/matchmaker. Peltz, who would work part-time for Main Events, took over most of the duties that Carl Moretti had handled. Russell had a working relationship with Main Events since their inception in 1979. Peltz would continue to run his own boxing promotional company in Philadelphia. Kathy Duva praised Russell's abilities as a matchmaker and boxing sage.[1421]

HBO planned on billing the July 14 show as Arturo's farewell fight. It was the final bout in the contract that Arturo signed with HBO five years prior. Arturo was planning his future on a fight-by-fight basis. Kathy Duva reminded reporters that Arturo's first fight with Micky Ward was supposed to be his farewell fight.[1422]

Kathy announced that Main Events would expand its business to cover sports and entertainment publicity, public relations, and marketing for corporations and educational institutions. Donald Tremblay was named president of the new Main Events Proactive Publicity company. Tremblay had been public relations director for Main Events for many years.

Pernell Whitaker's name began surfacing as a possible trainer for Arturo's next fight. Whitaker was now training Main Events fighters Calvin Brock and Jason Litzau. HBO advised Main Events that they would approve a match between Gatti and Paulie Malignaggi. Arturo and "The Magic Man" were close friends. Arturo was one of the first people to call Malignaggi after Paulie took a terrible beating from Miguel Cotto. Paulie suffered a broken orbital bone under his right eye during the bout. Gatti offered words of encouragement for the courageous Malignaggi. When asked about a possible Gatti match, Malignaggi revealed that he wouldn't want to fight his childhood idol unless the money was right.[1423] Malignaggi's promoter, Lou DiBella, commented that it might take twice as much as the $250,000 Paulie earned against Miguel Cotto, to make the Gatti match. Although Malignaggi was considered a light puncher, he was very fast with his hands and feet. Malignaggi was being trained by Buddy McGirt.

On March 10, Lovemore N'dou's name was mentioned as a possible opponent for Arturo. N'dou, 45-8-1 (30 KOs), was the current 140-pound IBF champion. N'dou would have to move up in weight for the match. By the end of March, N'dou's name was removed as a possible opponent.

On April 21, it was announced that Arturo had selected his new trainer. Arturo would be trained by none other than his old nemesis, Micky Ward.

On April 25, even though Arturo had not officially announced that he would fight again, an opponent had finally been agreed upon by Main Events, Lynch, and HBO. Alfonso Gomez, 16-3-2 (7 KOs), would face Arturo. The 26-year-old Gomez had participated in the first season of "The Contender" boxing show. Lynch and Main Events were pleased that HBO had accepted Gomez. They considered him a light-punching club fighter, though publicly they spoke differently.

What Main Events and Lynch failed to take into consideration was Gomez had been fighting in the 154-pound class during his previous few fights. Gomez, while not known for his power, had knocked out three of his last four opponents. Gatti and Gomez would be the TV co-main event, with the main bout pitting Antonio Margarito against Paul Williams. The Williams-Margarito bout would take place in California and be televised after the Gatti bout.

Ross Greenburg voiced his concerns over Arturo's health if he continued with his boxing career. But Greenburg also admitted that since HBO was obliged to pay Arturo $1 million for the bout, he required Gatti to face a capable opponent. Gomez had gone 4-0-1 since losing a decision to Peter Manfredo, at middleweight, on "The Contender" show in 2004. Gomez had never been stopped.

HBO and Main Events had difficulty reaching an agreement on Arturo's opponent. Sources revealed that 15 potential opponents were turned down by Arturo's handlers before Gomez was agreed upon. Some of the names turned down included Paul Spadafora, Paul Malignaggi, Steve Forbes, Demetrius Hopkins, Mike Stewart, Dmitriy Salita, Edgar Santana, Shamone Alvarez, and Lovemore N'dou.

Gomez was selected mainly because he was a straight forward fighter with little power. HBO agreed to Gomez primarily due to his popularity from "The Contender" boxing show. Gomez also was selected because he agreed to fight Arturo for $200,000. Paul Spadafora wanted $500,000. Arturo was expected to earn $1.7 million for the fight.

Even though this would be Arturo's last contracted fight with HBO, the network still had the first and last "rights of refusal" if Arturo continued fighting. HBO refused to comment on the negotiation process over the opponent selection. Kathy Duva appeared upset with HBO when she said that she had very different priorities from the cable company. Kathy was trying to put on the most entertaining fight she could for the fans, but the fighters HBO offered would not have made good matches. Duva felt HBO was more concerned with trying to satisfy boxing critics than they were with trying to put together a fight that was exciting and would sell tickets. Kathy added that if boxing fans wanted a chess match they would be better served watching the upcoming Bernard Hopkins-Winky Wright fight in July. Arturo Gatti, Kathy expressed, is there for the people who play checkers.[1424] Main Events wanted to avoid the fast Ivan Robinson type boxers, such as Spadafora and Forbes.

On April 26, Arturo had his first will and testament drawn up in New Jersey. In the 38-page document, he directed that his mother,

Ida Gatti, be his personal representative or executor. In the will, Ida was given responsibility over Arturo's daughter Sofia's $300,000 trust fund. Ida was also given guardianship over Sofia, with Fabrizio the alternate, if anything should happen to Ida. All of Arturo's vehicles and jewelry were willed to Fabrizio. All tangible items were willed to Ida, with Anna-Maria second in line. Ida was also left $500,000 in cash. If Sofia were to die, then Arturo's five siblings; Anna-Maria, Giuseppina, Joe, Fabrizio, and Mirella would split her trust equally five ways. However, it later was discovered that Arturo never signed the will after it was completed.

Arturo took some time off to relax. He traveled to the South American countries of Argentina and Brazil. When he returned, Arturo publicly confirmed that he would indeed fight again. He said that he felt fine physically and wanted to continue his career. The announcement unnerved many of those close to him. There was no reason for Gatti to continue fighting. He had won two world titles and had earned millions. There was nothing left to gain and quite a lot to lose. Boxing is akin to rolling the dice; eventually the numbers will go against you. It is a mathematical certainty. The question was, would Arturo be one of the few who would walk away with money in his pocket and his health intact or would he be one of the many who left the ring penniless, brain damaged, or God forbid, something even worse. There is no limit in boxing to the term "something even worse."

Retirement would have been the optimal choice for Gatti. The same could not be said for Main Events and the Atlantic City casinos, who craved the revenue that Arturo generated. Arturo was Main Events' only money maker at the time. Fernando Vargas had lost two straight, and all of their young prospects were struggling to reach stardom. Main Events was feeling the pressure of Top Rank, DiBella Entertainment, and Golden Boy Promotions, who had more funds to sign top amateur prospects. The aforementioned promoters, because of their deep rosters, grabbed more of the desired television slots.

Many boxing insiders felt that Arturo had given enough to HBO and Main Events, as well as the entire sport of boxing. The best reward he could be given at this point was a farewell victory in front of his loyal fans. Arturo deserved no less. The only question was, if Arturo was given an easy exit fight, would he exit? Would a win only stir up dreams of that elusive third world title and another big payday? It was like being in a brakeless car that was rolling towards a cliff, but the driver and occupants stayed in the car because they hoped the brakes might finally work. It was a dream ride that was doomed to have a horrific crash ending.

Main Events and Pat Lynch were still thinking of undefeated Miguel Cotto as a possible future opponent, as Mario Costa recalled. *"That Gomez fight, I can't believe they put him with Micky Ward [as his trainer]. Arthur's camps were not the best of camps. So Gomez was with his cutman, Miguel Diaz. And Miguel Diaz at the time was working with Cotto. Miguel Diaz and I were working with Sultan Ibragamov when he was fighting Holyfield. So while we were in Ibragamov's dressing room, Diaz said, 'You know who they got your boy fighting?' I said, 'What are you talking about?' 'Gatti, your boy Gatti.' I said, 'Who?' He said, 'If Gatti wins the Gomez fight they're going to try to put him in with Cotto.' I said, 'What? Are you kidding me! Are you fucking kidding me!' He goes, 'Yeah, I was talking to Bob Arum and Main Events.' I said, 'Listen, if Arthur beats Gomez I will go in the ring. I will come out this time with my name, not John O'Brien. That bullshit name I used before.' I said, 'He will never fight Cotto because he will get killed.' And that's how they think, see. All they care about is money."*[1425]

Arturo and Ward were expected to depart on April 29 for Florida, where they would begin training for Arturo's July 14 bout. Arturo's new training location would be Sultan Ibragimov's gym in Pompano Beach, Florida.

Micky Ward brought super lightweight Jeff Fraza with him from Massachusetts to spar with Arturo. Fraza had been on the "Contender" TV series with Alfonso Gomez and may have had insight into Gomez' strengths and weaknesses.

Travis Hartman, who was training in the gym at the time, recalled that there was an air of overconfidence regarding the Gomez match. Hartman recalled, *"It definitely appeared as though they felt that Gomez was an easy match. They were looking past Gomez."*[1426] One day during training, Arturo and Ward asked Hartman if he wanted to go out with them to a strip club. Hartman thought it was best if he declined the invitation as he wasn't sure if they were testing his dedication to training. The following day Arturo approached Hartman and said, *"Boy, you sure missed out last night."*[1427]

Boxing Insider reporter, Ron Scarfone, asked to be allowed into camp to video Arturo while he was training. Ward allowed Scarfone to video Arturo but asked him not to video Gatti while he was working out with a sauna suit on. Ward did not want Gomez' camp to know that Arturo was struggling to make weight.

Donny Jerie did not attend many of Arturo's training camps. Mikey Red was more involved with Arturo's training, while Donny usually hung out with Arturo in-between camps. Donny was invited to the Gomez camp, and decided to fly down. Donny recalled, *"I was in camp with Ward and Gatti. It was wild. I flew up there myself. Gatti and Mikey Ward picked me up at the airport and Teddy Cruz was there too. They picked me up and we went back to his place. We were doing the daily routine you know, the gym. He'd do his work out at the gym. Arturo would cook breakfast. He would cook in the morning for everybody, egg whites. He was a chef. He cooked pasta for us all the time down in Marlboro. He liked to cook a little bit here and there. He liked pasta, you know, he was Italian.*

"He wasn't stressed out. I'll never forget, I went out to get a movie called 'A Guide To Recognizing Your Saints.' They had this song in it, 'Back in the New York Groove' by Kiss's Ace Frehley. I'm like, 'You gotta come out to that song.' Because he was making a comeback... He said, 'You know what bro, I want you to get me the CD. And I'm gonna come out to that song.' Me, him and Teddy Cruz, we were watching this movie and he's sweating. He was dancing and jumping around and he had his full clothes on pretending that he was coming out for a fight. He had his weight in gold on. We watched that whole movie. Camp was good. We went to go see his nephew Davey. There were three of them. As a matter of fact, they were the Hilton's kids. I remember Anna-Maria used to bring the whole pack. I remember he had the Team Gatti [shirts] for everybody. All the little kids. It was beautiful."[1428]

On May 14, tickets for the Gatti-Gomez fight went on sale. Arturo started camp weighing 180-pounds. Arturo, a casual smoker when he drank, quit smoking when camp began. He stopped drinking alcohol a few weeks into camp. Gatti and Ward ran together and spent their down time playing golf. Ward appeared to be more of a support figure than an actual trainer. He looked uncomfortable in his new role as head trainer of the man who had defeated him twice. Ward did see enough speed, power, and reflexes from Arturo to convince him that Gatti could defeat Gomez.

A press conference for the upcoming Gatti-Gomez battle was held on May 22 at Spanky's BBQ in Manhattan. Arturo advised the press that he almost pulled out of the Baldomir fight because of hand problems and personal issues. Arturo commented on those who were saying that he should hang the gloves up by stating that he felt great.

Gatti added, *"I know I've been in a lot of wars, but most of my opponents got hurt worse than me. I seem to have this gift that keeps me from getting hurt. But I can talk all I want. It's my performance that will tell if I still belong in the ring or not. I want to prove to everyone and to myself that I'm still a world-class fighter. I want to show that I have what it takes to stick around and hopefully fight for the title again."*[1429]

Arturo was asked about hiring Micky Ward as his trainer. *"He's not here to teach me how to fight, but just to keep reminding me to do the things that I do best. Micky makes me work hard. He keeps working harder and harder and I have to follow him."*[1430] Ward advised the press that his job was to help Arturo keep the blinders on and work hard.[1431]

Gomez was not at the press conference but he gave a statement by teleconference call. He fully believed that his skills and training regimen would help him to win the fight.[1432] Boxing reporters were so certain that Arturo would blow through Gomez, they questioned him on his plans after the bout. Arturo cautioned that he had to take one fight at a time. Gatti added, *"Every fight I'm fighting now is my last fight."*[1433]

Gatti considered retiring for only about five seconds after the Baldomir loss. He blamed his performance against Baldomir on "outside the ring" distractions, including his legal dispute with Erika Rivera over his daughter Sofia Bella. Arturo commented, *"The reason I gave such a poor performance was I got involved with Satan's daughter and it poisoned me to the point where it nearly wrecked my life. That fight [against Baldomir] was the only time I've ever gone into the ring and not wanted to be there. It was the only time in my life I wanted to put out in the ring and couldn't."*[1434]

Arturo revealed that he was engaged to his new girlfriend, Amanda Rodrigues. Gatti felt that Amanda had opened his eyes to those who were using him for his money. Arturo confessed, *"I've been good to everybody who have worked for me, but I've had to cast a lot of people out. I've made a couple of bucks and a bunch of leeches came around trying to live off my sweat. No more."*[1435]

Arturo refused to elaborate on his split with McGirt, saying only that McGirt betrayed him.[1436] Micky Ward was impressed with Arturo's skills. Ward felt that Gatti still could perform at a high level, because he had his legs and his faculties.[1437] Ward admitted that he was shocked when Gatti first called to offer the training job to him.

As of May 27, many tickets were unsold for the Gomez match. Bob Arum felt that Gatti, the 2-1 betting favorite, was in an easy match. He was maneuvering for a Gatti-Julio Cesar Chavez Jr. match if Arturo defeated Gomez.[1438]

Gatti appeared motivated for the match. The *Star Ledger* reported that Arturo was *"no longer a serious contender. At 35, Gatti's reflexes aren't as quick, his punches not as hard."*[1439] For Arturo to read this in the press was bad enough, but for those in his entourage to be whispering it behind his back was treasonous. Gatti announced, *"I can't wait until after this performance, because a lot of people are going to have their foot in their mouth. I know a lot of those people are close to me... Boxing is a sport where a guy has a couple of losses and people say he is finished. They forget that we are human beings, and we have personal problems, and that was the cause of my performance."*[1440]

The issue with Erika Rivera over Sofia's child support and visitation was yet to be resolved, but Arturo assured everyone that it would not affect his training this time.

As of July 11, there were over 3,000 tickets available for the Gatti-Gomez match. It appeared as though this would be the first time since 2002 that Arturo failed to reach the 11,000 mark in ticket sales at Boardwalk Hall. Arturo appeared jovial at a press conference in New York City. Gomez appeared confident. Alfonso pointed to the fact that whenever Gatti moved up against bigger fighters, he lost.[1441] Gomez added that he had fought several middleweights who couldn't hurt or drop him.[1442]

Pat Lynch was confident that Arturo was not taking Gomez lightly. Lynch added that Arturo was fully aware that if he lost the Gomez fight, his career would be over.[1443] Ward was impressed with Arturo's training camp, his conditioning, and his mental state. Ward felt as though Gatti's experience would be the deciding factor in the battle.[1444]

Lou DiBella felt that Arturo was continuing to fight solely for financial reasons, and because he didn't know how to do anything else. DiBella pointed to the fact that most people felt that Alfonso Gomez would give Gatti a competitive fight, which was an indication of how far Arturo's skills had eroded. DiBella hoped that Gatti would retire after the Gomez fight.[1445]

Many on Arturo's team were perplexed at why he was continuing to fight. Arturo's close friend and former New York Jet, Wayne Chrebet, understood Arturo's desire to compete. Chrebet continued to play football even though family and friends pleaded with him to retire after he suffered several serious concussions. Chrebet finally retired in 2005, but he missed everything about professional football. He missed the competition, the fans' adulation, and most importantly, the money. Chrebet not only supported Arturo, he actually got in the ring and sparred with Gatti when one of Arturo's sparring partners was unavailable.

Arturo had considered Hector Roca and Pernell Whitaker as trainer before settling on Pat Lynch's choice of Micky Ward. Arturo commented, *"We were debating different guys and Micky just seemed like the best choice. We fought 30 rounds together, so he's more qualified than anyone to remind me to do the things that I do best. I know some people were surprised when I picked him, but I always felt like he would train me one day. It was always in my heart."*[1446]

Ward and Arturo trained in Pompano Beach for two months for the Gomez fight. Micky trained alongside Arturo, running and hitting the bag with Gatti. The only thing they didn't do is spar each other. Arturo commented on not sparring Ward. *"I respect Micky as a trainer now and I don't want to fight him. It wouldn't be very professional to do that. Besides, we would probably get some flashbacks. The thing about Micky is he is a competitor just like I am. If we sparred, it would be a war again."*[1447] Main Events was considering matching Arturo up against Julio Cesar Chavez Jr. on November 10, if Arturo were to be successful against Gomez.

When he was 10-years-old, Gomez moved with his family from Guadalajara, Mexico to Oakland, California. That's where Gomez Sr. started making doughnuts in the family kitchen. Alfonso recalled that selling donuts helped to keep the family's home from being foreclosed upon. Gomez Sr. wound up opening his own bakery, but he sold it a few years later to focus on training his son full time.[1448] Both of Gomez's parents quit their jobs to help their children pursue their dreams. Alfonso originally wanted to be an actor, while his younger brothers, Roberto and Jesus, worked towards becoming musicians. The Gomez family planned on celebrating Alfonso's victory with a doughnut party.[1449]

On July 13, the 35-year-old Arturo weighed in at 146-pounds while the 26-year-old Gomez weighed in at 147. Arturo entered the match with a 40-8 (31 KOs) record, while Gomez sported a 16-3-2 (7 KOs) record.

After the weigh-in, Gomez revealed that he planned on putting a lot of pressure on Gatti, to make Arturo brawl with him. Ken Condon admitted that there were question-marks over whether Arturo still could move tickets. Condon believed that Arturo would answer those questions if over 10,000 tickets were sold. Condon repeatedly commented that Arturo was the only fighter keeping boxing alive in Atlantic City.[1450]

Wayne Chrebet was interviewed on the day of the Gomez match. Chrebet understood Gatti not wanting to quit the ring. He believed Arturo would be devastated if he had to stop boxing, because it was all he knew. Chrebet added that he would be there to support Gatti when the day finally came for him to hang up the gloves, but Wayne knew that it would not be easy for Arturo to let go of the sport.[1451]

On July 14, 2007, 9,438 fans turned out to support Arturo as he battled Alfonso Gomez. It was a solid crowd by normal fight standards, but a substantial drop off from the usual 11,000-plus that normally attended Arturo's fights.

Many of Gatti's friends would meet Arturo's new girlfriend for the first time at the fight. Amanda's full name was Amanda Carina Barbosa Rodrigues. The 21-year-old Rodrigues was sitting ringside.

Gomez made his way into the ring wearing a Mexican bandana. Making their way into the ring with Gatti were his new trainer Micky Ward, Chuck Zito, Wayne Chrebet, and Teddy Cruz. "New York Groove" by Ace Frehley blared through Boardwalk Hall's speaker system as Arturo made his way into the ring.

The 35-year-old Gatti was nine years older than Gomez. Gomez held a 1½-inch height advantage over Arturo. Both boxers had the same reach. When Arturo took his robe off, it was plain to see that the added weight from his move up was mostly in his abdomen.

Working Arturo's corner with Ward were Teddy Cruz and cutman Joe Souza. Working Gomez's corner were his father Alfonso Gomez Sr., Pepe Correa, and cutman Ruben Gomez.

In an ominous premonition, announcer Michael Buffer, for the first time when announcing Arturo's name for a match, left out the ring name "Thunder" and simply introduced Gatti as *"Arturo Gatti."* Both boxers appeared confident as they waited for the bell to ring.

The 1st round began with Arturo jabbing. Gomez, though not a fast puncher, was landing jabs, rights, and hooks with ease. Gomez landed the cleaner, more effective punches in the round. As he walked back to his corner, Gomez raised his right arm as a show of confidence that he had won the round.

Ward asked Arturo to move his head after he jabbed. Ward also asked for combinations. Arturo started the 2nd by pressing forward. As the round settled in, Gomez landed several solid rights. Arturo tried to open up at the end of the round, but nearly every punch missed. Gomez's father asked his son to throw double jabs followed by hard rights to the body.

In the 3rd, Gomez snapped Arturo's head back with several straight rights. Gatti missed most of his attempts. His punches were slow and he took long breaks between throwing. Alfonso wasn't particularly fast or strong, but he kept throwing and landing. Ward asked for more speed and head movement. In Gomez's corner, Pepe Correa asked for more jabs.

Gomez landed punch after methodical punch in the 4th. Kathy Duva looked on as though she was attending the medieval execution of a loved one. Fans were shaking their heads side-to-side in disbelief with each crunching, head-turning blow that Gatti absorbed. After the round ended, Ward asked Arturo to sit on his punches and work the body more. Gatti's lip was swollen to twice its normal size. Gomez landed 38 punches in the 4th, compared to 11 by Arturo.

Gomez pounded on Arturo in the 5th. Arturo missed nearly every punch he threw, making the average Gomez look like a defensive wizard. Even Judge Steve Weisfeld looked disturbed at what he was witnessing. Ward begged Arturo to keep his hands up. In Gomez's corner, Correa asked Alfonso to make Arturo miss and counter with right hands.

A minute into the 6th, Arturo made Gomez miss a few shots. The pro-Gatti crowd, hungry for something to cheer, let out a roar. Arturo smiled, did the "Ali Shuffle" with his feet, and raised his right arm to acknowledge his loyal fans. The crowd started chanting his name, *"Gatti! Gatti! Gatti."* Gomez finished the round by backing Gatti up with jabs and rights. Amanda, who was sitting next to Anna-Maria, stood and cheered her boyfriend yelling, *"Gatti!"* She also had some choice words for Gomez, calling him a *"puta"* [whore] and yelling *"fuck you"* to him.

Forty seconds into the 7th, Gomez landed two chopping rights followed by a hard hook to the body. Gatti retreated, wincing in pain. Gomez drove Arturo into the ropes. Alfonso continued pouring in uppercuts, rights and lefts. Arturo's supporters grimaced with every punch that found its mark. Ken Condon surmised that everyone in the crowd was a Gatti fan, and everyone in the crowd felt every punch that Arturo was hit with.[1452] Gomez forced Gatti to slide across the ropes into a neutral corner. Arturo held onto Gomez after absorbing over twenty power shots.

Referee Randy Neumann broke the fighters. Max Kellerman lamented that they were watching the destruction of an action hero. Arturo landed two solid left hooks. He was desperate, so he reverted to the first move his father taught him when he was 6 years old, *"Sinistro!"*

Arturo was trapped along the ropes again. A perfectly timed right hand dropped the man that Micky Ward once called the indestructible Jason from *Friday The 13th*. As Randy Neumann picked up the count, Arturo grabbed onto a rope to pull himself up. Boxing commissioner Larry Hazzard, sensing that Neumann was going to let the slaughter continue, jumped into the ring. He had seen enough and called an end to the carnage.

While Arturo was being pummeled in the 7th, Amanda screamed for the bout to be stopped. One of the most noticeable things about Arturo's new girlfriend was her appearance. She had a beautiful face, with expertly dyed blonde hair. Her body had an hour-glass curve, but this was not the most noticeable thing about Amanda. She wore a white, low cut, knee-length dress. She wasn't wearing a bra, nor was she wearing underwear. Sky Sports 1 filmed Amanda and her revealing dress. After the fight was stopped, she hopped the metal barrier separating the ring from the spectators.

Sitting to the left of Amanda was Arturo's former sparring partner, Nasser Nettles. Nettles had worked the corner of welterweight Henry Crawford, who fought on the undercard. Nettles recalled Amanda's revealing appearance. He also recalled that Amanda kept screaming for the referee to stop the fight. According to Nettles, *"Amanda's body language showed how much she loved him."*[1453] Before Amanda jumped over the barricade, Nettles heard her say, *"He can't do this anymore."*[1454]

Arturo suffered a deep gash to his lip from the final barrage of punches. A corner stool was brought into the ring for Gatti to sit on. After sitting, Arturo closed his eyes, fell limp, and appeared to be drifting off into unconsciousness as the doctor treated the lip wound. The doctor called out, *"Arturo!"* Suddenly Gatti opened his glassy eyes, wide in disbelief. Arturo clearly had no idea where he was. All at once he recognized his surroundings, realized what was happening, and jumped up off of the stool. He started pushing people away, yelling, *"I can't believe this."* He was having trouble breathing. Hazzard grabbed Arturo and told him everything was all right. He held Gatti's arms, and like a father would a son, sat him back down.

Mikey Red, who was in the crowd, frantically jumped into the ring. He was visibly upset at seeing his friend in this condition. Arturo took several deep breaths and started smiling. Tears flowed freely from fans who sat ringside. Gomez had landed 216 of 471 punches to Arturo's 74 of 358.

Arturo departed the ring without being interviewed. Max Kellerman followed Gatti to the dressing room to interview him. Arturo told Kellerman that Gomez was younger, stronger, and hungrier than he was. Gatti revealed that the boxing ring appeared to shrink as the fight wore on. Arturo admitted that he no longer could take the physical abuse of professional boxing, and since he could no longer make 140-pounds, he was going to retire. Gatti ended by saying, *"Hasta la vista, baby."* Arturo's team applauded.

To his fans, Arturo said that he loved them and he tried real hard, but he just couldn't do it. He thanked his fans for supporting him and helping him to win a second world title. Amanda hugged and kissed Arturo. He started crying. Pat Lynch, Christian Santos, Teddy Cruz, Chuck Zito, Micky Ward, Kathy Duva, Mikey Red, and Joe Souza were all in the dressing room.

Family, friends, and fans alike all shed tears for their warrior. Gomez landed 40 of 62 power shots in the final round. Overall, Gomez landed 142 power shots compared to Gatti's 29. Arturo headed to the hospital for the final time in his career, to have his lip stitched.

The *Bergen Record* printed a scathing article wherein it asked and answered the question that everyone was thinking, *"Why was Gatti in the ring to begin with? Forget all the rhetoric about a farewell fight or Gatti's need for closure, this was all about money, the engine that runs the sport. With one bout left on his contract with HBO, Gatti, and his handlers, saw another $1 million-plus to be made. At what cost, however? Here's hoping a battered Gatti, 35, will be able to remember anything when his young daughter is grown and asks him about his boxing experiences... Sadly, this sport has few restrictions in place to prevent a boxer from doing himself harm. Many promoters, managers and trainers are sharks who openly talk about their concern for their boxers, and then match them against opponents that they know the fighters can't beat."*[1455]

Mario Costa recalled, *"His last fight with Alfonso Gomez, you could see the condition he was in was terrible. They thought that Gomez was easy but Arthur was so bad that he couldn't even beat*

Gomez. But even if he did beat Gomez you're gonna put him in with a guy like Cotto? Where's their minds? These people were crazy. They had no idea what they were doing with him. Especially when a manager is always supposed to look out for the well-being of their fighter. That's your job. But if you worry about the money, of course, you don't give a shit then. But Lynch should talk because he should defend himself. Pat should tell his side. But he has no side because if you look at the facts; he cared, but he never had the balls to say, 'Listen you can't fight. I got to call it off. I'm doing the right thing Arthur. I got to call it off.' But he didn't say that. Pat was afraid that Arthur would get rid of him too."[1456]

After his interview with Kellerman ended, Arturo joked, *"I'm coming back... as a spectator."*[1457] He then turned to Kathy Duva and confessed, *"I'm retired."*[1458] Arturo turned back to Amanda and said, *"I wanted you to be the champion's wife."*[1459] Amanda replied, *"Baby, you will always be my champion."*[1460]

Ken Condon admitted that the Gomez bout was very difficult to watch.[1461] As Gatti courageously rose while Neumann was counting, Hazzard had the mercy to jump up into the ring and end the slaughter, 2 minutes and 12 seconds into the 7th round. Hazzard waited for the referee or Gatti's corner to stop the fight, and when he saw that neither were going to end the bout, he felt it was his duty to step in and stop the one-sided affair. Hazzard added that it may have been a good thing that the fight ended as it did, because if Arturo had won or lost a close fight he might have decided to continue his career and risk serious injury.[1462]

Chuck Zito recalled meeting Amanda Rodrigues for the first time at the fight. He was shocked at her "truck driver" foul language during the bout. Zito added that Amanda was all caring in the dressing room while the cameras were on, but when Arturo went to the hospital to have his cut lip stitched up, only Zito accompanied him.[1463]

Men sometimes come to terms with aging, and their mortality, while sitting in a barber's chair watching their white hair follicles float onto the black barber's cape. A boxer realizes he is aging in a much different way. Most of the time, he realizes it while on his knees, or his back, in a padded canvas ring. For the lucky ones, it comes with their backs against the ropes being rescued by a referee. Even the rare ones who leave the ring for the final time with their hands raised in victory usually pay the same price in the end, either through dementia pugilistica, vision and arthritic hand issues, or a plethora of other physical ailments.

Unfortunately for Arturo, his ending came on his knees, in front of his adoring fans. Boxing, like life, rarely has fairytale endings. Immediately after the loss, the finger pointing began. It started with the referee letting the fight go too long. The blame then shifted to Lynch, Kathy Duva, and Carl Moretti for even allowing Arturo to enter the ring again.

Mario Costa commented on the loss. *"How the fuck is a Gomez, 16-3-2, gonna beat a guy like Gatti? Are you kidding me? He stopped Gatti. It's like stabbing Arthur in the back [losing on his knees in Atlantic City]."*[1464]

Gomez was even bewildered, questioning why both the referee and Micky Ward failed to stop the fight.[1465] Ward admitted that he thought about stopping the bout several times, but whenever he did, Arturo would come back. Chuck Zito yelled for Ward to stop the fight several times.

Kathy Duva had just lost her biggest meal ticket. The downward spiral of Main Events continued. Kathy believed that Arturo finally realized it was time to hang up the gloves. She predicted that five years down the road, when Arturo was elected into the Boxing Hall of Fame, the fans and reporters would remember his epic battles against Ward and Rodriguez and not the way his career ended.[1466]

Kathy admitted that she saw the end approaching, and tried to prevent Arturo from being knocked out in front of his loyal fans. She claimed that she was fighting her way through the crowd, but couldn't make it to Arturo's corner before Gomez dropped him with a right hand. Neumann took up the count and reached "four" when Larry Hazzard jumped into the ring to waive the fight over.

Neumann, a former heavyweight contender, had been criticized in the past for stopping bouts too soon. He may have allowed the carnage to continue for that reason, or because he was from the same area of North Jersey that Arturo fought out of. Neumann was from Ridgefield, N.J., approximately fifteen minutes north of Jersey City. He would have had a lot of explaining to do if it were perceived that he had stopped the fight too early. Neumann felt that Gatti had a puncher's chance and was fighting back. He didn't believe Arturo was seriously hurt until the final punch landed.[1467] If Arturo would have beaten Gomez either Julio Cesar Chavez, Jr. or Miguel Cotto would have been next. Many boxing insiders cringed at the thought of an aged Gatti trading punches with Cotto or Chavez Jr.

On July 22, *Star Ledger* reporter Franklin McNeil wasted no time lobbying for an Arturo Gatti Hall of Fame induction. McNeil believed that Gatti belonged in the Hall on the strength of his three world titles, in three different weight divisions [including the IBA belt], his three-fight trilogy against Micky Ward, and his impact on the New Jersey boxing scene by single handedly reviving big-time boxing in the Garden State.

Former professional football coach Bill Parcells was a huge Arturo Gatti fan. Parcells loved Arturo and was sad with the way his career ended. Parcells felt that Gatti's courage and heart appealed to everyone.[1468]

Chapter 29
Life After Boxing

In August 2007, Arturo and Amanda decided to wed. Amanda recalled that Arturo got down on his knee and proposed by saying that he was in love with her and wanted to give her the world.[1469] When Arturo spoke to Pat Lynch about his plans, Lynch wisely advised Arturo to have a pre-nuptial agreement drawn up. Arturo agreed with the pre-nup, which would protect all of the assets that Arturo amassed prior to the marriage, should the marriage end in divorce. Pat had his brother, attorney John Lynch, draw up the contract. At the time of the pre-nup, Arturo owned property at 2525 Riverview Court in Vero Beach, Florida and 354 Salinger Court in Morganville, New Jersey.

On August 22, Arturo and Amanda drove to John Lynch's law office in Union City. John Lynch later recalled that Amanda put on a big show in front of several secretaries, saying that she wasn't marrying Arturo for his wealth. Amanda stated that she had no issue with signing the prenuptial agreement, which she readily signed.[1470] The next day, August 23, the couple flew to Las Vegas.

On August 26, 2007 the pair were married in Las Vegas, with none of their family or friends present. The couple rented a helicopter which flew them to the Grand Canyon where they took wedding photos. Immediately after they wed, the issue of the pre-nup came up. Just hours after the wedding, Arturo was on the phone with John Lynch. *"John, whoever prepared this agreement left this girl without the shoes she came in with."*[1471] An argument between the couple allegedly ensued regarding the prenuptial agreement.

Pat Lynch had tried to talk Arturo out of marrying Amanda, but Arturo lived his life as he wanted. Lynch recalled that Arturo would yes him to death on one day regarding advice, only to change his mind the following day.[1472]

On September 13, Ken Condon announced that he was stepping down as chief executive of Bally's Atlantic City. Condon had held the title for nine years, since 1998. He oversaw some of the most significant boxing events that Atlantic City ever held. Condon had started his casino career at Resorts International in 1978. In 1989 he moved to the Trump Taj Mahal Casino. He had another brief stint at Resorts before joining Bally's in 1993. Five years later, he was promoted to president.

Condon was responsible for 17 of the 18 major boxing events held at Boardwalk Hall since its renovation. Besides boxing, Condon brought musical stars such as Elton John, Cher, Fleetwood Mac, Neil Diamond, Simon and Garfunkel, The Eagles, Madonna, Jimmy Buffet, and Paul McCartney to Atlantic City.

Larry Hazzard commented that Condon's departure was a knockout punch to boxing in Atlantic City. Hazzard added that Condon had been the main promoter of big-time boxing in the state of New Jersey. Top Rank's Bruce Trampler felt that Condon's resignation was a huge blow to boxing.[1473]

Nick Lembo, of the N.J. Athletic Control Board, expressed that Condon was a great asset because he understood the reasons why certain fights were good for Atlantic City, and he was very aggressive in pursuing them.[1474] Kathy Duva added that she hoped that whoever took his place would emphasize boxing the way Condon did.[1475]

In an interview years later, Condon fondly recalled how Arturo would always come back to greet his fans after he responded to the hospital after his fights, no matter what condition he was in.[1476]

Lynch moved on to managing other fighters. He signed three-time New York Golden Gloves champion Ronney Vargas and two-time National Golden Gloves champion Jeremy Bryan. Lynch also signed Jorge Diaz. Lynch co-managed Bryan and Diaz with Sal Alessi. Lynch's brother John obtained a boxing promotional license in November 2007. His new company was called "Pound for Pound Promotions." Pat tried to get Arturo to come on board as the head trainer, but Gatti had no interest in training fighters.

On November 14, 2007 at 4 p.m., long-time N.J. State boxing commissioner Larry Hazzard was fired by administrator Kim Ricketts. Ricketts was acting on orders from Attorney General Anne Milgram. Hazzard, who had run boxing in the state for nearly 22 years, was escorted out of the building. Hazzard was shocked that he was fired.[1477] Deputy commissioner Sylvester Cuyler was temporarily installed as the new commissioner until a permanent replacement could be found.

Hazzard's salary was $105,672. He oversaw boxing, MMA, wrestling, and other combative sports in the state. Hazzard said there was no warning given before he was let go.[1478] The Attorney General's Office would not elaborate on the rapid dismissal, saying only that the move was personnel related and had nothing to do with the recent sports-betting ring that was broken up at Borgata's Hotel and Casino. Attorney General spokesman, David Wald, commented that Commissioner Hazzard did nothing wrong. It just was time for a change.[1479]

Hazzard had many supporters, including Bernard Hopkins, who felt that Hazzard always had been about honesty, integrity, and the safety of boxers above all else. Hopkins admitted that Hazzard had his share of enemies because he was so outspoken.[1480]

Bob Arum was stunned and announced that he would not bring any of his fighters to New Jersey until he saw that the commission was operating efficiently and effectively. Arum questioned how politicians, who knew absolutely nothing about the sport, could fire someone like Hazzard without first consulting with people inside the boxing business.[1481]

Hazzard believed that his dismissal was due to his investigation into the shortcomings of one of his Athletic Control Board employees. Attorney General Anne Milgram advised Hazzard to stop his investigation, but he ignored her. Some in the boxing community felt that the always controversial Hazzard kept his Commissioner's position because of his close relationship with State Senator and Newark Mayor Sharpe James. James controlled a large portion of Democratic votes in the Essex County area. James left office as mayor in 2006 and announced he would not run for re-election as State Senator in 2007, due mostly in part to a federal investigation. The retirement of James left Hazzard without any political protection. Governor Jon Corzine, although a Democrat, owed nothing to Hazzard, and was more concerned with his own political career. The incoming Newark Mayor, Corey Booker, was a bitter enemy of James, and may have played a part in forcing Hazzard out. On April 16, 2008, a federal jury convicted James on five counts of fraud. He was sentenced to 27 months in prison.

On December 17, 2007, Arturo was driving to his home in Marlboro, N.J., in his 2006 Range Rover, when he rear ended another vehicle on Route 9 South in Old Bridge. The struck automobile, a 1994 Subaru, was stopped at a traffic light when Arturo drove his vehicle into the Subaru's rear bumper. There were no injuries from the accident and the Subaru only suffered minor damage. The officer who responded to the scene discovered that Arturo had an outstanding warrant from Secaucus, N.J. for $36, most likely for an unpaid parking ticket. Gatti was arrested and processed for the warrant. After he paid the $36 bail, Arturo was issued a summons for careless driving and released.

Amanda persuaded Arturo to enter a rehab for his substance abuse problems. Gatti entered a rehabilitation center for the first and only time in his life. However, Arturo left the Florida-based facility prior to completion of the program.[1482]

Costa commented, *"The girl [Amanda], she's the only one. She paid $10,000. Amanda paid for him to go to a rehab. She's probably the only one, his wife. Yeah, because he wanted to be normal. He told me that. And if Pat had tried at least one time. Call HBO and say, 'Listen, Arthur can't fight. He's on drugs. He's got to get help.' He didn't want to do that. Because of the money and the tickets. The money, money, money, and all the tickets sold. I don't hate Pat. It's just what he did was wrong, very wrong. Especially when you know your fighter has paperwork at Christ Hospital. We have paperwork from the Jersey City Medical Center. Paperwork from Saint Mary's Hospital in Hoboken. Three different places during his career. All the hospitals by us. One guy who was working for an ambulance called one time, Arthur was on the highway, on the Turnpike going into Secaucus. In the car on the side of the road. He didn't know where he was. He didn't know who he was, nothing. And somebody called me. A lady who worked for the Medical Center, she recognized him. She said, 'Arthur, I know who you are.' He didn't know who he was. He went completely blank. Somebody called that there was a car parked on the Turnpike. The ambulance went. Pat didn't know a fucking thing! Now you're telling me the manager didn't know about that? The manager didn't know the times he went to these hospitals overdosed?"*[1483]

On December 31, New Year's Eve, Arturo decided to stop by the Squeeze Lounge gentlemen's club to celebrate the new year. Amanda showed up. She observed Arturo talking with two of the female dancers from Brazil. According to barmaid Nehomy Prosperi, Amanda allegedly wanted to fight with the two dancers. Arturo did his best to calm Amanda down.[1484]

During one of Arturo and Amanda's domestic disputes, Arturo's Range Rover dash board, radio, and steering wheel were allegedly destroyed, causing thousands in damages.

In early January 2008, the couple celebrated a belated honeymoon. They flew to Hawaii and stayed at the five-star Ritz-Carlton hotel in Kapalua, Maui. Their honeymoon would be short-lived, however, as they engaged in another domestic altercation.

On January 8, the police were dispatched to a call of a couple fighting at the Ritz-Carlton. Amanda had thrown a lamp at Arturo during their dispute. When the police arrived, both Arturo and Amanda were outside the hotel. It was nearly 3 a.m. The officers separated the couple to investigate what had transpired. While Arturo was speaking to one officer, Amanda stepped into the face of another officer yelling, *"Fuck you, you fucking bitch. You don't know the fucking story."*[1485] Amanda was arrested for harassment and transported to the police station, where she was processed and released. Both Amanda and Arturo were visibly intoxicated. Amanda was carrying a Fendi handbag valued at a few thousand dollars. During their investigation, the police discovered that Amanda was in the United States illegally. Deportation proceedings were allegedly initiated against Amanda.

On January 29, Ken Condon, who recently resigned from Bally's, took a new position as head of Harrah's Entertainment.

On February 9, Pat and John Lynch held their first boxing show under the "Pound for Pound" boxing promotional banner. The show was held at the Park Theater in Union City, N.J. The 1,100-seat theater had been used by Main Events for two shows in 2002.

The brothers quickly learned that running a show was no walk in the park. The popular ticket-selling main eventer, Pawel Wolak, pulled out of the show. The main event slot was filled by Main Events fighter Henry Crawford. After barely breaking even on the show, the Lynch brothers planned a second show in North Jersey. Pat admitted that he had been spoiled by Arturo's popularity and his ability to sell tickets.[1486]

In mid-February, John Lynch's secretary received a surprise visit. Arturo and Amanda arrived at his law office unannounced. John was in court with a client. The couple wanted to see the original prenuptial agreement, even though both of them had been given a copy when it was signed. Apparently the pre-nup had been a continual source for bickering between the couple. John received a phone call from his secretary, asking him what she should do. John advised the secretary to give them another copy, not the original. Arturo took the copy and ripped it up in front of Amanda, to make it appear as though he was destroying the original.[1487] Arturo called Lynch's office a few days later to confirm that he had only destroyed a copy. John and Arturo shared a hearty laugh from the ruse. John recalled that Amanda was ecstatic that the pre-nup was allegedly destroyed.[1488]

Arturo confided to John that his rock-solid pre-nup made living with Amanda nearly impossible. Gatti was hopeful that tearing up the pre-nup copy would make life easier for him at home. Amanda was now facing possible deportation after the Hawaii incident. Arturo decided to move back to Montreal with her in May. Gatti may not have wanted to leave the United States but he had no choice if he was going to remain with Amanda.

The couple moved into one of Arturo's high-rise condominiums, in the Jarry section of Montreal. Arturo told the press in Montreal that he had always planned to move back, to be closer to his family. He had also previously spoken about plans to open a restaurant or bar in New Jersey. Did he really want to move back to Montreal?

As Arturo's career was winding down he started avoiding many members of his entourage. He had made statements that he had become aware that certain people were using him. Joe had stated that meeting Vikki helped him to open his eyes regarding those who hung around him for his money and status as a boxer. Did Amanda help enlighten Arturo regarding those who were using him? Being forced to end his career was obviously very painful for Arturo. Boxing was his life and it defined who he was. He may have isolated himself from his boxing associates because they reminded him of the career that he was forced to abandon. Moving back to Montreal may have been a way to further avoid the people, places and things that reminded him of the life he could no longer live.

Arturo landed a bit part, as a member of a gang, in the movie *Breaking Point* starring Tom Berenger and Armand Assante. In the movie, Arturo played the petty thug T-Bar.

In mid-March 2008, Floyd Mayweather Jr. sued Bob Arum over money owed him for his bouts against Arturo and Zab Judah. Mayweather felt that he was shortchanged the money owed him from the pay-per-view buys for each fight. Of the dispute, Arum agreed that there was no question that he owed Mayweather some money, but Arum added that Floyd also owed him a lot of money too.[1489]

Mario Costa excitedly telephoned Arturo. He asked Gatti if he had heard about the Mayweather lawsuit. Arturo replied that he had not. Gatti did not understand his connection to the lawsuit. Costa recalled, *"I said, 'Arthur, now you're gonna find out how much money HBO gave Main Events and how much money they paid you. You're gonna know how much they're fucking you. So Arthur goes, 'What do you mean?' I said, 'Mayweather is suing Bob Arum because he left him and he's disputing the money that Bob paid him for those fights. You are one of the fights. Arthur was like, 'Alright.'*

Arthur was all happy because he goes ,'I wanna see, I wanna see.'"[1490] Mayweather and Arum came to a confidential settlement before the documents were released.

The move to Montreal only served to add pressure to Arturo and Amanda's already fragile relationship. Arturo rekindled childhood friendships and spent time with his mother. Arturo's friends felt very uncomfortable around Amanda, and for the most part tried to avoid her. Arturo's Montreal friends felt that they were able to take liberties with Gatti that his Jersey friends wouldn't dare to take. Their loyalty to Arturo was based on childhood friendships, not on his status as a boxer. They spoke freely to Arturo and discussed their fears of him being in a relationship with someone so controlling.

Although Amanda and Arturo had a rocky relationship, Amanda tried to get Arturo to attend Alcoholics Anonymous classes. She also was known to flush Arturo's pills down the toilet. Amanda later revealed that all of her fights with Arturo were based on trying to get him to stop drinking. Tom Casino witnessed Amanda trying to help Gatti.

Arturo came home to Montreal as a hero, but his aura soon faded when friends and fans spotted him at erotic clubs such as Supersex, Wanda's, or Solid Gold. He would take the dance girls into limousines for trysts. The alcohol and drugs flowed freely.

Amanda recalled that Arturo took retirement hard. He was depressed that his career had ended.[1491] Gatti didn't know how to refocus his energy. He started drinking heavily. Amanda revealed that there were two Arturo Gattis. There was the man she fell in love with, the funny, romantic, loving husband and father. Then there was this aggressive, nasty person when he drank. Amanda blamed all of their fighting on alcohol.[1492]

Amanda called Anna-Maria and told her that she was pregnant and she didn't love Arturo anymore.[1493] Anna-Maria always advised Arturo to try and work out his problems with Amanda.

In early April 2008, Arturo flew to New Jersey. He headed to Atlantic City where Pat and John Lynch had a few of their fighters boxing on a Top Rank card at Tropicana Casino on April 11. When the casino found out that Arturo was coming, they offered to pay him $50,000 to meet and greet the high rollers in private poker rooms. Arturo told Pat that he would take the job, only to arrive late and miss the opportunity for some easy money. Arturo also turned down an offer from Carl Moretti to make some guest appearances for a few thousand dollars.

On April 12, Arturo attended the Miguel Cotto-Alfonso Gomez fight at Boardwalk Hall in Atlantic City. Cotto dominated the bout, winning by TKO in the 5th round. Gatti had put on weight, but he appeared content.

Arturo met up with former sparring partner Danny McDermott. The pair discussed opening a boxing gym together that they would name the Victory Boxing Gym. The gym's logo would mirror the tattoo Arturo had on his neck; boxing gloves with blood dripping off of them. The friends also discussed possibly opening a restaurant together.

Arturo spoke with *N.Y. Daily News* reporter Tim Smith. Arturo told Smith how distant his boxing career felt to him, now that he was retired. Arturo had no plans of a comeback. He was finished as a fighter.

It was rumored that Arturo was thinking of promoting boxing shows in Canada. After Gatti left New Jersey, he flew to Brazil where he met up with Amanda. She had flown directly to Brazil from Canada. The couple traveled to Brazil to celebrate Arturo's 36th birthday on April 15. They celebrated the event at the home of Brazilian boxer Acelino Freitas. Freitas, a former four-time world champion, had been trained by Paterson, N.J. native Oscar Suarez. Suarez was training boxers at the Lou Costello boxing gym when Arturo trained there early in his career.

In May 2008, Tony Rizzo visited Arturo's penthouse apartment in the 82-unit condo complex that they had built together. Rizzo allegedly witnessed a sight he never would forget. Arturo invited his childhood friend and business partner inside, but Rizzo was frozen in his tracks. He allegedly observed Amanda, naked and five-months pregnant, become unhinged. Amanda was shouting at Arturo in English with a thick Brazilian accent. She commented on Gatti's final fight against Gomez, calling Arturo's performance pathetic. She purportedly called Gatti's mother a whore, his brother Fabrizio a loser, and she finished by telling Arturo to go fuck his sisters.[1494] As Rizzo stood in shock, Arturo turned to him and calmly remarked, *"Tony, can you believe the mouth on this girl?"*[1495]

Rizzo then watched as Amanda smashed top-of-the-line crystal glass ornaments.[1496] Tony was forced to leave the scene. He could not handle seeing his friend and hero treated that way. Arturo remained silent as Amanda exploded. Either he was embarrassed that his friend had to witness the episode or he was numb to the behavior.

Rizzo believed that Arturo's partying habits were no different than anyone else's. Tony recalled that the couple fought constantly. On one occasion, Amanda allegedly struck Arturo over the head with a broom. She purportedly gave Gatti black eyes on several other occasions. She allegedly called Arturo a good-for-nothing junkie and alcoholic. Rizzo felt Arturo was fed up and it was only a matter of time before the relationship ended.[1497] Amanda also allegedly made negative remarks about Arturo's deceased father.[1498]

Rizzo recalled going out one evening with Amanda and a few other friends while Arturo was busy with another engagement. Amanda had offered to get Tony weight-loss pills that were mailed to her by her father, who worked in a hospital in Brazil. Rizzo recalled Amanda leaving the house dressed provocatively. Tony asked her to wear a sweater, in an effort to avoid upsetting Arturo. Amanda admitted that she liked dressing that way because Arturo hated it so much. She loved to see his reaction to her clothes.

During dinner that evening, the conversation turned to everyone's children. Amanda allegedly broke into the conversation and made negative, unkind comments about Arturo's daughter, Sofia. After leaving the restaurant, they went back to Arturo's condo, where Amanda allegedly continued to verbally attack Sofia. Amanda spent the remainder of the evening sending hateful texts and voice messages to Arturo's cell phone.

When out drinking with friends on another evening, Amanda bragged to Arturo's friend, Gisela Mineiro, that if Arturo thought his ex-girlfriends were bitches, she would show him what a real bitch is. According to Gisela, on several occasions Amanda allegedly said that she would end up killing Arturo.[1499]

Arturo's friends, even his brother Fabrizio, often kept away to avoid being around the verbal abuse that Arturo was experiencing. Humans were not the only target of Amanda's rage. She would twist Arturo's German Shepard's neck, causing the dog to yelp. Arturo would snap at Amanda when she did this.[1500] Fabrizio confessed that he never saw a couple fight like that in his life. They were always arguing, every day. Over stupid little things.[1501] Christen Santos recalled that the relationship was a disaster. Santos knew that sooner or later, it was going to end.[1502] Santos had been Arturo's closest childhood friend while growing up. Arturo's mother, Ida, recalled witnessing the couple fight while she was babysitting. She allegedly heard Amanda tell Arturo that she would kill him.[1503]

Arturo would often give Amanda between $500 and $1,000 a day to shop and get her hair done. Besides that, Amanda would allegedly max out Arturo's credit cards each month. Amanda was sending money to her mother in New Jersey, purportedly without Arturo's knowledge. She purchased a $30,000 Versace table, and Jimmi and Manolo shoes that ran for $400 a pair. She purchased umbrellas made by Gucci and Juicy Couture, and luggage from Louis Vuitton. Arturo spent $75,000 on a house for Amanda's father in Brazil. When a friend asked Arturo why he would do that, Gatti replied, *"Hey, if it shuts her up and keeps her quiet, it's worth it."*[1504]

Amanda reportedly was focused on persuading Arturo to change his will. Arturo's attorney, and his business partners, tried to talk him out of doing so. Amanda apparently dealt with the boredom of living in Montreal by attacking Arturo. Gatti had his own way of dealing with returning to Canada. He was frequenting strip clubs, drinking, womanizing, and using pills and cocaine. He would spend hours sitting at video lottery machines in Montreal bars.[1505]

On August 16, Pat Lynch received tragic news. Ronney Vargas, 8-0 (6 KOs), Lynch's up-and-coming junior middleweight prospect, was gunned down in the Bronx, N.Y. Vargas was only 20 years old. Besides being managed by Lynch, Vargas was promoted by Lynch's brother John's "Pound for Pound Promotions."

Vargas had stopped in a bodega at around 3:30 a.m. and started speaking to a lady customer. It was first believed, incorrectly, that the woman went outside and told her friends, who were gang members, that a boxer was flirting with her. It was later discovered that Vargas had a confrontation earlier in the evening with 31-year-old Jose Coimbre. Coimbre had confronted Vargas about Ronney dating his niece. Coimbre returned with a group. When Vargas exited the store with his friends, a surveillance camera captured Ronney trying to avoid a confrontation with Coimbre. Vargas attempted to drive away with his friends, but was blocked by Coimbre's car. Coimbre exited his vehicle and shot Vargas in the torso while Ronney was sitting in his car. Vargas crawled out of the vehicle and was pistol whipped by Coimbre. Vargas later died at St. Barnabas Hospital.

Lynch was in St. Petersburg, Florida, on vacation, when Vargas was murdered. Lynch had proudly touted Ronney as the next Arturo Gatti. Some who were close to Vargas were taken aback that Lynch did not cut his vacation short to come back for Vargas' funeral wake which was held on August 19 and 20.

On September 9, 2008 at Pierre-Le Gardeur Hospital in Quebec, Amanda gave birth to Arturo Gatti Jr. Junior was baptized at Montreal's lavish Notre Dame Basilica. Gatti's longtime friend, Anthony Ferrandino, later recalled seeing Arturo playing with Junior in a park in Montreal during an Italian festival. Ferrandino recalled how visibly obvious it was that Arturo loved his son.[1506] Arturo planned on teaching Junior to box at an early age.

Amanda and Arturo were observed arguing at the Christening party. Arturo was overheard saying, *"All you do is take money."*[1507]

Arturo was always with his son, according to friends. He would wake up in the middle of the night to feed Junior.[1508]

Mike Skowronski recalled that the final time he saw Arturo was at an airport with his son. Junior was strapped to Arturo with a chest harness. Arturo appeared happy and proud of Junior.

Gatti was very attached to Junior, and Amanda knew this. When Arturo mentioned that he wanted a divorce, Amanda allegedly used Junior as leverage. Tony Rizzo recalled that Amanda was continuously threatening Arturo, by stating that she was going to take Junior to Brazil. Rizzo felt that this was the reason why Gatti didn't leave her.[1509] Arturo started going out more. He would look for comfort with other women, but mostly he drank and wound up at his mother's house.

Arturo would sleep in a 10' x 20' room that was in the basement of his mother's home.[1510] Arturo often would sleep in his mother's house after a night of drinking, or when he fought with Amanda. Sometimes Arturo would crash at friends' houses as well, to spare his mother the stress of his family situation. Ida Gatti hated drunks, and she did not approve of Arturo's drinking.

Not long after Junior's birth, Arturo started speaking of a comeback bout. Local promoters wanted to pit him against fellow welterweight Antonin Decarie, who was born in Montreal and lived in nearby Laval, Quebec. When Pat Lynch heard of the comeback rumor he immediately called Arturo. Gatti promised Lynch that he would remain retired. Amanda, however, started taking boxing lessons three days a week from one of Arturo's friends, Angelo DiBella.

On November 29, 2008, Joe Gatti was in Montreal with his brother-in-law, Rocco Crispo. Joe was there to scout light middleweight prospect Phil Lo Greco. Joe was contemplating investing in the 16-0 (9 KOs) Italian-Canadian boxer. Lo Greco was taking on Roberto Valenzuela, 48-43-2, of Mexico. Joe and Rocco walked into the Montreal Casino to watch Lo Greco fight.

Not long after Joe and Rocco entered the casino ballroom, Arturo walked in with his mother Ida, Gerardo, Tony Rizzo, and his brother Fabrizio. Arturo was a special guest at the show. He was going to step into the ring, wave to the crowd, and watch a fight or two before leaving. Amanda was waiting for him outside in their truck with Junior. Arturo noticed Joe and went over to speak to him. Arturo asked Joe, *"Why don't you come over and talk to mommy?"* Joe replied, *"No, I'm outta here."*[1511] Joe was still upset with his mother over removing his children's photographs from her house wall. Vikki and Joe both felt that Ida didn't treat Versace and Gianni as well as she did her other grandchildren.

After Joe left the casino, he noticed a female sitting in a pick-up truck holding a baby. It looked like Amanda. The truck was parked on a curb, so Arturo definitely was not planning on staying at the fights too long. Joe called Vikki on his cell and told her, *"I think I just saw Junior."*[1512] Vikki asked Joe if he went over to say hi. Joe did not, because he felt funny approaching Amanda like that.

When Joe left the fights, Arturo went into a rage. He told everyone that he was leaving. Arturo said, *"That's it. We're not watching the fights. Let's go."*[1513] When Arturo entered his truck, Amanda was smiling at him. Arturo asked Amanda what she was smiling about. Amanda said, *"I just saw your brother."*[1514] Amanda had never met Joe, though she might have seen pictures of him. Arturo asked Amanda how she could be so certain that Joe was his brother. Amanda replied confidently, *"You guys look exactly alike. That's your brother."*[1515]

Ida told Arturo, *"See, I told you he didn't love you. He walked right by you. He didn't stay with you. You think that Joe loves you, but he doesn't love you."*[1516] Tony Rizzo agreed with Ida's remarks. Arturo was visibly upset. He started punching the window of the pick-up truck while he was driving. He yelled, *"Shut the fuck up! I'm gonna crash the car. Shut the fuck up!"*[1517] Arturo went out that night and comforted himself with drugs and alcohol.

On December 3, Arturo's home in the Morganville section of Marlboro, N.J., which had been on the market, sold for $1,125,000. Arturo had paid $1,250,000 for the 5 bedroom, 4.5 bath, 4,262 square foot home in May 2007. He took a loss on the sale.

On December 7, Amanda called the police to the couple's penthouse condo in Jarry. Amanda told the police that a drunken Arturo had come home at 7 a.m. and kicked in two doors. Both husband and wife displayed signs of a struggle, with scratches throughout their bodies. Amanda had a bloody nose. She told the police that Arturo punched and kicked her. Arturo was arrested and charged with assault. It appeared as though the relationship finally had reached a violent end, but there was more to come.

On January 15, 2009, Arturo moved in with his mother.

Joe still hadn't recovered from the debt he incurred when he was forced to pay for the custom motorcycle. Joe and Vikki were on the verge of losing their home from the mounting bills. The only family member with the type of finances to help Joe was Arturo. Joe swallowed his pride and called Arturo, begging for help. Joe promised to pay the loan back if Arturo would help him. Arturo said, *"You're like everybody else. You call me when you need money."* Joe replied, *"I'm not everybody else. I never asked you before, but I need help."* Arturo responded, *"Oh, I can't, my money's all invested."* Joe said, *"Alright, it doesn't matter. I just figured I'd ask."* Joe then asked Arturo how he was doing. Arturo said, *"Oh, I'm good."*[1518]

Joe was working three jobs just to pay the bills. Sometimes he would be driving home at 3 a.m. and he would close his eyes while driving, hoping to crash and end his suffering. It felt like his eyes were shut for five minutes, but it was more like five seconds. Joe would think of his family and snap out of his depression. Joe would arrive home, take a quick shower so he could sleep for an hour-and-a-half, and then get up to respond to his day job.

A few friends who were close to both brothers felt that Arturo and Joe really did love each other. It appeared as though they fought with each other to get each other's attention. Like most siblings, they most likely felt that there would come a time in the future when they would reconnect. Vikki felt that Arturo treated Joe negatively because addicts purposely pick on those they love. Arturo may have been jealous because although he was much more successful financially, he was unhappy in his personal life. He was known to tell people close to him that he wanted what Joe had; a nice wife, kids, and a stable family life. Arturo never grasped the fact that the reason he didn't enjoy those things was because he never came face to face with his own demons.

Amanda noticed that Tony Rizzo's wife, Karen, was working in the Gatti-Rizzo office. She asked Arturo if Karen was getting paid. Arturo said that she wasn't. Amanda told Arturo that she wanted to work in the office too. Amanda later discovered that Karen was making a six-figure salary. This was the source of yet another argument between the couple. Amanda felt that Arturo's friends were taking advantage of him.

Arturo never offered to let Joe in on his Gatti-Rizzo building company. Joe recalled, *"I never understood what I did to him. It bothered me so crazy."*[1519] Joe asked Arturo why he didn't give him an opportunity to invest with the company. Arturo told Joe, *"Well, you don't know nothing about construction."*[1520] Joe replied, *"And you do? You'll see how fast I'll learn [laughing]."*[1521]

On March 19, it was announced that Pat Lynch had signed welterweight boxer Henry Crawford. Crawford, promoted by Main Events, was a former two-time N.J. Golden Gloves champion.

On March 24, the police were called to the Gatti condo. Arturo was arrested for assault again. Arturo's friends felt the arrest was a setup. Arturo had been estranged from Amanda. She allegedly called him to the condo under the ruse that their son was sick and needed to be taken to the hospital. Once Arturo arrived at the apartment Amanda called the police and Arturo was arrested. Arturo was released from jail and ordered to stay at least 200 meters away from Amanda. He also was ordered to avoid alcohol and drugs. Arturo's court date was set for April 7.

Arturo and Amanda allegedly traded vicious text messages during this time. Amanda texted Arturo, calling him an embarrassment inside and outside of the ring. She also called him a loser and said she hoped he would crash his car.[1522]

On March 31, Arturo called his daughter Sofia, to wish her a happy 3rd birthday. Their communications with each other were so infrequent that Sofia allegedly did not even recognize his voice.[1523] Arturo was brought to tears from the incident.

Arturo started experiencing memory issues. There were times when he would forget the names of his children and even his own name. Chuck Wepner had confided in Mario Costa that he suffered from the same ailment, obviously from punches to the head. Wepner told Costa that he would wake up some mornings and not remember his own name or what he did for a living. On the days when this occurred, he would just sit and wait for his memory to return.

Arturo was taking medicine that was supposed to help with memory loss. He planned on enrolling in school. He discovered that working the brain helped to prevent memory loss. Arturo again spoke of a possible return to the ring.

Amanda called Arturo repeatedly, imploring him to help her

establish citizenship in Canada. Marrying Arturo, a Canadian citizen, did not automatically make Amanda eligible for Canadian citizenship. Arturo would need to sponsor Amanda for permanent residence prior to her applying for citizenship. Even though she was married to Arturo, Amanda feared that she would be labeled as an economic refugee and be subject to expulsion. She pleaded with Arturo to transfer a substantial amount of money into her bank account. Arturo promised to help her. Amanda was hopeful that if she established citizenship, she would be allowed to re-enter the United States legally to visit friends and relatives. Amanda texted Arturo, telling him that she was applying for an American visa. She told him that she needed a significant amount of money in her bank account to reflect her statement on her visa application that she was self-sufficient.[1524] Amanda may have been worried that Arturo was thinking of returning to the United States. She needed to regain legal entry into the U.S. to follow Arturo if he left her and headed back to New Jersey.

On April 4, at the Bell Centre in Montreal, Paterson native Kendall Holt, who had won the WBO light welterweight title in July 2008, met Timothy Bradley in a WBO/WBC unification bout. Arturo attended the match with Amanda even though there was an active restraining order barring Arturo from being near Amanda. Holt had trained in the same gym, Lou Costello, that Arturo attended early in his professional career. In fact, Arturo had driven the 11-year-old Holt home from the gym on several occasions in 1992. Kendall had later served as a sparring partner for Arturo's brother Joe. Arturo visited Holt in his dressing room before the match, to give him words of encouragement. During the fight, Arturo cheered Kendall on. Holt lost a decision and his WBO title to Bradley.

Arturo's friend Mike Moffa was now a boxing coach. Moffa recalled running into Arturo and Amanda at the Bell Centre during the Bradley-Holt fight. Moffa gave Arturo his cell phone number. While Arturo was attempting to enter Moffa's number into his phone, Amanda grabbed the phone away from Gatti and started typing the number in, while chastising Arturo for not knowing how to utilize a cellphone.[1525]

When April 7 arrived, Arturo was a no-show in court for his domestic incident. A warrant was issued for his arrest. Arturo would later claim that he failed to appear because he wanted to spare his mother the shame of having his personal problems aired in public. Arturo had been confronted by the police no less than five times in a seven-month stretch from December 2008 to June 2009.

On April 10, 2009, Arturo flew to Fort Lauderdale, Florida. He stayed there until April 12. He became romantically involved with Karen Brennan, who originally was from New Jersey. Brennan later stated that within fifteen minutes of meeting Arturo he confessed to her that he was married but separated, and was living in his mother's basement. He also told Brennan that he fought with his wife all the time, that he wasn't happy, and he feared losing his son to his wife.[1526]

On April 11 at 1:20 a.m., Arturo was involved in a street fight outside of a bar/restaurant at 208 Southwest 2nd Street in Fort Lauderdale. Nestor Fernandez was struck in the head by Arturo and spent the next five days in the North Broward Medical Center. A CAT scan revealed a fractured skull. Fernandez claimed he was sucker punched. A bystander recalled that Arturo was running around beating people up. Another witness stated that Arturo was intoxicated and belligerent.[1527] On April 13, Arturo was back in Montreal.

On April 15, Arturo was at a local strip club called Chez Pare, where he was celebrating his 37th birthday. The police received a tip that Arturo was there and responded. The heavily intoxicated Gatti was arrested shortly after midnight on April 16. He spent the night in jail. Arturo was charged with failing to appear in court and violating the restraining order that Amanda had taken out against him. He was released in the morning and given a new court date of June 5. Arturo was again advised not to have any contact with Amanda. Arturo was telling friends that he probably was going to get a divorce.[1528]

Arturo returned to Fort Lauderdale on April 25. He spent more time with the young and attractive Karen Brennan. Arturo stayed in Florida until April 28, when he again returned to Montreal.

Phil-Lan Doan was a childhood friend of Arturo's. Doan was a member of the Olympic Boxing Club with Arturo when they were kids. Arturo confided in Doan that although he still loved Amanda he planned on divorcing her. Arturo told Doan that the number one reason he wanted to end the relationship was not due to the fighting or her verbal abuse; it simply was because she never was satisfied or happy.

On May 7, Arturo hired a divorce attorney in Montreal. He finally had had enough. Gatti met with the attorney several times regarding divorcing Amanda. Amanda also hired an attorney. Arturo called

Pat Lynch to tell him his plans. Lynch was elated that Arturo was going to leave Amanda. Arturo had a copy of his pre-nup faxed from New Jersey to his divorce attorney. Pat Lynch later stated that Amanda became aware that the pre-nup was still valid and she would get nothing if the couple divorced. This may have motivated her to try and re-establish the relationship and work things out.[1529]

Arturo's friend Gisella Mineiro recalled that Arturo could not take the constant fighting any longer. He was fed up with living his life this way.[1530] Amanda was staring at a potential divorce and a valid pre-nup.

On May 11, Arturo's attorney gave a copy of the prenuptial agreement to Amanda's attorney. Additionally, Arturo's last will and testament left his entire estate to his mother, his siblings, and his daughter Sofia if he were to die. The will, created not long after Arturo met Amanda, did not mention her or Junior, as Junior was yet to be conceived.

On May 17, Arturo purchased a one bedroom condominium for himself and his son on Castelneau Street in Montreal for $510,000. Arturo had told friends that he planned on building more condominiums in Montreal with Tony Rizzo. He also revealed that he was interested in opening a gym in Montreal and possibly fighting in the UFC. Arturo asked his old friend, John Capone, to help him run the boxing gym when he opened it. Arturo had conversations with Pierre Bouchard and Stephan LaRouche in regards to a possible boxing comeback in 2010.

Arturo was telling friends that he was planning on bringing Karen Brennan to Montreal to live with him.

On June 5, Arturo responded to court. He appeared well dressed and groomed. The judge relaxed the restrictions against the couple seeing each other. Arturo left the courthouse claiming to love his wife. Amanda and Arturo decided to give their relationship one more try. Amanda pressed Arturo to keep the family together. Arturo acquiesced to her request. The newly reunited couple planned a second honeymoon in Europe.

In New Jersey, Pat Lynch heard the news of Arturo's reconciliation with Amanda. He was deeply disappointed. Now that Amanda had re-established contact with Arturo, the matter of the will and pre-nup likely would become an issue again. Donny Jerie recalled, *"You could see right through that she was a bad person."*[1531] But in the same breath, Jerie added, *"She tried to stop him from doing his drinking, but she just went crazy. She controlled him, she tried to change him and make him somebody that he's not. You can't change somebody. They are going to be who they are. He was getting ready to leave her for a fact, I know. He was getting ready to leave her."*[1532] On June 7, Arturo spoke to Karen Brennan by phone for the final time.

Arturo was arrested again. He spent several days in jail in Monteregie. The incident was not reported by the news. Arturo was very concerned about his mother hearing that he was in trouble again, as he had promised her that he would steer clear of problems.

Arturo was dealing with other matters besides his relationship with Amanda. The effects of 17 years of ring wars were taking their toll. Gatti confided in Phil-Lan Doan that his memory loss issues were worsening. Arturo played in an adult hockey league two to three nights a week to relax and get his mind off of his problems.

On June 10, it was announced that New York Giants running back Brandon Jacobs was entering into a boxing managerial partnership with Pat Lynch. Jacobs had fought as an amateur, posting a 30-2 record. The first fighter that the pair signed was New York and National Golden Gloves champion Steven Martinez. Jacobs planned on making boxing management his career after he retired from football.[1533] Lynch added Passaic junior middleweight Glen Tapia to his stable of young prospects. Jacobs and Lynch planned on debuting Martinez on the June 25th "Pound for Pound" promoted card being held at Schuetzen Park in North Bergen, N.J.

On June 15, Arturo and Amanda had a verbal dispute in their condo. Amanda had discovered that Arturo was having an affair with Karen Brennan. Their neighbor allegedly heard Amanda yell at Arturo to go to Brazil so she could show him what she was going to do. To which Arturo replied that he would indeed go down to Brazil to see what she was going to do to him.[1534]

On June 17, 2009, Amanda and Arturo responded to the office of Bruce Moidel, a notary public. Moidel had in his possession a will that had allegedly been prepared by Amanda and her lawyer. It was waiting in the notary's office. Arturo signed the will and it was notarized. The new will left nearly everything to Amanda, and if she were to die, everything would be turned over to her mother, Rosilene Barbosa, and her sister Flavia Luana Barbosa. The will was drafted in English. Arturo's daughter Sofia would receive a $100,000 college trust fund and another $500,000 trust that already was in place. Sofia's mother, Erika, also was receiving $4,640 a month in child support for Sofia, which would end on Sofia's 18th birthday.

The new will awarded Amanda "the universality of the residual of all" of Arturo's earnings. The new will also gave two-thirds of Arturo's alleged six to ten-million dollar estate to Amanda. In the new will, if both Arturo and Amanda died, Pat Lynch would control a trust fund for Junior.

Missing from the new will were Ida, Fabrizio, and Anna-Maria. Amanda would later state that Arturo changed the will because he now had his own family and he wanted to demonstrate his love for them. Amanda added that she and Arturo made the will just prior to leaving on vacation because of the Air France plane crash on June 1. The plane crashed after departing from Rio de Janiero, Brazil. Even though Arturo had changed his will, his prenuptial agreement was still valid. As long as Arturo was alive, if the couple divorced, Amanda would receive almost nothing. With the new will, however, if Arturo died, Amanda would get millions. Amanda was adamant that she did not pressure Arturo into signing the new will.

In early June, Sylvia Fagnani ran into Arturo. She noticed he was not the same Arturo. He was not as full of life as he usually was. Arturo told Sylvia that he was going through rough times and having trouble with his marriage. He added that the age difference between him and his wife, 14 years, did not help.

Arturo's friends in Montreal felt that Amanda forced him to sign the new will by threatening to take Junior to Brazil if he didn't sign the document.[1535] Amanda later denied that she threatened to take Arturo's son away. She said she wanted Arturo to stop drinking. Amanda admitted that when she was mad at Arturo she would tell him that she would leave him if he didn't change his ways. She added that she never meant what she said.[1536] Amanda acknowledged that Arturo was a great father, the best ever.[1537]

Tony Rizzo recalled that Arturo had spoken to him on several occasions regarding his fear of losing his son. Arturo told Rizzo, *"Tony, I have to see my son. I have to stick with this no matter what."* Rizzo felt that Arturo's relationship with Amanda was built on money. Rizzo recalled that Arturo told him that he met Amanda at the Squeeze Lounge gentlemen's club.[1538]

Chapter 30
Tragedy in Brazil

On June 18, 2009, Arturo and Amanda left for Europe on a second honeymoon. They spent time in Amsterdam and Paris. Amanda's mother, Rosie Barbosa, watched Junior in New Jersey. Amanda later recalled that it was the best vacation of her life. She described it as beautiful and perfect.[1539] Arturo apparently did not feel the same way. He called Tony Rizzo while he was in Amsterdam and told Rizzo that the vacation was a nightmare and he planned on returning to Montreal sooner than expected.[1540] Rizzo believed that Amanda was unbalanced and had no desire to be a mother. He felt that Arturo should have divorced her.

Amanda recalled that Arturo renewed his vows to her at the Eiffel Tower by proposing on one knee with a champagne glass. Inside the glass was a new wedding ring. After Paris, Arturo flew to New Jersey to pick up Junior. Amanda flew straight from Paris to Brazil. When Arturo arrived in New Jersey at Newark Airport, he had two black eyes. Arturo met with his old friend, Donny Jerie. When Jerie asked about the swollen eyes, Arturo replied, *"You know Donny, I gotta get out of this shit man, I gotta get out of this relationship. I can't do it no more."* [1541]

On June 25, Amanda sent an e-mail, in Arturo's name, from Brazil to Merrill Lynch in New Jersey, requesting $300,000. Merrill Lynch replied by sending a written release form for Arturo to sign. The form was never signed. Arturo wasn't even in Brazil. Arturo allegedly was unaware that Amanda sent the e-mail. Amanda later stated that the funds were needed for vacation spending money.

On July 1, at 1 a.m., Alexis Arguello committed suicide in his home in Managua, Nicaragua. Arguello, a former three-division world champion, pointed a gun at his chest and pulled the trigger. Authorities at first felt that foul play was involved, but all the evidence pointed towards suicide. Arguello was disenchanted with politics and was feeling the pressure that came from his role as mayor. The sports world was shocked. It was not common knowledge that Arguello had talked about committing suicide in the past. In 1984, while on his boat in the ocean, he placed the barrel of a loaded pistol in his mouth. He later confessed that he would have pulled the trigger if his 12-year-old son had not been on the boat. Arguello had lost his rematch to Aaron Pryor a few months prior to the boating incident. In a 1985 interview with *Sports Illustrated*, Arguello spoke of his suicidal thoughts.

There were many similarities between Arturo and Arguello. Both lost their fathers at an early age. Both boxers went from modest backgrounds to becoming millionaire superstars. Both had trouble with relationships and splurged their money on family and friends. Both frequented night clubs and bars at all hours of the night while sleeping all day. Both, although known for their courage, received severe beatings and were forced to submit in the ring. And both fell victim to drug and alcohol abuse.

Arturo's voice could be heard ringing through Arguello's lips in 1985 when Alexis discussed why he was making a comeback. Arguello confessed that boxing was the only thing he knew how to do. It was the only way he could generate money and buy himself nice things. Arguello had trouble articulating why, but he felt fulfilled when he was in the ring fighting. He likened himself to a reincarnated gladiator. Arguello felt that everyone around him was selfish. He added that he cared nothing for the world.[1542]

Arturo most certainly would have known of Arguello's suicide, as it was broadcast worldwide through media outlets.

Arturo returned to Montreal for a week after picking up Junior, before flying with his son to Brazil.[1543] While in Montreal, Arturo asked his step-father, Gerardo di Francesco, to go with him to Brazil. The rest of Arturo's family was in Florida for his sister Anna-Maria's upcoming wedding. Di Francesco remained behind in Montreal to keep an eye on the house. Arturo confided to Gerardo that he did not feel comfortable going to Brazil alone. Gerardo turned down Arturo's offer, but later questioned whether Arturo would still be alive if he had accompanied him to Brazil.[1544]

Amanda recalled that she and Arturo planned on staying in Brazil for two months. The couple decided on Porto de Galinhas, which had a beach area. Amanda stated that she had never been to that part of Brazil before.[1545] Arturo most likely would not have been able to spend two months in Brazil, as Amanda stated, unless he flew back and forth to the United States. He was scheduled to testify in New York City, in Joey Gamache's civil trial, the following week. Arturo had been called to testify by both the plaintiff and defendants. Amanda later told ESPN's "E:60" that she and Arturo planned on staying in the resort for six weeks.

Arturo called Micky Ward before he boarded his plane for Brazil. Ward had just left Mark Wahlberg's house, where he was helping

Wahlberg prepare for his role in the movie *The Fighter*. Ward later recalled that Gatti told him he was going to visit Ward in Lowell, Massachusetts, when he returned from Brazil.[1546]

Arturo had vacationed in Brazil several times prior to meeting Amanda. Amanda was later asked whose idea it was to travel to Brazil. She first commented, *"To tell you the truth it was a surprise. I think he surprised me."*[1547] Amanda would later state that the trip was planned, to see her sister graduate from medical school.

On July 10, Arturo and Junior arrived at the small beach resort town of Porto de Galinhas. Amanda was there already. The family stayed at the Doris-Ancorar Resort, in a two-story condominium. The resort had no video cameras and limited security. Friends of Arturo would later state that he would never stay at such a resort. Arturo always stayed at five-star hotels.

After settling into their rental, the family headed by taxi to the center of the village. They walked the tourist area, with Junior in a stroller, then entered a pizzeria at around 9 p.m. Arturo ordered two large pies, one for his family, and one for a group of children who were playing in the street outside of the restaurant. Arturo drank two bottles of wine and appeared intoxicated. The manager of the pizzeria recalled that the couple seemed happy.

Around midnight, the couple left the pizzeria and continued walking the small village. They came upon another restaurant at around 12:30 a.m. Arturo went in and bought himself a beer. Amanda stated that everything was fine up until that moment. The baby was sleeping in the stroller. Amanda recalled that she wanted to go back to the hotel, but Arturo didn't want to go home.[1548] The pleasant evening suddenly turned ugly. The couple began arguing. Arturo slammed his beer down and chastised Amanda by stating, *"You'll never change!"*[1549]

Either Arturo or Amanda wanted to go to the Santeria dance club, depending on which version you believe. Amanda stated that she wanted to take Junior back to the condo to sleep. They went into the club and an argument between the couple ensued. Witnesses claimed that Amanda was dancing with other men in the club while Arturo was holding the baby and wanted to go home.

According to police detective Josedite Ferreira, Amanda was wearing a bustier dress with no bra or underpants.[1550] Arturo was sitting in the club watching his wife, who was wearing a short dress with no underwear or bra, dancing with other men.[1551] This scenario obviously would have enraged Arturo.

After the couple left the club, Amanda stepped onto the sidewalk and accidentally exposed her genitalia. Bystanders started laughing, making fun of her.[1552] Amanda and Arturo began cursing at each other in English, which prompted bystanders to laugh more at the couple. Arturo asked Amanda why the people were laughing at them. She didn't respond, and started walking away. Gatti pushed Amanda and pulled her by her hair. Amanda fell to the ground, injuring her chin and elbow. Brazilian investigator Paulo Alberes revealed that witnesses at the scene stated that Amanda *"skidded on the asphalt"* after being pushed by Arturo, which caused her to fall.[1553]

When Amanda was later interviewed, she failed to mention the fact that the couple went to a dance club after leaving the pizzeria.[1554] There are those who believe that Amanda purposely staged the dance club scenario, fully knowing that Arturo would explode and attack her in public.

After Amanda fell to the ground, Arturo flagged down a taxi and put Junior in the back seat. A local doorman, Jorge Soares, tried to intercede in the altercation. Arturo struck him three times, in the head, jaw and chest, knocking Soares down and out. Amanda rose to her feet and fled on foot. The taxi driver, Manu Barros, ran from the cab, searching for a police officer. Witnesses on scene confirmed that Amanda left the area.

A crowd had gathered and began throwing debris at Arturo for pushing Amanda. One bystander threw a bicycle at Gatti. Another threw a brick that struck Arturo in the back of his head, opening a gash. Manu Barros returned to the scene without the police. Arturo demanded to be driven to his condo. Junior was still sitting in the back seat of the cab. Arturo stepped into the cab. He angrily told Barros that if it weren't for his son, he would've killed everyone. Barros had noticed that the back of Arturo's head was bleeding, and asked Gatti if he wanted to go to the hospital. Arturo replied that he was fine. Barros was later interviewed by ESPN, but he refused to allow himself to be identified, nor did he want his face shown on TV.

Upon returning to the condo, Arturo noticed that Amanda was not there. He demanded that Barros take him back to the village. Barros refused. Arturo hailed another cab and went back to the village. Witnesses told police that Arturo left his son in the apartment while he returned to the city center to look for his wife. Arturo had the taxi stop at the Santeria dance club. Like a wild man, he entered the club throwing chairs and threatening the patrons. When he realized that Amanda was not in the club, Arturo jumped back into the cab and returned to the condo.

When Arturo arrived back at the condo, Amanda was waiting there with her own taxi driver. Amanda had left her purse at the condo and had asked a taxi driver to take her home, where she could pay for the ride.[1555]

At the hotel, the desk clerk recalled that when Arturo came back the second time he observed the tattoo on the back of Arturo's neck, but he did not see any blood coming from his head. The driver of the second cab that dropped Arturo off stated that there was some blood on the head rest where Arturo was sitting. When Arturo walked up the stairs he handed Amanda's driver a $20 bill. Amanda's driver, who later refused to give his name or be shown on TV, did not leave the property for another 45 minutes. Where did he go? Some questioned whether the taxi driver could have been involved in the tragedy that would follow.

Amanda described the scene when they entered the condo with Arturo's pass key at 2:26 a.m. She said that Arturo explained that he had fought with four men in the street.[1556] Arturo noticed Amanda's bleeding chin and asked her if he was responsible for the injury. Amanda told him that he was. Arturo panicked and asked Amanda if she was going to leave him. Amanda answered that she was going to divorce him. Did Amanda also threaten to call the police on Arturo? If she did she never mentioned this in subsequent interviews. She recalled that Arturo showed her his injured head, but she didn't care to see it because she was angry with him. When she told Arturo that he had hurt her, Gatti stated, *"I guess that's it."* Amanda later recalled that those were the last words that he ever spoke to her. She told Arturo that it was over between them.[1557]

Amanda should have been fully aware that if she divorced Arturo she would receive nothing but child support, but if Arturo died, the newly signed will would leave her millions.

Amanda described Arturo's emotions as sad, not angry. Amanda said that she was fed up. She recalled that Arturo became sullen when he observed her standing there, injured and hysterical.[1558] Amanda took Junior up the stairs to the second floor bedroom of the condo. She locked the door and went to sleep. She would later state that this was the final time that she saw Arturo alive.

Arturo's brother Joe believes that Arturo found himself in a very dark place. One of Arturo's favorite songs by Journey was "Wheels in the Sky." The song's lyrics stated, *"Ooh, I can't take this very much longer, I'm stranded in the sleet and rain. Don't think I'm ever gonna make it home again."*[1559] Another one of Arturo's favorite bands, Metallica, wrote a song about suicide called "Fade to Black." *"I have lost the will to live, simply nothing more to give. There is nothing more for me, need the end to set me free."*[1560] Were these the types of thoughts that were going through Arturo's mind?

Amanda stated that she woke up around 6 a.m. and went downstairs to the kitchen to warm up milk for Junior. She noticed Arturo on the floor in a fetal position, but she thought he was sleeping. Amanda claimed that she did not notice the pool of blood around Arturo's head. Nor did she notice the lividity in his body, that gave a red and purple color to Arturo's side, hands and feet. The blood pooled out around Arturo's head, in all directions, filling the tile floors' grouted seams, turning them crimson. Amanda later recalled that Arturo had slept on the floor in the past when he was drunk, so she didn't think much of his position. Joe confirmed that he and Arturo had both slept on the floor many times as adults.

Amanda recalled that she didn't say anything to Arturo because she was still angry at him from the night before. Amanda boiled water for Junior's milk. Apparently she didn't notice Arturo's gold and diamond chain, which was later recovered by police in a pot on the stove.

Amanda said that she walked back upstairs and fed Junior. Looking at the crime scene photos it is clear to see that a significant amount of blood had pooled around Arturo's head. Enough to make anyone concerned. Also, the color of the lividity in his hands, feet and legs were plain to see. Anyone who lives with or knows someone well should recognize that the skin color was severely abnormal. Amanda would later say that she didn't look at the floor behind his head to see if there was blood.[1561]

Arturo was below the second floor stair case, on the right. The stove and refrigerator were on the left. There was a small, 3' x 5' island in the middle of the kitchen. Amanda admitted that she did indeed look at Arturo. She claimed that there was no blood there at that time.[1562] She recalled that she then walked to her left, to get Junior's bottle, and returned back upstairs.

Amanda returned back downstairs at around 9 a.m. It was at that time that she claimed she noticed the blood on the floor around Arturo. Amanda recalled that she shook Arturo in an attempt to wake him up, and noticed that he felt cold. While recalling the scene in a later ESPN interview, she stated that she hoped that he had just passed away. The interviewer had to correct Amanda by asking her if she meant passed out.[1563] Amanda nodded yes. Tears started streaming down Amanda's face during the interview.

When Amanda went back upstairs the first time she changed her clothes and freshened up before coming back down, recognizing her husband was dead, and screaming for help. The clothes she wore on the night of the incident were not taken into evidence.

Arturo had semen in his briefs, but Amanda was not examined by authorities to confirm if she had sexual intercourse with Arturo. An examination may have helped the investigators who were reconstructing the timeline of events by confirming Amanda's account that after returning to the condo she locked herself in the room with Junior, and that she was not intimate with Arturo after returning to the condo.

In crime scene photos, it appears as though there were footprints all over Arturo's body.[1564] Were these marks actual footprints, and if so, how did they get there?

Amanda would later state that she believed Arturo wanted to punish himself.[1565]

After touching Arturo and feeling how cold he was, Amanda started shaking him. When he didn't move she started calling out his name. She pleaded with him to wake up and told him that she forgave him. When there was no reaction from Arturo she opened the door to the condo and started screaming that her husband was dead.[1566]

Amanda originally had told the police that she believed someone had broken into the house and murdered her husband. Police advised her that they would check the electronic key device to determine if the door had been opened during the night. The next day, Amanda changed her opinion, saying that she believed Arturo had killed himself. Amanda would later state that she would never do anything to hurt her husband.[1567]

The police investigation revealed that Arturo's estimated time of death was 3 a.m. on July 11. This was only 28 minutes after he arrived at the condo. There were seven empty beer cans in the kitchen. Was it possible that Arturo had consumed seven cans of beer in 28 minutes, and then hung himself? Did Arturo drink the beers prior to going out for the evening?

Amanda recalled that she ran out of the condo and knocked on a neighbor's door, screaming that her husband was dead. Witnesses would later state that if Amanda was acting, she gave an Academy Award-winning performance. The hotel administrator, Wiliton Vincente, heard Amanda scream and came running over. Amanda pleaded with Vincente to come to her condo, telling him that her husband had fallen down, hit his head, and wouldn't get up. Vincente checked Arturo for a pulse but found none. He was stiff and cold. Vincente realized immediately that Arturo was deceased.

The police were called and arrived at the scene. Their immediate impression was that a homicide had occurred. Arturo's neck had bruises that were consistent with strangulation. He also had a wound on the back of his head. In the kitchen, there was a bloody towel and a steak knife. Amanda's chin and arm injury led police to believe that a domestic assault had occurred and that Arturo had been murdered.

The stool that was near Arturo's body was actually underneath the staircase. Brazilian investigator Paulo Alberes would later state that he believed Arturo had kicked the chair out from under him. Arturo's head was underneath the kitchen cabinet. The investigators that Pat Lynch later hired dropped a test dummy dozens of times. The dummy never fell even close to the position that Arturo was found in.

Amanda's purse was found on the floor, under a kitchen cabinet. The purse strap had been removed and was wrapped around Arturo's neck.

The lead investigator of Arturo's death was Moises Texeira of the Porto de Galinhas Police. He was assisted by Josedith Ferreira. Amanda was interrogated for six hours.

Texeira did not believe that Amanda's responses to his questions were truthful. She did not appear distraught about her husband's death. She had a cold and emotionless expression. Amanda's explanation of the events that took place did not match up with the evidence. She contradicted her own statements and mumbled when she answered questions.

Josedite Ferreira recalled that Amanda answered all of his questions evasively and even laughed while replying to some of his questions. At one point, Amanda went to the refrigerator and offered Ferreira a beer, which he declined. Ferreira later revealed that he did not find any evidence on the scene that led him to believe that Arturo committed suicide.[1568]

According to Paul Ciolino, a private investigator later hired by Pat Lynch, Amanda allegedly gave three different stories on the morning of the tragedy. First she stated that her stepbrothers may have been involved in the tragedy. Then she stated that Arturo had been with strange men, and they all left the apartment together while she went to bed. Lastly, she stated that after she told Arturo she was leaving him, he became so depressed that he killed himself.[1569] It should be noted that the stories that Ciolino stated Amanda gave regarding her stepbrothers and strange men were never mentioned by Amanda, the police or the media in the months that followed.

Amanda told police that she did not wear a bra or underwear on the night before Arturo's death. She added that she was a virgin when she met Arturo. She denied that she had ever worked as an exotic dancer in New Jersey, because she was only 20 years old when she met Gatti. It should be noted that in New Jersey an exotic dancer is required to be 18 years of age or older. Amanda said that she could not remember when Arturo signed his new will. How could that be? Arturo signed the new will only 24 days prior, in Amanda's presence, right before they left for their second honeymoon. Amanda said that Arturo never talked about suicide, but he did say that he would never be separated from her. She also stated that Arturo had told her the only thing that could separate them was death.

Amanda was asked point blank if she had anything to do with her husband's death. She replied that she did not.[1570]

There were no video surveillance cameras at the complex. Although authorities were confident that no one had entered the rental with a card key after 2:26 a.m., could someone have been waiting in the condo and committed the crime? Did the authorities check if anyone had entered the condo during the time that Arturo and Amanda were walking in the village center? Not all electronic coded key entry systems registered when the door was opened from the inside without a key. This would mean that the system might not have registered if someone had been let in or exited from the interior. Additionally, a window could have been used to enter and exit the rental unit.

The crime scene was a disaster. No one secured the scene by logging who entered and exited the scene, as is customary in suspicious death investigations. Hotel employees, Emergency Medical Technicians, and everyone else who was on the scene were not logged in by police. During the two-day investigation, the Brazilian forensic authorities spent only 2 hours and 46 minutes on the scene.

No fingerprints were taken off of the stool that Arturo allegedly used to hang himself. Nor were fingerprints or DNA samples taken from the empty beer cans at the scene. There were limited crime scene photos taken, and none of the photos were of Amanda's clothing or Arturo's hands. No DNA testing was conducted on the purse strap, the bloody rag in the kitchen, or underneath Arturo's finger nails.

More importantly, no DNA testing was conducted on the bedsheets even though there were traces of blood on the sheets. Arturo had been found in his underwear. Pat Lynch was convinced that Gatti would never take his clothes off and hang himself with his son upstairs in a bedroom.[1571]

Oddly enough, crime scene photos did not show Arturo wearing his prized $30,000 white gold chain with a diamond cross pendant. The chain subsequently reappeared around Arturo's neck in morgue photos. It was later revealed that when police arrived on the scene the chain had been placed in a pot on the stove. It took months for this information to be released. Was Amanda even questioned about this? Arturo cherished the expensive chain, and would never remove it from his neck except to box.

Cell phones were not confiscated. Amanda may have made phone calls when she left Arturo at the club. A search of her phone would have revealed if Amanda had called family or friends in Brazil. Arturo's $40,000 Rolex watch was missing and has never been recovered. $40,000 or $50,000 in missing cash also was unaccounted for. The purse strap was not matched to the purse by brand. A similar strap, in later testing, was unable to hold Arturo's weight, or even half of his weight. Arturo's pancreas, half of his heart, and a piece of his brain were taken for lab testing. All three of the samples would disappear.

Michael Baden was later hired by the Gatti family. He called the Brazilian autopsy "sloppy." Arturo's hyroid bone was fractured. When death comes from this type of injury, it usually is from manual strangulation, not hanging. Brazilian doctors later admitted that they inadvertently broke the hyroid bone during their autopsy. Baden stated that it was possible for the hyroid bone to break during an autopsy.

By the afternoon on the day of Arturo's death, the interrogation of Amanda was complete, and she was released. News of Arturo's death had not yet been made public. Most of Arturo's family were in Florida for Anna-Maria's second wedding. Pat Lynch was vacationing in Italy. Mario Costa was vacationing in Portugal and Micky Ward was vacationing in New Hampshire. Joe Gatti was at home, back in New Jersey.

At 3:35 p.m., after her release, Amanda called Anna-Maria in Florida. It was 1:35 p.m. Florida time when Anna-Maria received the call. Amanda told Anna-Maria that something bad had happened. Anna-Maria asked what had happened. Amanda told her that Arturo had died. Ida Gatti was holding onto Anna-Maria's arm and she immediately screamed, *"She did it!"*[1572] Ida then fainted.

Anna-Maria demanded to know how her brother had died. Amanda said that she did not know what happened. Anna-Maria would later state that Amanda's voice was emotionless. Anna asked Amanda what she meant when she said that she did not know what happened. Hysterically, Anna demanded to talk to Arturo. If her prior nightmare marriage to Davey Hilton wasn't bad enough, her second wedding day would be marred by this tragedy. Arturo's sister, Giuseppina, entered the room. All three women started crying. News quickly spread throughout the family via cell phones. The media soon picked up on the information and news of Arturo's death spread throughout the United States, Canada, and the rest of the world. Anna-Maria later recalled that Amanda seemed very cold during the conversation. Anna initially thought Amanda was joking.[1573] Anna-Maria added that Amanda always talked about money. She was convinced that Amanda used her brother for his wealth.[1574]

Pat Lynch was contacted in Italy via phone. He stated that he felt like he lost a son or a younger brother. Lynch admitted that he never felt comfortable around Amanda. He added that Arturo gave her a life she could never have dreamed of in a million years.[1575]

Mario Costa, after initially hearing of the tragedy, thought that maybe Arturo had been murdered. At the same time, Costa knew that Arturo had talked about killing himself, especially after the Mayweather fight. Costa recalled Arturo stating, *"I want to die. I'm tired. I want to check out."* Costa recalled that Arturo hadn't spoken to many people in New Jersey during his final two years. One of the few people he kept in touch with was photographer Tom Casino. Costa felt that Arturo had no structure in his life. Gatti had repeatedly told Costa that he just wanted a normal life with a family and children. Costa tried to convince Arturo that he could have all of the things he wanted if he stopped using drugs.[1576]

By 4 p.m., everyone had heard of the news. Joe Gatti was watching his two daughters swim in their backyard pool when his phone started ringing off the hook. First his brother-in-law, Rocco Crispo, called. Then Ivano Scarpa called. Both left messages for him to call them immediately. Joe called Crispo back and Rocco told Joe that Arturo was found dead in Brazil. Joe became enraged. He felt that his brother had been killed. Vikki would later recall that she never saw her husband in such an angry state. Joe reportedly told boxing trainer Howard Grant that he thought Amanda set his brother up.[1577]

Joe called Costa and cried, *"Mario, they finally managed to kill my brother."*[1578] Joe called John Lynch, who was at his home in Union City, N.J., and told him, *"I hope that with all the money you made on his back, you will send the world to Brazil to clear up his death. And don't tell me that your brother cares. He did not care about Arturo when he was alive. Do you think he will worry about him in death?"*[1579]

Joe finally reached Pat Lynch in Italy. Joe recalled, *"Pat goes, 'There is nothing I can do right now. I'm on vacation'. Arturo made this guy a millionaire. I would have stopped everything. This is my prodigy. This is the kid that made me what I am today. I would have said, 'Pack it up. We're leaving.' Get a flight, cause he has the money to do anything. He stood there. He finished his vacation."*[1580] Coincidentally, Lynch was on vacation when Arturo died, just as he had been when Ronney Vargas was murdered.

Mike Sciarra recalled, on the day of Arturo's death, that although there wasn't a cloud in the sky, thunder could be heard overhead, without any lightning or rain.

The first official statement from the Brazilian police was carefully worded, so as not to lay blame anywhere, until more evidence was collected. Rumors were circulating that Gatti had been murdered, and that Arturo might have been accidentally strangled during wild sex. When Pat Lynch first heard the news of Arturo's death, he turned to his wife Lisette and told her that he was sure that Amanda had killed Arturo, or knew who did. In Montreal, some of Arturo's friends believed that Amanda had set Arturo up by bringing him to Brazil.

Arturo's close friend Donny Jerie was in a theater in New York City, watching the movie *The Hangover*. Jerie had shut his cell phone off. He didn't notice the missed calls until he exited the theater. He saw that two of his close friends, Roland and Eric Ortense, had called him. Micky Ward also called. Before listening to the messages, Jerie knew something terrible had happened to

Arturo. Jerie listened to Ward's message first. *"Yo Donny B, Arturo, his girlfriend murdered him."*[1581] Jerie could not believe it was true. Jerie later suggested, *"She reels him in, changes the will, gets him down to where she's from, and got him murdered."*[1582]

Main Events released a statement saying that they mourned Arturo's untimely death and wondered if boxing ever would be as much fun without him.[1583] Buddy McGirt had just landed in Orlando on a flight from Reno when he turned his cell phone on and noticed that he had 30 voice mails and 25 texts. Before he listened to his voice mails or looked at his texts, he called his wife Gina. Gina told McGirt that she had bad news, that Arturo was found dead. Pat Lynch called to ask if Buddy was okay.[1584] McGirt started receiving phone calls from the press. Buddy stated that Arturo had the heart of a lion, but also the heart of a pussycat. McGirt added that he would miss the hell out of Arturo.[1585]

Buddy later stated that Arturo had a roller coaster ride in life and boxing, and he just wished that people would let him rest in peace. McGirt recalled how Arturo used to tell Buddy that McGirt was a lucky man because he had a beautiful family. Gatti told McGirt that when he retired, he wanted a family life just like Buddy had.[1586]

On July 11, only hours after Arturo's death, Main Events held a boxing card at the Prudential Center in Newark, N.J. The featured bout was Tomasz Adamek versus Bobby Gunn. Sal Alessi recalled the night. *"Ron Katz came over to my house. He met me in Bayonne to go up to the Prudential Center and we found out that Arturo had died earlier in the day. We had to go pick up Mikey Red, who loved Arturo. I got a feeling that they weren't talking at the time and that made it even worse, even more painful. When we picked up Mikey Red he had these big black sunglasses on and he was doing his best to keep himself together. All I could think is, 'How are we going to get through this night.' It was Kathy Duva's show. Jolene Mizzone, who loved Arturo, organized the events for Main Events. We get to the arena. I take one look at Jolene and she looks at Mikey Red and I don't know how we got through that night, Mikey and Jolene and Kathy and everybody. I wasn't part of the Gatti camp during his career, but later on I got to know him a little bit. But at the time I was very close to Mikey Red and it was just heart breaking, heart breaking."*[1587]

Alessi described Pat Lynch's reaction to Arturo's death. *"Well, there's a couple of different ways of looking at it. The fact that everybody knew that that kid didn't kill himself. They were determined to clear his name. I know that John Lynch and Pat moved heaven and earth. They brought Doctor Baden in. They hired special investigators from Chicago who were top notch guys, that had done work for '60 Minutes.' They were in constant contact with the Gatti family. They did everything they could to try and clear that kid's name. They felt that they didn't want a kid who would never quit in a fight to go down in history as a guy who killed himself. So you know it was painful. It was painful because they were trying to mourn and at the same time trying to clear this guy's name. So it was a mixed bag of emotions. There was broken hearts and there was anger, a lot of anger over that, because people were gonna believe what they wanted to believe. But those guys, they knew that Arturo didn't kill himself."*[1588]

Before the Adamek fight took place, the bell was tolled ten times, symbolizing the ten-count for both Arturo Gatti and Alexis Arguello. Highlights of Arturo's fights were shown on the jumbo screens. When the highlights of his matches against Micky Ward were displayed the crowd of almost 6,000 roared in applause. Referee Randy Neumann, who was working the Newark show, recalled that he never saw a crowd show so much love for someone like they did for Arturo when he fought in Atlantic City.[1589]

Kathy Duva called Arturo's death an unspeakable tragedy, a horror. She recalled how Arturo would be surprised when fans were excited to meet him. He didn't grasp how appreciative his fans were of his performances. Kathy added that when Arturo entered the ring in Atlantic City, it was absolute magic.[1590] Duva sadly revealed how much she would miss Arturo's annual phone calls on the morning of December 25, to wish her and her family a Merry Christmas.

Heavyweight prospect Monte Barrett was at the Newark show. He commented that Arturo definitely was the ultimate warrior.[1591] Retired light heavyweight champion and current trainer, Eddie Mustafa Muhammad, who was working a corner at the show, was visibly upset. He surmised that there would be a lot of sadness in the arena.[1592]

Ivan Robinson, who also had a fighter boxing on the Newark card, said that he was devastated and crushed.[1593] Robinson added that Arturo was a great human being, a gentleman who would give you the shirt off his back if he could.[1594]

Gabe Ruelas recalled Arturo. *"I was here at home. I was stunned, I just couldn't believe it. I had to search the internet to see if it was a rumor or really true. They said he killed himself. I still don't believe that. He had too much to live for and he was too much a fighter in every way to do that. I think of a great fighter and I wish we could have gotten to know each other as friends. I am good friends with quite a few of my former opponents. I wish I would have had the same chance with Gatti. I think we would have gotten along very well. But if I ever see him again, wherever he is, I'm gonna ask him for a rematch [smiles]."*[1595]

Although Lou DiBella didn't expect Arturo to live to be 80 years old, he certainly was shocked that he was dead at 37. DiBella called Gatti the greatest fan-friendly TV fighter he had ever been associated with in his 20-plus years in boxing. DiBella added that Arturo fought hard, lived hard, played hard, and partied hard. He raced through his life like a shooting star or a fast-moving comet.[1596] DiBella did not believe that Gatti killed himself.[1597] In a *New York Times* interview back in 1999, DiBella made a statement that would forebode the tragedy that unfolded. In the interview, he revealed that Arturo had always frightened him, because he was reckless. DiBella added that Gatti didn't think of the consequences when he was having a good time. DiBella predicted that Arturo's recklessness wouldn't hurt anyone but himself.[1598]

Teddy Cruz recalled hearing of the death of his friend. *"I was in my friend's house, in Jersey City on North Street, when Mark Breland called me. It was like any one of those things when a close person or a sibling dies. When you hear something like that, you're like, 'What! No way! Come on!' And then shortly after that I turned on ESPN and they were flashing it across the news. My thoughts were like, 'No way it was suicide.' There was no way for him to do that. Especially since I had seen him maybe a few months before that. I know that Amanda didn't do it personally, but she knows what happened, is what I feel in my heart. I really hope that justice comes because I feel really bad, because I know he's not resting. I pray to God for him all the time. It's hurtful. It's very hurtful."*[1599]

Edilson Alves, a local Brazilian police investigator, announced that it was unclear how Arturo had died. The death was being ruled suspicious. Alves added that it was still too early to say anything concrete, although the entire incident appeared very strange.[1600] There were no reported stab or bullet wounds to Arturo's body. Arturo had suffered wounds to his neck and the back of his head.

Jersey City's legendary St. Anthony's High School basketball coach, Bob Hurley, tried to put what Arturo meant to Jersey City into perspective. Hurley felt that the people of Jersey City connected with Gatti because he was like them in that he would be back on his heels, bleeding and hurt, but somehow he would come back again because he had a puncher's chance.[1601] Hurley added that Arturo was proud to say he was from Jersey City. He was the poster child for never giving up.[1602]

Mikey Red fondly recalled Arturo's popularity in Jersey City. *"He knew people in the Heights, he knew people in Marion, on the West Side, Greenville. We could go everywhere and we knew everyone in Jersey City."*[1603] When Mikey was asked his thoughts on Amanda, he recalled that he got bad vibes from her.[1604]

Carl Moretti expressed his feelings by calling Arturo a friend who would always be there if you needed him. He was the kind of guy you would have wanted in your foxhole during a battle. Although he came from Canada, Moretti felt that Arturo was North Jersey through and through.[1605]

Ken Condon was saddened by the news. He reminisced on how Gatti sold out Boardwalk Hall six times in a row, mostly against guys nobody had ever heard of. Condon recalled when Arturo had to go to the hospital after fights, how he always came back to mingle with his fans and sign autographs.[1606]

The person in the best position to give his opinion on what Atlantic City meant to Gatti was Arturo himself, when he said, *"Atlantic City has always been a special place to me because of the way people receive me. They are always so nice to me and it's been that way since the beginning. I really enjoy Atlantic City, the whole atmosphere. I honestly don't see myself ever fighting anywhere else again."*[1607]

Larry Hazzard recalled that Arturo singlehandedly revived boxing in the state of New Jersey, especially in Atlantic City. There were times when Hazzard thought Arturo was walking that fine line between life and death in the ring. Hazzard recalled that with all the adoration and fame he attained, Gatti still was a very humble person and a nice guy.[1608]

Russell Peltz, when asked for his most fond memory of Arturo, stated, *"His smile. Arturo was always very polite to me and very friendly. The most special moment was watching ref Wayne Kelly let the Rodriguez fight go long enough for Arturo to come back and win."*[1609] When asked his opinion on how Arturo died, Peltz surmised, *"Obviously, he was murdered. Those were my first thoughts and they remain today."*[1610]

Alfonso Gomez stated, *"I always admired Arturo Gatti's heart. I could only pray on giving the fans epic performances like he did. It was an honor to have fought him, and to be the last fighter to ever face him will give me a place in his memory forever."*[1611]

Micky Ward was in shock and couldn't believe it was true. Buddy McGirt found it difficult to put his feelings into words.[1612]

Pete Maino surmised Arturo's life, *"He lived like he fought, furious. He fought like every round was his last and he lived like every day was his last. It was only going to last so long and he was gonna burn out. It was a shame, but there was no other way because there was never gonna be an old Arturo."*[1613]

Arturo's family in Florida believed that Amanda convinced him to go to Brazil. Arturo originally had planned to attend his sister's wedding in Florida, but they believed Amanda persuaded him to change his plans.[1614] At the time of the wedding Amanda would not have been able to attend, due to her immigration issues, and she knew that Arturo had been seeing a woman in Florida. It would be in Amanda's best interest to prevent Arturo from going to Florida. Arturo's step-father, Gerardo, recalled that he overheard Arturo arguing with Amanda in June. He heard her say that she would kill him one day. Di Francesco recalled that Ida tried to stop Arturo from going to Brazil. She was afraid something bad might happen to him; that he might fall into a trap.[1615]

Most of the guests at Anna-Maria's wedding wept openly for Arturo. Arturo's sister, Giuseppina, previously had a confrontation with Amanda late in 2008. She and Amanda had been neighbors in the same condominium complex where Arturo and Amanda resided. Giuseppina argued with Amanda about her marriage to Arturo. She recalled that Amanda said that she was going to benefit from her marriage to Arturo and that Arturo would pay.[1616] The family recalled that Arturo constantly complained about the way Amanda dressed.

Gerardo, who was in Montreal, revealed that his wife Ida was too shaken up to speak about the tragedy.[1617] Gerardo was haunted by the thought that Arturo might still be here if he had taken Arturo's offer to go to Brazil with him.[1618] Di Francesco revealed that Arturo had been living with him and Ida for a while because he was experiencing difficulties with Amanda.[1619]

Gerardo recalled that Arturo was living a more calm lifestyle of late, even though his friends always wanted him to go out with them to drink. Gerardo fondly recalled how after every boxing match, Arturo would come home to Montreal and spend a week with his mother.[1620]

As of July 12, Amanda still was being interrogated by police because of contradictions in her statements. Authorities announced that they were preparing formal charges against her. She would be held in a local prison, in Pernambuco, pending charges. Rodrigues could not explain how she spent nearly six hours in the condo without noticing her husband was dead. The police were told that Amanda and Arturo were extremely jealous of each other and that Arturo complained about the clothing that Amanda wore when they traveled to Brazil. Acelino Freitas admitted that he knew the couple were having problems and were about to separate.[1621]

The Brazilian police felt the following had occurred; Amanda and Arturo had gotten into a violent fight in public. Back at the hotel Amanda struck a drunk Arturo in the back of the head with a meat clever, knocking him out. After Arturo was knocked out, he was strangled by Amanda with her 48-inch purse strap. The police did not believe that Amanda could spend nearly six hours in the apartment with a deceased Arturo, including walking past his body, and not realize he was dead.

Amanda said that she never heard Arturo's body fall. There were two air conditioners on the second floor that may have drowned out the noise. Lynch admitted that if Arturo did kill himself, alcohol would have played a part. Amanda believed that Arturo killed himself because she was leaving him. The police discounted a third person being involved, because the computerized locking mechanism to the front door showed that no one had entered the rental unit with a pass key from 2:26 a.m. until 9 a.m. Again, it is not known if the locking mechanism in use at the resort in 2009 was the type to register if the door was opened from the inside.

Amanda's sister, Flavia, went on a local Brazilian TV station and defended her sister by saying that she was very religious and was incapable of killing anyone.[1622]

Back in New Jersey, the news of Arturo's death was still numbing those who knew him. Local boxing promoter Gabe LaConte said Arturo had more heart than boxing ability. LaConte added that the only way Arturo was coming out of a ring was if he was counted out.[1623] Kathy Duva called the tragedy senseless.[1624] Kathy recalled that she only met Amanda once, when the couple were still engaged. She added that she spoke to Arturo a few months prior to his death and he seemed happy.

Buddy McGirt was under the impression that Arturo was enjoying his retirement, because Gatti was one of the few boxers who was able to retire with no financial concerns. Buddy recalled Arturo's desire to have a family and children. McGirt added that Arturo was at least able to have the son that he always wanted to have. McGirt was mystified by the apparent domestic violence in Arturo's relationship with Amanda.[1625]

Many close to Arturo weren't surprised to hear that Amanda was being held in his death. The marriage was inundated with arguments and physical altercations caused by jealousy. Carl Moretti commented that although the news of Arturo's death was shocking, the circumstances surrounding it weren't shocking. He had heard that there were prior domestic incidents between the two in Canada.[1626]

Mike Skowronski spoke of the violence that seemed to permeate all of Arturo's relationships. *"I've personally driven him to the emergency room to get stitches from domestic incidents either with his wife or one of his former girlfriends. She just didn't seem like she was with Arturo for the right reasons, from the conversations I did have with her. Him being 37 and her being 23, they didn't have a whole lot in common."*[1627]

Amanda's attorney was insisting that his client was too fragile to kill Arturo. The police were ruling nothing out, except that they were certain that only Arturo and Amanda were in that apartment with their son. Moises Teixeira, the lead investigator, felt that it was impossible for a third person to have been in the condo. This led Teixeira to believe that Amanda committed the crime alone.[1628]

John Lynch believed that Amanda was involved in Arturo's death, and if she didn't do it herself, she was there and had help.[1629] Doctor Frank Rotella felt differently about Amanda. He felt that Amanda appeared very bubbly and in love with Arturo.[1630]

Amanda would later state that her living conditions in the Colonia Penal Femina Bom Pastor, or Good Shepard prison in Pernambuco, were deplorable. She stated that cockroaches crawled all over her body at night. Twenty women were cramped into a cell that had only four beds. An Amnesty International report in 2007 claimed that the prison system in Brazil was overpopulated and had poor sanitary conditions. The prisoners were exposed to torture and ill-treatment. Gang violence and riots were common in the prison. Women were reported to have been violated in the prison where Amanda was held, and detainees were forced to sleep on the floor and in shower stalls, due to a lack of bedding. Women who had given birth while in prison were kept in the cells with their newborn babies. The justice system in Brazil was slow and reportedly corrupt. There were allegations of slave labor. Many of Brazil's municipal jails housed women and men together, with females frequently being raped by males. In 2007, a 15-year-old female was kept, uncharged, in a cell with twenty males for a month. She was raped and tortured repeatedly over the month, only being given food in exchange for sex.

The Gatti family chose to send Fabrizio to Brazil to identify and retrieve Arturo's body. Fabrizio left Montreal on July 13 with Freddy Robb, his niece Anne-Marie's husband. They arrived in Brazil the following day. At the morgue, when police pulled the sheet off of the body, Fabrizio immediately recognized the cross tattoo on Arturo's left bicep. He positively identified his brother then quickly turned away, stating that he could not bear to look anymore.

On July 13, the Joey Gamache trial began in New York. The judge, Melvin Schweitzer, contemplated suspending the starting date because Arturo was scheduled to testify for both sides. The judge decided to begin the trial as scheduled. Gamache had fired his first attorney and his second attorney committed suicide. Gamache was on his third attorney by the time the trial started.

On July 14, Amanda asked to be released from prison. Her lawyer, Celio Avelino, petitioned the court for her release while the investigation continued. He expected the court in Recife to make a decision on his request by July 15. Avelino pointed to the fact that Amanda called the police when she discovered Arturo, which he believed showed her willingness to help with the investigation.

Police were still looking at Amanda as the prime suspect. Police spokeswoman Milena Saraiva revealed that Rodrigues may have planned the murder in advance by encouraging Arturo to drink heavily so that he would not be able to fight her off. Saraiva believed that Arturo was sleeping when he was murdered.[1631] Police added that Arturo had marks on his throat from strangulation and a knife wound to the back of his head.

Star Ledger reporter Sid Dorfman spoke of why Arturo was so popular. He recalled that fans adored Gatti because he tempted death when he fought.[1632] Floyd Mayweather recalled his bout with Arturo and how Gatti refused to quit. Mayweather called Arturo a warrior.[1633] Lou Duva added that Gatti would take punishment, more punishment, and more punishment, and then he'd come back.[1634]

While the boxing world grieved, Amanda was speaking out through a letter she released. She stated that the malicious accusations against her were causing her intolerable pain. Amanda added that it hurt her to know that her husband would not be in her house waiting for her return.[1635]

Arturo's mother spoke to the Associated Press by phone. She reiterated that the couple fought all the time, and she recalled Amanda saying that she was going to kill Arturo.[1636]

On July 17, Fabrizio flew back to Montreal with Arturo's body in the luggage compartment.

On July 18, news of the autopsy findings were released. The autopsy revealed that Arturo's body was suspended and hanged, indicating that he may have committed suicide, but murder or accidental death could not be ruled out.[1637] The findings also revealed that Arturo's head wound could have come from his fall after hanging. Under Brazilian law, authorities had until July 22 to turn over their evidence to prosecutors, who would then decide if charges were appropriate.

Chapter 31
Burying a Legend

On July 19, 2009 at Maison Funeraire Magnus Poirier in Montreal, over 5,000 family, friends, and fans attended the wake for Arturo Gatti. The hours of the wake were 1 p.m. to 10 p.m. The line to see the champ one last time was steady throughout the day. Near his coffin were a pair of boxing gloves, along with his USBA super featherweight belt. The coffin color was black with gold trim. A massive floral arrangement spelled out "THUNDER."

As a sign of kinship, Micky Ward threw a left hook at Arturo's coffin as he passed. While Ward tapped the coffin with his left he thought to himself, *"I got you last."* Ward sadly admitted that he had lost his dancing partner.

Among those attending the Montreal funeral were Joe & Vikki Gatti, Pat Lynch, Buddy McGirt, Chuck Zito, Mike Skowronski, Lou DiBella, and Mario Costa. Costa read a letter from Jersey City Mayor Jerramiah Healy, which expressed, *"He was a great man, a great champion. He was a source of pride to the people of Jersey City."*[1638]

Ivano Scarpa read two letters, one from Mike Tyson and one from Jose Sulaiman. Mario Costa empathetically replaced Davey Hilton Jr.'s name with Matthew's, in Tyson's letter, to avoid the Gatti family from having to reflect on the other family tragedy. Mario read his own letter, and one from the N.J. Boxing Hall of Fame. Tyson's letter stated, *"We never knew he would be such a great fighter. I was always happy to see his success, to see him walk in the gym a boy and become a great man."*[1639]

Pat Lynch took Arturo's death extremely hard. He cried at Arturo's wake. Lynch seemed fixated on preventing Amanda from receiving Arturo's inheritance. Lynch discussed Arturo's estate, and the actions he was taking to prevent Amanda from acquiring it, with anyone who would listen. Arturo's brother-in-law, Rocco Crispo, grew tired of listening to Lynch talk about Arturo's estate and the dispute over the two wills. Crispo turned to Lynch at the wake and bluntly asked, *"Could you at least wait until the end of the funeral before discussing [Arturo's] inheritance?"*[1640]

Some of Arturo's family found it indecent that several people from New Jersey, who were in town for Arturo's funeral, commemorated Arturo's passing by attending strip clubs in Montreal. They were overheard stating that they were visiting the clubs because that was what Arturo would have wanted.[1641]

Joe Gatti was enraged at his brother's death. He felt that Pat Lynch, as much as anyone or anything, was directly responsible for his strained relationship with his brother. Joe felt that Lynch isolated Arturo from him in order to control Arturo.

One of Arturo's close friends felt the rift between the brothers was more complex. The friend recalled that early on Joe would sometimes tease Arturo and boss him around, as is the tendency between an older and younger sibling, especially when the siblings are competitive in nature. Girls that Arturo would meet would sometimes gravitate towards Joe. Some of Arturo's friends would go as far as to say that Joe pilfered some of the girls that Arturo met.

As Arturo became more successful, and his star status eclipsed Joe's, it would be normal for Arturo to want to avoid being the "little brother" in front of the entourage who adored him as a champion boxer. It would also be normal for Joe to have difficulty accepting his new role as the older brother of the champ, having to live in the shadow of his now famous brother, especially since Joe had once been labeled as a can't miss prospect who was destined for stardom.

Jealousy between siblings is normal, but if it turns into envy the consequences can be relationship altering. As Arturo's celebrity status grew, the sycophants, enablers, and yes-men who gravitated towards Arturo acquiesced to any and all of his whims, no matter how self-destructive they might be. Joe would not fit into this new group of "bugs" as he had called them. Of course, separating himself from his older brother would have consequences for Arturo. Joe would not have sat around silently while Arturo self-destructed with drugs. Nor would he have remained silent while Arturo was throwing away his hard earned money on the spongers who always seem to gravitate around superstars like magnets to steel. Joe's domineering attitude towards Arturo was accompanied with a love and affection that was unmatched by any of Arturo's friends.

Vikki pleaded with Joe not to confront Lynch. She recalled when Joe and Lynch crossed paths at the wake. *"At the funeral, Pat saw Joe. You would have thought Pat saw a ghost. He didn't know what to do when he saw Joe."*[1642] Joe admitted that he had to hold back his emotions and avoid Lynch.

When famous athletes and entertainers succumb to drugs, alcohol, and depression, outside observers point to the fact that those close to the celebrity did not do enough to help the superstar. Michael

Jackson, Whitney Houston, Elvis Presley, Prince, John Belushi, Kurt Cobain, Robin Williams and Marilyn Monroe are just a few in the long line of celebrities who fell victim to their addictions and mental health issues. It is rather unfair to blame those close to the celebrity because ultimately it is the celebrity, with their wealth, power, and fame, who control their own destiny. Mike Skowronski said it best when he stated that those around Arturo constantly walked on eggshells because they feared saying or doing the wrong thing that would lead to them being expelled from Arturo's inner circle.

While Joe was in Montreal, he stated that he observed three men removing a safe from Arturo's condominium. The safe allegedly contained Arturo's jewelry, diamonds, and cash. The three men were known to Joe. The condominium was ransacked. Photographs, clothing, entertainment items, and anything else of value was allegedly removed.[1643]

Police in Brazil still believed the crime scene may have been altered to give the appearance of a suicide. The police reconstructed the scene using an 80-pound dummy with a similar purse strap. The dummy fell to the floor in five seconds, clearly not enough time for someone to die from hanging. The police would later claim that Arturo hung by the strap for nearly three hours before it broke.

The autopsy report conflicted with the police investigation's findings. Brazilian police spokeswoman Milena Saraiva told the press that they were convinced that the crime scene had been altered prior to their arrival, to make it appear as though Arturo committed suicide. While the investigation continued, Amanda remained in a jail cell in Recife.

On July 18, the *Quebec Star* printed an article that painted a picture of a stormy and sometimes violent relationship between Arturo and Amanda. Chris Santos, Gatti's childhood friend, recalled Arturo erupting during a dinner at a sports bar over comments Amanda made about Arturo's daughter. Santos recalled that Amanda provoked Arturo any way that she could and she treated him extremely poorly. She would allegedly say that Arturo was a second-rate fighter, which hurt Gatti, because he was proud of his boxing career.[1644]

Montreal sports journalist Jeremy Filosa was a close friend of Arturo's. Filosa recalled that Arturo spent large amounts of money on Amanda. He purchased her a Cadillac Escalade. He bought her family a house in Brazil and he paid $30,000 for Amanda to fix her teeth. Filosa added that Arturo's credit cards were always maxed out. According to Filosa, Arturo feared that Amanda was hoarding his money behind his back.

When Arturo and Amanda first moved to Montreal, their neighbor Vanessa recalled Amanda being left alone on many occasions while Arturo went out with his friends. Vanessa felt sorry for Amanda.[1645] Vanessa acknowledged that Amanda appeared to take good care of Junior, but she also stated that Amanda could be aggressive, and she was not afraid to give her opinions.[1646]

Amanda's sister, Flavia, maintained her sister's innocence. Flavia stated that there was no way Amanda could have strangled a man of Arturo's size.[1647] Rodrigues' attorney, Celio Avelino, agreed with Flavia's assessment. Amanda remained in jail, even though police were now backing away from their original statement that Amanda had positively killed her husband. The autopsy report obviously had influenced their change in position.

Arturo's burial Mass was held on July 20 at the Notre Dame De La Defense church in Montreal. Over a thousand mourners attended the Mass. The church stands in the heart of Montreal's Italian community. Ida Gatti received Arturo's WBC championship belt at the ceremony. Friends and family gave Ida a standing ovation as she received the posthumous championship belt in Arturo's honor.

Vikki Gatti did not place the blame for her brother-in-law's death solely on Amanda's shoulders. She felt that Pat Lynch did not have the experience to deal with Joe and Arturo, being that they were two of his first fighters. Vikki also questioned how Arturo had 21 appearances on HBO yet had a fraction of what other fighters, such as Oscar De La Hoya and Roy Jones, Jr., earned. Vikki asked, *"You tell me why Oscar De La Hoya has an empire and my brother-in-law has a pot. Where's the rest of the money?"*[1648] Joe added that Arturo never made any real money.

It should be noted that Arturo headlined one pay-per-view event while fighters such as De La Hoya and Jones Jr. headlined multiple pay-per-view shows. De La Hoya is estimated to have grossed $500 million dollars in his career while Jones grossed approximately $55 million. Arturo, in comparison, grossed approximately $16 million from his ring career.

Vikki felt that Arturo became enlightened after his retirement. He had opened up to Amanda after his career ended. He started understanding some of the things that were done to him and the things that people had coerced him into doing, such as being isolated from his brother Joe.

Joe recalled the first Patterson match, when he was forced to sit in the bleachers. Joe questioned how Arturo could let Lynch treat him that way. Joe didn't even have clearance to go into his brother's dressing room. When Joe questioned Arturo about the ticket issue, Arturo didn't seem to think it was a big deal.[1649] Vikki felt that Arturo was completely controlled by Lynch during his career. After Arturo retired, Vikki felt he started realizing what had happened. Vikki recalled Tom Casino telling her, *"Vik, he was waking up."*[1650]

Joe recalled that during the subsequent estate lawsuit in Canada, they tried to get Lynch to hand over records of Arturo's earnings and expenses during his career. They were unable to get Lynch to turn over the records because the lawsuit was in a different country.[1651]

Joe fondly recalled Lynch's father, John Lynch Sr., who was affectionately known as "Pops," telling him that he had the best left hook he ever saw.[1652] Mikey Red recalled that Pops was a passionate boxing fan. Pat appeared to be more interested in the business aspect of the sport. Pops told Joe a story of when he took Pat to get an autograph from a N.Y. Yankee player. Joe recalled, *"Pops told me this story. Yankee player sitting at the end of the table over there and all the kids are 9 years old, in line to go to him to get an autograph picture signed. Pat shows up, the baseball player is starting a conversation with the kids. 'Would you like to be a baseball player?' Pat gets to the baseball player and the player asked Pat, 'So you like to play baseball?' Pat replied, 'No, I don't want to play baseball.' 'Oh you want to be a manager?' 'No, I want to own the team.' Right there they should have known. All he had in mind was to make money."*[1653]

Vikki felt that Main Events and Lynch would never have been able to maneuver other stars, such as Mayweather and De La Hoya, like they did Arturo. Vikki sarcastically stated that Lynch and Main Events told Arturo, *"Here's your little money and here's your case of beer. Have a good day."*[1654] Unfortunately, in boxing, it is common for fighters to be exploited. Arturo ending his career with several million dollars in the bank was not common. Buddy McGirt, who has been in the boxing business his entire life, said it best when he stated that Arturo was one of the rare fighters who retired without any financial concerns. Although it can be argued that Arturo should have received a larger percentage of his career earnings, it could also be argued that with Lynch's investment guidance, Arturo was able to end his career with generational wealth.

Boxing promoter Yvon Michel, who had known Arturo for 30 years and coached him on the Canadian national amateur team, spoke of Arturo. *"He had the same personality when he was boxing in the ring and in his life; he gave it his all."*[1655] Arturo's friend Ivano Scarpa added, *"Nobody believes whatsoever that there's even a one percent chance of a suicide. He lived life to the fullest."*[1656]

Initially, Arturo's family and friends in Canada had gotten along well with Amanda. After a short period of time, Arturo and Amanda's fighting, coupled with the rumors that Amanda was with Arturo for money, led Arturo's family and friends to begin avoiding Amanda. Amanda complained to neighbors about Arturo buying condos for his siblings, Giuseppina and Fabrizio. The condos were part of the construction project Arturo partook in with Tony Rizzo.

Investigators in Brazil now surmised that Amanda stabbed Arturo while he was drunk and then strangled him with her purse strap. She had not yet been charged with Arturo's death, but she was still in police custody. Lynch recalled that he had spoken to Arturo right before he left for his European vacation. Lynch knew that Amanda was trying to change Arturo's will, and that worried him.

On July 22, Mike DePompe, boxer Scott DePompe's father, wrote an anonymous online post regarding Arturo and Joe. In the post he spoke of Arturo's big heart. He felt that Arturo never had a chance to truly get away from the boxing groupies, or bugs as he called them, that surrounded him during his career. DePompe recalled how Joe tried to help his brother deal with fame. *"I know that his older brother, Joe Gatti, who was there in the beginning when Arturo arrived in Jersey City, who supported Arturo while he was getting the experience and exposure that propelled him to the limelight, and was always trying to be the big-brother that had to endure the 'bugs' that tried to come between them, is hurting the most today. I know how much Joe loved Arturo, and as a boxer himself, Joe knew exactly what that life is about."*[1657]

DePompe advised Joe and Vikki not to beat themselves up over what they could have done differently to help Arturo, because, as DePompe recalled, *"You tried so hard, and it was always from your hearts. Joe, your love of Arturo came before everything else. You never backed off trying to give him the good advice. The same advice that helped get him started, and perhaps the advice, had he listened a little more, that could have changed the ending to his journey through this world."*[1658]

DePompe's own special memory was not about boxing or the great fights Arturo partook in. DePompe recalled a sunny day in Sussex County, New Jersey, when Arturo and Joe were galloping down a wheat field on horseback, laughing and enjoying a simple day as loving brothers, away from the boxing crowd.[1659]

Many of Arturo's friends in Jersey City and Hudson County were unable to attend Arturo's wake and funeral because of the travel expenses and/or lack of a passport. Mario Costa organized a memorial Mass on July 25 at St. Nicholas' Church in Jersey City. Joe Gatti attended the ceremony, which started at 11:30 a.m.

Both Pat Lynch and Joe refused to believe that Arturo had killed himself. Joe spoke of the suicide allegations. *"Are they kidding me? Everything points to Amanda. No doubt they're trying to get her off."*[1660] Pat Lynch agreed with Joe. He believed that Arturo was happy and enjoying his retirement and his children.[1661] Mike Skowronski added, *"Absolutely, 100 percent I couldn't see him ever commit suicide. He loved life."*[1662]

Costa wasn't sure of what to believe as the latest developments in Arturo's investigation unfolded, but he was saddened by all of the controversy. Costa admitted, *"I'm hurt and sad he was alone when he died. I'll wait to see what exactly happened, but despite all his fans, he died in a foreign country with no one by his side."*[1663]

Pat Lynch, who remained estranged from Costa and Joe, organized his own Mass for Arturo on July 30, at 7 p.m., at St. John the Baptist Roman Catholic Church on Kennedy Boulevard in Jersey City. Mike Skowronski helped to organize the Mass with Lynch.

Over a hundred of Arturo's friends and relatives attended Costa's Mass. Erika Rivera attended, as did Arturo's 3-year-old daughter, Sofia Bella. Erika carried Sofia in her arms up to the podium. Sofia grabbed the microphone and started to sing the alphabet song. She faltered in the beginning, but like her father, she showed determination in finishing the song. As Sofia sang confidently, she reduced the attendees to tears. Sofia spoke to the crowd, *"My daddy is in the clouds. I want to sing with him."*[1664] Joe Gatti, who was sitting in a pew in the front row, wept openly.

Jersey City Mayor Jerramiah Healy attended the Mass and spoke of Arturo. *"His spirit, in and out of the ring, was similar to the spirit of our city; a great, tough actor. We applauded his great courage and fighting spirit, and we're certainly going to miss him."*[1665]

Joe spoke to a local reporter. He expressed his disbelief that a professional boxer, with the power that Arturo had, could be murdered. Joe described his younger brother as a devoted father and a good-natured prankster. Joe recalled that Arturo would be the first to throw popcorn in a movie theater, but Joe added that in the ring he was a different person. He took care of business in the ring, while outside of it he was a comedian. Joe confessed that Arturo kept him young.[1666]

The final bell count was rung in Arturo's honor. Henry Hascup, president of the N.J. Boxing Hall of Fame, tolled the "nine count." Hascup did not toll ten because the ten count is considered final. Hascup was confident that the memory of Arturo would remain alive *"in the hearts and minds of his family, friends and fans."*[1667]

Mario Costa spoke at the Mass and read a letter from Mike Tyson. Tyson first met Arturo when Gatti was 9 years old. In the letter, Tyson revealed, *"We never saw him coming. We were always going to his brother Joe's fights- we never knew he would be such a great fighter."*[1668]

The altar was lined with photos of Arturo. Gatti's promotional photo, taken by Tom Casino in 1991, showed a young Arturo with a determined look, wearing hand wraps. Several photos of Arturo with his daughter Sofia were also on display, courtesy of Erika Rivera. In one photo, Arturo was feeding Sofia, while in another he was playfully pinching her cheeks. Arturo's WBC and IBF championship belts were propped up on display, as was a typed note, signed in capital letters by his daughter Sofia. The letter read, *"The beautiful butterflies that you got me are mounted on my wall forever. You drove for hours to get those for me the day I was born. You always wanted my room decorated in butterflies, and that's how I'll keep it. I will never forget you."*[1669]

Costa was very outspoken about Arturo's tragic ending, and who he felt was responsible. *"Arthur, for the last years he fought, was a shell of himself. He would always try to stop, try to be normal, a father, husband, regular guy, but the drugs, the pills would make him very paranoid. He was real nice, and then towards the end he was nasty. Because he lived that life of the go-go bars and the nightlife. He changed. He wasn't nice. I heard he used to fight in the streets. He used to look at guys across the bar from him, 'What, you looking at my girl?' He'd want to fight the guy. Bahama Mama's in Hoboken, most of the bars in Hoboken, they wouldn't let him in towards the end because he used to fight with everybody. And he was very insecure. I guess his mind would play with him. Very paranoid. One time, one of his best friends, Ivan, right in my bar,*

[Arturo] came to the kitchen. Ivan worked in the kitchen. He said to Ivan, 'Are you looking at my girl?' And the guy knew Arthur since he came here. And he started to really see things that were not there. Paranoid, very insecure.

"With Buddy, he said that Buddy fucked one of his girls. So at the fights he wouldn't even look at Buddy in the face. He would cry. He would hug me. He told me, 'Nobody loves me.' He told me his breakfast was four Percocets. And he would just go to go-go bars. He had no structure to his life. He was always drinking, doing drugs, always out.

"The mother of his daughter, Erika, came here after he passed away and she said, 'I knew something was wrong, you couldn't stay in the house with him for 24 hours. And he was always going into the bathroom. There's something wrong with him.' She went to see Pat Lynch with her dad and told him, 'Your fighter is on drugs.' But he'd brush her off. Nobody would ever do anything, they didn't want to stop the gravy train. I understand. Pat's business, Curtain Call, was selling tickets.

"To call a fight off would have been bad for Pat. If they called a fight off maybe Arthur would still be here to see his son. But what was important was to make millions. Every time he fought they brought him closer to his death. The destruction cycle just continued.

"He was so obsessed with killing himself, and dying, and being with his father who died when he was 45. He told me many times he wanted to die. One time Arthur came in around 1 a.m. and stayed till 4 in the afternoon the next day. He stayed all those hours, no drinking, doing no drugs, telling us that we will never see him again. He was saying it to all of us, me, Manny, Nunzio, Fernando [workers at the Ringside Lounge]. He said goodbye to everybody.

"He said he had the gun but no bullets. He said he wanted me to get him a bullet. 'I know you have bullets.' I said, 'No.' I know if I gave him the bullets he was going to kill himself. He said, 'Every time I try to kill myself [meaning overdosing], they always brought me back. I'm too strong. By blowing my brains out, that's it, I'll never come back.' That's how obsessed he was that time. I got really scared. I called Tyson. I told Mike what happened, that he's really going to do it. I asked if I should call the Commission, the network. Mike told me, 'Yes' and he also said, 'But nobody cares about the fighter.'

"Then I called the Commission again. And I went to see Pat again.

I think Pat said he had a problem with his girlfriend or baby momma and he was okay already and he won't kill himself. That day, Arthur made a will [April 26, 2007]. He said to 'give my watch to my brother Fabrizio. I want all my posters on the wall and then put my belts here [on display at the Ringside Lounge].'

"He was never able to get away from Pat Lynch, Main Events. And they always tell you how great a job they did, how much money he made. Their main focus was the millions, the sellouts, but they knew there was a big problem with the fighter. But him being a true gladiator, he never refused a fight. He would have fought King Kong or Mike Tyson, anybody. If you don't stop him, he'd never stop himself. This is why he fought right to the end. This is why fighters have to have somebody with them, a father, a family, but Arthur didn't have that. He didn't have anybody to protect him. They kept me away. They kept his brother Joe away. They had him all to themselves. The fighter needs someone that cares about the fighter first. They never stopped or postponed any of the fights. Sometimes they couldn't find him at training camps, he would disappear. They'd find him and put him back in the ring.

"With the De La Hoya fight, Arthur said, 'He never hurt me to the head but he killed me to the body.' When you don't take care of yourself, when you are doing drugs and drinking alcohol, you can't take those shots to the body. He said, 'I wasn't even 50%.' But despite all the problems they did the fights for the money. This is why he's in the box."[1670] Costa added, "And what really pains me is that he was alone. So many people loved him, and in the end he was alone. No one was there to help him."[1671]

Costa recalled Arturo's depression. "He told me, 'I want to die Mario.' A lot of times I thought he really wanted to die, because I felt his heart was really broken when he used to lose, because he couldn't take defeat well. Like Pat says, HBO told him Arthur's a 'B' fighter not an 'A' fighter. So I said, 'Did you tell Arthur that?' Of course he never told him. But Arthur felt in some way those people were using him." Costa recalled meeting Micky Ward at the funeral. "Ward said, 'Mario I heard about you. You helped Arthur.' I said, 'Yeah, when he first came to America he came to my house. He lived with me.'"[1672]

On Thursday, July 30, Brazilian police shockingly announced that Arturo's death would be ruled a suicide. Amanda was released from jail the same day. When she was released, Amanda announced that she was going to sue the Brazilian authorities for unjust imprisonment. Paulo Alberes, the lead investigator, offered no details regarding the announcement of Judge Ildete Verissino de Lima's decision. Verissimo de Lima stated that the investigation excluded the possibility of murder. The judge felt that Arturo committed suicide by hanging.[1673] The judge also felt it would have been impossible for Amanda to suspend and hang a man of Arturo's size.[1674]

Joe was livid. He immediately called John Lynch after Amanda was released, saying, *"You guys, for all the money my brother made you guys, you don't have the bananas to send somebody out there to investigate?' [Lynch replied], 'It's not like that Joe. It's not what you're thinking. It's different over there.' I said, 'Bull crap it's different. You make it happen.'"*[1675] Joe demanded that Lynch conduct his own investigation into the death of his brother. He felt that was the least Lynch could do, being that Arturo made him so many millions of dollars.

Amanda walked out of the Brazilian prison smiling, just as an Academy Award nominee would while walking on the red carpet. She wore oversized Hollywood-style designer sunglasses, an Ed Hardy t-shirt, designer jeans, and freshly painted nails. She did not appear as though she spent 19 days in a hardened Brazilian prison. Amanda was later asked why she looked so elated upon her release. Although she was a widow, she said that she was thrilled to be out of prison and heading home to her child.[1676]

When she walked out of the jail, cheers erupted in the street. Amanda responded with a wide grin. There was an Olympic event type feeling in the air. Brazil had defeated the United States and Canada. To the Brazilian people, their Amanda was the victim. She was the abused spouse who was beaten in the street by the rich Canadian/American boxer.

Amanda's smile was a grin of victory. Russell Peltz had said that what he remembered most about Arturo was his smile. The memorable Arturo smile was now erased from this world and replaced by the bright, radiant smile of his widow as she was released from prison.

Chuck Zito, upon Amanda's prison release, said that he would never forget her face when she was released, coming out with a smile. Zito felt that the smile was very disrespectful, given her husband's recent death.[1677]

As Amanda was released from jail, she suggested that Arturo may have killed himself after having a violent argument with her in public. She felt that Arturo may have thought that she was going to leave him because he had assaulted her.[1678] Amanda's attorney, Lasso, felt that it was improper to lock Amanda up so quickly, especially since the investigation led to the conclusion that Arturo had killed himself.[1679]

The Gatti family retained Brazilian attorney Eduardo Trinidade. He had a different outlook on the investigation's conclusion. Trinidade found it hard to believe that Amanda didn't notice that her husband was dead until the second time she came downstairs.[1680] Trinidade questioned the police investigation, calling it incomplete. He commented on the police not taking DNA samples of the bloody towel, as well as their failure to sample blood stains on the bed sheets. Amanda had stated that Arturo did not enter the bedroom that night. Trinidade also commented on the authorities' "resistance test" of an 80-pound mannequin, using a similar purse strap. The strap broke in five seconds. Trinidade questioned whether five seconds was enough time for a person to die from asphyxia.[1681]

The Brazilian authorities gave their new version, and sequence of events, for what they believed happened on July 11. Arturo took the strap off of Amanda's purse. He climbed up onto a stool and tied the purse strap to the second floor railing. He slipped his neck over the strap and kicked out the stool. He hung suspended in that position for three hours until the strap gave way.

The Brazilian authorities' synopsis did not make any sense. There was a significant amount of blood on the floor around Arturo's head, but there was none on the staircase, the stool he allegedly used, or the floor directly under where he supposedly hung himself. Nor did they explain how he was suspended for so long without the strap breaking. If the strap could not hold an 80-pound dummy, how could it hold a man over twice that weight?

Vanja de Oliviera Coehlo, a scientific criminal pathologist for the Pernambuco Department of Public Safety, claimed the blood found around Arturo's body was the result of the impact he took from the brick earlier in the evening. Coehlo stated that blood from the earlier trauma was retained in Arturo's head, and exited through the wound after he hung himself and fell to the floor. Coehlo's statement completely contradicted studies on Livor Mortis. According to studies, circulation of the blood stops at death and blood starts to move towards dependent regions due to gravity. This means that if Arturo did die from hanging, and remained elevated for several hours as authorities had stated, all of his blood would have settled in the lower portion of his body and could not have leaked out of the wound in his head as Coehlo had stated.[1682] The amount of blood around Arturo's head would mean that either his heart was still pumping while he was on the ground, or that he died moments before hitting the ground.

Ida Gatti felt that the authorities were siding with Amanda because she was Brazilian. Fibers found on the purse strap matched fibers on the staircase baluster. There also were marks on the wood staircase that were consistent with the metal clasp on the purse strap. Brazilian investigator Josedith Ferreira had stated that a strip of Arturo's skin had been violently ripped from his neck with the purse strap. He was convinced that this could not be from a suicidal hanging.

On the same day as Amanda's release, Lynch's Mass to honor Arturo was held in Jersey City. Several hundred people attended the ceremony including Chuck Wepner, Carl Moretti, Mickey Rourke, Joey Gamache, Micky Ward, Tracy Harris Patterson, Chuck Zito, Lou DiBella, Ivan Robinson, John Lynch, Anna-Maria Gatti, and Kathy Duva.

Lynch did not explain why he decided to hold a separate Mass but it was most likely due to his strained relationship with Mario Costa and Joe Gatti. Lynch did comment on why he organized the event. He felt that since it was not possible for so many of Arturo's friends and fans in the U.S. to attend his funeral in Montreal, it was conscientious to give them the opportunity to celebrate Arturo's life and pay their respects. Lynch added that he was humbled and honored by the fact that Arturo considered him to be his second father. He was unsure if he ever would get over losing Arturo.[1683] Lynch commented on the ruling that Arturo took his own life. He considered the theory of Arturo committing suicide almost laughable, if it weren't so sad. He questioned how it was possible for Arturo to stab himself in the back of the neck and then hang himself. Lynch added that no one who knew Arturo believed that he took his own life.[1684] He felt that the coroner's finding was so far from the truth, it was unbelievable.[1685]

The mourners at St. John's refused to believe that Arturo had committed suicide. Lou DiBella was one of three people who were selected to speak at the event. DiBella recalled that Arturo fought with passion and lived with passion. DiBella added that Arturo never quit in the ring, and he did not quit in Brazil.[1686] Most of the attendees stood and applauded the comment.

Kathy Duva spoke of the Brazilian court's ruling. She did not believe that Arturo took his own life. Duva recently had written a letter to the United States Immigration and Naturalization Service, at Arturo's request, to help him gain a permanent residence card. She announced that Arturo's family was in the process of conducting their own investigation into Arturo's death.[1687]

Carl Moretti spoke of violating one of boxing's unwritten rules when it came to Arturo; never falling in love with a fighter. That rule seemed virtually impossible for everyone in the boxing business to uphold when it came to Arturo.[1688]

Mike Skowronski stated, *"If they told me he hit a wall, drunk at 100 miles per hour, I would believe it. But killing himself, he would never do that."*[1689] Pat Lynch felt that there was no way Arturo would commit suicide. He believed that Arturo loved his baby boy too much. Lynch added that the saddest part of the tragedy was that Arturo's children were going to grow up believing that their father had committed suicide when it was so far from the truth. Lynch promised not to rest until the truth was revealed.

Arturo's blood had not been checked for alcohol levels. His brain tissue was not sampled for signs of abnormalities from the trauma he suffered while boxing. Dr. Baden commented on the shoddy autopsy, and how the Brazilian pathologists failed to inspect Arturo's organs. Baden questioned how the Brazilian authorities did not have the facilities to perform an alcohol test, when that was the easiest test to perform.[1690] Baden revealed that the ligature mark on Arturo's neck was less than 180 degrees, not 360. In other words, the strap was not completely wrapped around Arturo's neck. This is not consistent with suicide by hanging.[1691] Baden added that prison inmates commonly make murders appear as though they are suicides by hanging their victims. Baden admitted that it would have taken more than one person to pick a drunk or deceased Arturo up and hang him.[1692]

Arturo's family and friends could not believe that a fighter so full of heart and courage would give up and take his own life. Pat Lynch admitted that it would have been believable if Arturo had died in a street altercation or in a bar fight, but never in a million years would he be convinced that Arturo would hang himself while with his son.[1693]

Arturo had many reasons to live, even if his marriage was ending. Arturo was planning on opening up two gyms, one with his old friend John Capone. He had the 325-unit real estate project with

Tony Rizzo. Donny Jerie had just restored a candy apple red 1974 Corvette for Gatti. Jerie was convinced that Arturo's death was premeditated murder. *"This was planned. The will was changed. When he signed that will, he signed his life away."*[1694]

Amanda's mother, Rosie Barbosa, disagreed with the theory that her daughter killed Arturo. She said that she and her husband gave Amanda a good education. She added that Amanda's sister was a doctor in Brazil.[1695]

Although the coroner's report revealed that Arturo may have killed himself, the report did not rule out the possibility that someone may have killed Gatti. Micky Ward asked for the investigation to be reopened. He refused to believe that Arturo would kill himself.[1696] Mike Skowronski was 100% sure that it was not a suicide. Skowronski expressed that if Amanda was given Arturo's money, it would be blood money.[1697]

Joe Gatti revealed publicly that his family might seek to exhume Arturo's body and have an autopsy conducted in Canada. Joe and Vikki pondered over what may have occurred in Brazil. Joe felt that Arturo found himself in a very dark place. The thought of never seeing his son again may have been too much for him to deal with.[1698]

Vikki felt that when Amanda said she was going to leave Arturo, and locked herself in the bedroom, he kept drinking. Vikki believed that Arturo may have been trying to get Amanda's attention by feigning suicide, waiting for her to open the door to look. Vikki added that it probably was more of an accidental death because Arturo was drunk. Vikki admitted that another possible conclusion was that Arturo simply had had enough. He had vision problems, crippled hands, and his body was always in pain. He was estranged from his brother, was fighting with his wife, and might be losing his son.

Would Joe have fallen into the same death spiral if he had been as successful as Arturo? His wife Vikki believes so. Vikki surmised, *"Yeah, 100%. Of course he would have. Yes, 150%."*[1699] Joe agreed with Vikki. *"Because we were crazy. And that's why I left Canada."*[1700]

It was obvious that Giovanni's death still had a huge impact on Joe. In death, Giovanni still had dominion over Joe and Arturo. Both brothers lived their lives to try and please their father. Giovanni had navigated the two brothers lives so intensely that when he died, they did not know how to direct their own lives. Joe fell into a year of partying and mischief after his father died. Finally he snapped out of it in 1988, as he explained. *"And then I woke up. I said, 'What am I doing? I gotta get outta here.' That's when I called Mario, because I already met him. And that's when I came here to America."*[1701]

Joe and Vikki had different opinions on how Arturo met his demise. Vikki felt that Arturo craved attention. Joe now believed that Amanda could not have killed his brother. After hearing that there were bruises all over Arturo's body Joe thought that Amanda had him killed, but Vikki convinced him otherwise because she felt that Arturo was too strong to be overwhelmed. Joe felt that the only way they would have been able to kill Arturo was if they shot him or stabbed him in the back. Vikki didn't believe that anyone in Brazil would take an offer to kill Arturo for money with their bare hands. She admitted that when she first heard of Arturo's death, she thought that Amanda had killed him.[1702]

Arturo's old sparring partner, Danny McDermott, recalled that when Arturo went out drinking, many times he would get into fights. McDermott recalled an incident in the Bronx where Arturo knocked a man out. After Gatti knocked the man out Arturo was knocked out by another male. Arturo woke up on the sidewalk alone. Besides his many knockout victories in the streets, Arturo occasionally would find himself on the losing end of his drunken battles. If Arturo was extremely intoxicated in Brazil he most definitely could have been overwhelmed.

Tom Casino, the boxing photographer, knew that if Arturo continued drinking something bad would happen. It was inevitable. Casino recalled that he would receive phone calls when Arturo did something crazy. Everybody that Casino met in the tri-state area had a party story with Arturo.[1703] Mario Costa commented that Arturo lost the fight with himself.[1704]

Tony Rizzo felt that Amanda was a hustler and she was all about the money. Rizzo pointed to the fact that Arturo signed a new will and then three weeks later he was dead.[1705]

Amanda addressed the comments regarding the last minute will change by stating that she knew it looked bad. She did not have an explanation for that. She added that if the family didn't agree with the Brazilian authorities, they should open their own investigation.[1706] Amanda did not know it at the time, but Pat Lynch and the Gatti family already had hired investigators to re-examine the evidence.[1707]

On July 31, Arturo's body was exhumed. The Quebec coroner's office performed a new autopsy at the Gatti family's request. Michael Baden would assist with the new autopsy on August 1 in Montreal. Baden would not be able to perform the autopsy, as he was not licensed to practice in Canada. Gilles Ethier, the deputy chief coroner for the western part of the Province of Quebec, felt that it was necessary to pursue the investigation. Ethier added that it would be a little complex for the pathologist, because the body had already been embalmed.

Canada's Foreign Minister, Lawrence Cannon, announced that Canadian government officials would seek more information from Brazilian authorities regarding Arturo's death investigation. Ellen Haley, a spokeswoman for Main Events, announced that the company did not believe that Arturo took his own life. Haley added that the company was confident that once the results of the new investigation were revealed, the truth would come to light and justice would be served.[1708]

Amanda's attorney, Celio Avelino, remarked that the exhumation of the body didn't surprise him at all. Avelino felt that it made perfect sense, since the authorities had told the Gatti family conflicting stories. Avelino was certain that the second autopsy would reconfirm that Arturo committed suicide.[1709]

Spokeswoman Milena Saraiva, of the Brazilian Recife police, gave more insight into Arturo's death. The police believed that Arturo hung himself from a wooden staircase column that was 7.3 feet off of the ground. They surmised that Gatti stood on the stool and kicked it out from underneath himself. The autopsy report stated that Arturo was suspended for approximately three hours before the purse strap gave way and he fell to the floor.

Saraiva revealed that when the first investigators arrived at the scene, they only saw his body on the floor and the bloody strap near his body. They assumed that his wife had strangled him.[1710] Saraiva added that Arturo had consumed seven cans of beer at the apartment, along with two bottles of wine during dinner and his bar visit.

Witnesses told authorities that Arturo started arguing with Amanda in the street. He picked her up by her chin with his right hand and tossed her to the ground. Saraiva stated that a security guard from a local hotel tried to break up the fight, but Arturo punched him in the face. An angry crowd gathered around the couple, with some throwing stones and one throwing a bicycle at Arturo. One of the stones hit Arturo in the back of his head. The blow caused the wound that police originally thought was caused by a steak knife that was found near Arturo's body. Saraiva expressed that the case had been resolved. She added that while the evidence at the scene first led authorities to think Gatti was murdered, the autopsy results and a detailed crime scene analysis simply pointed to a different outcome.[1711]

The second autopsy ordered by Arturo's family did not rule out homicide. Michael Baden, host of the HBO series "Autopsy," believed that the Brazilian autopsy was incomplete. Baden was a former chief pathologist for the New York State Police. He felt that there definitely were injuries that had not been documented by the Brazilian authorities. Baden added that additional information was needed, including a toxicology test, which wasn't available yet, to come to a conclusion as to whether the death was a homicide or a suicide.[1712] Toxicology tests were scheduled to be performed in Montreal.

On August 3, the Quebec coroner's office asked Brazilian authorities to share their files on the initial autopsy. Quebec's coroner's office spokeswoman, Genevieve Guilbault, revealed that her office had asked Canada's federal government to help the coroner obtain the initial autopsy results, as well as files describing the death scene.

On August 5, the details of Arturo's new will were revealed. The CBS News website "Crimesider" announced that Arturo left everything to Amanda. Fabrizio Gatti confirmed the report. *Canadian Press* journalist, and friend of Arturo, Jeremy Filosa, revealed that everything that Arturo owned, past, present, and future, went to his wife. Nothing was left for his mother, his brothers, or sisters.[1713] Amanda also was named executor of Arturo's will.

On August 13, the *Journal de Montreal* published a letter sent to them by Amanda. *"I have been waiting for all the questions to be answered and all the accusations made against me to be corrected. I always knew that the truth would come out as to my innocence. I believe in justice, especially the justice of God. It is very hard to stay away from my baby, as well as to see my friends and family suffering from the injustice of humans. I was in shock, and I still have problems believing in this entire nightmare. I still don't know how I will cope from this loss. Arturo was my life! He was included in all my dreams and goals. I don't know how I can restart my life again. My son and my faith in God is what keeps me going. The worst* accusations came from Arturo's family. Family with whom I have never had any intimacy. Not because I didn't want to or because I didn't like them. This intimacy never existed because my own husband was never 'that' close with his own family.

Arturo left home [Montreal] at age 19 to train in the United States. He returned from the U.S. at age 36. While living all these years in the U.S. Arturo never had any close relationship with his family. When I heard that they want the custody of my child, I was in shock. I didn't believe it in the beginning. The reason I didn't believe it is because none of them had ever had any relationship with my son. My son knows only four people from his father's family: Arturo's brother Fabricio Gatti, his sister Pina Gatti, his mother and his stepfather. Only Arturo's mom and stepfather showed care and love for my baby. They never bothered to come to my house. I had my son far away from my family. Arturo was the only person who helped me with all aspects of my son. I have never received any visits or help from any member of his family. Arturo's family are not in any condition to take care of my son, neither psychologically nor financially.

Arturo's struggle with depression came at a very young age. He grew up in a very violent home. His father was an alcoholic and a very aggressive man who not only used to hit his mother but the kids as well... Arturo's brother Fabricio Gatti never had respect or affection for my son. That just makes clear that the only reason they would want custody of my son would be for financial reasons.

I just want to make it clear that Arturo and I have documents signed by both of us which gives my family the custody of my son in case both of us die. Arturo, more than me, knew that our son would be better off being raised by my family. He would never want Junior to be raised in the same way and environment that he was.

Arturo had a very hard time with drugs and alcohol, and I was the only person who ever helped him in this matter. I checked him into rehab, and during this time I didn't hear from his family. I just heard from his sister [Anna-Maria] when she picked him up three days before he was supposed to finish his treatments. His family was never involved in any of his problems or struggles. Even after our marriage and the birth of our child, I have not met his other sister and his other brother, which just shows how close he was with his family.

My only problem regarding Arturo and his family, especially his brother Fabricio Gatti, was that he wanted to be supported by my husband. For that, it is more than normal that I, his wife, wouldn't accept the situation. All the accusations and false statements made about me from anybody or by the media, my lawyer will be taking care of. It obviously upsets me that people that don't even know us make up their own stories and judgements about me. But in the end of the day, I know I have my son, my friends and my family, people that really know me and care for me for the right reason.

I totally agree that his family should ask for another autopsy on Arturo's body. This will only count for my benefit, reassuring my innocence for his family and everyone else who still doesn't believe that I am innocent. I was told that his family wanted to know how my baby is doing. If they really wanted to know, they would have contacted me or anyone from my family.

They have my sister's, my mother's number and my e-mail address. We did not receive any phone calls. While Fabricio Gatti stayed in Brazil [not] in any moment did he ask to speak with me, to ask me any questions, to find out any details about what happened or to hear my version of the story. Fabricio called my sister once, and the only question he asked my sister was, 'Where is Arturo's watch?' What I find very strange is that if it was my sister, I would want to know every little detail about the incident. In his police report, the only thing he mentioned was about my financial life. Everything that came from his family so far was about financial issues.

It is more than normal that my husband had a will done, and that me and my son were the main beneficiaries on that will. His family was me and Junior. Strange would be if in that will he would have included another woman or his brothers, for instance. I was his wife, not his girlfriend. I never heard of any father that has a family putting brothers and sisters as beneficiaries. What really bothers Arturo's family is not the fact that he is not here anymore, or the reason why he is not here. It's the simple fact that they are not included in the will. I know that even after the private autopsy, when it is proven for the second time that I did not do any harm to my husband, they will still be against me, claiming and fighting in the expectation of receiving anything regarding Arturo's estate.

I also want to make clear that Arturo's daughter, Sofia Bella Gatti, has her future guaranteed. Arturo would never let anything miss for his daughter. The will explains in detail what she gets, Sofia Bella Gatti owns two accounts- one for her college fund, and another as her trust account. Regarding Arturo not being present in Sofia's life, that has nothing to do with me. The problem that he had with Sofia's *family started way before I met him. Arturo was supervised and monitored during all the visits that he made to his daughter. As a dad, he felt uncomfortable with that situation. This issue and other problems that he had with his daughter's mother changed his behavior towards his daughter. Obviously, he loved her, but he had to deal with a lot of drama to see Sofia. I have documents from attorneys that can prove what I am stating. Also, Arturo did want to have more contact and a closer relationship with his daughter. Everyone that doesn't know the story and even some that do just find it convenient and easier to blame me for all the problems, but the reality is very different. I never asked Arturo or his family members [who also had no contact with his daughter] to stop seeing his daughter, because before anything I am still a mother.*

It has been very hard to wake up every day, knowing that my husband is no longer here with me. It comes down to the point that nobody knows my pain, unless you go through the same nightmare that I did. Nobody knows what it feels like to be accused of the death of a loved one. Worse than that, I didn't even have the chance to go to my husband's funeral.

For the friends that really care, here is some news of Junior. Even though he is little, I know that he misses his father a lot. Arturo was very present in Junior's life. Even when he was away, he would talk to him on the phone, and Junior would just listen and scream on the other side of the phone. Junior's first word was 'papa' and he still keeps saying 'papa' every single day. I am sure he will miss his father forever, but around great people that love him for the right reasons he will be fine. He has unconditional affection, love and care around my family and I. It has been an unexplainable pain for both Junior and I. We want to thank every single person that has been praying for us. We know the truth would come out because our GOD is faithful. (Psalm 35)." Amanda Rodrigues.[1714]

Chapter 32
Amanda Returns to Canada

Amanda returned to Canada to begin a long legal battle over Arturo's estate.

On August 28, 2009, Main Events announced that they would be honoring Arturo on their September 19 Atlantic City card at Bally's Casino. The card was billed, "Night of Thunder: A Tribute to Arturo Gatti."

On the September 19 show, highlights of Arturo's most memorable fights were shown in-between the bouts. Earlier in the day, during a public ceremony, Atlantic City councilman George Tibbit renamed Georgia Avenue "Arturo 'Thunder' Gatti Place." Friends, family members, and fans attended the afternoon ceremony. Atlantic City officials declared Arturo's birthday, April 15, "Arturo Gatti Day."

On September 24, CBS aired a "48 Hours Mystery" episode on Arturo's death. On the show, private investigator Paul Ciolino, who was hired by Pat Lynch, stated that Arturo was unequivocally murdered by Amanda. Mario Costa and Joe Gatti were both interviewed. Joe revealed that Arturo had problems with drugs and alcohol. Costa recalled that Arturo had mentioned wanting to kill himself. Amanda was interviewed. She maintained that she had nothing to do with Arturo's death and that she missed her husband. Amanda was sure that Arturo had killed himself. She added that when she met Arturo she did not know that he was a boxer. That statement contradicted accounts by employees of the Squeeze Lounge who said that Amanda was told Arturo was a fighter when he walked into the club with his dog.[1715] Amanda noted that Arturo became nasty and aggressive when he drank.

When Amanda was asked if she ever had worked in a gentlemen's club, she stated that she did many things that she was not proud of, but she insisted that she had never stepped foot in, nor worked in, the Squeeze Lounge.[1716] The workers at the Squeeze Lounge presented a photograph of Amanda on stage, in the club, in a bikini. Four employees came forward and acknowledged that Amanda had indeed worked there, including barmaid Nehomy Prosperi. Amanda countered that she was too young, 20 years old, to dance in the club. According to the NJ Alcohol Beverage Control Handbook age limits section, although a customer must be 21 years old, employees, including entertainers, can be as young as 18 years old.

Additionally, as previously stated, exotic dance clubs such as the Squeeze Lounge were known to hire dancers that did not possess bar card licenses. Some clubs would contract companies in the tri-state area to transport dancers to the club. There would be no official records of the dancers who were unlicensed. The dancers, or the companies who supplied the dancers, were always paid in cash.

On November 5, Amanda's request for $140,000 from Arturo's estate was turned down by Superior Court Justice Paul Chaput. Amanda had requested the money to help cover her legal expenses and child care costs while the fight against Arturo's family over his estimated $5.6-million estate continued. Judge Chaput awarded Amanda $37,500 to cover expenses. Chaput allowed Amanda to enter the condominium she shared with Arturo, to retrieve her belongings.

When Amanda entered the condo she was shocked. Besides the safe being missing, all of her and Arturo's clothes were gone. Everything was taken. The photographs of Arturo and Junior were all missing, with only empty picture frames remaining on the walls. Amanda filed a police report, but the burglary remains unsolved.

Amanda was angry that Arturo's family, friends, and boxing associates were saying that she was responsible for his death. She countered that it was they who stood by silently and watched Arturo self-destruct. Amanda declared that they had Arturo's blood on their hands for not stepping in to help him battle his alcohol and drug addictions. Now, out of guilt, they were using her as a scapegoat.[1717] Amanda was contemplating taking Junior and leaving Canada.

Arturo's family contended that his will from New Jersey in 2007 was valid, while the one he signed in Quebec in 2009 was signed under duress. Chaput asked both sides to talk before returning to court on November 17.

On November 11, ESPN's E:60 aired a segment titled "Death of a Champion." On the segment, the owner of the Squeeze Lounge, Michael Sciarra, spoke directly to Amanda via television, telling her that she would pay for Arturo's death.[1718] A different Amanda emerged when she was told of the club owner's comments. Amanda responded by stating that all of Arturo's friends talked too much shit. She added that everyone loved her and kissed her ass when Arturo was alive, but after he died, she became a witch.[1719]

On November 12, 2009, Arturo was inducted into the New Jersey Boxing Hall of Fame. Four of the bouts in his career were voted "Fight of the Year" by the Boxing Writers Association of America.

Arturo's trilogy with Micky Ward was voted the second greatest boxing trilogy of all time, by fans, in an ESPN sports poll. Gatti-Ward came in second only to Muhammad Ali's battles against Joe Frazier.

On November 20, another friend of Arturo's, Jimmy Cassano, died from a drug overdose. Cassano, of Bowers Street in Jersey City, was only 40 years old when he died. He was the third close friend of Arturo who died from a drug overdose.

On March 26, 2010, the Joey Gamache vs. the State of New York civil case was decided. Judge Schweitzer ruled that the State of New York indeed was negligent in their handling of the weigh-in for the Gatti-Gamache bout, but the Judge awarded no monetary damages to Gamache, stating that the weigh-in did not affect the bout's outcome. Gamache announced that the lawsuit was not about money. He just wanted the truth to come out.[1720] How Judge Schweitzer, who had no experience in boxing, could make the determination that weigh-in negligence could not affect a bout's outcome, is shocking. A boxer who is having severe trouble making the contracted weight, and who is allowed to avoid losing the last few pounds or ounces, could absolutely affect the fight's outcome. Losing weight and dieting on the final few days when a boxer has finished his training camp is called "drying out." This is when a boxer drastically reduces or eliminates food and liquids. The process saps the energy and strength from a fighter. "Drying out" can also strip away a fighter's muscle mass and reduce the liquid around his brain. This would affect the boxer's punching power as well as his ability to absorb a punch. If Gatti did indeed avoid having to lose extra weight, it might have benefited him during the bout, although it might not have changed the outcome.

On April 1, 2010, Dr. Michael Baden was a guest on HBO's "Real Sports With Bryant Gumbel." On the show, Baden announced that he did not believe Arturo Gatti committed suicide. He added that the autopsy performed in Brazil was incomplete and failed to prove that Arturo committed suicide.[1721] Baden believed that the marks around Arturo's neck did not match the purse strap.[1722] Baden's findings gave Lynch and the Gatti family hope that Brazilian authorities would continue the investigation into Arturo's death. Amanda declined a request to be interviewed on "Real Sports."

Lynch commented on the findings, stating that he hoped Dr. Baden's conclusions would lead to a reopening of the case.[1723] Lynch and Arturo's brother, Fabrizio, were among the many family and friends who felt that Amanda murdered Arturo. Fabrizio confessed that Arturo had been addicted to pain-killers for many years. He recalled that Arturo partied until sunrise every second night of the week. He also revealed that Arturo would get into fist fights with patrons at local bars.[1724]

Vikki and Joe felt that Arturo's manager and promoter should have done more to help Arturo with his addiction issues. Vikki felt that it was easy to blame Amanda, but she was only with Arturo for three years. Main Events and Lynch had been with Arturo for sixteen years. Vikki questioned what Arturo's manager and promoter had done in all that time to help Arturo with his drug and alcohol issues.[1725]

Joe questioned how Arturo's brain sample went missing. The sample might have shown that he was suffering from a traumatic brain injury.[1726] Vikki added that it was visibly clear that Arturo was suffering from some sort of dementia. Vikki saw the signs when Arturo's daughter Sofia was born. Arturo's memory was fading in and out at that time. Vikki recalled that Arturo's eyes appeared cloudy and his thoughts seemed to drift off.[1727]

Joe had a strained relationship with Arturo during the final years of his life. Arturo also cut ties with Mikey Red and others who were a part of his career. Joe and Vikki never had the opportunity to forge a relationship with Amanda.[1728] Joe felt that his mother could have done more to bring him and his brother back together.

Joe recalled that his siblings were close to him when he was winning and sending them money, but when he started losing and didn't have money to send, they avoided him. He suddenly became the family villain. During the end of his career, Joe heard rumors that his siblings were saying that they were glad that his boxing career was not as successful as Arturo's. According to Joe, this was when his family grew closer to the financially successful Arturo.[1729]

On April 1, the Quebec Superior Court awarded Amanda $100,000 to pay for her mounting legal fees. Ida and Fabrizio were the main beneficiaries of the first will, and they were the two plaintiffs contesting the second will.

On April 12, 2010, Pat Lynch sat down with Lem Satterfield of FanHouse boxing. Satterfield asked Lynch if he was comfortable discussing Arturo's death, being that HBO was airing a story on Arturo, Alexis Arguello, and Vernon Forrest. Lynch remarked that there were many inconsistencies with the police investigation. He believed that Arturo was murdered by more than one person. Lynch pointed to Dr. Baden's second autopsy, which surmised that Arturo was severely beaten with a baseball bat or some other blunt instrument. The beating was more severe on the left side of his body. This injury was not reported in the first autopsy.[1730]

Fabrizio led Keith Greenberg, of *Maxim* magazine, into the world where Arturo spent many of his nights during the final months of his life. Fabrizio led Greenberg down a set of stairs to Ida's basement. Around a dark corner, Fabrizio unlocked a door to a 10' x 20' room where Arturo often slept. On the bed rested Arturo's two world championship belts. The green leather WBC belt and the red leather IBF belt. Next to the belts was a photograph of Arturo fighting Micky Ward. On many nights Arturo might have laid in bed alone, in the dark, damp basement room, after a night of partying, staring at his two world championship belts and the photo, wondering how his life had come to this. A laundered pile of exercise clothing was stacked nearby, as was a box of Arturo's personal items. On top of the box was a photograph of heavyweight champion Rocky Marciano. Like Arturo, Marciano was a boxer of Italian descent, with great heart, who also met a tragic and early death when he died in a plane crash.[1731]

On April 15, 2010, the city of Atlantic City again commemorated Arturo's birthday with "Arturo Gatti Day." The ceremony took place at 4 o'clock outside of Boardwalk Hall. Councilman George Tibbitt presented Arturo's mother Ida, and his daughter Sofia, with plaques commemorating the event. Arturo Jr. did not attend the event, nor does it appear as though he was invited.

On April 19, WBC light welterweight champion Edwin Valero committed suicide by hanging himself in a Venezuelan prison. At the time of his death, Valero, who suffered from alcohol and cocaine abuse, was being held on charges of murdering his wife.

In May, Joe spoke of his family's lawsuit against Amanda by stating that his family should be ashamed of themselves. Joe felt that his family knew that Amanda was innocent.[1732] Joe originally felt that Arturo was murdered, until he came face to face with Amanda. He decided to stay friendly with Amanda so he could visit with his nephew. Joe had many regrets about his relationship with Arturo and he did not want to make those same mistakes with Junior. Joe added that if Amanda needed him to go to Montreal to testify on Junior's behalf, he would.[1733] Amanda felt that Joe treated Junior like a son. She added that Joe was the only family member who was interested in Junior.[1734]

On June 13, Larry Hazzard was inducted into the International Boxing Hall of Fame along with Shelly Finkel and Bruce Trampler.

On July 3, 2010, Fabrizio held firm in his belief that his brother was murdered. He did not want Arturo's children to think that their father was a coward who left them to grow up alone. Fabrizio vowed that he would find a way to prove that Arturo did not kill himself.[1735] Fabrizio revealed that Amanda had threatened Arturo before the couple left on their second honeymoon. He added that a neighbor heard the couple fight outside of Ida's garage in Montreal. The neighbor allegedly heard Amanda state, *"Come to Brazil! You're going to see what I'm going to do to you!"*[1736]

The courtroom battle between Fabrizio and Ida against Amanda continued. Amanda demanded that she be given custody of the family dog.[1737] Brazilian authorities still were withholding the basic crime scene and autopsy information that Baden and the Quebec coroner's office requested back in August 2009.[1738]

Fabrizio was hoping to have Arturo's estate split evenly between his two children and put in trust funds for when they became adults. Fabrizio believed that Arturo's children, not Amanda, deserved the money for which Arturo had fought and bled.[1739]

As of July 8, 2010, the Canadian superior court had yet to rule on Arturo's estate.

Amanda filed a civil libel lawsuit against the *NY Post, NY Daily News,* and *Maxim* magazine in a New Jersey District Court, because of statements they had made claiming that she was a stripper who either killed or was suspected of killing her husband.[1740] Amanda sought $500,000 in damages. In 2012, Amanda reached a confidential settlement with all three news outlets. In regards to the libel settlement, Amanda's attorney Mark Casazza stated, *"I truly believe that justice has been served today. Amanda is a young woman who tragically became a widow to her beloved husband and a single parent to their son, Arturo, Jr. What she has been forced to endure since her husband's passing has been unthinkable. I hope she can get the closure she deserves."*[1741]

A Mass was held on July 10 at St. Nicholas' Church in Jersey City, on the one-year anniversary of Arturo's death. Mario Costa organized the Mass, which was presided over by Reverend Kevin Carter. Pat Lynch did not attend the Mass, but he commented on the anniversary by stating that he never would be convinced that Arturo committed suicide.[1742]

On December 6, 2010, the movie *The Fighter* opened in theaters. The movie displayed the life and career of Micky Ward up until, but not including, the Gatti fights. The story focused on Ward's dysfunctional family, with an emphasis on his mother and brother. The movie starred Mark Wahlberg as Micky and Christian Bale as his brother and trainer, Dickie Eklund. Mickey O'Keefe was asked to audition for the role of himself, and he won the role. O'Keefe, a 30-year veteran of the Lowell Police Force, had trained both Dickie and Micky in the amateurs. O'Keefe was also a former amateur New England Golden Gloves champion at 147-pounds. Ward still lived in Lowell and owned a gym. He was part owner of an outdoor hockey rink and he drove trucks for the Teamsters Union.

On December 14, 2010, the movie *The Fighter* earned seven Oscar nominations.

Many critics wondered why the Gatti fights were not mentioned in the movie. Several movie producers approached Arturo's family and Pat Lynch in regards to making a movie on Arturo's life and career.

Christian Bale and Melissa Leo both won Golden Globe awards for their performances in *The Fighter*. Bale won for his portrayal of Dickie Ecklund, while Leo won for her performance as Ward's mother Alice.

On February 25, 2011, both Bale and Leo took home best supporting actor and actress Oscars at the 83rd annual Academy Awards.

One day in 2011, out of the blue, Amanda called Joe and Vikki. She asked if they wanted to see Junior. The Gattis excitedly said, *"Sure."*[1743] They figured that they would have to drive up to Canada to see their nephew. Amanda told the couple that she was in Canada, but Junior was in Elizabeth, N.J., at her mother's house.[1744] Joe and Vikki were shocked. They couldn't believe that their nephew was in the United States. They drove to Elizabeth, still doubting whether Junior was really there.

When they arrived at the house, Amanda's mother opened the door and said, *"Hi, how are you?"*[1745] She stepped aside and standing there was little Arturo Junior. Joe and Vikki took Junior into their car and drove home. They were astounded that Junior actually was in the car with them. When they arrived home with Junior they were *"in heaven."*[1746] The family bond was instantaneous. Junior took to them immediately. It was at that moment that Vikki felt in her heart that Amanda couldn't have killed Arturo, because she trusted them with her child. Vikki believes that she is very adept at reading people. When she saw Amanda in person, she watched her movements very carefully, as Amanda was talking to Joe. Vikki recalled that she did not see any signs of nervousness or twitching around Joe.

On August 8, 2011, over two years after Arturo's death, and 10 months after they were hired by Pat Lynch, investigators Paul Ciolino of Chicago and Joseph Moura of Boston finally finished their investigation. Ciolino announced that after their press conference was complete it would be clear that Arturo's death was not a suicide.[1747] The 300-page report, with 76 crime scene photos, included disturbing shots of Arturo lying in his own blood. Ciolino's report included interviews and expert opinions from around the United States, Canada, and Brazil. The report also included phone records, bank records, and social interactions, as well as Amanda Gatti's arrest report. A press conference was planned for 11 a.m. on August 30 at the Global Boxing Gym in North Bergen, N.J.

The investigators planned on displaying animated scenes which, in their eyes, would prove that Arturo could not have killed himself. Ciolino believed that the Brazilian investigation was half-assed and the autopsy was totally incomplete.[1748] Ciolino added that scientific expert witnesses from across the country would be on hand, making brief presentations which would conclusively lay to rest the mystery surrounding Gatti's cause of death.[1749]

Amanda issued a direct challenge to those who thought she was guilty of murder. She said that she would love to get together with the investigators, Pat Lynch, and Arturo's family. She was also willing to take a lie detector test.[1750]

Arturo's brother Joe did not agree with the murder theory. *"My brother is me. We talk the same. We laugh, we joke the same. Just hate to say it, but it came to this. That people need to know the truth. He was on drugs. He was on pain killers. And he was an alcoholic. I believe it was suicide. I believe it. That night in Brazil he found himself in a dark place. What changed my mind is when I got Amanda to my house. She showed up and I'm looking at her. There was no sign of anything. She looked into my eyes. It was nothing."*[1751]

Joe's feelings may have been influenced by his nephew, Arturo Junior, and Joe's desire to spend time with him. *"He wouldn't let me go [crying]. He was just hugging me. He wouldn't let me go. I put him down. He wanted to play with me. It was something else."*[1752]

Pat Lynch's press conference date was moved back to September 7, due to travel interruptions caused by Hurricane Irene. The time and location remained the same.

On September 2, 2011 the Gatti family requested a delay in the civil trial so they could have attorneys study the new information gathered by Pat Lynch's investigation. The estate trial would begin on September 8 in Montreal. Lynch informed the media that the results of the investigation he commissioned would prove that Arturo did not commit suicide.

Lynch confessed that he paid for an independent investigation because he would never accept the verdict that Arturo would take his own life, ever. The main reason Lynch was doing this was to let Arturo's children know that Arturo did not quit on them.[1753] A *Star Ledger* article questioned why Lynch thought it would be better to show Arturo Junior that his mother was a murderer rather than affirm that his father had committed suicide. The article acknowledged that Lynch's actions spoke of the closeness between he and Arturo. When Lynch first heard that Arturo had died in the hotel room, he called Amanda an evil person and he hoped she would rot in hell.[1754] Lynch was now more reserved with his comments.

Brazilian authorities announced that they would reopen the case and take a look at the new evidence. Ciolino was excited that a new judge and prosecutor, whom he believed were incorruptible, would be looking over the new evidence. Ciolino revealed that he was doing the investigation mostly "pro bono."

A *Star Ledger* article brought up an interesting hypothetical scenario. If Arturo was from another country and he came to the United States and beat his female companion, who was a U.S. citizen, in public, and he was later discovered dead, would anyone blame his companion for defending herself? Most would call the act justifiable, and rightly so. The article played devil's advocate by also stating that the crime would be murder if Arturo was strangled, not while fighting with Amanda, but in a drunken haze.

Lynch was asked his thoughts on eyewitness accounts that Arturo had struck Amanda. He answered that he did not know if that were true.[1755] Lynch also was asked if Amanda's threats to take Junior away from Arturo could lead him to commit suicide. Lynch replied that he did not believe that threatening to take Junior away from Arturo would lead him to take his own life, especially with his son sleeping upstairs.[1756] Ciolino was absolutely sure that Arturo did not hang himself, but instead that he was strangled. Ciolino reminded reporters that Arturo had his son in his arms when he pushed Amanda and she fell to the floor.[1757]

Although Arturo's close friends spoke publicly of his benevolence, there was another side, a dark side, especially when he was under the influence of alcohol and drugs. He was known to be angry and abusive. His temper could be explosive. Lynch commented on Arturo's gremlin or Sybil-like personality by stating that we all have our demons. Lynch added that Arturo was a great, big-hearted guy, who gave his fans everything they could want inside of the ring.[1758]

On September 7, Paul Ciolino introduced his assembled experts one at a time. Each took to the podium and gave their expert opinions. One and all attacked the Brazilian police investigators, the Brazilian judicial system, the autopsy doctors, and the main target, Amanda Gatti. Each presentation was geared towards disproving the suicide theory, yet not one of the experts could say with any type of certainty how Amanda performed the act of murder, if she indeed committed it. The nearly three-hour press conference was held while Arturo's famous fights played on flat screen TVs in the background.

Brent Turvey, a forensic scientist, felt that the injury to the back of Arturo's head was not a fatal blow, but it proved that he was attacked by an assailant from behind while in the apartment. Turvey believed that Arturo was then strangled with a ligature while in a dazed/drunken state.[1759] Cyril Wecht, a forensic pathologist, called the autopsy horrible. She added that it was deliberately bungled to support the Brazilian authorities' conclusion of suicide.

Alfred Bowles, a biodynamic expert, noted that the purse strap that Arturo allegedly used to hang himself with was not strong enough to support his 160-pound frame. Bowles felt that the strap was too long to secure around Arturo's body. He also pointed out several other inconsistences. Bowles believed that the position that Arturo was found in, with his head under a cabinet, was not consistent with where he would have fallen after hanging himself. Additionally, the ligature marks on Arturo's neck did not form the "V" mark that would be expected from hanging. The marks were straight and more consistent with strangulation. FBI agent Stephen Moore surmised that the Brazilian investigation was not evidence-driven, but conclusion-driven.[1760]

Lynch and his experts were confident that Brazilian authorities would change their opinion once they received this new report. The report was translated into Portuguese and forwarded to Eduardo

Trinadade, the Gatti family attorney in Brazil. Trinadade commented on the report by saying that he expected the prosecutor to start a process against Amanda.[1761] Trinadade presented the investigation's findings to the prosecutor in Ipojuca, Brazil.

Dominick Gatti, Arturo's cousin who lived in New Jersey, attended the press conference. Dominick felt that he had heard enough to be convinced that Arturo was murdered.[1762] Dominick came to know Amanda when she and Arturo moved into their Morganville home, which was near Dominick's home. He recalled how Arturo wanted to move Amanda away from Hoboken and Jersey City. Dominick added that in the beginning Amanda was really nice, but she started changing her manners, even the clothing she wore, to the point where Dominick felt something bad was going to happen.[1763] Dominick recalled talking to Arturo when it was first believed that actor Heath Ledger took his life in 2008, before it was ruled that his death was the result of an accidental overdose. Arturo asked Dominick why someone would commit suicide. Dominick was convinced that Arturo never would contemplate taking his own life.[1764]

The only people who were paid in Lynch's investigation were Ciolino and Moura. This is probably why the other specialists wrote such small reports on the case. It was announced that Lynch had spent thousands of dollars on the investigation.

The civil trial over Arturo's estate was ongoing. While the two wills were at the center of the trial, the couple's troubled relationship was also garnering attention. Carmine Mercadente was representing the Gatti family at the civil trial, while Pierre-Hughes Fortin represented Amanda. Lynch had hoped that his investigation's findings would help delay the civil trial, but more importantly, he wanted to prove that Arturo was murdered.

On September 8, only one day after the press conference, Lynch and the Gatti family received hopeful news. The Brazilian prosecutors announced that they would re-examine Arturo's death. Spokesman Jacques Cerqueira predicted that prosecutor Paula Ismail would ask for the private investigation's findings.[1765]

On September 9, 2011, Brazilian investigator Paulo Alberes announced at a news conference that he still believed that Arturo had killed himself. Nevertheless, Alberes confirmed that he would re-examine the evidence. Alberes had not seen any evidence that persuaded him to believe that Arturo was murdered.[1766]

Alberes surmised that it would have taken three or four people to pick up the 160-pound Arturo and hang him from a strap. Alberes suggested that Arturo would have fought against this. That is true, if he were conscious. It later was revealed that Arturo had the muscle relaxant Carisoprodol in his system, which coupled with alcohol, could have left Arturo in a very vulnerable state. Alberes believed that it was impossible for Arturo to have been hanged. What Alberes did not contemplate was, if the hanging had been staged, Arturo would not need to be lifted up and hung. He could have been strangled on the floor, after which the purse strap could have been rubbed around the railing to leave enough trace evidence, which would lead investigators to believe that Arturo had hung himself. It should be noted that there was no trace of blood on the staircase.

Alberes believed the private investigation had been triggered by the fight over Arturo's estate. That statement was factually incorrect. Pat Lynch triggered the investigation, and he did not stand to profit financially if the will was reversed.

Alberes unprofessionally suggested that Arturo's family were dissatisfied that Amanda and Junior would inherit the millions of dollars left by Arturo's estate.[1767]

Brazilian prosecutor, Paula Ismail, announced that she would look into the private investigation's findings and might order a reinvestigation of the case. She added that she would file murder charges if applicable. Canadian officials had yet to release the findings of their autopsy. Amanda dismissed the private investigation because it was funded by Pat Lynch.

Also on September 9, attorney Anthony Pope, representing 5-year-old Sofia Bella Gatti, filed a wrongful-death lawsuit against Amanda in Middlesex County, N.J. The suit sought damages and restraints on Arturo and Amanda's New Jersey assets. The lawsuit claimed that Amanda violently bludgeoned and asphyxiated Arturo, resulting in his death.

On September 14, Amanda rejected Montreal Judge Claudine Roy's suggestion to reach a settlement with Arturo's family over his estate. The family was willing to split the estate fifty-fifty. Amanda went home and called Vikki and Joe. She asked for their advice. She told them that she was tired of fighting with Ida and Fabrizio and just wanted the case to end. She asked if she should take the deal. Vikki told Amanda that if she gave in, and gave them half, that it would look as though she was guilty. Vikki added, *"Well that's funny Amanda. They said you murdered him, but if you give them half the money they don't mind that you murdered him? Don't give in to them. That money belongs to Junior."*[1768] Amanda agreed with Vikki and decided that she would continue fighting even if it meant spending every last penny on lawyers.

Amanda must have known that Fabrizio and Ida had a poor case if they were willing to negotiate. Outside the courthouse, Amanda revealed that she did not want to negotiate, while her attorney, telling her not to comment, led her away. Her lawyer later confirmed that Amanda was not willing to discuss a deal. The judge had hoped that both sides would agree to attend a settlement conference before an independent judge. Joe couldn't believe what his family was doing. He was thoroughly embarrassed. How could his family say that they believed Amanda killed Arturo and then make a deal with her to settle for half of Arturo's estate? Fabrizio and Ida announced that they wanted the money for Junior, yet Junior was living with Amanda.

Judge Roy noted a pending legal action in Florida, outstanding income taxes, and the newly filed wrongful death suit on behalf of Sofia Bella. Judge Roy also added that she did not believe that Arturo would want his fortune to be squandered away in multiple court proceedings. Roy revealed that new documents from Amanda's lawyers estimated Arturo's estate to be worth $3.4 million, not the $5.6 million originally calculated. Ida and Fabrizio were standing by their claim that Amanda pressured Arturo into changing his will, leaving everything to Amanda.

During the civil trial, the Gatti family called attorney John Lynch's secretary to the stand. The secretary confirmed that Arturo tore up a copy of the prenuptial agreement to appease Amanda, and then called a week later to confirm that the original pre-nup was still intact. The secretary also confirmed that Arturo called and asked for a copy of the pre-nup to be sent to a Montreal lawyer he had consulted with about divorcing Amanda in May 2009.

On September 16, Amanda took the stand for the third consecutive day. She was asked why she did not attempt to contact Arturo's mother after his death. Amanda started crying, stating the reason she did not attempt to contact Ida after Arturo died was because she was afraid that Ida thought that she had killed Arturo.[1769] She started sobbing again when the Gatti family lawyer questioned her as to why she wouldn't let her in-laws see Junior. Amanda replied that she was worried that the Gatti family would try to take her son away. Amanda admitted, *"I was not the perfect wife. I could have been better. I did a lot of bad things."*[1770] She added that her marriage wasn't perfect, but she loved Arturo and he loved her.[1771]

Amanda was questioned as to why Arturo's regular notary, one that was close to their home and one that he used frequently, wasn't used to notarize the new will and fidelity agreement. Amanda stated, *"I wanted to have my own [notary]."*[1772] Amanda had stated that Arturo accompanied her to Bruce Moidel's office on their initial visit to the notary. The notary contradicted her testimony, stating that Amanda initially came to the office alone. Amanda also stated that it was Moidel who recommended Arturo prepare a new will, when previously she had stated that she and Arturo had decided to compose a new will after a plane crashed in Brazil.

When questioned, Amanda admitted that she had keyed Arturo's truck while he and Junior were sitting inside of the vehicle. The incident caused over $4,000 in damages. Arturo completed a police report on the day of the incident. In the report, he referred to Amanda as his ex-wife. When Amanda was questioned about the incident, she stated, *"I know it sounds ridiculous. That's how my relationship was. We were never mad at each other for too long."*[1773]

On September 19, Fabrizio took the stand. He testified that he was not fighting over Arturo's estate for his own gain, but rather to ensure that Sofia and Arturo Junior were the recipients of his brother's estate. Fabrizio was asked if he ever attempted to reach out to Amanda, to arrange visiting with his nephew. He admitted that he had not. Fabrizio would later state that Amanda wanted everything.[1774]

Arturo's friend Tony Rizzo took the stand. Rizzo recalled that Arturo rarely if ever read contracts that he signed. Arturo's family added that he had a limited education, dropping out of school in the eighth grade. Rizzo believed that Arturo never would have left his estate to Amanda. Rizzo testified that he discussed with Arturo how his will should split his estate between his daughter and his son. Rizzo recalled that Gatti revealed that Amanda wanted him to leave everything to her. The promiscuous Arturo also had signed a "fidelity promise" when he signed the second will, which if broken, would reward Amanda with a million dollars. When Judge Roy asked Amanda about the fidelity agreement, Amanda stated that she thought the agreement *"was cute."*[1775] The Judge, astounded by Amanda's answer, asked her to repeat her answer a second time.

The civil trial was suspended for a day, until September 21. It appeared that a settlement between Arturo's family and Amanda was being discussed. Amanda confessed that she was tired of fighting her in-laws. She sobbed as she described how difficult it was for her to relive her tumultuous relationship with Arturo, day after day. The Gatti family attorney, Carmine Mercadante, said a deal would not be possible until he discussed a few issues with his clients.

On September 24, Judge Roy ruled that Amanda could no longer be questioned about the evening before Arturo's death. Amanda's attorney argued, and the judge agreed, that the events on the night that Arturo died were not relevant to the civil trial over Arturo's estate. Before the judge's ruling, Amanda was forced to describe how an intoxicated Arturo struck her in public, and ignited a street brawl, only hours before his death. When leaving the courthouse on one of the days of the trial, Amanda advised a reporter, *"I'm sure the end is going to be good for me. I deserve this."*[1776]

In court, Amanda commented on Arturo's family by stating that they were not normal.[1777] Amanda recalled that Arturo could hardly make a fist from all the trauma his hands endured during his career. Arturo frequented warm vacation areas because his joints ached in the cold weather. Jacques Ponthier, who wrote a book in French about Arturo, believed that Gatti had triple vision in one eye and blurred vision in the other.

On September 24, the season premiere of CBS's "48 Hours" examined the mysterious death of Arturo. The episode was titled "Arturo Gatti's Last Fight." The show included interviews with Amanda, Joe Gatti, Mario Costa, and Micky Ward. Ward called Arturo his dancing partner in the ring. Ward's gut feeling was that Arturo did not kill himself. He felt that Amanda knew what happened.[1778]

Mario Costa commented on the "48 Hours" episode. *"Lynch said, 'Oh, how can he be champion if he's partying like that?' I said, 'You guys knew he was a functional junkie.' And Arthur and his brother, they didn't even have a father. Their mother was in Canada. They were here, two young guys, by themselves. And Lynch and Main Events did whatever the fuck they wanted with them.*

"I didn't care about the money, so they couldn't have me around, or Joe around. And Joe, now they say all he wanted was money. What did they want? They didn't want money? All Joe wanted was money? Joe never really got no money from his brother. Never, nothing to make sense of. And Joe works two or three jobs now. And he's been doing it for the last ten years. Joe will tell you he did drugs for a while. Now he won't touch them. Now he's got two girls. He

picks them up from school. Works two, three jobs. He calls me sometimes at 4 or 5 in the morning, 'Mario, I love you. I'm going to work.' It's a shame. I feel bad. Sometimes I feel like I want to cry by myself. I got the pictures up in the bar and it's a shame, what happened, because he was such a good kid. And it's a shame the way his life went and the way things happened to him. He was a real good kid."[1779]

Nestor Fernandez, who Arturo assaulted in April 2009 in Florida, filed a civil suit against Arturo's estate seeking $5 million in damages. Amanda and Fernandez reached an out-of-court settlement. Amanda, who was not with Arturo during the assault, believed that Arturo was only defending himself after being attacked.

On November 9, the long-awaited coroner's report from Quebec was released. The report stated that there was no clear evidence that a third party was involved in Arturo's death. The report also stated that suicide still remained a plausible explanation. The report added that Brazilian authorities mishandled the crime scene, which made it nearly impossible to draw a definitive conclusion.

Montreal's chief coroner, Jean Brochu, stated, *"The conclusion of the Montreal pathologists to the effect that there is no clear evidence of foul play in Mr. Gatti's death means I cannot dismiss the formal conclusions reached by the authorities of the country where it occurred."* Brochu added, *"The methods used by Brazilian investigators in examining the scene of Arturo Gatti's death can raise doubts, and so the circumstances of death cannot be determined with certainty."*[1780]

Brochu consulted with Martin Laliberte, an expert toxicologist, who noted the presence of the drug Carisoprodol in Arturo's system. Carisoprodol is a muscle relaxant that is not available in Canada but is widely available around the world. Laliberte added that the drug is highly addictive and has frequently been involved in cases of death and suicide. The drug is known to cause anxiety, confusion, and psychosis. After hearing of the Quebec coroner's findings, Amanda's lawyer, Pierre-Huges Fortin, stated that Amanda hoped the report would put an end to any speculation that she was involved in her husband's death.[1781]

On December 16, 2011, Judge Roy ruled in favor of Amanda and awarded her Arturo's entire estate. The judge ruled that the will Arturo signed with Amanda was legitimate.

On January 20, 2012, a Middlesex County Superior Court judge ruled that he reserved the right to decide where Sofia Gatti's wrongful death case should be heard. Amanda's lawyer argued that the case should be heard in either Brazil or Canada. Erika Rivera's attorney argued that the case should be heard in the county where she lived with her daughter Sofia. Rivera and Sofia lived in Sayreville in Middlesex County, New Jersey. Amanda's attorney, Mark Casazza, reminded the court that Erika's relationship with Arturo occurred before his marriage. He also reminded the court that Arturo's 2009 will included a trust fund and college fund for Sofia.

On February 10, 2012, a Middlesex County Superior Court judge dismissed the wrongful death suit filed by Erika Rivera on behalf of Sofia Bella Gatti. Erika did not believe the suicide allegations. She revealed that Arturo could get a little bit crazy, and he was very superstitious, but he was not suicidal. Erika added that Arturo was a free spirit who loved life.[1782]

Erin Moriarty, a correspondent for the CBS show "48 Hours," commented that Erika must have forgotten that she filed court records in 2006. In the documents, she stated that Arturo had tried to commit suicide in 2005. Moriarty added that she had records that showed Arturo had overdosed on cocaine and a number of other drugs. She expressed that there was substantial evidence that Arturo was suicidal for years.[1783] Moriarty also revealed that Paul Ciolino's investigation left out the fact that Arturo's body had lividity, or blood pooling, that was consistent with suicide. She claimed that Arturo had the classic "boots and gloves" lividity found in hanging victims. Moriarty felt that Amanda did not help Arturo emotionally on the night of his death. She added that Amanda knew where Arturo's weak points were when they fought.[1784] Was Moriarty suggesting that Amanda may have encouraged Arturo to commit suicide? Moriarty believed that since Arturo and Amanda were alone, that he killed himself. She did say that if evidence surfaced to show that another person had been in the condo to assist Amanda, it might have been a homicide. Erika Rivera was shocked that Amanda had not been arrested again. She promised that if Amanda was not arrested, she would make sure that Amanda would not get any of Arturo's money, not one red cent.[1785]

Chapter 33
The Hall of Fame

Arturo would be eligible for induction into the International Boxing Hall of Fame in 2013. The debate regarding his potential induction started in October 2012. Those opposed to his induction argued that Arturo lost too many fights, took too many punches, and lost to all of the elite opponents that he faced. They also argued that Arturo was not considered a top ten pound-for-pound fighter during any year in his career. Additionally, Arturo was not considered the top fighter in his weight class at any time during his career. There were some who believed that the only reason Arturo was being considered for the Hall of Fame was because of the tragic way he died.

Buffalo, N.Y. matchmaker and Hall of Fame voter, Rick Glaser, did not support Arturo's entry. He stated that Arturo never won a fight he wasn't supposed to win.[1786]

Larry Merchant thought Gatti's induction was appropriate. Merchant felt that it was much easier to become a champion in boxing than it was to become a star. He felt that Gatti had the "IT" factor that was needed to be a superstar. Merchant added that Arturo helped to make the HBO "Boxing After Dark" series a success. Merchant admitted that Gatti wasn't on the highest level of the sport, but you were pretty much guaranteed to see drama and blood when he fought.[1787]

Russell Peltz, a Hall of Fame voter, supported and cast a vote for Arturo. Peltz commented that although Arturo wasn't the most talented fighter, he was special. Peltz added that Gatti was just as exciting when he lost as he was when he won. Peltz, however, felt that Gatti might be the most controversial selection in the history of the Hall of Fame.[1788]

Henry Hascup, boxing historian and Hall of Fame voter, recalled the Arturo nomination controversy, *"There's two ways you could look at it, his boxing record or what he meant to boxing. His boxing record didn't compare to some of the other guys that were on the ballot, but what he meant for boxing, selling out Atlantic City, the excitement of an Arturo Gatti fight was second to none... In the end I did vote for him."*[1789]

Pat Lynch reflected on how he believed Arturo should be remembered. Lynch felt that Gatti was the rare exception who could lose a fight on HBO and still be asked back because he brought so much excitement to an event. Lynch felt that the average fight fan connected with Arturo because he was a working-class guy just like them. Lynch admitted that Gatti wasn't the most talented fighter, but the most talented boxers knew if they got in the ring with him they'd have to go through hell to beat him. Lynch recalled that early in Arturo's career he had to win his fights to keep his contract with HBO. HBO had a clause in the contracts with all of their fighters, that if the fighter lost, the contract could be voided. HBO never enforced the clause with Gatti, because Arturo's fights, win or lose, were entertaining. Lynch recalled that Arturo would ask him if he thought Arturo could get into the Hall of Fame someday.[1790]

The most significant aspect being scrutinized pertained to what exactly the criteria was for entrance into the Hall of Fame. Was it skill, world titles, wins, or impact on the sport? If promoters, managers, referees, matchmakers and writers were inducted solely on the basis of their impact on the sport, shouldn't this criteria also apply to fighters? No one doubted that Arturo contributed to boxing in a tremendous way, especially the fact that he single-handedly brought boxing back to life in Atlantic City. It was Boardwalk Hall, more affectionately known as "The House of Gatti," where Arturo attracted over 100,000 supporters during his many memorable fights there. His supporters pointed to the fact that he gave his all in the ring and was involved in four *Ring* magazine "Fights of the Year." Arturo was showcased twenty-two times on HBO. Kathy Duva commented on the Hall of Fame controversy by stating that people needed to ask themselves one question. Was Arturo Gatti a legend? Duva felt that everyone could agree that he was.[1791]

On November 10, 2012, Arturo's friend Joey Perrenod died at the age of 37 from a drug overdose. Perrenod was the step-son of Arturo's doctor, Frank Rotella. Joe Gatti felt that his brother's friends were dying off because they had enabled Arturo's drug use. Joe felt that Arturo was speaking from the grave, saying, *"Hey you, come here, because of you I'm here."*[1792] Although Joe felt that others enabled Arturo's drug use it appears likely that Arturo's drug issues would have existed regardless of his choice of friends.

On December 10, the Hall of Fame voting committee released their induction class for 2013, which included Arturo "Thunder" Gatti. The voting committee included members of the Boxing Writers Association, along with a panel of international boxing historians. The induction ceremony would be held on June 9, 2013, in

Canastota, N.Y. Micky Ward gave his thoughts on Arturo's induction by stating that Gatti gave his all in the ring.[1793]

Others who were voted into the Hall with Arturo included 1984 U.S. Olympian and five-time world champion Virgil Hill, Myung-Woo Yuh, Jeff Smith, and Mills Lane. Pat Lynch reflected on Arturo's induction by stating that it was an honor and a privilege for him to have managed Arturo for his entire career.[1794] Lynch was happy for Gatti's family, friends, and children.[1795] Lynch received the call that Arturo would be a first-ballot entry from Ed Brophy, executive director of the International Boxing Hall of Fame.

Amanda opened a fashion boutique on trendy Saint-Denis Street in Montreal. She named the business A.G. Boutique. Her legal battles were now in the past. She was awarded Arturo's $3.4 million estate. Amanda stated that she had learned to love Montreal.[1796] She was very happy to be opening up her new store. She added that her boutique was created with a tremendous amount of energy and love.[1797] Montreal boxing trainer and retired fighter, Otis Grant, felt that it was very gutsy for Amanda to live in Montreal after all that had happened.[1798]

Amanda hoped that her mother-in-law Ida would put aside her suspicions and let Amanda, and by extension, Arturo, Jr., be a part of her life.

Brazilian authorities planned on revisiting the death of Arturo in March, with a court hearing. A spokesperson for the Pernambuco prosecutor's office, Gilvan Oliveira, announced that prosecutor Paula Catherine Ismail was studying the process.[1799]

Paul Ciolino revealed that new evidence had turned up that pointed to Amanda as a suspect. He stated that a bribe was paid to a Brazilian investigator to hide evidence. He also believed that the bribe was the reason Amanda was released from prison. Ciolino added that the original lead investigator had confessed on tape that evidence at the crime scene was destroyed, and that bribes were offered. Ciolino felt that Arturo finally would get the justice that he deserved.[1800] He added that he thought that Amanda would be arrested and the truth eventually would come out.[1801]

Amanda insisted that her husband committed suicide. She called Ciolino a liar. She denied the allegations and challenged those who felt she was guilty to try and send her back to Brazil. Amanda added that she really didn't care about anything that came out of Ciolino's mouth. She had nothing to hide.[1802] The tape that Ciolino spoke of most likely never existed, as it was never revealed to the public. The

Brazilian authorities reviewed the new evidence and decided it was not valid enough to re-open the case. Pat Lynch believed that the Brazilian authorities were not cooperating with his investigators.[1803]

On March 28, 2013, HBO sports announced that it would air a documentary of Arturo's trilogy against Micky Ward under its "Legendary Nights" series. The one-hour documentary was titled, "The Tale of Gatti-Ward." In the documentary, Larry Merchant commented that both Gatti and Ward emptied themselves in the ring. Pat Lynch added that it was sad that Ward and Gatti would not be able to grow old together and tell war stories.

In the documentary, Micky Ward recalled receiving a phone call from the Port Authority Police that Arturo had fallen asleep at the wheel and hit the Holland Tunnel. The officer wanted Ward to come and take Arturo's car before they towed it. Ward told the officer that he was in Massachusetts, and there was no way he could come pick up the car. Arturo had crashed his car into a concrete divider at the toll booth outside of the tunnel. Arturo was unresponsive when police arrived, which was why the police were scrolling through his cell phone looking for someone to pick his car up. After Ward said he couldn't come down, the officer called Omar Sheika. Sheika called Pat Lynch, but Lynch was in Atlantic City and couldn't drive up. Arturo's car was towed and he was taken to the Jersey City Medical Center for evaluation. Arturo later told friends that he was trying to get to Kennedy Airport. Lynch asked Mikey Red to pick up Arturo from the hospital.

On April 3, the New Jersey Boxing Hall of Fame announced its class of 2013. Among those voted in was Arturo's brother Joe Gatti. Inducted with Joe was Arturo's long-time matchmaker, Carl Moretti. Mike Tyson, Gabe LaConte, Ray Mercer, and Marvin Hagler also were voted in. The event was held at the Venetian in Garfield, N.J. on November 14. Voted professional fighter of the year was Pat Lynch-managed junior middleweight Glen Tapia. Tapia and Lynch did not attend the event on November 14. Tapia was in camp in Middletown, N.J., training for his upcoming fight with James Kirkland. When Joe Gatti was called up to the podium, he broke down when reminiscing about his brother. Mike Tyson stood up and comforted Joe as Carl Moretti sat nearby.

On March 13, A&E's Bio channel aired an episode in their "Prenup to Murder" series that was titled "Arturo Gatti's Final Bout." In the episode, it was revealed for the first time that Arturo's white gold and diamond chain with the cross pendant was discovered in a pot on the stove when the police arrived.

On June 6, 2013, just three days before Arturo's induction into the International Boxing Hall of Fame, several of Arturo's closest boxing associates were interviewed. Carl Moretti was asked about those who felt Arturo was not deserving of Hall of Fame entry. Moretti called them ignorant haters. He added that the Hall of Fame was not a pound-for-pound list.[1804]

On June 9, 2013, Arturo was inducted into the International Boxing Hall of Fame. On hand were his manager Pat Lynch, promoter Kathy Duva, matchmaker Carl Moretti, Erika Rivera, Arturo's daughter Sofia Bella, Ida Gatti, Micky Ward, Angel Manfredy, and even actress Rosie Perez. Lynch, Duva, Ward, and Sofia all spoke at the event. Mikey Red drove four hours to the ceremony, but was not invited to sit with Lynch's group. The 7-year-old Sofia was brought up to the podium and was held up by a beaming Pat Lynch as she spoke the words, *"Thank you from my daddy."*[1805] Sofia was holding Arturo's plaque in her hands. Ken Condon recalled that it was a very emotional day.[1806]

A tearful Lynch commented that it was wonderful that Arturo's mother and daughter were on hand to celebrate his tremendous accomplishments. He added that Sofia would have the memory of this event forever.[1807] Kathy Duva added that Arturo was in Heaven. She hoped he knew that one of his dreams had come true.[1808]

Ward took to the podium and acknowledged that he thought about Arturo every day, and felt that Arturo's presence was on hand. Ward then turned to Sofia and added that Arturo's little girl being in attendance meant more than anything. Ward was happy for Arturo's entire family.[1809]

Those who could not attend gave their thoughts on Arturo. Tracy Patterson stated, *"I had over 100 amateur fights and 73 professional fights. Gatti was one of the toughest men that I stepped in the ring against. I fought guys like Daniel Zaragoza, Jesse Benavides, and Steve Cruz, and many other tough competitors in the ring. Arturo Gatti did not quit in the ring and he did not quit on life. I salute the boxing Hall of Fame and Ed Brophy for putting him in the boxing Hall of Fame. Congratulations to Arturo Gatti, Gatti's family and his fight fans."*[1810]

Russell Peltz gave his thoughts on Arturo's induction. *"He was the franchise in Atlantic City for years, he drew big crowds, he was never in a bad fight. It was a no-brainer that he get inducted. He was the most exciting fighter of his era, what else can you say? It's *the Hall of Fame.*"[1811]

Gabriel Ruelas stated, *"It is a great accomplishment for Arturo Gatti, someone that gave so much of himself to the sport and to the fans. I totally agree and I am not surprised that he is going into the boxing Hall of Fame. To this day, it was very memorable to me because of the intensity and drama of the fight. Even though I came up short, as no fighter wants to, people still talk about the fight to me in a complementary way... We never spoke to each other during the fight, there was no bad blood between Arturo and I."*[1812]

Unbeknownst to many, Arturo Junior was sitting in the back of the audience. The precious memory that Sofia would have would not be shared by her half-brother. Junior was sent to the ceremony with Amanda's friend, Victoria Purchio. Purchio and Junior drove eight hours from Montreal to Canastota. Amanda wanted Junior to be at the event to celebrate his father's achievements. The International Boxing Hall of Fame was allegedly advised that Junior would be attending the event. Junior and Purchio sat in the back and were not invited up to the podium. Junior sat at a rear table dressed in a crisp black suit. He had curly hair and a smile that was undeniably Arturo. Arturo Jr. was not even acknowledged at the event.

Amanda stated that she had contacted the International Boxing Hall of Fame via phone, telling them that Junior wanted to attend his father's induction. After she received no response, Amanda wrote the Hall a letter on June 7. In the letter, she explained that Arturo would have wanted his son and his wife to attend the induction ceremony. She added that she was deeply saddened by the Hall of Fame's decision not to contact her. She felt that the Hall of Fame's actions showed a serious lack of respect towards her late husband, herself, and most importantly, Arturo Gatti, Jr., who would have been honored to have officially participated in the induction ceremony.[1813] Amanda wrote that she would be unable to attend the event due to her immigration status. She added that she sent Junior down to the ceremony to appreciate how much his father was loved by his boxing fans.[1814]

Pat Lynch had commented that Arturo never would have killed himself while in the same condo as his son. That he loved his son too much. If that were true, wouldn't Arturo want his son to participate in the greatest honor of his career? Although it is understandable that Amanda attending the event would have made for a very uncomfortable situation due to the various opinions regarding Arturo's demise, personal feelings should have been set aside for Arturo Jr.'s sake. It is unknown who ultimately made the decision to exclude Arturo Jr. from the event, but it was obviously a poor decision.

N.Y. Post reporter George Willis discovered that Junior had been at the event when he stopped at a McDonald's across the street from the ceremony after the event had ended. It was there that he ran into Junior and Purchio by accident. Junior told Willis that he came to see his daddy.[1815] While Arturo Jr. ate his chicken nuggets, Purchio explained to Willis that she brought Junior to the event at his mother's request. Purchio added that this was a very special occasion for Junior to remember about his dad.[1816]

Joe was not told that his nephew was attending the ceremony. He would have made sure that Junior was brought to the stage had he been there. Joe did not attend the ceremony because he felt that Lynch would be there controlling every detail. Joe was perplexed as to why Amanda did not tell him that she was sending Junior to the event. Joe would have attended had he known that Junior would be there.[1817]

Mario Costa recalled the ceremony controversy. *"Amazingly, Arturo's son had a hard time getting into the Hall of Fame that day. Can you believe they were made to wait almost a half hour? And when they finally let him in, they gave him a seat in the back. They never brought young Arturo up to introduce to the audience. If George Willis didn't, by chance, bump into young Arturo and his host at McDonald's, nobody would have ever known he was there. The presentation was all set up to show the daughter. George Willis wrote his column in the New York Post about little Arthur being kept in the back and someone called him and said, 'Why are you taking sides?' George Willis said, 'I'm not taking sides. I'm writing what I saw.' I actually believe it was some kind of intervention for George Willis to go to McDonald's and meet little Arthur before driving home. I think it was Arturo Gatti who made George Willis go to McDonald's to meet his son."*[1818]

Costa believed that the Gatti camp was trying to showcase Arturo's daughter, Sofia, as a symbol of their devotion to Arturo. At the same time, they could not bring themselves to invite the son that Arturo cherished. It appears likely that Junior was shut out to hurt Amanda, which it obviously did. But at what cost? Junior was Arturo's son. His father loved him dearly. This was the moment that Arturo dreamed of. He most certainly would have wanted both of his children to experience the event in his honor.

On October 8, 2013, *Variety Magazine* announced that former NFL player Michael Strahan was teaming up with Mark Wahlberg and Pat Lynch to produce a biopic on Arturo's life. Actor Jerry Ferrara was slated to play Arturo in the movie. The project would later be shelved, possibly due to the fact that those involved in the project didn't want to expose the darker events in Arturo's life. Without touching on those events there wasn't much of a story to be told. Some of the most entertaining aspects of the Micky Ward movie were the segments related to his dysfunctional family.

On October 16, a private screening of the HBO documentary on the Gatti-Ward trilogy was shown at HBO's headquarters in Manhattan. Among those in attendance were Pat Lynch, Buddy McGirt, Lou DiBella, and Micky Ward. At the event, DiBella confessed that Arturo might not have been the greatest fighter, but he was the most exciting television fighter of the modern age.[1819]

On October 19, the Gatti-Ward documentary aired on HBO. Micky Ward was brought to tears by the film. He stated that he just tried to remember all of the great times they had together.[1820] Kathy Duva commented on the Gatti-Ward wars by saying that they looked like scenes from *Rocky*.[1821]

Epilogue

How did Arturo Gatti die in Brazil on July 11, 2009? Was it murder, suicide, or a delicate weave of both murder and suicide? The Brazilian autopsy report alluded to a suicidal death by hanging, but they did add that murder or accidental death could not be ruled out.[1822] The Canadian autopsy report could not dismiss Brazil's findings, however they added third party involvement was unlikely. They also added that the crime scene was mishandled which made it nearly impossible to draw a definitive conclusion.[1823] Listed below are several possible theories on how Arturo may have met his demise. These are unproven theories, which are presented to the reader for analysis, they are not presented as fact.

<u>Devil Worship.</u>

Arturo had told Joe years earlier that if he wanted to be successful and a champion, he would have to sell his soul to the devil. Joe and Vikki recalled feeling an evil presence in Arturo's Weehawken apartment. If Arturo truly did sell his soul to the devil, eventually Satan would come calling for his property. Is that why Arturo's gold and diamond encrusted cross and necklace was found at the bottom of a pot on the stove? Was this a message from Arturo that he had surrendered his soul to the force that had given him his worldly desire of being a world champion? Donny Jerie recalled that Arturo started talking about God and how he wanted to get closer to him.

<u>Contracted Hit.</u>

Johnny Bos, who was Joey Gamache's adviser, had his own theory on Arturo's demise. Bos felt that Arturo was killed to prevent him from testifying the following week in the Gamache lawsuit against the New York State Athletic Commission. Arturo was set to testify for both the plaintiff as well as the defense. Bos felt that the powers-that-be in world-class boxing wanted to silence Arturo before he testified. If anyone knew what really happened during the weigh-in, it would have been Arturo. World-class boxing generates large scale betting and is inundated with unsavory characters. Bos felt that Arturo was the victim of a contract killing, and claimed to know who the hit man was. He stated that it was a retired Brazilian boxer who drove a white van. He added that the boxer, who lived in the United States, was in Brazil at the same time that Arturo was murdered. Bos was convinced that Arturo was murdered by this hit man. This author was scheduled to interview Bos and obtain the name of the alleged hit man. On the week of the scheduled interview, in May 2013, Bos died suddenly of an apparent heart attack.

Erotic Asphyxiation.

The closing of an airway during sexual climax allegedly leads to a magnified euphoria. The rumor of erotic asphyxiation spread immediately after Arturo's death was made public. The possibility of this occurring is highly unlikely because Amanda simply could have explained what had happened. Unless, of course, she was too embarrassed to do so. During the investigation it was discovered that Arturo had semen in his briefs. Was this due to erotic asphyxiation? It has been documented that a male can ejaculate during the moment of death, which would explain the semen.

Suicide from Depression.

Arturo was undoubtedly suffering from depression. He told friends that he felt depressed and had suicidal thoughts. Arturo was known to struggle with relationships his whole life. On July 11, he was faced with the humiliation of what had transpired with his wife. Amanda told him that their relationship was over. Arturo might have felt that this meant she would be taking his son, whom he cherished, away from him. This situation, coupled with drug and alcohol abuse, could have led Arturo to feel that his life was no longer worth living.

Suicide from Brain Injury.

The trauma that Arturo received to his brain throughout his career is plain to see by watching his fights. What effects this may have had in regards to Gatti's depression will never be fully known, as he never sought help. Arturo suffered a traumatic event when he fought with his wife. This was magnified by the alcohol and drugs he was using. What may have been overlooked was the injury to the back of Arturo's head that was caused by a brick. Severe head trauma in and of itself can lead to feelings of isolation, depression, and paranoia. The combination of alcohol, drugs, depression, possible CTE, a physical confrontation with his wife, a fresh head injury, and being confronted with possibly losing his son could have created an avalanche of emotions that might have led him to make a suicidal decision that he normally would not have made.

Murder.

Amanda could have orchestrated the entire incident leading up to the physical altercation outside the club. Arturo's jealousy was very predictable. Amanda was fully aware of how Arturo would react to her revealing clothing choice. Couple this with Arturo's drinking, and an explosive situation was created. After the public scene,

Arturo went back to the condo and continued drinking, as evidenced by the seven empty beer cans. He also had the muscle relaxant Carisoprodol in his system. When he was in this helpless intoxicated state, it would have been possible to slip the purse strap around his neck, end his life, and stage the scene as though it were a suicide. The fact that Arturo had made suicidal comments in the past would help to make this scenario more believable. The purse strap markings on the staircase, however, make this scenario unlikely.

Murdered with Assistance.

Amanda arrived in Brazil ahead of Arturo. She had plenty of time to prepare a trap. She was aware that he was seeing Karen Brennan in Florida. She may also have been aware that Arturo was applying for a permanent resident card in the U.S. It was also rumored that Arturo was planning on bringing Brennan to Canada. Arturo had recently changed his will. After provoking Arturo, which triggered the fight outside of the club, and returning to the condo, Amanda could have let others in to kill the intoxicated Gatti. Arturo had traces of semen in his briefs. Amanda may have had sex with the intoxicated Arturo while her accomplices came in and struck him on the head from behind, strangled him, and staged the scene, as private investigator Paul Ciolino suggested. There was trace evidence of blood on the bed sheets. This blood was not tested. Amanda also allegedly stated, when first interviewed by police, that her stepbrothers may have been involved in Arturo's death.[1824] What would lead her to make such a comment? She later retracted the comment and insisted that Arturo committed suicide.

Did the electronic key mechanism at the resort register every time the door was opened or did it only register every time the door was opened with a pass card? Were there first floor windows that someone could have entered and exited from? Could someone have been waiting inside the condo? There were those who claimed that Amanda came back to the condo accompanied by three males. Amanda had family and friends in the country. Her family was not happy about the way Arturo treated her and she may have told them that Arturo was planning on leaving her and that he had a valid prenup. Amanda enjoyed showing off her financial status through designer clothing and high end jewelry. Losing that lifestyle for someone of Amanda's disposition would have been devastating. There also was the issue of the missing money, nearly $50,000, as well as Arturo's gold watch. Other persons being involved might have been the reason Arturo's necklace had been on the stove. They may have been trying to destroy DNA evidence. This scenario is also unlikely as neighbors, when interviewed, stated they did not observe any other persons entering or exiting the condo.

Inflicted/Induced Suicide.

Amanda could have possibly induced Arturo into killing himself by her threats of taking Junior away or by threats of remaining in Brazil with Junior. These threats, coupled with the alcohol and drugs, could have led Arturo to end his life. Arturo might have expressed his feelings of suicide to Amanda, perhaps even threatening to commit the act. She could have pushed him over the edge by telling him that he was too much of a coward to go through with the act. Covert psychological murder or inflicted suicide is under research, and does occur. The victim can turn to drug or alcohol abuse when they are dehumanized by their partner. Amanda was known to ridicule the most sacred thing in Arturo's life next to his children; his boxing career. Arturo could have been made to feel worthless and unwanted. The life and soul of a victim of induced suicide is gradually destroyed much like the sand on a beach is eroded from the constant pounding of a storm. This type of gradual eradication of the soul is also referred to as soul murder.

In 2011, a male nurse, William Melchert-Dinkel of Faribault, Minnesota, was convicted of aiding and encouraging suicides. He had targeted depressed people online and aided them in committing the act. One of his victims hung himself in 2005, while another drowned himself in 2008. Dinkel entered into suicide pacts with his victims and gave instructions on how the victims could end their lives. Dinkel stated that he actually talked five people into committing the act. Of his decision to convict Dinkel, Judge Thomas Neuville wrote that the predisposition of a suicidal victim actually makes the victim more vulnerable to encouragement or advice, and their death more imminent and foreseeable.[1825]

Accidental Suicide.

Arturo was known to reach out to others when he was depressed. He visited Mario Costa several times, seeking advice, when he was suicidal. People who are depressed, and/or suicidal, seek out help. When Arturo allegedly called his manager and told him goodbye right before overdosing, he was crying out for help. Arturo may have put the purse strap around his neck, stood on the stool and yelled up to Amanda that he was going to kill himself, not in an attempt to commit suicide, but rather as a cry for help. Being in the obvious intoxicated state he was in, he may have slipped and accidentally hung himself. This would explain why the stool was underneath the staircase. As Arturo slipped, the stool might have been knocked out from under him. Joe felt that Arturo may have feigned suicide in an attempt to get Amanda's attention, with the hope that Amanda would open the door, and seeing Arturo, would forgive him for the events that transpired earlier in the evening. While staging this scene, Arturo could have accidentally slipped and ended his life.

Failed or Accidental Suicide Attempt Followed by Murder.

If Arturo indeed attempted to hang himself with the purse strap or feigned hanging himself with the purse strap and it broke, as it did when a similar strap was tested, Arturo would have been lying on the floor, still alive. He might have been knocked unconscious from the fall, coupled with his alcohol and drug use. This would explain his position on the floor, as well as the blood flow in the tile grout. This would also explain the abrasion under his chin and the belt marks on the staircase. When Amanda came down the stairs to retrieve Junior's milk, she would have observed Arturo in this groggy or unconscious state. Amanda would have had two choices, help him get medical attention, or help him complete the failed suicide he had attempted.

Arturo had retained a divorce attorney, was seeing Karen Brennan in Florida, and recently applied for his U.S. residency card prior to the second honeymoon. Amanda was aware of all of these things. She was aware that a divorce would leave her with nothing because of the prenup. The new will that she had allegedly prepared, and that Arturo had signed, would guarantee that his entire estate would fall into her lap if he died prior to a divorce.

Amanda could have tightened or pulled on the strap around Arturo's neck until he died of asphyxiation. This would also explain why the marks on Arturo's neck were not consistent with the V-shape normally associated with hanging. She could have then gone back upstairs, changed her clothes, and prepare for the story that she would tell authorities. It should be noted that Amanda waited hours after initially seeing Arturo on the floor before returning back downstairs, screaming, and running outside for help.

Which scenario, or combination of scenarios, actually occurred probably never will be known with 100% certainty. The one thing that can be agreed upon is that the world tragically lost a much beloved legend way too soon.

Boxers' careers rarely, if ever, have fairytale endings. Arturo Gatti's story is no different. F. Scott Fitzgerald stated, *"Show me a hero and I will show you a tragedy.*"[1826] Arturo's life was both a tragedy and a triumph. He streaked across the sky like a comet, and much like the fantastic glow of a comet, Arturo's memorable fights will forever be etched in the hearts and minds of all those who were lucky enough to have witnessed them. His life was short, but the memories he created will last for generations to come.

Joe Gatti has come close to having a fairytale finish. He has a loving wife and two beautiful daughters. For anyone looking in from the outside, he has "made it." Unfortunately, his life is not a fairytale. Not a day goes by that he doesn't think about his younger brother and what he could have done differently to prevent his demise. Unfortunately, reflecting on the past is not the same as when you are living in the moment.

In 2013, New Jersey Governor Chris Christie reinstated Larry Hazzard as commissioner of boxing for the state. At the time, the Atlantic City casino business was failing. Several casinos were forced to close due to bankruptcy. Hazzard was rehired to restore Atlantic City to the glory years of the Gatti era. This would be an impossible task without Arturo. Ten years after returning to his position, world class boxing is virtually non-existent in Atlantic City. Boxing is barren in the city, with the exception of lower and mid-level club shows.

Pat Lynch continues to look for the next Arturo Gatti but so far he has come up empty. He continues to try and duplicate the once-in-a-lifetime find he enjoyed when Joe brought Arturo to him. Every time Lynch signs a new fighter, he states that the boxer reminds him of Arturo. In reality, the odds of him finding another gem like Gatti are highly unlikely. Lynch has tried to build up his prospects in Atlantic City to recapture that "Thunder" magic, but again, the boxing electricity at Boardwalk Hall abruptly switched off with Arturo's departure and is unlikely to return. The last three fighters that Lynch managed, Glen Tapia, Julian Rodriguez, and Clarence Booth, all failed to reach world title contention. Lynch was inducted into the N.J. Boxing Hall of Fame in 2016. He declined to attend the event, stating that he had previous commitments. He sent Sal Alessi to accept the award on his behalf.

Carl Moretti currently is vice-president of boxing operations for Bob Arum's Top Rank. He maintains a close relationship with Pat Lynch. Kathy Duva still runs Main Events. She partnered with Russell Peltz on an NBC boxing series before it was cancelled. Her promotional company's roster includes former heavyweight champion Evander Holyfield's son Evan, who is 11-1 with 7 KOs. As of this book's completion, Main Events has no world champions on its slim seven-fighter roster.

Pernell "Sweet Pea" Whitaker was killed on July 14, 2019 when he was struck by a car in Virginia Beach. Whitaker was 55 years old. The millions he had earned in the ring had mostly evaporated.

In 2020, Kathy Duva was inducted into the International Boxing Hall of Fame. She followed her father-in-law Lou, who was inducted in 1998, and her husband Dan, who was inducted in 2003.

Amanda still resides in Montreal, as does Ida and all of her children with the exception of Anna-Maria and Joe. Anna-Maria lives in Florida, where she is a real estate agent. Joe and Vikki moved to Florida from New Jersey, where they are helping their daughters pursue their quests to become professional tennis players. Amanda had opened a women's clothing store called AG Boutique in 2013. The business, which was located on Rue Saint-Denis in Montreal, is now permanently closed. Since July 2019 she has worked for Prime luxury auto sales and leasing on Chemin de la Cote-de-Liesse in Montreal.

At the Ring 83 Boxing Club in Montreal, a young Arturo Jr. has been observed taking boxing lessons from Moe Latif. In December 2019, Junior had his first amateur boxing match, winning by 1st round TKO. Maybe, just maybe, Arturo Jr. is thinking of following in his father's footsteps. Perhaps the passion for boxing that flowed through his grandfather, father, and uncle's veins, might someday flow through his veins as well. Vikki Gatti revealed that Amanda told her that she talks to her son every night. *"Every night before Junior goes to bed. She whispers in his ears, exactly who and what they did to his father."*[1827]

On January 3, 2023 Hector Roca passed away at the age of 82. The pain of the vicious accusations levied against Roca years earlier were apparently still fresh in the minds of those who loved Hector. In press interviews with those close to Roca, and again at a memorial service held in his honor at Gleason's Gym by Hector's close friend Bruce Silverglade, Gatti was omitted as one of the fighters that Roca had worked with during his successful career as a trainer.

In central New Jersey, 17-year-old Sofia Bella Gatti is living the life of an average teen. Her appearance is a striking cross between her mother Erika and her father Arturo. Not a day goes by that her father does not cross her mind, even as the memories of the moments she shared with him fade into the hazy memories of childhood.

Arturo traveled hours to bring his daughter butterfly decorations when she was born. Some believe that butterflies represent an ever-abiding presence while others believe that the sight of a butterfly signifies forgiveness, hope and faith or that an angel has been sent to look over you. Sofia is confident that her father, Arturo "Thunder" Gatti, is watching over her and those whom he loved.

Before his battles with Arturo, Micky Ward had cautioned it was yet unknown what heavy price both he and Arturo would pay from the physical damage they both received in their many ring wars.[1828] Within two years of retiring, in 2005, Ward started experiencing symptoms of chronic traumatic encephalopathy (CTE). Ward stated, *"It's terrible. It makes you nauseous, it's like a thump in the back of my head. You just feel drained all day."* Ward added that the headaches wake him up in the middle of the night. He uses over-the-counter medication but confessed that, *"nothing takes it away completely."* Ward works with the Concussion Legacy Foundation on trying to find ways to make sports safer for athletes. He has also agreed to donate his brain and spinal column to the CTE Center at Boston University after his death. He recommends that parents should refrain from allowing their children to participate in boxing and football until the child is at least 14 years old. Ward cautioned, *"If one of the mothers or fathers could get inside my head for a day and know what my head feels like from taking so many blows in boxing. They would think twice about letting their kids get hit under 14 years old."*[1829]

On August 5, 2023, in Florida, Anna-Maria organized a family get-together for her birthday. She wanted to use the occasion to help bring her family closer together. Ida and Fabrizio attended the event, as did Joe, Vikki, Versace, Gianni, Sophia, and Erika Rivera. Joe felt that the tragedy of losing Arturo and the emotions involved had in part fueled the family discord. According to Joe, at Anna-Maria's get-together, he made peace with his mother and his siblings. They were ready to move forward as a family once again.

As of this book's completion, Danny McDermott and Ray McCline, president of the Atlantic City Boxing Hall of Fame, were organizing for a statue of Arturo "Thunder" Gatti to be placed in Atlantic City to honor the man who, for a short time, like a rolling rumble of thunder, single handedly energized the city with a jolt of electrifying excitement that has not been seen since.

ENDNOTES

[1] Interview with Wayne Witkowski 2014.
[2] *Edmonton Sun* July 13, 2009.
[3] Interview with Joe Gatti 2013.
[4] *Winnipeg Sun* July 13, 2009.
[5] *Winnipeg Sun* July 13, 2009.
[6] *Winnipeg Sun* July 13, 2009.
[7] *Winnipeg Sun* July 13, 2009.
[8] Interview with Joe Gatti 2013.
[9] 'Hooks and Splatters' *Sports Illustrated* July 26, 2004.
[10] Interview with Joe Gatti 2013.
[11] Interview with Joe Gatti 2013.
[12] Interview with Joe Gatti 2013.
[13] *NY Daily News* March 21, 1996.
[14] Interview with Joe Gatti 2013.
[15] Interview with Joe Gatti 2013.
[16] Interview with Joe Gatti 2013.
[17] Interview with Joe Gatti 2013.
[18] Interview with Joe Gatti 2013.
[19] *Quebec Star* July 18, 2009.
[20] Interview with Joe Gatti 2013.
[21] Associated Press July 12, 2009.
[22] Interview with Joe Gatti 2013.
[23] *Newark Star Ledger* February 20, 1997.
[24] Interview with Joe Gatti 2013.
[25] Interview with Joe Gatti 2013.
[26] Interview with Joe Gatti 2013.
[27] Interview with Joe Gatti 2013.
[28] *Arturo Gatti: Le Dernier Round* by Jacques Pothier.
[29] *KO* magazine October 1996.
[30] Interview with Joe Gatti 2013.
[31] Interview with Eric Huard 2014.
[32] Interview with Joe Gatti 2013.
[33] *Arturo Gatti: Le Dernier Round* by Jacques Pothier.
[34] Interview with Joe Gatti 2013.
[35] Interview with Joe Gatti 2013.
[36] *Los Angeles Times* November 2, 1988.
[37] Interview with Don Elbaum 2014.
[38] *New York Times* July 7, 1981.
[39] Interview with Mario Costa 2013.
[40] *Montreal Gazette* May 17, 1984.
[41] *Montreal Gazette* May 17, 1984.
[42] *Montreal Gazette* June 4, 1984.
[43] *Jersey Journal* April 27, 1999.
[44] Mario Costa Eulogy Speech for Arturo Gatti, Montreal Canada 2009.
[45] Interview with Mario Costa 2013.
[46] Boxing Insider 2009.
[47] Boxing Insider 2009.
[48] Interview with Mario Costa 2013.
[49] Interview with Mario Costa 2013.
[50] Interview with Mario Costa 2013.
[51] Interview with Joe Gatti 2013.
[52] Interview with Joe Gatti 2013.
[53] *Bergen Record* December 12, 1985.
[54] *Bergen Record* December 12, 1985.
[55] *Bergen Record* December 12, 1985.
[56] *Bergen Record* May 25, 1986.
[57] *Bergen Record* May 25, 1986.
[58] *Bergen Record* May 25, 1986.
[59] *Bergen Record* May 25, 1986.
[60] *Bergen Record* May 25, 1986.
[61] *Newark Star Ledger* February 20, 1997.
[62] *Newark Star Ledger* February 20, 1997.
[63] Interview with Joe Gatti 2013.
[64] Interview with Joe Gatti 2013.
[65] Interview with Joe Gatti 2013.
[66] Interview with Joe Gatti 2013.
[67] Interview with Mike Skowronski 2013.
[68] Interview with Mike Skowronski 2013.
[69] Interview with Mike Skowronski 2013.
[70] Interview with Sal Alessi 2013.
[71] Interview with Pete Maino 2023.
[72] Interview with Pete Maino 2023.
[73] Interview with Sal Alessi 2013.
[74] Interview with Mike Skowronski 2013.
[75] Interview with Mike Skowronski 2013.
[76] Interview with Pete Maino 2023.
[77] Interview with Buddy McGirt 2013.
[78] Interview with Pete Maino 2023.
[79] Interview with Mike Skowronski 2013.
[80] Interview with Sal Alessi 2013.
[81] Interview with Buddy McGirt 2013.
[82] Interview with Buddy McGirt 2013.
[83] Interview with Joe Gatti 2013.
[84] Interview with Mario Costa 2013.
[85] Reg Gutteridge: Commentator known as ITV's 'Voice of Boxing' The Independent January 27, 2009.
[86] Interview with Michael Strange 2013.
[87] Q &A Kathy Duva: 'She's An Incredible Person' by Lem Satterfield July 12, 2010.
[88] *Newark Star Ledger* April 30, 2006.
[89] Q &A Kathy Duva: 'She's An Incredible Person' by Lem Satterfield July 12, 2010.
[90] *Newark Star Ledger* April 30, 2006.
[91] A Fighting Life by Lou Duva with Tim Smith.
[92] Conflicts of Interest by Thomas Hauser SecondsOut.com August 8, 2013.

[93] Conflicts of Interest by Thomas Hauser SecondsOut.com August 8, 2013.
[94] Interview with Andre Kut 2016.
[95] *Newark Star Ledger* July 15, 2009.
[96] Thirty Dollars And A Cut Eye by J. Russell Peltz 2021.
[97] *The Press of Atlantic City* October 23, 1990.
[98] Interview with Michael Strange 2013.
[99] Interview with Joe Gatti 2013.
[100] Interview with Mario Costa 2013.
[101] Interview with Mario Costa 2013.
[102] Interview with Mario Costa 2013.
[103] Interview with Mike Skowronski 2013.
[104] Interview with Pete Maino 2023.
[105] *Jersey Journal* May 4, 1991.
[106] Interview with Mario Costa 2013.
[107] Interview with Joe Gatti 2013.
[108] Interview with Mario Costa 2013.
[109] Interview with Mario Costa 2013.
[110] Interview with Mike Skowronski 2013.
[111] Interview with Vikki Gatti 2013.
[112] Interview with Mike Skowronski 2013.
[113] Interview with Joe Gatti 2013.
[114] Interview with Wayne Witkowski 2014.
[115] Interview with Mario Costa 2013.
[116] *Newark Star Ledger* February 12, 1997.
[117] Interview with Mario Costa 2013.
[118] *Boxing Monthly* September 2002.
[119] *The Bergen Record* June 11, 1991.
[120] Interview with Joe Gatti 2013.
[121] Interview with Mario Costa 2013.
[122] *He's Bloody Good* Sports Illustrated November 6, 2000.
[123] SecondsOut "The Matchmakers" by Thomas Hauser.
[124] *Boxing Examiner* July 11, 2009.
[125] Thirty Dollars And A Cut Eye by J. Russell Peltz 2021.
[126] *Newark Star Ledger* July 15, 2009.
[127] Interview with Donnie Jerie 2014.
[128] Interview with Joe Gatti 2013.
[129] Interview with Joe Gatti 2013.
[130] Interview with Joe Gatti 2013.
[131] Interview with Joe Gatti 2013.
[132] *Newark Star Ledger* April 23, 1992.
[133] ESPN *"Johnny Bumphus..Dies at Age 59"* by Dan Rafael February 5, 2020.
[134] *Boxing Monthly* July 1996.
[135] *Newark Star Ledger* October 6, 2010.
[136] Interview with Joe Gatti 2013.
[137] Interview with Diego Rosario 2013.
[138] Interview with Nasser Nettles 2014.
[139] Mike DePompe quote.
[140] Interview with Diego Rosario 2014.
[141] Interview with Diego Rosario 2014.
[142] Interview with Diego Rosario 2014.
[143] Interview with Diego Rosario 2014.
[144] Interview with Joe Gatti 2013.
[145] *Newark Star Ledger* August 12, 1992.
[146] *Newark Star Ledger* August 12, 1992.
[147] *Newark Star Ledger* August 12, 1992.
[148] *Newark Star Ledger* August 12, 1992.
[149] *Newark Star Ledger* August 12, 1992.
[150] *Newark Star Ledger* August 12, 1992.
[151] *Newark Star Ledger* August 12, 1992.
[152] *Newark Star Ledger* August 12, 1992.
[153] Thirty Dollars And A Cut Eye by J. Russell Peltz 2021.
[154] Interview with Diego Rosario 2014.
[155] Interview with Diego Rosario 2014.
[156] Interview with Russell Peltz 2013.
[157] Interview with Russell Peltz 2013.
[158] *Herald News* July 21, 2006.
[159] Interview with Mike Skowronski 2014.
[160] Interview with Mike Skowronski 2014.
[161] Interview with Diego Rosario 2014.
[162] Interview with Diego Rosario 2014.
[163] Interview with Diego Rosario 2014.
[164] Interview with Mario Costa.
[165] Interview with Joe Gatti 2013.
[166] Interview with Joe Gatti 2013.
[167] *The Sweet Science* Edgar Santana learns boxing from Hector Roca.
[168] Interview with Donnie Jerie 2014.
[169] *Newark Star Ledger* April 30, 2006.
[170] *Newark Star Ledger* April 2, 1993.
[171] *Newark Star Ledger* April 2, 1993.
[172] Interview with Joe Gatti 2013.
[173] Interview with Donnie Jerie 2014.
[174] Interview with Donnie Jerie 2014.
[175] "Don't Stop Believing" by Journey 1981.
[176] *The Matchmakers* by Thomas Hauser June 30, 2006.
[177] Interview with Joe Gatti 2013.
[178] *Newark Star Ledger* September 7, 1998.
[179] Interview with Joe Gatti 2013.
[180] Interview with Mario Costa 2013.
[181] Interview with Mike Skowronski 2014.
[182] Interview with Mario Costa 2013.
[183] Interview with Mike Skowronski 2013.
[184] Interview with Vikki Gatti 2013.
[185] Interview with Vikki Gatti 2013.
[186] Interview with Joe Gatti 2013.

[187] Interview with Joe Gatti 2013.
[188] Interview with Vikki Gatti 2013.
[189] Interview with Vikki Gatti 2013.
[190] Interview with Joe Gatti 2013.
[191] Interview with Mario Costa 2013.
[192] Interview with Mario Costa 2013.
[193] Interview with Mike Skowronski 2013.
[194] Interview with Diego Rosario 2014.
[195] *Newark Star Ledger* October 8, 1994.
[196] *Thirty Dollars And A Cut Eye* by J. Russell Peltz 2021.
[197] Interview with Joe Gatti 2013.
[198] Interview with Joe Gatti 2013.
[199] *Newark Star Ledger* June 29, 1994.
[200] Interview with Buddy McGirt 2013.
[201] Interview with Mario Costa 2013.
[202] Interview with Mario Costa 2013.
[203] Interview with Donnie Jerie 2014.
[204] Interview with Joe Gatti 2013.
[205] Interview with Joe Gatti 2013.
[206] *Newark Star Ledger* October 8, 1994.
[207] *Newark Star Ledger* October 8, 1994.
[208] *The Bergen Record* October 16, 1994.
[209] *Newark Star Ledger* October 8, 1994.
[210] *Newark Star Ledger* October 8, 1994.
[211] *Newark Star Ledger* October 9, 1994.
[212] *Newark Star Ledger* October 9, 1994.
[213] *Newark Star Ledger* October 9, 1994.
[214] *Newark Star Ledger* October 9, 1994.
[215] *Newark Star Ledger* October 9, 1994.
[216] *Philadelphia Daily News* October 24, 1994 by Bernard Fernandez.
[217] *Philadelphia Daily News* October 24, 1994 by Bernard Fernandez.
[218] *Philadelphia Daily News* October 24, 1994 by Bernard Fernandez.
[219] Interview with Sal Alessi 2013.
[220] *The Life and Times of Luis Sarria* by Enrique Encinosa.
[221] Interview with Wayne Witkowski 2014.
[222] *Newark Star Ledger* November 23, 1994.
[223] *Newark Star Ledger* January 16, 1998.
[224] *The Bergen Record* February 12, 1995.
[225] *The Bergen Record* March 12, 1995.
[226] *The Bergen Record* April 30, 1995.
[227] Interview with Buddy McGirt 2013.
[228] Interview with Joe Gatti 2013.
[229] Interview with Joe Gatti 2013.
[230] Interview with Joe Gatti 2013.
[231] Interview with Joe Gatti 2013.
[232] Interview with Joe Gatti 2013.
[233] *Newark Star Ledger* July 13, 1995.
[234] *Newark Star Ledger* July 13, 1995.
[235] *Newark Star Ledger* July 13, 1995.
[236] *The Press of Atlantic City* July 13, 1995.
[237] *The Press of Atlantic City* July 13, 1995.
[238] *Newark Star Ledger* July 13, 1995.
[239] SecondsOut "The Matchmakers" by Thomas Hauser.
[240] Interview with Barrington Francis 2013.
[241] *Newark Star Ledger* July 14, 1995.
[242] *Newark Star Ledger* July 14, 1995.
[243] *Newark Star Ledger* July 14, 1995.
[244] *Newark Star Ledger* July 14, 1995.
[245] Interview with Joe Gatti 2013.
[246] Interview with Donnie Jerie 2013.
[247] *Press of Atlantic City* October 8, 1995.
[248] *New York Times* September 20, 1995.
[249] *Boxing Monthly* July 1996.
[250] HBO interview for Angel Manfredy fight.
[251] *Boxing 96* May 1996.
[252] *Boxing 96* May 1996.
[253] *Boxing 96* May 1996.
[254] *Boxing 96* May 1996.
[255] *Boxing 96* May 1996.
[256] *Boxing 96* May 1996.
[257] *Quebec Star* July 18, 2009.
[258] A&E's *Prenup to Murder: "Arturo Gatti's Final Bout."* March 19, 2013.
[259] Interview with Vikki Gatti 2013.
[260] Interview with Joe Gatti 2013.
[261] Interview with Joe Gatti 2013.
[262] Interview with Vikki Gatti 2013.
[263] *Le Dernier Round* by Jacques Ponthier.
[264] Interview with Lou Duva 2013.
[265] Interview with Joe Gatti 2013.
[266] Interview with Vikki Gatti 2013.
[267] Interview with Sal Alessi 2013.
[268] Interview with Lou Duva 2013.
[269] Interview with Mike Skowronski 2013.
[270] Interview with Donny Jerie 2014.
[271] *Newark Star Ledger* April 30, 2006.
[272] *Bergen Record* February 14, 1996.
[273] *NY Daily News* March 21, 1996.
[274] *NY Daily News* March 21, 1996. Allegedly, the pin would be removed eight months later.
[275] *Newark Star Ledger* March 21, 1996.
[276] *Newark Star Ledger* March 21, 1996.
[277] *Newark Star Ledger* March 21, 1996.
[278] *Newark Star Ledger* March 21, 1996.
[279] *Gatti-Mayweather* Official Program.
[280] HBO interview for Angel Manfredy fight.
[281] *NY Daily News* February 22, 1997.
[282] *KO* magazine October 1996.

283 *NY Daily News* February 22, 1997.
284 *Newark Star Ledger* March 25, 1996.
285 "Gatti's Guts, Devotion will be Missed" by Dan Rafael July 18, 2009.
286 Interview with Donnie Jerie 2014.
287 *USA Today* November 20, 2002.
288 *Boxing Monthly* July 1996.
289 *Boxing Monthly* July 1996.
290 *Boxing Monthly* July 1996.
291 *Boxing Monthly* July 1996.
292 *Boxing Monthly* July 1996.
293 *Boxing Monthly* July 1996.
294 *Boxing Monthly* July 1996.
295 *Boxing Monthly* July 1996.
296 *Boxing Monthly* July 1996.
297 *Boxing Monthly* July 1996.
298 Interview with Donnie Jerie 2014.
299 *KO* magazine October 1996.
300 *KO* magazine October 1996.
301 *KO* magazine October 1996.
302 *KO* magazine October 1996.
303 *KO* magazine October 1996.
304 *KO* magazine October 1996.
305 *KO* magazine October 1996.
306 Interview with Donnie Jerie 2014.
307 *KO* magazine October 1996.
308 *KO* magazine October 1996.
309 *KO* magazine October 1996.
310 *KO* magazine October 1996.
311 *KO* magazine October 1996.
312 *KO* magazine October 1996.
313 *KO* magazine October 1996.
314 *Newark Star Ledger* July 12, 1996.
315 *Newark Star Ledger* July 12, 1996.
316 Interview with Joe Gatti 2013.
317 Interview with Joe Gatti 2013.
318 Interview with Donny Jerie 2014.
319 *Newark Star Ledger* August 16, 1996.
320 Interview with Donny Jerie 2014.
321 *Newark Star Ledger* September 27, 1996.
322 *Newark Star Ledger* September 27, 1996.
323 *New York Times* January 15, 1997 by Frank Litsky.
324 *New York Times* January 15, 1997 by Frank Litsky.
325 *Newark Star Ledger* February 22, 1997.
326 *Atlantic City Press* January 15, 1997.
327 *Atlantic City Press* January 15, 1997.
328 *Atlantic City Press* January 15, 1997.
329 *Atlantic City Press* January 15, 1997.
330 *Newark Star Ledger* February 22, 1997.
331 Interview with Ivan Robinson June 2013.
332 Interview with Joe Gatti 2013.
333 *Newark Star Ledger* February 20, 1997.
334 *Newark Star Ledger* February 20, 1997.
335 *Atlantic City Press* February 20, 1997.
336 *Atlantic City Press* February 20, 1997.
337 *Atlantic City Press* February 21, 1997.
338 *Atlantic City Press* February 21, 1997.
339 *Atlantic City Press* February 21, 1997.
340 *Atlantic City Press* February 22, 1997.
341 *Atlantic City Press* February 22, 1997.
342 *Atlantic City Press* February 22, 1997.
343 *Atlantic City Press* February 24, 1997.
344 *KO* magazine July, 1997.
345 *KO* magazine July, 1997.
346 *KO* magazine July, 1997.
347 *KO* magazine July, 1997.
348 *Atlantic City Press* February 24, 1997.
349 *Atlantic City Press* February 24, 1997.
350 *Atlantic City Press* February 24, 1997.
351 *KO* magazine July, 1997.
352 *KO* magazine July, 1997.
353 *KO* magazine July, 1997.
354 *KO* magazine July, 1997.
355 *Newark Star Ledger* May 4, 1997.
356 *Newark Star Ledger* May 4, 1997.
357 *Press of Atlantic City* May 4, 1997.
358 *Press of Atlantic City* May 5, 1997.
359 *Press of Atlantic City* May 5, 1997.
360 *Press of Atlantic City* May 5, 1997.
361 Interview with Joe Gatti 2013.
362 Interview with Vikki Gatti 2013.
363 Interview with Joe Gatti 2013.
364 Interview with Donny Jerie 2014.
365 Interview with Omar Hernandez 2014.
366 Interview with Omar Hernandez 2014.
367 Interview with Omar Hernandez 2014.
368 Interview with Omar Hernandez 2014.
369 Interview with Omar Hernandez 2014.
370 Interview with Omar Hernandez 2014.
371 Interview with Omar Hernandez 2014.
372 Interview with William Peer 2014.
373 Interview with Omar Hernandez 2014.
374 Interview with Omar Hernandez 2014.
375 *Newark Star Ledger* July 3, 1997.
376 Interview with Joe Gatti 2013.
377 Interview with Joe Gatti 2013.

[378] Interview with Joe Gatti 2013.
[379] Interview with Vikki Gatti 2013.
[380] Interview with Joe Gatti 2013.
[381] Interview with Donny Jerie 2014.
[382] Interview with Donny Jerie 2014.
[383] Interview with Joe Gatti 2013.
[384] Interview with Joe Gatti 2013.
[385] Interview with Joe Gatti 2013.
[386] Interview with Joe Gatti 2013.
[387] *Newark Star Ledger* October 4, 1997.
[388] *Newark Star Ledger* October 4, 1997.
[389] Interview with Joe Gatti 2013.
[390] Interview with Vikki Gatti 2013.
[391] Interview with Vikki Gatti 2013.
[392] Interview with Vikki Gatti 2013.
[393] Interview with Vikki Gatti 2013.
[394] Interview with Joe Gatti 2013.
[395] *New York Times* May 19, 1995.
[396] *Boxing News* October 10, 1997.
[397] Eastside Boxing Gabriel Ruelas Interview by James Slater July 31, 2009.
[398] *New York Times* January 15, 1998.
[399] Interview with Mario Costa 2013.
[400] Interview with Mario Costa 2013.
[401] Macho: The Hector Camacho Story. 2020
[402] HotBoxin' with Mike Tyson. November 11, 2020.
[403] *Atlantic City Press* October 1, 1997.
[404] *Atlantic City Press* October 2, 1997.
[405] *Chicago-Sun Times* October 2, 1997.
[406] *Chicago-Sun Times* October 2, 1997.
[407] *Atlantic City Press* October 4, 1997.
[408] *Atlantic City Press* October 4, 1997.
[409] *KO* magazine February 1998.
[410] *Newark Star Ledger* September 28, 1997.
[411] HBO interview for Angel Manfredy fight.
[412] HBO interview for Angel Manfredy fight.
[413] Interview with Benjy Esteves 2013.
[414] *Gatti-Mayweather* Official Program.
[415] *Atlantic City Press* October 5, 1997.
[416] *Press of Atlantic City* October 5, 1997.
[417] *Boxing News* October 10, 1997.
[418] *KO* magazine February 1998.
[419] *KO* magazine February 1998.
[420] Interview with Mario Costa 2013.
[421] Eastside Boxing Gabriel Ruelas Interview by James Slater July 31, 2009.
[422] MaxBoxing.com "Exciting Gatti Gives Fans Their Moneys Worth" by Thomas Gerbasi July 21, 2004.
[423] HBO Interview for Angel Manfredy fight.
[424] Murphy 2002 Pg. 143.
[425] Interview with Donnie Jerie 2014.
[426] Interview with Donnie Jerie 2014.
[427] *Le Dernier Round* by Jacques Ponthier.
[428] Interview with Joe Gatti 2013.
[429] Interview with Joe Gatti 2013.
[430] Interview with Joe Gatti 2013.
[431] *Press of Atlantic City* January 15, 1998.
[432] *Press of Atlantic City* January 15, 1998.
[433] *New York Times* January 15, 1998.
[434] *New York Times* January 15, 1998.
[435] *New York Times* January 15, 1998.
[436] *Press of Atlantic City* January 16, 1998.
[437] *Press of Atlantic City* January 16, 1998.
[438] *Press of Atlantic City* January 16, 1998.
[439] *Boxing News* January 16, 1998.
[440] *To Hell and Back* Gatti-Manfredy Official Program.
[441] *To Hell and Back* Gatti-Manfredy Official Program.
[442] *To Hell and Back* Gatti-Manfredy Official Program.
[443] *To Hell and Back* Gatti-Manfredy Official Program.
[444] *To Hell and Back* Gatti-Manfredy Official Program.
[445] *To Hell and Back* Gatti-Manfredy Official Program.
[446] *Press of Atlantic City* January 17, 1998.
[447] *Press of Atlantic City* January 17, 1998.
[448] *Press of Atlantic City* January 17, 1998.
[449] *Press of Atlantic City* January 17, 1998.
[450] *Press of Atlantic City* January 17, 1998.
[451] *Press of Atlantic City* January 18, 1998.
[452] *New York Times* January 15, 1998.
[453] Interview with Joe Gatti 2013.
[454] Interview with Joe Gatti 2013.
[455] *Newark Star Ledger* January 16, 1998.
[456] *Newark Star Ledger* January 16, 1998.
[457] *Newark Star Ledger* January 16, 1998.
[458] *Newark Star Ledger* January 16, 1998.
[459] *New York Times* January 17, 1998.
[460] *New York Times* January 17, 1998.
[461] *New York Times* January 17, 1998.
[462] *Boxing Monthly* May 1998.
[463] HBO prefight interview for Angel Manfredy fight.
[464] Interview with Mike Skowronski 2013.
[465] HBO prefight interview for Angel Manfredy fight.
[466] Interview with Joe Gatti 2013.
[467] Interview with Vikki Gatti 2013.
[468] Interview with Joe Gatti 2013.
[469] Interview with Joe Gatti 2013.
[470] *Ring* magazine Summer 2005.
[471] *Press of Atlantic City* January 18, 1998.
[472] *Press of Atlantic City* January 18, 1998.
[473] *Press of Atlantic City* January 19, 1998.

[474] *Newark Star Ledger* January 18, 1998.
[475] *Newark Star Ledger* January 19, 1998.
[476] *New York Times* January 19, 1998.
[477] Interview with Vikki Gatti 2013.
[478] Interview with Joe Gatti 2013.
[479] Interview with Joe Gatti 2013.
[480] Interview with Mario Costa 2013.
[481] Interview with Mario Costa 2013.
[482] Interview with Mike Skowronski 2013.
[483] Interview with Joe Gatti 2013.
[484] Interview with Donny Jerie 2014.
[485] Interview with Steve Sandoval 2014.
[486] Interview with Steve Sandoval 2014.
[487] Interview with Mario Costa 2013.
[488] Interview with Steve Sandoval 2014.
[489] Interview with Steve Sandoval 2014.
[490] Interview with Steve Sandoval 2023.
[491] Interview with Joe Gatti 2013.
[492] Interview with Joe Gatti 2013.
[493] Statement by Mike DePompe.
[494] Interview with Joe Gatti 2013.
[495] Interview with Mike Skowronski 2013.
[496] Interview with Mike Skowronski 2013.
[497] Interview with Mike Skowronski 2013.
[498] Interview with Mike Skowronski 2013.
[499] *Le Dernier Round* by Jacques Ponthier.
[500] Interview with Mike Skowronski 2013.
[501] *New York Times* January 19, 1998.
[502] Interview with Donny Jerie 2014.
[503] Interview with Donny Jerie 2014.
[504] Interview with Donny Jerie 2014.
[505] *Miami Herald* April 27, 1998.
[506] Police Incident Report.
[507] Police Incident Report.
[508] Police Incident Report.
[509] Police Incident Report.
[510] Police Incident Report.
[511] Police Incident Report.
[512] Police Incident Report.
[513] Police Incident Report.
[514] Police Incident Report.
[515] *Miami Herald* April 27, 1998.
[516] *Le Dernier Round* by Jacques Ponthier.
[517] *Newark Star Ledger* June 21, 1998.
[518] *Newark Star Ledger* June 21, 1998.
[519] Interview with Ron Katz 2014.
[520] Interview with Mario Costa 2013.
[521] Interview with Dan Goosen 2013.
[522] Interview with Donnie Jerie 2014.
[523] *Newark Star Ledger* July 14, 1998.
[524] *Newark Star Ledger* July 14, 1998.
[525] *Newark Star Ledger* July 14, 1998.
[526] *Newark Star Ledger* July 14, 1998.
[527] *Newark Star Ledger* July 14, 1998.
[528] *Newark Star Ledger* August 23, 1998.
[529] Interview with Mario Costa 2013.
[530] *Newark Star Ledger* June 19, 2005.
[531] *Newark Star Ledger* June 19, 2005.
[532] *Press of Atlantic City* August 24, 1998.
[533] *Press of Atlantic City* August 21, 1998.
[534] *Press of Atlantic City* August 22, 1998.
[535] *Press of Atlantic City* August 22, 1998.
[536] Interview with Mike Skowronski 2013.
[537] *Press of Atlantic City* August 22, 1998.
[538] *Press of Atlantic City* August 22, 1998.
[539] Interview with Ivan Robinson 2013.
[540] *Le Dernier Round* by Jacques Ponthier.
[541] *Le Dernier Round* by Jacques Ponthier.
[542] *Gatti vs. Robinson* Official Program.
[543] *Gatti vs. Robinson* Official Program.
[544] *Gatti vs. Robinson* Official Program.
[545] *Gatti vs. Robinson* Official Program.
[546] *Gatti vs. Robinson* Official Program.
[547] *Gatti vs. Robinson* Official Program.
[548] *Gatti vs. Robinson* Official Program.
[549] *Gatti vs. Robinson* Official Program.
[550] *Boxing Monthly* October 1998.
[551] *Le Dernier Round* by Jacques Ponthier.
[552] Interview with Ivan Robinson 2013.
[553] Interview with Ivan Robinson 2013.
[554] *Newark Star Ledger* August 24, 1998.
[555] *Press of Atlantic City* August 24, 1998.
[556] *Press of Atlantic City* August 24, 1998.
[557] *Press of Atlantic City* August 24, 1998.
[558] *Boxing Monthly* October 1998.
[559] *Boxing Monthly* October 1998.
[560] *Newark Star Ledger* August 24, 1998.
[561] *Newark Star Ledger* August 24, 1998.
[562] Interview with Vikki Gatti 2013.
[563] Interview with Joe Gatti 2013.
[564] Interview with Joe Gatti 2013.
[565] Interview with Mike Skowronski 2013.
[566] *Boxing News* December 11, 1998.
[567] *Boxing News* December 11, 1998.
[568] *Boxing Monthly* October 1998.
[569] *Newark Star Ledger* September 7, 1998.

[570] *Bergen Record* October 4, 1998.
[571] Interview with Donny Jerie 2013.
[572] *Le Dernier Round* by Jacques Ponthier.
[573] *Newark Star Ledger* June 19, 2005.
[574] *Newark Star Ledger* June 19, 2005.
[575] *Newark Star Ledger* November 3, 1998.
[576] *Press of Atlantic City* December 11, 1998.
[577] *Press of Atlantic City* December 11, 1998.
[578] *It Had to Happen Again* Gatti-Robinson II Official Program.
[579] Interview with Lou Duva 2013.
[580] *Press of Atlantic City* December 11, 1998.
[581] *Press of Atlantic City* December 11, 1998.
[582] *It Had to Happen Again* Gatti-Robinson II Official Program.
[583] *It Had to Happen Again* Gatti-Robinson II Official Program.
[584] *It Had to Happen Again* Gatti-Robinson II Official Program.
[585] *Press of Atlantic City* December 12, 1998.
[586] *Press of Atlantic City* December 12, 1998.
[587] *Press of Atlantic City* December 12, 1998.
[588] *It Had to Happen Again* Gatti-Robinson II Official Program.
[589] *It Had to Happen Again* Gatti-Robinson II Official Program.
[590] Interview with Benjy Esteves 2013.
[591] Interview with Benjy Esteves 2013.
[592] HBO Sports
[593] *Press of Atlantic City* December 14, 1998.
[594] *Press of Atlantic City* December 13, 1998.
[595] *Le Dernier Round* by Jacques Ponthier.
[596] *Press of Atlantic City* December 14, 1998.
[597] *Boxing 99* May 1999.
[598] *Boxing 99* May 1999.
[599] *Boxing 99* May 1999.
[600] *Boxing 99* May 1999.
[601] *Boxing 99* May 1999.
[602] *Boxing 99* May 1999.
[603] Interview with Mario Costa 2013.
[604] Interview with Vikki Gatti 2013.
[605] Interview with Joe Gatti 2013.
[606] Interview with Joe Gatti 2013.
[607] Interview with Vikki Gatti 2013.
[608] Interview with Joe Gatti 2013.
[609] Interview with Donny Jerie 2013.
[610] Interview with Donny Jerie 2013.
[611] Interview with Donny Jerie 2013.
[612] Interview with Donny Jerie 2013.
[613] Interview with Donny Jerie 2013.
[614] Interview with Donny Jerie 2013.
[615] Interview with Donny Jerie 2013.
[616] Interview with Donny Jerie 2013.
[617] *Jersey Journal* March 24, 1999.
[618] *Jersey Journal* March 24, 1999.
[619] Interview with Joe Gatti 2013.
[620] Interview with Vikki Gatti 2013.
[621] Interview with Joe Gatti 2013.
[622] Interview with Joe Gatti 2013.
[623] Interview with Joe Gatti 2013.
[624] Interview with Joe Gatti 2013.
[625] Interview with Joe Gatti 2013.
[626] Interview with Joe Gatti 2013.
[627] Interview with Joe Gatti 2013.
[628] Interview with Vikki Gatti 2013.
[629] *KO* magazine November 1999.
[630] *KO* magazine November 1999.
[631] *KO* magazine November 1999.
[632] *KO* magazine November 1999.
[633] *KO* magazine November 1999.
[634] *KO* magazine November 1999.
[635] *KO* magazine November 1999.
[636] *KO* magazine November 1999.
[637] *KO* magazine November 1999.
[638] *KO* magazine November 1999.
[639] *Jersey Journal* August 6, 1999.
[640] *Jersey Journal* August 6, 1999.
[641] *Jersey Journal* August 6, 1999.
[642] *New York Times* August 18, 1999.
[643] *New York Times* August 16, 1999.
[644] Interview with Mike Skowronski 2013.
[645] Interview with Donnie Jerie 2013.
[646] *Jersey Journal* August 23, 1999.
[647] Interview with Joe & Vikki Gatti 2013.
[648] *Newark Star Ledger* April 30, 2006.
[649] *Newark Star Ledger* December 5, 1999.
[650] *Newark Star Ledger* December 5, 1999.
[651] *Newark Star Ledger* December 5, 1999.
[652] *Newark Star Ledger* December 5, 1999.
[653] *Newark Star Ledger* December 5, 1999.
[654] *Newark Star Ledger* December 5, 1999.
[655] *Newark Star Ledger* December 5, 1999.
[656] *Newark Star Ledger* December 5, 1999.
[657] *Jersey Journal* December 16, 1999.
[658] *Jersey Journal* December 16, 1999.
[659] *Jersey Journal* December 16, 1999.
[660] *Jersey Journal* December 16, 1999.
[661] *Le Dernier Round* by Jacques Ponthier.
[662] Interview with Vikki Gatti 2013.
[663] *Jersey Journal* February 9, 2000.
[664] *Newark Star Ledger* February 6, 2000.
[665] *Jersey Journal* February 17, 2000.

[666] *Jersey Journal* February 17, 2000.
[667] *Jersey Journal* February 17, 2000.
[668] *Jersey Journal* February 17, 2000.
[669] *Jersey Journal* February 17, 2000.
[670] *Jersey Journal* February 17, 2000.
[671] *Jersey Journal* February 17, 2000.
[672] *Jersey Journal* February 17, 2000.
[673] *Jersey Journal* February 17, 2000.
[674] *Le Dernier Round* by Jacques Ponthier.
[675] *New York Times* March 9, 2000.
[676] *Newark Star Ledger* February 26, 2000.
[677] *Newark Star Ledger* February 26, 2000.
[678] Interview with Scott DePompe 2014.
[679] *New York Times* March 11, 2000.
[680] *New Jersey Monthly* 2006.
[681] *Newark Star Ledger* March 12, 2000.
[682] *Jersey Journal* March 17, 2000.
[683] Interview with Joe Gatti 2013.
[684] Interview with Donny Jerie 2014.
[685] *Ring* magazine April 2003.
[686] *Ring* magazine April 2003.
[687] *Ring* magazine April 2003.
[688] *Sports Illustrated* July 26, 2004.
[689] Interview with Joe Gatti 2013.
[690] Interview with Joe Gatti 2013.
[691] Interview with Donnie Jerie 2014.
[692] Interview with Vikki Gatti 2013.
[693] Interview with Joe Gatti 2013.
[694] Interview with Joe Gatti 2013.
[695] Interview with Vikki Gatti 2013.
[696] Interview with Vikki Gatti 2013.
[697] Interview with Vikki Gatti 2013.
[698] Interview with Joe Gatti 2013.
[699] Interview with Joe Gatti 2013.
[700] Interview with Joe Gatti 2013.
[701] Interview with Vikki Gatti 2013.
[702] Interview with Joe Gatti 2013.
[703] Interview with Joe Gatti 2013.
[704] Interview with Joe Gatti 2013.
[705] Interview with Joe Gatti 2013.
[706] Interview with Joe Gatti 2013.
[707] Interview with Joe Gatti 2013.
[708] Interview with Joe Gatti 2013.
[709] Interview with Joe Gatti 2013.
[710] Interview with Vikki Gatti 2013.
[711] Interview with Joe Gatti 2013.
[712] Interview with Vikki Gatti 2013.
[713] Interview with Joe Gatti 2013.
[714] Interview with Mario Costa 2014.
[715] *Jersey Journal* April 4, 2000.
[716] *Jersey Journal* April 4, 2000.
[717] *Jersey Journal* April 14, 2000.
[718] *Jersey Journal* April 14, 2000.
[719] *Jersey Journal* April 21, 2000.
[720] *Jersey Journal* April 21, 2000.
[721] *Jersey Journal* April 21, 2000.
[722] *Jersey Journal* April 21, 2000.
[723] *Jersey Journal* April 21, 2000.
[724] *Jersey Journal* April 29, 2000.
[725] *Jersey Journal* April 29, 2000.
[726] *Jersey Journal* May 1, 2000.
[727] *Jersey Journal* May 1, 2000.
[728] *Jersey Journal* May 1, 2000.
[729] *Wonder of Thunder* by Wayne McCullough July 14, 2009.
[730] *Jersey Journal* May 1, 2000.
[731] *Jersey Journal* June 22, 2000.
[732] *Jersey Journal* September 7, 2000.
[733] *Le Dernier Round* by Jacques Ponthier.
[734] *Le Dernier Round* by Jacques Ponthier.
[735] *Jersey Journal* September 1, 2000.
[736] ESPN 2 Pre-fight Interview.
[737] ESPN 2 Pre-fight Interview.
[738] *Thirty Dollars And A Cut Eye* by J. Russell Peltz 2021.
[739] *Arturo Gatti: Le Dernier Round* by Jacques Pothier.
[740] Interview with Joe Gatti 2013.
[741] *Sports Illustrated* November 6, 2000.
[742] *Arturo Gatti: Le Dernier Round* by Jacques Pothier.
[743] *Arturo Gatti: Le Dernier Round* by Jacques Pothier.
[744] *Jersey Journal* December 2, 2000.
[745] *Sports Illustrated* November 6, 2000.
[746] *Sports Illustrated* November 6, 2000.
[747] *Jersey Journal* November 6, 2000.
[748] Interview with Mike Skowronski 2014.
[749] *Newark Star Ledger* February 4, 2001.
[750] Interview with Joe Gatti 2013.
[751] Interview with Joe Gatti 2013.
[752] *Newark Star Ledger* December 10, 2000.
[753] *Jersey Journal* December 2, 2000.
[754] Interview with Mike Skowronski 2014.
[755] *Jersey Journal* February 8, 2001.
[756] *Montreal Gazette* March 2, 2001.
[757] *Montreal Gazette* March 2, 2001.
[758] *Montreal Gazette* March 2, 2001.
[759] *Bergen Record* July 20, 2006.
[760] *Jersey Journal* March 23, 2001.
[761] *Jersey Journal* March 23, 2001.

[762] *Jersey Journal* March 23, 2001.
[763] *Jersey Journal* March 24, 2001.
[764] *Newark Star Ledger* March 23, 2001.
[765] Interview with Buddy McGirt 2013.
[766] Interview with Joe Gatti 2014.
[767] *De La Hoya vs. Gatti* Official Program.
[768] *De La Hoya vs. Gatti* Official Program.
[769] *Newark Star Ledger* February 25, 2001.
[770] *Newark Star Ledger* March 23, 2001.
[771] *Boxing News* March 30, 2001.
[772] CBS Sports March 22, 2001.
[773] CBC News March 17, 2001; *Montreal Globe and Mail* May 10, 2001.
[774] CBS Sports March 22, 2001.
[775] CBS Sports March 22, 2001.
[776] Interview with Mike Skowronski 2014.
[777] *Boxing Monthly* May 2001.
[778] *Newark Star Ledger* March 25, 2001.
[779] *Newark Star Ledger* March 25, 2001.
[780] Interview with Joe Gatti 2014.
[781] *Jersey Journal* March 26, 2001.
[782] Interview with Mike Skowronski 2014.
[783] Interview with Steve Sandoval 2014.
[784] Interview with Steve Sandoval 2014.
[785] Interview with Steve Sandoval 2014.
[786] Mario Costa Interview with Mark Malinowski 2013.
[787] Interview with Joe Gatti 2014.
[788] Interview with Mario Costa 2013.
[789] *Jersey Journal* May 1, 2001.
[790] *Newark Star Ledger* April 15, 2001.
[791] *Newark Star Ledger* April 15, 2001.
[792] *Newark Star Ledger* April 15, 2001.
[793] *Newark Star Ledger* April 15, 2001.
[794] *Newark Star Ledger* April 15, 2001.
[795] *Newark Star Ledger* April 15, 2001.
[796] *Newark Star Ledger* April 15, 2001.
[797] *Newark Star Ledger* April 15, 2001.
[798] *Newark Star Ledger* April 15, 2001.
[799] *Newark Star Ledger* April 15, 2001.
[800] *Newark Star Ledger* June 21, 2005.
[801] *Newark Star Ledger* June 19, 2005.
[802] *Herald News* July 24, 2004.
[803] *Jersey Journal* July 25, 2001.
[804] Interview with Joe Gatti and Vikki Gatti 2014.
[805] Interview with Teddy Cruz 2013.
[806] Interview with Teddy Cruz 2013.
[807] Interview with Teddy Cruz 2013.
[808] Interview with Teddy Cruz 2013.
[809] Interview with Teddy Cruz 2013.
[810] Interview with Teddy Cruz 2013.
[811] *Jersey Journal* December 13, 2001.
[812] *Jersey Journal* December 26, 2001.
[813] *Jersey Journal* December 26, 2001.
[814] *Jersey Journal* December 26, 2001.
[815] *Jersey Journal* December 26, 2001.
[816] Mike Skowronski Interview 2013.
[817] *Jersey Journal* January 15, 2002.
[818] Interview with Vikki Gatti 2014.
[819] *Jersey Journal* January 24, 2002.
[820] *Jersey Journal* January 24, 2002.
[821] *Jersey Journal* January 24, 2002.
[822] *Jersey Journal* January 24, 2002.
[823] *Jersey Journal* January 24, 2002.
[824] *World Boxing* July 2002.
[825] *Jersey Journal* January 28, 2002.
[826] *World Boxing* July 2002.
[827] *World Boxing* July 2002.
[828] *World Boxing* July 2002.
[829] *World Boxing* July 2002.
[830] *World Boxing* July 2002.
[831] *World Boxing* July 2002.
[832] *Boxing Monthly* November 2002.
[833] *Boston Globe* March 10, 2002.
[834] *Boston Globe* March 24, 2002.
[835] *Boston Globe* March 26, 2002.
[836] Interview with Buddy McGirt 2013.
[837] Interview with Buddy McGirt 2013.
[838] Interview with Buddy McGirt 2013.
[839] Interview with Buddy McGirt 2013.
[840] *Boston Globe* May 12, 2002.
[841] *Boston Globe* May 12, 2002.
[842] *Boston Globe* May 12, 2002.
[843] *Boston Globe* May 18, 2002.
[844] *Boxing Monthly* November 2002.
[845] Interview with Mike Skowronski 2014.
[846] *The Ring* October 2002.
[847] *The Ring* November 2003.
[848] Interview with Mike Skowronski 2014.
[849] *Maxim* March 2010.
[850] *Maxim* March 2010.
[851] *Boston Globe* May 19, 2002.
[852] *The Ring* October 2002.
[853] *The Ring* October 2002.
[854] *Boston Globe* May 20, 2002.
[855] *Boxing Monthly* November 2002.
[856] *Boston Globe* May 22, 2002.
[857] *Bergen Record* June 2, 2002.

[858] *Bergen Record* June 2, 2002.
[859] *Bergen Record* June 2, 2002.
[860] *Bergen Record* June 2, 2002.
[861] *Bergen Record* June 2, 2002.
[862] *Boxing Monthly* September 2002.
[863] *Boxing Monthly* September 2002.
[864] *Boxing Monthly* September 2002.
[865] *Boxing Monthly* September 2002.
[866] *Boxing Monthly* September 2002.
[867] *Boxing Monthly* September 2002.
[868] *Boxing Monthly* September 2002.
[869] *Boxing Monthly* September 2002.
[870] *Boxing Monthly* September 2002.
[871] *Boxing Monthly* September 2002.
[872] Interview with Teddy Cruz 2013.
[873] Interview with Joe Gatti 2013.
[874] *Herald News* September 2, 2005.
[875] *Press of Atlantic City* August 29, 2002.
[876] *Press of Atlantic City* August 29, 2002.
[877] *Press of Atlantic City* August 29, 2002.
[878] *Boston Globe* September 8, 2002.
[879] *USA Today* November 20, 2002.
[880] *USA Today* November 20, 2002.
[881] *USA Today* November 20, 2002.
[882] *USA Today* November 20, 2002.
[883] *Boxing Monthly* November 2002.
[884] *The Ring* December 2002.
[885] *Ring* magazine April 2003.
[886] *Boxing Monthly* November 2002.
[887] *KO* magazine May 2003.
[888] *Boxing Monthly* November 2002.
[889] *Boxing Monthly* November 2002.
[890] *Jersey Journal* November 21, 2002.
[891] *Jersey Journal* November 21, 2002.
[892] *Boxing Monthly* November 2002.
[893] *Ward-Gatti II* Official Program.
[894] *Boxing Monthly* November 2002.
[895] *Press of Atlantic City* November 23, 2002.
[896] *Washington Post* November 23, 2002.
[897] *Boston Globe* November 23, 2002.
[898] *Boxing News* November 22, 2002.
[899] *Washington Post* November 23, 2002.
[900] *Boston Globe* November 23, 2002.
[901] Interview with Michael Nestor 2013.
[902] Interview with Mike Skowronski 2013.
[903] *Jersey Journal* November 25, 2002.
[904] *USA Today* November 26, 2002.
[905] *Jersey Journal* November 25, 2002.
[906] *Jersey Journal* November 25, 2002.
[907] *Press of Atlantic City* November 25, 2002.
[908] *Press of Atlantic City* November 25, 2002.
[909] *Press of Atlantic City* November 25, 2002.
[910] *Boston Globe* November 24, 2002.
[911] *Boston Globe* December 15, 2002.
[912] *Boston Globe* November 25, 2002.
[913] *KO* magazine May 2003.
[914] *Boston Globe* July 12, 2009.
[915] *USA Today* November 26, 2002.
[916] *KO* magazine May 2003.
[917] *KO* magazine May 2003.
[918] *Boston Globe* November 29, 2002.
[919] Interview with Paul Dunleavy 2022.
[920] *Newark Star Ledger* February 2, 2003.
[921] *Newark Star Ledger* March 2, 2003.
[922] *Newark Star Ledger* February 2, 2003.
[923] *Newark Star Ledger* March 16, 2003.
[924] *Newark Star Ledger* March 16, 2003.
[925] *Newark Star Ledger* March 16, 2003.
[926] *Newark Star Ledger* March 16, 2003.
[927] *Newark Star Ledger* March 16, 2003.
[928] *KO* magazine May 2003.
[929] *Herald News* April 8, 2003.
[930] *Herald News* April 11, 2003.
[931] *Boston Globe* April 6, 2003.
[932] *Boston Globe* April 6, 2003.
[933] *Boston Globe* April 6, 2003.
[934] *Boston Globe* April 6, 2003.
[935] *Press of Atlantic City* April 8, 2003.
[936] *Press of Atlantic City* April 8, 2003.
[937] *Boston Globe* April 20, 2003.
[938] NY Fights "A Response to the Thomas Hauser Story On How Arturo Died" September 30, 2020 by Peter Carvill.
[939] *KO* magazine May 2003.
[940] *Newark Star Ledger* May 25, 2003.
[941] *Newark Star Ledger* June 6, 2003.
[942] *Newark Star Ledger* June 6, 2003.
[943] *Herald News* June 6, 2003.
[944] *Herald News* June 6, 2003.
[945] *Boston Globe* June 6, 2003.
[946] *Boston Globe* June 7, 2003.
[947] *Press of Atlantic City* June 6, 2003.
[948] *Press of Atlantic City* June 6, 2003.
[949] *Press of Atlantic City* June 6, 2003.
[950] *Press of Atlantic City* June 13, 2003.
[951] *Sports Illustrated* June 16, 2003.
[952] *Sports Illustrated* June 16, 2003.
[953] *Press of Atlantic City* June 9, 2003.

[954] Interview with Mike Skowronski 2013.
[955] *Press of Atlantic City* June 8, 2003.
[956] *Press of Atlantic City* June 9, 2003.
[957] ESPN's E:60 "Death of a Champion" November 11, 2009.
[958] *Press of Atlantic City* June 8, 2003.
[959] *The Ring* November 2003.
[960] *Press of Atlantic City* June 8, 2003.
[961] *Newark Star Ledger* July 13, 2009.
[962] *Boston Globe* June 9, 2003.
[963] *Boston Globe* June 9, 2003.
[964] *Boston Globe* June 9, 2003.
[965] *Boston Globe* June 9, 2003.
[966] *Press of Atlantic City* June 8, 2003.
[967] *Boston Globe* June 9, 2003.
[968] *Boston Globe* June 9, 2003.
[969] *Boston Globe* June 9, 2003.
[970] *Boston Globe* June 9, 2003.
[971] *Boxing Digest* August 2003.
[972] *Jersey Journal* June 9, 2003.
[973] *New York Times* June 9, 2003.
[974] *New York Times* June 9, 2003.
[975] *The Ring* November 2003.
[976] *The Ring* November 2003.
[977] *Herald News* June 9, 2003.
[978] *Herald News* June 9, 2003.
[979] *Newark Star Ledger* June 15, 2003.
[980] *Newark Star Ledger* June 15, 2003.
[981] Interview with Steven Sandoval 2015.
[982] *KO* Winter 2003.
[983] *KO* Winter 2003.
[984] *KO* Winter 2003.
[985] *KO* Winter 2003.
[986] *KO* Winter 2003.
[987] *KO* Winter 2003.
[988] *KO* Winter 2003.
[989] *KO* Winter 2003.
[990] *KO* Winter 2003.
[991] *KO* Winter 2003.
[992] *KO* Winter 2003.
[993] *KO* Winter 2003.
[994] *KO* Winter 2003.
[995] *KO* Winter 2003.
[996] *KO* Winter 2003.
[997] *KO* Winter 2003.
[998] *Newark Star Ledger* October 12, 2003.
[999] *Newark Star Ledger* November 9, 2003.
[1000] *Newark Star Ledger* November 16, 2003.
[1001] *New York Times* November 12, 2003.
[1002] *Herald News* Friday November 14, 2003.
[1003] *Boston Globe* November 13, 2003.
[1004] *KO* February 2004.
[1005] *KO* February 2004.
[1006] *The Ring* March 2004.
[1007] *The Ring* March 2004.
[1008] *The Ring* March 2004.
[1009] *The Ring* March 2004.
[1010] *Herald News* January 22, 2004.
[1011] *Herald News* January 22, 2004.
[1012] *Esquire* December 17, 2010.
[1013] *Herald News* January 16, 2004.
[1014] *Jersey Journal* January 21, 2004.
[1015] *The Record* January 22, 2004.
[1016] *The Record* January 22, 2004.
[1017] *Boxing Monthly* March 2004.
[1018] *Herald News* January 22, 2004.
[1019] *Gatti-Branco* Official Program.
[1020] *Gatti-Branco* Official Program.
[1021] *Press of Atlantic City* January 23, 2004.
[1022] Interview with Omar Sheika 2014.
[1023] *Press of Atlantic City* January 24, 2004.
[1024] *Press of Atlantic City* January 24, 2004.
[1025] *Jersey Journal* January 28, 2004.
[1026] *The Record* January 26, 2004.
[1027] *Jersey Journal* January 28, 2004.
[1028] *Boxing News* January 30, 2004.
[1029] *Boxing News* January 30, 2004.
[1030] *Boxing Monthly* March 2004.
[1031] *Herald News* May 2, 2004.
[1032] Interview with Joe Gatti 2013.
[1033] *Arturo Gatti: Le Dernier Round* by Jacques Pothier.
[1034] *Newark Star Ledger* April 4, 2004.
[1035] *Herald News* May 20, 2004.
[1036] *The Ring* March 2004.
[1037] *Newark Star Ledger* May 23, 2004.
[1038] *Newark Star Ledger* May 30, 2004.
[1039] *Newark Star Ledger* May 30, 2004.
[1040] Interview with Buddy McGirt 2013.
[1041] Interview with Buddy McGirt 2013.
[1042] Interview with Buddy McGirt 2013.
[1043] Interview with Buddy McGirt 2013.
[1044] *Newark Star Ledger* May 30, 2004.
[1045] *Sports Illustrated* July 26, 2004.
[1046] *Sports Illustrated* July 26, 2004.
[1047] *Sports Illustrated* July 26, 2004.
[1048] *Maxboxing.com* July 21, 2004.

[1049] *The Record* July 22, 2004.
[1050] *Newark Star Ledger* May 30, 2004.
[1051] *Press of Atlantic City* July 21, 2004.
[1052] *Press of Atlantic City* July 21, 2004.
[1053] *Press of Atlantic City* July 23, 2004.
[1054] *Press of Atlantic City* July 23, 2004.
[1055] *Press of Atlantic City* July 24, 2004.
[1056] *Press of Atlantic City* July 24, 2004.
[1057] *Herald News* July 22, 2004.
[1058] *Herald News* July 22, 2004.
[1059] *Herald News* July 24, 2004.
[1060] *Herald News* July 24, 2004.
[1061] *Herald News* July 24, 2004.
[1062] *Newark Star Ledger* July 24, 2004.
[1063] *Jersey Journal* July 24, 2004.
[1064] *Newark Star Ledger* July 23, 2004.
[1065] *Jersey Journal* July 24, 2004.
[1066] *Press of Atlantic City* June 20, 2005.
[1067] *Press of Atlantic City* June 20, 2005.
[1068] *Newark Star Ledger* July 25, 2004.
[1069] *The Record* July 25, 2004.
[1070] *Herald News* July 26, 2004.
[1071] *The Record* July 25, 2004.
[1072] *Press of Atlantic City* July 26, 2004.
[1073] *Press of Atlantic City* July 26, 2004.
[1074] *Jersey Journal* July 26, 2004.
[1075] *Press of Atlantic City* July 26, 2004.
[1076] *Newark Star Ledger* July 26, 2004.
[1077] Interview with Mario Costa 2013.
[1078] *The Telegraph* November 23, 2012.
[1079] *Los Angeles Times* August 31, 2011.
[1080] BOXING.com August 31, 2011.
[1081] BOXING.com August 31, 2011.
[1082] Life After Peak Experiences June 5, 2014.
[1083] The Finish Line July 31, 2014.
[1084] BBC Sport December 18, 2012.
[1085] *New York Times* January 3, 2014.
[1086] *Boston Globe* September 10, 2003.
[1087] *Only In America* by Jack Newfield.
[1088] *N.Y. Daily News* July 14, 2009.
[1089] *Canadian Press* October 18, 2004.
[1090] *Canadian Press* October 18, 2004.
[1091] *Press of Atlantic City* January 21, 2005.
[1092] *Press of Atlantic City* January 21, 2005.
[1093] *The Record* January 27, 2005.
[1094] *The Record* January 27, 2005.
[1095] *Gatti vs. Leija* Official Program.
[1096] *Gatti vs. Leija* Official Program.
[1097] *Newark Star Ledger* January 29, 2005.
[1098] *Newark Star Ledger* January 29, 2005.
[1099] *Newark Star Ledger* January 29, 2005.
[1100] *Press of Atlantic City* January 28, 2005.
[1101] *Press of Atlantic City* January 29, 2005.
[1102] *Newark Star Ledger* January 30, 2005.
[1103] *Jersey Journal* January 31, 2005.
[1104] *Herald News* January 30, 2005.
[1105] *Press of Atlantic City* January 30, 2005.
[1106] Interview with Mike Skowronski 2013.
[1107] *Press of Atlantic City* January 30, 2005.
[1108] *Boxing* July 2005.
[1109] *The Record* January 31, 2005.
[1110] *Boxing* July 2005.
[1111] *Boxing* July 2005.
[1112] *Boxing* July 2005.
[1113] Interview with Joe Gatti 2013.
[1114] *Press of Atlantic City* March 5, 2005.
[1115] *Press of Atlantic City* March 11, 2005.
[1116] *Press of Atlantic City* March 11, 2005.
[1117] *Herald News* May 14, 2005.
[1118] *Herald News* May 14, 2005.
[1119] *Newark Star Ledger* March 24, 2005.
[1120] *The Record* March 24, 2005.
[1121] *Press of Atlantic City* March 24, 2005.
[1122] *Press of Atlantic City* March 24, 2005.
[1123] *Press of Atlantic City* March 24, 2005.
[1124] *Press of Atlantic City* March 25, 2005.
[1125] *Press of Atlantic City* March 25, 2005.
[1126] *Newark Star Ledger* April 3, 2005.
[1127] *Press of Atlantic City* March 24, 2005.
[1128] *Press of Atlantic City* March 25, 2005.
[1129] *Newark Star Ledger* June 12, 2005.
[1130] *Arturo Gatti: Le Dernier Round* by Jacques Pothier.
[1131] *Arturo Gatti: Le Dernier Round* by Jacques Pothier.
[1132] *Razor* magazine June 2005.
[1133] *Razor* magazine June 2005.
[1134] *Razor* magazine June 2005.
[1135] *Press of Atlantic City* June 25, 2005.
[1136] *Newark Star Ledger* June 19, 2005.
[1137] *Newark Star Ledger* June 19, 2005.
[1138] *Press of Atlantic City* June 20, 2005.
[1139] Interview with Mike Skowronski 2013.
[1140] *Press of Atlantic City* June 25, 2005.
[1141] *The Bergen Record* June 26, 2005.
[1142] *Maxim* March 2010.
[1143] *Maxim* March 2010.
[1144] *Newark Star Ledger* June 19, 2005.

[1145] Interview with Teddy Cruz 2013.
[1146] Press of Atlantic City June 24, 2005.
[1147] Press of Atlantic City June 19, 2005.
[1148] Press of Atlantic City June 20, 2005.
[1149] Press of Atlantic City June 19, 2005.
[1150] Bergen Record June 21, 2005.
[1151] Bergen Record June 21, 2005.
[1152] Bergen Record June 21, 2005.
[1153] Herald News June 23, 2005.
[1154] Press of Atlantic City June 19, 2005.
[1155] Press of Atlantic City June 19, 2005.
[1156] Press of Atlantic City June 19, 2005.
[1157] Press of Atlantic City June 19, 2005.
[1158] Press of Atlantic City June 21, 2005.
[1159] Press of Atlantic City June 21, 2005.
[1160] Press of Atlantic City June 22, 2005.
[1161] Press of Atlantic City June 22, 2005.
[1162] Press of Atlantic City June 22, 2005.
[1163] Herald News June 17, 2005.
[1164] Herald News June 17, 2005.
[1165] Newark Star Ledger June 24, 2005.
[1166] Newark Star Ledger June 24, 2005.
[1167] Newark Star Ledger June 24, 2005.
[1168] Newark Star Ledger June 24, 2005.
[1169] Newark Star Ledger June 24, 2005.
[1170] The Bergen Record June 26, 2005.
[1171] Boxing News June 24, 2005.
[1172] Herald News June 17, 2005.
[1173] Ring magazine Summer 2005.
[1174] Newark Star Ledger June 24, 2005.
[1175] Newark Star Ledger June 24, 2005.
[1176] Newark Star Ledger June 24, 2005.
[1177] Newark Star Ledger June 24, 2005.
[1178] Newark Star Ledger June 24, 2005.
[1179] Press of Atlantic City June 23, 2005.
[1180] Press of Atlantic City June 23, 2005.
[1181] Newark Star Ledger June 24, 2005.
[1182] Newark Star Ledger June 21, 2005.
[1183] Newark Star Ledger June 21, 2005.
[1184] Newark Star Ledger June 21, 2005.
[1185] Newark Star Ledger June 24, 2005.
[1186] Newark Star Ledger June 24, 2005.
[1187] Newark Star Ledger June 19, 2005.
[1188] Newark Star Ledger June 24, 2005.
[1189] Press of Atlantic City June 25, 2005.
[1190] Press of Atlantic City June 25, 2005.
[1191] Press of Atlantic City June 25, 2005.
[1192] Newark Star Ledger June 25, 2005.
[1193] Newark Star Ledger June 25, 2005.
[1194] Newark Star Ledger June 24, 2005.
[1195] The Bergen Record June 25, 2005.
[1196] New York Times June 24, 2005.
[1197] New York Times June 24, 2005.
[1198] New York Times June 24, 2005.
[1199] New York Times June 24, 2005.
[1200] New York Times June 24, 2005.
[1201] The Bergen Record June 25, 2005.
[1202] Interview with Joe Gatti 2013.
[1203] Newark Star Ledger June 27, 2005.
[1204] Newark Star Ledger June 27, 2005.
[1205] Newark Star Ledger June 27, 2005.
[1206] Newark Star Ledger June 27, 2005.
[1207] Arturo Gatti: Le Dernier Round by Jacques Pothier.
[1208] Arturo Gatti: Le Dernier Round by Jacques Pothier.
[1209] Newark Star Ledger June 27, 2005.
[1210] Newark Star Ledger June 27, 2005.
[1211] Newark Star Ledger June 27, 2005.
[1212] Interview with Joe Gatti 2013.
[1213] Press of Atlantic City June 26, 2005.
[1214] Newark Star Ledger June 27, 2005.
[1215] Newark Star Ledger June 27, 2005.
[1216] Press of Atlantic City June 26, 2005.
[1217] Interview with Mike Skowronski 2013.
[1218] Newark Star Ledger June 27, 2005.
[1219] Press of Atlantic City June 26, 2005.
[1220] Press of Atlantic City June 26, 2005.
[1221] Interview with Mike Skowronski 2013.
[1222] Boxing News July 1, 2005.
[1223] Ring magazine Volume 5, 2005.
[1224] Arturo Gatti: Le Dernier Round by Jacques Pothier.
[1225] Newark Star Ledger June 26, 2005.
[1226] Boxing News July 1, 2005.
[1227] Newark Star Ledger June 26, 2005.
[1228] Press of Atlantic City June 26, 2005.
[1229] Press of Atlantic City June 26, 2005.
[1230] Newark Star Ledger June 27, 2005.
[1231] Interview with Joe Gatti 2013.
[1232] Interview with Joe Gatti 2013.
[1233] Interview with Joe Gatti 2013.
[1234] Interview with Joe Gatti 2013.
[1235] Mario Costa Interview 2013.
[1236] Press of Atlantic City June 27, 2005.
[1237] Press of Atlantic City June 30, 2005.
[1238] Newark Star Ledger July 14, 2009.
[1239] Newark Star Ledger July 14, 2009.
[1240] Interview with Buddy McGirt 2013.

[1241] Interview with Teddy Cruz 2013.
[1242] Interview with Teddy Cruz 2013.
[1243] Interview with Teddy Cruz 2013.
[1244] Interview with Teddy Cruz 2013.
[1245] Interview with Teddy Cruz 2013.
[1246] Interview with Teddy Cruz 2013.
[1247] Interview with Teddy Cruz 2013.
[1248] Mike Sciarra interview with Ryan Songalia September 7, 2011.
[1249] Interview with Donnie Jerie 2014.
[1250] Mike Sciarra interview with Ryan Songalia September 7, 2011.
[1251] *Newark Star Ledger* August 7, 2005.
[1252] *Press of Atlantic City* September 24, 2005.
[1253] *Press of Atlantic City* September 24, 2005.
[1254] Interview with Danny McDermott 2022.
[1255] Interview with Mario Costa 2013.
[1256] Interview with Mario Costa 2013.
[1257] *Arturo Gatti: Le Dernier Round* by Jacques Pothier.
[1258] Interview with Joe Gatti 2013.
[1259] Mario Costa Interview with Mark Malinowski 2013.
[1260] Interview with Mario Costa 2013.
[1261] Interview with Mike Skowronski 2013.
[1262] Interview with Mike Skowronski 2013.
[1263] Interview with Mike Skowronski 2013. It should be noted that the waiving of Lynch's managerial fees never was confirmed.
[1264] *Newark Star Ledger* October 16, 2005.
[1265] *Herald News* October 21, 2005.
[1266] *Jersey Journal* October 21, 2005.
[1267] *Herald News* October 28, 2005.
[1268] *Herald News* November 11, 2005.
[1269] *Herald News* December 2, 2005.
[1270] *Press of Atlantic City* December 16, 2005.
[1271] *Herald News* December 16, 2005
[1272] *Press of Atlantic City* December 16, 2005.
[1273] Interview with Joe Gatti 2013.
[1274] *Arturo Gatti: Le Dernier Round* by Jacques Pothier.
[1275] *Le Dernier Round* by Jacques Ponthier.
[1276] Interview with Donnie Jerie 2014.
[1277] *Le Dernier Round* by Jacques Ponthier.
[1278] *Newark Star Ledger* January 9, 2006.
[1279] *Newark Star Ledger* January 9, 2006.
[1280] *Herald News* January 11, 2006.
[1281] *Bergen Record* January 26, 2006.
[1282] *Bergen Record* January 26, 2006.
[1283] *Bergen Record* January 26, 2006.
[1284] *Bergen Record* January 26, 2006.
[1285] *Press of Atlantic City* January 26, 2006.
[1286] Interview with Mario Costa 2013.
[1287] *Press of Atlantic City* January 26, 2006.
[1288] *Herald News* January 26, 2006.
[1289] *Herald News* January 26, 2006.
[1290] *Herald News* January 26, 2006.
[1291] *Jersey Journal* January 27, 2006.
[1292] *Jersey Journal* January 27, 2006.
[1293] *Jersey Journal* January 27, 2006.
[1294] Interview with Pete Maino 2023.
[1295] *Herald News* January 27, 2006.
[1296] *Herald News* January 28, 2006.
[1297] *Herald News* January 28, 2006.
[1298] *Press of Atlantic City* January 28, 2006.
[1299] *Press of Atlantic City* January 28, 2006.
[1300] *Press of Atlantic City* January 28, 2006.
[1301] *Newark Star Ledger* January 28, 2006.
[1302] *Jersey Journal* January 30, 2006.
[1303] *Newark Star Ledger* January 30, 2006.
[1304] *Newark Star Ledger* January 29, 2006.
[1305] *Newark Star Ledger* January 30, 2006.
[1306] *Newark Star Ledger* January 30, 2006.
[1307] *Press of Atlantic City* January 30, 2006.
[1308] *Boxing Digest* April 2006.
[1309] *Boxing Digest* April 2006.
[1310] *Press of Atlantic City* January 30, 2006.
[1311] *Press of Atlantic City* March 18, 2006.
[1312] *Press of Atlantic City* March 18, 2006.
[1313] *Press of Atlantic City* March 18, 2006.
[1314] *Press of Atlantic City* March 18, 2006.
[1315] *Press of Atlantic City* March 18, 2006.
[1316] *Ring* magazine June 2006.
[1317] *Herald News* January 30, 2006.
[1318] *Herald News* January 30, 2006.
[1319] *Ring* magazine June 2006.
[1320] *Herald News* February 24, 2006.
[1321] *Newark Star Ledger* April 30, 2006.
[1322] *Newark Star Ledger* April 30, 2006.
[1323] *Newark Star Ledger* April 30, 2006.
[1324] *Newark Star Ledger* April 30, 2006.
[1325] *Newark Star Ledger* April 30, 2006.
[1326] *Newark Star Ledger* April 30, 2006.
[1327] Interview with Nettles Nasser 2014.
[1328] *Herald News* March 17, 2006.
[1329] *Ring* magazine August 2006.
[1330] *Ring* magazine August 2006.
[1331] *Bergen Record* April 13, 2006.
[1332] *Newark Star Ledger* July 22, 2006.
[1333] *Newark Star Ledger* July 22, 2006.
[1334] *Bergen Record* April 13, 2006.
[1335] *Bergen Record* April 13, 2006.
[1336] *Bergen Record* April 13, 2006.

[1337] *Le Dernier Round* by Jacques Ponthier.
[1338] *Press of Atlantic City* June 6, 2006.
[1339] *Press of Atlantic City* June 6, 2006.
[1340] *Press of Atlantic City* June 6, 2006.
[1341] *Press of Atlantic City* June 6, 2006.
[1342] *Press of Atlantic City* June 6, 2006.
[1343] *Press of Atlantic City* April 13, 2006.
[1344] Interview with Teddy Cruz 2013.
[1345] *Press of Atlantic City* April 13, 2006.
[1346] *Press of Atlantic City* April 13, 2006.
[1347] *New Jersey Monthly* 2006.
[1348] *New Jersey Monthly* 2006.
[1349] *New Jersey Monthly* 2006.
[1350] *New Jersey Monthly* 2006.
[1351] *New Jersey Monthly* 2006.
[1352] *New Jersey Monthly* 2006.
[1353] *New Jersey Monthly* 2006.
[1354] *Newark Star Ledger* July 10, 2006.
[1355] *Press of Atlantic City* July 19, 2006.
[1356] *Press of Atlantic City* July 19, 2006.
[1357] *Press of Atlantic City* July 19, 2006.
[1358] *Press of Atlantic City* July 20, 2006.
[1359] *Bergen Record* July 20, 2006.
[1360] *Press of Atlantic City* July 20, 2006.
[1361] *Bergen Record* July 20, 2006.
[1362] *Bergen Record* July 20, 2006.
[1363] *Bergen Record* July 20, 2006.
[1364] *Bergen Record* July 22, 2006.
[1365] *Jersey Journal* July 20, 2006.
[1366] *Jersey Journal* July 20, 2006.
[1367] *Bergen Record* July 22, 2006.
[1368] *Newark Star Ledger* July 21, 2006.
[1369] *Herald News* July 21, 2006.
[1370] Interview with Mike Skowronski 2013.
[1371] *Bergen Record* July 22, 2006.
[1372] *Press of Atlantic City* July 21, 2006.
[1373] *Press of Atlantic City* July 21, 2006.
[1374] *Press of Atlantic City* July 21, 2006.
[1375] *Press of Atlantic City* July 22, 2006.
[1376] Interview with Mike Skowronski 2013.
[1377] *Boxing News* July 28, 2006.
[1378] *Bergen Record* July 24, 2006.
[1379] *Bergen Record* July 24, 2006.
[1380] *Jersey Journal* July 24, 2006.
[1381] *Press of Atlantic City* July 24, 2006.
[1382] *Press of Atlantic City* August 3, 2006.
[1383] Everlast Equipment Catalog, Fall 2006.
[1384] Everlast Equipment Catalog, Fall 2006.
[1385] Everlast Equipment Catalog, Fall 2006.
[1386] Everlast Equipment Catalog, Fall 2006.
[1387] Everlast Equipment Catalog, Fall 2006.
[1388] Everlast Equipment Catalog, Fall 2006.
[1389] Everlast Equipment Catalog, Fall 2006.
[1390] Everlast Equipment Catalog, Fall 2006.
[1391] Everlast Equipment Catalog, Fall 2006.
[1392] *Newark Star Ledger* August 6, 2006.
[1393] *World Boxing* Winter 2006.
[1394] *Herald News* September 20, 2006.
[1395] *Le Dernier Round* by Jacques Ponthier.
[1396] *Maxim* March 2010.
[1397] *Bergen Record* November 9, 2006.
[1398] *Herald News* September 20, 2006.
[1399] *Herald News* September 20, 2006.
[1400] *Herald News* September 20, 2006.
[1401] *World Boxing* Winter 2006.
[1402] *World Boxing* Winter 2006.
[1403] *Newark Star Ledger* November 26, 2006.
[1404] *Press of Atlantic City* November 30, 2006.
[1405] *Press of Atlantic City* November 30, 2006.
[1406] *Press of Atlantic City* November 30, 2006.
[1407] "Faithfully" written by Jonathan Cain 1982.
[1408] Interview with Joe Gatti 2013.
[1409] *Arturo Gatti: Le Dernier Round* by Jacques Pothier.
[1410] *Maxim* March 2010.
[1411] *Maxim* March 2010.
[1412] *Maxim* March 2010.
[1413] Interview with Omar Shieka 2014.
[1414] A&E's *Prenup to Murder: "Arturo Gatti's Final Bout."* March 19, 2013.
[1415] A&E's *Prenup to Murder: "Arturo Gatti's Final Bout."* March 19, 2013.
[1416] *Maxim* March 2010.
[1417] Interview with Omar Shieka 2014.
[1418] *Maxim* March 2010.
[1419] *Maxim* March 2010.
[1420] *Herald News* January 5, 2007.
[1421] *Herald News* January 26, 2007.
[1422] *Press of Atlantic City* February 8, 2007.
[1423] *Newark Star Ledger* March 18, 2007.
[1424] *Press of Atlantic City* April 27, 2007.
[1425] Interview with Mario Costa 2013.
[1426] Interview with Travis Hartman 2023.
[1427] Interview with Travis Hartman 2023.
[1428] Interview with Donnie Jerie 2014.
[1429] *Press of Atlantic City* May 23, 2007.
[1430] *Jersey Journal* May 24, 2007.
[1431] *Jersey Journal* May 24, 2007.
[1432] *Jersey Journal* May 24, 2007.

[1433] *Jersey Journal* May 24, 2007.
[1434] *Press of Atlantic City* May 23, 2007.
[1435] *Press of Atlantic City* May 23, 2007.
[1436] *Press of Atlantic City* May 23, 2007.
[1437] *Press of Atlantic City* May 23, 2007.
[1438] *Newark Star Ledger* June 3, 2007.
[1439] *Newark Star Ledger* July 8, 2007.
[1440] *Newark Star Ledger* July 8, 2007.
[1441] *Herald News* July 12, 2007.
[1442] *Boxing News* July 13, 2007.
[1443] *Herald News* July 12, 2007.
[1444] *Herald News* July 12, 2007.
[1445] *Herald News* July 12, 2007.
[1446] *Press of Atlantic City* July 12, 2007.
[1447] *Press of Atlantic City* July 12, 2007.
[1448] *Press of Atlantic City* July 13, 2007.
[1449] *Press of Atlantic City* July 13, 2007.
[1450] *Press of Atlantic City* July 14, 2007.
[1451] *Herald News* July 14, 2007.
[1452] *Press of Atlantic City* July 16, 2007.
[1453] Interview with Nasser Nettles 2014.
[1454] Interview with Nasser Nettles 2014.
[1455] *Bergen Record* July 16, 2007.
[1456] Mario Costa Interview with Mark Malinowski 2013.
[1457] *Press of Atlantic City* July 15, 2007.
[1458] *Press of Atlantic City* July 15, 2007.
[1459] *48 Hours: Arturo Gatti's Last Fight* September 24, 2011.
[1460] *48 Hours: Arturo Gatti's Last Fight* September 24, 2011.
[1461] *Press of Atlantic City* July 15, 2007.
[1462] *Press of Atlantic City* July 16, 2007.
[1463] *The Chaunce Hayden Show* January 24, 2013.
[1464] Mario Costa interview 2013.
[1465] *Newark Star Ledger* July 15, 2007.
[1466] *Newark Star Ledger* July 16, 2007.
[1467] *Jersey Journal* July 16, 2007.
[1468] *Herald News* July 27, 2007.
[1469] A&E's *Prenup to Murder: "Arturo Gatti's Final Bout."* March 19, 2013.
[1470] *Maxim* March 2010.
[1471] *Maxim* March 2010.
[1472] *Bergen Record* July 20, 2009.
[1473] *Press of Atlantic City* September 14, 2007.
[1474] *Press of Atlantic City* September 14, 2007.
[1475] *Press of Atlantic City* September 14, 2007.
[1476] *Press of Atlantic City* July 13, 2013.
[1477] *Press of Atlantic City* November 16, 2007.
[1478] *Press of Atlantic City* November 16, 2007.
[1479] *Press of Atlantic City* November 16, 2007.
[1480] *Press of Atlantic City* November 16, 2007.
[1481] *Press of Atlantic City* November 18, 2007.
[1482] *The Globe and Mail* September 6, 2012.
[1483] Interview with Mario Costa 2013.
[1484] Murder In Paradise: Season 1 Episode 2 "Brazilian Knockout" 2013.
[1485] Kapalua, Maui, Police Report.
[1486] *Herald News* June 5, 2008.
[1487] *Maxim* March 2010.
[1488] *Quebec Star* July 18, 2009.
[1489] *New York Daily News*, March 18, 2008.
[1490] Interview with Mario Costa 2013.
[1491] A&E's *Prenup to Murder: "Arturo Gatti's Final Bout."* March 19, 2013.
[1492] *48 Hours: Arturo Gatti's Last Fight* September 24, 2011.
[1493] Murder In Paradise: Season 1 Episode 2 "Brazilian Knockout" 2013.
[1494] *Maxim* March 2010.
[1495] *Maxim* March 2010.
[1496] *Maxim* March 2010.
[1497] *48 Hours: Arturo Gatti's Last Fight* September 24, 2011.
[1498] *Le Dernier Round* by Jacques Ponthier.
[1499] ESPN'S E:60 "Death of a Champion" November 11, 2009.
[1500] *Le Dernier Round* by Jacques Ponthier.
[1501] ESPN'S E:60 "Death of a Champion" November 11, 2009.
[1502] ESPN'S E:60 "Death of a Champion" November 11, 2009.
[1503] *Maxim* March 2010.
[1504] *Le Dernier Round* by Jacques Ponthier.
[1505] *Le Dernier Round* by Jacques Ponthier.
[1506] A&E's *Prenup to Murder: "Arturo Gatti's Final Bout."* March 19, 2013.
[1507] A&E's *Prenup to Murder: "Arturo Gatti's Final Bout."* March 19, 2013.
[1508] *Le Dernier Round* by Jacques Ponthier.
[1509] ESPN'S E:60 "Death of a Champion" November 11, 2009.
[1510] *Maxim* March 2010.
[1511] Interview with Joe Gatti 2013.
[1512] Interview with Joe Gatti 2013.
[1513] Interview with Joe Gatti 2013.
[1514] Interview with Joe Gatti 2013.
[1515] Interview with Joe Gatti 2013.
[1516] Interview with Joe Gatti 2013.
[1517] Interview with Joe Gatti 2013.
[1518] Interview with Joe Gatti 2013.
[1519] Interview with Joe Gatti 2013.
[1520] Interview with Joe Gatti 2013.
[1521] Interview with Joe Gatti 2013.
[1522] *48 Hours: Arturo Gatti's Last Fight* September 24, 2011.
[1523] *Le Dernier Round* by Jacques Ponthier.
[1524] *Maxim* March 2010.
[1525] *Quebec Star* July 18, 2009.
[1526] Murder In Paradise: Season 1 Episode 2 "Brazilian Knockout" 2013.
[1527] Nestor Fernandez vs. The Estate of Arturo Gatti November 22, 2010.
[1528] *Press of Atlantic City* July 16, 2009.

[1529] *Maxim* March 2010.
[1530] *48 Hours: Arturo Gatti's Last Fight* September 24, 2011.
[1531] Interview with Donnie Jerie 2014.
[1532] Interview with Donnie Jerie 2014.
[1533] *Newark Star Ledger* June 11, 2009.
[1534] A&E's *Prenup to Murder: "Arturo Gatti's Final Bout."* March 19, 2013.
[1535] *The Chauncey Hayden Show* January 24, 2013.
[1536] A&E's *Prenup to Murder: "Arturo Gatti's Final Bout."* March 19, 2013.
[1537] A&E's *Prenup to Murder: "Arturo Gatti's Final Bout."* March 19, 2013.
[1538] *48 Hours: Arturo Gatti's Last Fight* September 24, 2011.
[1539] *48 Hours: Arturo Gatti's Last Fight* September 24, 2011.
[1540] *Maxim* March 2010.
[1541] Interview with Donnie Jerie 2014.
[1542] *Sports Illustrated* October 21, 1985.
[1543] *Le Dernier Round* by Jacques Ponthier.
[1544] *The Globe and Mail* July 13, 2009.
[1545] A&E's *Prenup to Murder: "Arturo Gatti's Final Bout."* March 19, 2013.
[1546] *USA Today* December 8, 2010.
[1547] *48 Hours: Arturo Gatti's Last Fight* September 24, 2011.
[1548] A&E's *Prenup to Murder: "Arturo Gatti's Final Bout."* March 19, 2013.
[1549] *Journal de Montreal*.
[1550] Murder In Paradise: Season 1 Episode 2 "Brazilian Knockout" 2013.
[1551] A&E's *Prenup to Murder: "Arturo Gatti's Final Bout."* March 19, 2013.
[1552] Murder In Paradise: Season 1 Episode 2 "Brazilian Knockout" 2013.
[1553] ESPN's E:60 "Death of a Champion" November 11, 2009.
[1554] A&E's *Prenup to Murder: "Arturo Gatti's Final Bout."* March 19, 2013.
[1555] A&E's *Prenup to Murder: "Arturo Gatti's Final Bout."* March 19, 2013.
[1556] *48 Hours: Arturo Gatti's Last Fight* September 24, 2011.
[1557] A&E's *Prenup to Murder: "Arturo Gatti's Final Bout."* March 19, 2013.
[1558] ESPN's E:60 "Death of a Champion" November 11, 2009.
[1559] "Wheels in the Sky" by Robert Fleischman, Neal Schon & Diane Valory.
[1560] "Fade to Black" by James Hetfield, Lars Ulrich, Cliff Burton & Kirk Hammett.
[1561] A&E's *Prenup to Murder: "Arturo Gatti's Final Bout."* March 19, 2013.
[1562] *48 Hours: Arturo Gatti's Last Fight* September 24, 2011.
[1563] ESPN's E:60 "Death of a Champion" November 11, 2009.
[1564] A&E's *Prenup to Murder: "Arturo Gatti's Final Bout."* March 19, 2013.
[1565] A&E's *Prenup to Murder: "Arturo Gatti's Final Bout."* March 19, 2013.
[1566] *48 Hours: Arturo Gatti's Last Fight* September 24, 2011.
[1567] *48 Hours: Arturo Gatti's Last Fight* September 24, 2011.
[1568] Murder in Paradise. Season 1 Episode 2 "Brazilian Knockout" 2013.
[1569] Murder In Paradise: Season 1 Episode 2 "Brazilian Knockout" 2013.
[1570] ESPN's E:60 "Death of a Champion" November 11, 2009.
[1571] ESPN's E:60 "Death of a Champion" November 11, 2009.
[1572] ESPN'S E:60 "Death of a Champion" November 11, 2009.
[1573] *Boxing News* July 17, 2009.
[1574] *Boxing News* July 17, 2009.
[1575] *Boxing News* July 17, 2009.
[1576] Interview with Mario Costa 2013.
[1577] *Boxing News* July 17, 2009.
[1578] Interview with Joe Gatti 2013.
[1579] Interview with Joe Gatti 2013.
[1580] Interview with Joe Gatti 2013.
[1581] Interview with Donnie Jerie 2014.
[1582] Interview with Donnie Jerie 2014.
[1583] *Boxing News* July 17, 2009.
[1584] Interview with Buddy McGirt 2013.
[1585] *Boxing News* July 17, 2009.
[1586] Interview with Buddy McGirt 2013.
[1587] Interview with Sal Alessi 2013.
[1588] Interview with Sal Alessi 2013.
[1589] *Newark Star Ledger* July 12, 2009.
[1590] *Herald News* July 12, 2009.
[1591] *Newark Star Ledger* July 12, 2009.
[1592] *Newark Star Ledger* July 12, 2009.
[1593] *Herald News* July 12, 2009.
[1594] *Boxing News* July 17, 2009.
[1595] Gabe Ruelas Interview 2013.
[1596] *New York Daily News* July 14, 2009.
[1597] *Boxing Insider* August 8, 2011.
[1598] *Boxing Insider* August 8, 2011.
[1599] Interview with Teddy Cruz 2013.
[1600] *Newark Star Ledger* July 12, 2009.
[1601] *Newark Star Ledger* July 13, 2009.
[1602] *Jersey Journal* July 14, 2009.
[1603] *Jersey Journal* July 14, 2009.
[1604] *Jersey Journal* July 14, 2009.
[1605] *Newark Star Ledger* July 13, 2009.
[1606] *Press of Atlantic City* July 12, 2009.
[1607] *Press of Atlantic City* July 13, 2009.
[1608] *Press of Atlantic City* July 13, 2009.
[1609] Interview with Russell Peltz 2013.
[1610] Interview with Russell Peltz 2013.
[1611] Interview with Alfonso Gomez 2013.
[1612] Interview with Buddy McGirt 2013.
[1613] Interview with Pete Maino 2023.
[1614] *The Globe and Mail* July 13, 2009.
[1615] *The Globe and Mail* July 13, 2009.
[1616] *The Globe and Mail* July 13, 2009.
[1617] *The Globe and Mail* July 13, 2009.
[1618] *The Globe and Mail* July 13, 2009.
[1619] *The Globe and Mail* July 13, 2009.
[1620] *The Globe and Mail* July 13, 2009.
[1621] *Newark Star Ledger* July 13, 2009.
[1622] *Maxim* March 2010.

[1623] *Newark Star Ledger* July 13, 2009.
[1624] *Newark Star Ledger* July 13, 2009.
[1625] *Newark Star Ledger* July 15, 2009.
[1626] *Bergen Record* July 13, 2009.
[1627] *Bergen Record* July 13, 2009.
[1628] *Jersey Journal* July 13, 2009.
[1629] *Jersey Journal* July 14, 2009.
[1630] *Jersey Journal* July 14, 2009.
[1631] *Newark Star Ledger* July 15, 2009.
[1632] *Newark Star Ledger* July 15, 2009.
[1633] *Herald News* July 17, 2009.
[1634] *Herald News* July 17, 2009.
[1635] *Press of Atlantic City* July 16, 2009.
[1636] *Press of Atlantic City* July 16, 2009.
[1637] *Newark Star Ledger* July 19, 2009.
[1638] *Jersey Journal* July 22, 2009.
[1639] *Jersey Journal* July 21, 2009.
[1640] *Arturo Gatti: Le Dernier Round* by Jacques Pothier
[1641] *Arturo Gatti: Le Dernier Round* by Jacques Pothier
[1642] Interview with Vikki Gatti 2013.
[1643] Interview with Joe Gatti 2013.
[1644] *Quebec Star* July 18, 2009.
[1645] *Quebec Star* July 18, 2009.
[1646] *Quebec Star* July 18, 2009.
[1647] *Jersey Journal* July 20, 2009.
[1648] Interview with Vikki Gatti 2013.
[1649] Interview with Joe Gatti 2013.
[1650] Interview with Vikki Gatti 2013.
[1651] Interview with Joe Gatti 2013.
[1652] Interview with Joe Gatti 2013.
[1653] Interview with Joe Gatti 2013.
[1654] Interview with Vikki Gatti 2013.
[1655] *Jersey Journal* July 21, 2009.
[1656] *Press of Atlantic City* July 21, 2009.
[1657] Online post by Mike DePompe July 22, 2009.
[1658] Online post by Mike DePompe July 22, 2009.
[1659] Online post by Mike DePompe July 22, 2009.
[1660] *Jersey Journal* July 23, 2009.
[1661] *Jersey Journal* July 23, 2009.
[1662] *Newark Star Ledger* July 31, 2009.
[1663] *Jersey Journal* July 23, 2009.
[1664] *Newark Star Ledger* July 26, 2009.
[1665] *Newark Star Ledger* July 26, 2009.
[1666] *Newark Star Ledger* July 26, 2009.
[1667] Interview with Henry Hascup 2023.
[1668] *Newark Star Ledger* July 26, 2009.
[1669] *Newark Star Ledger* July 26, 2009.
[1670] Mario Costa Interview with Mark Malinowski 2013.
[1671] Mario Costa Interview 2013.
[1672] Mario Costa Interview 2013.
[1673] *Newark Star Ledger* July 31, 2009.
[1674] *Jersey Journal* July 31, 2009.
[1675] Interview with Joe Gatti 2013.
[1676] A&E's *Prenup to Murder: "Arturo Gatti's Final Bout."* March 19, 2013.
[1677] *The Chaunce Hayden Show* January 24, 2013.
[1678] *Newark Star Ledger* July 31, 2009.
[1679] *Maxim* March 2010.
[1680] *Maxim* March 2010.
[1681] *Maxim* March 2010.
[1682] *Postmortem Changes* July 27, 2020 by R.Shedge, K.Krishan, V.Warrier, T.Kanchan.
[1683] *Jersey Journal* July 30, 2009.
[1684] *Newark Star Ledger* July 31, 2009.
[1685] *Jersey Journal* July 31, 2009.
[1686] *Newark Star Ledger* July 31, 2009.
[1687] *Newark Star Ledger* July 31, 2009.
[1688] *Jersey Journal* July 31, 2009.
[1689] *Boxing Digest* October 2009.
[1690] *Maxim* March 2010.
[1691] *Maxim* March 2010.
[1692] *Maxim* March 2010.
[1693] *Maxim* March 2010.
[1694] *Maxim* March 2010.
[1695] *Maxim* March 2010.
[1696] *Bergen Record* July 31, 2009.
[1697] *Bergen Record* July 31, 2009.
[1698] Interview with Joe Gatti 2013.
[1699] Interview with Vikki Gatti 2013.
[1700] Interview with Joe Gatti 2013.
[1701] Interview with Joe Gatti 2013.
[1702] Interview with Vikki Gatti 2013.
[1703] *48 Hours: Arturo Gatti's Last Fight* September 24, 2011.
[1704] *48 Hours: Arturo Gatti's Last Fight* September 24, 2011.
[1705] *48 Hours: Arturo Gatti's Last Fight* September 24, 2011.
[1706] *48 Hours: Arturo Gatti's Last Fight* September 24, 2011.
[1707] *48 Hours: Arturo Gatti's Last Fight* September 24, 2011.
[1708] *Newark Star Ledger* August 1, 2009.
[1709] *Newark Star Ledger* August 1, 2009.
[1710] *Newark Star Ledger* August 1, 2009.
[1711] *Newark Star Ledger* August 1, 2009.
[1712] *Newark Star Ledger* August 2, 2009.
[1713] *Jersey Journal* August 6, 2009.
[1714] *Journal de Montreal* August 13, 2009.
[1715] *ESPN.com* September 25, 2011.
[1716] *48 Hours: Arturo Gatti's Last Fight* September 24, 2011.
[1717] *Maxim* March 2010.

[1718] ESPN'S E:60 "Death of a Champion" November 11, 2009.
[1719] ESPN'S E:60 "Death of a Champion" November 11, 2009.
[1720] *New York Daily News* April 3, 2010.
[1721] *Herald News* April 13, 2010.
[1722] *Newark Star Ledger* July 4, 2010.
[1723] *Newark Star Ledger* July 4, 2010.
[1724] *The Globe and Mail* September 6, 2012.
[1725] Interview with Vikki Gatti 2013.
[1726] Interview with Joe Gatti 2013.
[1727] Interview with Vikki Gatti 2013.
[1728] Interview with Vikki Gatti 2013.
[1729] Interview with Joe Gatti 2013.
[1730] Fanhouse Boxing April 12, 2010.
[1731] *Maxim* March 2010.
[1732] Boxinginsider.com May 6, 2010.
[1733] Boxinginsider.com May 6, 2010.
[1734] Boxinginsider.com May 6, 2010.
[1735] *Newark Star Ledger* July 4, 2010.
[1736] *Newark Star Ledger* July 4, 2010.
[1737] *Newark Star Ledger* July 4, 2010.
[1738] *Newark Star Ledger* July 4, 2010.
[1739] *Newark Star Ledger* July 4, 2010.
[1740] *Courthouse News Service* July 14, 2010.
[1741] *Sportsnet* February 10, 2012.
[1742] *Jersey Journal* July 10, 2010.
[1743] Interview with Joe Gatti 2013.
[1744] Interview with Joe Gatti 2013.
[1745] Interview with Joe Gatti 2013.
[1746] Interview with Joe Gatti 2013.
[1747] *Jersey Journal* August 9, 2011.
[1748] *Jersey Journal* August 9, 2011.
[1749] *Jersey Journal* August 9, 2011.
[1750] A&E's *Prenup to Murder: "Arturo Gatti's Final Bout."* March 19, 2013.
[1751] Interview with Joe Gatti 2013.
[1752] *48 Hours: Arturo Gatti's Last Fight* September 24, 2011.
[1753] *Newark Star Ledger* September 6, 2011.
[1754] *Newark Star Ledger* September 6, 2011.
[1755] *Newark Star Ledger* September 6, 2011.
[1756] *Newark Star Ledger* September 6, 2011.
[1757] *Newark Star Ledger* September 6, 2011.
[1758] *Newark Star Ledger* September 6, 2011.
[1759] *Newark Star Ledger* September 8, 2011.
[1760] *Newark Star Ledger* September 8, 2011.
[1761] *Jersey Journal* September 8, 2011.
[1762] *Newark Star Ledger* September 8, 2011.
[1763] *Newark Star Ledger* September 8, 2011.
[1764] *Newark Star Ledger* September 8, 2011.
[1765] *Newark Star Ledger* September 9, 2011.
[1766] *Jersey Journal* September 10, 2011.
[1767] *Jersey Journal* September 10, 2011.
[1768] Interview with Vikki Gatti 2013.
[1769] *Jersey Journal* September 17, 2011.
[1770] *The Canadian Press* September 16, 2011.
[1771] *USA Today* September 22, 2001.
[1772] *The Canadian Press* September 16, 2011.
[1773] *The Canadian Press* September 16, 2011.
[1774] *48 Hours: Arturo Gatti's Last Fight* September 24, 2011.
[1775] *The Canadian Press* September 16, 2011.
[1776] Murder in Paradise. Season 1 Episode 2 "Brazilian Knockout" 2013.
[1777] *The Globe and Mail* September 6, 2012.
[1778] *48 Hours: Arturo Gatti's Last Fight* September 24, 2011.
[1779] Interview with Mario Costa 2013.
[1780] SPORTNET "Coroner: No Evidence of Murder in Gatti Case November 9, 2011.
[1781] SPORTNET "Coroner: No Evidence of Murder in Gatti Case November 9, 2011.
[1782] *The Globe and Mail* September 6, 2012.
[1783] *USA Today* September 22, 2011.
[1784] *USA Today* September 22, 2011.
[1785] *The Globe and Mail* September 6, 2012.
[1786] *The Ring* April 2013.
[1787] *The Ring* April 2013.
[1788] *The Ring* April 2013.
[1789] Interview with Henry Hascup 2023.
[1790] *The Ring* April 2013.
[1791] *Herald News* October 27, 2012.
[1792] Interview with Joe Gatti 2013.
[1793] *Newark Star Ledger* December 12, 2012.
[1794] *Newark Star Ledger* December 12, 2012.
[1795] NorthJersey.com December 10, 2012.
[1796] *The Canadian Press* February 26, 2013.
[1797] *The Canadian Press* February 26, 2013.
[1798] *Global Montreal* February 25, 2013.
[1799] *The Canadian Press* February 26, 2013.
[1800] *The Canadian Press* February 26, 2013.
[1801] *The Canadian Press* February 26, 2013.
[1802] *Global Montreal* February 25, 2013.
[1803] Boxingscene.com October 18, 2013.
[1804] *Herald News* June 7, 2013.
[1805] *Newark Star Ledger* June 10, 2013.
[1806] *Press of Atlantic City* July 13, 2013.
[1807] *Newark Star Ledger* June 10, 2013.
[1808] *Press of Atlantic City* June 10, 2013.
[1809] *Press of Atlantic City* June 10, 2013.
[1810] Interview with Tracy Patterson 2013.
[1811] Interview with Russell Peltz 2013.

[1812] Interview with Gabriel Ruelas 2013.
[1813] *N.Y. Post* June 10, 2013.
[1814] *N.Y. Post* June 10, 2013.
[1815] *N.Y. Post* June 10, 2013.
[1816] *N.Y. Post* June 10, 2013.
[1817] Interview with Joe Gatti 2013.
[1818] Mario Costa Interview with Mark Malinoski 2013.
[1819] *Herald News* October 18, 2013.
[1820] *Herald News* October 18, 2013.
[1821] *Herald News* October 18, 2013.
[1822] *Press of Atlantic City* July 16, 2009.
[1823] SPORTNET "Coroner: No Evidence of Murder in Gatti Case November 9, 2011.
[1824] Murder in Paradise. Season 1 Episode 2 "Brazilian Knockout" 2013.
[1825] *Associated Press* March 15, 2011.
[1826] *Notebook E* by F. Scott Fitgerald 1945.
[1827] Interview with Vikki Gatti 2013.
[1828] *Boston Globe* May, 12, 2002.
[1829] *Boxer Micky Ward Talks CTE and the Mental Health Effects* by Meghan Blackford FHE Health December 20, 2021.

About The Author

Born in Jersey City and raised in Union City, New Jersey, Joe Botti has been involved in the sport of boxing since 1977. He has boxed as an amateur and trained and managed amateur and professional fighters. Botti founded and directed the Union City Boxing Club from 1989 to 2013. Under Botti's direction, the Club won 7 first-place state team trophies. In 1995, the N.J. Golden Gloves Association named Botti coach of the year. He has trained 34 N.J. Golden Glove champions and multiple successful professional boxers. Botti's boxers have been featured on HBO, Showtime, ESPN, and MSG networks. In 1993, Botti promoted the first ever USA Boxing sanctioned female amateur boxing match in the NY-N.J. tri-state area. He is a member of the Ring 14 Veteran Boxer Association and the Hudson County Boxing Association. Botti was voted into the N.J. Boxing Hall of Fame in 2023. Botti's first book, *Joe Jennette: Boxing's Ironman* was a fascinating story about one of the 20th Century's greatest boxers. Botti currently is working on his third book, on the life and boxing career of International Boxing Hall of Fame inductee Don Elbaum. Botti served as a police officer from 1997 to 2021, earning numerous awards and retiring at the rank of Captain. He studied at William Paterson University in Wayne, N.J.

Also by the Author

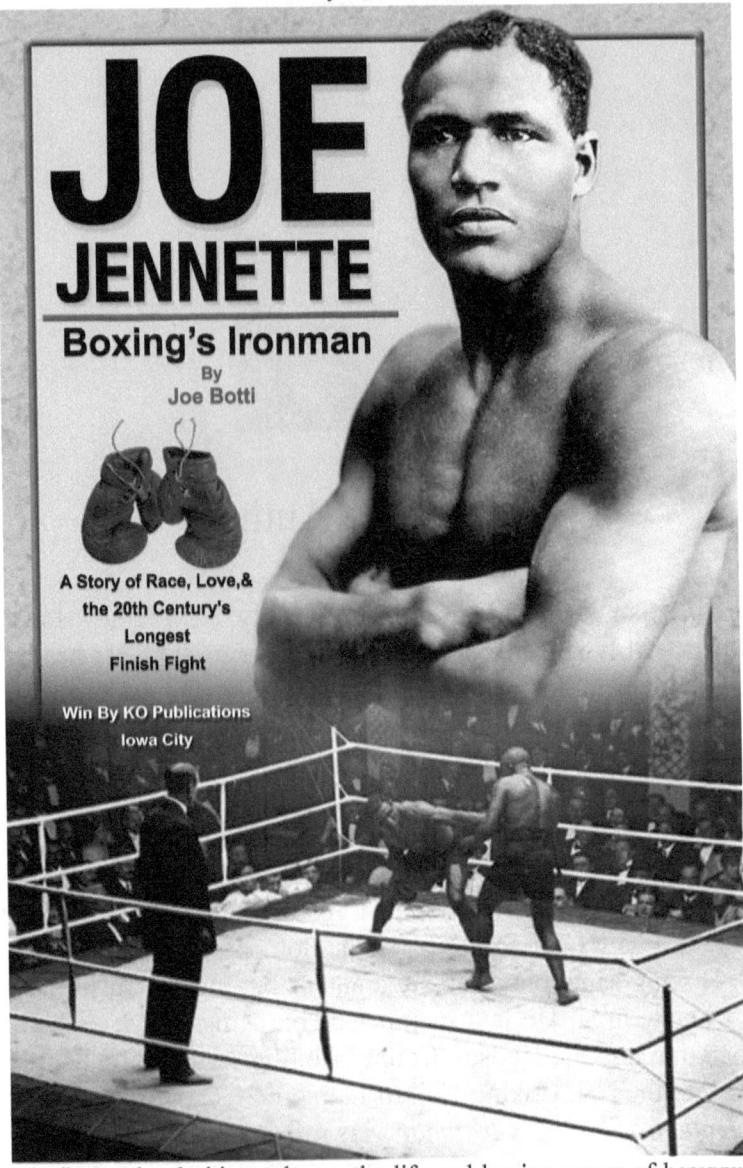

In this first and only biography on the life and boxing career of heavyweight boxing contender Joe Jennette, author Joe Botti chronicles the life and career of this interracial athlete who competed in the longest boxing contest of the twentieth century. From 1904 to 1922 Jennette faced and defeated the most dangerous fighters of his era, including Jack Johnson, Sam Langford, and Sam McVea. Jennette was unable to secure a title shot due to the fact that the world was fixated with finding a Caucasian boxer to defeat Jack Johnson in the "great white hope" era. The story deals with the struggles of interracial romance, racism, and the world of boxing in the early twentieth century.

www.ingramcontent.com/pod-product-compliance
Lightning Source LLC
Chambersburg PA
CBHW022004300426
44117CB00005B/32